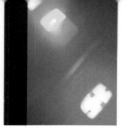

# map page

G000167754

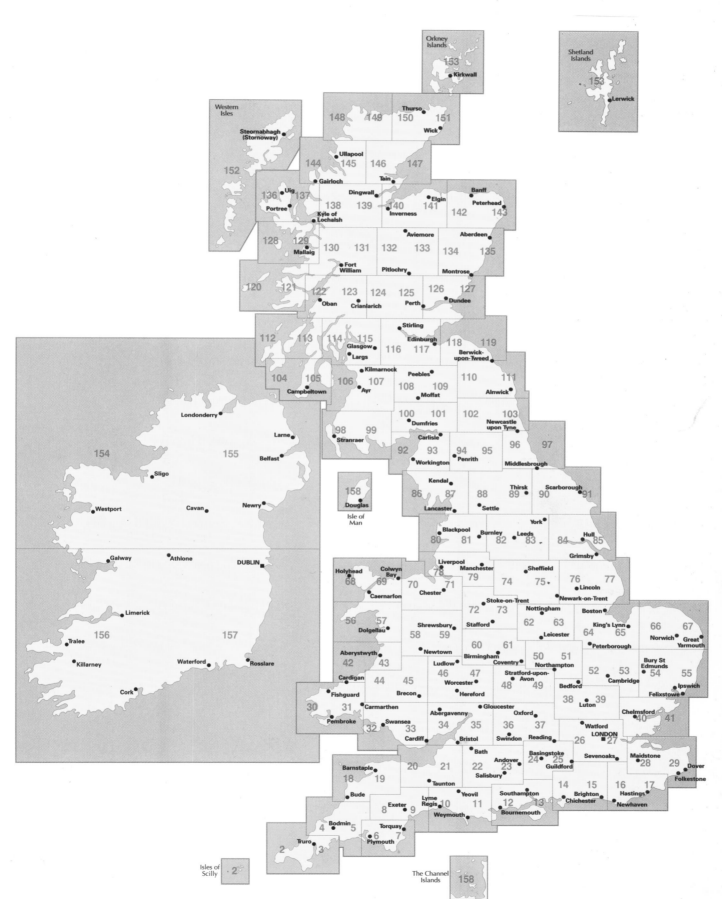

# Road Atlas of the
# British Isles
## 1999

# Helping Members ...that's the job of the AA

# contents

**9th edition August 1998**
8th edition August 1997
7th edition September 1996
6th edition September 1995
5th edition September 1994
4th edition September 1993
Reprinted October 1993
3rd edition October 1992
Reprinted October 1992
2nd edition September 1987
Reprinted October 1991
1st edition September 1990

© The Automobile Association 1998

Published by AA Publishing (a trading name of Automobile Association Developments Limited, whose registered office is Norfolk House, Priestley Road, Basingstoke, Hampshire RG24 9NY. Registered number 1878835).

Mapping produced by the Cartographic Department of The Automobile Association. This atlas has been compiled and produced from the Automaps database utilising electronic and computer technology.

ISBN 0 7495 1866 9

A CIP catalogue record for this book is available from The British Library.

Printed in Italy by Pizzi, Milan

The contents of this atlas are believed to be correct at the time of the latest revision. However, the publishers cannot be held responsible for loss occasioned to any person acting or refraining from action as a result of any material in this atlas, nor for any errors, omissions or changes in such material. The publishers would welcome information to correct any errors or omissions and to keep this atlas up to date. Please write to the Cartographic Editor, Publishing Division, The Automobile Association, Fanum House, Basing View, Basingstoke, Hampshire RG21 4EA.

Information on National Parks provided by the Countryside Commission for England and the Countryside Council for Wales.

Information on National Scenic Areas in Scotland provided by Scottish Natural Heritage.

Information on Forest Parks provided by the Forestry Commission.

The RSPB sites shown are a selection chosen by the Royal Society for the Protection of Birds.

National Trust properties shown are a selection of those open to the public as indicated in the handbooks of the National Trust and the National Trust for Scotland.

# THE TOURIST'S BRITISH ISLES
## ·SYMBOLS·

*Rochester Castle, in Kent, is a fine example of Norman military architecture.*

WHETHER you are looking to spend an afternoon with the family or want to plan a holiday, knowing exactly where to go and what you can see when you get there can often be a problem. The following pages have been designed to give you an idea of what is on offer wherever you happen to be visiting.

Your needs could be as simple as locating a suitable place to enjoy a picnic, where to launch your boat for a day's sailing or where you can find further information about the area.

Whatever your requirement, some 50 symbols, highlighting over 8,000 features of interest, give you a chance to choose what interests you.

Pages 6 to 48 give a taste of what can be seen and where to find it.

Each place located on the atlas by the use of red symbols, has been chosen because it is open and has reasonable access for the public. Although some places may not be

open to the public, they have been included simply because they are an interesting feature or landmark, waterfall, windmill etc.

The AA is constantly checking and updating these entries in its atlases and other publications to ensure accurate, up-to-date information is given. All the attractions featured in *Days Out in Britain*, published annually by the AA, are highlighted in this atlas by the red symbols. The atlas, however, includes even more places and the information on locations such as country parks, nature reserves, nature trails, RSPB sites and Forest Parks, is supplied by the numerous authorities and national bodies such as the Countryside Commission, the Forestry Commission and many others.

There is a wide range of interests to choose from.

For cultural tastes, museums, art galleries, historic houses, castles, abbeys and cathedrals are featured. A stately home like Stourhead, in Wiltshire, may be more famous for its garden than its house and will therefore be depicted by the red

garden symbol. Others, like Chatsworth in Derbyshire, which are better known for the architectural splendour of the house, even though they are also renowned for their garden features, will be indicated by the red house symbol. Larger, specific garden features, classified as arboreta, are depicted accordingly. Major sporting venues such as athletics stadiums, county cricket grounds and horse racing courses are located by appropriate symbols. It is not possible to indicate league football grounds because of their large numbers and the limitations of the map scale. However, some are shown on the town plans at the back of the atlas where appropriate.

For those who like to participate rather than spectate, outdoor and leisure-type facilities, such as ski slopes, golf courses and coastal launching sites for boats are located.

If you have a particular interest in Ancient Britain, you can choose from the various hill-forts, Roman antiquities and prehistoric monuments which are found throughout the country. Even battle

*The places behind Portsmouth's tourist symbols.* Left *Tourist Information at The Hard.* Below left *Industrial Interest with restored steam pumping engines at Eastney.* Below right *The Cathedral.* Right *HMS Warrior, just one of the city's many Museums.*

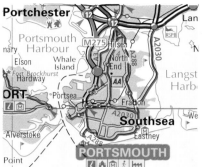

sites, where the course of history has often been changed, are shown. Some of these have interpretative centres which help you to relive and understand the events that occurred there.

Animal lovers can visit the major wildlife collections (both mammals and birds), zoos, and aquariums, or see nature in the wild at one of the numerous nature reserves, Forest Parks and RSPB sites. Another option is to follow one of the nature trails through the countryside. The more adventurous can attempt part or all of one of the national trails which traverse some of Britain's most spectacular scenic areas.

Industrial interest covers a wide spectrum from heritage centres and museums to mills, mines and slate caverns. Old railways, many of which served these industries in the past, now delight the public with a taste of the golden days of steam.

Family days out are catered for by the theme parks. The AA has selected eight of these for inclusion on the basis that they provide multi-purpose entertainment and leisure facilities

and have numerous fairground attractions that are unnervingly described as 'white knuckle' rides. Along with the country parks, they make ideal places to spend the whole day rather than just a quick visit.

Picnic sites are selected and inspected by the AA on a regular basis and are easily accessible, being sited on or by A and B roads. Viewpoints are shown if they offer vistas of at least 180 degrees, and many have panoramic 360 degree views.

Other places of interest which are worth visiting but do not fall easily into the categories symbolised are indicated by a small red star alongside their name. There is a great variety of these – waterfalls, water mills, visitor centres and market crosses, among others.

New additions for the 1990s include the National Parks of England and Wales and the National Scenic Areas of Scotland, along with 930 miles of Heritage Coasts along the shores of England and Wales.

When the red symbols are boxed, this indicates the attractions are in

urban areas. Some of these places may seem bare compared to the surrounding countryside. However, it may be that one symbol for a museum covers several museums in the town, but it is not practical to include them all because of space limitations.

Ireland is included in this special tourist section, and places of interest are located in the atlas, but the scale of mapping does not allow a large selection. Nevertheless, all the most important of Ireland's many tourist attractions are clearly marked.

Wherever possible, the red pictorial symbols used in the atlas are based on the Department of Transport's brown tourist signposts, so that the maps correspond with the road signs. In addition to all this information in the special tourist spreads, a month by month calendar on pages 46 and 47 tells you which customs and events occur throughout the year. This can assist you in deciding when to go. Page 48 describes the services offered by Britain's Tourist Information Centres to help you get the most out of your visits

Abbey, cathedral
or priory

Ruined abbey,
cathedral or
priory

Top *Tintern Abbey: majestic roofless ruin beside the River Wye in Gwent.* Above *St David's Cathedral, Dyfed, where the bones of St David lie.*

**Abbeys
Cathedrals
Priories**
Augustinian, Benedictine, Cistercian and Dominican – the monastic orders which preserved ideals and scholarship after the fall of Rome have left a rich heritage in stone across Britain. Each imposing ruin or active place of worship tells its own story. All evoke a sense of wonder at the faith and industry of the medieval builders and monks. Which of any of them is the loveliest, however, will for ever be a matter of personal preference.

Burnt down in 1174, four years after Becket's murder, the choir of **Canterbury Cathedral** was rebuilt in a manner worthy of the martyr and appears today much as it was in the early 16th century. The 'Altar of the Sword's Point' and a modern cruciform sculpture, dedicated in 1986, mark the site of Becket's martyrdom. The long vistas back to the nave, at a lower level than the choir aisles, show the evolution of Gothic style over three centuries.

The west front of **York**, the largest Gothic church north of the Alps, presents an almost 13th-century 'French' outline, with its glorious façades. The Minster contains the largest single collection of medieval stained glass in England – the West Window painted in 1339 by Master Robert and the East Window, the work of John Thornton of Coventry, between 1405 and 1408. The Pilgrim Window dates from about 1312 and the Bellfounders' Window was given by Richard Tunnoc, buried in the Minster in 1330.

A fire, started by lightning on 9 July 1984, destroyed much of the south transept. Craftsmen, incorporating 20th-century improvements for future safety, restored the medieval beauty of the transept, reopened by the Queen in October 1988.

Embodiment of the spirit of the nation, **Westminster**, the Norman abbey of Edward the Confessor, took on its Gothic appearance after its rebuilding by Henry III. Fortunately, when the 600-year-old Benedictine community was disbanded, the buildings were spared. The Lady Chapel houses the Confessor's shrine, ringed by the tombs of five kings and three queens. In the centre is the Coronation Chair and below the oaken seat the Stone of Scone.

In the Sanctuary beyond the choir every monarch since the Conqueror has been crowned, with the exception of Edward V and Edward VIII. Early Parliaments met in the Chapter House, and the Henry VII Chapel has a superb fan-vaulted roof – the most glorious, some would say, in the country. Near the West Door lies the 'Unknown Warrior', brought back from France after World War I to sleep among the nation's great.

On its rocky promontory dominating the city and a loop in the River Wear, the Norman architecture of **Durham Cathedral** gives an impression, inside as well as out, of overwhelming power. Huge, deeply grooved columns alternating with massive piers support gallery, clerestory and beautiful vault. The Early English Chapel of the Nine Altars is a 13th-century addition, its tall lancet windows paralleled only in the now ruined Fountains Abbey. In the Treasury are evocative relics of the 7th-century St Cuthbert, including his tiny portable altar, his delicate gold pectoral cross and the remains of his original carved oak coffin.

One of the most delicate of England's cathedrals must be **Salisbury**, built in the 40 years following 1220 in local silver-grey limestone with pointed arches and soaring windows. The spire, at 404 feet (123m), is the tallest in the country. It is such inspired work that it blends perfectly with the rest, though crossing piers of clustered black marble had to be reinforced in the 15th century to support the added 6,500 tons of the spire.

**Wells** is the first cathedral church in the Early English style. Its west front is still, despite Puritan vandalism, one of England's richest displays of 13th-century sculpture. Inside, the most striking feature is the inverted arches, built from 1338 to 1348 to combat subsidence of the tower.

The Norman crypt and transepts of **Winchester Cathedral** survive, the rest being 13th and 14th century. At 556 feet (169m) it is the longest Gothic church in Europe. Saved from demolition in 1652 by a petition of the citizens, it was again saved at the beginning of this century by a diver, William Walker. Working alone, from 1906 to 1912, in pitch dark waters of the marshy foundations, he replaced the rotting 13th-century beech tree raft (on which the cathedral had originally been built) with cement.

Near York are three jewels – Beverley, Selby and Ripon. **Beverley Minster** houses the Percy Tomb, the most splendid of British Decorated funerary monuments. It shares, with St Mary's Church nearby, wonderful misericords and the largest collection of carvings of medieval musical instruments anywhere in the world.

Benedictine **Selby Abbey**, founded in 1069, predates Durham. The west front ranges in style from strength and simplicity to later elegance. The easternmost arches of the nave have distorted spectacularly, due to a high water table. High up above the south side of the choir is a 14th-century window with the arms of the Washington family – the 'Stars and Stripes' motif of the American flag.

**Ripon Cathedral** is built over the tiny 11 by 8 ft (3.4 x 2.4m) Saxon crypt of St Wilfrid's Church, one of the few Saxon structures left in England. The cathedral has a beautiful Early English west front. One woodcarver, working from 1939 to 1945, replaced all the 'idolatrous images' on the choir screen, destroyed by Puritans in 1643.

There are modern cathedrals, too. The new **Coventry Cathedral** appears to grow out of the old St Michael's and the overwhelming impression is of height, light and colour. South-facing angled windows enable sunlight to flood the nave with colour. Dominating the whole cathedral is the huge tapestry designed by Graham Sutherland, *Christ in Glory*.

Liverpool's **Anglican Cathedral** is, in the words of Sir John Betjeman, 'vastness, strength and height no words can describe'. Sir Giles Gilbert Scott designed Britain's largest cathedral in medieval style but on a scale which no medieval builder would have attempted. His memorial is set in the floor of the central space under the tower. He, a Catholic, is buried just outside the West Door.

The **Metropolitan Cathedral of Christ the King** in Liverpool, often irreverently called 'Paddy's Wigwam', stands above the huge crypt of the cathedral which Sir Edwin Lutyens started before the war. Inside the 194ft (59m) circular nave, completed by Sir Frederick Gibberd, every member of the 2,300 congregation has an uninterrupted view of the white marble high altar.

A cathedral conveys 'city status' on a town, however small. Pass through the gatehouse at **St David's,** Dyfed, and the lichen-encrusted purple stone of Wales's greatest church is dramatically revealed. It was restored in Decorated Gothic style after an earthquake in 1248 and the whole building slopes upwards some 14 feet (4m) from west to east – an unnerving first glimpse for the visitor entering at the western end

of the nave. The relics of St David rest in an oak and iron reliquary, hidden at the Reformation and discovered during restoration work in 1866.

**St Asaph Cathedral**, in Clwyd, is on the site of a monastic community founded in AD570. It houses the tomb of Bishop William Morgan, translator of the Bible into Welsh, and the 16th-century Bible itself, which was used at the Investiture of the Prince of Wales in 1969.

Henry VIII's Dissolution left a legacy of ruined religious centres across the country, many of which still survive today in all their shattered glory.

Perhaps one of the most magnificent monastic ruins is **Rievaulx Abbey**, two miles north-west of Helmsley. It was founded in 1131 and is the first Cistercian house in the north of England. The name, pronounced 'Reevo', comes from Rye Vallis or valley of the River Rye, above which it stands, surrounded by wooded hills. Its chief glory is its choir built *c.* 1225. The scale of the buildings gives an idea of the activities and work of the 600 and more monks and lay brothers who lived here in the 13th century.

The Cistercian community of **Fountains Abbey**, near Ripon, became the centre of an enormous enterprise, with fish-farms, forestry,

*Right The ancient kings of Northumbria lie buried near Tynemouth Priory. Below Cistercian Fountains Abbey, now part of the Studley Royal estate.*

iron-workings and, above all, sheep, which funded its building. It was one of the first foundations to be sold by Henry VIII in 1540. In 1768 the Aislabie family bought it as a picturesque addition to their Studley Royal estate.

The condition of the Benedictine **Whitby Abbey** cannot wholly be blamed on King Henry. The gaunt ruins of the clifftop site, chosen by St Hilda in AD657, became the setting for Bram Stoker's *Dracula* and suffered further indignity when they were bombarded by German warships during World War I.

The 7th-century buildings at **Much Wenlock** were destroyed by the Danes and later refounded by Leofric, husband of Lady Godiva. Today's ruins are the remains of the church built in the 1220s by Prior Humbert, whose lodging is one of the finest examples of English domestic architecture from around the 1500s.

*Abbey, cathedral or priory*

*Ruined abbey, cathedral or priory*

*Castle*

## Castles

Maiden Castle to Balmoral, Mousa Broch to Dover – Britain is rich in castles dating from Bronze to Victorian ages. The very name 'castle', conjuring up visions of power, of menace and later of opulence, has often been affected by builders of lesser dwellings.

Castles begin with the hillforts of the Bronze Age and stone brochs of pre-Christian Scotland, primarily refuges for men and cattle in time of local warfare. The ruins of Norman timber-built motte and bailey castles – a stone keep on a mound, surrounded by a defensive wall – later converted by the Plantagenets to stone fortresses, still dominate many towns, river crossings and strategic points across the country.

These were not solely refuges, but administrative headquarters, stores and living quarters. Even in times of peace they would have been bustling centres of activity; in time of war, life must have been pretty chaotic, with garrisons, stores, cattle and weaponry increased and as many of the local population as

*Below* Orford Castle, *in Suffolk, has a remarkable 18-sided polygonal keep.* Inset *The Welsh border castle of* Goodrich, *in the Wye Valley.*

could be squeezed in taking refuge in the bailey. Castles were not designed for passive defence but for vigorous action. They were not safe refuges in which to avoid conflict, but ingeniously contrived to make the enemy fight at a disadvantage – they were meant to be costly to capture – both in time and in lives. Henry II (1154-1189), after the mayhem of Stephen's reign 'took every castle of England into his hands', destroyed about 500 unlicensed castles and founded a line of castle-building kings – Richard, John, Henry III, Edward I and III.

Visiting some of these castles, it needs only a little imagination to bring to life the history of their times. The castles of Edward I (1272-1307) around the coast of North Wales are symbols of the organising ability and engineering skills as well as reminders of the vast expense of castle building in the Middle Ages.

Norman and Plantagenet castles vary to suit the site on which they are built but the first criterion was always that of aggressive defence. Where possible a ditch or moat – dry or flooded – was dug to prevent besiegers tunnelling under the walls. Towers without sharp

corners were less likely to be undermined, and so became the fashion.

From about 1268, the date of **Caerphilly Castle** in Mid Glamorgan, the defenders of the outer curtain wall and its towers would be supported by covering fire from higher inner walls. A formidable array of outworks defends gateways and sluices, further protected by drawbridge and portcullis. Barbicans and towers ensured that attackers were subjected to murderous flanking crossfire before they got anywhere near anything so flammable as a wooden gate.

Caerphilly, at 30 acres the largest castle in Wales, surpassed only by **Dover** and **Windsor**, is sufficiently well preserved to give a vivid idea of the way these defensive ideas worked together. It has wide water defences, in imitation of those which Henry III had built at **Kenilworth** and which Simon de Montfort held so successfully against him. Edward I, on his return from the Crusades, liked what he saw at Caerphilly and began to turn the **Tower of London** into a concentric castle. He also introduced at **Caernarfon** and **Conwy** an idea from his campaigns in Gascony –

the 'bastide' – an extension of the bailey to enclose a small town in which traders, labourers and craftsmen could live under the protection of the castle.

Edward I's castle building in North Wales is well documented and throws fascinating light on the feudal power and organisation at the King's command. Ditch diggers were recruited from the Fens and marched across by mounted serjeants – to discourage deserters – to dig the canal around **Rhuddlan Castle.**

At **Conwy**, Edward's young Spanish queen, Eleanor, homesick for the courts and fountains of her native Castile, had a small garden and fishpond built in the castle's east barbican. In the hot summer of 1283 a labourer hauled water from the well, to 'water the Queen's new grass'. Here at Conwy it is believed that Eleanor introduced one of our favourite summer flowers – the sweet pea.

At **Caernarfon Castle** where his son, later Edward II, was born on 25 April 1284, Edward sought to bring Arthurian and Welsh legends to life and make the seat of his government in Wales a new imperial Constantinople. Octagonal towers are set in a single curtain wall, banded with red sandstone in imitation of those of the 5th-century Turkish capital. Defended passages within the thickness of the masonry and ingenious triple arrow slits allowed three bowmen a wide angle of fire through only one external opening.

The more settled times of the Tudor dynasty after the Wars of the Roses reduced the military significance of the castle. Gunpowder played no little part in this. Castles continued to be built, but design changed. Henry VIII began a series of symmetrically planned coastal 'artillery forts' from the Thames to Dorset in 1538. **Deal, Walmer** and **Sandgate** are three, but these were garrisoned rather than lived in – the garrisons complaining that 'they stank of gunpowder and dogs'. Comfort and elegance dictated the style of Elizabethan and Jacobean buildings, though many were still castellated and defensible.

The Civil War saw many castles used again as strongpoints. They stood up so well, even to improved 17th-century firepower, that the victorious Parliamentarians decreed that those which had been so vigorously defended should be 'slighted' – demolished so as to make them useless for military purposes. Some of these 'ruins Cromwell knocked about a bit', if not too badly damaged, became the

*Castle*

local prison and the Norman word for the keep – *donjon* – became the English dungeon.

In Scotland, Northumberland, Cumbria and the troubled lands of the Borders, there are over 1,100 'castles' of one sort or another, excluding the baronial houses of the last 200 years. Most are tower houses or 'peles', built in stone, for timber was always short in the region, and usually several storeys high. **Craigievar**, west of Aberdeen, is the masterpiece of this uniquely Scottish style. Seven storeys high with, even today, few windows in its pink granite walls, it must have been a formidable sight for any would-be attacker.

Many peles have been absorbed into later houses. **Traquair House** west of Galashiels, now more 'château' than castle, claims to be the oldest continuously inhabited house in Scotland. Buried within the north-east corner is a pele tower dating back to the reign of Alexander I (1107-24).

**Stirling Castle,** which looked down on Edward II's ignominious defeat at Bannockburn in 1314, was still an earthen and timber construction. The 'Gateway to the Highlands' was transformed under the Stuarts, first into a stone fortress, then into a splendid Renaissance royal palace.

Castles lived on in the romantic imaginations of later centuries. Sir Charles Cavendish, son of Bess of Hardwick, built his mansion at **Bolsover**, Derbyshire, in the 1620s with the turrets, crenellations and medieval fancies so popular with the Elizabethans. As tastes began to rebel against Classical symmetry and long for 'the good old days', mock medieval 'castles' were built

*Above Caernarfon Castle, Gwynedd, built by Edward I to subdue the Welsh. Right St Andrews' 13th-century castle overlooks the North Sea.*

and some genuine 14th-century castles, such as **Croft**, in Shropshire, were 'gothicised'.

William Burges built two for the Marquess of Bute, at **Cardiff** and **Castell Coch**, reconstructing the motte and bailey castle the Normans had built at Cardiff within a Roman fort into an extravaganza rivalling the creations of Ludwig of Bavaria – with a medieval tower suite complete with smoking room, Gothic chapel and banqueting hall. At Castell Coch, to the north of Cardiff, Burges transformed the ruins of a keep destroyed in the 15th century into a mock 13th-century retreat. Its conical roofs recall the illustrations in the Duc de Berry's 'Book of Hours' but the thick walls have arrow slits and 'murder holes' and a portcullis and drawbridge which function.

The last such conceit built in Britain was designed by Edwin Lutyens, who in 1901 had made a comfortable home for the publisher of *Country Life* magazine within the ramparts of **Lindisfarne**, off the Northumbrian coast. For 20 years, from 1910, **Castle Drogo**, Lutyen's composite Norman and Tudor 'castle' arose overlooking the River Teigne in Devon, home to the founder of the Home & Colonial Stores and is – to date, at any rate – Britain's 'last castle'.

*Historic house*

*National Trust
properties*

## Historic Houses

The Greek historian, Thucydides said 'Men, not walls, make a city'. The same holds true for a house and the human stories of the builders, owners or residents add interest to it, however humble, however grand. Membership of the National Trust and English Heritage – an outlay quickly recouped if you are going to visit even half a dozen properties in a season – will give you a wonderful selection from which to choose, rich in architecture and in treasures, but above all in personalities.

The name 'Mote' at **Ightham Mote** in Kent recalls the 'moot', the council which met here, in the Great Hall, dating from 1340. Three centuries of continuous ownership by the Selby family have left their mark, from Jacobean fireplaces through 17th-century wallpaper to Victorian bedrooms. All told there are 600 years of England's history to be discerned at Ightham.

*Ightham Mote, Kent, is one of the best examples of a medieval manor house.*

Built in 1340 by a Lord Mayor of London, the Great Hall at **Penshurst Place** in Kent is the finest to have survived. Birthplace of the Elizabethan courtier, soldier and poet, Sir Philip Sidney, the house remains in the same family today. Later ranges of building have left it light and airy. The Long Gallery marries house to garden and medieval to Renaissance, a fitting memorial to the man who personified all that was best in the Elizabethan age.

The Elizabethan house Bess of Hardwick built with Sir William Cavendish at **Chatsworth** in Derbyshire has been absorbed into the present house. Chatsworth is the home of the Cavendish family, the Dukes of Devonshire, the first of whom, in the early 1700s, transformed the house into a baroque palace, a second Versailles. Treasures are everywhere – in the Painted Hall, the State Rooms, Sculpture Gallery – works by famous artists, painters and sculptors abound. The Library has over 17,000 volumes, among them those of Henry Cavendish, the 18th-century discoverer of hydrogen. Capability Brown laid out much of the garden, but retained Grillet's 1696 Cascade, the sound of the water varying as it falls over steps of different height. Joseph Paxton, too, worked here, and his Great Conservatory was the forerunner of the Crystal Palace.

**Montacute** in Somerset is one of the least altered of late Elizabethan houses. Begun in the year of the Armada, it expresses the rise to power of an astute lawyer, Edward Phelips. He led the prosecution of Guy Fawkes and became Speaker of the House of Commons. The house, with its mullioned front and statues standing in their lofty niches, is the masterpiece of a local genius, William Arnold. No one, though, who has seen the charming Elizabethan pavilions can ever doubt the delicacy and humour of this Elizabethan mason who has so completely captured his master's wish to display his continuing good fortune.

After a spell in the Tower and a stiff fine, Sir John Thynne retired to his Wiltshire estate at **Longleat**, following his support of the disgraced Lord Protector to Edward VI. He began Longleat in about 1546, and today it is still home to the Thynne family, now the Marquesses of Bath. The Great Hall, with its 16th-century fireplace and hunting scenes, is the least altered part of the house. Sir John broke from the tradition of the Elizabethan 'E-shaped' house and built around two inner courts. The top floor of the house was the library and home of Thomas Ken, Bishop of Bath and Wells, who was given refuge

here when he fell foul of both James II and William and Mary. Lord Bath, an innovator like his ancestor, opened his house to the public in 1949 and in 1966 introduced the 600-acre safari park, a 'drive-through' reserve of giraffes, rhinoceroses, elephants, tigers – and the well-known 'lions of Longleat'.

Bess of Hardwick married four times, each time increasing her fortune. She married Sir William Cavendish when she was 27 and their second son inherited Chatsworth. She left her fourth husband, the Earl of Shrewsbury, for his alleged infatuation with his prisoner, Mary, Queen of Scots. Then, aged 70, she began to build **Hardwick Hall**. The accounts of the building reflect the imperiousness of the owner who, living a hundred yards away in her old hall, strode across to inspect and criticise every day. Her descendants preferred Chatsworth and Hardwick remained, frozen in time, one of the purest examples of 16th-century design and decor in the country, a memorial to the indomitable woman whose portrait stares down from the tapestried wall of the Long Gallery.

Robert Cecil, first Earl of Salisbury, builder of **Hatfield House**, Hertfordshire, was adviser to both Elizabeth I and James I. James suggested that Robert Cecil exchange the house his father, Lord Burghley, had built at Theobalds, for the palace at Hatfield – a 'suggestion' he could scarcely refuse. Between 1607 and 1611, Cecil built himself a vast new house nearby.

Great Halls and Long Galleries were by then going out of fashion, but Hatfield would have lost much had Cecil not been traditionalist enough to include them. His own quarters and the guest wing, however, have smaller rooms. Here conversation and gracious living could flourish. The style of the great house was changing. It was a later Cecil, Marquess of Salisbury, three times Prime Minister to Queen Victoria and amateur scientist, who installed electricity in 1881 and it is reported that 'the naked wires on the Gallery ceiling tended to burst into flame, being extinguished by members of the family who threw cushions a them before returning to their conversation'.

By the time **Petworth** was built, 70 years or so after Hatfield, Long Galleries and Great Halls had gone completely from the English building scene. The house passed by marriage from the Percys to the 'Proud Duke' of Somerset, who began building – using his wife's fortune – in 1688. The name and skill of Grinling Gibbons will always be associated with Petworth. His mastery of limewood carving is complete. The house also

*Historic house*

*National Trust properties Scotland*

boasts excellent tracery work by Jonathan Ritson, and the Marble Hall has wonderful carving by John Selden, the Duke's estate carpenter.

Just to the south of Wrexham lies **Erddig**. It was completed by a local mason in 1689 and owned by the Yorke family since 1733, who collected much and threw little away! Subsidence from coal mining almost destroyed the house and restoration began in 1973. The interest of the house is not in its architecture or its treasures, but in the relationship that a local family maintained with their servants. Portraits of master and servant hang in drawing room and servants' hall, many with little poems and descriptions. There are frequent group photographs of the whole staff, enabling us to follow some servants right through their careers. Erddig is one of the few houses to show the public the maids' bedrooms as well as the public rooms. Here, 200 years of the running of a self contained estate come vividly to life.

Soldier turned dramatist on his return to England in 1692, John Vanbrugh came to the notice of Charles Howard, 3rd Earl of Carlisle, perhaps through his popular and bawdy plays. Howard chose this enthusiastic amateur to build him a home fitted to the position of an Earl, and so Castle Howard came about. Vanbrugh was widely helped by one of Sir Christopher Wren's assistants, Nicholas Hawksmoor, who turned Vanbrugh's ideas into working drawings. Castle Howard impresses

but does not overawe, as does their later work at Blenheim. At the heart of the house is the Great Hall, rising 70 feet (21m) through two storeys into the painted dome. It is the most light-hearted but impressive concept of English architecture. Treasures and portraits abound, including one of a stricken Henry VIII, painted by Holbein just after the execution of Catherine Howard, and a portrait of her uncle, Thomas Howard, who escaped the block because the king died on the day of his execution.

The story of **Blenheim Palace** is full of powerful men and women. It was built for John Churchill, Duke of Marlborough. Queen Anne instigated the idea of the palace as a reward for Churchill's victory over the French and Bavarians at the battle of Blenheim. She later quarrelled with Sarah, Duchess of Marlborough, as did Vanbrugh, the architect. Sarah wanted a comfortable country house and Vanbrugh wanted something even greater than Castle Howard. Sir Winston Churchill, born here, became Prime Minister at a time when a man of Marlborough's character was again needed.

William Adam began to build **Mellerstain** in the Scottish borders for George Baillie in 1725 and his son, Robert, finished it in 1770. It is the interiors, by Robert, that are the main attraction, for William was never able to finish the exterior as planned and it lacks a noble central block. The colours Adam used in his decorations make the rooms particularly attractive.

Above *Vanbrugh's spectacular Castle Howard, in North Yorkshire.*
Right *The beautiful Georgian mansion of Mellerstain, in the Borders.*

**The National Trust**
Many of the historic houses mentioned on these two pages are in the care of the National Trust of England, Wales and Northern Ireland and the National Trust for Scotland. Apart from maintaining many of Britain's finest buildings the Trust also owns gardens such as the renowned Hidcote Manor Garden near Chipping Campden, ruins such as **Fountains Abbey** in North Yorkshire, tracts of especially scenic shoreline, such as 110 miles of spectacular Cornish coast, follies, windmills, locks and even pubs, of which *The Fleece Inn* at Bretforton, on the edge of the Cotswolds, is a particularly attractive example. The letters 'NT' designate where the Trust owns property or land.

Museum or art gallery

*Concorde 01 is on show at the Imperial War Museum, Duxford, Cambridgeshire.*

## Museums
## Art Galleries

Among the prized possessions of the British Museum in its early days were a landscape painted on a spider's web, a two-headed chicken, Chinese shoes, figures of King William III and Queen Mary carved out of walnut shells and various unpleasant-looking things preserved in spirits and hidden in the basement in case they might frighten pregnant women. A far cry from the British Museum of today with its Elgin Marbles, Assyrian winged bulls and the Sutton Hoo treasure included in its fabulous array of objects from every corner of the globe.

The ancestors of today's museums and art galleries were the collections of classical sculptures and antiquities formed during the Renaissance period by rulers, wealthy churchmen and merchant princes like the Medicis of Florence. They were inspired by the devouring interest which had sprung up in ancient Greece and Rome. With interest also rapidly developing in science, others assembled natural history collections and 'cabinets of curiosities', which contained animal bones, weapons, coins, shells, oddly shaped plants or stones – anything that took the collector's fancy.

In England the two John Tradescants, father and son, who were keen naturalists, plant-hunters and gardeners to Charles I in the 17th century, formed a substantial collection, or 'museum' as it was called: one of its star pieces was a stuffed dodo. The collection passed to Elias Ashmole, the antiquary, herald and pioneer Freemason, who added to it and passed it on in turn to Oxford University. Twelve wagon loads of objects were conveyed to Oxford, to form the nucleus of the **Ashmolean Museum**, opened to the public in 1683 and the oldest museum in Britain.

The Ashmolean today glories in its Egyptian mummy cases and medieval jewellery, its Old Master paintings and British art, but it still honours Ashmole's memory and items from the original Tradescant collection can be seen, with other curiosities such as Guy Fawkes's lantern.

The **British Museum** opened its doors in London to 'studious and curious persons' in 1759, the word 'museum' now meaning the building in which a collection was kept rather than the collection itself. It was established by Parliament and funded by a state lottery to house the collections of Robert Harley, Earl of Oxford, and the books and manuscripts assembled by Sir Robert Cotton – which included the Lindisfarne Gospels and two copies of Magna Carta. Also included was the astonishing collection of no less than 79,575 objects put together by Sir Hans Sloane. A successful London doctor, Sloane's fanatical zeal as a collector extended to classical antiquities, coins, jewels, fossils, plants, butterflies, zoological specimens and oddities of every kind. Those who came to feast their eyes on these items consisted, as the Trustees reported in 1784, 'chiefly of Mechanics and persons of the lower Classes'.

Zeal to improve and educate 'persons of the lower classes' gained strength in the 19th century, especially in the heavily populated towns created by the industrial revolution, and prompted the establishment of numerous museums and art galleries. The splendid **City Art Gallery** in Manchester, for example was opened in 1834 and is today noted for its superb Victorian and Pre-Raphaelite paintings. The **Birmingham Museum and Art Gallery** was founded in 1867 and the building it now occupies was opened in 1885. Approximately a hundred museums opened in Britain in the 1870s and '80s.

The Victorian boom in museums and art galleries was also stimulated by an ambition to promote scientific and technological advance and to improve standards of design. This was why the **Victoria & Albert Museum** in London was founded by the Prince Consort in 1852, originally as a 'museum of manufactures', in the wake of the Great Exhibition of the previous year.

National and civic pride were also a factor. The **National Gallery** in

London is now the country's premier collection of Western painting down to 1900 (developments since then are the preserve of the **Tate Gallery**). It was founded in 1824 to emulate the national art galleries already established in Vienna, Paris, Berlin and other European capitals. The government bought 38 paintings to start it off from the collection of a banker, Sir John Julius Angerstein: they included the Rubens *Rape of the Sabine Women*, two Rembrandts and Raphael's *Portrait of Julius II.*

Major museums and galleries generally have two functions and there is often a tension between them. The obvious function is to instruct and entertain the public. The other, carried on out of the public eye, is the advancement of scholarship. An example of this dual role is the **National Museum of Wales** in Cardiff, opened in 1927 (in a building which has leaked ever since). It was founded to inform both the Welsh and the rest of the world about Wales, which it does. However, its own staff and visiting academics also work behind the scenes on collections far too voluminous for public display – 230,000 pressed plant specimens, more than 300,000 fossils, serried multitudes of dead beetles.

The museum is also a good example of the fact that the functions of an institution of this kind today go far beyond the display of objects in showcases. Activities include lectures, the loan of items to schools, and guided family walks with experts from the staff discoursing learnedly along the way.

Museums like this take a wide range of subjects for their province. Others concentrate on specialised areas. There is a museum of Scottish tartans at **Comrie**, for example, of stained glass at **Ely**, of horse racing at **Newmarket**. Military museums concentrate on regiments: the **Durham Light Infantry** in Durham, the **Staffordshire Regiment** in Lichfield, the **Royal Green Jackets** at Winchester. Some museums concentrate on World War II, such as the **German Occupation Museum** in Guernsey. Portsmouth has an unrivalled battery of naval attractions, with the excellent **Royal Naval Museum**, Nelson's flagship **HMS** *Victory*, the Tudor warship *Mary Rose* and the **Submarine Museum** in Gosport among others.

There are museums which concentrate on a single famous person: **John Bunyan** in Bedford, **Jane Austen** at Chawton, **Captain Cook** in Middlesbrough, **Barbara Hepworth** at St Ives. There are also galleries which preserve a collection

formed by a single person or family – the enchanting **Lady Lever Art Gallery** at Port Sunlight, for instance, or the gorgeous **Bowes Museum** at Barnard Castle. Some of the most rewarding preserve a collection accumulated by a business firm: **Colman's Mustard** in Norwich, the **Harvey's Wine Museum** in Bristol, the **Pilkington Glass Museum** in St Helen's, the **Bass Museum of Brewing** at Burton upon Trent, treasures of **Minton** at Stoke-on-Trent, **Wedgwood** at Barlaston, **Royal Crown Derby** in Derby.

There are agricultural museums, costume museums, museums which collect whole buildings, like the **Weald and Downland Museum** in Sussex. So does the sparkling **Welsh Folk Museum** in St Fagans, founded in 1947 and an example of the growing post-war interest in the lives of ordinary people in the past.

The **North of England Open Air Museum** at Beamish in County Durham, which is showered with awards like confetti, re-creates the way of life of working-class people in the North around the turn of the century.

Since the 1950s there has been a second museum boom, on a far greater scale than the first. There were perhaps 700 museums all told in Britain when World War II ended. There are now more than 2,000. A substantial number of these, about a third, are independent institutions, not set up by the government or the local authorities, but by private operators. To survive, they depend on their ability to attract and please paying customers and among them are some of the best museums in the country. The **National Motor Museum** at Beaulieu in Hampshire has more than 250 historic vehicles on show and visitors are carried in moving 'pods' past displays which show how motoring developed in Britain from the late 19th century on and how it may develop in the future. In Shropshire there is the marvellous **Ironbridge Gorge** complex of museums, bringing one of the key sites of the industrial revolution to life. In the old canal docks at Gloucester is the immensely enjoyable and nostalgic **Robert Opie Collection** of packets, wrappers, tins and advertising material, a museum of all our domestic yesterdays.

The best independents have contributed to the general enlivening of museums over the last 20 years. The old, musty institution of yore, full of mournful stuffed birds, prehistoric flint implements and dauntingly uninformative captions, is now a collector's item, if you can find one.

Some of the newest museums and galleries have been encouraged or funded by local authorities bent on developing tourist attractions to bring visitors and money into an area. In Bradford, for example, the **National Museum of Photography, Film and Television** opened in 1983, with the biggest cinema screen in Britain. It has galleries with 'interactive displays', where you can see yourself reading the news on TV!

There are teapots to admire in **Norwich**, trams to ride at **Crich** in Derbyshire, pork pies in **Melton Mowbray** and buns in **Abingdon**, voices in Lincolnshire dialect to listen to on the telephone in **Lincoln**, while the **Town Docks Museum** in Hull echoes to the voices of whales moaning in the deep. Certainly no one could sensibly complain of a lack of variety and interest in Britain's museums and galleries today.

*Museum or art gallery*

Below *The ship's wheel of HMS* Warrior *on show at Portsmouth.* Bottom *One of the locomotives at the National Railway Museum, in York.*

13

Industrial interest

Tourist railway
or steam centre

## Industrial Interest
## Tourist Railways
## and Steam Centres

Agriculture, industry and transport are the three principal activities through which successive generations have altered the appearance and character of Britain's landscape. Far back in the Stone Age there were axe factories in the Lake District and men wielding deer antlers as picks were digging shafts 40ft (12m) deep to mine for flint in Norfolk and Sussex. Since then the face of the land has been scarred wherever opportunity offered, by quarrying for building stone and mining for coal, iron ore, copper, lead and tin.

The great majority of Britain's sites of industrial interest today are legacies from the industrial revolution. They date roughly from the 1750s on, when water power and subsequently steam power were harnessed to the mass production of goods in mills and factories. The products were efficiently transported to customers along

Below *Handsome 18th-century Quarry Bank Mill, at Styal in Cheshire.* Bottom *The splendid iron bridge in Ironbridge in Shropshire.*

improved roads, later by canals and in the 19th century by railways.

Interest in preserving what was left of the old industrial heritage gathered strength after World War II. The term 'industrial archaeology' was coined in about 1950 and since then some exceptionally impressive sites have been rescued from dereliction or threatened destruction.

Perhaps the single most important one is the **Ironbridge Gorge** in Shropshire, where the River Severn cuts its way through steep, wooded hills. Here in the mining village of Coalbrookdale, the Darby dynasty of ironmasters succeeded in 1709 in smelting iron with coke – a fundamental advance in technology which led to the mass production of iron. It was in Coalbrookdale that the great Iron Bridge across the Severn was cast, the first important iron bridge in the world. The bridge is still there and the complex of museums and sites in the area today includes blast furnaces and engines, and a charmingly restored 1890s industrial community at Blists Hill, with a working foundry, a candle mill, other installations and railway exhibits.

The Darby family and other ironmasters pressed on to exploit the use of steam. One of the pioneers was John Wilkinson, known as 'Iron-Mad Wilkinson' because of his passionate advocacy of iron for every conceivable use. He wore an iron hat, was buried in an iron coffin when he died in 1808, and an iron obelist was raised to his memory. It was Wilkinson who patented the method of boring cylinders which made James Watt's steam engine a practical proposition. His ironworks at **Bersham**, near Wrexham in North Wales, is today the centrepiece of an industrial heritage centre. This itself is on an eight-mile trail which traces the industrial history of this area from Roman times to the present day.

Another pioneer was Richard Arkwright, the Lancashire barber turned textile magnate, who built a water-powered cotton mill in the 1770s at **Cromford** in Derbyshire, with model housing for his factory hands. The site is being restored by the Arkwright Society. In Cheshire the National Trust owns **Quarry Bank Mill** at Styal, where another factory town was created round the cotton mill by the Greg family from the 1780s on. The machinery is running again, cotton goods woven in the mill are on sale and visitors can see the huge 85ft (26m) water-wheel, the village and the house where the pauper children lived.

The vast, dinosaur-like wheels and engines of the early industrial

age always attract and awe visitors. Lead mining was long an important industry on the northern moors and an enormous wheel is the most striking feature of the **Killhope Lead Mine** in Weardale, County Durham. In Cornwall giant engines were needed to pump water out of the shafts of tin mines driven 2,000ft (610m) deep and sometimes far out under the sea. The ruined engine houses and chimney stacks of abandoned tin mines are a dramatic and melancholy feature of the Cornish landscape. The National Trust preserves two of the engines at **East Pool Mine**, near Camborne. North of St Austell, in the strange white moonscape of china clay heaps, the 19th-century **Wheal Martyn** pit is a museum of the industry.

The titanic 1876 steam engine which pumped Brighton's water up from 160ft (49m) below ground has been restored, with many other engines, at the **British Engineerium** in Hove. Machinery clatters and rattles energetically away at the **Stott Park Bobbin Mill** in Cumbria, now in the care of English Heritage. This bobbin factory built in the 1830s is virtually unchanged. Wheels turn and fan-belts flap alarmingly at **Camden Works** in Bath, in the former brass foundry of J B Bowler. Here the most elementary safety precautions were ignored. The firm also made dubious aerated soft drinks. Nothing was ever thrown away at Bowler's and the whole ramshackle place is a delight.

Scotland is not as rich in industrial sites as it might be, but drinks of quite a different kind can be sampled in a clutch of whisky distilleries in the Dufftown area. There is a 70-mile, eight-distillery Whisky Trail for enthusiasts, who are urged to let someone else do the driving.

Coal mining and ironworking were carried on for centuries on a small scale in the Forest of Dean. One of the eerier experiences in Britain is to make your way down into the echoing tunnels and caverns of the **Clearwell Caves Iron Mine**, which had its heyday between 1850 and 1900.

In Wales, among the mountains of Snowdonia, there are dramatic sites where the hillsides are torn and broken by quarrying for slate, the principal industry of the area for 200 years until quite recently. At the **Llechwedd Slate Caverns** near Blaenau Ffestiniog, visitors are taken deep underground into the tunnels and caverns, and there are demonstrations of the skilled art of slate-splitting. Close by is the **Gloddfa Ganol Slate Mine**, once the biggest in the world. At Llanberis there is a museum of the

industry in the workshops of the now-closed **Dinorwic Quarry**.

The country's most dramatic and convincing coal mining museum is in South Wales. This is **Big Pit**, near Blaenafon in Gwent, in a colliery which closed in 1980. You go down almost 300ft (90m) in the cage, wearing your miner's helmet with lamp – which you need – and an ex-miner guides the party through the tunnels.

The application of steam power to transport created the great age of railways in Britain in the 19th and 20th centuries. The landscape was changed for every by the Herculean works involved; the construction of embankments, cuttings and tunnels, the throwing of noble bridges and soaring viaducts across rivers and valleys. The sight of a powerful steam locomotive hammering along the rails at full tilt under a plume of smoke, the screaming of its whistle echoing across country, became part of the right order of things. When steam gave way to diesel and electric power, and much-loved branch lines were closed down in the 1950s and '60s, preservation societies were formed to keep steam lines running or restore them to operation.

Many of the preserved lines go through particularly attractive stretches of country. The **Severn Valley Railway** runs more trains than any other, for 16 miles close to the River Severn between Bridgnorth, Bewdley and Kidderminster. Among its steam warhorses are some fine old Great Western locomotives.

The **Bluebell Railway** in Sussex has five miles of track between Sheffield Park and Horsted Keynes, through woods shining with bluebells in the spring. The **North Yorkshire Moors Railway** steams the 18 miles from Pickering to Grosmont through superlative scenery in the North York Moors National Park and runs a Pullman service regularly. There are gaslit stations on the **Keighley and Worth Valley Railway**, whose headquarters are at Haworth in the Brontë Country. The **Lakeside & Haverthwaite Railway** puffs amicably through the Cumbrian woods to connect with the steamers on Lake Windermere.

In 19th-century England and Scotland the standard gauge of 4ft $8\frac{1}{2}$in held sway, but elsewhere, especially in mountainous areas, a narrow gauge might be better suited

to the terrain – the **Isle of Man Railway's** 15-mile line from Douglas to Port Erin, has a 3ft gauge. Wales has a special reputation for its 'great little trains', on which the traveller can enjoy the steam, the shining paintwork and polished brass, and extremely spectacular scenery.

The **Vale of Rheidol Railway**, for instance, which opened in 1902, clanks its way along the mountainsides and round sharp bends from Aberystwyth to the famous beauty spot of the Devil's Bridge. The **Ffestiniog Railway**, originally built to haul slate, clambers up into Snowdonia from the harbour of Porthmadog past lakes and waterfalls and into the mountains. Some of its genial, round-faced engines have been making the trip for a hundred years. The **Talyllyn Railway**, which has been running since 1865, travels seven miles inland from Tywyn on Cardigan Bay, with splendid mountain prospects. This was the first railway in Britain to be saved by volunteers from destruction. It set an example many were glad to follow.

*A vintage steam engine on the Brecon Mountain Railway near Merthyr Tydfil.*

*Industrial interest*

*Tourist railway or steam centre*

*Garden*

*Arboretum*

## Gardens
## Arboreta

'An Englishman's home is his castle' and round his castle he creates a garden. Despite – or perhaps because of – the vagaries of our climate, the closeness of the Gulf Stream and the collections brought back from all over the world particularly in the 18th and 19th centuries, Britain has a wonderful heritage of gardens and arboreta.

The **Royal Horticultural Society**, inaugurated in 1804, has gardens at **Wisley**, near Woking, **Rosemoor**, in Devon, as well as close affiliations with the College of Horticulture, at **Pershore** and Liverpool University Botanic Garden, at **Ness**, on the Wirral. The RHS has, since 1889, published *'The Garden'*, describing what can be seen, when and where. At all these places, keen gardeners can readily obtain advice and information.

The **Royal Botanic Garden** at Kew was established in 1759, in the reign of George II. Joining the traditional Victorian Palm and Temperate Houses, is Kew's latest feature, the Princess of Wales Conservatory, a

*The gardens at Bodnant, Gwynedd, are among the most beautiful in Britain.*

complex of 10 independently controlled climatic environments, growing a range of plants from desert to tropical forest species.

Since 1965 the National Trust property at **Wakehurst Place**, near Ardingly, has been 'Kew in the country' and it is here that a national seed bank is maintained.

As we become increasingly aware of the fragile nature of our planet's eco-system, plant collections and gene banks are more and more a vital part of horticulture. The National Council for the Conservation of Plants and Gardens has, since 1982, co-ordinated collections such as the magnolias at **Savill Garden**, near Windsor, violas at **Leicester University,** clematis at **Tenbury**, peonies at **Hidcote** and rhododendrons at **Leonardslee, Nymans** and at **Exbury. Abbotsbury,** in Devon, looks after eucalyptus and in scores of smaller gardens, amateurs as well as professionals nurture border plants, primroses, celandines, buddleias and asters. For bigger specimens, arboreta play their part. Seventeen miles of pathways lead through the 500 acres of the Forestry Commission's **Westonbirt Arboretum** in Gloucestershire, where plantings have been

continuous for 150 years. Oak, chestnut, pine and beech shelter more exotic specimens, such as acers and willows, azaleas and rhododendrons.

The **Granada Arboretum**, in Manchester, and the National Trust's **Winkworth Arboretum**, in Surrey, maintain sorbus and malus. Winter-flowering plants such as daphnes, honeysuckle, camellias and viburnum can be seen at the **Hillier Arboretum**, near Romsey, and plants which flourish on chalky soils are the specialty of **Hidcote Manor Garden**, north of Chipping Campden.

Many of the gardens lovingly tended in the past have now been restored. At **New Place,** in Surrey, the Edwardian garden of Gertrude Jekyll was recovered from beneath couch grass and poppies. At East Grinstead, the mullioned windows of 16th-century **Gravetye Manor** now reflect the glory of a Victorian garden created by William Robinson. At **Erddig**, near Wrexham, another 18th-century design has been re-created in the grounds of the National Trust house and **Culpeper Flower Garden** now flourishes at **Leeds Castle**, in Kent, 17th-century home of the Culpeper family. The 18th-century garden at

**Painshill Park** in Surrey was laid out in the 1740s by Charles Hamilton. Sadly decayed, the combination of classical architecture, lake and landscaping is being restored and it may once again rival the garden of Hamilton's friend, Henry Hoare at Stourhead.

Gardens stretch the length and breadth of the British isles. **Inverewe,** in Wester Ross, despite its northern latitude, enjoys frost-free conditions, due to the warm North Atlantic Drift, and **Tresco Abbey Gardens** in the Scilly Isles, created and maintained since 1834 by successive generations of the same family, relishes mild, moist weather. In the 1790s garden of 13th-century **Drum Castle**, near Aberdeen, a collection illustrating the development of roses from the 17th-century has recently been created by the National Trust for Scotland.

The **University Botanic Gardens** at St Andrews, training ground for future professionals, also provide a well laid out and informative garden for the visitor. Its high point is the peat, water and rock complex simulating the natural progression from mountain crag to scree to meadow and bog. The **Royal Botanic Garden**, in Edinburgh, second oldest in the country after Oxford, also has a superb rock garden and, like the new conservatory at Kew, grows the astonishing *Victoria Amazonica* water lily, its huge leaves capable of supporting a small child, but which grow from seed annually.

Across on the west coast are the gardens of **Brodick Castle**, on the Isle of Arran. Sir John Ramsden, then owner of **Muncaster Castle**, in Cumbria, after a visit to Brodick sent his hostess some rhododendrons for her garden – in all 80 tons! In 1953 an expedition to Burma brought back hundreds more plants and yet more varieties, most of which flourish in the mild climate.

At **Belsay**, north of Newcastle, English Heritage has restored the gardens, partly in the quarry used by Charles Monck, a keen member of the Horticultural Society. At **Thorp Perrow**, near Ripon, there is a cherry avenue which is a riot of blossom in May. Several 'autumn bays' provide colour from September to November and there is a rowan avenue, with spring blossom and autumn berries.

John Aislabie, Chancellor of the Exchequer at the time of the South Sea Bubble, retired to his estate at **Studley Royal**, in Yorkshire, albeit under something of a cloud. The garden he designed is a work of true inspiration, anticipating

Stourhead by 40 years. It now incorporates the ready-made 'folly', so essential to Romantic landscaping, acquired when his son purchased the nearby Fountains Abbey.

**Harlow Carr Botanical Garden**, near Harrogate, has been since 1948 the headquarters of the Northern Horticultural Society, working closely with the RHS and offering a similar range of walks, workshops and demonstrations as Wisley. **Newby Hall,** near Ripon, has something to delight the eye all year round, but is best known for its display of roses in early summer and its herbaceous border plants.

At **Eaton Hall**, Eccleston, near Chester, there is an unheated glasshouse 360 feet (110m) long, with camellias which are usually at their best in April. **Bodnant**, near Llandudno, always associated with the Aberconway family, has rhododendrons, azaleas, magnolias and camellias. Here, too, there is a wonderful laburnum walk where, on a sunny day in May, you can walk through a tunnel of glorious yellow blossom. Near Welshpool is **Powis Castle**, once the home of Clive of India. Its terraces are one of the few remaining medieval-style gardens in the country.

**Doddington Hall,** south-west of Lincoln, was built by the Elizabethan architect, Smythson, who designed Longleat and Hardwick Hall. The garden, even as late as 1919, had cattle grazing on the lawns, but now the walled west garden is full of the old-fashioned roses for which Doddington is famous, as well as a profusion of irises.

Near Colchester, **Beth Chatto's Garden** covering 12 acres, has developed into a centre where gardeners can pick up hints on what grows best in hard-baked sandy soil, sour silt or waterlogged clay. At **Sissinghurst**, in Kent, the garden of this Tudor house is a monument to Vita Sackville-West who, in the 1930s, created walks where each of the gardens opening off had its own colour scheme.

In **Sheffield Park**, near East Grinstead, famous for its autumn colours, you can wander away from the lakeside rhododendrons and discover the wonderful collection of conifers. One group of maritime pines is reputed to have been planted by Sir Joseph Banks, a founder of the RHS. David Douglas, after whom the Douglas fir is named, brought Monterey pines here from California and there is a dwarf Siberian pine planted in the 1920s, which has just about reached five feet (one and a half metres) and can thus be highly recommended for the small garden!

The National Trust property at **Kingston Lacy** in Dorset, has a delightful fernery planted with snowdrops for an early effect and the Cedar Walk has carefully recorded plantings by the Duke of Wellington, King Edward VII, the Kaiser and King George V, who planted an oak here to commemorate his Coronation. At **Stourhead**, north of Shaftesbury, lake, bridge, temples and grottoes combine to achieve one of the finest 'landscaped' gardens in the world, the creation of Henry Hoare in the 1740s, a generation before Capability Brown began diverting rivers and moving mountains around many of the great houses of his day.

**Penjerrick**, in Cornwall, was begun in the 1830s and many exotic plants here were grown from seed brought into nearby Falmouth by clipper captains, but rhododendrons remain one of its glories.

Wherever you go, at no matter what season of the year, there are gardens to be enjoyed all over Britain. Provided you do not pick a Bank Holiday weekend, in most cases you will find someone ready to pass on the secret of their success to you.

*Garden*

*Arboretum*

*Hillier Arboretum in Hampshire.*

*Country park*

*The forested slopes at Afan Argoed resemble those in Switzerland.*

## Country Parks

In the 1960s and '70s, increasing affluence, more leisure time, more cars and faster roads combined to bring the open countryside within the reach of far more people. The number of townspeople and suburbanites driving out for a day in the country was growing rapidly and there was a need to accommodate the demand without spoiling the countryside which everyone was eager to enjoy.

In 1966 a government white paper on 'Leisure in the Countryside' suggested the establishment of country parks and the idea was taken up in the Countryside Acts which followed. The two Countryside Commissions, one for England and Wales, the other for Scotland, were given the responsibility for stimulating the creation of country parks, providing advice and grants of taxpayers' money to projects they approved.

Most of the country parks have been set up by local authorities. One of their fundamental functions is to make available country places where visitors know they have a right to be. Opinion polls and studies have shown time and time again that people are held back from enjoying the countryside by an uneasy feeling that they may be trespassing or at least not wanted. A country park is a place where you are welcome. It is also a place where there will be toilets and somewhere to park the car.

There are now more than 200 country parks in Britain, varying considerably in size and character. The larger ones have visitor centres where you will find information about the landscape, the wildlife and often the area's history; wardens or rangers who keep an eye on things and provide help and information when needed; way-marked paths; amusements for children, and refreshments.

Country parks are usually open every day during daylight hours, and in the great majority of them admission is free, though boating, bowls or other special facilities may have to be paid for. Activities vary from one park to another – from riding, fishing, hang-gliding and grass-skiing to orienteering, golfing, boating and sailing.

Some of the earliest country parks were areas which were already heavily visited and where better facilities were needed. An example is **Box Hill**, near Dorking in Surrey, named after the rare wild box trees on the chalk hill. For centuries past people have loved to walk there and admire the views of the Weald. Much of the area is owned by the National Trust and there is a car park, information room and shop.

Another case in point is **Butser Hill**, a much-visited beauty spot on the A3 south of Petersfield where

Hampshire County Council created the **Queen Elizabeth Country Park,** opened by the Queen in 1976. The park covers 1,400 acres of downs, Forestry Commission beechwoods and stands of yew at the western edge of the South Downs Way footpath. There are splendid views from the top of Butser Hill, a nature reserve and waymarked trails, with downland plants and flowers to see, woodpeckers, butterflies and deer. The Ancient Farm Research Project here farms the way Iron Age man did 2,000 years ago and the park has an information centre with an audio-visual programme, a café and a picnic area.

Another heavily visited area is the **Brimham Rocks Country Park** on the moors near Pateley Bridge in North Yorkshire. The rocks, weathered into strange shapes over the centuries, drew sightseers in such numbers that the area was in danger of being badly damaged. It is owned by the National Trust and the threat to the rocks has been brought under control.

Since country parks were intended primarily for town dwellers, they tend to be more numerous close to heavily populated urban areas. They are not thick on the ground in Norfolk and Suffolk, for example, but there is quite a concentration of them in Essex, nearer London. One of these is the attractive **Hatfield Forest Country Park**, near Bishop's Stortford, an area of ancient hunting forest which was only just rescued from the developer's grasp in the 1920s and which is famous for its hornbeams and its nightingales.

Similarly, there are fewer country parks in North and Central Wales than in the former mining and industrial areas of South Wales. One of the biggest and best is **Margam Country Park**, near Port Talbot. Its 850 acres include what were once the stately grounds of the Mansel family's fine house. There are landscaped gardens, a deer park, a handsome orangery which is used for concerts, a theatre, a large maze and boating on the lake, which is also occupied by swans, coots and moorhens. A herd of Glamorgan cattle and an Iron Age hillfort with commanding views over the Bristol Channel add to its enormous appeal. There is an adventure playground, a heronry in the nature reserve and there are skylarks and buzzards. Just outside the park is the ruined church of 12th-century Margam Abbey.

Many other parks have solved the problem of what to do with fine country estates the owners can no longer keep up. **Mount Edgcumbe Country Park**, which looks out over Plymouth Sound, preserves the formal gardens with their statues and fountains laid out for the Edgcumbe family in the 18th century. Stretching for miles along the coast, it boasts follies, woods, a deer park and a fabulous collection of camellias.

Many country parks, by contrast, have contributed to the reclamation of derelict industrial wasteland. East of Sheffield, on the border of Yorkshire and Derbyshire, the **Rother Valley Country Park** has arisen phoenix-like from an area of opencast coal mining, with 350,000 freshly planted trees and no less than three lakes for fishing and watersports. There are footpaths and visitors can hire cycles to ride along the network of bicycle tracks.

The **Strathclyde Country Park** in the south-eastern outskirts of Glasgow was formally opened in 1978. Millions of pounds were spent to take a derelict, stagnant wasteland of exhausted colliery workings and desolate spoil heaps and turn it back into pleasant countryside. The River Clyde was diverted to create a 200-acre loch, trees and shrubs and long stretches of grass were planted, paths were laid out by the loch and picnic areas and car parks provided.

Now the trees have matured. The loch, almost two miles long, is a watersports centre for sailing, canoeing and waterskiing. There is a golf course and sports pitches, an interpretation centre and a nature reserve which attracts wintering whooper swans and other waterfowl. Also inside the park are the remains of a Roman fort and a peculiar 19th-century mausoleum, which was constructed for the Dukes of Hamilton but turned out to have such a noisy echo in the chapel inside that it was impossible to use it.

Country park landscapes vary from the heath and scrub of **Cannock Chase** in Staffordshire to the giant trees in **Sherwood Forest**, the ducal landscape by Capability Brown not far away in **Clumber Park** in Nottinghamshire and on to the deer and rugged rocks of **Bradgate Park** in Leicestershire, with the ruins of the house in which the tragic Lady Jane Grey grew up. On top of **Ham Hill** in Somerset, the grassed-over stone quarries make a wonderful arena for hide-and-seek. On **Berry Head**, south of Torbay in South Devon, towering cliffs command bracing views of the English Channel and the nests of kittiwakes and guillemots. The need to protect the wild orchids and other rare plants here was one reason why the local council bought the land in 1968. Further on along the Channel coast, at the **Lepe Country Park** in Hampshire, you can look across the Solent to the Isle of Wight and idly watch the ships and the black-headed gulls go by.

One question which remains is: are the visitors at country parks enjoying real countryside or a mock-up? Nowadays the Countryside Commission believes that the parks should be treated less as ends in themselves and more as gateways to the true countryside beyond.

*Brimham Rocks, in North Yorkshire, where the rocks form weird shapes.*

*Country park*

*Theme park*

*The 'Thunder River' rapid-water ride, for all the family, at Thorpe Park.*

## Theme Parks

The British theme park has its spiritual ancestor across the Atlantic. Disneyland, which opened in Anaheim in the southern suburbs of Los Angeles in 1955, combined four basic characteristics. First there was a central theme – the world of Disney cartoons and films. Second, there were illusions, using the latest technology, and visitors experienced a simulated river trip in the African jungle, or thought they were going deep underwater in a submarine, when in fact they were only a few inches beneath the surface. Next, there were 'white knuckle' rides – an exciting roller-coaster, a terrifying helter-skelter and other thrilling fairground rides, again using the latest technology. And last, Disneyland catered for the motor car, the family with children and modern mass tourism, with a parking lot of gargantuan proportions and an ample supply of toilets and places to eat.

The lessons of Disneyland were absorbed and put to use at **Alton Towers**, the 500-acre 'leisure park' in Staffordshire which is now attracting two and a half million visitors a year. Alton Towers employs a staff of 1,400 people during the summer and has six different restaurants, of varying types and price levels, with innumerable kiosks scattered about the grounds selling ice-creams and soft drinks. There is no single central theme, but six 'themed areas', which include Fantasy World, Aqualand and Kiddies Kingdom. Among the 'white knuckle' rides are the gravity-defying Corkscrew Roller-coaster, which lives up to its name, as well as the New Black Hole, the Alton Beast, and the water-based Log Flume

and Grand Canyon Rapids Ride.

There are gentler rides for those of nervous disposition or with small children, with a beautiful carousel, and a mass of indoor attractions and Disney-style parades with bands, floats and performers in life-size animal costumes.

In addition to all this is a wonderful Victorian Gothic ruin and some of the most spectacular gardens in the country, inherited from the Earls of Shrewsbury, whose country seat Alton Towers used to be. The 15th and 16th Earls constructed an enormous pseudo-medieval fantasy palace here, replete with towers and spires, turrets and battlements. A W Pugin himself, the high priest of Victorian Gothic, was called in to preside over the interior decor. Outside, meanwhile, a fortune was spent to lay out a magnificent park and gardens. Lakes and pools were dug out, fed by water brought from a spring two miles off. Terraces, miles of walks, giant stairways and grand glasshouses were built at colossal expense by an army of workmen.

The future Queen Victoria visited Alton in 1832, at the age of 13, and was entertained to luncheon on gold plates. The Chinese-style Pagoda Fountain was built, and shoots a jet of water 70ft (21m) high. A Swiss cottage was erected on the hillside to provide a fine prospect over the grounds while a blind Welsh harper was stationed there to play soothing music. Today it is a restaurant.

In later years it proved impossible to keep the house up and the mansion fell into the condition of picturesque ruin in which visitors see it now. The gardens were properly maintained, however, and are a delight to walk in today.

More 'white knuckle' rides can be found by the adventurous at the **Chessington World of Adventures**, in Surrey. 'This Ride Is Not For The

Faint-Hearted' one sign warns. There is a blood chilling roller-coaster called the Vampire, which zooms along at tree-top height and dives underground. It is set in a 'Transylvania' village which also has a bubble works fantasy ride for children through a simulated fizzy pop factory, and a restaurant wittily named the Black Forest Chateau.

The theme areas at Chessington feature encounters with horrible science fiction monsters, and Calamity Canyon, where there's a Wild West trading post, a shooting gallery and a roller-coaster called the Runaway Mine Train. In the Mystic East area visitors see the Palace of the Nine Dragons, the Giant Buddha and the Cambodian temple of Angkor Wat, and go on a 'dragon river' water ride through a bamboo jungle, where the boat is attacked by a crocodile. In addition, Chessington has a zoo, a circus, a miniature railway, plenty of eating places and live entertainment with bands, dancers, clowns, street performers and 'madcap' characters in costume.

Halfway between Derby and Nottingham may seem an odd place to meet cowboys and shoot-outs, but the Wild West is one of the main themes at the **American Adventure**, near Ilkeston in Derbyshire. Pistol-packing posses career through town, bullets fly and saloon girls squeal as badmen get their come-uppances. There is live entertainment in Lazy Lil's Saloon and jazz on a Mississippi riverboat.

The numerous rides include a double-drop log flume in Thunder Canyon and a charge through the raging torrents of the Great Niagara Rapids. Or you can take a triple-looping roller-coaster called the Missile and blast off to the stars from Space Port USA. There are special attractions to keep small children happy in Pioneer Playland, including a cartoon cinema.

At the **Pleasurewood Hills American Theme Park**, near Lowestoft in Suffolk, southern fried chicken is on the menu, and attractions range from the evil Rattlesnake roller-coaster and the New Tempest, which hangs you upside down 100ft (30m) in the air, to a waterborne voyage to Aladdin's Cave, a land of dinosaurs, fairground big wheels, a spooky haunted castle and shows by performing sea lions and parrots.

In Yorkshire, near Ripon, the **Lightwater Valley Theme Park**, in the 1970s a peaceful pig farm, prides itself on the sheer appalling terror of its 'white knuckle' rides. It opened the longest roller-coaster ride in the world in 1990, at a cost of over £5 million, running close to

1¹/₂ miles (2.4km) with a drop of 158ft (48m) and a top speed of about 60mph. This joined a nightmare ride called The Rat, which runs entirely underground in pitch darkness, 'through smelly sewers alive with the shrieks and shrills of rats' – rated tops for sheer horror by the *Daily Mirror*.

There are calmer pleasures at Lightwater Valley, too – a nine-hole golf course, three boating lakes, an old-fashioned fairground, a miniature railway and a shopping centre. There is skateboarding, a go-kart track, an adventure playground for smaller children and a theatre with live entertainment.

At Charnock Richard in Lancashire, there awaits 'an enchanted day out for the whole family' in 'the magical kingdom' of **Camelot.** The theme here is the world of King Arthur and his heroic knights of the Round Table. Knights in full armour thunder into combat on their chargers in the jousting arena. Jesters and grotesque animal figures wander about. A chilling roller-coaster hurtles into the Tower of Terror, where something unspeakable called the Beast lurks in its dark lair. Guinevere's swan ride negotiates Merlin's magic mountain, the Grail trail crosses a swinging rope bridge and Sir Bedevere's Bridge leads to the enchantments of the Wild Wood.

You can eat at the Round Table Burger Bar, naturally, but altogether Camelot has 28 outlets selling food and drink. It reckons to cook 2¹/₂ miles of sausages every season, as well as 250,000 pounds of dragon burgers and 315,000 pounds of chips.

The 'family leisure park' at **Thorpe Park**, near Chertsey in Surrey, is close to both the M3 and the M25. It opened in 1979 on the site of old gravel workings, which gave it plenty of lakes and pools. Water skiing, windsurfing and other watersports rank high among its pleasures, water barges carry visitors from one area of the park to another and there are river-boat restaurants.

The original theme was Britain's maritime history, but now, with the need to attract repeat visitors, the emphasis has changed. 'White knuckle' rides are not particularly important here and the park concentrates more on entertainments and amusements which families with children aged about four to 14 can all enjoy together. There is live entertainment at two theatres, lots of street entertainment, musicians, clowns and giant sub-Disney animal grotesques, and a large amusement centre with video games and one-armed bandits. The log flume ride in the Canadian Rockies theme area has a drop of 50ft and there is a fast Space Station Zero ride, but more typical is the complete working farm, which operates as it did in the 1930s. A simulated medieval town square has a double-decker carousel and other attractions include a nature trail, miniature railway, roller skating rink, crazy golf and a cartoon cinema.

All theme parks are geared to a safe, enjoyable family day out, and you pay once, on entry, and get the rides and other attractions thrown in. Alton Towers is the kingpin in terms of visitor figures, but the numbers rung up at the other parks – over a million and a quarter at Thorpe Park and a similar figure at Chessington – suggest that this type of transatlantic family attraction is in Britain to stay.

*The 'Runaway Mine Train' at Chessington World of Adventures.*

*Theme Park*

*Zoo*

*Wildlife collection – mammals*

*Wildlife collection – birds*

*Aquarium*

## Zoos
## Wildlife Collections
## Aquariums

The oldest picture of an elephant in England is in Exeter Cathedral, a 13th-century wood carving under one of the choir seats. It is quite likely to be a portrait of a real African elephant, the one which was presented to Henry III by the King of France in 1253. Its arrival in England created a sensation and people flocked to see the great beast as it tramped from the port of Sandwich to London.

### Zoos
The century before, Henry I had established a menagerie at Woodstock in Oxfordshire. It was later moved to the Tower of London and survived there until well into the 19th century. The public was let in to see the animals, which in 1609 consisted of 11 lions, two leopards, a jackal, two mountain cats, three eagles and two owls.

Kings and noblemen continued to keep private menageries, but the 19th century saw the creation of public zoological gardens – zoos for short – as part of the same educational and improving impulse responsible for the establishment of so many museums. The first in the field was the **Regent's Park Zoo** in London, laid out by Decimus Burton and opened in 1828 by the recently founded Zoological Society of London. The animals from the Tower were moved here.

Municipal zoos now opened, combining serious study of animals with public instruction and entertainment. In Dublin, for example, the Royal Zoological Society of Ireland opened a zoo in **Phoenix Park** in 1830. It gained a substantial reputation for breeding lions, as **Glasgow Zoo** breeds porcupines and Edinburgh Zoo is famous for its penguins.

### Wildlife Collections
After World War II, a tide of disapproval set in against the old-fashioned 19th-century zoo, which seemed little better than a prison with its cramped cages and unnatural conditions, and against the whole attitude to animals which this type of zoo was felt to represent. The consequence was the modernisation of many zoos and the coming of the safari park and a new style of wildlife collection. The development of the open-range zoo, where animals roam in large enclosures instead of being penned in cages, had begun in 1931, when the Zoological Society of London opened a country branch at **Whipsnade Park** in Bedfordshire, near Dunstable. Whipsnade covers

*The famous lions of Longleat.*

more than 500 acres, most of the animals live in herds in sizeable paddocks and well over 90 per cent of them were born in the zoo. In the last 30 years many other zoos have moved closer to the open-range system.

Britain's first safari park opened in 1966 at **Longleat** in Wiltshire, the palatial Elizabethan seat of the Marquess of Bath. The prime movers in the enterprise were the Marquess himself and Jimmy Chipperfield, of the well-known circus family, an experienced supplier of wild animals to zoos. The idea was for visitors to drive through the spacious enclosures where the animals roamed: in other words, for a change, the animals would be free and the public confined. The project proved extremely popular.

Lions were the first and have always been the foremost attraction at Longleat, but many other animals can be seen there today – including the country's only white Bengal tiger, as well as white rhinos, camels, giraffes and gorillas. The monkeys enjoy riding on visitors' cars and there are boat trips to see hippos and sea lions. In some areas visitors can leave their cars and stroll about or even have a picnic among the animals. Like other safari parks, Longleat depends on and provides for the motor car and there is plenty of parking with no problem about finding a restaurant or a toilet.

The Duke of Bedford was not far behind in opening a safari park of his own at his stately Bedfordshire mansion of **Woburn**. Jimmy Chipperfield was again involved. But Woburn already had a distinguished history of keeping and breeding wild animals. Père David's deer are named after a French missionary, who saw the only remaining herd of them in the imperial park outside Peking where they were kept in the 19th century. A few animals were grudgingly shipped out to European zoos and

*Flamingoes at Slimbridge Wildfowl Trust*

when the Chinese herd was wiped out, the 16 Père David's deer in Europe were the only ones left. The 11th Duke of Bedford rounded all 16 up in 1894 and settled them in his park at Woburn, where they prospered and multiplied. All the Père David's deer in the world are descended from them, and in 1985 some were sent back to China, to the same park outside Peking.

Woburn also played a part in saving the European bison from extinction. The Père David's deer are still there, and so are the bison, and the **Woburn Wild Animal Kingdom** today is Britain's largest drive-through collection of wild creatures. A ride in aerial cars gives a bird's eye view of the park and there are performing sea lions, and even performing macaws.

A wildlife collection of an entirely different flavour can be enjoyed at **Chillingham**, in Northumberland, where visitors can cautiously inspect the 50-strong herd of wild white cattle. With their wicked, curving horns, they are the nearest thing to prehistoric cattle still in existence. They have been kept in the park at Chillingham for centuries and have never been crossbred.

John Aspinall has set up two Kent

*Zoo*

*Wildlife collection – mammals*

*Wildlife collection – birds*

*Aquarium*

zoo parks: **Howletts**, near Canterbury, famous for breeding gorillas and African elephants, and its sister at **Port Lympne**, near Hythe. Here magnificent Siberian tigers, black rhino and the country's only breeding colony of majestic Barbary lions loll about in aristocratic splendour.

Breeding animals, and especially breeding species which in the wild are threatened with extinction, has become an important function of zoos, safari parks and wildlife collections, and a key justification of their existence. **Chester Zoo**, for example, which ranks second only to London in its tally of visitors and has a wide range of animals in attractive grounds, has successfully bred orang-utans, Madagascan tree boas and rare fruit bats, among other species. **Bristol Zoo**, where the creatures on view range from tigers to tarantulas and penguins to piranhas, counts gorillas and orang-utans, Persian leopards, colobus monkeys and long-tailed macaques among its breeding successes. **Twycross Zoo**, near Atherstone in Warwickshire, a small zoo with a remarkable collection of apes and monkeys, has a notable breeding record and **Marwell**, near Winchester, breeds rare Sumatran tigers and the endangered oryx.

In 1947 there were only 50 breeding pairs of the Hawaiian geese (called nene) left in the world, all of them in Hawaii. The species was saved by successful breeding at the Wildfowl & Wetlands Trust reserve at **Slimbridge** in Gloucestershire, founded by the late Sir Peter Scott. Some of the birds from here were later sent back to Hawaii in the hope of re-establishing them in their native land.

The splendid Slimbridge reserve is on the bank of the River Severn. Other Wildfowl Trust reserves include those at **Arundel** in Sussex, **Washington** in Tyne and Wear, and **Caerlaverock**, near Dumfries in Scotland. At **Stagsden** in Bedfordshire is one of the first specialist bird collections in Britain. The Bird Gardens concentrate on cranes, but there are 150 species or more on view in all. **Birdworld**, near Farnham in Surrey, has a collection ranging from tiny hummingbirds to outsize ostriches, and is successfully breeding Humboldt penguins.

**Aquariums**

The first public aquarium in Britain opened in London in 1853. It was not until a hundred years later that the first massive sea aquariums, or oceanariums, opened in the United States, with huge tanks containing

*The 'Penguin Parade' – the star attraction at Edinburgh Zoo.*

hundreds of fish of different species swimming together. The example has been followed in Britain, for example at the **Sea Life Centre** in Weymouth, which opened in 1983 with the biggest display tank in Europe. Visitors can see dolphins and porpoises, British sharks, octopus and squid and evil-looking conger eels, and fish in drifting droves. There is a special flatfish tank and a tank with a simulated sunken wreck and the marine life that would gather around it. There are also 'touch pools' and plenty of fun for children.

Of the same genre, but on a much more modest scale, is **Anglesey Sea Zoo**, near Brynsiencyn, close to the shore of the Menai Strait, with its tanks of fish, lobsters and crabs from the local waters and 'touch tanks' for the children.

There is plenty of enjoyment and discovery at other sea life centres in seaside towns, like Brighton, Blackpool and Southsea and at Barcaldine in Scotland where young seals can be viewed prior to their release back into the wild. While wildlife is increasingly threatened in the wild, it flourishes in British zoos, safari parks and aquariums.

23

*Nature reserve*

*RSPB site*

**Nature Reserves**
**Nature Trails**
**RSPB Sites**

**Brownsea Island** is a much-treasured Dorset beauty spot, a 500-acre island in Poole Harbour, accessible only by boat. It has an honoured place in the history of the Boy Scouts, as it was here in 1907 that General Baden-Powell held his first scout camp. A succession of wealthy and sometimes eccentric owners preserved the island from contamination by development until, with the death of the last of them in 1961, it passed to the National Trust. It was then a wildly overgrown paradise for red squirrels, the late owner's peacocks, Sika deer, herons and seabirds. The National Trust has protected it ever since and thousands of visitors go there every year to enjoy the beaches, walk the heathland and woodland glades and admire stunning views of the Dorset coast.

A substantial area of the island is sealed off against casual visitors dropping in, though parties are guided round at regular intervals. This is a nature reserve, managed by the Dorset Trust for Nature Conservation, with a heronry, two lakes and a marsh fringed with reeds, where wildfowl congregate in

*A view from a hide overlooking Welney Wildfowl Refuge, in Norfolk.*

safety – terns and oystercatchers, godwits and sandpipers, dunlins and redshanks.

**Nature Reserves**

Unlike a National Park or a country park, a nature reserve is not protected for the sake of human visitors, but for the sake of the wild creatures, birds, insects and rare plants, and the habitats and conditions they need to survive and flourish. Many nature reserves are open to the general public; at others a permit may be needed or access may be limited, but some are closed altogether.

As long ago as 1912 the need to set aside areas in which threatened species could survive was recognised with the founding of the Society for the Promotion of Nature Reserves by the pioneering naturalist Charles Rothschild. When he died the movement lost impetus. After World War II, however, the pressure of expanding population and expanding leisure time bore so heavily on the country's wildlife that something plainly needed to be done. In 1949 the government set up the Nature Conservancy Council (NCC) as its wildlife protection arm, and one of the new body's responsibilities was 'to establish, manage and maintain nature reserves'.

At the same time vigorous county and local wildlife protection trusts were forming and establishing nature reserves of their own. Charles Rothschild's society re-emerged into the limelight as the national organisation and mouthpiece of these groups, as the Royal Society for Nature Conservation.

Today Britain has more than 2,000 nature reserves, occupying more than half a million acres of land between them. Some are managed by the NCC, but a far larger number are run by the county or local trusts for nature conservation, naturalists' trusts or wildlife trusts. Others are owned and managed by the Forestry Commission, others again by local authorities and conservation bodies.

From a visitor's point of view, nature reserves supply a way of seeing and coming close to the full range of Britain's wildlife and plant life without any danger of trespassing or going where one is not wanted. They can be found on the coast and inland, on high ground and on low, in a great variety of countryside.

At **Caerlaverock**, for instance, on the Solway Firth coast of Scotland, the NCC established a reserve in 1957 on the low-lying saltmarshes among muddy flats and creeks. Multitudes of birds feed and roost there: golden plovers in legions,

greylag geese, pintail and all manner of ducks and waders. Thousands of barnacle geese fly in from the Arctic every winter, and there are birds of prey, as well as saltmarsh plants in abundance. This is also one of the breeding grounds of the rare and noisy natterjack toad. Visitor access is limited, partly because the flats and creeks are dangerous when the tide sweeps in suddenly. There is also a Wildfowl Trust refuge close by and the romantic pink ruin of Caerlaverock Castle to visit.

By contrast, not so many miles away inland, east of Newton Stewart, the NCC runs the **Cairnsmore of Fleet** nature reserve, largely a trackless waste of peat and heather moorland, bog and mountainside. It is important as the home of the red deer, wild goats and ravens. Access is again restricted.

Similarly, there is a cluster of contrasting nature reserves in the Gower Peninsula of South Wales, which is famed for packing a remarkable variety of scenery into a small area, and for the accompanying wealth of wildlife. At **Cwmllwyd Wood**, west of Swansea, for instance, West Glamorgan County Council has a reserve of oak woods, grassland and marsh, with hides from which to watch snipe and woodcock. At **Oxwich** on the south coast there is an NCC reserve of quite different character in an area of sand dunes, wooded headlands and marshes, explored by nature trails. Keep an eye out for adders on the slopes.

### RSPB Sites

Some of the most rewarding nature reserves in the country belong to the Royal Society for the Protection of Birds (RSPB). Founded in 1889, the RSPB is devoted to the conservation of wild birds. It has built up a portfolio of well over a hundred reserves in which the habitats of breeding and wintering birds and birds of passage are preserved.

Some of the RSPB reserves are as far flung as the **Orkneys** and **Shetlands**, but most of them are more accessible. There is one at **Dungeness** on the Kent coast, where the nuclear power station broods over a desolate landscape of shingle beach, ponds and abandoned gravel workings, and tangled gorse and brambles. But there is plenty of life here – marsh frogs, plants like viper's bugloss, and waterfowl in huge numbers, with many migrating birds making a landfall at this point.

Up in Lancashire, at **Leighton Moss** near Silverdale, the RSPB preserves an area of swamp,

*The 300ft (91m) high cliffs of Marwick Head's RSPB reserve, Orkney.*

shallow meres and scrubland. Here bitterns boom and breed among the reeds and marsh harriers pass by in spring, while below are otters, deer, bats and beautiful wild orchids.

The Forest of Dean is one of the few remaining ancient royal forests left in England. Although commercial forestry plantations have replaced much of the original oak woods, there are still a few areas where magnificent oaks over 150 years old can be found. One of these is at the RSPB **Nagshead Reserve** which covers some of the best remaining oak woodland and has a rich bird community. Summer visitors include wood warblers, redstarts and pied flycatchers as well as the whole range of woodland species including all three species of woodpecker, sparrowhawks, treecreepers and nuthatches.

At **Nene Washes** in Cambridgeshire the RSPB reserve, saved from drainage and ploughing, is an example of a landscape now nearly lost. Once, hay meadows like these – rich in flowers in spring and full of birds in winter – were common; now there are only scattered remnants left. It is ironic that the washes are entirely man-made, created in the 18th century as part of flood control and drainage schemes. Breeding birds here include redshanks, snipe, sedge warblers, yellow wagtails and shovelers. Winter brings Bewick's swans, wigeon, teal and pintails in large numbers.

On the north-west tip of Holy Island, is the RSPB reserve of **South Stack Cliffs**. This reserve consists of two separate areas: the dramatic sea cliffs and heathland of Holyhead Mountain make up the northern part, while the maritime heathland of Penrhosfeilw Common is the

southern section. The most numerous seabirds are guillemots but there are razorbills, puffins and kittiwakes. The reserve is one of the foremost migration watchpoints in North Wales, both for landbirds and seabirds. On most summer days, especially with a westerly wind, Manx shearwaters and gannets may be seen flying past, while in spring and autumn large movements of passerines can be recorded in suitable weather conditions. Hundreds of wheatears and swallows may pass through daily, with smaller numbers of willow and grasshopper warblers, whinchats and ring ouzels. In early winter thousands of starlings, chaffinches and other species pass westward to the warmer climate of Ireland.

One of the RSPB's most celebrated reserves is **Bempton Cliffs** near Goole. These spectacular 445ft chalk cliffs hold the largest breeding colony of seabirds in England. Puffins and guillemots nest here but the most famous of Bempton's seabirds is the gannet, whose colony is the only mainland one in Britain. Seawatching can be exceptionally good, especially in the autumn, when the terns and skuas are moving south. The narrow band between the cliffs and the cliff-top fields is an excellent place for wild flowers.

Though the primary purpose of a reserve is protection, the RSPB welcomes visitors – the general public as well as its own members – in order to encourage public sympathy and support for conservation. Trails and hides are provided to help visitors see as much as possible, while interfering as little as possible with the birds.

## National Trails

Enthusiasm for long distance walking has grown apace in Britain since World War II, as part of a general quickening of appetite for exploring and enjoying the countryside at first hand, away from main roads and crowded tourist spots. The first national long distance walking route, the Pennine Way, was declared open in 1965. Since then many more paths have been established. Ten of them are now classified by the Countryside Commission as 'national trails'. These are continuous routes over substantial distances, which can take a week or more to traverse though, of course, many people enjoy walking for only a few hours or a day or two on part of one of the routes.

The ten national trails in England and Wales are: the Cleveland Way; the North Downs Way; the Offa's Dyke Path; the Peddars Way and Norfolk Coast Path; the Pembrokeshire Coast Path; the Pennine Way; the Ridgeway Path; the South Downs Way; the South

*Below* Offa's Dyke Path *traces the 8th-century English – Welsh boundary.* *Bottom* The 50 miles of the Peddar's Way, in Norfolk, follow a Roman road.

West Coast path; and the Wolds Way. Placed end to end, these 10 routes together cover approximately 1,750 miles. Three of them are in the South of England, one is in East Anglia, two are in Wales and the Marches, and three in the North. There are also three more long distance walking routes in Scotland.

The founding father of this whole network was the late Tom Stephenson of the Ramblers' Association, who in 1935 put forward the idea of a continuous public footpath running the whole length of the Pennine Chain to the Cheviots and the Scots Border. It took 30 years during which much opposition had to be overcome, but he lived to see his brainchild brought safely to birth as the Pennine Way.

The **Pennine Way** runs 250 miles up the backbone of England from the High Peak in Derbyshire to the Scottish border. It starts in the Peak District National Park and crosses two other National Parks – the Yorkshire Dales and Northumberland – as well as an Area of Outstanding Natural Beauty in the North Pennines.

You can walk it either way, naturally, but travelling from south to north keeps the weather at the walker's back and the route is usually described in this direction. It starts at Edale in the delectable valley of the River Noe, close to Castleton and its deep, eerie limestone caverns. The Way goes up across the Kinder Scout plateau (there are alternative routes here and elsewhere along the trail) to the aptly named wasteland of Bleaklow. It then passes by Blackstone Edge, with its exceptionally well preserved stretch of Roman road, and across the Calder Valley close to Hebden Bridge, where the rows of millhands' houses cling to the steep hillsides, to the beauty spot of Hardcastle Crags. North from here are the wild moors of the Brontë Country, near Haworth, and the bleak scenery and atmosphere of *Wuthering Heights* at the ruined farmhouse at Withins.

The Way crosses the Craven district to reach the tremendous limestone scenery of the Yorkshire Dales National Park: 'a strange landscape,' as the great fell-walker Wainwright has written, 'almost lunar, in places awesome, in places beautiful, and everywhere fascinating.' From Malham, the beetling gorge of Gordale Scar is a mile or so off the path, which scrambles up the sheer curving cliff of Malham Cove, close to 250ft (76m) high, to the cracked and fissured limestone 'pavement' on top. Malham Tarn is the lake where Charles Kingsley was inspired to

create *The Water Babies*. Further on is the isolated hump of Pen-y-ghent, 2,273ft (693m).

On to Ribblesdale and to Wensleydale, at Hawes, and close to Hardraw Force, where the water tumbles over a 100ft (30m) rock. Further on is Middleton in Teesdale and the Way follows the swirling, rock-strewn Tees to three spectacular waterfalls in succession: Low Force, High Force and Cauldron Snout, where the river boils and rages down the rock ledges for 200ft (61m). At the stupendous horseshoe of High Cup Nick an immense abyss opens, whose sides are sheer for almost 1,000ft (305m).

Northwards again, up the valley of the South Tyne to Hadrian's Wall, getting on for 1,900 years old now, but still swooping athletically over the crags. The Way follows it for nine miles, passing Housesteads, where there are the remains of a substantial Roman fort, with legionary latrines and a museum. Then the route lies on north over heathery moors to Bellingham, across Redesdale and through the forest to the high Cheviots, the lonely open spaces of the Northumberland National Park, and the Border at last, coming to a final grateful halt at Kirk Yetholm.

The **Wolds Way** in the old East Riding of Yorkshire is about as unlike the Pennine Way as two walking routes in the same country could conceivably be. In length, by comparison, the Wolds Way is a mere pygmy of 79 miles all told. It is easy going where the Pennine Way is hard. And instead of daring the wild and lonely places, and scenes of spectacular grandeur, the Wolds Way walker is in placid, pretty country and never far from a small town or a village, a bed, a meal, a drink.

Open since 1982, the Wolds Way begins at Hessle on the north bank of the Humber and runs under the northern end of the mighty Humber Suspension Bridge. Then the route heads north to the Yorkshire Wolds, rounded chalk hills with attractive valleys. The path lies through farming country and woods, over gentle slopes, along farm tracks and roads. A point of special interest is the deserted village of Wharram Percy, north of Thixendale. It was abandoned in Tudor times and only the ruined church is still standing.

From the northern scarp of the Wolds there are fine views across the Vale of Pickering to the North York Moors, and later to the North Sea as the footpath comes to the Victorian seaside resort of Filey. It passes close to Filey Brigg, a mile-long finger of rock protruding into the sea, going on along the cliffs to join the Cleveland Way.

The **Cleveland Way** was the second long distance footpath to be opened, in 1969. It steers its course northwards along the Yorkshire coast by Scarborough and Whitby to Saltburn. There it turns inland and changes course to the south-west, to spend the rest of its energies in the Cleveland Hills and the North York Moors National Park before coming to an end at Helmsley, not far from the haunting ruins of Rievaulx Abbey.

The **Pembrokeshire Coast Path**, 180 miles round Wales's south-western corner, and the **South West Coast Path** both take the walker through heroic coastal scenery of massive sea-beaten cliffs, coves and sandy beaches, lighthouses, vast seaward panoramas and superlative sunsets. The South West Coast Path follows the entire coastline from Minehead on the Bristol Channel in Somerset, along the North Devon shore, all round Cornwall by Land's End and the Lizard, back along the South Devon coast and the Dorset shoreline to finish on the edge of Poole Harbour.

The longest of the Scottish long distance paths is the **Southern Upland Way**, 212 miles clear across the country between Cockburnspath, east of Dunbar on the North Sea shore, and Portpatrick, looking out over the Irish Sea from the Rhinns of Galloway. This is a demanding route over a great variety of Border landscape, and positively dripping in history – passing through the Lammermuirs and the Scott Country, by the austere Jacobite mansion of Traquair, past St Mary's Loch and across the wild country of the Galloway Forest Park.

The 95 miles of the **West Highland Way**, opened in 1980, also make a romantic pilgrimage. The route is by Loch Lomond, across bleak Rannoch Moor and past the grim mountain gates of Glen Coe to Kinlochleven and Fort William, in the shadow of Ben Nevis.

The English and Welsh paths, too, have historic roots. **Offa's Dyke Path**, which is quite heavily trampled in some sections but satisfactorily lonely in others, runs the whole length of the Welsh Marches for 168 miles. From Chepstow on the River Severn it goes up the entrancing Wye Valley and long the edge of the Brecon Beacons National Park, then makes its way through the solitary, eerie Shropshire Hills and over the Clwydian Range to reach the coast of North Wales at Prestatyn. For about one-third of a distance it follows the line of the formidable bank and ditch constructed by Offa, 8th-century King of Mercia, to mark and defend his frontier with the Welsh.

The **North Downs Way**, similarly, 140 miles from Farnham to Dover and Folkestone, in part runs along the traditional medieval pilgrims' route to Canterbury, to the shrine of St Thomas à Becket. The **South Downs Way** runs 106 miles on pre-historic tracks from towering Beachy Head across Sussex and Hampshire to Winchester, commanding on the way wonderful views over the English Channel and across the Sussex Weald. The **Peddars Way**, again, follows an ancient track from the Suffolk border across Norfolk to the coast, and the **Ridgeway Path** across Wiltshire is an immensely ancient route, passing close to the important prehistoric monuments of Avebury, Wayland's Smithy and the White Horse of Uffington. On these timeworn, well-trodden ways, today's walkers tread in the footsteps of travellers of long ago.

*National trail*

*A view from Benbrack Hill, along the Southern Upland Way in Galloway.*

*Cave*

*Prehistoric monument*

*Hillfort*

*Roman antiquity*

*Stonehenge is one of the most famous prehistoric monuments in Europe.*

**Caves**
**Prehistoric Monuments**
**Hillforts**
**Roman Antiquities**

As the last great Ice Age held Britain in its grip, early man and the animals he hunted with increasingly sophisticated stone weapons followed shifts of climate. Small family groups took refuge from the sleet-lashed tundra in many natural limestone caverns.

**Caves**
**Creswell Crags**, in Derbyshire, one of the most important Palaeolithic sites in Britain, has a visitor centre which illustrates the life they must have led, both in the main cave and in nearby **Pin Hole** and **Robin Hood's Cave**. At **Cheddar Gorge**, Gough's Cave and Cox's Cave have displays in a nearby museum. Other caves worth visiting are the remains of mine workings for lead and later for semi-precious fluorspar near Castleton, Derbyshire – the **Treak Cliff** and **Speedwell Caverns**, near Buxton, as well as the **Blue John Cavern** itself.

**Prehistoric Monuments**
Long after the retreating glaciers and rising sea levels had submerged the mud flats to the east of Britain, agriculturalists arrived from Europe.

By about 5000BC, they had given the British upland landscape a basic appearance which was to remain largely unchanged until the introduction of intensive farming methods in the 20th century. But in that landscape began to appear burial mounds and much larger monuments.

Most famous must be **Stonehenge**, but from **Callanish**, on the Isle of Lewis, through **Arbor Low** and the **Nine Ladies**, near Matlock, to the **Rollright Stones**, north of Oxford, similar circles have filled later generations with awe. Possibly built, like **Castlerigg** in Cumbria and the **Ring of Brodgar** on Orkney, in connection with solar or lunar observation and associated rituals, the 'alignments' so often attributed to these circles, and to groups such as the **Devil's Arrows**, near Boroughbridge, should be treated with caution. Stonehenge pre-dates the Druid cult by 3,000 years and yet, in the Romantic age and the 19th century was thought to have been a Druid temple. In today's 'computer climate' it has become, for some, an astronomical calculator.

Orientation to the rising and setting sun does appear to have influenced the builders of most of the megalithic burial mounds in Britain. One of these, at **Newgrange**, north of Dublin, a splendid example of Neolithic

carving in its own right, is so aligned that the midwinter sunrise casts a beam directly into the tomb chamber. Newgrange predates Stonehenge by a thousand years and the positions of earth and sun, of sunrise – midwinter or midsummer – have changed, but the east–west alignments remain an intriguing facet of the study of all these monuments.

The village of **Avebury**, in Wiltshire, is set within another huge stone circle and earthwork rampart. A museum here displays finds and explains the way in which rampart and circle were constructed.

**Stonehenge** has seen many phases in its construction, from its origins in 3000BC to its present form, which dates from around 1800BC. The sheer manpower involved is amazing. Four million cubic feet of chalk were dug out at Avebury, using antler picks. This and the hauling on raft and sledge of the Stonehenge bluestones from the Preseli Mountains in Wales and the transport of the 80 huge sarsens from the Marlborough Downs, tells us something of the beliefs and about the organisational ability of the builders of both monuments. Illiterate agriculturalists they may have been – certainly they were ignorant of the use of iron – and yet their kings and priests were able to organise and plan huge civil engineering projects.

Associated with Stonehenge is the huge circular timber building – **Woodhenge**. It is not difficult to imagine a conical thatched roof supported by timber uprights, their positions now marked by concrete posts. When was it built? Around 2750BC – that at least is known. Why was it built? Who used it? There is no scatter of the usual debris associated with hut circles and their domestic middens, so Woodhenge and the nearby **Durrington Walls** site would seem to have a public and ceremonial function. Perhaps the forest of tree trunk pillars recalled forest groves which had long had religious significance. At Woodhenge a three-year-old child, its skull split, was buried, perhaps as a dedication, at the centre of the complex. When the timbers at last decayed, a memorial stone was placed at the centre of the circle.

**Silbury Hill**, near Avebury, has so far yielded up few of its secrets. Why this 130ft (40m) mound, covering over five acres at its base, was raised is still a mystery. Trenches have been dug, seeking a burial somewhere within, but all these excavations have found is that it was very carefully built. Inside the turf mound is a stepped cone of compacted chalk rubble, each layer being finished with smooth chalk blocks. The steps were later filled with earth except for the topmost one, still visible as a terrace. The fact that the whole of the Stonehenge circle would fit comfortably within this topmost terrace gives an idea of the scale of the mound.

Carbon-14 dating has placed its construction at around 2600BC – and the trenches have told us that it was started in July or August, for right at the core have been found winged ants – but maybe there is a more important burial still to be discovered. Nearby is **West Kennet Long Barrow** and its sarsen façade – burial chamber perhaps, of the chieftains who commanded the building of Avebury.

## Hillforts

The 'Beaker Folk', so called from the distinctive pottery vessels found in their graves, arrived in Britain around 2700BC. They brought with them the Aryan roots of our language and their knowledge of metal working was gradually learnt by the established communities into which they merged. By 1800BC the British climate was deteriorating and tribes vied for workable land. Local chiefs gained power and protected their arable land and pasture from the safety of upland hillforts, which gradually became tribal 'capitals'

rather than merely bolt holes in case of war.

Thousands of these hillforts dot the landscape, and many were inhabited well into the Roman age. **Ingleborough**, just north of the National Park Centre at Clapham, North Yorkshire, is the highest in Britain. Life must have been very hard on this high windswept plateau. Earlier settlers in the area possibly make themselves a warmer home in the cave systems nearby, at **Ingleborough Show Cave** and **Gaping Gill**. One of the largest and most important hill-forts in Britain is **Maiden Castle**. Built initially around 300BC, it finally fell to Vespasian's troops in AD43. Boards around the two-mile perimeter provide much information and the museum in nearby Dorchester displays finds from the site.

Often associated with these hill-forts are the figures carved into the chalk hillsides – horses and giant figures – but only a handful can be said with certainty to be 'pre-historic'. **Uffington White Horse**, between Swindon and Wantage, certainly is. Overlooking the Ridgeway Path, an ancient trade route across the north Berkshire Downs, its disintegrated simplicity resembles the horses – tribal totems, perhaps – which feature on Celtic coinage. The **Cerne Abbas Giant,** north of Dorchester, is probably not more than 1,500 years old, but its club-wielding phallic figure possibly represents Hercules, part of a god-cult which flourished around AD100. The iron Age enclosure above him was used for May Day and fertility ceremonies long after the foundation of the nearby Benedictine priory in the 10th century. **Wilmington Long Man**, near Alfriston, inland from Beachy Head, could well be Romano-British, too.

From 700BC onwards, Celtic settlers brought their language, their chariots and a love of finery, gold and ornaments. Iron swords gave them an ascendancy in battle over the native Britons, who were pushed westwards. Celtic immigrant groups shared a common dialect but their lack of any concept of 'nationhood' left their society an easy prey to the civilising might of Rome.

## Roman Antiquities

The lure of corn, gold, iron, slaves and hunting dogs was enough to make the Romans decide that an invasion of Britannia in the summer of AD43 was worthwhile. By AD70 50 or more towns were linked by a network of roads. *Lex Romana* tamed the unruly land and Latin became yet another rootstock from

which English would eventually spring. Evidence of Roman military occupation is everywhere – from **Hadrian's Wall** and the lighthouse in **Dover Castle**, to the legionary fortress at **Caerleon** in Gwent.

Many of the civilising influences of Rome can still be seen today – an aqueduct which supplied fresh water 12 miles along the Frome Valley to Dorchester, sewers in Lincoln, Colchester and York, and bath houses. The finest of these, at **Bath**, is rivalled by the complex of baths and exercise halls at Viroconium, near **Wroxeter**. Theatres such as those of Verulamium and Caerleon, and the busy shopping centres which developed around the forum or the town gates, attracted people to the towns. Mosaic floors like those at **Aldborough**, in Yorkshire, reflect a very comfortable style of life. This wealth is mirrored, too, by the remains of many Roman villas such as those at Lullingstone, near **Eynsford** in Kent, **Fishbourne** in Sussex and **Chedworth** in Gloucestershire.

Below *Westbury White Horse, on Bratton Down, Wiltshire.*
Bottom *Housesteads Fort along Hadrian's Wall, in Northumbria.*

*Cave*

*Prehistoric monument*

*Hillfort*

*Roman antiquity*

THE BATTLE OF FLODDEN FIELD
9th September 1513

Above *The site of the Battle of Flodden. Inset A display board at Flodden chronicles the battle which was fought here.* Top right *According to tradition, men watched London's Great Fire from Outwood Mill, Surrey.* Bottom *Porthcurno's Minack open-air theatre.*

*Windmill*

*Other place of interest*

## Battlefields
## Windmills
## Other Places of Interest

Normans and Plantagenets, wars in Scotland and Wales, the Wars of the Roses, the Civil War and the Jacobite risings, have all left the map of Britain dotted with 'crossed swords' symbols. In the 250 years that separate us from Culloden, in 1746, the last battle on British soil, farming, roads and railways, canals and houses have changed the fields on which the history of the nation was written.

### Battlefields

We do not commemorate our battles as lavishly as the Visitor Centres at places such as Waterloo or Gettysburg, but there are still fields where there is something to be seen today. Facilities are available, mainly in the tourist season, for organised groups to be taken round and it is worth telephoning to see whether you can join one.

The Battle of **Hastings**, on 14 October 1066, certainly changed things in England. Stories of the battle are well enough known – Harold's forced march of 250 miles from battle against the Norwegian king at Stamford Bridge, near York, to meet the Norman invaders; the Norman minstrel Taillefer charging

the shield-wall; the hail of arrows harassing the axemen; the final stand of the house-carles around the royal standard of Wessex. All are vividly recalled in an audio-visual presentation in the Tourist Office on the green just opposite the gateway of the Abbey which William founded, its altar traditionally on the spot where Harold fell. Now an English Heritage property, the pathways around and overlooking main sectors of the battlefield are well signposted, with information boards at regular intervals.

In the **Bannockburn** Heritage Centre the full story of the battle of 24 June 1314, is graphically told in an audio-visual entitled *The Forging of a Nation*. On the field itself is preserved the Borestone, where Robert the Bruce raised his banner before this decisive culmination of the Wars of Independence.

From the top of the Durham Cathedral tower the battlefield of **Neville's Cross** can be seen as it was by the monks who gave 'moral support' by singing hymns there in 1346. A leaflet explaining the battle is available from the Tourist Office and a half mile walk from the city brings the visitor to the battlefield itself.

An exhibition is mounted on **Bosworth** battlefield, near Sutton

Cheney, with an audio-visual presentation including scenes from Laurence Olivier's *Richard III*. There is a battlefield trail, with another information centre halfway round at Shenton Station. Here, Richard of Gloucester, uncle of the Princes in the Tower, met his end, having found no one to answer his cry 'My kingdom for a horse!'

At a call from France for help from the 'auld alliance', James IV of Scotland marched into England. On Pipers' Hill, at **Flodden Edge**, is a monument 'To the Brave of both Nations', with the battlefield spread out below. A booklet and map from nearby Coldstream enable you to follow the course of the battle. King Henry VIII had left the old Earl of Surrey, a veteran of Bosworth, to defend the north. Surrey had borrowed the banner of St Cuthbert, obviously a powerful morale raiser, from Durham Cathedral. But it was artillery fire that stung the Scots into premature offensive action, allowing English archers to reach the crest of Pipers' Hill and pour a murderous arrow storm into the massed pikemen below. Flodden was the last major battle won largely by the longbow.

The Castle Inn, in **Edgehill,** was built on the spot where King Charles raised his Standard. There

is a memorial on the field below and a map and guidebook will enable you to follow the course of the fighting. Neither side seemed willing to strike the first blow until a Parliamentary gunner spotted the King on the hill, fired – and missed. Prince Rupert charged – found an ally in the inaptly named Sir Faithful Fortescue, one of the Parliamentary cavalry commanders – and they all dashed the two miles or so to Kineton, where they rested their horses and indulged in a little light looting. Roundhead foot soldiers were about to finish off the exhausted Royalists when they were attacked owing to the opportune return of Prince Rupert and the cavalry. Captain John Smith, of the King's Lifeguard, met a party of Roundheads escorting a Royalist prisoner and the Royal Standard which they had just captured. The prisoner recognised Smith and called to him. Smith charged, killed one Roundhead, wounded another and the other four fled. He was knighted on the spot by the King for recovering the Standard, which had not been in Parliamentary hands above fifteen minutes.

In the village of **Naseby** is a museum with dioramas and a ten minute commentary of different stages of the battle of 14 July 1645.

Should the museum be closed, then try the village shop or the church for the descriptive leaflet and map, which will make the whole encounter more easy to follow.

A drive up the Naseby-Sibbertoft road takes you to a monument marking the position from which Cromwell led his cavalry to win the day and from where there is a good view over the whole battlefield.

Information about the battle of **Worcester**, 3 September 1651, is available from both the Tourist Office and the Civil War Centre at the Commandery. Worcester was the scene of the first and last battles of the war. During the summer, frequent 're-enactments' are staged by several groups, particularly in September.

**Sedgemoor**, the last battle fought on English soil, on 6 July 1685, followed the landing by the Duke of Monmouth, illegitimate son of Charles II, to claim the throne of James II. A stone monument marks the site of the battle, and information can be obtained from the Admiral Blake Museum in Bridgwater.

The Battle of **Culloden**, on the moors outside Inverness, ended the Jacobite Rising in 1746. Bonnie Prince Charlie, with the help of Flora Macdonald, escaped 'over the sea to Skye' and the Stuart cause was swept away. The whole story is graphically told in the visitor centre on the battlefield, which has been restored to its 18th-century appearance, but now dotted with emotive memorial cairns and the Graves of the Clans, on which no heather ever grows.

Since Culloden, we may be thankful that no armies have fought on British soil – only *above* it, in 1940. Aerial bombardment brought the realities of war much closer to the public than did any of the very localised combats of the previous 700 years.

**Windmills**
Few things add as much atmosphere to the countryside as a windmill. They have drained marshlands and ground corn since medieval times. One tradition suggests that they were introduced by crusaders returning home from the wars. Whether or not this is true, we know for a fact that they were first built here some eight centuries ago. None of the original structures remain, but some have survived a few hundreds years. Still in working order is **Berney Arms Mill**, in Norfolk, from the top of which there is a splendid view and the working wind pump at **Wicken Fen**, a remnant of the wetlands drained by Dutch engineers, which

became England's first nature reserve, in 1899. **Bourn Mill**, near Cambridge, is a 17th-century 'post mill', the oldest surviving mill in the country. Unlike the conical tower windmills with a rotating cap, here the sails and machinery all turn together, revolving round a central post. A tide mill has stood on the river bank at **Woodbridge** in Suffolk since the 12th century and the present one was working until 1956, when the shaft of the waterwheel broke. Careful restoration has successfully restored it to working condition.

**Other Places of Interest**
There is a wide range of other places of interest which are well worth visiting. From waterfalls, wells, bridges and towers to dovecotes, follies, monuments and parks, Britain has something to offer every visitor.

Not far from Land's End, on the cliffs near Porthcurno, is the **Minack Theatre**, carved out of the living rock in the 1930s, with the sea as a backdrop for the stage. North of Tavistock is **Lydford Gorge**, a deep wooded gorge with the lovely White Lady Waterfall at the end of a mile or so walk.

Further along the coast, north-west of Weymouth, the extraordinary Chesil Beach, a 12-mile long pebble bank, shelters the **Abbotsbury Swannery**, where swans were bred for the table by the monks as long ago as the 14th century. Today it is a breeding haven for hundreds of wild mute swans. At St Fagans, to the west of Cardiff, is the **Welsh Folk Museum,** a collection of rural buildings from the 17th century onwards from all over Wales, carefully re-erected in the grounds of St Fagans Castle, an elegant Elizabethan mansion.

Waterfalls abound, but one not to be missed is **Hardraw Force**, north of Hawes, North Yorkshire, a spectacular 90ft (27m) drop into a glen which has been used for brass band contests – a great local tradition – on account of its splendid acoustics. Further north, near Moffat on the A708, is one of Scotland's highest falls, the **Grey Mare's Tail**, where Loch Skeen plunges 200ft (61m) to meet Moffat Water.

Shire horses, Clydesdales and Suffolk Punches have ploughed England's fields – and delivered England's beer – for centuries. In the **National Shire Horse Centre**, at Plymouth, there is stabling dating back to 1772 and three parades a day are staged in summer. Courage Breweries have a **Shire Horse Centre** near Maidenhead, as do Whitbread at their **Hop Farm**, on the B2015, east of Tonbridge.

*Battle site with year*

*Windmill*

*Other place of interest*

*Viewpoint*

*Picnic site*

*Agricultural showground*

**Viewpoints**
**Picnic Sites**
**Agricultural Showgrounds**
The **Clee Hills** of Shropshire, in the Welsh Marches, are in a remote and exceptionally attractive area of the country – an official Area of Outstanding Natural Beauty, in fact. They are 'young' hills, geologically, jagged and more impressive than their official height statistics would suggest, and in the past were heavily quarried for coal, building stone, iron and copper. A wealth of folklore still attaches to them, with sinister tales of witches and evil forces. They are also the site of a spectacular viewpoint.

**Viewpoints**
The viewpoint is on the A4117, six miles east of Ludlow. In the immediate foreground to the north is the bulk of Titterstone Clee, 1,750ft (533m) with its aerials and radar dishes, and one of the biggest Iron Age hillforts in Britain on its summit. Beyond the hill is the long,

Below *The picnic site at David Marshall Lodge, Aberfoyle.*
Bottom *View of South Stack lighthouse from the viewpoint on Anglesey.*

wooded ridge of Wenlock Edge and to the west beyond Ludlow rise the mountains of Wales.

Viewpoints, as marked in AA Road Atlases, are all easily accessible by car and have a plaque to identify landmarks and places of interest in the area. Each viewpoint has a prospect of at least 180 degrees and some command wider vistas still. The **Cockleroy** viewpoint, two miles south of Linlithgow in the Lothian region of Scotland, has marvellous views over the full 360 degrees. To the east the eye ranges over Edinburgh to the Firth of Forth, to the south-east lie the Pentland Hills, in the west is Glasgow and in the north the outlying bastions of the Highlands.

The viewpoint is in the Beecraigs Country Park, among the Bathgate Hills, with trails through the woodland, a reservoir with hides for watching the numerous waterfowl and a deer farm with a viewing platform. At Linlithgow are the romantic ruins of the palace of the Stuart kings, where Mary, Queen of Scots was born, and the church where she was christened. Not far away is Torphichen Preceptory, once the Scottish base of the crusading order of the Knights of St John of Jerusalem. A little to the south there are superlative views again, from Cairnpaple Hill, where prehistoric men buried their dead over a period of 2,500 years and more.

On the other side of Glasgow, the **Lyle Hill** viewpoint is just outside the former shipbuilding town of Greenock, the birthplace of James Watt, and during World War II the principal Free French naval base. The viewpoint is near the war memorial to those sailors, an anchor surmounted by a Cross of Lorraine. Down below is the Firth of Clyde and its swarming ferries. To the north and north-west lie Holy Loch and the woods and mountains of the Argyll Forest Park on the Cowal Peninsula, with the serrated crests of The Cobbler in the distance. West and south-west are the Isle of Bute, separated from the mainland by the narrow Kyles of Bute, the Isle of Arran rising to Goat Fell and, beyond Arran, the Kintyre Peninsula.

Far away at the other end of the country, in Cornwall, the majestic harbour of Carrick Roads was an important United States Navy base during the war. The viewpoint is on **Pendennis Point**, outside Falmouth, commanding a sweeping prospect of the harbour and out to the English Channel and the Lizard Peninsula. Close at hand is the round keep of Pendennis Castle,

one of the artillery strongpoints built along the coast in Henry VIII's time against attack by the French. Across the water is its other half, St Mawes Castle. These twin fortresses have done their job, and no enemy force has ever attempted to penetrate Carrick Roads.

Another viewpoint with naval connections lies eastward along the coast, on **Portsdown Hill** in Hampshire, a mile north of Cosham. Immediately to the south sprawls Portsmouth, with its historic harbour and the Royal Navy dockyard where Nelson's HMS *Victory* rests in honourable retirement. Birds wheel above the Farlington Marshes at the northern end of Langstone Harbour and the eagle eye pierces 10 miles across the Solent to the Isle of Wight. For visitors who would like something to eat as well as watch, there is a picnic site here.

So there is at the viewpoint at **David Marshall Lodge**, the Forestry Commission visitor centre in the scenic Trossachs area, in the Central region of Scotland, a mile north of Aberfoyle on A821. There are spectacular views here of Ben Lomond, the Highland mountains and the valleys of the Forth.

The haunting beauty of the Trossachs – 'So wondrous wild, the whole might seem the scenery of a fairy dream' – with its lochs, peaks and 'wildering forest' – was praised by Sir Walter Scott in 1810 in his immensely popular poem *The Lady of the Lake*. To add to its romantic attractions, much of the area was Rob Roy country.

Strictly speaking, the Trossachs ('the cross places' in Gaelic) means the narrow belt of land between Loch Katrine and Loch Achray, but the name is more often used broadly for the whole area between Loch Lomond and Callander. Much of it is now in the Forestry Commission's enormous Queen Elizabeth Forest Park. After Scott, tourists began to flock to the area in such numbers that the local landowner, the Duke of Montrose, built the road north from Aberfoyle which is now the A821, or Duke's Road. There are parking places and a picnic site along it, and more along the Forestry Commission's one-way Achray Forest Drive, which leaves the Duke's Road to make its way seven miles through the woods, by Loch Drunkie and Loch Achray. There are more scenic viewpoints here and a waymarked forest walk.

**Picnic Sites**
One of the Countryside Commission's achievements has been to stimulate local authorities to

provide places where motorists could pull off the road to enjoy a picnic. Opinion surveys and studies repeatedly made it clear that many people were deterred from enjoying the countryside by an uneasy fear of trespassing or going where they were not wanted; an official picnic spot is somewhere where you know you are entitled to be. Although most sites have been organised by county councils, many have been provided by the Forestry Commission, others by the National Trust and by private landowners.

Many sites provide a view of attractive scenery or are close to an outstanding attraction. There is one near the ruins of **Mount Grace Priory**, for instance, the medieval Carthusian monastery near Osmotherley in North Yorkshire (where each of the tiny hermit-like cells had running water, incidentally) and there is one close to the **Hardraw Force** waterfall, off the Pennine Way. In Wales there are several with views of **Llyn Clywedog**, near Llanidloes in Powys, a three-mile long reservoir. An old iron mine can also be visited here, and not far away is another picnic site beside the infant River Severn, as it starts its long journey to the sea from the high moors of Plynlimon. There are more looking over **Lake Vyrnwy** in Powys, a beautiful 1880s reservoir with wooded shores and a striking Victorian Gothic tower. In England too, reservoirs make pleasing picnic spots, as at **Rutland Water** in Leicestershire, or **Grafham Water** in Cambridgeshire.

## Agricultural Showgrounds

The 'traditional' English landscape of green fields, hedgerows and narrow lanes was created by the agricultural revolution of the 18th century, which introduced improved farming methods. County agricultural societies were formed to spread knowledge of the new ways and raise standards. They organised annual county shows at which farmers and breeders showed off their achievements and competed against each other. For 200 years and more these agricultural shows have been part of the accustomed round of country life, with their marquees and bands, their displays of the latest farm machinery and equipment, and their classes for heavy horses, cattle and sheep. One of the oldest is the **Royal Bath and West Show**, which can trace its history back to 1777 and draws 100,000 people every year to its permanent showground near Shepton Mallet in Somerset. Before the War, the county shows normally moved around from one

*Viewpoint*

*Picnic site*

*Agricultural showground*

country estate or farmer's fields to another, year by year. After 1945 the cost of staging a show escalated alarmingly. Some shows folded up, some amalgamated and others established permanent showgrounds. The leader in the field was the Yorkshire Agricultural Society, which planted its **Great Yorkshire Show** on a permanent site at Harrogate. The **Royal Highland Show** chose a location at Ingliston, a few miles west of Edinburgh, for its shows.

Other leading shows which have equipped themselves with fixed locations include the **Three Counties** at Great Malvern (the three counties being Herefordshire, Worcestershire and Gloucestershire), the **South of England** at Ardingly in Sussex, the **Royal Cornwall** at Wadebridge, the

*A plaque marking the viewpoint on Sugar Loaf Mountain in Wales.*

**East of England** near Peterborough and the **Royal Welsh** at Builth Wells. The Royal Agricultural Society of England, founded in 1838, held its first show at Oxford the following year. The 'Royal' moved about the country every year until 1963, when it settled at Stoneleigh in Warwickshire, in a permanent home where the **National Agriculture Centre** evolved in the 1970s. The agricultural shows have had heavy weather to come through in recent years, but they have survived, and altogether are estimated to attract about three million visitors a year to share country triumphs and pleasures.

**Horse Racing
Show Jumping and
Equestrian Circuits
Athletics Stadiums
Motor Racing Circuits**

*Horse racing*

*Show jumping
and equestrian
circuit*

Becher's Brook . . . Valentine's . . .
the Canal Turn . . . the Chair. The
familiar litany of names conjures up
**Aintree** on Grand National Day –
the jostle at the start, the crash and
crackle of horse meeting thorn-and-
fir fence, horses and jockeys falling,
the clamour of the crowd. The early
history of the great race is obscure,
but it is usually traced back to the
Grand Liverpool Steeplechase of
1839. That race was won by a horse
appropriately named Lottery and
that was the year the gallant
Captain Becher, a well-known
gentleman rider of the day, fell into
the brook that bears his name. His
horse, named Conrad, fell in as
well.

### Horse Racing

A steeplechase as the name
implies, did not originally take place
on a course at all. A by-product of
hunting, it was a wild pell-mell
gallop across country over hedges
and ditches, towards a distant
steeple or other agreed marker. Not

*World famous Derby Day, at Epsom
Race Course in Surrey.*

until the 19th century did organised
racing over artificial jumps on a set
course begin. Racing started at
Aintree in 1829, on the course
owned by the Earls of Sefton for
another 120 years. The course, in a
dreary northern suburb of
Liverpool, has the most formidable
fences in the sport and in 1928 a
horse named Tipperary Tim won
the Grand National simply by being
the only finisher of 42 starters. Far
and away the most famous horse
associated with Aintree and the
National, however, is Red Rum, the
only three-time winner (in 1973,
1974 and 1977).

The most prestigious steeplechase
course in England is at **Cheltenham**,
in a delightful country situation
outside the town, at Prestbury Park,
under the looming Cotswold
bulwark of Cleeve Hill. It is a
testing track on heavy clay. The
major event of the year is the
Cheltenham Gold Cup in March,
first held in 1924. The great horse
Golden Miller won it five years in
succession from 1932 to 1936 (and in
1934 won the Grand National as
well). The Champion Hurdle at
Cheltenham is the premier hurdle
event in the country.

The capital of the flat racing
industry is across the other side of
the country at **Newmarket**. The

town developed as a racing and
breeding centre for 'the sport of
kings' under royal patronage.
Charles II rode his own horses in
races there: hence the name Rowley
Mile for one of Newmarket's two
courses, from the king's nickname,
Old Rowley. In the mid-18th
century the aristocratic Jockey Club
was founded at Newmarket. It owns
the two courses and Newmarket
Heath, the open country around the
town on which strings of
staggeringly valuable racehorses can
be seen exercising. It occupies a
suitably august red brick building in
the centre of the town, and nearby
is the highly enjoyable National
Horseracing Museum, which
opened in 1983.

Two of the five 'classic' races are
held at Newmarket: the Two
Thousand Guineas, and the One
Thousand Guineas for fillies only,
inaugurated in 1809 and 1814
respectively. Both are run on the
Rowley Mile course, which has a
long flat straight, followed by a dip
and rise to the finish. Long races
cannot easily be seen from the
grandstands because the course was
laid out long before the days of
packed modern race crowds.

The most famous race in the
world is run early in June every year
at **Epsom.** It is named after the

12th Earl of Derby, though it might easily have been called the Bunbury. Lord Derby and Sir Charles Bunbury tossed a coin in 1780 to decide the name of a new race for three-year-old colts and fillies. As if in compensation, Bunbury's horse Diomed won the first Derby, and Lord Derby had to wait until 1787 to win with Sir Peter Teazle.

The other classic race at Epsom, the Oaks, restricted to fillies, was first run in 1779 and was named after a house which Lord Derby had taken nearby.

W P Frith's well-known painting *Derby Day* gives a vivid impression of the occasion in Victorian times, when it was virtually a public holiday. Huge numbers of people swarmed to enjoy a day out and all the fun of the fair on Epsom Downs. The Derby course is more or less level for the first three-quarters of a mile and then drops to a sharp turn at Tattenham Corner before the run-in.

The last of the classics, in September, is the oldest; the St Leger, which goes all the way back to 1776 and is named after a prominent Yorkshire sportsman of the time. It is run at **Doncaster,** on the Town Moor, the common land outside the town which, as at Epsom, was the natural place for the races.

One of the oldest courses in the country, and one of the oddest, is the Roodee at **Chester,** where there was apparently organised racing in Henry VIII's time. The course has the River Dee on one side with the old city wall on the other and is circular, with almost no straight. At **York**, there was racing on the Knavesmire, common land outside the city, early in the 18th century. Here in August is contested the Gimcrack Stakes, named in honour of a famous grey. The sport's most attractive setting is claimed by **Goodwood**, near Chichester in Sussex, where the course was laid out by the 3rd Duke of Richmond with the first meeting staged in 1801.

The smartest social occasion of the racing year is the **Royal Ascot** meeting in June, attended by the Queen, with a royal procession up the straight in carriages and much media fuss about fashionable hats. Races were first held at Ascot, in Berkshire, in 1711. The King George VI and Queen Elizabeth Diamond Stakes, run in July with the richest prize money in the sport, was inaugurated in 1951 to mark the Festival of Britain.

### Showjumping and Equestrian Circuits

The first show jumping contest on record was held in London in 1869. From 1912 the sport was regularly included in the Olympic Games, but it is only since 1945 that it has attracted strong public and media interest. The popular Horse of the Year show, at **Wembley Arena** in London, dates from 1949. The same year saw the first horse trials at **Badminton,** in Avon, on a testing course laid out in the grounds of his palatial mansion by the Duke of Beaufort. Himself a redoubtable huntsman, the duke was determined to do something about the indifferent showing of the British equestrian team in the 1948 Olympics. The three day event at Badminton in the spring now draws spectators in thousands. In 1984 Lucinda Green won Badminton for a record sixth time, on six different horses. Another stately home course is the one at **Burghley House**, near Stamford, in the grounds of the palace of the Cecils, right-hand men to Elizabeth I and James I. The Marquess of Exeter, a former Olympic athlete, offered a home for a three day event here, first held in 1961. The Burghley Horse Trials in September are now firmly established as a prestigious occasion in the show jumping calendar.

The sport's equivalent of Aintree and Epsom combined is the course at **Hickstead** in Sussex, opened in 1960 at his home by a leading rider, Douglas Bunn, to provide a permanent arena with formidable obstacles. The first British Show Jumping Derby was held there in 1961.

### Athletics Stadiums

Athletics is less well equipped with tracks and grounds than other major sports. The principal arena for international athletics is at the **Crystal Palace** in South London, where a 12,000-seater stadium was opened in 1964. Ten years later, an all-weather track was installed in the town stadium at **Gateshead**, and home-town athlete Brendan Foster set a new 3,000m world record to celebrate. The cross-country course at Gateshead is also well known.

### Motor Racing Circuits

The magic name from the early history of motor racing in England is **Brooklands**, the track near Weybridge in Surrey which, sadly, closed in 1939. Every great figure of the early days raced there and John Cobb set a lap record of 143mph in a Napier-Railton in 1935. Another leading venue was **Donington Park**, near Derby, where Grand Prix events were held in the 1930s. During the war the site was taken over by the Army. Years later the circuit was reopened for racing, in the 1970s. The Motor Museum there has a notable collection of Grand Prix racing cars.

Since 1945 the two major British circuits have been Silverstone and Brands Hatch. **Silverstone**, in Northamptonshire near Towcester, opened in 1948 on a former airfield, hence the name Hangar Straight for part of the course. The British Grand Prix is staged there, but for many years it alternated with Brands Hatch, near Farningham in Kent. It opened for Formula Three racing in 1949 and in 1960 opened the Grand Prix course.

*A rider in the TT races, held every June on the Isle of Man.*

*Athletics stadium*

*Motor racing circuit*

*Golf course*

*County cricket ground*

*National rugby ground*

*A scene at Lord's, the home of Middlesex County Cricket Club.*

**Golf Courses**
**County Cricket Grounds**
**National Rugby Grounds**
**Ski Slopes**
**Coastal Launching Sites**
Of all the world's great golf courses, the most august is the venerable and venerated Old Course at **St Andrews** in Scotland, where the Victorian clubhouse of the Royal and Ancient Golf Club is the temple and citadel of the game. A links, or seaside course – as all the country's top courses are – the Old Course is four miles in length and so many golfers are keen to play it that it normally opens at six o'clock in the morning. The notorious par 4 17th, or Roadhole, is said to have driven

more great golfers to rage and bitter despair than any other golf hole in the world.

**Golf Courses**
Golf was played at St Andrews on the springy turf beside the North Sea as long ago as the 15th century, it seems, and when 22 noblemen and gentlemen founded the Society of St Andrews Golfers in 1754, they described the game as an 'ancient and healthful exercise'. The club was dubbed 'royal' in 1834 by King William IV and became the governing body of the game.

Another illustrious club is the Honourable Company of Edinburgh Golfers, which was founded in 1744 (as the Gentlemen Golfers of Leigh), ten years before the Royal and Ancient. It drew up the first set of

rules, which the R and A adopted. The club now has its headquarters at **Muirfield**, a famous championship course on the outskirts of the village of Gullane, east of Edinburgh. It is close to the shore of the Firth of Forth, whose invigorating breezes are claimed to account for the great age which the Edinburgh Golfers commonly attain. The course is known for its meticulously constructed bunkers. Jack Nicklaus won his first British Open at Muirfield in 1966 and Nick Faldo won there in 1987.

There is a clutch of notable courses across on the Ayrshire shore, on hillocky ground on the sandy turf and coarse grass beside the sea. The **Prestwick** club organised the first British Open championship in 1860 and it was played there many times, but after 1925 the course was no longer big enough for the crowds which the event was beginning to attract. Few of them are these days.

**Royal Troon,** just to the north, has holes with names – they start with Seal and to on to Postage Stamp and Rabbit. In the 1973 Open two holes-in-one were scored at Postage Stamp. One was by the veteran American Gene Sarazen and the other by the amateur David Russell, who happened to be respectively the oldest and the youngest players in the field.

There is another group of redoubtable courses in England along the Lancashire coast. **Royal Lytham and St Anne's**, near Blackpool, was in open countryside when the club was founded in 1886, but is now an oasis in a desert of housing estates. Here, the first Ladies Open was played in 1893 and Tony Jacklin had his Open triumph in 1969. Near Southport is another crack course, **Royal Birkdale,** and further south on the tip of the Wirral Peninsula, is **Hoylake,** where the first British Amateur championship was contested in 1885. The demanding course is no longer considered adequate to cope with Open crowds. The Open is still played over the **Royal St George's** course at Sandwich on the Kent coast, one of the toughest in Britain, and the scene of a famous fictitious match in Ian Fleming's *Goldfinger*.

Other courses are celebrated not for the championships fought out over them, but for their associations with heroic figures of the past. The legendary James Braid, five times Open champion, was professional at **Walton Heath** in Surrey for 45 years until he died in 1950 at the age of 80. On his birthday he invariably went out and played the course in as many strokes as his age or less.

His contemporary, the incomparable John Henry Taylor, learned his golf at the **Royal North Devon's** links at Westward Ho!, on the bumpy sandy ground of the Burrows, frequented by horses, cows and sheep as well as golfers.

Speaking of animals on a course, in 1934 the professional at the **St Margaret's at Cliffe** club in Kent killed a cow with his tee shot to the 18th. And in 1975 at **Scunthorpe**, Humberside, a drive at the 14th hole, named the Mallard, hit and killed a mallard duck in flight.

## Cricket Grounds

Cricket, like golf, emerged from the mists of obscurity into the light of history in the 18th century. The most famous ground in the country, and the world, is **Lord's** in the St John's Wood district of London. It takes its name from its original proprietor, a Yorkshireman named Thomas Lord, who came to London in 1787, was instrumental in the founding of the MCC (Marylebone Cricket Club) and opened the St John's Wood ground in 1812. Lord's is also the home of the Middlesex County Cricket Club. The original pavilion, a one-room hut, and the tavern provided by Thomas Lord have been replaced over the years by a Victorian pavilion and modern stands. The grand entrance gates to the ground were specially designed in 1923 as a memorial to W G Grace, the greatest cricketer of his age, and Lord's now has a good museum of cricket.

The other famous London ground is the **Oval,** in Kennington, south of the river. Originally a market garden, and long famed for a fine view of the local gasometers, the ground has been the headquarters of the Surrey county club since its formation in a nearby pub in 1845. Like Lord's, the Oval is a regular Test match arena. The highest innings ever recorded in Test cricket was notched up there in 1938, when England scored 903 for 7 declared, with Len Hutton making 364.

One of cricket's most attractive settings is the county ground at **Worcester,** where the cathedral rises nobly in the background across the Severn. The drawback is that when the river floods, as in 1990, the pitch is covered with tons of thick black mud. Another attractive county cricket arena is the St Lawrence ground at **Canterbury** in Kent. The Canterbury Week cricket festival has been held since 1847.

The ground at **Old Trafford** in the southern suburbs of Manchester has seen many a Test match and many a tussle between the red rose of Lancashire and the white rose of Yorkshire. The principal Yorkshire ground is at **Headingley,** a couple of miles from the centre of Leeds. Two other grounds regularly used for Test cricket are **Trent Bridge** in Nottingham, where cricket has been played since 1838, and **Edgbaston,** the Warwickshire county ground in Birmingham.

## Rugby Grounds

Rugby's equivalent of Lord's is the 'cabbage patch' at **Twickenham,** a market garden bought by the Rugby Union in 1907. The choice was fiercely criticised for being too far from Piccadilly Circus, but the motor car changed all that and the ground has been developed into a spanking modern arena. For Welsh rugby men, however, the holy of holies of their national game is **Cardiff Arms Park,** beside the River Taff close to the heart of the city, where the stands echo on great occasions to the impassioned sound of Welsh singing. The Cardiff Football Club began to practise on a piece of meadow here beside the river in 1876. Today it is a thoroughly up-to-date arena with

*Above The clubhouse at St Andrew's. Right Skiing in the Cairngorms, one of Scotland's busiest resorts.*

two stadiums. The two other home international grounds are Murrayfield in Edinburgh and Lansdowne Road in Dublin.

## Ski Slopes

Increasing affluence since 1945 has brought skiing within the reach of far more people than before, and although all the major ski slopes are abroad, a skiing industry has developed in Scotland. The Highland village of **Aviemore,** a quiet haven for anglers and mountaineers, was transformed into a thriving winter sports resort in the 1960s. There are ski schools and dry-ski slopes, and Aviemore is the base for the nearby Cairngorms ski area, with its chairlifts and ski tows.

There are cross-country ski trails of varying degrees of difficulty in this area, too. The other main Scottish ski areas are **Glenshee,** south of Braemar on the A93, Britain's highest main road, the **Lecht** area on the A939 near Tomintoul and the **Glencoe** area above the A82, where the road crosses Rannoch Moor.

## Coastal Launching Sites

Sailing has also become more popular. Most of its enthusiasts are weekend sailors, who do not go far from shore, and there are boat launching sites at harbours and marinas all round the coast, from **St Ives** harbour in Cornwall to **Thurso Bay** on the north coast of Scotland. They vary from the broad, sheltered expanses of **Carrick Roads** or **Plymouth Sound** to the flat shingle shore at **Deal** in Kent, close to the historic anchorage of The Downs, or the exposed Suffolk coastline at **Walberswick** or **Southwold.**

*Natural ski slope*

*Artificial ski slope*

*Coastal launching site*

Heritage Coast

## Heritage Coasts

For centuries the white cliffs of Dover have stood as symbols of English nationhood, independence and pride, confronting foes across the Channel with unyielding defiance. It was the sight of the white cliffs which told generations of weary English travellers that they were nearing home. Today, to keep the white cliffs unspoiled, they have to be protected as two four-mile stretches of Heritage Coast, either side of Dover.

## Heritage Coasts

Before World War II, concern was growing about the substantial areas of coastline which had been ruined by commercial development and the threat that what was left would go the same way, disappearing under an ever-rising tide of cliff-top bungalows and caravan sites. The

Above *Looking across Embleton Bay, a view for Dunstanburgh Castle.*
Left *Spectacular rock formation at Elegug stacks, Pembrokeshire.*

Coastal Preservation Committee mounted a campaign in the 1930s. During the War, the distinguished geographer J A Steers surveyed the coast for the government, and his work would later be the basis on which Heritage Coasts were chosen.

In 1965 the National Trust, thoroughly alarmed, launched Enterprise Neptune, a campaign to raise money to buy threatened coastline. This campaign continues and the Trust now owns and protects more than one mile in every six along the shoreline of England, Wales and Northern Ireland, including the **Giant's Causeway** on the scenic North Antrim seacoast of Northern Ireland and more than a quarter of the entire coast of **Cornwall.**

In 1970 the Countryside Commission recommended to the government that scenically outstanding stretches of undeveloped coast should be designated as Heritage Coasts and protected against undesirable development. This was duly set in train and by the end of the 1980s there were some 850 miles of Heritage Coast in total, amounting to a little over 30 per cent of the coastline of England and Wales. In Scotland more than 20 stretches of coastline of scenic, ecological or environmental importance have been designated by the Scottish

Development Department as Preferred Conservation Zones.

The Heritage Coasts reflect much of the wide variety of scenery and wildlife of the shores of England and Wales. Atop the sheer chalk cliffs of **Dover**, **Beachy Head** and the **Seven Sisters** orchids grow, and they make good places to watch jackdaws and swallows as well as seabirds. Right across on the other side of the country, the granite **Isles of Scilly** lie 28 miles out to sea off Land's End. In legend the islands are all that is left above the surface of the lost land of Lyonesse, which sank beneath the waves when King Arthur's reign came to an end.

The local environmental trust manages 40 miles of Heritage Coast in the Scillies, where the long Atlantic rollers cream on sandy beaches and rocky coves. The mild climate fosters a wealth of wildlife – snails and worms, sea urchins and anemones in the sand or in rock pools, seaweed trailing and undulating in the waves. Here Manx shearwaters, stormy petrels and puffins breed and there are multitudes of terns and gulls. Marram and sand sedge grow in the dunes, with the dwarf pansy – found only here and in the Channel Islands.

The **Suffolk** Heritage Coast is altogether different. This is an understated shore of low cliffs under enormous skies, and shingle beaches where the sea's melancholy retreating roar rattles the pebbles. The sea has swallowed up stretches of this coast, but contrariwise has constructed the shingle bulk of Orford Ness and the long shingle spit that runs six miles down the North Weir Point. Martello towers stud the shoreline. The country's principal breeding colony of avocets has been established by the RSPB in the reserve at Havergate Island. Further north is the Sizewell nuclear power station and beyond is the RSPB reserve at Minsmere. Here among the marshes and shallow 'scrapes', or lagoons, are more avocets, as well as bitterns, marsh harriers, nightingales and nightjars, all told the largest number of breeding bird species on any British reserve.

Bird sanctuaries are again a feature of the **North Norfolk** Heritage Coast between Holme-next-the-Sea and Weybourne. This is a hauntingly desolate coast and another shifting shoreline, which has left places 'next the sea' – like Holme, Cley and Wells – marooned some distance inland. Along the shore an almost unbroken succession of nature reserves protects the saltmarshes, sand dunes and shingle spits, where mats of sea lavender edge the muddy inlets. Hundreds of species of moths gladden the hearts of entomologists here, and there are birds in millions. Rarities sometimes seen include hoopoes and ospreys. The nature reserve on Scolt Head Island is famous for its nesting terns and there are more at Blakeney Point.

Though it faces the same North Sea, the **North Yorkshire and Cleveland** Heritage Coast is a different matter altogether. Lying north of Scarborough and on either side of Whitby, this is the seaward edge of the North York Moors National Park, a line of high cliffs and bays, dramatic headlands and narrow, wooded ravines. Fishing villages huddle in deep clefts, and this is where the great explorer Captain Cook first learned his seamanship. Geologically it is an area of unusual interest and pieces of jet picked up along the shore are the foundation of the trade in Whitby jet ornaments. At Robin Hood's Bay the village houses crowd above each other on a 1-in-3 gradient.

Further up the same coast is the **North Northumberland** area, where there is a different landscape again, with miles of delectable sandy beaches, many of them owned by the National Trust. There are no titanic cliffs here, but low, rocky headlands thrust into the sea. On one of them sprawls ruined Dunstanburgh Castle, lazily menacing like a lion lying in the sun. Bamburgh Castle looks out seawards to the Farne Islands bird

sanctuaries and there are memories here of gallant Grace Darling, the lighthouse keeper's daughter who in 1838 rowed out in a storm to rescue shipwrecked sailors. The tides race in across the gleaming mudflats to cut Lindisfarne off from the mainland.

The only Heritage Coast in Cumbria and Lancashire is the short section round **St Bees Head.** The sheer red sandstone cliffs here command views of the Isle of Man on a clear day and the seabirds wheel and cry – fulmars, herring gulls, black-headed gulls and kittiwakes. Thrift, harebell and wild thyme grow by the cliff path.

**The Great Orme** is another dramatic headland with stark cliffs looming above Llandudno on the North Wales coast. Further south, miles more of formidable cliff scenery have been designated as Heritage Coasts: around the **Lleyn Peninsula**, along the **Pembrokeshire** shore and in **Devon, Cornwall** and **Dorset**.

Heritage Coasts have a great variety of owners, not all of whom are equally conscientious in their stewardship: from the National Trust, the RSPB and other conservation bodies to county councils, local authorities, farmers, private estates and individuals. The Countryside Commission itself gives advice and financial help, but does not own any of the land.

Where a piece of Heritage Coast is owned by an organisation like the National Trust or the RSPB, the public can feel entirely certain there will be proper protection. Matters are not as straightforward along the other Heritage Coasts. Here, each area has a Heritage Coast plan,

drawn up by the local authority on Countryside Commission guidelines. The aim is to involve all local interests in a common approach to the management of the area, to conserve it and to encourage locals and visitors to take tender care of it.

**Pollution Free Beaches**
Quite apart from the physical constitution of the coastline, there is concern about polluted beaches. In 1988 one-third of the bathing beaches in England, Wales and Northern Ireland failed to meet EEC standards of cleanliness: sewage levels in the water were too high. This was at least an improvement on 1986, when half the beaches had failed the test. The great majority of bathing beaches in Cornwall, Devon, Dorset, East Anglia, Wales and Northern Ireland were passed as clean. Along the Kent, Sussex and Hampshire shore, in southern Northumberland and especially in the North-West, the situation was not so good.

Large amounts of money are being spent on the problem. The Marine Conservation society publishes *The Good Beach Guide*, which gives lists and details of the country's cleanest beaches. These include most of those which have won a Blue Flag award from the Tidy Britain Group. The Blue Flag winners were mostly town beaches; those which are cleaned every day during the season and where water cleanliness is high. More beaches in Britain are clean than are not, but there is still work to be done.

*Alum Bay, Isle of Wight, whose colourful sands are sold as souvenirs.*

*Heritage Coast*

## National Parks

Wordsworth, in his *Guide to the Lakes* wrote: 'the Lakes are a sort of national property, in which every man has a right and interest who has an eye to perceive and a heart to enjoy'. In the 19th century 'being outdoors' was seen as being good for body and soul.

Earlier this century, on many wild moors shooting took precedence over amenities for walkers. In the Peak District, an area much appreciated by those wishing to escape for a while from nearby large industrial communities, a mass trespass took place on Kinder Scout in 1932 and five men were arrested and imprisoned.

The Standing Committee on National Parks (SCNP) met for the first time on 26 May 1936, the start of an organised effort to protect and to make available to all the wild landscapes of Britain. The Council for National Parks now oversees the 11 National Parks in Britain, which have been set up since the National Parks and Access to the Countryside Act became law in 1949.

Reservoirs, power lines, roads, quarrying, forestry, TV transmitter

*A spectacular view towards Derwent Dale, in the Peak District.*

masts, power boats, caravan sites, even the tourists themselves by eroding footpaths are all potential threats to the preservation of the National Parks. But, provided informed and responsible public opinion and a spirit of co-operation prevail, all these amenities will be available to future generations.

It is fitting that, after the Kinder Scout protest, the **Peak District** should have been established as the first National Park. The Pennine Way was opened on the anniversary of the protest in 1965 and follows the backbone of England from Edale in Derbyshire, across Hadrian's Wall, to Kirk Yetholm, in the Cheviots. Seventeen million people live within a couple of hours' drive of the park and many come to enjoy walking the deep dales of the White Peak or the dramatic moors and peat bogs of the Dark Peak. Fishing, cycling and rock climbing on the gritstone edges have been joined as leisure activities by gliding and hang-gliding. An Iron Age fort on Man Tor overlooks Roman lead workings and the mine near Castleton, where deposits of decorative fluorspar – blue john – have been worked since Roman times. Heather covers one third of the Park and provides food for the red grouse.

Largest of the National Parks, the **Lake District** combines mountain and lake, woodland and farmland. Moving ice shaped these troughs and corries and glacial rubble dammed the valleys, but the underlying rock dictated whether the hills were softly rounded, like Skiddaw, or wildly rugged, like Scafell and Helvellyn. Broad-leaved woodland like the Borrowdale and Witherslack woods, of great interest to conservationists, cover about five per cent of the Park.

The Snowdon massif is the heartland of the **Snowdonia National Park** and Cader Idris is one of the most popular areas. Half a million people reach Snowdon Summit each year and only a quarter of them admit to using the railway! Many fewer visit the Aran Mountains in the south, or the rugged Rhynogydd. Harlech Castle lies on part of the park's 20 or so miles of sweeping sandy coastline, backed by beautiful mountain scenery. For the 'railway buff' there are six narrow-gauge railways to enjoy and to the 5,000 acres of ancient broad-leaved woodland have been added another 5,000, which with commercial forestry, now cover over 10 per cent of the Park.

Two plateaux make up **Dartmoor,** the largest and wildest stretch of open country in southern Britain, rising to over 2,000ft (610m). Covered with

blanket bog and heather moorland, they are divided by the River Dart. Granite tors protrude near the edges, where other rivers have eroded deep valleys. Over a third of the Park is farmland and the high northern moors have been a military training area since the 1870s. The Dartmoor pony – descendant of ponies turned out to graze in the Middle Ages – grazes much of the lower lying heather moorland. There are hundreds of ancient sites – chambered tombs, hillforts and stone circles – in the Park and medieval crosses and waymarks can still be useful to today's traveller.

The **Pembrokeshire Coast National Park**, the smallest of the Parks, hugs the coast and is only three miles wide along most of its length. Steep cliffs display spectacularly folded and twisted rock formations, while sheltered bays invite bathing, and scuba diving. Offshore, islands such as Skomer and Skokholm support huge colonies of seabirds, among them the world's largest concentration of Manx shearwaters and puffins. Inland from the Milford Haven oil terminal, with its facilities for 300,000-ton tankers, is the Daugleddau, a drowned river valley with dense woodlands and in the north, the windswept moorlands of the Preseli Hills, source of the 'bluestones' of Stonehenge.

Though Middlesbrough and York are not far away, the **North York Moors** is a relatively quiet Park. The moors rise sharply from Pickering in the south, Teesside in the north and the Vale of York in the west. The eastern boundary is the sea, with Staithes, home of Captain Cook, and Whitby (outside the Park boundaries), famous for its clifftop Abbey and its jet – a fossilised black amber – so popular with the Victorians. Rievaulx and Rosedale Abbeys are within the Park, as is Mount Grace Priory, the best preserved Carthusian priory in Britain. Evidence of man's occupation of the high moors ranges from the burial mounds of the neolithic farmers who first cleared the land to the giant golf ball-like radar domes of the Fylingdales early warning system.

Nearly half of the **Yorkshire Dales** is farmland, but there is little woodland. Over four centuries the monasteries' sheep walks developed into the start of a road system across the fells, the best known today being the green lane between Kilnsey and Malham. Miles of dry stone walling are a man-made feature of the landscape, as is the Settle–Carlisle railway with its spectacular Ribblehead Viaduct. Public transport facilities being poor,

National Park

the Dalesrail scheme makes recreational use of this line for walkers, who form the second largest group of visitors, after the touring motorist. As well as a part of the Pennine Way, there are popular areas for walkers and day trippers around Malham Cove and Tarn, with its fascinating limestone pavement 'grikes' – sheltered habitats for lime- and shade-loving plants. Aysgarth Falls, in Wensleydale, attract over half a million visitors a year. There is a 'Bunk House Barns' project, offering basic shelter for walkers in field barns which used to over-winter the dairy cattle.

R D Blackmore's *Lorna Doone* has made **Exmoor** known to many, as has Williamson's *Tarka the Otter*. The heartland, rising to 1,500ft (460m), from Chapman Barrows to Dunkery Beacon is still the windswept haunt of falcon and hawk. The 'hog's back' cliffs along the coast are broken by deep valleys with waterfalls which make protected breeding sites for seabirds. Exmoor is known for its Bronze and Iron Age sites, and a recent aerial survey has added over 2,000 fresh areas to be investigated. The medieval Tarr Steps bridge in the Barle Valley is a popular tourist attraction. With the Quantocks, Exmoor is the last secure habitat in the south of

England for the red deer. The number of Exmoor ponies, adapted to rough grazing and wild winters, is declining, but a small herd has been established to maintain the breed.

Cheviot sheep graze the open moorland which makes up most of the **Northumberland National Park.** Remote from all settlements and mostly above 1,000ft (300m), it is often a harsh environment and must have seemed the end of the world to Roman legionaries from sunny Spain and Italy who manned Hadrian's Wall, part of which runs along the southern edge of the Park. Housesteads fort and Vindolanda have interesting visitor centres and museums. Otterburn and other battles over the 300 years up to the Union of Crowns in 1603 have given rise to many a Border ballad.

The **Brecon Beacons,** four high red sandstone mountain blocks, divide the ancient rocks of mid-Wales from the coalfields and industrialisation further south. From the Black Mountains, near Hay-on-Wye, through the Brecon Beacons and Fforest Fawr, the Park stretches to Black Mountain in the west. Along its southern edge a limestone belt provides a dramatic change in scenery with hundreds of sink-holes and cave systems. The most

spectacular are the Dan-yr-Ogof Caves, on the A4067, at the head of the Tawe valley. The ruins of Carreg Cennen Castle, a 13th-century stronghold on sheer limestone cliffs, lie just off the A40, near Llandeilo.

The **Broads Authority** was rejected together with the Sussex Downs from the twelve candidates in 1949, but was established as a National Park on 1 April 1989. We owe Britain's most famous stretch of inland waterways to the peat-digging activities of our ancestors in the 9th century, which caused flooding in the 14th, and its survival as a recreational area to the strenuous efforts of the Broads Authority, in the 1980s, to halt the environmental degradation. Algae flourished on increased nutrients from effluents and fertilisers, the water 'died', reed cover was lost and the banks became eroded. Much has been done, but care is still needed.

The **New Forest** is the latest area to be granted the status of a National Park, although, as it is administered by the Forestry Commission, the status is not 'real'.

*Hound Tor, an example of Dartmoor's striking landscape.*
Inset *The deep waters of Llyn Cau, from Cader Idris, Gwynedd.*

*National Park*

*National Scenic Area (Scotland)*

**National Scenic Areas (Scotland)**
Where England and Wales have National Parks, Scotland has National Scenic Areas. There are 40 of them, designated in 1978 by the Countryside Commission for Scotland, established to conserve Scotland's natural beauty and improve public access to and enjoyment of it. Though the Commission's stated policy is not 'to see land in Scotland managed as though it were a museum', the National Scenic Areas are protected from development which would harm their scenic qualities. Between them they cover close to one eighth of the total area of Scotland.

Inevitably, the great majority of these National Scenic Areas lie in the Highlands and Islands, along or north of the Highland Line, the geological fault which separates Highland from Lowland Scotland. It runs diagonally from south-west to north-east clear across the country from the Isle of Arran to Stonehaven on the east coast. North and west of this line Scotland's wilder, more solitary, most spectacular and least spoiled landscapes are to be found. The land to the south and east is far more given to farming and industry, and some of it is heavily populated.

A few of the areas lie south of the Highland Line, however. In the Borders, for instance, the **Eildon and Leaderfoot** area includes the uncannily beautiful Eildon Hills. The Leader Water runs south to join the River Tweed below the three volcanic Eildon peaks, the highest rising to 1,385ft (422m). These

*Looking out to Scarista Bay, from Borve on the west coast of Harris.*

shapely hills are steeped in legend and romance. King Arthur and his gallant knights of the Round Table are said to lie sleeping beneath them, under an enchantment, awaiting the time of their recall to life. It was here that Thomas the Rhymer, the 13th-century poet and prophet, encountered the Queen of Fairyland. Dressed all in green, and very fair, she took him away to her magic realm for seven years and gave him the power to see into the future. Here, below the hills, lies ruined Melrose Abbey, where the heart of Robert the Bruce was buried, and close by is Abbotsford, the house Sir Walter Scott built for himself in the countryside he loved.

Scott's immensely popular poems and novels whetted the appetite of prospective tourists for his native land. The process was helped along by Queen Victoria and Prince Albert, who made themselves a Highland retreat at Balmoral in the 1840s. They loved to go stalking deer in the mountains, picnicking at the remote shielings, or shepherds' huts, and fishing for trout in a lumbering rowing boat on Loch Muick.

The region today is the **Deeside and Lochnagar** National Scenic Area, which is the only one in the Grampian Region. The high granite ridge of Lochnagar, a favourite with climbers, rises to 3,786ft (1,154m) to the south of Braemar, in an area of mountain and forest where the River Dee flows past Balmoral Castle on its way to the North Sea at Aberdeen. Lord Byron wrote rhapsodically of 'the crags that are wild and majestic, the steep frowning slopes of dark Lochnagar'. Ever since Queen Victoria's time,

the Highland Gathering at Braemar has been regularly attended by the royal family and marks the annual apogee of the Highland Games season.

From Deeside westwards, the pass called the Lairg Ghru runs through another National Scenic Area, negotiating the heart of the **Cairngorm Mountains** on its way to Speyside. This is the largest tract of land above 3,000ft (915m) in Britain. Rearing up between Braemar and the valley of the Spey, the lofty granite summits of Ben Macdhui, Braeriach, Cairn Toul and Cairn Gorm itself all clear 4,000ft (1,220m) and are outstripped in height only by Ben Nevis.

The lures of hill walking, rock climbing and wintersports draw visitors here. The Forestry Commission manages an extensive Forest Park and near Loch an Eilein are Scots pines at least 250 years old. A hundred square miles of nature reserve lie to the south of Glen More and includes both Braeriach and Cairn Toul. Arctic and alpine plant rarities grow here, with all sorts of mosses and ferns. Reindeer were reintroduced a few years ago and red deer and wildcat roam the mountainsides. Golden eagles soar above the corries and in the woods capercaillies make popping noises like corks.

Scottish scenery is renowned not only for its breathtaking grandeur, its harmony of sky and mountain and water, but for the romantic and often violent history which seems to cling still to every peak and corrie, every pass and glen. The **Ben Nevis** and **Glen Coe** areas contain both the highest mountain in Britain at 4,408ft (1,344m) and one of the most notorious localities in all Scotland's bloody and tragic past. Ben Nevis, which is more of a hump than a peak, can be climbed fairly easily in good weather, though it will take a good many hours up and down, and there are colossal views from the top on a clear day. In Fort William, down below the mountain, the West Highland Museum illuminates the natural and the human history of the district.

To the south are the peaks which tower above Glen Coe, on an overcast day one of the bleakest and most melancholy places in the British Isles. The celebrated and treacherous massacre of the local Macdonalds by a party of Campbell soldiery occurred on a bitter February night in 1692. The site of the Macdonald settlement and much of the surrounding country is now owned by the National Trust for Scotland, which has a visitor centre in the glen. There is also a folk museum in Glencoe village. Further

south still, and part of the National Scenic Area, is the brooding wasteland of Rannoch Moor, with its peaty bogs and lochans, vividly described in an episode of Robert Louis Stevenson's *Kidnapped*.

Famed again in song and story are the **Cuillin Hills** of the Isle of Skye, which reach up in savage splendour above dramatic Loch Coruisk. These are black, jagged, precipitous, sinister mountains, the highest peak being Sgurr Alasdair at 3,309ft (1,009m). The Cuillins are an irresistible magnet to rock climbers, but they have an old reputation for treachery – compasses go oddly astray, mists descend suddenly, climbers are lost and cut off. Among marginally safer attractions on Skye are Talisker malt whisky and the MacLeods' ancestral castle at Dunvegan with its singularly daunting dungeon.

There is wonderful mountain and loch scenery again to the north, where six massive ranges rear their peaks to the sky in the National Scenic Area of **Wester Ross.** The sun glitters on Loch Maree and its islands, and the warmth of the North Atlantic Drift fosters a subtropical paradise in the luxuriant gardens at Inverewe, at the head of Loch Ewe. The gardens were created from the 1860s on by Osgood Mackenzie on what was initially barren peat wasteland.

The island of Foula is included in the Shetlands National Scenic Area, and so is Fair Isle, familiar from weather forecasts. In the Orkneys

the island of **Hoy** is protected, with its dramatic isolated 450ft (137m) stack, the Old Man of Hoy. Man-made Orkney attractions include the Stone Age village of Skara Brae and the enormous Stone Age tomb of Maes Howe, as well as the cathedral of St Magnus in Kirkwall.

Though most of the National Scenic Areas protect mountain scenery, one of them is centred on the old town of **Dunkeld** in the Tayside Region, where the River Tay sweeps past the ruined cathedral among its lawns and sheltering trees. There are memorials in the church to a renowned Scottish regiment, the Black Watch, and to the Scottish Horse, a regiment raised by the Duke of Atholl to fight in the Boer War. An attractive walk through the woods by the River Braan leads to a waterfall and an 18th-century folly. Not far away in the opposite direction is the Loch of the Lowes nature reserve, run by the Scottish Wildlife Trust, where visitors who are lucky may see ospreys. *Macbeth's* Birnam Wood is not far away either.

Lying across the Highland Line are the 'bonnie banks' of **Loch Lomond,** 24 miles long and the largest stretch of inland water in Britain. This is another National Scenic Area. The narrow northern end of the loch protrudes into the Highlands between Ben Vorlich and Ben Lomond, both over 3,000ft (915m). The southern end, with its numerous islands, lies in more

Top *The rocks and tumbling waters of the River Dee, in Royal Deeside.*
Above *Beinn Alligin's peak, with Upper Loch Torridon in the foreground.*

placid country. The burial place of the outlawed Clan MacGregor is on the island of Inchaillach, which is part of the nature reserve at the lower end of the loch.

To the south-west there is a return to mountain landscape in the National Scenic Area of **North Arran**, among the jagged heights of this island in the Firth of Clyde. The highest is Goat Fell at 2,866ft (874m), which can be climbed from the town of Brodick and offers wonderful views, stretching on a clear day to England, Ireland and the Isle of Man. It is to be hoped that the National Scenic Areas will continue to reward Scots and their visitors for many generations to come.

*Forest Park*

*Forest Drive*

**Forest Parks**
**Forest Drives**

Long ago, before man began to make his mark, most of the land surface of Britain was thickly covered with trees. Far back in the New Stone Age, 6,000 years ago or more, farmers began to fell and burn the woodlands to make clearings for crops and pasture stock. By the Middle Ages more than 80 per cent of the original woodland cover had been cleared. Little is left today of the tangled Wealden forest through which the defeated English were chased by William the Conqueror's Normans after Hastings, or of the oaks and glades of Sherwood Forest where Robin Hood and his outlaws hunted.

In this century huge new man-made forests have been created by the Forestry Commission, set up in 1919 to repair the ravages of World War I, when no timber was imported. The Commission's principal purpose has always been a commercial one, to grow saleable timber. It planted pine, larch and spruce – fast-growing softwood trees that thrive in poor soil and are ready for harvesting in 25 or 30 years – and it has been fiercely criticised for its regimented ranks of

*This vast, wooded region of Argyll became Scotland's first Forest Park.*

conifers marching monotonously over hill and dale. Increasingly, however, the Commission has recognised the importance of its role as a provider of recreation and its responsibility to the environment.

**Forest Parks**
In Scotland, where it is the largest landowner, the Commission began to create Forest Parks in scenically attractive areas. The first of them, set under way as far back as 1935, was the **Argyll Forest Park,** extending over 100 square miles of the Cowal Peninsula in the Strathclyde region. Lying between Loch Fyne and Loch Long, it is mountain country, long dominated by the Campbell clan, who feuded with the local Lamonts. The ruined Campbell hold of Carrick Castle glowers out over Loch Goil and the churchyard of Kilmun on Holy Loch was the traditional burying place of the Campbell chiefs.

Visitors can enjoy driving the forest roads, walking on miles of tracks, pony trekking, fishing, sailing and waterskiing. Deer, wildcats, otters, golden eagles and ravens live here. Near the head of Loch Long are fine peaks, including The Cobbler at 2,891ft (881m) and the pass called 'Rest and be Thankful' on the A83, named from the inscription on a stone seat that used to be there. Close to the

southern end of Loch Eck, Benmore House, weirdly and wonderfully Scots Baronial, was given to the Forestry Commission in 1928. The Younger Botanic Garden here is open to the public and is celebrated for its marvellous azaleas and rhododendrons. A brook runs through Puck's Glen, a narrow cleft among the rocks with rare mosses and ferns.

Further south and more than twice as big in area is the **Galloway Forest Park,** designated in 1943, a wild area of wooded mountains, moorland, lochs and streams lying to the north of Newton Stewart. There are ten peaks above 2,000ft (610m), the highest being Merrick, 2,766ft (843m) near the centre of the park. There is climbing, walking, fishing and swimming to enjoy, and a tremendous richness of wildlife – deer, wild goats, pine martens, wildcats, red squirrels, golden eagles and hen harriers.

There are miles of trails for walkers, but motor roads are few and far between in this part of the world. North of Newton Stewart, Loch Trool, bowered among wooded slopes, has a good forest trail. The main road in the park is the Queen's Drive, or more prosaically the A712, from New Galloway to Newton Stewart. Bruce's Stone marks the place where Robert the Bruce scored an early

victory over the English and the man-made Clatteringshaws Loch is part of a hydro-electric scheme. The Galloway Deer Museum is informative not only about the deer but the park and its wildlife in general. The Raiders' Road Forest Drive turns off to the south and follows an old cattle thieves' route through the woods for 10 miles beside the Black Water of Dee, with bathing places and picnic spots.

The **Glen More Forest Park** is in the National Scenic Area of the Cairngorms. The **Queen Elizabeth Forest Park,** designated in 1953, links two National Scenic Areas, Loch Lomond and the Trossachs. In the Tayside Region there is pony trekking, mountain biking and fishing in the **Tummel Forest Park,** with numerous walks of varying length and degrees of difficulty. Forestry Commission walks are graded as 'Easy', 'Strenuous' or 'Difficult'. There are camp sites, picnic sites and plenty of car parks, with deer, red squirrels and capercaillies to watch. The forest here has mostly been planted since World War II, but a specially enticing attraction is a guided walk through the magically named Black Wood of Rannoch. On the south shore of Loch Rannoch, this is one of the rare remaining fragments of the great Caledonian pine forest, which once stretched for hundreds of miles. The visitor centre for the Forest Park is above Loch Tummel at the Queen's View, where you can stand in the footsteps of Queen Victoria, who admired the prospect in 1866. She also admired the Pass of Killiecrankie, not far away, a wooded gorge and battlefield where the National Trust for Scotland has a visitor centre.

The Forest Park idea spread from Scotland south into England. The **Border Forest Park,** designated in 1955, straddles the high sparse moors on both sides of the Anglo-Scots border, where so many raiding and rustling parties rode about their nefarious business in past centuries. Ruins of pele towers and castles testify to a violent history of feuding and marauding. At the heart of the park lies Kielder Water, a spectacular man-made reservoir seven miles long in the valley of the North Tyne, holding 40 million gallons of water. Ferry boats ply across it in the summer, and it is reached by the 12-mile Kielder Forest Drive from the A68. The drive runs past viewpoints and picnic spots to the Forestry Commission's visitor centre at Kielder Castle. In the remoter areas, you may catch sight of red deer, wild goats, blue hares and red squirrels.

On a much smaller scale is the **Grizedale Forest Park,** occupying a slice of Lake District scenery between Coniston Water and Esthwaite Water, south-west of Hawkshead. There are walks and guided tours, orienteering courses, cycle trails, a disabled trail, and a theatre. A trail bears witness to past industries: bloomeries where iron ore was smelted, charcoal pits, potash pits for soap-making, kilns, a tannery and a blast furnace.

The **North Riding Forest Park** lies north-east of Pickering in the rolling landscape of the North York Moors. Centred on the Dalby Valley, in the Middle Ages it was part of the much larger royal hunting forest of Pickering. A nine-mile forest drive takes the motorist gently through the woodland today, with an ample supply of parking pull-offs and places for a picnic. Leaflets detail forest walks for those who want to stretch their legs. Part of the drive follows the Staindale Beck, which was dammed to create an attractive lake, and there is a walk from here to the strange rock formations called the Bridestones, in a nature reserve run by the National Trust and the Yorkshire Wildlife Trust.

**Forest Drives**

Where there is no Forest Park, there is still occasionally a forest drive: as in the **Hamsterley Forest,** the largest area of woodland in County Durham. It covers 5,000 acres west of Bishop Auckland, off the A68. The Forestry Commission bought the estate from the last Surtees owner, a descendant of the famous Victorian sporting novelist R S Surtees. The drive runs for four miles along the Bedburn Beck and the Spurlswood Beck, through

Right *Helpful information at the Visitor Centre in the Borders Forest Park.* Below *Kielder Forest Drive, between Kielder Castle and Redesdale.*

woodland which sports much pine and fir, spruce and larch. There are no less than 60 varieties of tree here all told, with oak and ash, beech and thorn among them. Red squirrels and roe deer, bats and lizards frequent these woods and there are large numbers of woodpeckers and fungi. There are waymarked walks, though more adventurous visitors can explore wherever they like.

In South Wales, meanwhile, it takes a tough cyclist to manage the splendid **Cwmcarn Forest Drive.** The seven-mile drive starts at an excellent new visitor centre south of Abercarn, near Newport. Higher up are picnic places and barbecue spots with commanding views across country and to the Bristol Channel. Walks lead off at intervals, including one which climbs to the summit. The trees are mostly spruce, larch and pine, but oaks, beeches and rowans temper the conifers.

The drive runs through part of the Forestry Commission's Ebbw Forest, a distant man-made descendant of the ancient forest of Machen, which was eaten away over the centuries by sheep and charcoal burners and finally fell victim to the devouring demand for timber in the South Wales coal mines. So here man has put back something of what he has destroyed.

Forest Park

Forest Drive

# THE TOURIST'S BRITISH ISLES
## · CALENDAR ·

## SPRING

### MARCH

**Whuppity Scoorie**
Lanark, Strathclyde
(March 1)

**Ideal Home Exhibition**
Earls Court, London
(early March to early April)

**Belfast Musical Festival**
Belfast
(March – 3rd week)

**Oxford v Cambridge Boat Race**
Putney to Mortlake,
London
(late March or early April)

### APRIL

**Midgley Pace Egg Play**
Calder Valley, West
Yorkshire
(Good Friday)

**Nutters Dance**
Bacup, Lancashire
(Easter Saturday)

**Easter Parade**
Battersea Park, London
(Easter Monday)

**Harness Horse Parade**
Regent's Park, London
(Easter Monday)

**Hare Pie Scramble and Bottle Kicking**
Hallaton, Leicestershire
(Easter Monday)

**Hocktide Festival**
Hungerford, Berkshire
(Easter Tuesday)

**Northumbria Gathering**
Morpeth, Northumbria
(week after Easter)

**The Grand National**
Aintree, Merseyside
(April – 2nd Saturday)

**Shakespeare's Birthday Celebrations**
Stratford-upon-Avon,
Warwickshire
(April 21)

**Spring Flower Show**
Harrogate, North Yorkshire
(late April)

**Badminton Three Day Event**
Badminton, Avon
(late April or early May)

### MAY

**May Morning Ceremony**
Oxford
(May 1)

**Royal May Day Celebrations**
Knutsford, Cheshire
(May – 1st Saturday)

**Flower Parade**
Spalding, Lincolnshire
(early May)

**Furry Dance**
Helston, Cornwall
(May 8)

**Garland Day**
Abbotsbury, Dorset
(May 13)

**Goat Fell Race**
Isle of Arran, Strathclyde
(May – 2nd or 3rd Saturday)

**Bath International Festival of the Arts**
Bath, Avon
(late May to early June)

**Chelsea Flower Show**
Royal Hospital, Chelsea,
London
(late May to early June)

**TT Motorcycle Races**
Isle of Man
(late May to early June)

**Arbor Tree Day**
Aston on Clun, Shropshire
(late May)

**Garland Day**
Castleton, Derbyshire
(May 29)

**Dickens Festival**
Rochester, Kent
(late May or early June)

**Royal Bath and West Show**
Shepton Mallet, Somerset
(late May or early June)

**Woolsack Races**
Tetbury, Gloucestershire
(Spring Bank Holiday)

## SUMMER

### JUNE

**The Derby**
Epsom, Surrey
(June – 1st Wednesday)

**Scuttlebrook Wake**
Chipping Campden,
Gloucestershire
(Saturday following Spring
Bank Holiday)

**Appleby Horse Fair**
Appleby, Cumbria
(June – 2nd Tuesday and
Wednesday)

**Trooping the Colour**
Horse Guards Parade,
London
(June – 2nd Saturday)

**Royal Cornwall Show**
Wadebridge, Cornwall
(June – 2nd week)

**Aldeburgh Festival of Music and the Arts**
Aldeburgh, Suffolk
(June – 2nd to 4th weeks)

**Selkirk Common Riding**
Selkirk, Borders
(mid-June)

**Three Counties Agricultural Show**
Great Malvern, Hereford &
Worcester
(mid-June)

**Stour Music Festival**
Boughton Aluph, Kent
(June – 2nd half)

**Royal Highland Show**
Ingliston, Lothian
(June – 3rd week)

**Royal Ascot Race Meeting**
Ascot, Berkshire
(late June)

**Wimbledon Lawn Tennis Championships**
Wimbledon, London
(late June to early July)

### JULY

**Tynwald Day**
Isle of Man
(July 5)

**Henley Royal Regatta**
Henley on Thames,
Oxfordshire
(July – 1st week)

**Cheltenham International Festival of Music**
Cheltenham,
Gloucestershire
(July – 1st and 3rd weeks)

**British Rose Festival**
Gardens of the Rose,
Chiswell Green,
Hertfordshire
(July – 1st or 2nd week)

**Royal International Agricultural Show**
Stoneleigh, Warwickshire
(early July)

**Great Yorkshire Agricultural Show**
Harrogate, North Yorkshire
(July – 2nd week)

**International Musical Eisteddfod**
Llangollen, Clwyd
(early July)

**Sham Fight**
Scarva, Co Down
(July 13)

**Royal Welsh Show**
Builth Wells, Powys
(July – 3rd week)

**Black Cherry Fair**
Chertsey, Surrey
(July – 3rd Saturday)

**Royal Tournament**
Earls Court, London
(mid-July)

**Buxton International Arts Festival**
Buxton, Derbyshire
(mid-July to early August)

**Tweedmouth Salmon Feast**
Tweedmouth,
Northumberland
(Sunday after July 18)

**Tolpuddle Martyrs Procession**
Tolpuddle, Dorset
(July – 3rd Sunday)

**Durham Miners Gala**
Durham
(July – Saturday of 2nd
week)

**Croagh Patrick Pilgrimage**
Near Westport, Co Mayo
(July-last Sunday)

## AUGUST

**Royal National Eisteddfod**
Varying locations in Wales
(August – 1st week)

**The Burry Man Festival**
Queensferry, Lothian
(August – 2nd Friday)

**Cowes Week**
Cowes, Isle of Wight
(August – 2nd week)

**Puck Fair**
Killorglin, Co Kerry
(August 10–12)

**Marymass Festival**
Irvine, Strathclyde
(August – 2nd or 3rd
weeks)

**Edinburgh International
Festival**
Edinburgh
(August – last three weeks)

**Priddy Sheep Fair**
Priddy, Somerset
(mid-August)

**Grasmere Sports**
Grasmere, Cumbria
(Thursday nearest
August 20)

**Burning of Bartle**
West Witton, North
Yorkshire
(Saturday nearest
August 24)

**Oul' Lammas Fair**
Ballycastle, Co Antrim
(August – last Tuesday)

**Plague Sunday Service**
Eyam, Derbyshire
(August – last Sunday)

**Navy Days**
Plymouth and Portsmouth
(August Bank Holiday)

### AUTUMN

## SEPTEMBER

**Ben Nevis Hill Race**
Fort William, Highland
(September – 1st Saturday)

**Braemar Gathering**
Braemar, Grampian
(September – 1st Saturday)

**Hop Hoodening**
Canterbury, Kent
(early September)

**St Giles's Fair**
Oxford
(September – 1st full week)

**Horn Dance**
Abbots Bromley,
Staffordshire
(Monday after 1st Sunday
following September 4)

**Burghley Horse Trials**
Burghley House, Stamford
(early September)

**Blackpool Illuminations**
Blackpool, Lancashire
(early September to early
November)

**International Air Show**
Farnborough, Hampshire
(September – 1st week)

**Clarinbridge Oyster
Festival**
Clarinbridge, Co Galway
(early or mid-September)

**World Carriage Driving
Championships**
Windsor, Berkshire
(September – 3rd week)

**Victorian Festival**
Llandrindod Wells, Powys
(September – 3rd week)

**Great Autumn Flower
Show**
Harrogate, North Yorkshire
(mid-September)

**Dr Johnson's Birthday**
Lichfield, Staffordshire
(on or near September 18)

**Egremont Crab Fair**
Egremont, Cumbria
(Saturday nearest
September 18)

**Barnstaple Old Fair**
Barnstaple, Devon
(September – 3rd week)

**Painswick Church
Clipping**
Painswick, Gloucestershire
(September – 3rd week)

**Dublin Theatre Festival**
Dublin
(late September to early
October)

## OCTOBER

**Nottingham Goose Fair**
Nottingham
(early October)

**Tavistock Goose Fair**
Tavistock, Devon
(October 10)

**Pack Monday Fair**
Sherborne, Dorset
(1st Monday after
October 10)

**Border Shepherds Show**
Alwinton, Northumberland
(October – 2nd week)

**Horse of the Year Show**
Wembley Arena, London
(mid-October)

**Stratford Mop Fair**
Stratford-upon-Avon,
Warwickshire
(mid-October)

**Wexford Opera Festival**
Wexford, Co Wexford
(late October to
mid-November)

## NOVEMBER

**London to Brighton
Veteran Car Run**
Hyde Park Corner, London
(November – 1st Sunday)

**Guy Fawkes Night**
Lewes, East Sussex, and
elsewhere
(November 5)

**Tar-Barrel Rolling**
Ottery St Mary, Devon
(November 5)

**Lord Mayor's Show**
Guildhall to the Strand,
London
(November – 2nd Saturday)

**Belfast Festival at Queen's**
Belfast
(mid to late November)

**Contemporary Music
Festival**
Huddersfield, West
Yorkshire
(late November)

### WINTER

## DECEMBER

**Royal Smithfield Show**
London
(early December)

**Festival of Carols and
Lessons**
King's College Chapel,
Cambridge
(December 24)

**Ba' Games**
Kirkwall, Orkney Islands
(December 25 and
January 1)

**Greatham Sword Dance**
Greatham, Cleveland
(December 26)

**Allendale Tar-Barrel
Ceremony**
Allendale, Northumberland
(December 31)

**Fireball Ceremony**
Stonehaven, Grampian
(December 31)

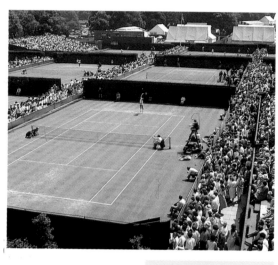

**Flambeaux Procession**
Comrie, Tayside
(December 31)

## JANUARY

**Haxey Hood Game**
Haxey, Humberside
(January 5 or 6)

**Straw Bear Festival**
Whittlesey, Cambridgeshire
(Friday and Saturday
before Plough Monday)

**Plough Stots Service**
Goathland, North
Yorkshire
(Monday after January 6)

**Burning the Clavie**
Burghead, Grampian
(January 11)

**Wassailing the Apple Tree**
Carhampton, Somerset
(January 17)

**Up Helly Aa**
Lerwick, Shetland Islands
(January – last Tuesday)

## FEBRUARY

**Jorvik Viking Festival**
York, North Yorkshire
(February – whole month)

**Pancake Day Race**
Olney, Buckinghamshire
(Shrove Tuesday)

**Shrovetide Football**
Ashbourne, Derbyshire
(Shrove Tuesday)

**Shrovetide Skipping**
Scarborough, North
Yorkshire
(Shrove Tuesday)

*Left Traditional maypole
dancing at Chipping Campden
in Gloucestershire.
Inset A familiar sight in The
Mall, the Household Cavalry.
Above Wimbledon draws the
crowds each summer.
Below May Day celebrations
in Oxford, which were started
in the mid-17th century.*

*Tourist Information Centre*

*Tourist Information Centre (Summer only)*

### Tourist Information Centres

With over 800 offices nationwide, Britain's Tourist Information Centres offer a free service, welcoming calls both in person and by phone.

Whatever your query – whether you are looking for something new to do on a Sunday, somewhere to take the family for the day or simply a good place to eat, your local Tourist Information Centre is only too willing to help.

The staff at each centre have details on just about everything within a 50-mile radius and this is backed up by a comprehensive range of brochures, pamphlets and guides both free and for sale.

They can help with excursions and outings, giving you details and route directions to a variety of places, from castles and craft centres to model villages and museums, tell you which bus to catch, the best place for a picnic, or a walk or a scenic drive. They can even advise on which restaurant is likely to provide a high-chair for the baby or which stately home involves a lot of walking about. They also have details of local events: concerts, carnivals, festivals and fêtes and what is on in town in the evenings.

Another invaluable service is to offer on-the-spot help with finding places to stay. Most centres have up-to-date lists of all kinds of holiday accommodation in the area such as hotels, holiday homes and campsites. They can make local reservations for you, if available, or reservations at any other town which has a centre offering this facility, for the same or the following day. A fee or deposit may be payable for these services.

Most of the centres keep regular office hours from 9 to 5, Monday to Friday, but many are also open at weekends or for longer periods, especially in the summer. Some, however, are open from Easter to September only, but you can always refer your enquiries to the nearest all-year-round centre.

Britain's Tourist Information Centres are at your service and are always happy to help, no matter what the query.

*Inside the London Tourist Board Information Centre at Victoria.*

---

The following signs indicate where you will find a Tourist Information Centre in a town.

 – directional sign for road traffic

 – sign for pedestrians

 – this sign means a Tourist Information Centre is just a few yards away

# Road Atlas of the
# British Isles
# 1999

# using this atlas

## Route planner (pages VIII–XIII)

Maps to help you plan long journeys, showing principal routes and pin-pointing major towns and cities throughout the country.

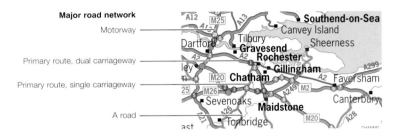

**Major road network**
Motorway
Primary route, dual carriageway
Primary route, single carriageway
A road

## Motorways – restricted junctions (pages XVI–XVII)

A selection of motorway junctions displayed as clear diagrams to help you pin-point individual restrictions.

Motorway junction number
Exit destinations

## Road maps (pages 2–158)

Clear, easy-to-read road mapping enables you to plan detailed journeys. A wealth of motoring information including motorways, primary roads, A and B roads, unclassified roads, interchanges and roundabouts, vehicle ferries, the rail network and numerous places of interest.

**Motoring information**
Motorway junction with restricted access
Motorway
Primary route
A road
Distance in miles between symbols
Roundabout
Interchange
B road
Road number
Unclassified road

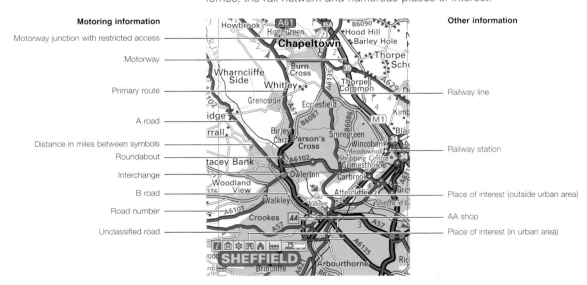

**Other information**
Railway line
Railway station
Place of interest (outside urban area)
AA shop
Place of interest (in urban area)

IV

## Town plans (pages 159–231)

84 fully indexed town plans provide you with essential town centre motoring information plus a wide selection of places of interest.

**Motoring information**

- AA-Recommended road
- Restricted road
- One-way street

**Other information**

- Building of interest
- Car park
- Shopmobility
- Pedestrian only
- Public convenience

## District maps (pages 232–243)

Unique planning maps designed to help you navigate through and around major urban areas.

**Motoring information**

- B road, single carriageway
- A road, single carriageway
- Primary route, dual carriageway
- Motorway

**Other information**

- Railway station
- Railway line

## Central London (pages 244–261)

Comprehensive, fully indexed maps of inner London provide a simple guide to finding your way around the city.

**Motoring information**

- Banned turn
- Classified road
- Restricted road
- One-way street

**Other information**

- Underground railway station
- Garage parking
- Major place of tourist interest

## Ports and airports (pages 264–267)

Plans of major airports and seaports that indicate approach roads and provide you with valuable car-parking information.

**Motoring information**

- Approach road

**Other information**

- Public transport stop
- Car park

# how the AA can help you

**The AA is Britain's largest motoring organisation, providing accurate and up-to-date information services for all motorists – just give us a call**

All 09003 prefixed numbers are charged at 50p per minute at all times (correct at time of going to press)

## Check the traffic before you leave

**Call AA Roadwatch** for the latest reports on traffic hold-ups and roadworks

**Call 09003 401** plus the 3 digits for the relevant area on the map

**London and the South East area**
**401 122** Area within M25
**401 123** Essex, Herts, Beds, Bucks, Oxon, Berks
**401 125** Hants, Surrey, Sussex, Kent
**401 127** M25 and link roads

**National motorway network**
**09003 401 110**

**Continental Roadwatch  09003 401 904**
For traffic conditions to and from ferry ports, ferry news and major European events

## Prepare for the weather

**Call AA Weatherwatch** for the latest weather report followed by a 4-day forecast

**Call 09003 401** plus the 3 digits shown on the relevant area of the map

**Latest national forecast**
**09003 401 130**

**Weather reports for crossing the Channel and for Northern France**
**09003 401 361**

## Travelling abroad

**Just dial 09003** followed by the numbers shown

**Seaports** – how to get there, parking and other essential information
**401 891** Hampshire/Dorset/Kent ports

**The Channel Tunnel  401 362**
Le Shuttle boarding details, terminal facilities, restrictions, passport control, journey times and general travel information

**Airports** – how to get there, parking, air-links and other essential information

**401 935** Birmingham, Edinburgh, Gatwick, Heathrow, Luton, Manchester, Stansted and London City Airport

**Taking your car abroad** – be prepared for different laws, paperwork and driving conditions

**401 866** for the information line and a report on your destination

## Calling on the move

**Mobile Phones** (dial 6 digits only) **401 110**
A special service for VODAFONE or CELLNET users
VODAFONE connects you to the local Roadwatch traffic message
CELLNET connects you to a cellular menu from which you select the appropriate
message (Calls cost 50p per minute at all times in addition to your mobile call tariff)

**Vodafone 'Fast Dial'** (dial 4 digits only) **2222**
A special service for VODAFONE users for easy access to AA motoring advice and other
travel information (Calls cost 41p per minute at all times. Call charges correct at time of
going to press)

## Need expert advice?

Access the expertise of the AA, **call 09003** followed by the numbers shown

**Motoring hints and advice**

**401 505** Checks before you start, route planning and motorway driving
**401 506** Child seats and harnesses
**401 508** Safe motorway driving

**401 509** Motoring for disabled drivers
**401 522** Towing: matching the vehicle to the load
**401 526** Motorway breakdowns

**Motoring and the law**

**401 841** Accidents: reporting to police, exchanging details
**401 847** Drinking and driving: what is the law and penalties?
**401 850** Lights: use in daytime, rear, high-intensity (fog) lights
**401 851** MoT: who needs one, what is tested, penalties and checks

**401 852** Wheel clamping
**401 853** Parking: restrictions and enforcements
**401 855** Seat belts
**401 856** Speed limits in the UK: what is the law?
**401 857** Tyre safety: keeping safe and within the law

The material contained in these 09003 recorded information services has been researched by the AA.
While every effort is made to ensure that it is accurate, no liability can be accepted arising from
inaccuracies or omissions. © The Automobile Association 1998

## Useful numbers

**AA The Driving School 0800 60 70 80**
Book your driving lessons anywhere in mainland Britain

**Road User Information Line (Highways Agency) 0345 50 40 30**
For information on motorways and trunk roads, to make a complaint or comment
on road conditions or roadworks, for MoT and vehicle licence enquiries

**Trace Service (Greater London only) 0171 747 4747**
Track down your car if it has been towed away

## Exclusive services for AA Members

All 0990 prefixed numbers are charged at BT's National Rate

**AA Hotel Booking Service 0990 05 05 05** (8.30am–7.30pm, Mon–Sat)
Free reservation service for business or leisure travel. Take advantage of the many
special offers available at over 8,000 AA-inspected hotels, guest houses, inns and
farmhouses in Britain and Ireland

**UK Route Planning 0990 500 600** (24 hours, 7 days a week)
Free personalised itineraries for routes within Great Britain and Ireland

**Special Offers and AA Services 0990 500 600** (24 hours, 7 days a week)
Expert advice and assistance on legal and technical aspects of motoring.
Details of discounts on AA services and other exclusive offers negotiated to help
AA members keep the cost of motoring down

**AA Membership Administration 0990 444 444** (8am–8pm, Mon–Fri; 8am–noon, Sat)
All Membership enquiries, including renewal, upgrades and name or address changes

**If you are not an AA Member and would like to be – call 0800 444 999
for details on how to join**

## Visit our web site

# www.theaa.co.uk

# route planner

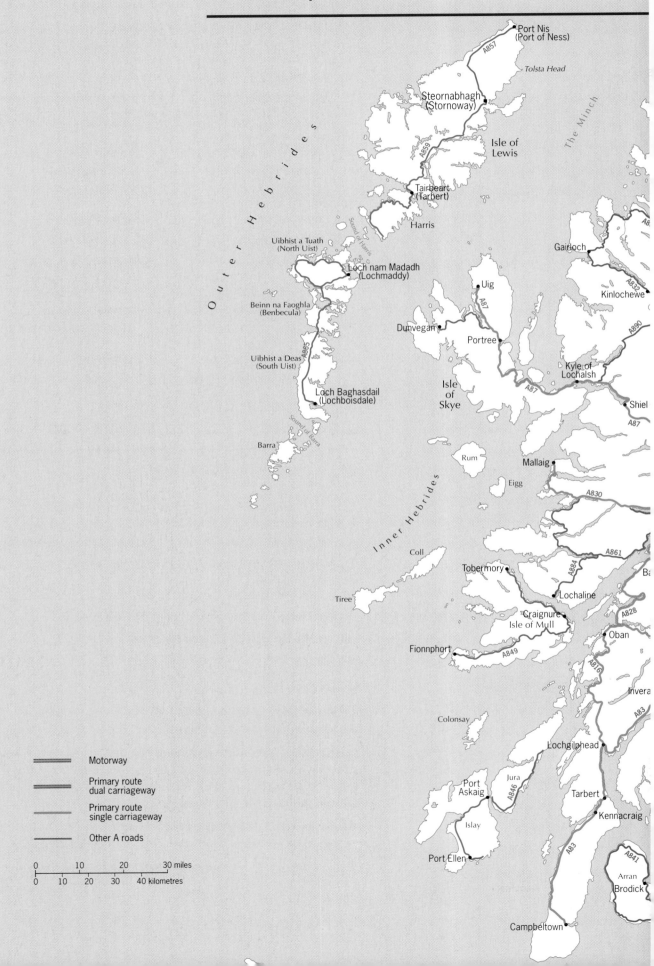

Port Nis
(Port of Ness)

*Tolsta Head*

Steornabhagh
(Stornoway)

Isle of
Lewis

*The Minch*

*Outer Hebrides*

Tairbeart
(Tarbert)

Harris

Gairloch

Uibhist a Tuath
(North Uist)

Loch nam Madadh
(Lochmaddy)

Uig

Kinlochewe

Beinn na Faoghla
(Benbecula)

Dunvegan

Portree

*Sound of Harris*

Uibhist a Deas
(South Uist)

Kyle of
Lochalsh

Shiel

Loch Baghasdail
(Lochboisdale)

Isle
of
Skye

Barra

*Sound of Barra*

*Inner Hebrides*

Rum

Mallaig

Eigg

Coll

Tobermory

Lochaline

Tiree

Craignure
Isle of Mull

Oban

Fionnphort

Colonsay

Invera

Lochgilphead

Port
Askaig

Jura

Tarbert

Kennacraig

Islay

Port Ellen

Arran

Brodick

Campbeltown

| | Motorway |
| --- | --- |
| | Primary route dual carriageway |
| | Primary route single carriageway |
| | Other A roads |

0    10    20    30 miles

0   10   20   30   40 kilometres

Stromness
Kirkwall
Orkney Islands
John O'Groats
Thurso
A836
Melvich
Tongue
A838
Scourie
A894
Altnaharra
A897
A9
A882
Wick
A99
Latheron
Helmsdale
Lairg
A839
Bonar Bridge
A835
Ullapool
A837
Tain
Moray Firth
Alness
A832
Cromarty
Dingwall
Achnasheen
Nairn
Elgin
Cullen
Banff
Macduff
Fraserburgh
A98
A95
A96
A940
A941
Forres
Keith
Turriff
Peterhead
A947
A952
A90
Inverness
Aberlour
Huntly
Drumnadrochit
A82
Tomatin
Grantown-on-Spey
Oldmeldrum
Ellon
Invermoriston
A938
Tomintoul
Inverurie
Aviemore
A939
Aberdeen
A887
A87
Invergarry
Kingussie
Newtonmore
A93
Braemar
Ballater
Banchory
A86
Stonehaven
Fort William
A92
Pitlochry
Brechin
Montrose
Aberfeldy
Blairgowrie
Forfar
A827
A826
A94
Coupar Angus
Arbroath
Killin
Carnoustie
Dundee
A85
Tyndrum
Lochearnhead
Perth
Newport-on-Tay
Crianlarich
Crieff
St Andrews
A819
Auchterarder
M90
A91
Cupar
A915
A917
A84
Callander
Tarbet
Dunblane
Kinross
Glenrothes
M9
Alloa
A977
Buckhaven
A811
Stirling
Dunfermline
Kirkcaldy
A815
Firth of Forth
A985
M80
NORTH SEA
Gourock
Dumbarton
Falkirk
Edinburgh
EDINBURGH
Dunbar
Dunoon
A80
Linlithgow
A1
Greenock
Cumbernauld
Musselburgh
M8
Glasgow
M73
Airdrie
Livingston
Dalkeith
Eyemouth
A78
A8
Paisley
GLASGOW
A71
A702
Largs
Motherwell
M77
A68
A737
A77
East Kilbride
A703
Berwick-upon-Tweed
A73
A7
Kilwinning
Strathaven
Lanark
A721
A701
A697
Ardrossan
M74
Peebles
Coldstream
A698
Biggar
A72
Galashiels
Irvine
Firth of Clyde
Lesmahagow
Kilmarnock
Kelso
Troon
A76
Wooler
Prestwick
Selkirk
A708
Cumnock
Ayr
A74(M)
Jedburgh
A70
New Cumnock
Hawick
Alnwick
Maybole
A713
A74
A1068
Amble

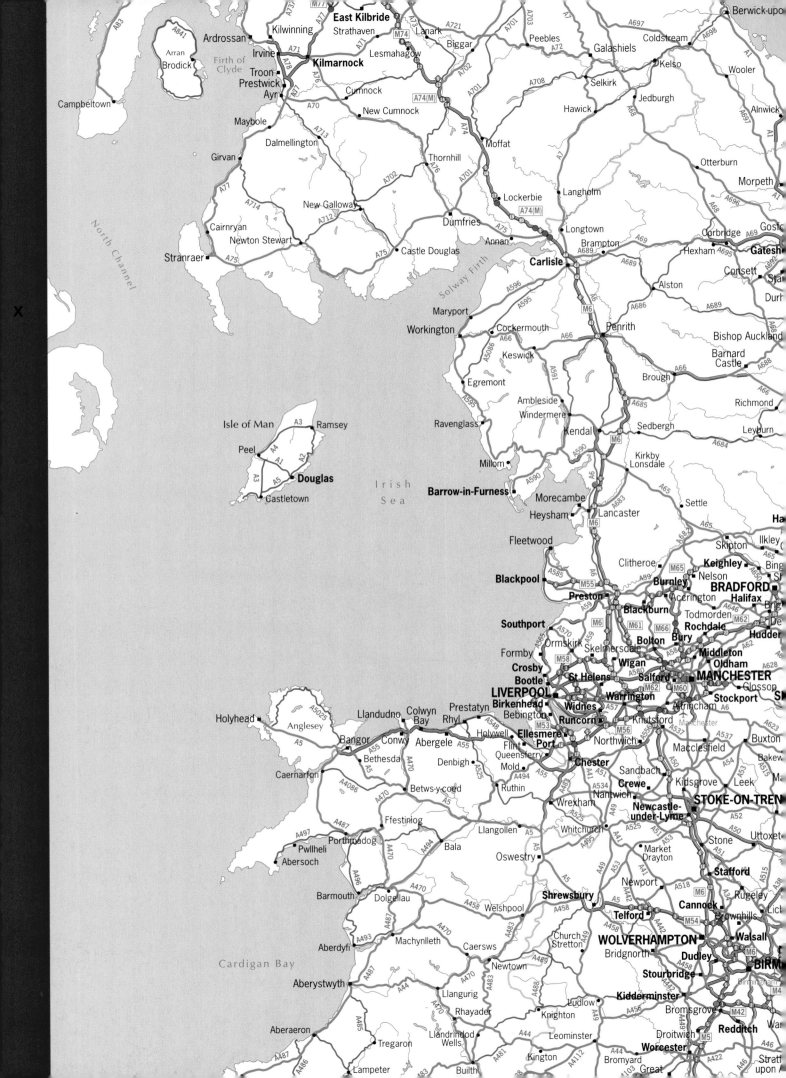

# AA Hotel Booking Service

Call now to book Business or Leisure accommodation
0990 050505

Motorway
Primary route dual carriageway
Primary route single carriageway
Other A roads

0   10   20   30 miles
0  10  20  30  40 kilometres

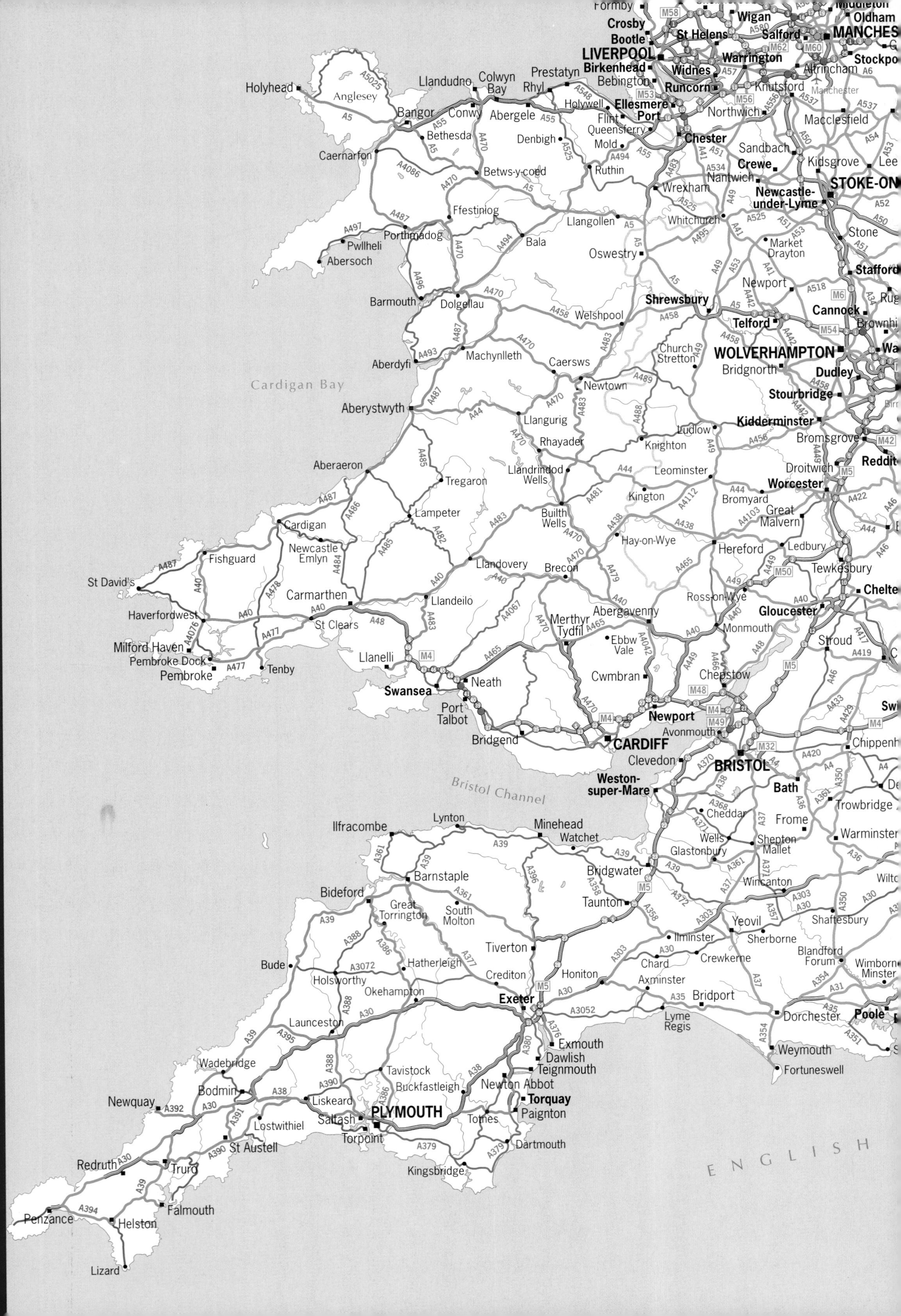

Formby
Crosby
Bootle
Wigan
St Helens
Salford
Oldham
MANCHESTER
Stockport
LIVERPOOL
Birkenhead
Warrington
Widnes
Altrincham
Bebington
Runcorn
Knutsford
Holyhead
Anglesey
Llandudno
Colwyn Bay
Prestatyn
Rhyl
Holywell
Ellesmere Port
Flint
Queensferry
Northwich
Macclesfield
Bangor
Conwy
Abergele
Bethesda
Denbigh
Mold
Chester
Sandbach
Crewe
Kidsgrove
Caernarfon
Betws-y-coed
Ruthin
Nantwich
Wrexham
Newcastle-under-Lyme
STOKE-ON
Ffestiniog
Llangollen
Whitchurch
Stone
Pwllheli
Porthmadog
Bala
Oswestry
Market Drayton
Abersoch
Stafford
Newport
Barmouth
Dolgellau
Shrewsbury
Cannock
Welshpool
Telford
Machynlleth
Church Stretton
WOLVERHAMPTON
Aberdyfi
Caersws
Bridgnorth
Dudley
Cardigan Bay
Newtown
Stourbridge
Aberystwyth
Llangurig
Kidderminster
Ludlow
Rhayader
Knighton
Bromsgrove
Aberaeron
Llandrindod Wells
Leominster
Droitwich
Tregaron
Kington
Worcester
Bromyard
Lampeter
Builth Wells
Great Malvern
Cardigan
Hay-on-Wye
Newcastle Emlyn
Fishguard
Hereford
Ledbury
Llandovery
Brecon
Tewkesbury
St David's
Carmarthen
Llandeilo
Ross-on-Wye
Abergavenny
Gloucester
Haverfordwest
St Clears
Merthyr Tydfil
Ebbw Vale
Monmouth
Stroud
Milford Haven
Pembroke Dock
Llanelli
Pembroke
Tenby
Neath
Cwmbran
Chepstow
Swansea
Port Talbot
Newport
Avonmouth
Bridgend
CARDIFF
Chippenham
Clevedon
BRISTOL
Weston-super-Mare
Bath
Bristol Channel
Trowbridge
Cheddar
Frome
Ilfracombe
Lynton
Minehead
Watchet
Wells
Shepton Mallet
Warminster
Glastonbury
Barnstaple
Bridgwater
Bideford
Great Torrington
South Molton
Taunton
Wincanton
Yeovil
Shaftesbury
Ilminster
Sherborne
Tiverton
Chard
Crewkerne
Blandford Forum
Bude
Hatherleigh
Holsworthy
Crediton
Honiton
Axminster
Wimborne Minster
Okehampton
Exeter
Bridport
Launceston
Lyme Regis
Dorchester
Poole
Exmouth
Dawlish
Teignmouth
Weymouth
Wadebridge
Tavistock
Fortuneswell
Buckfastleigh
Newton Abbot
Torquay
Newquay
Bodmin
Liskeard
PLYMOUTH
Paignton
Lostwithiel
Saltash
Totnes
Torpoint
St Austell
Dartmouth
Redruth
Truro
Kingsbridge
ENGLISH
Falmouth
Penzance
Helston
Lizard

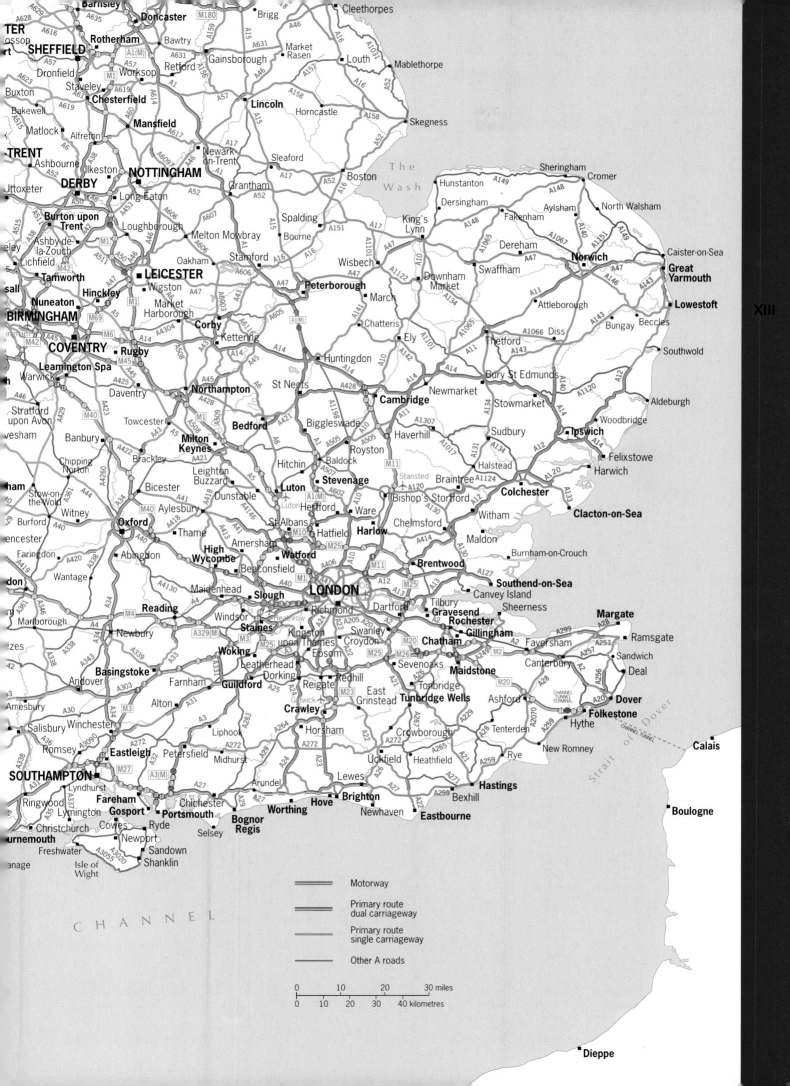

# road signs

## Classes of signs

Our road system has a consistent and comprehensive set of road signs that provide you with information, instructions and warnings.

| Circles order and prohibit | Triangles warn | Rectangles provide information |

## Junctions and roundabouts

These signs provide you with important information about the nature of the junction or the roundabout ahead.

| Distance to 'STOP' line ahead | Distance to 'GIVE WAY' line ahead | Give way to traffic on major road | Stop and give way | Crossroads | T-junction | Staggered junction | Roundabout | Mini-roundabout (roundabout circulation) | No through road |

## Traffic behaviour

Signs which must be obeyed. They indicate the speed or action you are required to take in particular situations.

| No stopping (clearway) | National speed limit applies | Maximum speed | Give priority to vehicles from opposite direction | No overtaking | Motor vehicles prohibited except for access | No entry for vehicular traffic | No U-turns | No right turn | No left turn |

| Turn left ahead | Turn left | Vehicles may pass either side to reach same destination | Ahead only | Keep left |

## The road ahead

Advance warning of the road layout ahead enables you to plan a safe approach.

| Bend to left | Double bend, first to left | Bend to right | Double bend, first to right | Road hump or series of road humps ahead | Worded warning sign | Dual carriageway ends | Steep hill downwards | Steep hill upwards |

| No goods vehicles over maximum gross weight shown (in tonnes) | Axle weight limit (in tonnes) | No vehicles over height shown | Sharp deviation of route | Two-way traffic straight ahead | Traffic merges from left | Traffic merges from right | Road narrows on left | Road narrows on both sides |

# Hazards ahead

These signs warn you of potential hazards on the road ahead.

| Hospital ahead with accident and emergency facilities | Pedestrian crossing | Cycle route ahead | Slippery road | Road works | Uneven road | Wild animals | Falling or fallen rocks | Other danger |
|---|---|---|---|---|---|---|---|---|

| Children | Children going to or from school | School crossing patrol ahead | School crossing patrol | Traffic signals | Hump bridge | Opening or swing bridge ahead | Quayside or river bank |
|---|---|---|---|---|---|---|---|

# On the motorway

These signals are used to warn you of conditions ahead and the lanes affected. They may be located overhead, on the central reservation or over the nearside lane. Drivers must observe the advisory speed limits and should remember that the red circle means a mandatory speed control.

| Temporary maximum speed limit and information message | Change lane | Leave motorway at next exit | Do not proceed further in this lane |
|---|---|---|---|

| Reduced visibility ahead | Lane ahead closed | Temporary maximum speed limit | End of restriction | National speed limits apply | Traffic building up ahead. Reduce speed to a maximum of 60mph to help maintain flow | Traffic getting heavier ahead. Reduce speed to a maximum of 50mph or lower if incidents occur | Traffic improving. Maximum speed increased to 60mph | Traffic is lighter. Flow easier. Return to national speed limits. This will appear for 3 minutes before going blank |
|---|---|---|---|---|---|---|---|---|

# Motorway diversions

Where the motorway is closed, special signs advise you of the recommended diversion route around the incident.

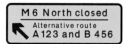      

Symbols showing emergency diversion route for motorway traffic

# motorways – restricted junctions

Diagrams of selected motorway junctions which have entry
and exit restrictions

## M1 London–Leeds

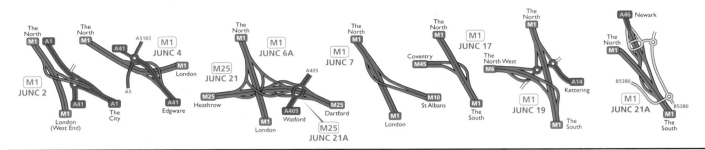

## M1 London–Leeds | M2 Rochester–Faversham | M3 Sunbury–Southampton

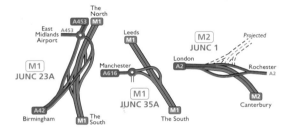
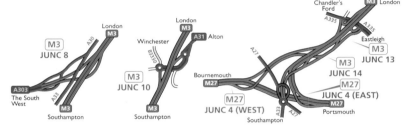

## M4 London–South Wales | M5 Birmingham–Exeter

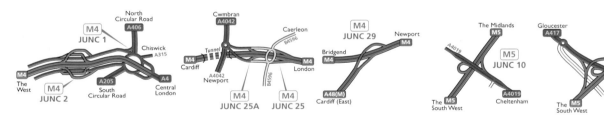

## M5 Birmingham–Exeter | M6 Rugby–Carlisle

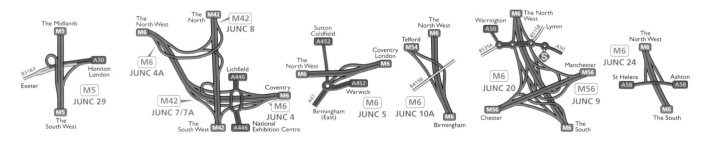

## M6 Rugby–Carlisle | M8 Edinburgh–Bishopton

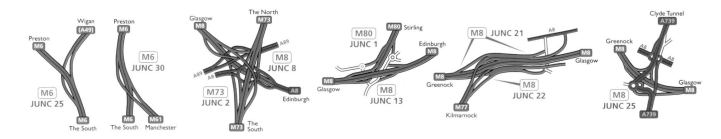

## M8 Edinburgh–Bishopton

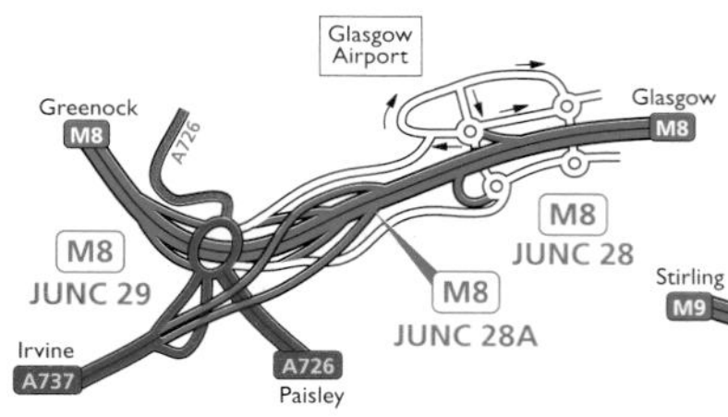

Glasgow Airport

Greenock M8
A726
Glasgow M8
M8 JUNC 29
M8 JUNC 28
M8 JUNC 28A
Irvine
A737
A726
Paisley

## M9 Edinburgh–Dunblane

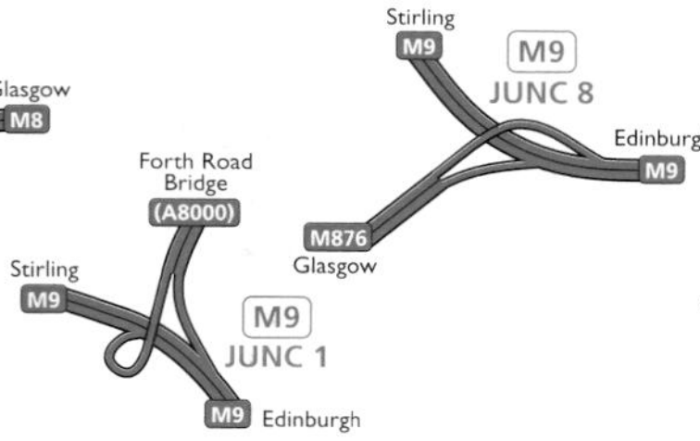

Stirling M9
M9 JUNC 8
Edinburgh M9
Forth Road Bridge (A8000)
M876 Glasgow
M9 JUNC 1
Stirling M9
M9 Edinburgh

## M11 London–Cambridge

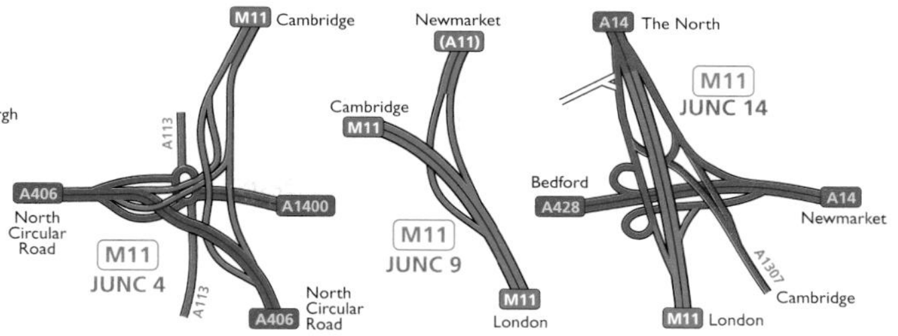

M11 Cambridge
A113
A406 North Circular Road
A1400
M11 JUNC 4
A113
A406 North Circular Road

Newmarket (A11)
Cambridge M11
M11 JUNC 9
M11 London

A14 The North
M11 JUNC 14
Bedford A428
A14 Newmarket
A1307 Cambridge
M11 London

## M20 Swanley–Folkestone

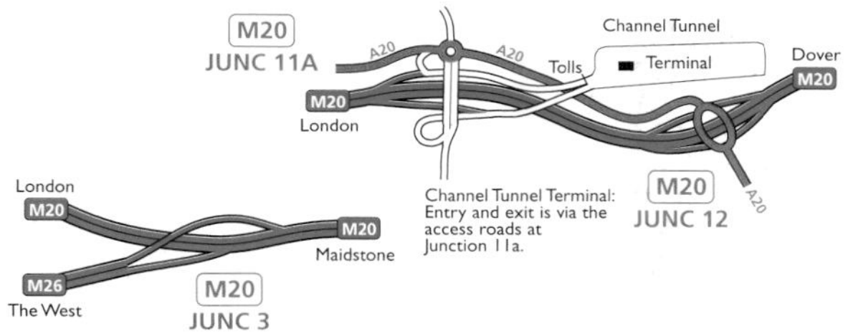

M20 JUNC 11A
A20
A20
Tolls
Channel Tunnel ■ Terminal
Dover M20
M20 London
Channel Tunnel Terminal: Entry and exit is via the access roads at Junction 11a.
M20 JUNC 12
A20
London M20
M26 The West
M20 Maidstone
M20 JUNC 3

## M25 London Orbital

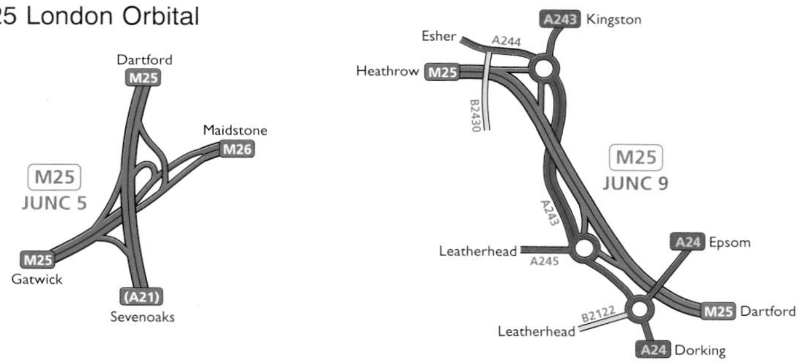

Dartford M25
Maidstone M26
M25 JUNC 5
M25 Gatwick
(A21) Sevenoaks

Esher A244 Kingston A243
Heathrow M25
B2430
M25 JUNC 9
A243
Leatherhead A245
B2122
A24 Epsom
M25 Dartford
Leatherhead
A24 Dorking

## M25 London Orbital

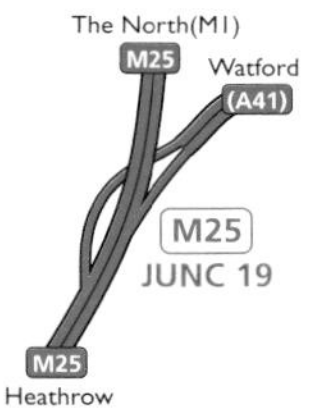

The North(M1)
M25 Watford (A41)
M25 JUNC 19
M25 Heathrow

## M27 Cadnam–Portsmouth

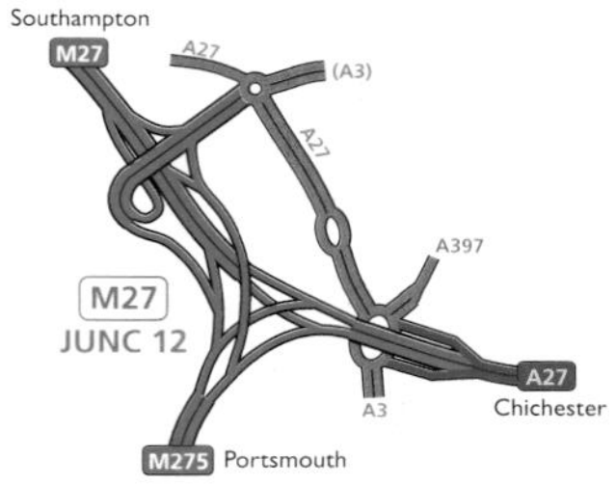

Southampton M27
A27 (A3)
A27
A397
M27 JUNC 12
A3
A27 Chichester
M275 Portsmouth

## M40 London–Birmingham

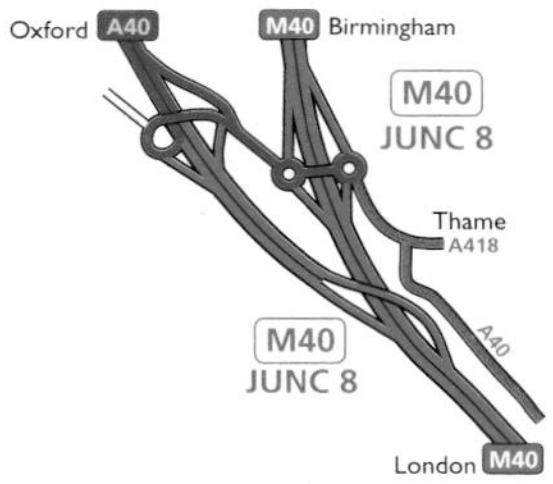

Oxford A40
M40 Birmingham
M40 JUNC 8
Thame A418
M40 JUNC 8
A40
London M40

## M42 Bromsgrove–Measham

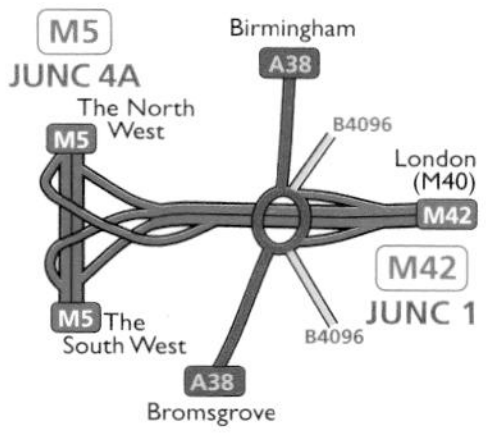

M5 JUNC 4A
Birmingham A38
M5 The North West
B4096
London (M40)
M42
M5 The South West
M42 JUNC 1
A38 Bromsgrove
B4096

## M56 North Cheshire Motorway

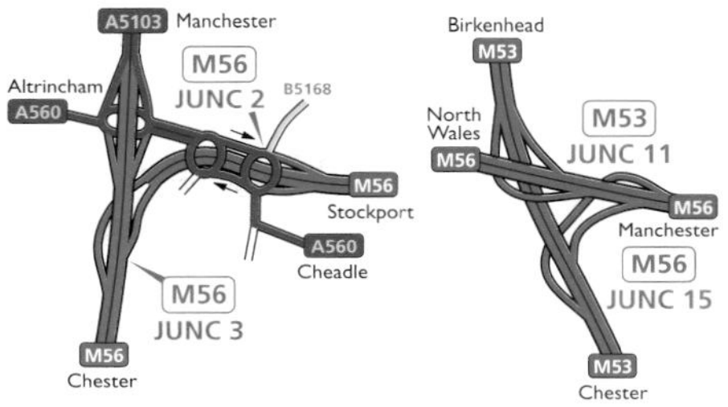

A5103 Manchester
M56 JUNC 2
B5168
Altrincham A560
M56 Stockport
A560 Cheadle
M56 JUNC 3
M56 Chester

Birkenhead M53
North Wales M56
M53 JUNC 11
M56 Manchester
M56 JUNC 15
M53 Chester

## M60 Greater Manchester

Preston (M61) M60
A34 Manchester
M60 JUNC 3
Stockport M60
M56 JUNC 1
M60 Chester
A34 Wilmslow

Manchester A5103
M60 Preston (M61)
Stockport M60
A5103 Chester (M56)
M60 JUNC 5

M61 (A666) Bolton
M61 JUNC 3
M61 JUNC 2
M61 Preston
M61 JUNC 1
M60 Leeds
M60 JUNC 14
A580 St Helens
Liverpool M60
M60 JUNC 15
A580 Manchester

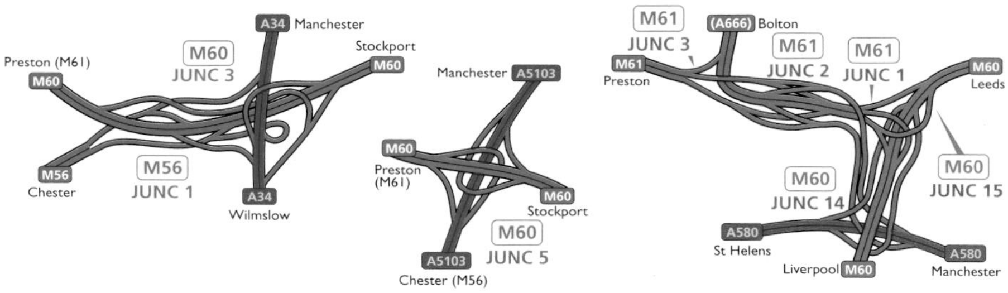

## M60 Greater Manchester

M60 JUNC 16
Bolton A666
Leeds M60
M60 Liverpool
A666 Swinton
M60 JUNC 27
A626
Chester (M56) M60
A560
A626 Stockport
B6104
Ashton M60
A6017
M60 JUNC 25
A560 Bredbury
B6104
M60 JUNC 26

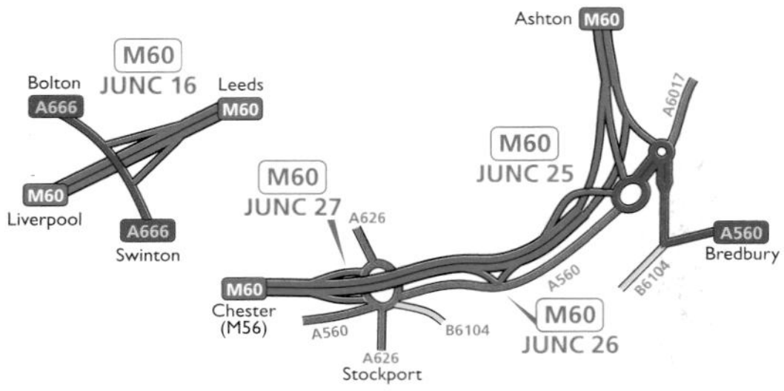

## M62 Liverpool-Humberside

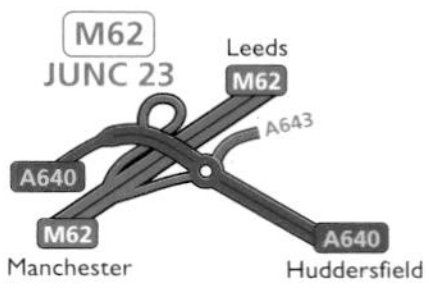

M62 JUNC 23
Leeds M62
A640
A643
M62 Manchester
A640 Huddersfield

## M73 East of Glasgow

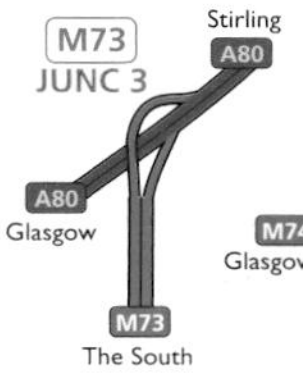

M73 JUNC 3
Stirling A80
A80 Glasgow
M73 The South

## M74 Glasgow–Gretna

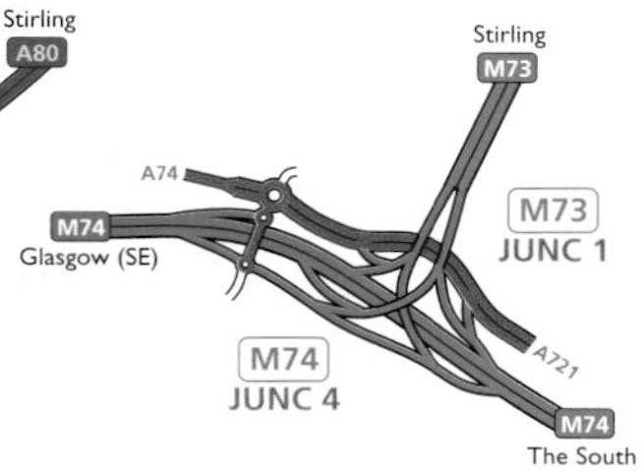

Stirling M73
A74
M74 Glasgow (SE)
M73 JUNC 1
A721
M74 JUNC 4
M74 The South

## M74, A74(M) Glasgow–Gretna

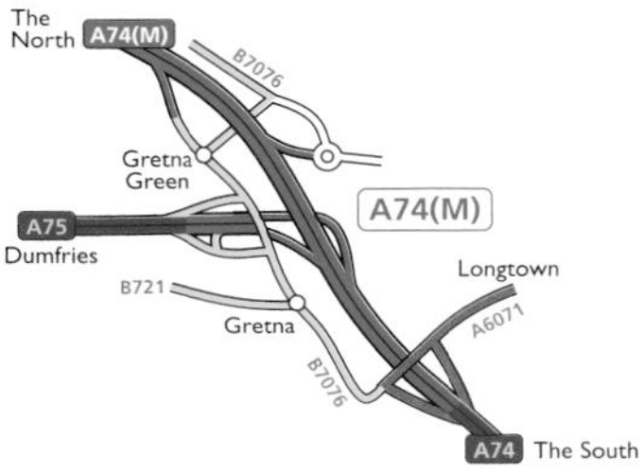

The North A74(M)
B7076
Gretna Green
A75 Dumfries
B721
Gretna
B7076
A74(M)
Longtown
A6071
A74 The South

## M80 Glasgow–Stirling

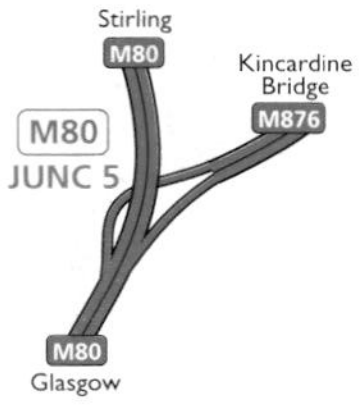

Stirling M80
Kincardine Bridge M876
M80 JUNC 5
M80 Glasgow

## M90 Forth Road Bridge–Perth

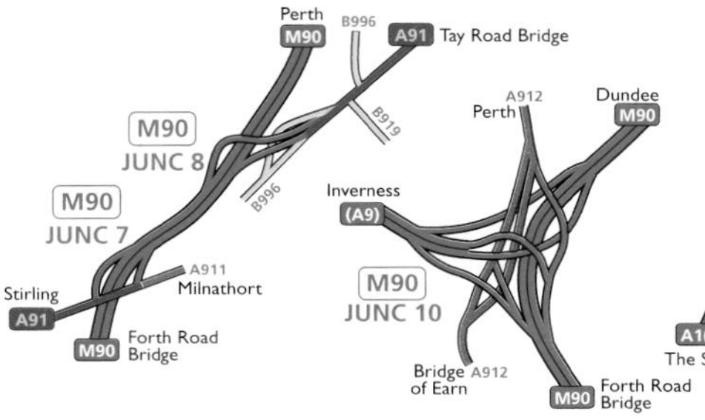

Perth M90
B996
A91 Tay Road Bridge
M90 JUNC 8
A912 Perth
Dundee M90
Inverness (A9)
B996
M90 JUNC 7
Stirling A91
A911 Milnathort
M90 JUNC 10
Bridge of Earn A912
Forth Road Bridge M90
M90 Forth Road Bridge

## A1(M) Scotch Corner–Tyneside

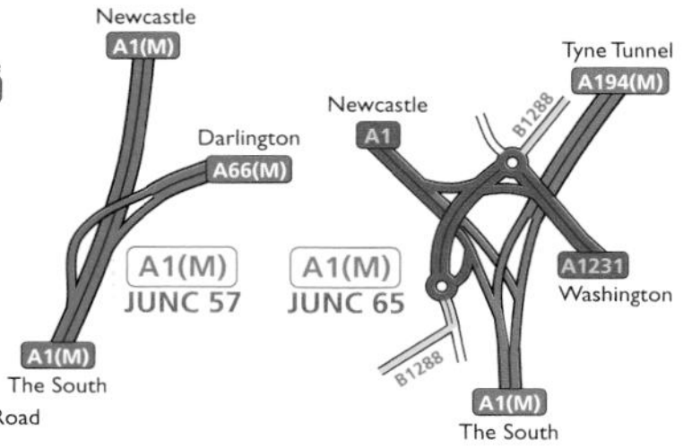

Newcastle A1(M)
Darlington A66(M)
A1(M) JUNC 57
A1(M) The South

Newcastle A1
Tyne Tunnel A194(M)
B1288
A1(M) JUNC 65
A1231 Washington
A1(M) The South
B1288

# map symbols

## motoring information

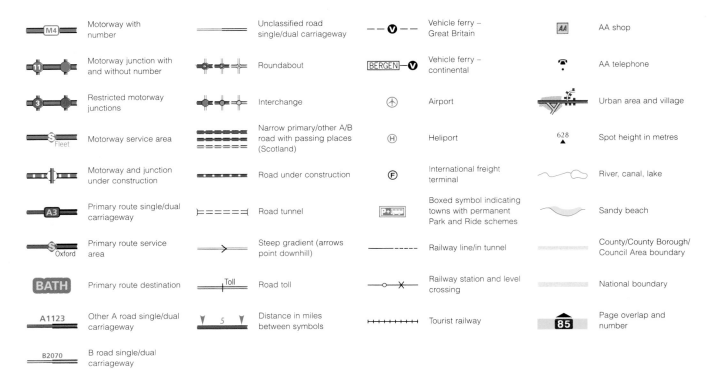

| | | | | | | | |
|---|---|---|---|---|---|---|---|
| M4 | Motorway with number | | Unclassified road single/dual carriageway | — V — | Vehicle ferry – Great Britain | AA | AA shop |
| 11 | Motorway junction with and without number | | Roundabout | BERGEN — V | Vehicle ferry – continental | ☎ | AA telephone |
| 3 | Restricted motorway junctions | | Interchange | ✈ | Airport | | Urban area and village |
| S Fleet | Motorway service area | | Narrow primary/other A/B road with passing places (Scotland) | H | Heliport | 628 ▲ | Spot height in metres |
| | Motorway and junction under construction | | Road under construction | F | International freight terminal | | River, canal, lake |
| A3 | Primary route single/dual carriageway | ⊨=====⊨ | Road tunnel | P+ | Boxed symbol indicating towns with permanent Park and Ride schemes | | Sandy beach |
| S Oxford | Primary route service area | → | Steep gradient (arrows point downhill) | —  — — | Railway line/in tunnel | | County/County Borough/ Council Area boundary |
| BATH | Primary route destination | Toll | Road toll | —o—X— | Railway station and level crossing | | National boundary |
| A1123 | Other A road single/dual carriageway | ▼ 5 ▼ | Distance in miles between symbols | +++++++ | Tourist railway | 85 | Page overlap and number |
| B2070 | B road single/dual carriageway | | | | | | |

## tourist information

| | | | | | | | |
|---|---|---|---|---|---|---|---|
| i | Tourist Information Centre | ⊠ | Theme park | 🐎 | Roman antiquity | 🏁 | Motor-racing circuit |
| i | Tourist Information Centre (seasonal) | 🐘 | Zoo | ⚑ | Prehistoric monument | ✈ | Air show venue |
| 🏛 | Abbey, cathedral or priory | 🐗 | Wildlife collection – mammals | ✕ 1066 | Battle site with year | ⛷ | Ski slope – natural |
| ⚭ | Ruined abbey, cathedral or priory | 🐦 | Wildlife collection – birds | 🚂 | Steam centre (railway) | ⛷ | Ski slope – artificial |
| ♜ | Castle | 🐟 | Aquarium | ⊙ | Cave | NT | National Trust property |
| 🏠 | Historic house | 🐋 | Nature reserve | 🐞 | Windmill | NTS | National Trust for Scotland property |
| M | Museum or art gallery | RSPB | RSPB site | ⚐ | Golf course | ★ | Other place of interest |
| ⚒ | Industrial interest | .......... | Forest drive | 🏏 | County cricket ground | ☐ | Boxed symbols indicate attractions within urban areas |
| ❀ | Garden | — — — | National trail | 🏉 | Rugby Union national ground | | National Park (England & Wales) |
| ♣ | Arboretum | ☀ | Viewpoint | 🏃 | International athletics ground | | National Scenic Area (Scotland) |
| ⚘ | Country park | ♠ | Picnic site | 🐴 | Horse racing | | Forest Park |
| ⚘ | Agricultural showground | ⌬ | Hill-fort | 🐎 | Show jumping/equestrian circuit | | Heritage Coast |

XVIII

## Ireland (see pages 154–157) For tourist information see opposite page

| | | |
|---|---|---|
| M1 Motorway | N17 National primary route (Republic of Ireland) | A4 Primary route (Northern Ireland) |
| 7 Motorway junction with and without number | N54 National secondary route (Republic of Ireland) | A21 A road (Northern Ireland) |
| 3 Restricted motorway junctions | R182 Regional road (Republic of Ireland) | B75 B road (Northern Ireland) |

Road under construction

5 Distance in miles between symbols

International boundary

## district maps (see pages 232–243)

| | | | |
|---|---|---|---|
| Motorway | Road under construction | Outer London Regional Transport (LRT) station | Crem Crematorium |
| Primary route single/dual | Restricted road | Railway station/LRT interchange | Place of interest |
| Other A road single/dual | Railway line/in tunnel | Light railway/tramway station | Golf course |
| B road single/dual | Railway station | Sports stadium | AA AA shop |
| Unclassified road single/dual | Inner London Regional Transport (LRT) station | H Hospital | |

## Central London (see pages 244–254)

| | | | |
|---|---|---|---|
| Motorway | Restricted road (access only/private) | Banned turn (restricted periods only) | PO Post Office |
| Primary route single/dual | Footpath | Ahead only | POL Police station |
| Other A road single/dual | Track | Mini-roundabout | Steps |
| B road single/dual | Pedestrian street | Barrier | Church |
| Unclassified road single/dual | Railway line/in tunnel | Railway station | AA AA shop |
| Unclassified road wide/narrow | One-way street | London Regional Transport (LRT) station | i Tourist Information Centre |
| Road under construction | Compulsory turn | Docklands Light Railway station | i Tourist Information Centre (seasonal) |
| Road tunnel wide/narrow | Banned turn | P Parking | |

**Royal Parks (opening and closing times for traffic)**
Green Park        Constitution Hill: closed Sundays, 08.00–dusk
Hyde Park         Open 05.00–midnight
Regent's Park     Open 07.00–midnight
St James's Park   The Mall: closed Sundays, 08.00–dusk

New traffic regulations in the City of London include security checkpoints and restrict the number of entry and exit points.

**Note:** Oxford Street is closed to through-traffic (except buses & taxis) 07.00–19.00, Monday–Saturday

## The Isles of Scilly

White Island

King Charles's

ST.MARTIN'S

BRYHER
Old Grimsby
Cromwell's
Old Blockhouse
42
Higher Town
49 St Martin's Head
38

Lizard Point

New Grimsby

Isles of Scilly Heritage Coast

Pool

Great Ganilly

TRESCO
Tresco
Tresco Abbey

Innisidgen Tomb

Great Arthur

Crow Sound

Samson

Bant's Carn Burial

North West Channel

A3110

Harry's Walls

ST MARY'S
Longstone Heritage Centre

Hugh Town
Deep Point
Porth Hellick Downs Tombs
Garrison Walls
Isles of Scilly (St Mary's)

Old Town

Peninnis Head

Annet

St Mary's Sound

Broad Sound

Middle Town
Gugh

ST.AGNES
Horse Point

Smith Sound

Western Rocks

| 0 | 1 | 2 | 3 | 4 | 5 miles |
|---|---|---|---|---|---|
| 0 | 1 2 | 3 4 | 5 | 6 | 7 kilometres |

**9**

St Agnes Heritage Coast

ST AGNES HEAD
Agnes
Wheal Coates
St Agnes's Wond
Goonvrea

Porthtowan

South West Coast Path

Menagissey

Godrevy-Portreath Heritage Coast

Portreath
B3300
Bridge
Cambrose
Wheal R
Illogan
North Country
Poynter's Lane End
Cornish Engines

Godrevy Island
Navax Point

Coombe
Park Bottom
Tehidy
Tuckingmill A3047 Pool
Red

Godrevy Point

Gwealavellan
Reskadinnick
Roscroggan

Carn Brea
Carn Brea

Carn Naun Point
The Island or St Ives Head
St Ives Bay
Gwithian
Kehelland
Upton Towans
A30
Roseworthy
Penponds
Camborne

Zennor Head
Treveal
Hellesveor
St Ives

Gurnards Head
Trendrine
Carbis Bay
The Towans
Phillack
Connor Downs
Barripper
Bolenowe
Four Lanes

South West Coast Path
Zennor
B3306
Halsetown
Hayle
Angarrack
Carnhell Green
Troon

Treen
Towednack
Lelant
Copperhouse
High Gwinear
Rosewarne

Porthmeor
14
Cripplesease
Merlin's Magic Land
Brunnion
Lanes
St Erth Praze
Trenerth
Praze-an-Beeble
Burras

Pendeen Watch
Georgia
Nancledra
St Erth
Fraddam
Kerthen Wood
Horsedown
Blackrock
Carnkie

Penwith Heritage Coast
Mulfra Quoit
Chysauster
Canonstown
Whitecross
Townshend
Leedstown
Crowan
Lezerea
Edgcum

Morvah
Men-An-Tol
Mulfra
Castle Gate
River Hayle
Drym
Releath
Nancegollan
Crelly

Lower Boscaswell
Geevor Tin Mines
Bojewyan
Boskednan
Boswarthan
Cockwells
Trannack
Relubbus
Trescowe
Godolphin Cross
Prospidnick
Trenear
Podark Mine

Levant Steam Engine NT
Pendeen
Trewellard
New Mill
Badger's Cross
Ludgvan
Crowlas
Penzance
Tolver
B3280
Wendron
Manhay
Treba

Carnyorth
Great Bosullow
Lanyon Quoit
Bone
Gulval
Longrock
St Hilary
Relubbus
Carleen
Crowntown
Trenear

Kenidjack
Botallack
Trengwainton Garden NT
Boswarthan
Marazion
St Michael's Mount NT
Millpool
Balwest
Green Lower Coverack
Town Bridges
Trewennack

Cape Cornwall
St Just
Madron
Heamoor
Chyandour
Perranuthnoe
Newtown
Germoe
Ashton
Breage
Sithney
Common
Helston

Ballowall Barrow
Newbridge
Tremethick Cross
Sellan
Tredavoe
Newlyn
Rosudgeon
Prussia Cove
Kenneggy
Trew
Antron
Tolvan

Bosavern
Kelynack
Grumbla
Carn Euny
Sancreed
Drift
Catchall
St Michael's Mount NT
RSPB
Cudden Point
Rinsey Croft
A394
Gweek

Nanquidno
Whitesand Bay
Land's End
Brane
10
Kerris
Paul
Mousehole
Praa Sands
Rinsey
Methleigh
Mellangoose
Flambards
Mawga

Sennen Cove
Escalls
Crows-an-Wra
Toldavas
Sheffield
Trevithal
Raginnis
Castallack
Cudden Point
Rinsey Head
Trewavas Head
Porthleven
Carminowe
Mawgan

LAND'S END
Land's End
Sennen
Trevorgans
St Buryan
Trewoofe
The Merry Maidens
Lamorna
Higher Pentire
Cross

Trevescan
Trebehor
Trengothal
Bottoms
Boskennal
Lamorna Cove
Chyvarloe
Tregiddle
Bereppa
Gwealeath
Garra

Polgigga
Trethewey
B3315
Treen
Merthen Point
MOUNT'S BAY
Gunwalloe
Chyanvounder
Tregoose

Rockesta
Raftra
Porthcurno
White Cross
Cross La

Porthgwarra
St Levan
Minack Open Air Theatre
Cribba Head
Cury
Bochym

Gwennap Head
Angrouse
Poldhu Point
Marconi Memorial
Trewoon
Penhale
GOON DOW

Mullion
B3296
Trenance

Mullion Cove
Mullion Island
Mullion Cove
Mullion
Ruan Major
Ruan

Predannack Wollas

Predannack Head
Mount Hermon
St Ruan

Vellan Head

The Lizard Heritage Coast
South West Coast Path
Grade

Lizard Head
Lizard
La

LIZARD POINT

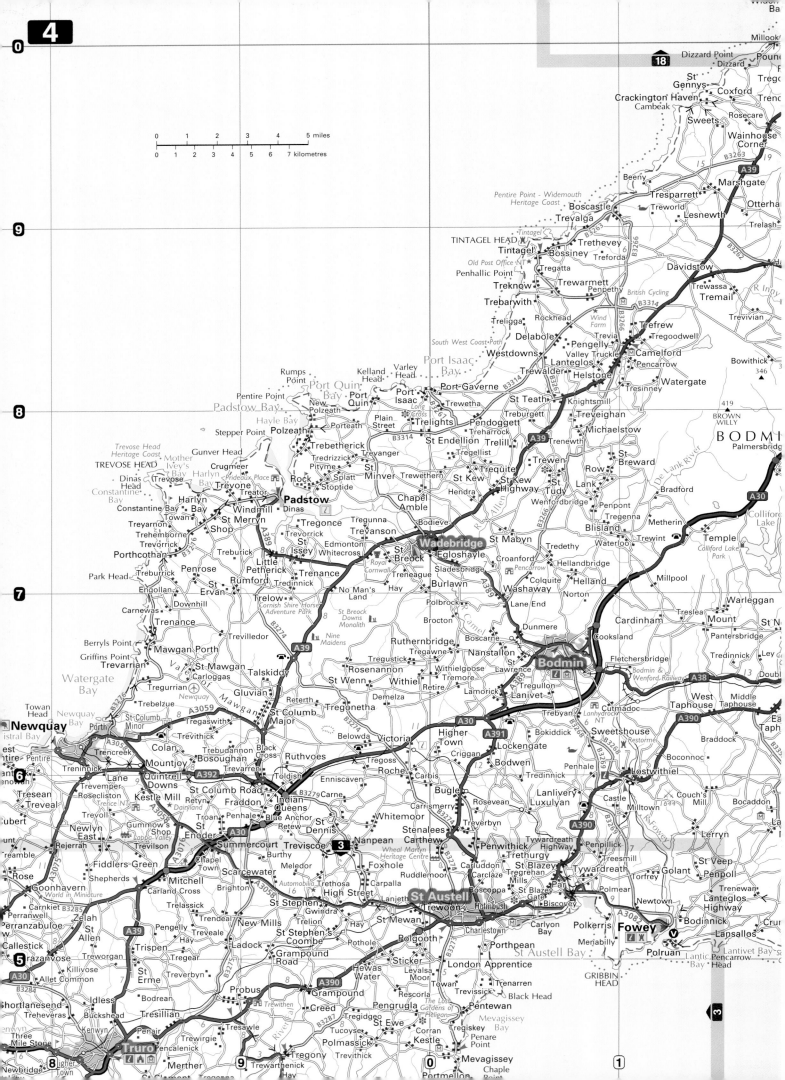

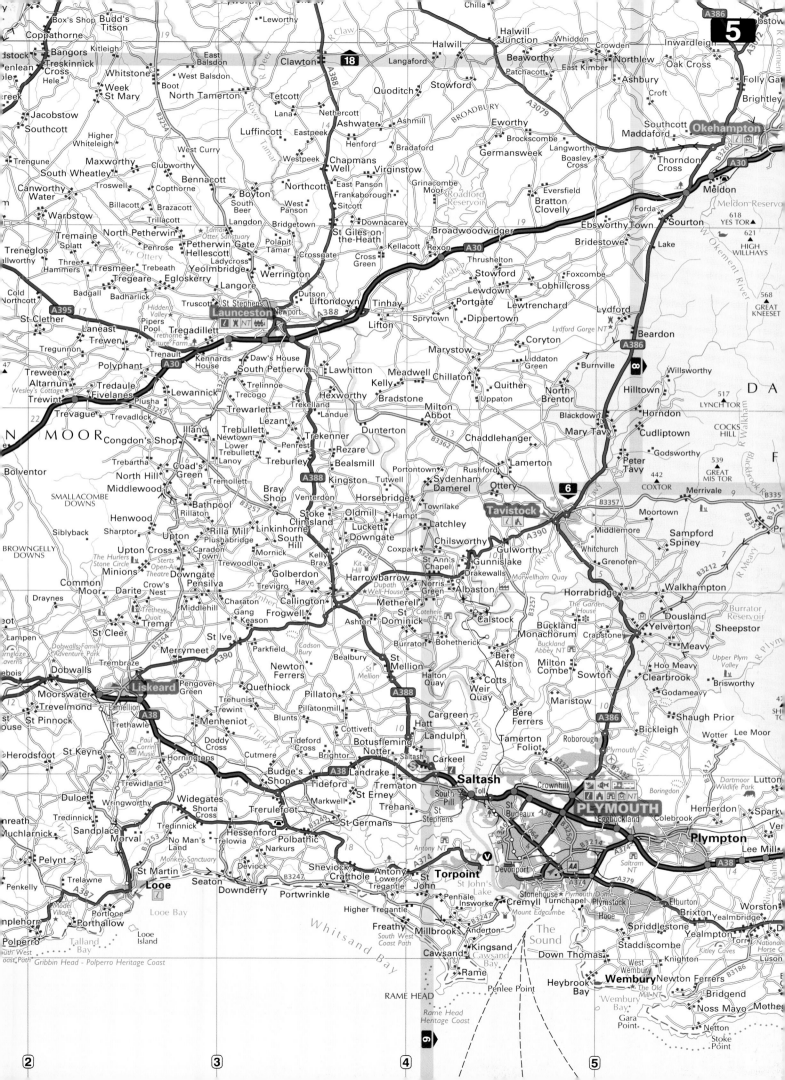

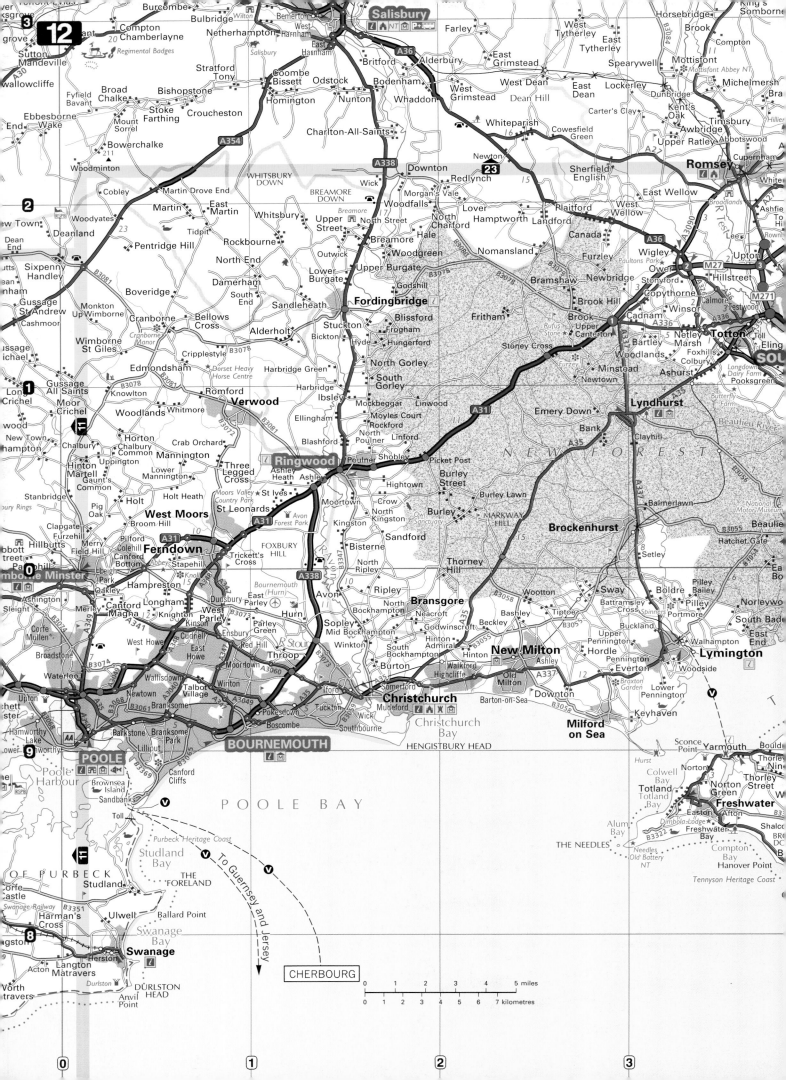

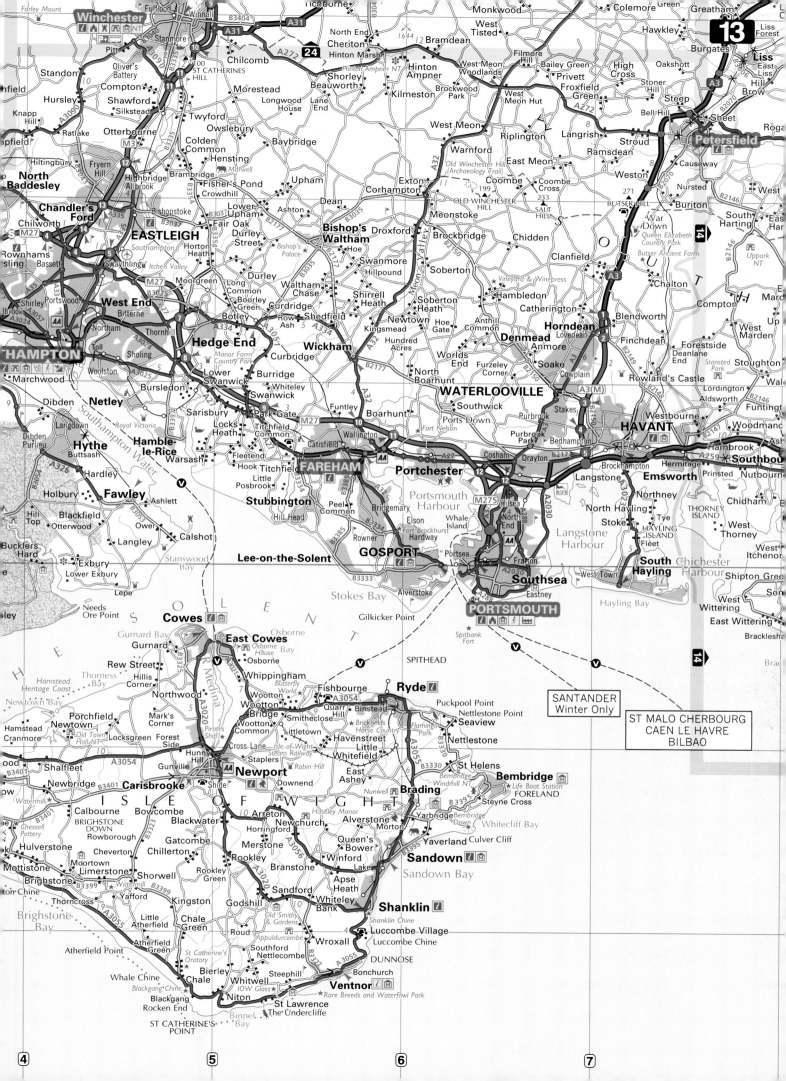

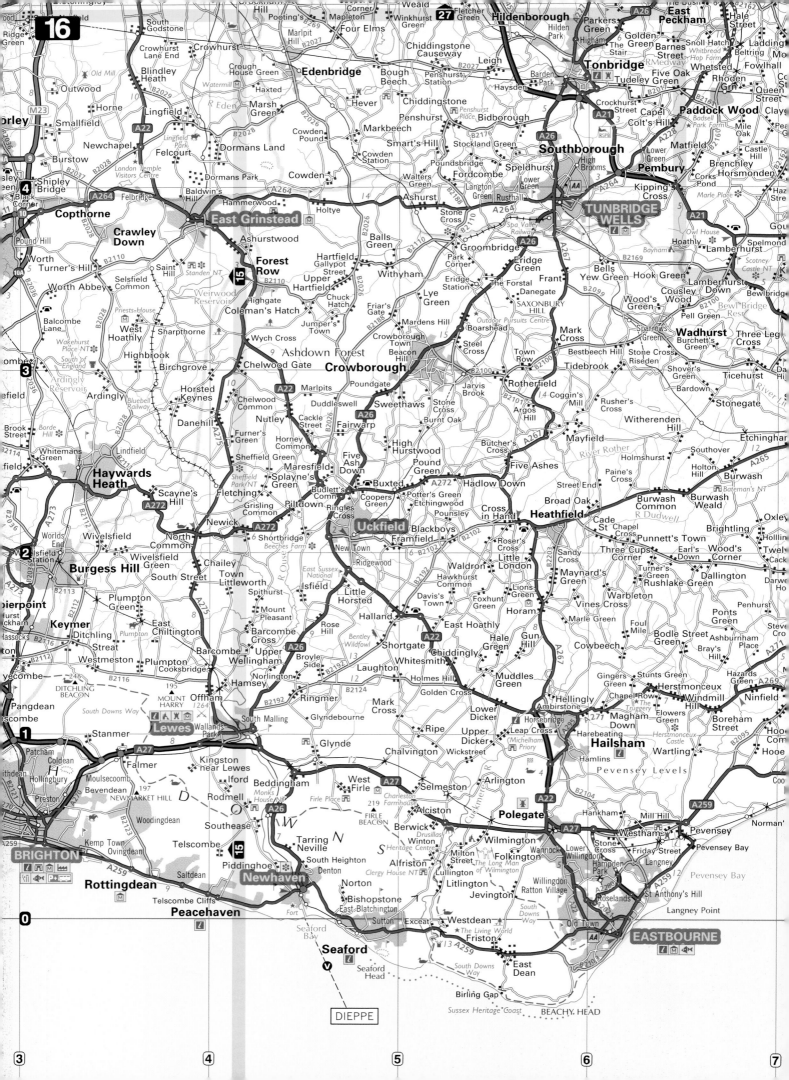

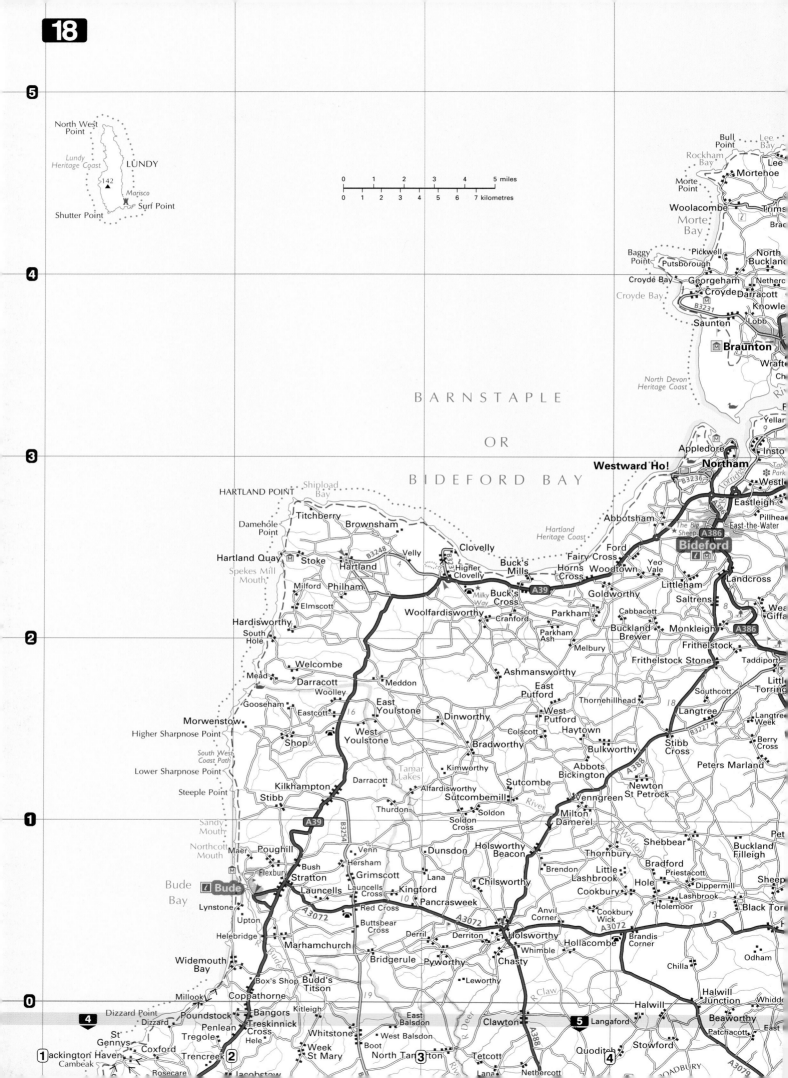

North West
Point

*Lundy*
*Heritage Coast*

LUNDY

▲ 142

*Marisco*

Surf Point

Shutter Point

0  1  2  3  4  5 miles

0  1  2  3  4  5  6  7 kilometres

Bull
Point

Lee
Bay

Rockham
Bay

Lee

Morte
Point

Mortehoe

Woolacombe

Trims

Morte
Bay

Brac

Baggy
Point

Pickwell

North
Buckland

Putsborough

Netherc

Croyde Bay

Georgeham

Croyde

Darracott

Croyde Bay

B3231

Knowle

Saunton

Lobb

**Braunton**

Wraft

Ch

B A R N S T A P L E

North Devon
Heritage Coast

Yellar

O R

Appledore

Insto

B I D E F O R D   B A Y

**Westward Ho!**

**Northam**

Westl

HARTLAND POINT

Shipload
Bay

Hartland
Heritage Coast

Abbotsham

B3236

The Big
Sheep

East-the-Water

Pillhea

Titchberry

Brownsham

Velly

Clovelly

Ford

A386

**Bideford**

Damehole
Point

Higher
Clovelly

Buck's
Mills

Fairy Cross

Horns
Cross

Woodtown

Yeo
Vale

Littleham

Landcross

Hartland Quay

Stoke

Hartland

B3248

A39

Goldworthy

Saltrens

Wea

Speke's Mill
Mouth

Milford

Philham

Buck's
Cross

Cranford

Parkham

Cabbacott

Buckland
Brewer

Giffa

Woolfardisworthy

Monkleigh

Elmscott

Milky
Way

Parkham
Ash

A386

Hardisworthy

Melbury

Frithelstock

Taddiport

South
Hole

Ashmansworthy

Frithelstock Stone

Littl
Torri

Welcombe

Meddon

East
Putford

Thornehillhead

Southcott

Mead

Darracott

Woolley

West
Putford

Langtree

Langtre
Week

Gooseham

Eastcott

16

East
Youlstone

Dinworthy

Haytown

A386

Berry
Cross

Morwenstow

Colscott

Stibb
Cross

B3227

Peters Marland

Higher Sharpnose Point

Shop

West
Youlstone

Bradworthy

Bulkworthy

South West
Coast Path

Kimworthy

18

Lower Sharpnose Point

Darracott

Abbots
Bickington

A388

Newton
St Petrock

Steeple Point

Kilkhampton

Tamar
Lakes

Alfardisworthy

Sutcombe

Venngreen

Stibb

Sutcombemill

River

Milton
Damerel

Thurdon

Soldon

Waldon

Sandy
Mouth

Soldon
Cross

Shebbear

Buckland
Filleigh

A39

B3254

Holsworthy
Beacon

Thornbury

Pet

Northcott
Mouth

Maer

Poughill

Venn

Dunsdon

Brendon

Little
Lashbrook

Bradford

Priestacott

Dippermill

Sheep

Hersham

Lana

Chilsworthy

Hole

Lashbrook

**Bude**

Flexbury

Bush

Grimscott

Cookbury

Holemoor

Black Tor

Bude
Bay

Stratton

Launcells

Launcells
Cross

Kingford

10

Pancrasweek

Anvil
Corner

Cookbury
Wick

13

Lynstone

Red Cross

A3072

A3072

Holsworthy

Brandis
Corner

Upton

Buttsbear
Cross

Derril

Derriton

Hollacombe

Helebridge

Marhamchurch

Bridgerule

Pyworthy

Whimble

Chasty

Chilla

Widemouth
Bay

Box's Shop

Budd's
Titson

19

Leworthy

Odham

Millook

Coppathorne

Kitleigh

R Deer

Halwill
Junction

Whiddo

Dizzard Point

Bangors

East
Balsdon

Clawton

A388

Halwill

**4**

Dizzard

Poundstock

Treskinnick
Cross

R Claw

**5**

Langaford

Beaworthy

St
Gennys

Penlean

Hele

West Balsdon

Boot

Clawton

Patchacott

East

ackington Haven

Tregole

Whitstone

North Tarrton

Tetcott

Stowford

Cambeak

Coxford

Week
St Mary

Quoditch

Lana

**1**

Trencreek

**2**

**3**

**4**

Rosecare

Jacobstow

Nethercott

A3079

Ilfracombe · Hele Bay · Water Mouth · Combe Martin Bay · Watermouths · Chambercombe Manor · Hele · Hele Mill · Haggington Hill · Sterridge · Berrynarbor · Combe Martin · Ruggaton · Bodstone Barton Farmworld · Dean · Parracombe

Elwill Bay · Martinhoe · Woody Bay · Trentishoe · Hunter's Inn · Heale · Kemacott · Killington · Woolhanger · Churchtown · Woody Bay · Toll · Dean · Barbrook · West Lyn · East Ilkerton · West Ilkerton · Cheriton · Furzehill

Lynmouth Bay · Foreland Point · Countisbury Cove · Lynton · Lynbridge · Lynmouth · Wilsham · Countisbury · Brass Rubbing Centre · Watersmeet House NT · Rockford · Brendon · Tippacott · Oare · Malmsmead · Culbone · Porlock Weir · West Porlock · Bossington · Hurtstone Point · Porlock Bay · Porlock · Horner · Lucott · Luccombe

Two Pots · Mullacott Cross · West Down · Bittadon · East Down · Churchill · Berry Down Cross · Patchole · Kentisbury · Kentisbury Ford · Arlington Beccott · Stowford · Arlington · Exmoor Zoological Park · Arlington Court NT · Loxhore · Knightacott · Leworthy · Fullaford

Wistlandpound Reservoir · Swincombe · Challacombe · Barton Town · HOAROAK HILL 474 · EXMOOR FOREST · River Exe · DRY HILL 444 · DUNKERY BEACON 519 · DUNKERY HILL · Edgcott · Luckwell Bridge · Exford · Newland · Blackland · River Barle · Simonsbath · B3358 · Withypool · NATIONAL PARK · Great Nurcott · North Quarme

Halsinger · Higher Muddiford · Milltown · Muddiford · Upcott · Loxhore Cott · Lower Loxhore · Bratton Fleming · Benton · Lydcott · Whitefield · SPAN HEAD 493 · Kinsford Water · 410 · North Quarme

Vinsham · Boode · Pippacott · Marwood · Marwood Hill · Prixford · Guineaford · Kingsheanton · Shirwell · Shirwell Cross · Northleigh · Stoke Rivers · Gunn · Brayford · R Bray · High Bray · Bentwichen · North Radworthy · South Radworthy · WORTH HILL · WINSFORD HILL · Winsford · Knaplock · Liscombe · Tarr Steps · Tarr · Hawkridge

Heanton Punchardon · Ashford · Bradiford · Pilton · Derby · Goodleigh · Willesleigh · Bradninch · Accott · Whitsford · Charles · Heasley Mill · North Heasley · North Molton · Twitchen · Molland · West Anstey · Slade · East Anstey · Northmoor

Barnstaple · Bickington · Newport · Lake · Brannams Pottery · Tawstock · St John's Chapel · Landkey Town · Swimbridge Newland · Bishop's Tawton · Hannaford · Landkey · Yarnacott · Swimbridge · Stoodleigh · West Buckland · Elwell · East Buckland · Castle Hill · Bremridge · Filleigh · South Molton · Aller · Bish Mill · Newtown · Bishop's Nympton · Ash Mill · Knowstone · East Knowstone · Roachill · Oldways End · Sowerhill · Crooked Oak

Horwood · Newton Tracey · Harracott · Week · Herner · Ensis · Chapelton · Hiscott · Delley · Cobbaton · Chittlehampton · Traveller's Rest · East Stowford · Umberleigh · Warkleigh · Clapworthy · George Nympton · Quince Honey Farm · Radley · Alswear · Mariansleigh · Yard · Rose Ash · Molland · A361

Yarnscombe · Atherington · Langridge Ford · High Bickington · Chittlehamholt · Satterleigh · River Mole · Romansleigh · Meshaw · Creacombe · Rackenford · Queen Dart · Westcott · Loxbeare

Great Torrington · Rosemoor · St Giles in the Wood · Kingscott · High Bullen · Huntshaw · Huntshaw Cross · King's Nympton · Cadbury Barton · Week · Little Dart River

Roborough · Beaford · A3124 (B3220) · Burrington · Colleton Mills · Elstone · Witheridge · Drayford · Edgeworthy · Nomansland · Templeton

Winswell · Little Marland · Merton · Huish · Dolton · Riddlecombe · Ashreigney · Bridge Reeve · Chulmleigh · Cheldon · Worlington · Thelbridge Cross · Washford Pyne · Pennymoor · Cruwys Morchard · Withleigh

Meeth · Dowland · Hollocombe · Chittlehampton · Ashley · Chawleigh · Leigh · Filleigh · Hele Lane · Littleborough · Puddington · Way Village · Well Town · A386

R Torridge · Fishleigh · Iddesleigh · Ingleigh Green · Wembworthy · Eggesford · Moor End · Nymet Rowland · Lapford · Morchard Bishop · Black Dog · Woolfardisworthy · Poughill · Upham · Cadeleigh

Monkokehampton · Broadwood Kelly · Winkleigh · Barwick · Brushford Barton · Coldridge · Weeke · Kennerleigh · Stockleigh English · East Village · Cheriton Fitzpaine · Uppincott

Hatherleigh · Splatt · Bondleigh · Lowton · West Leigh · East Leigh · Loosebeare · Down St Mary · Zeal Monachorum · Clannaborough · Newbuildings · Copplestone · Woolsgrove · West Sandford · Sandford · Chilton · Stockleigh Pomeroy · West Raddon

Honeychurch · Barons Wood · Sutton · Bow · Coleford · Nymet Tracey · Knowle · Lower Creedy · Creedy Park · Shobrooke · Little Silver · Thorver...

Exbourne · North Tawton · Broadnymett · Colebrooke · Penstone · Woodland Head · Yeoford · Neopardy · Posbury · Crediton · Upton Hellions · Pennicott · Wyke · Shute

Jacobstowe · Sampford Courtenay · Trecott · Itton · Highfield · Hillerton · Spestos · Coleford · Fordton · Uton · Sweetham · Venny Tedburn · Hookway · Newton St Cyres · Smallbrook · Nettacott

Inwardleigh · Northlew · Oak Cross · Ashbury · Croft · Brightley · Chichacott · Corscombe · Folly Gate · Taw Green · Rowden · Spreyton · R Yeo

A377 · A3072 · A361 · A386 · A3124

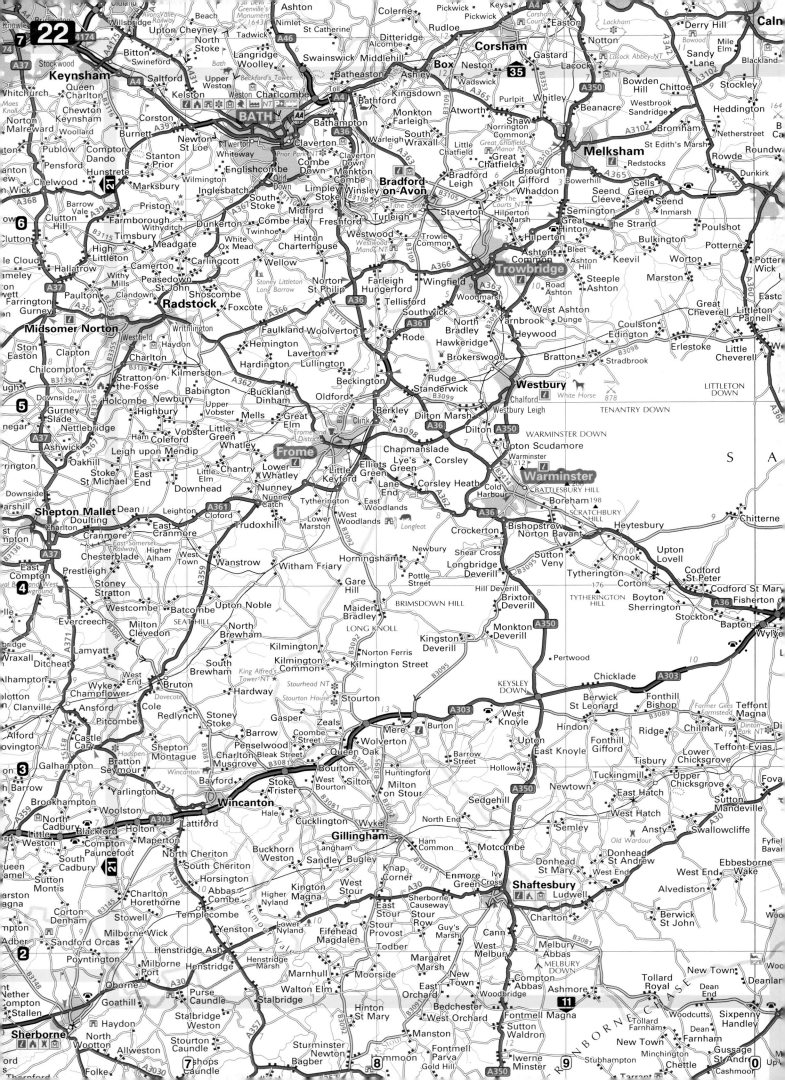

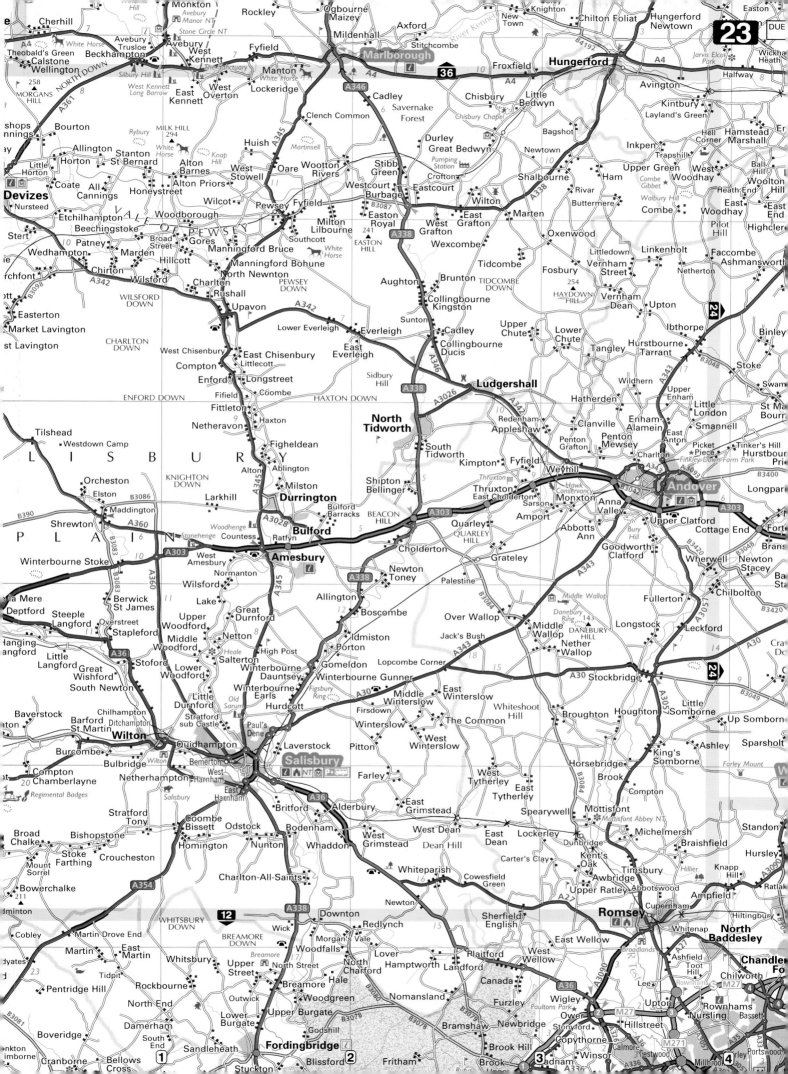

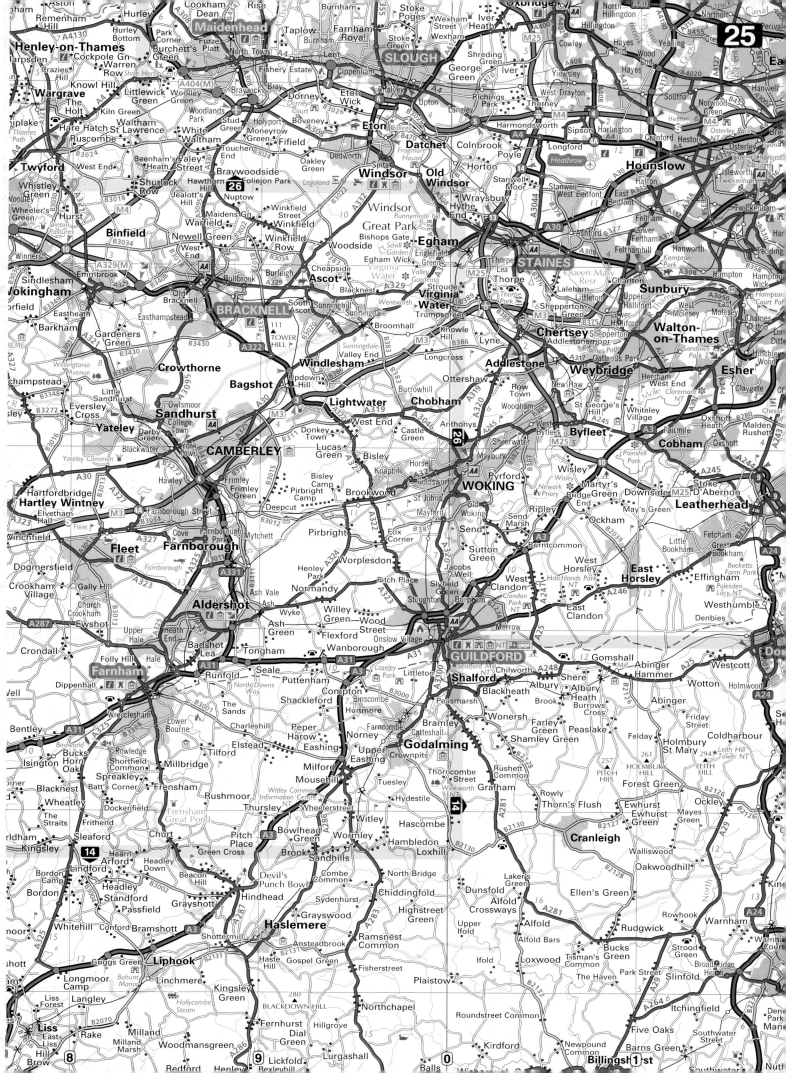

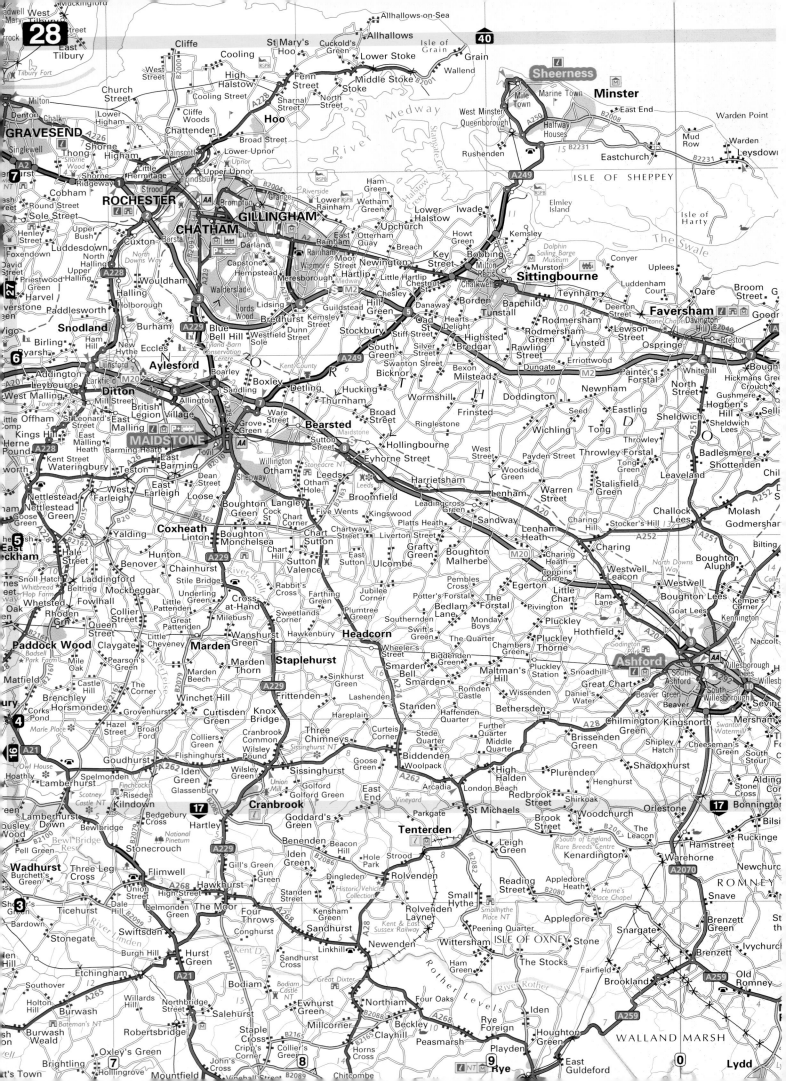

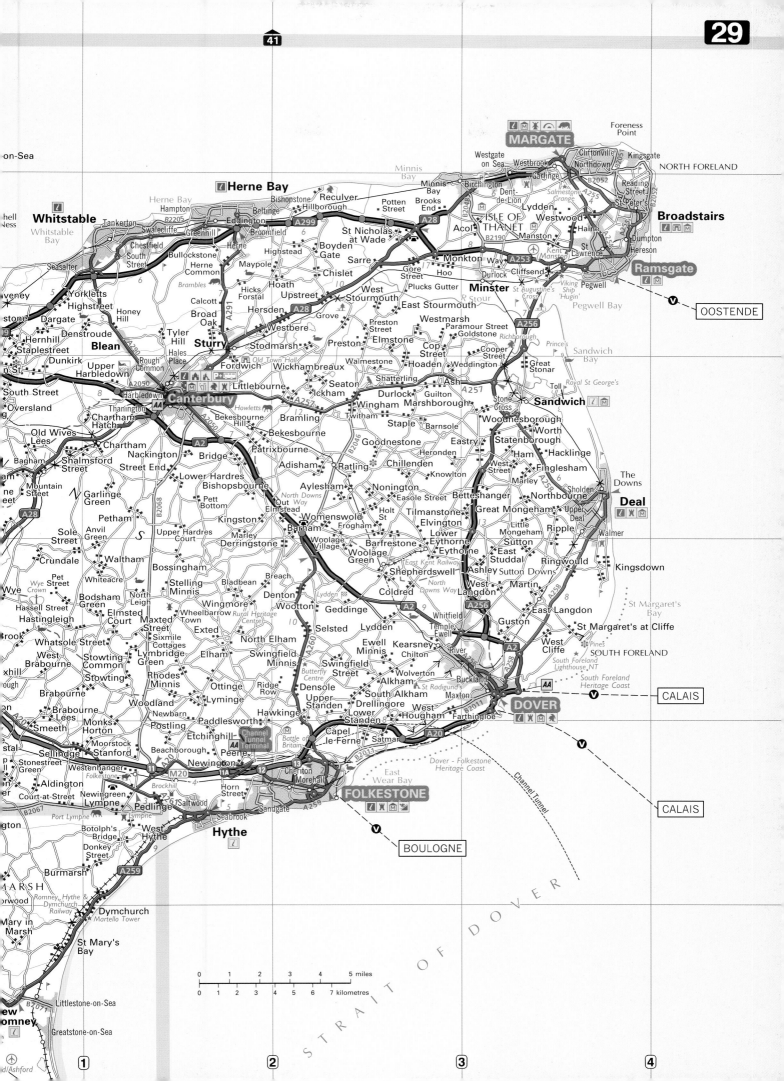

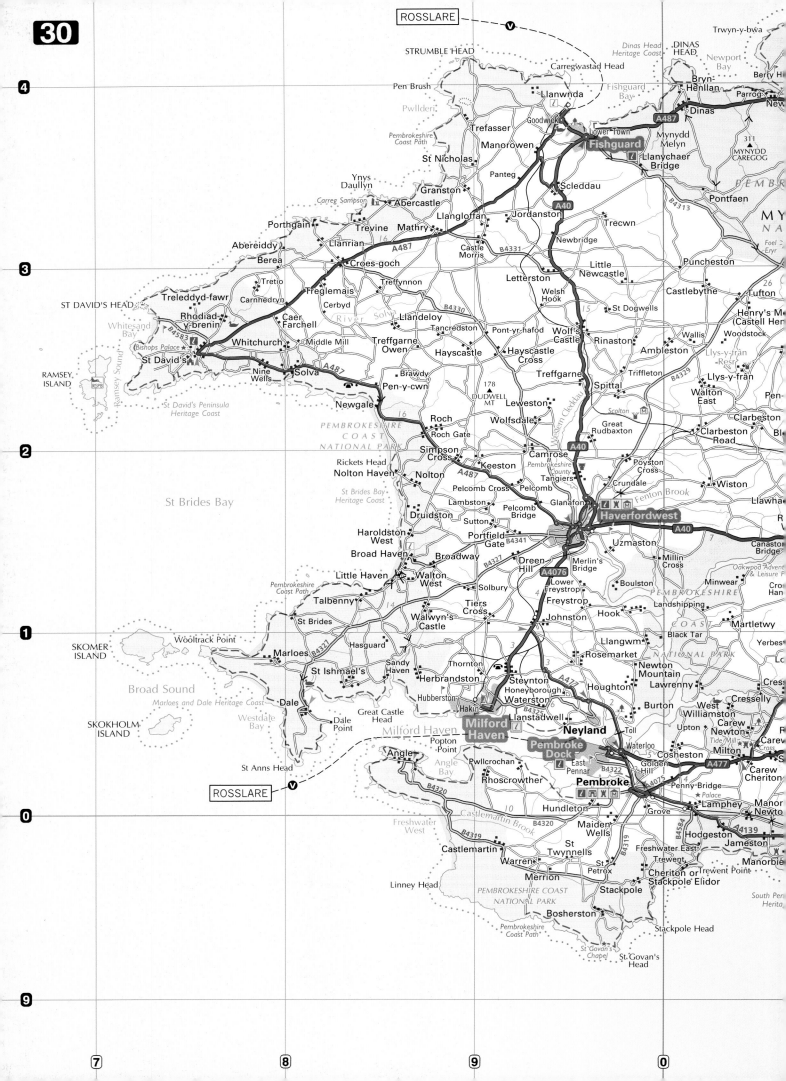

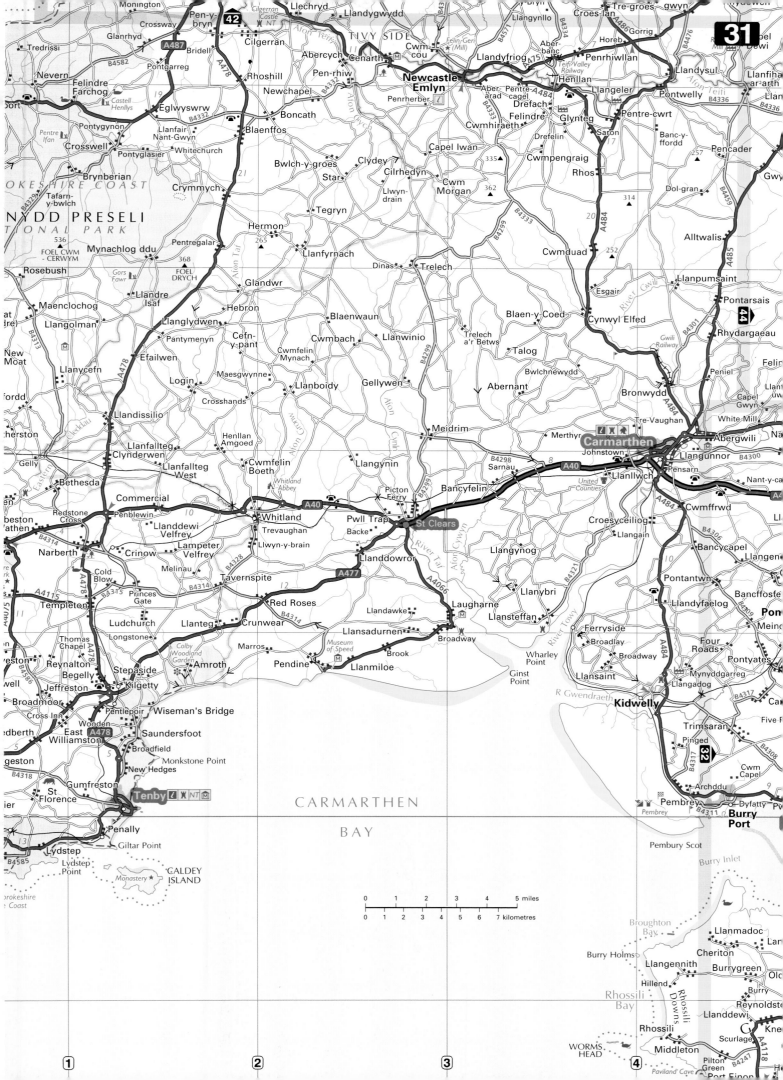

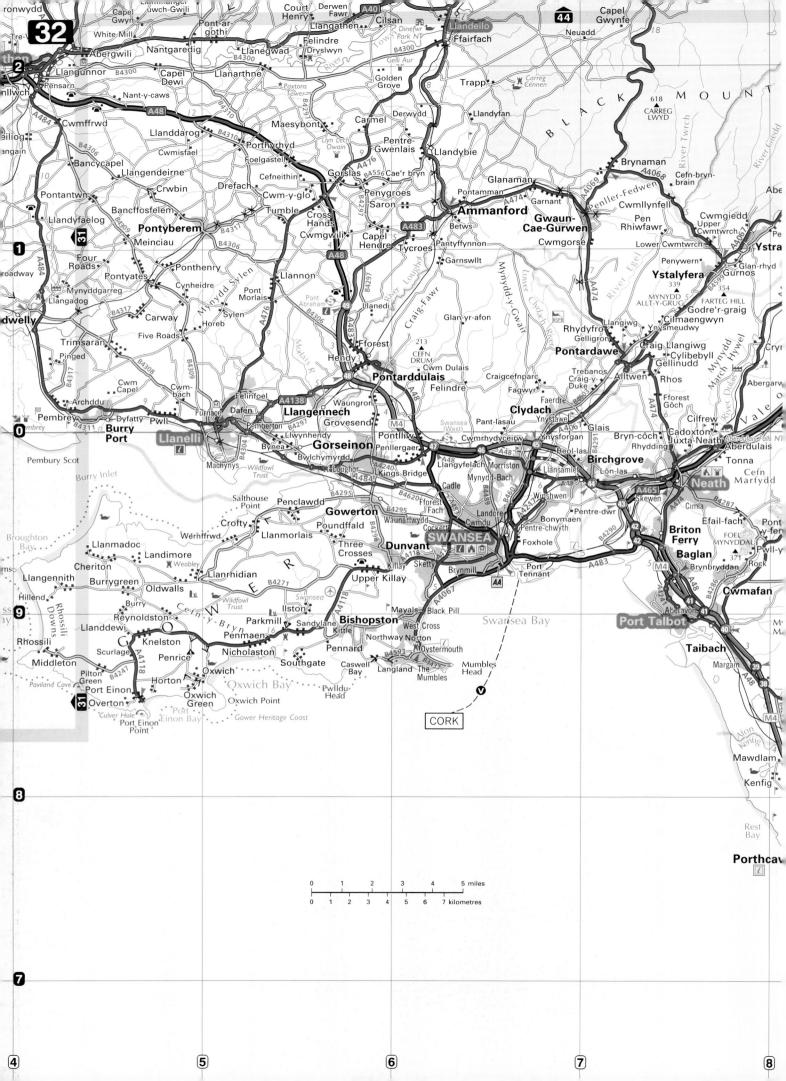

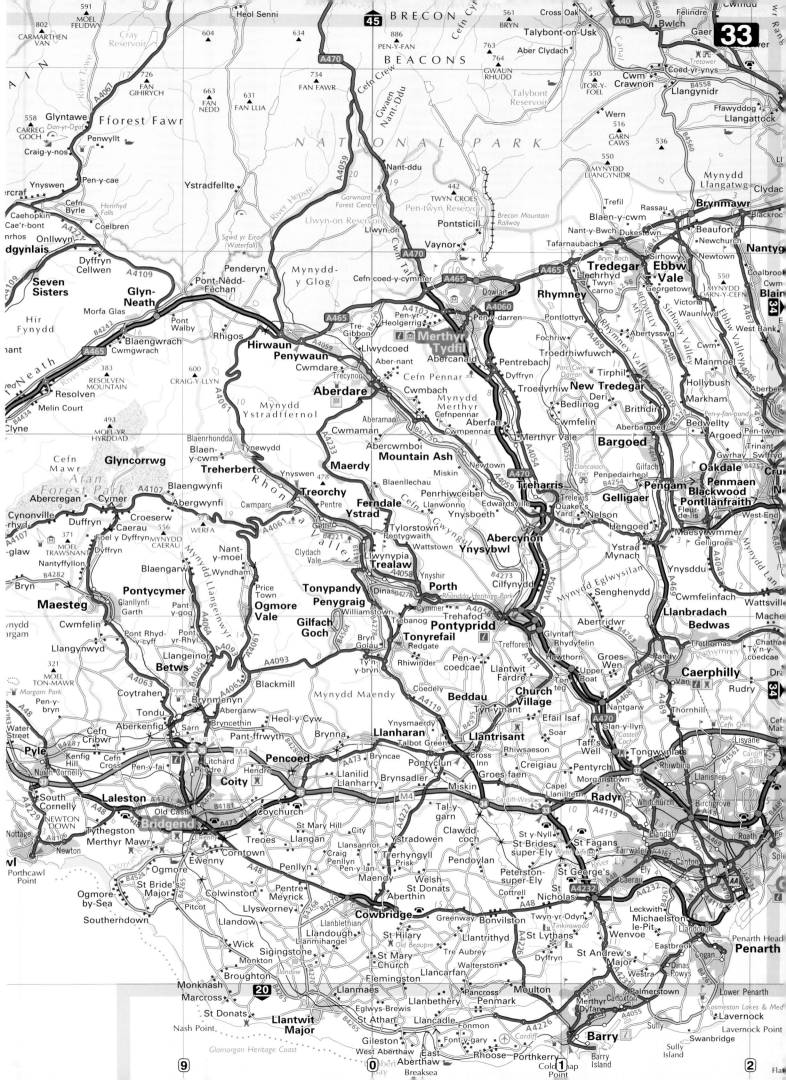

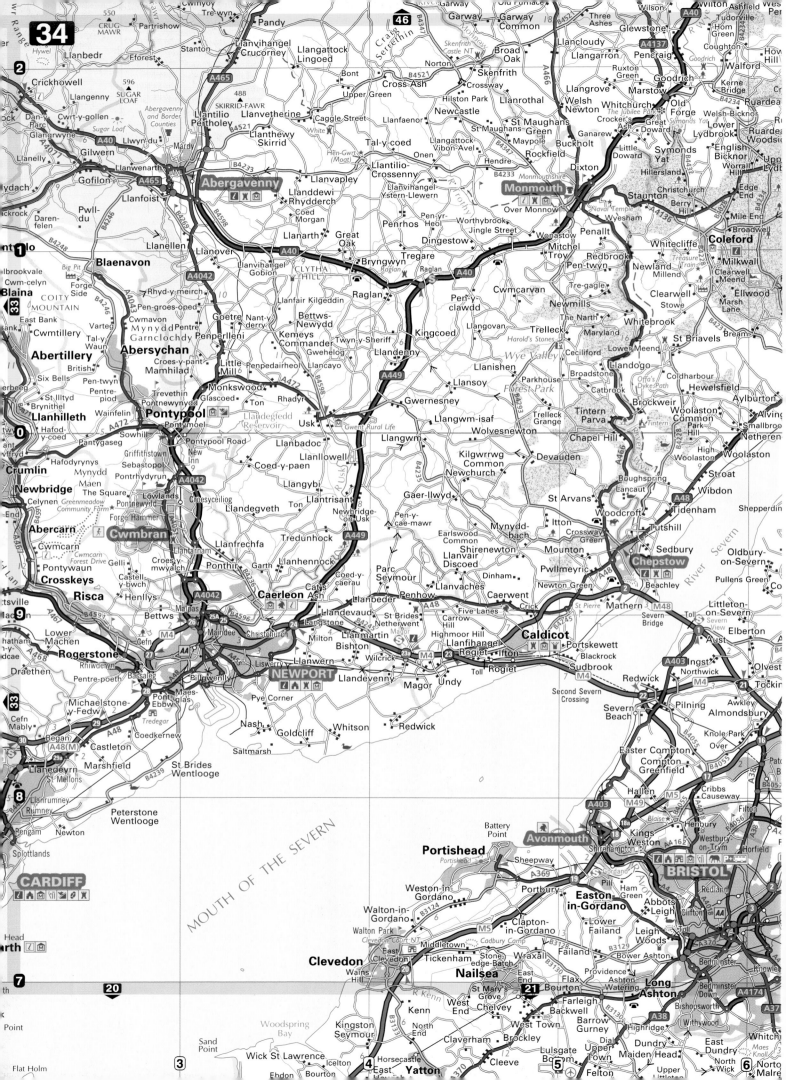

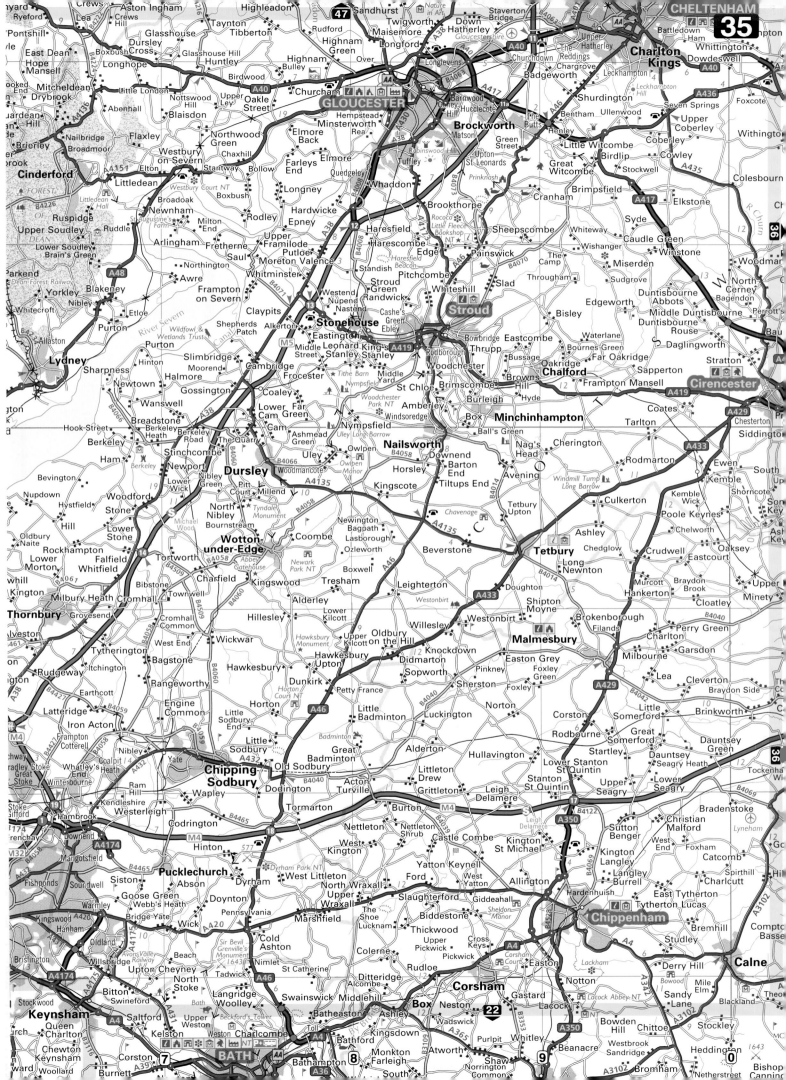

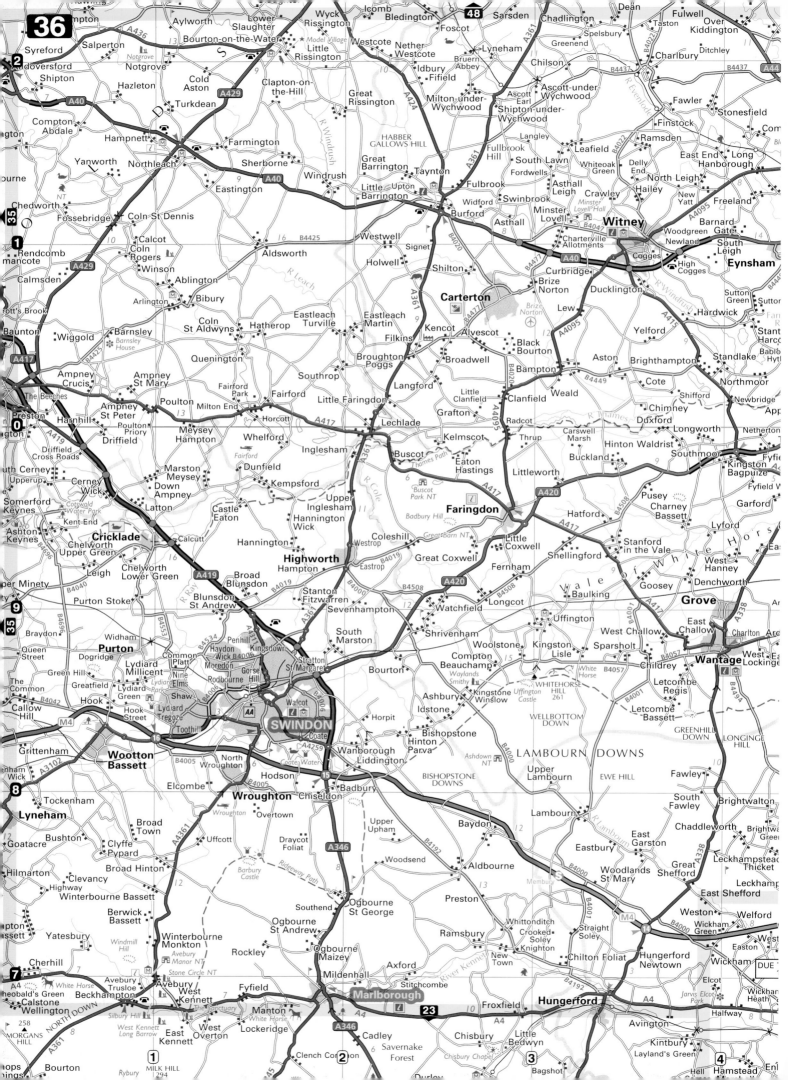

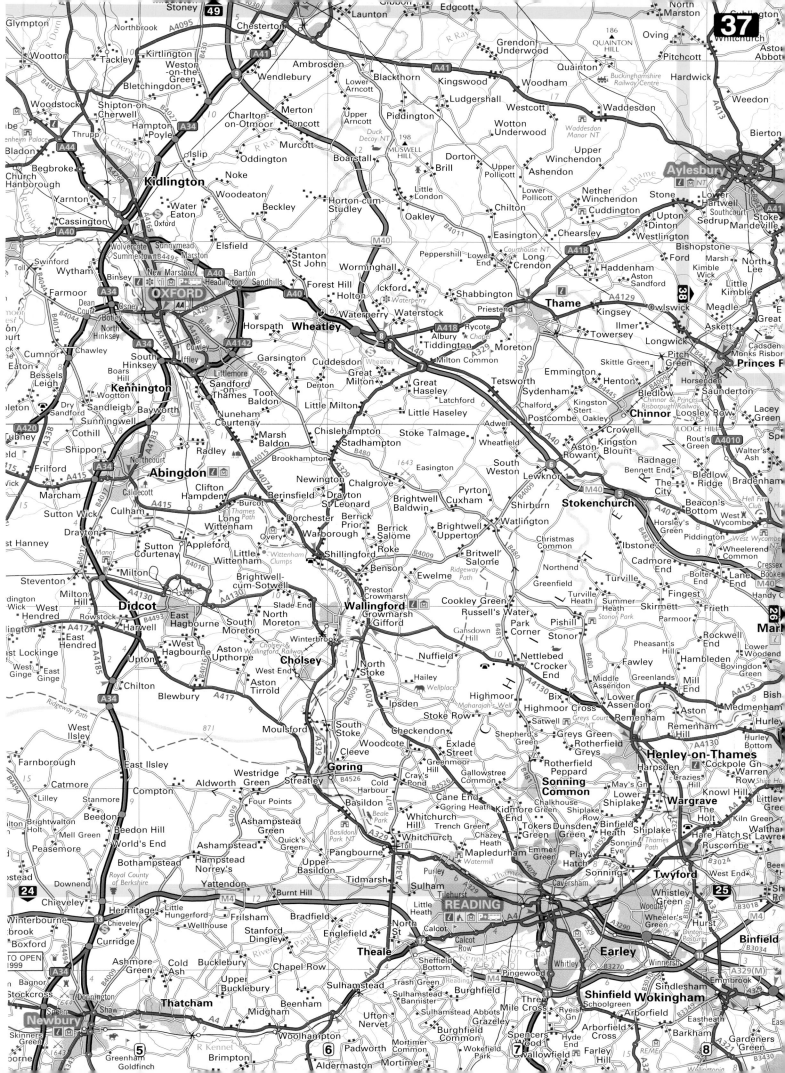

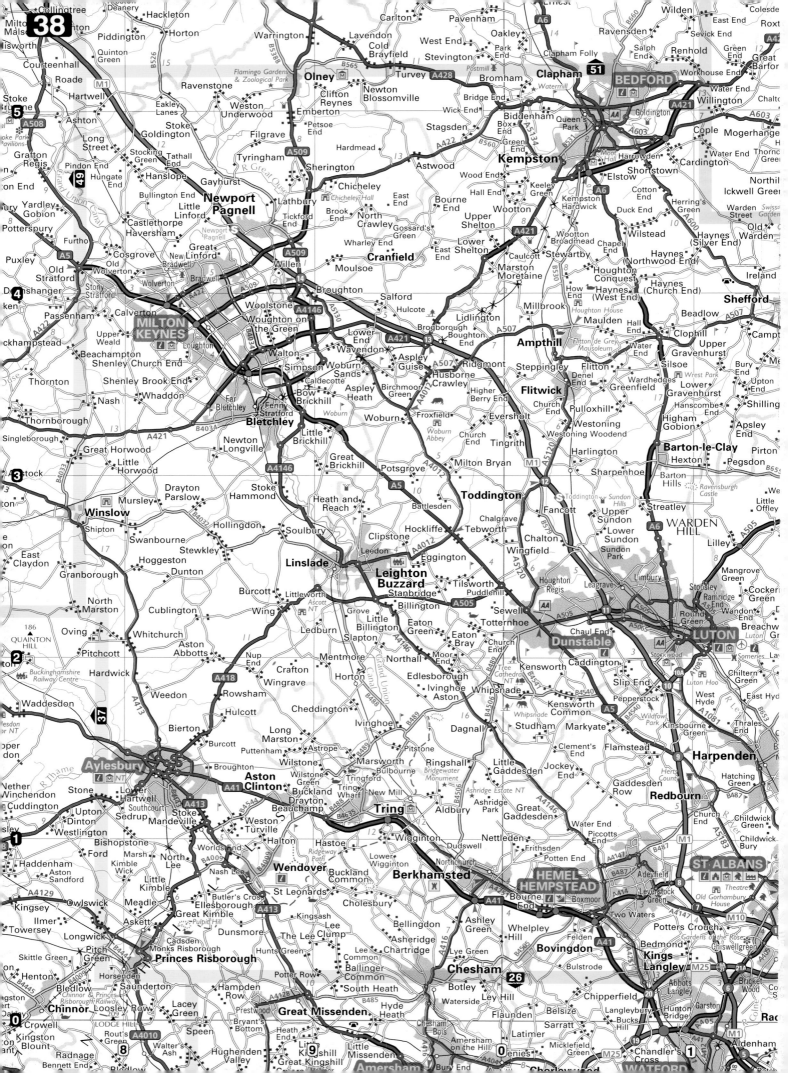

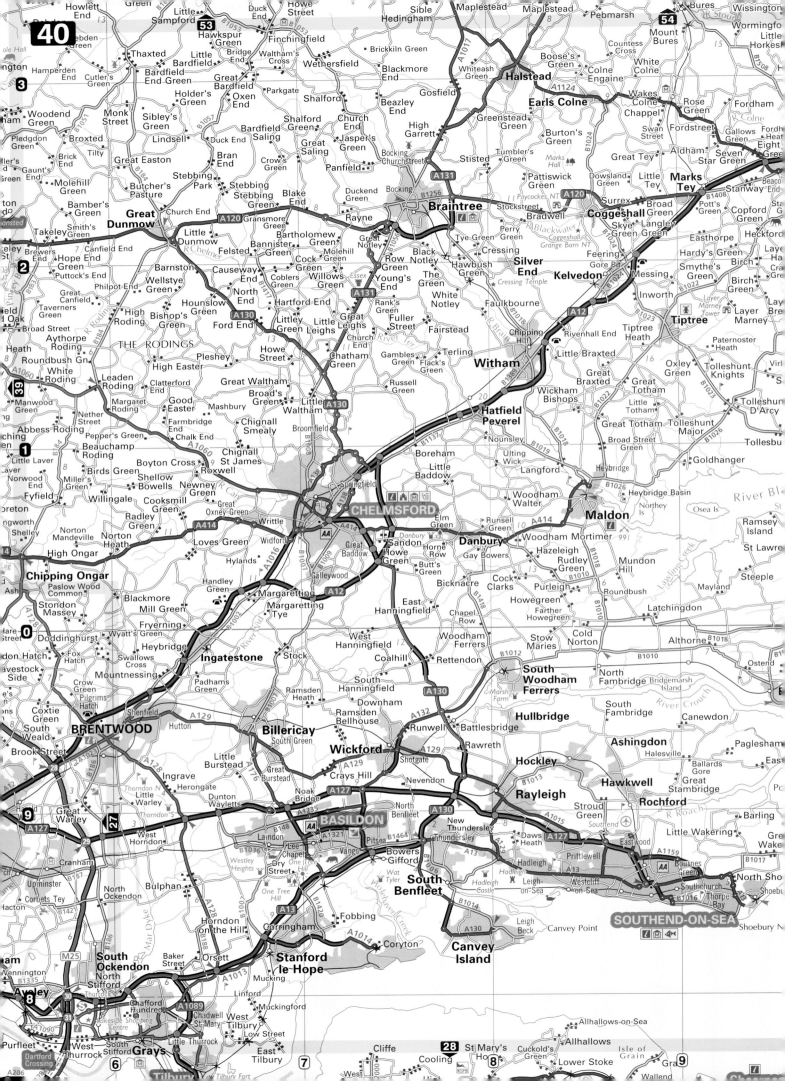

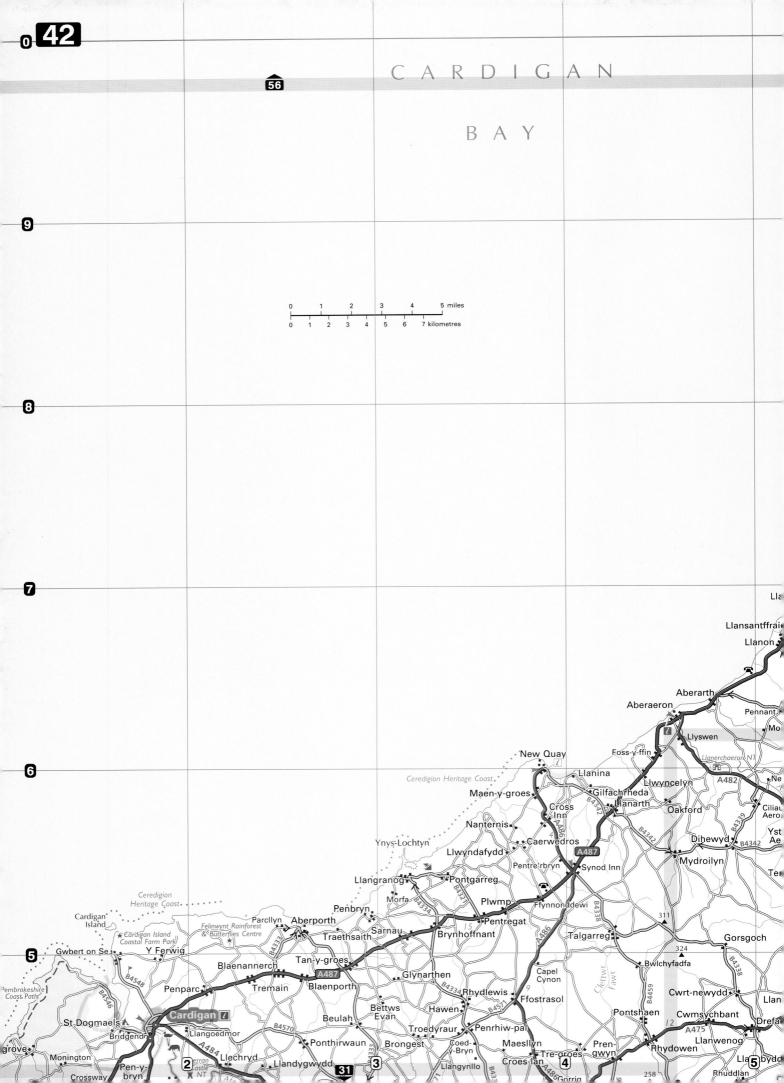

C A R D I G A N

B A Y

9

```
0    1    2    3    4    5 miles
0  1  2  3  4  5  6    7 kilometres
```

8

7

6

Llansantffrai

Llanon

Aberarth

Aberaeron          Pennant

Llyswen          Mo

New Quay          Foss-y-ffin          Llanerchaeron NT

Llanina          A482

Ceredigion Heritage Coast          Llwyncelyn          Ne

Maen-y-groes          Gilfachrheda

Cross          Llanarth          Oakford          Cilia

Inn          Aero

Nanternis          Caerwedros          Dihewyd          Yst

Ynys-Lochtyn          Llwyndafydd          B4342          Ae

Pentre'rbryn          A487          Mydroilyn

Llangranog          Pontgarreg          Synod Inn          Te

Morfa          Plwmp

Penbryn          Ffynnonddewi          311

Ceredigion          Pentregat

Heritage Coast          Brynhoffnant          Talgarreg          Gorsgoch

Cardigan          Parcllyn          Aberporth          Sarnau

Island          Felinwynt Rainforest          324          Bwlchyfadfa

& Butterflies Centre          Traethsaith          Capel

Cardigan Island          Tan-y-groes          Glynarthen          Cynon          Cwrt-newydd

Gwbert on Sea          Coastal Farm Park          A487          Rhydlewis

Y Ferwig          Blaenannerch          Bettws          Hawen          Pontshaen          Llan

Penparc          Tremain          Blaenporth          Evan          Penrhiw-pal          Cwmsychbant

Pembrokeshire          Troedyraur          Ffostrasol          Drefa

Coast Path          St Dogmaels          Beulah          Maesllyn          Prengwyn          A475

Bridgend          Llangoedmor          Coed-          Tre-groes          Rhydowen          Llanwenog

Cardigan          Ponthirwaun          Brongest          y-Bryn          Croes-lan          Lla

grove          Monington          Llechryd          Llandygwydd          Gorrig          Rhyddlan

Pen-y-          Llangynllo          bydr

Crossway          bryn          258

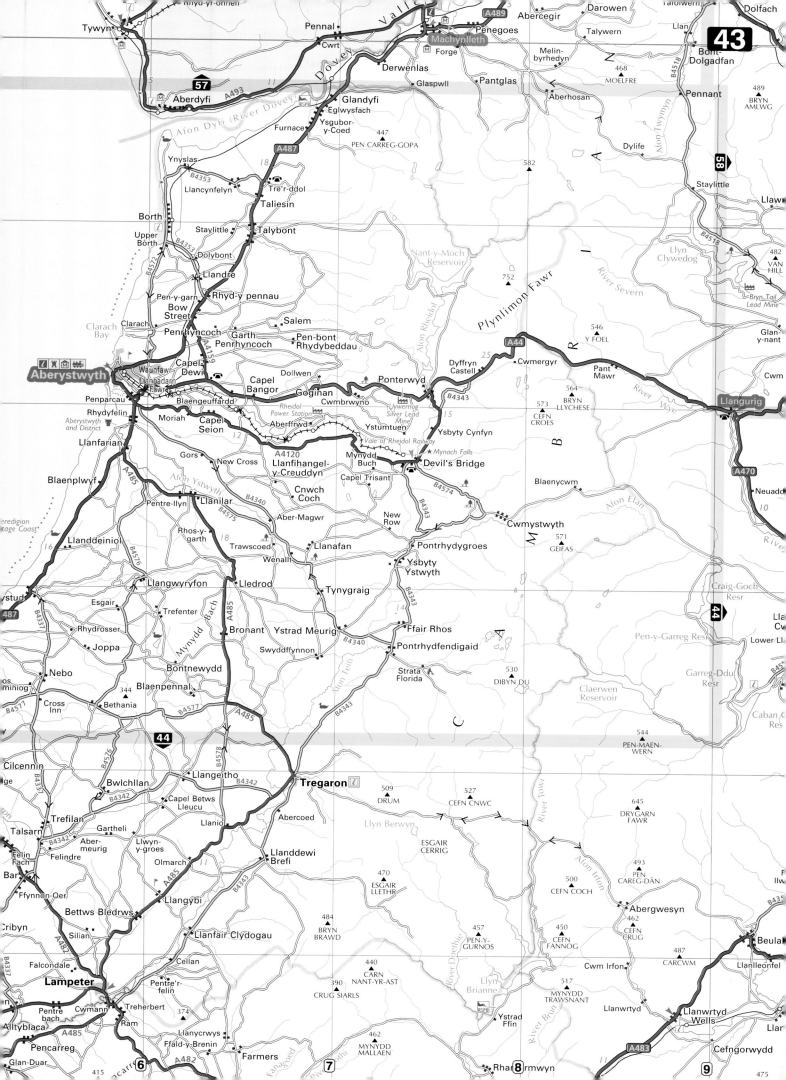

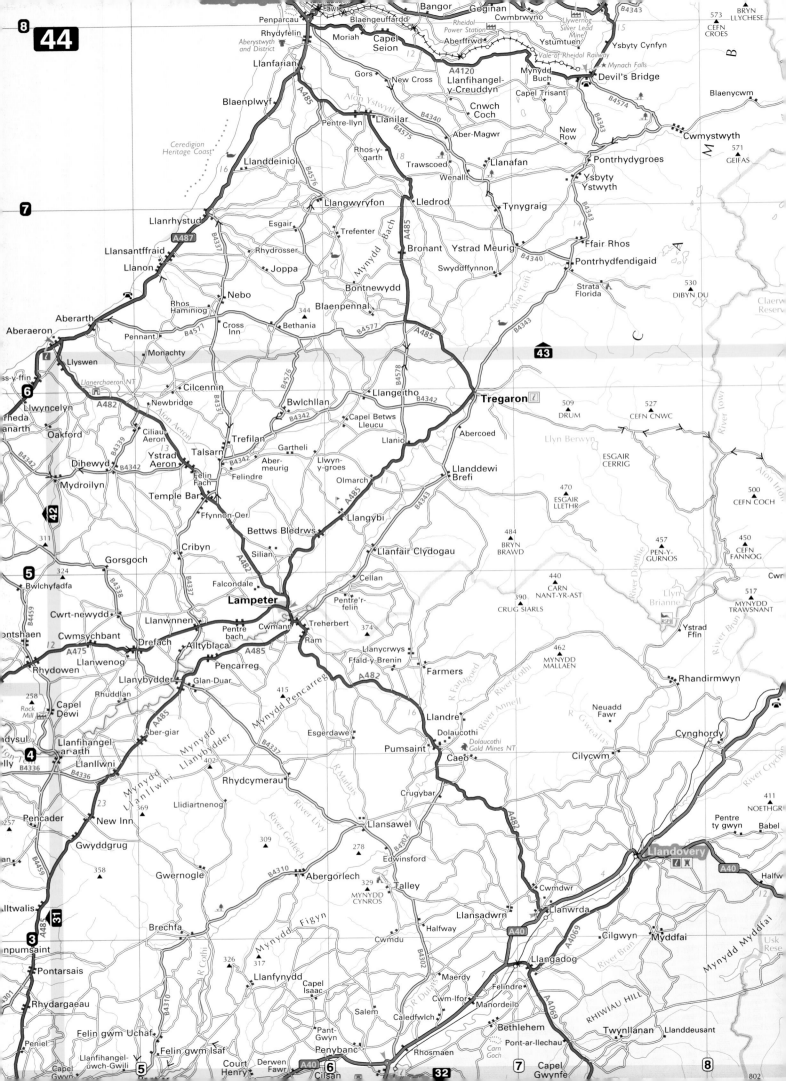

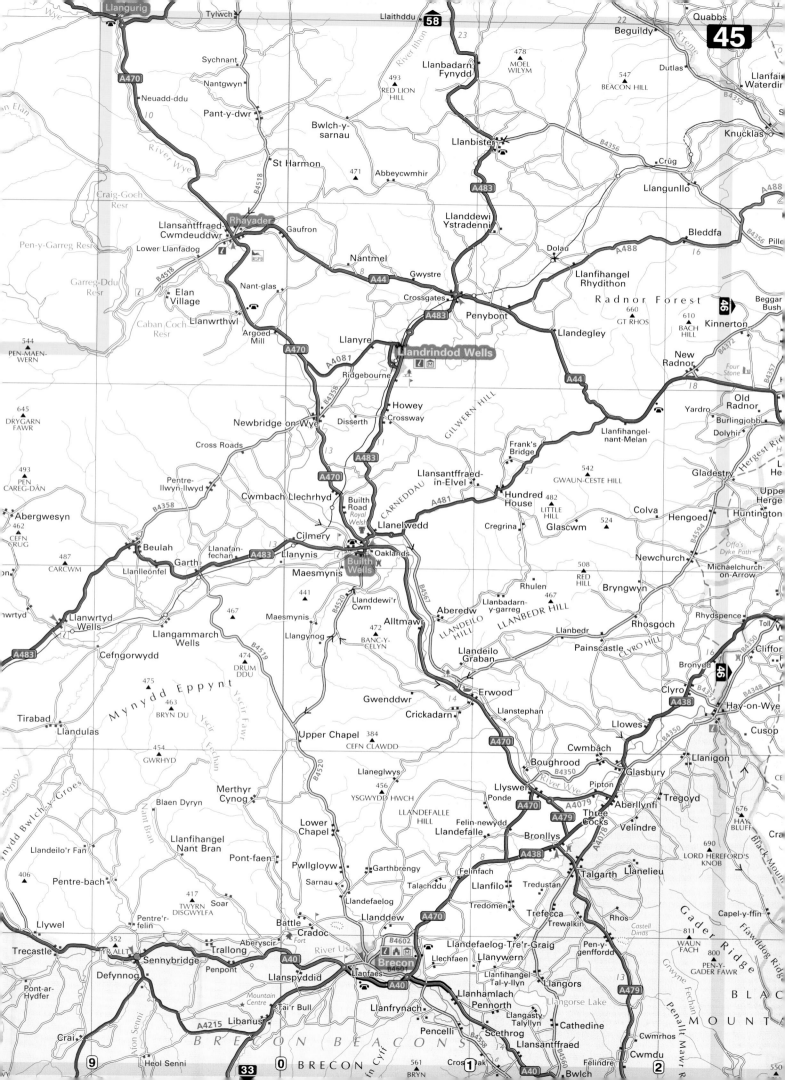

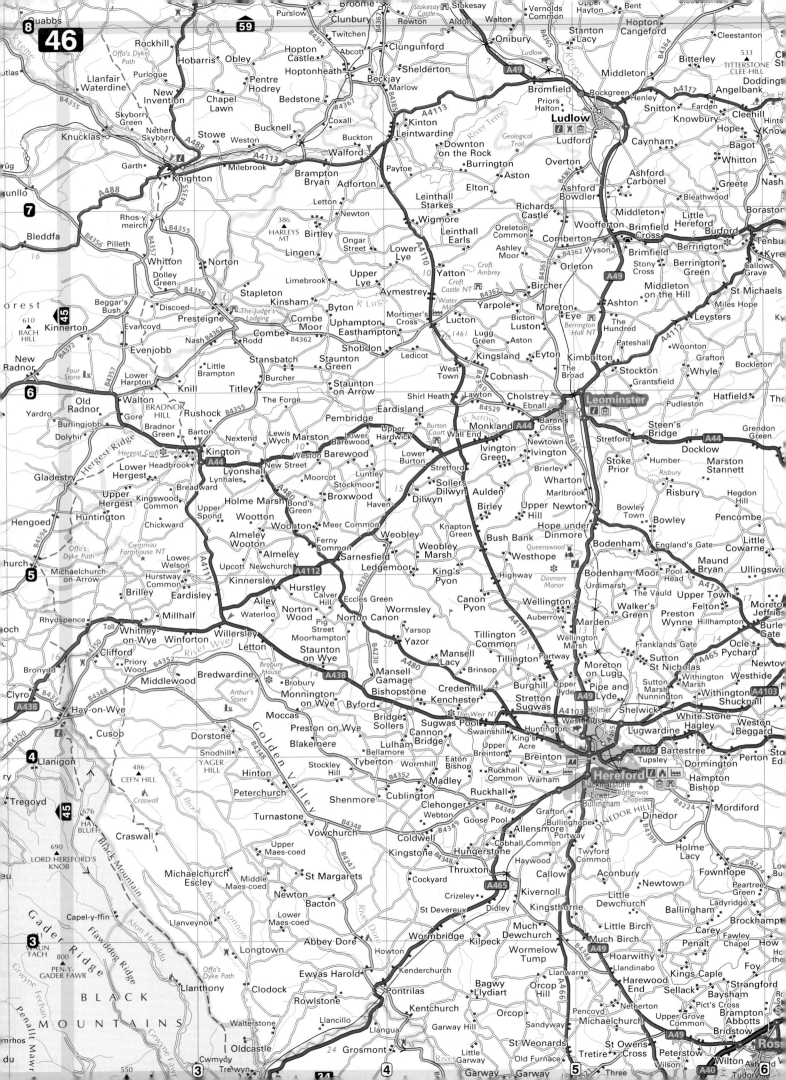

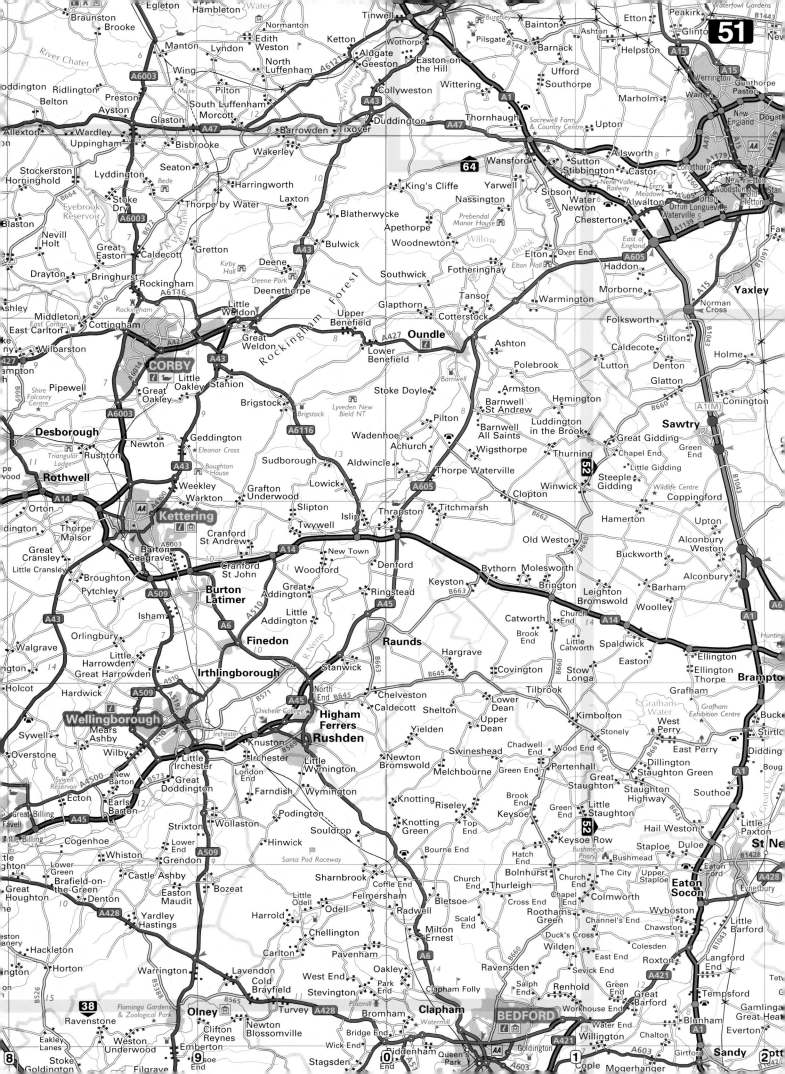

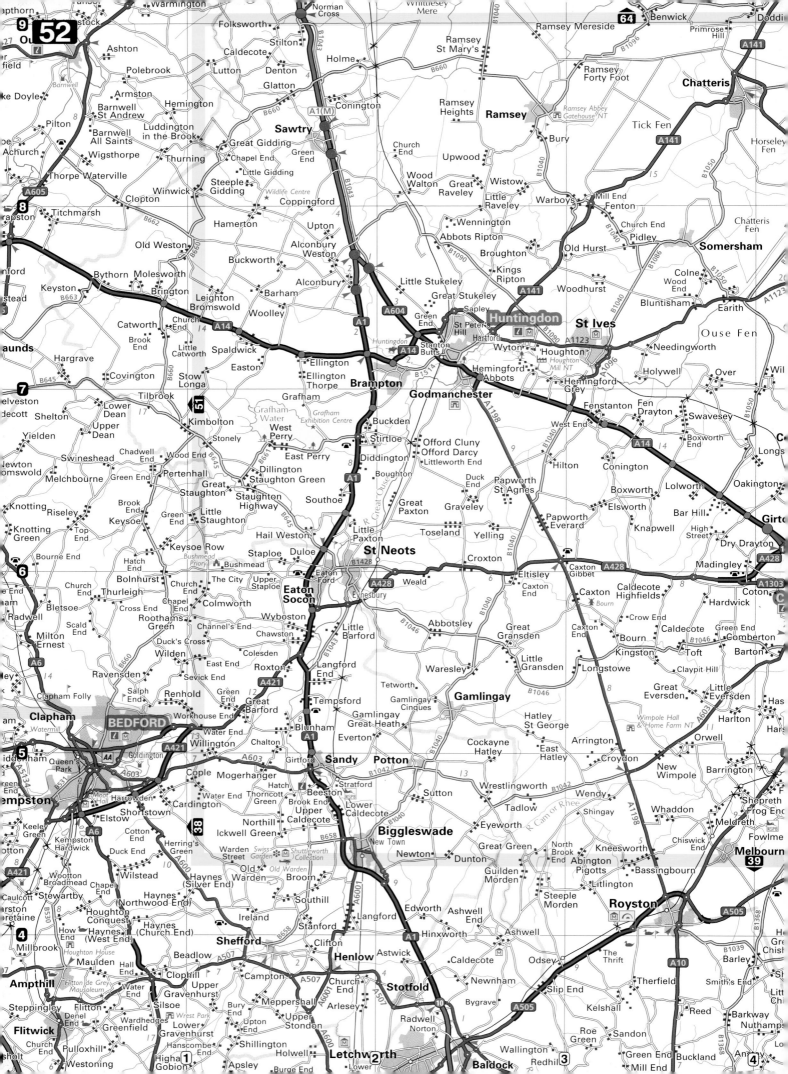

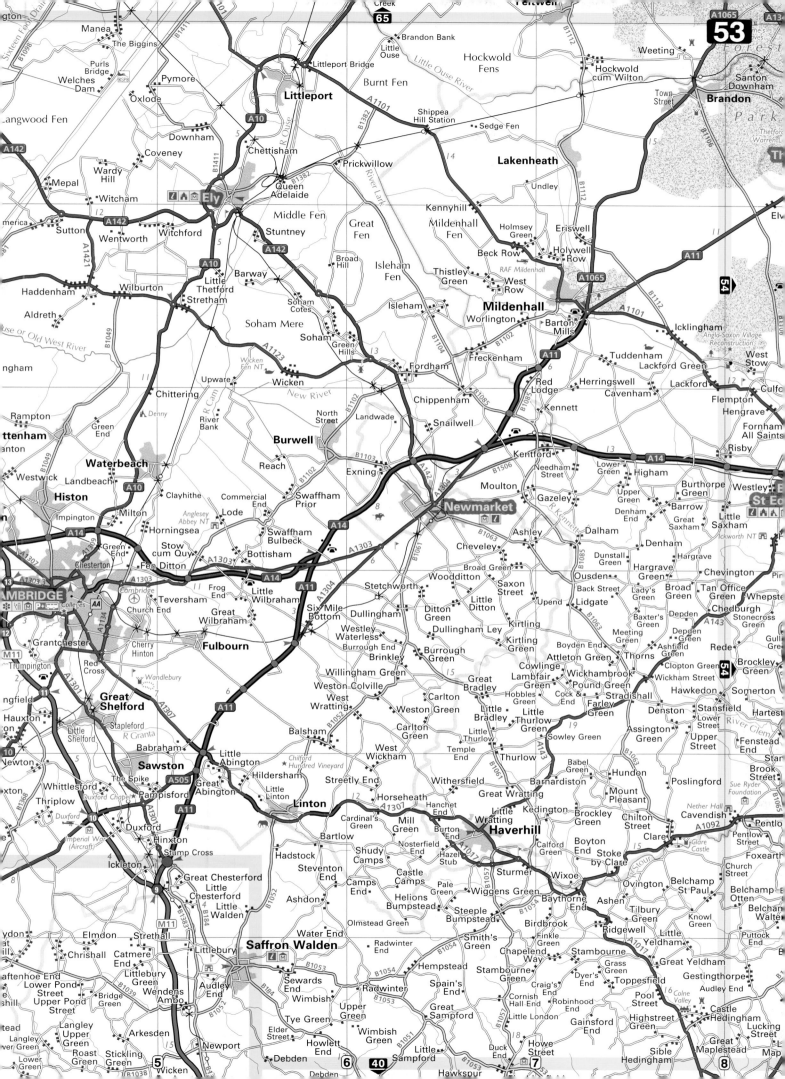

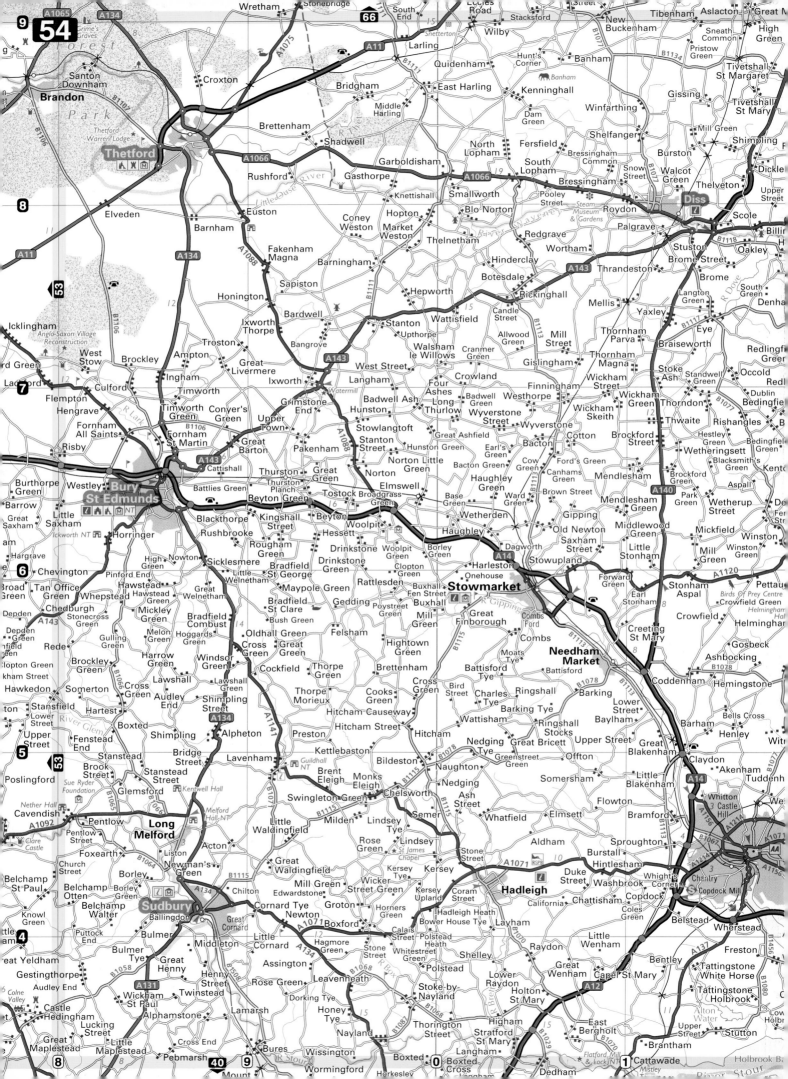

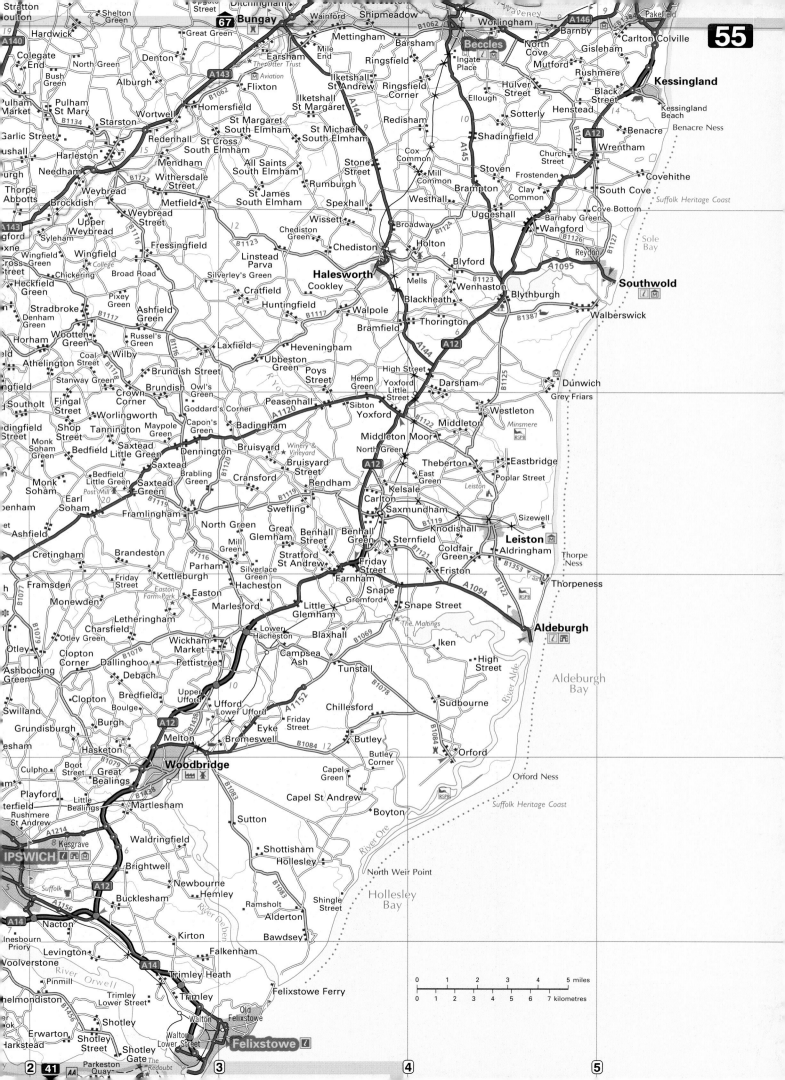

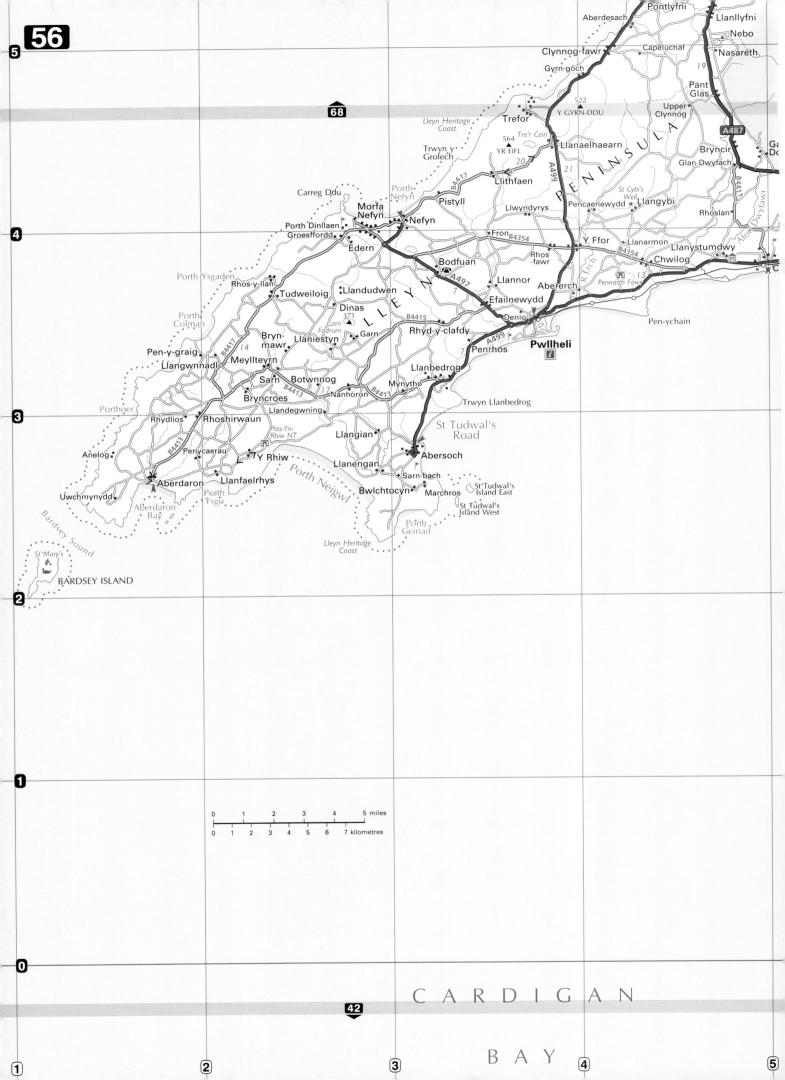

CARDIGAN

BAY

Pontlyfni
Llanllyfni
Aberdesach
Nebo
Clynnog-fawr
Capeluchaf
Nasareth
Gyrn-gôch
Pant Glas
522
Y GYRN-DDU
Upper Clynnog
Trefor
Trwyn y Grolech
564
Tre'r Ceiri
YR EIFL
Llanaelhaearn
Bryncir
Glan-Dwyfach
20
21
Llithfaen
Llwyndyrys
St Cybi's Well
Rhoslan
Carreg Ddu
Pistyll
Pencaenewydd
Llangybi
Porth Nefyn
Morfa Nefyn
Nefyn
Fron
Y Ffor
Llanarmon
Llanystumdwy
Porth Dinllaen
Groesffordd
Rhos-fawr
Chwilog
Edern
Bodfuan
Abererch
Pennarth Fawr
Porth Ysgaden
Rhos-y-llan
Llannor
13
Tudweiliog
Llandudwen
Efailnewydd
Pen-ychain
Dinas
Denio
Llaniestyn
Garn
Rhyd-y-clafdy
Pwllheli
Pen-y-graig
Bryn-mawr
Penrhos
Meyllteyrn
Llanbedrog
Llangwnnadl
Sarn
Botwnnog
Mynytho
Trwyn Llanbedrog
Bryncroes
Nanhoron
Rhydlios
Llandegwning
St Tudwal's Road
Rhoshirwaun
Llangian
Abersoch
Anelog
Penycaerau
Llanengan
Sarn-bach
St Tudwal's Island East
Y Rhiw
Bwlchtocyn
Marchros
Uwchmynydd
Aberdaron
Llanfaelrhys
Porth Neigwl
Porth Geiriad
St Tudwal's Island West
Aberdaron Bay
Porth Ysgo
Lleyn Heritage Coast
Bardsey Sound
St Mary's
BARDSEY ISLAND

LLEYN PENINSULA

Plas-Yn-Rhiw NT
Porthoer
Porth Colman
Lleyn Heritage Coast

0  1  2  3  4  5 miles
0  1  2  3  4  5  6  7 kilometres

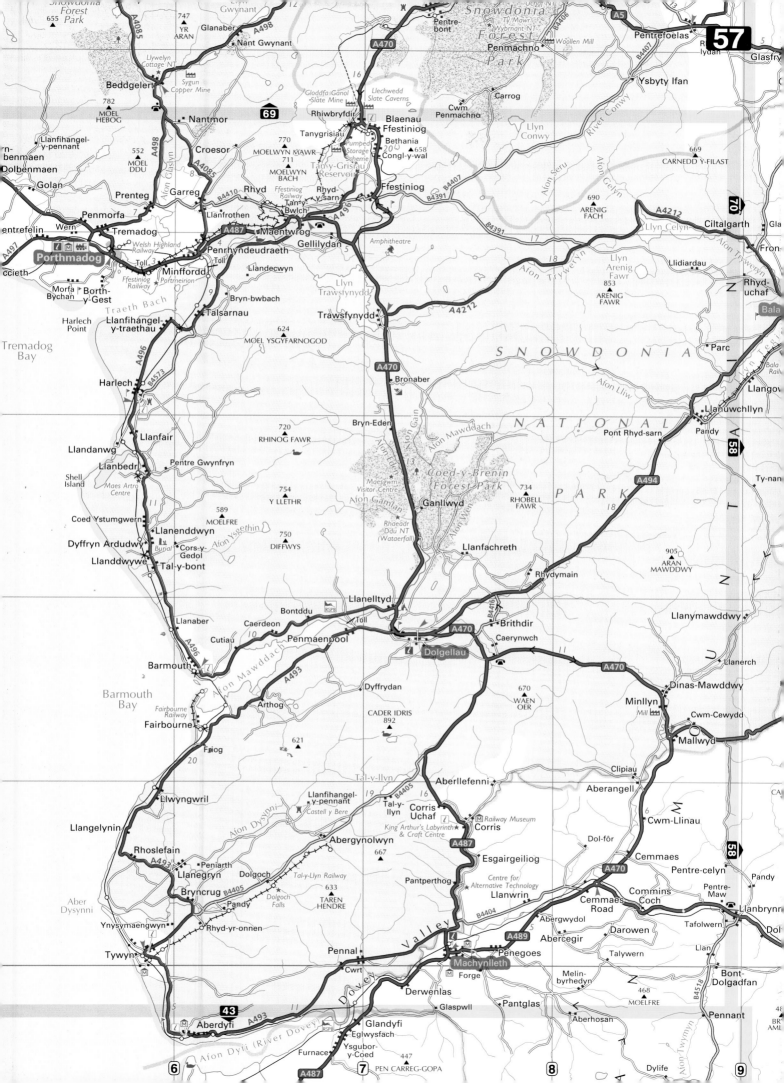

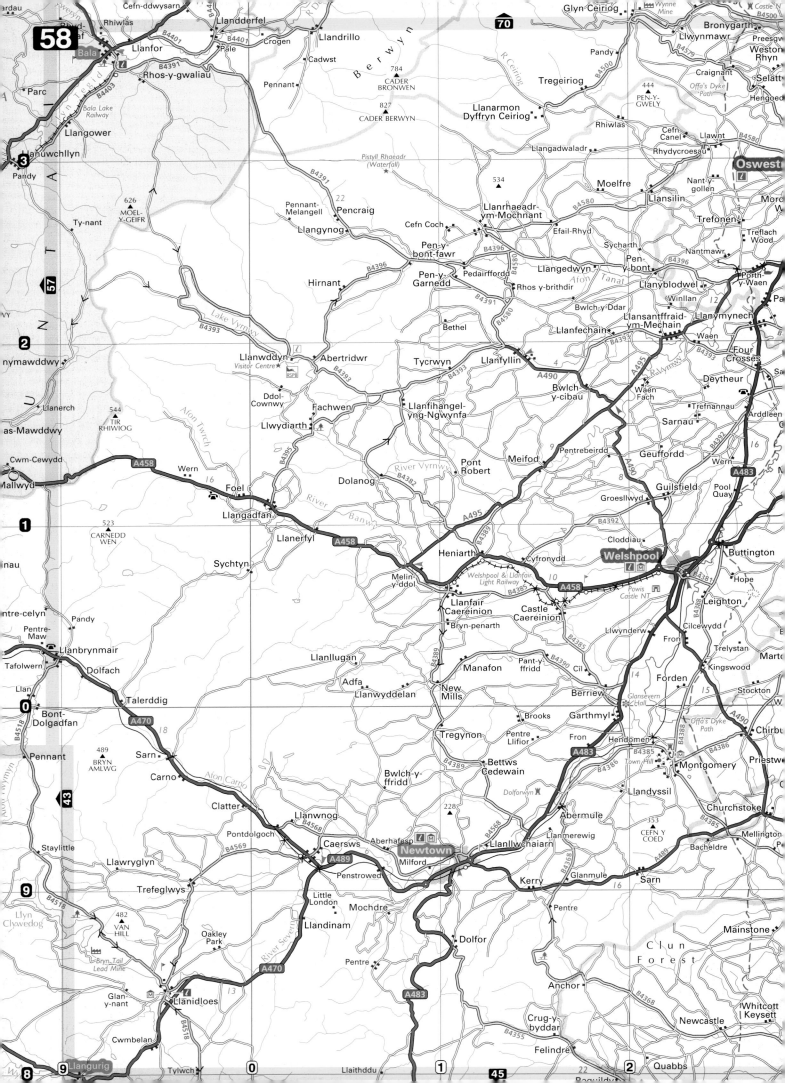

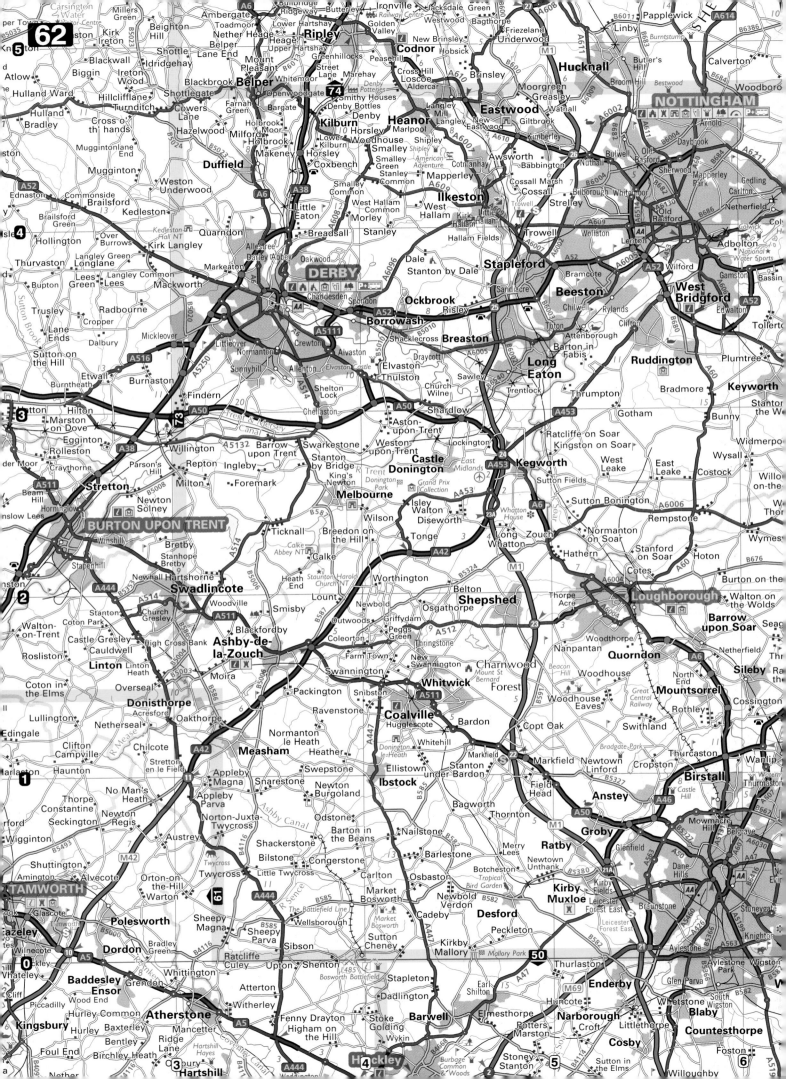

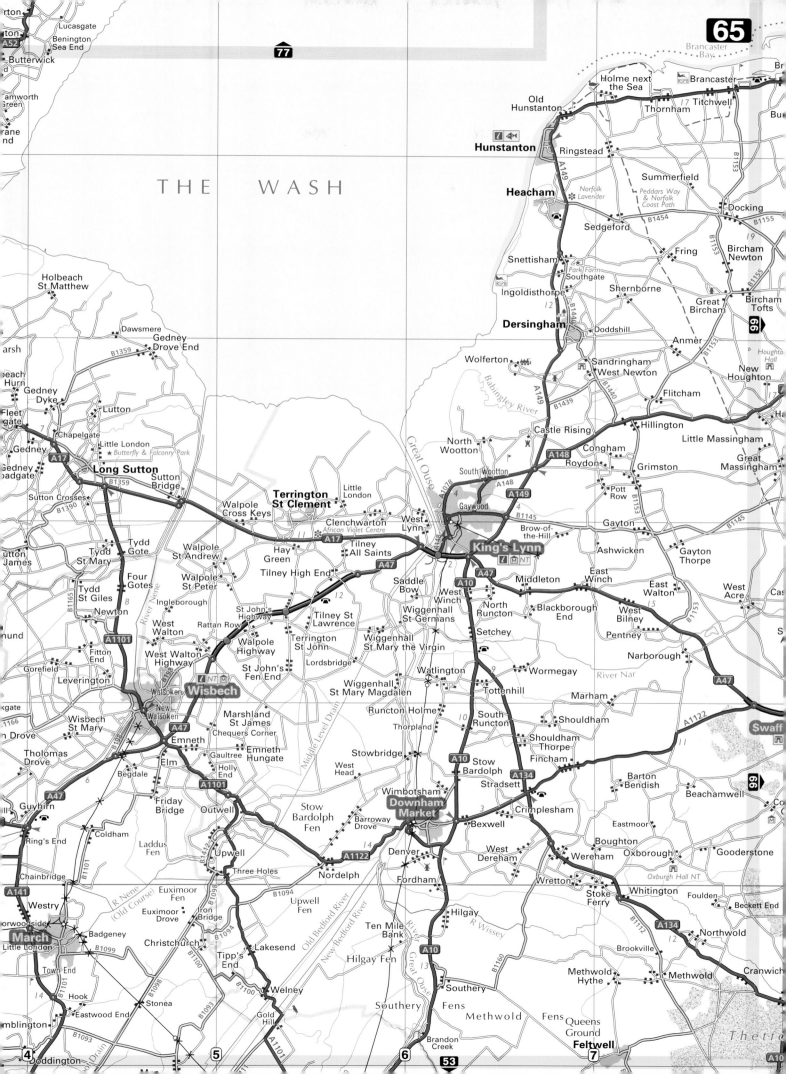

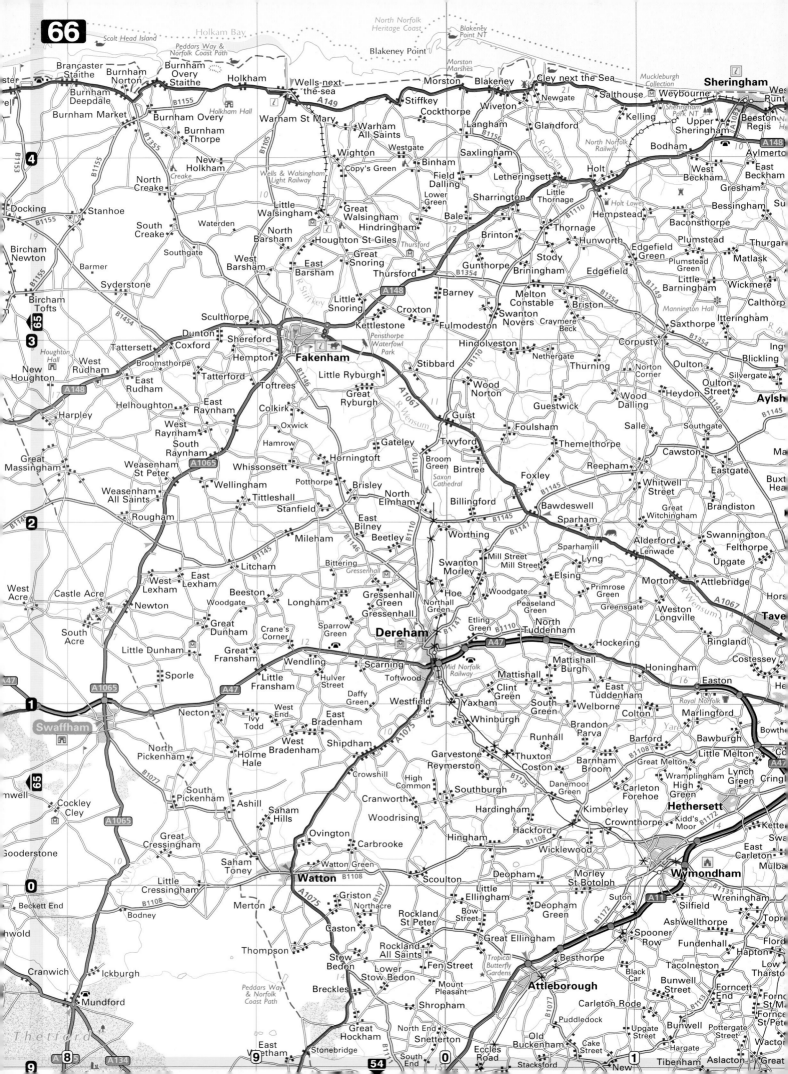

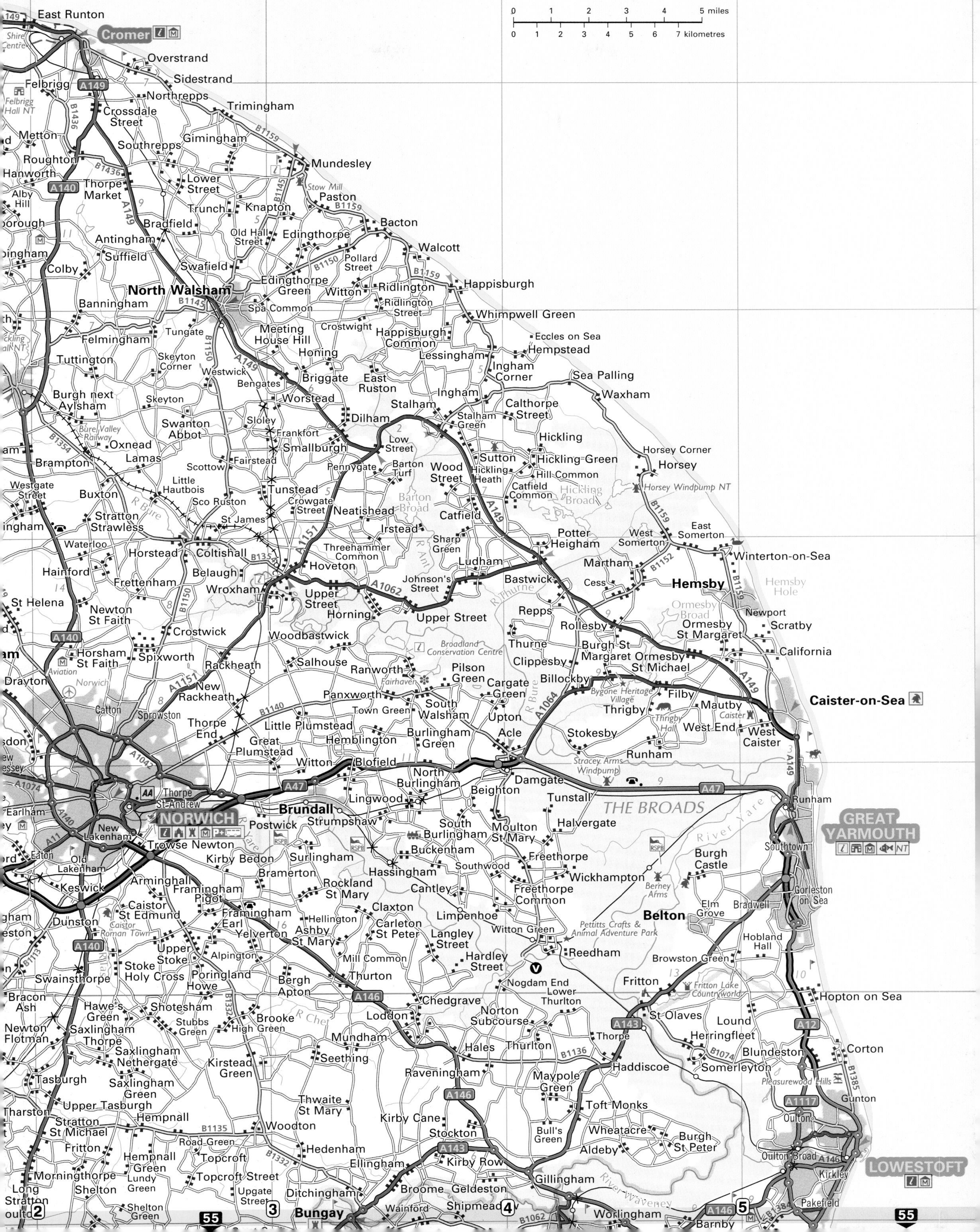

0  1  2  3  4  5 miles
0  1  2  3  4  5  6  7 kilometres

East Runton
Cromer
Overstrand
Sidestrand
Felbrigg
A149
Northrepps
Trimingham
Shire Centre
Felbrigg Hall NT
Crossdale Street
Southrepps
Gimingham
Metton
B1436
Mundesley
Roughton
Hanworth
Thorpe Market
Lower Street
Stow Mill
Paston
Alby Hill
Trunch
Knapton
Bacton
borough
A140
A149
Bradfield
Old Hall Street
Edingthorpe
Antingham
Suffield
Swafield
Walcott
Colby
Edingthorpe Green
Pollard Street
Happisburgh
Banningham
North Walsham
B1145
Ridlington
Whimpwell Green
Witton
Spa Common
Ridlington Street
Eccles on Sea
Felmingham
Tungate
Meeting House Hill
Crostwight
Happisburgh Common
Hempstead
Skeyton Corner
Honing
Lessingham
Ingham Corner
Sea Palling
Tuttington
Westwick
Briggate
East Ruston
Ingham
Waxham
Burgh next Aylsham
Skeyton
Bengates
Worstead
Stalham
Calthorpe Street
Bure Valley Railway
Sloley
Dilham
Stalham Green
Hickling
Horsey Corner
Oxnead
Lamas
Swanton Abbot
Frankfort
Low Street
Hickling Green
Horsey
Brampton
Scottow
Smallburgh
Barton Turf
Sutton
Hill Common
Horsey Windpump NT
Westgate Street
Little Hautbois
Fairstead
Pennygate
Wood Street
Hickling Heath
Catfield Common
Hickling Broad
Buxton
Sco Ruston
Tunstead
Crowgate Street
Neatishead
Barton Broad
Catfield
Potter Heigham
West Somerton
East Somerton
Stratton Strawless
St James
Threehammer Common
Irstead
Sharp Green
Ludham
Martham
Cess
Winterton-on-Sea
Waterloo
Horstead
Coltishall
Hoveton
Johnson's Street
Bastwick
Hemsby
Hainford
Belaugh
B1354
Wroxham
Upper Street
Repps
Rollesby
Ormesby St Margaret
Hemsby Hole
Frettenham
Horning
Thurne
Burgh St Margaret Ormesby St Michael
Newport
Scratby
Newton St Faith
A1062
Upper Street
Clippesby
Billockby
California
St Helena
Crostwick
Woodbastwick
Repps
Filby
Mautby
Caister
Horsham St Faith
Spixworth
Rackheath
Salhouse
Broadland Conservation Centre
Pilson Green
Thrigby
West End
Caister-on-Sea
Aviation
Norwich
New Rackheath
Ranworth
Fairhaven
Cargate Green
Bygone Heritage Village
Thrigby Hall
West Caister
Drayton
Catton
Sprowston
Panxworth
Town Green
South Walsham
Upton
Stokesby
Runham
Thorpe End
Little Plumstead
Hemblington
Acle
Great Plumstead
Witton
Blofield
Burlingham Green
Stracey Arms Windpump
Runham
A1074
Thorpe St Andrew
North Burlingham
Damgate
A47
NORWICH
AA
Brundall
Lingwood
Beighton
Tunstall
THE BROADS
New Lakenham
Postwick
Strumpshaw
South Burlingham
Moulton St Mary
Halvergate
Great Yarmouth
Trowse Newton
Kirby Bedon
Surlingham
Buckenham
Freethorpe
Southtown
A11
Bramerton
Rockland St Mary
Cantley
Southwood
Freethorpe Common
Wickhampton
Burgh Castle
Gorleston on Sea
Keswick
Hassingham
Berney Arms
Arminghall
Framingham Pigot
Claxton
Carleton St Peter
Langley Street
Witton Green
Belton
Elm Grove
Bradwell
Caistor St Edmund
Framingham Earl
Yelverton
Ashby St Mary
Limpenhoe
Pettitts Crafts & Animal Adventure Park
Dunston
Caistor Roman Town
Hellington
Mill Common
Hardley Street
Reedham
Hobland Hall
Eaton
Old Lakenham
Upper Stoke
Alpington
Thurton
Nogdam End
Lower Thurlton
Browston Green
Swainsthorpe
Stoke Holy Cross
Poringland Howe
Bergh Apton
A146
Chedgrave
Fritton
Fritton Lake Countryworld
Hopton on Sea
Bracon Ash
Hawe's Green
Shotesham
Brooke
High Green
Loddon
Norton Subcourse
St Olaves
Lound
A12
Newton Flotman
Saxlingham Thorpe
Stubbs Green
Mundham
Thorpe
Herringfleet
Blundeston
Corton
Tasburgh
Saxlingham Nethergate
Kirstead Green
Seething
Hales
Thurlton
A143
Haddiscoe
Somerleyton
A1117
Gunton
Upper Tasburgh
Saxlingham Green
Raveningham
B1136
Maypole Green
Pleasurewood Hills
Tharston
Stratton St Michael
Hempnall
B1135
Woodton
Thwaite St Mary
Kirby Cane
Toft Monks
Wheatacre
Burgh St Peter
Oulton
LOWESTOFT
Fritton
Hempnall Green
Topcroft
Hedenham
Stockton
Bull's Green
Aldeby
Oulton Broad
A146
Long Stratton
Shelton
Lundy Green
Topcroft Street
Upgate Street
Ellingham
Kirby Row
Gillingham
River Waveney
Kirkley
Shelton Green
Ditchingham
Broome
Geldeston
Shipmeadow
Worlingham
Barnby
Pakefield
Bungay
Wainford
B1062
55

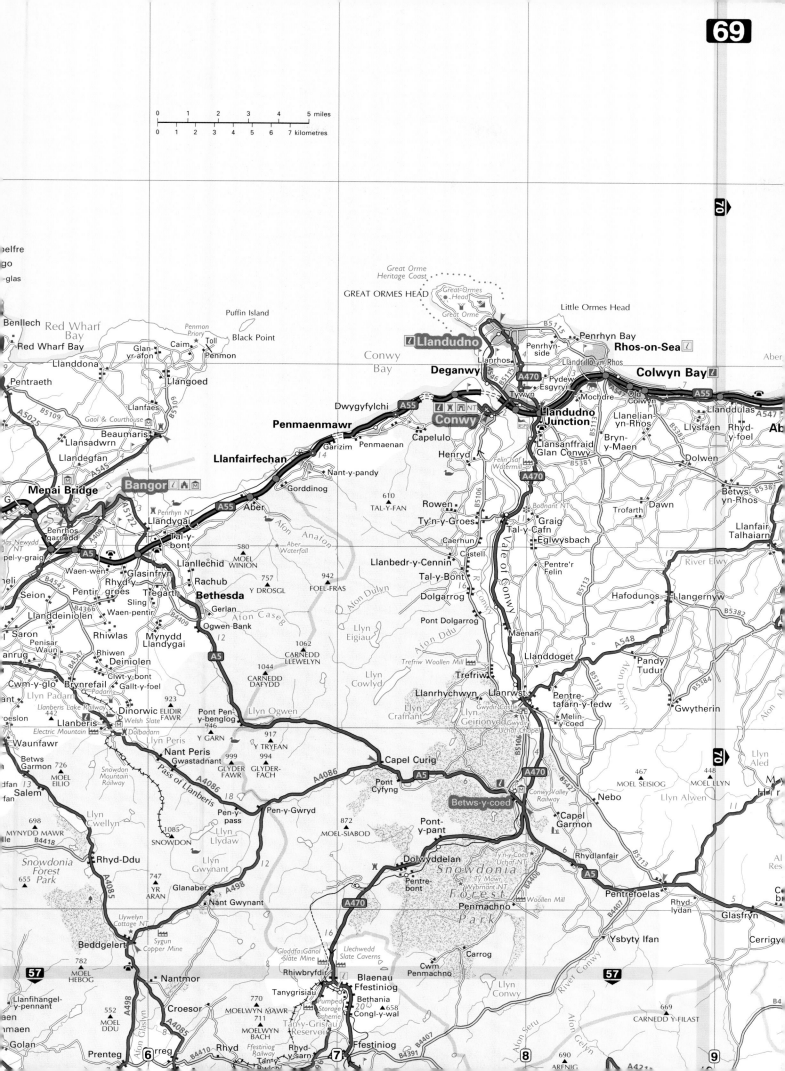

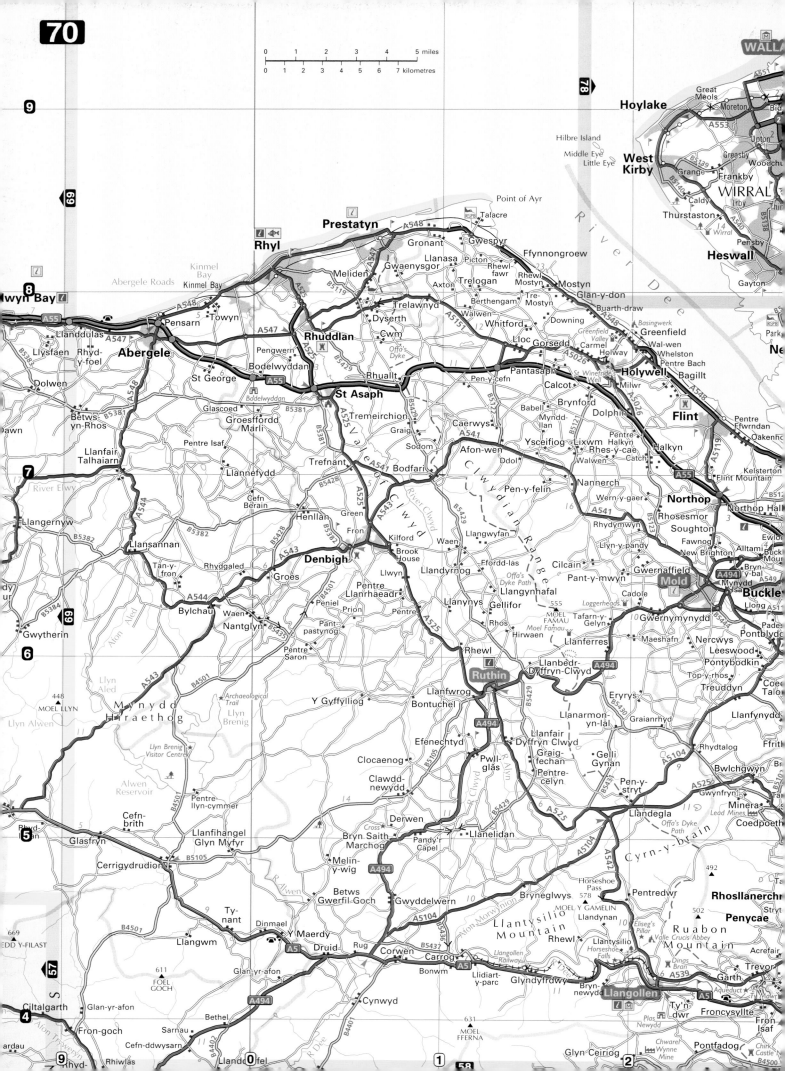

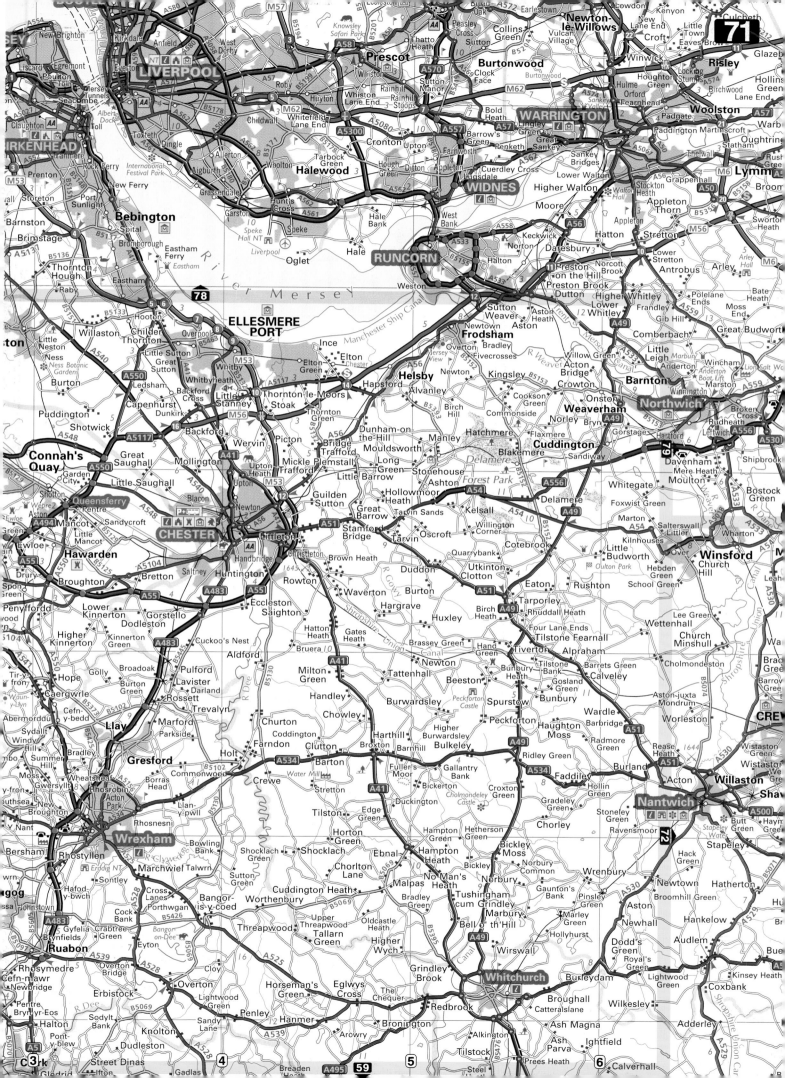

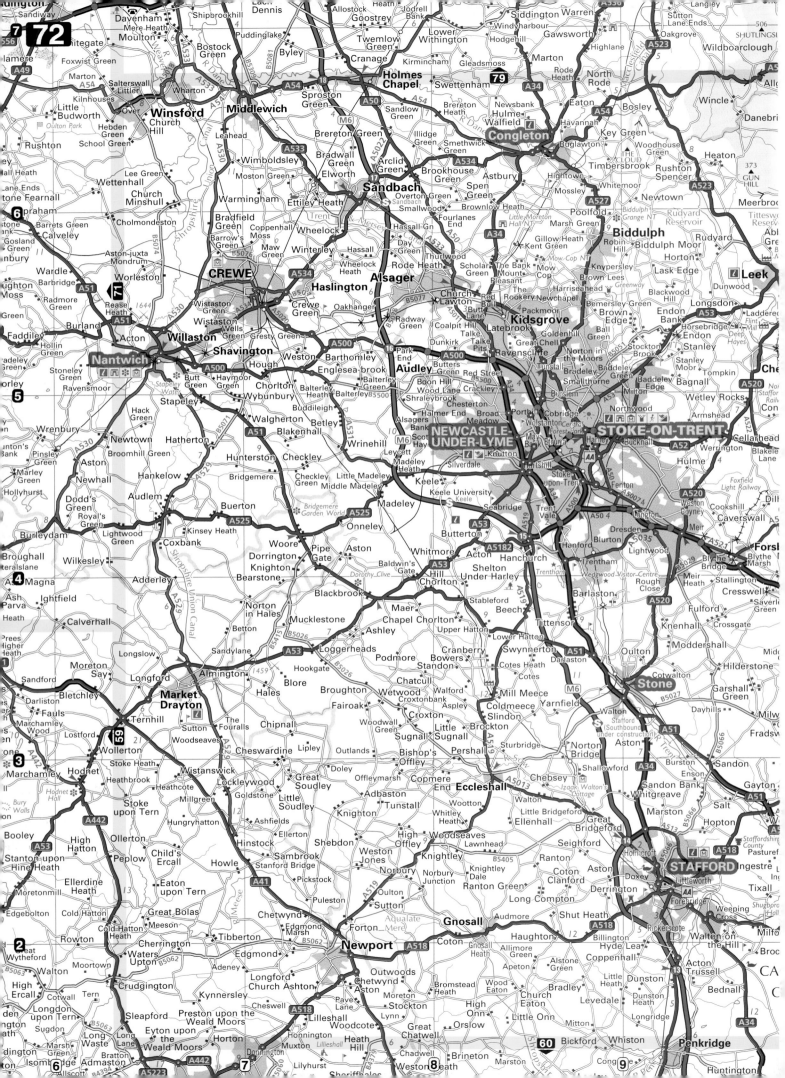

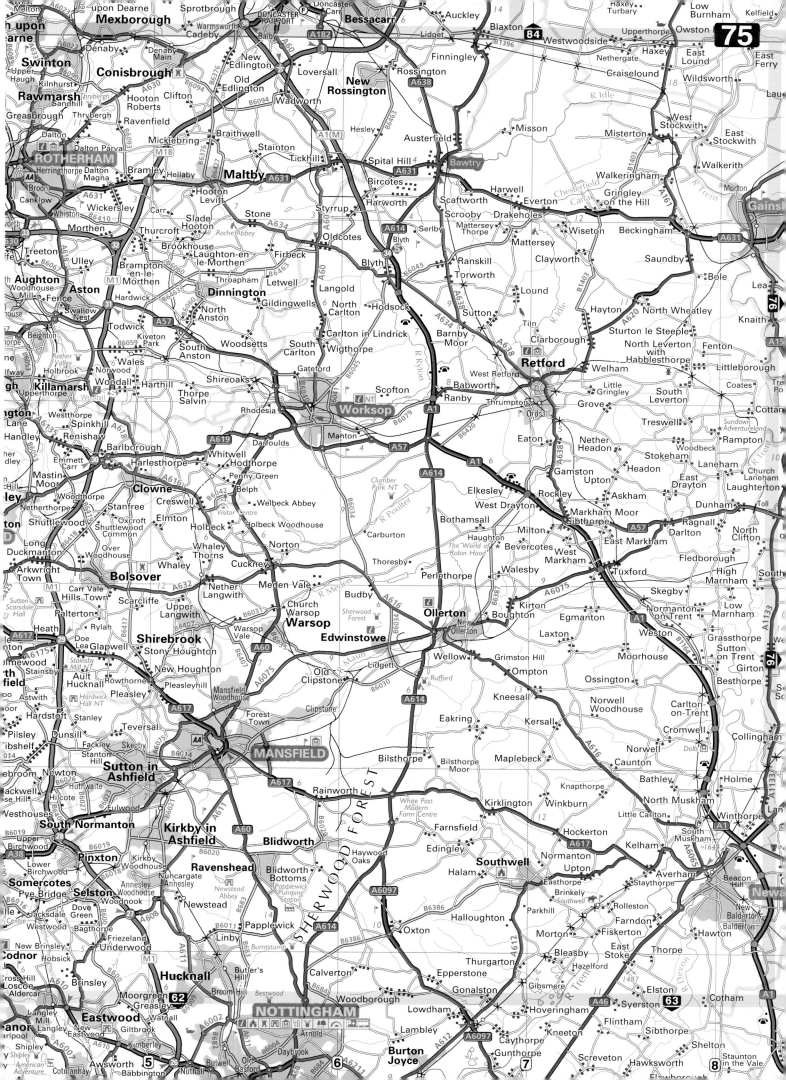

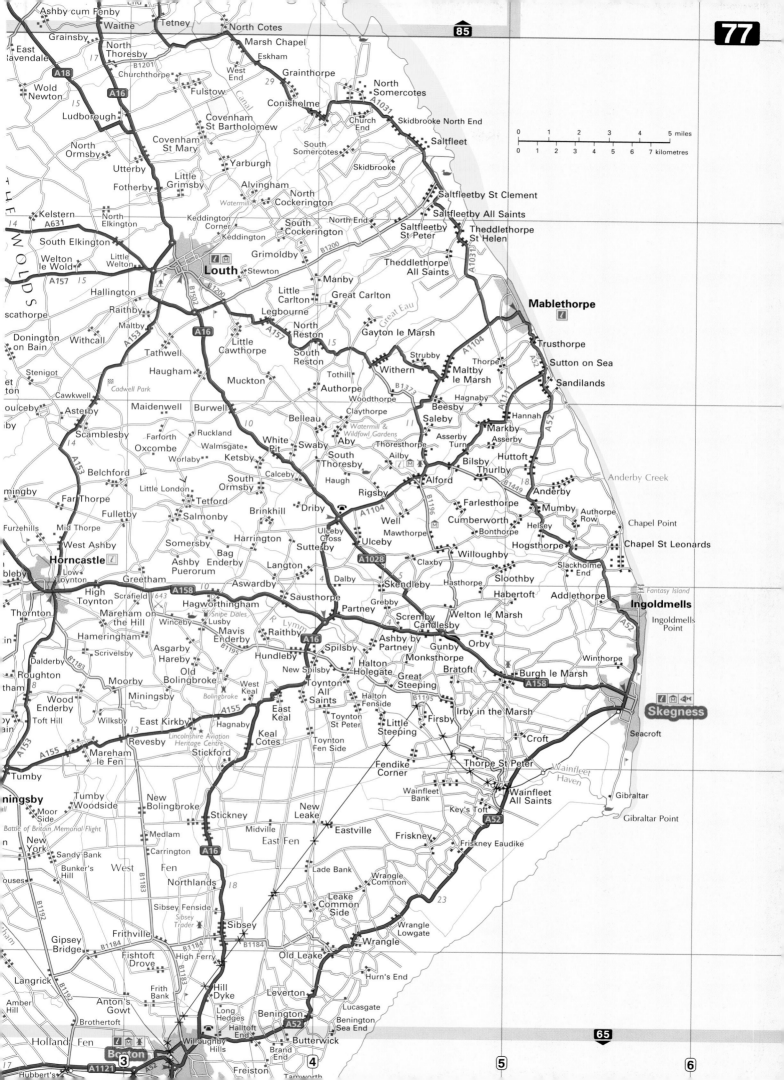

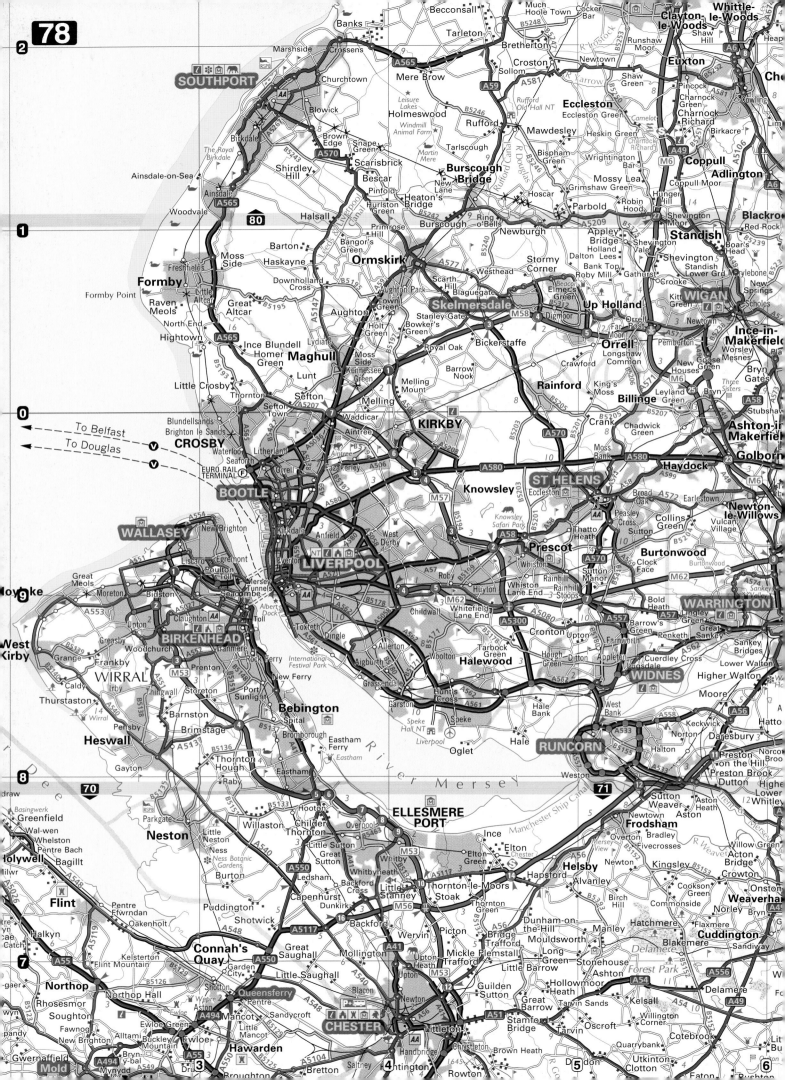

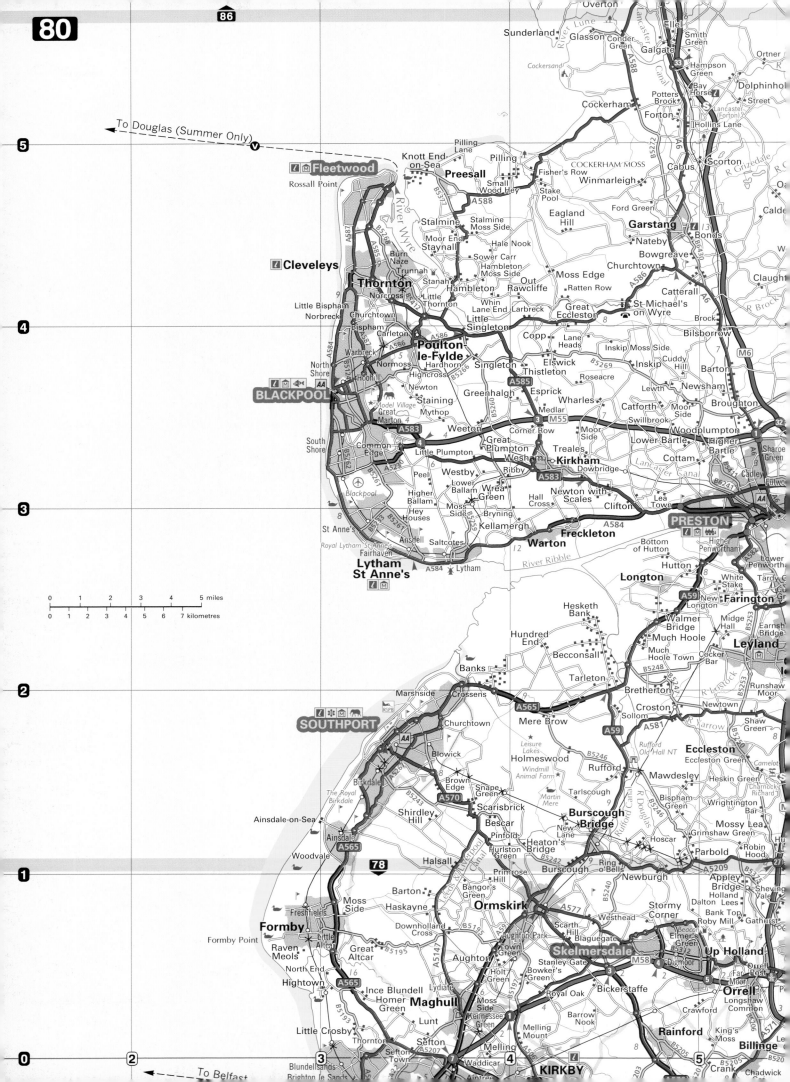

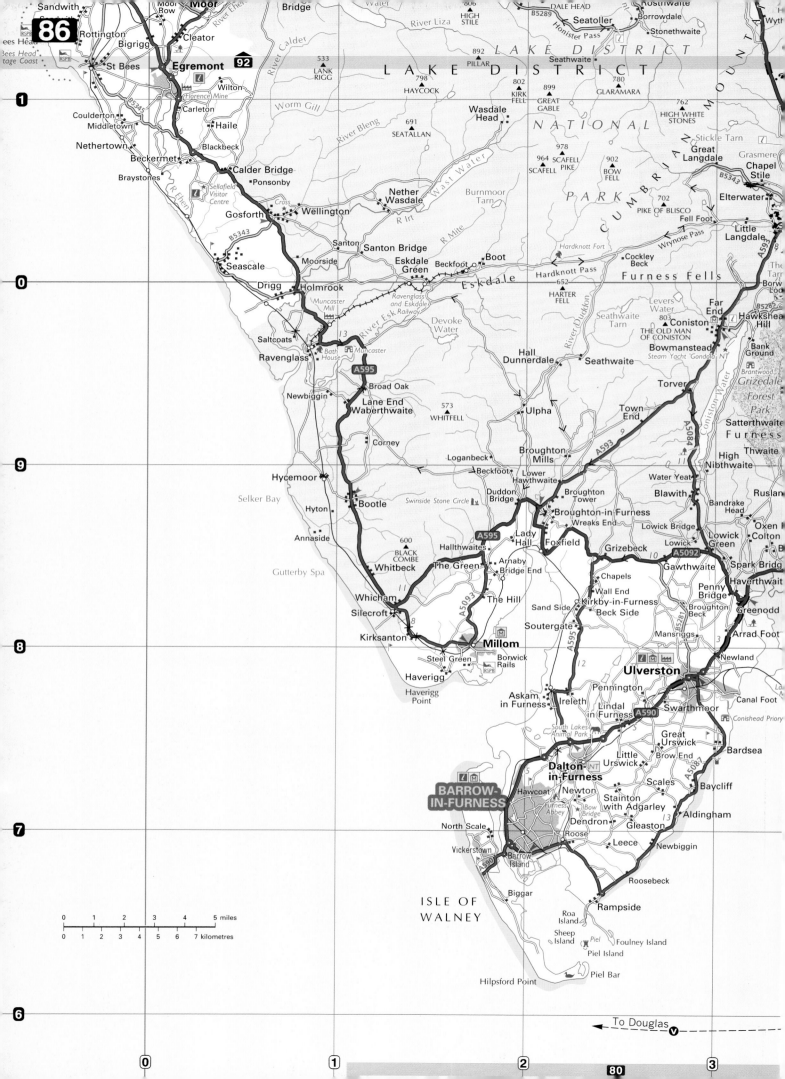

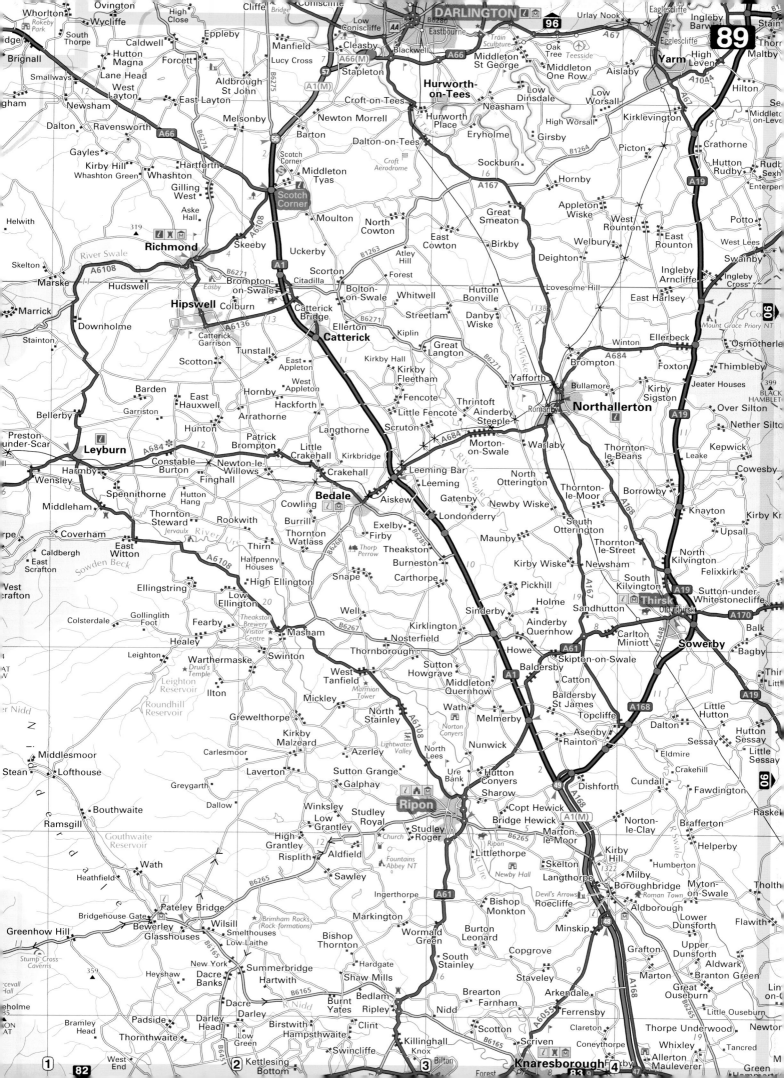

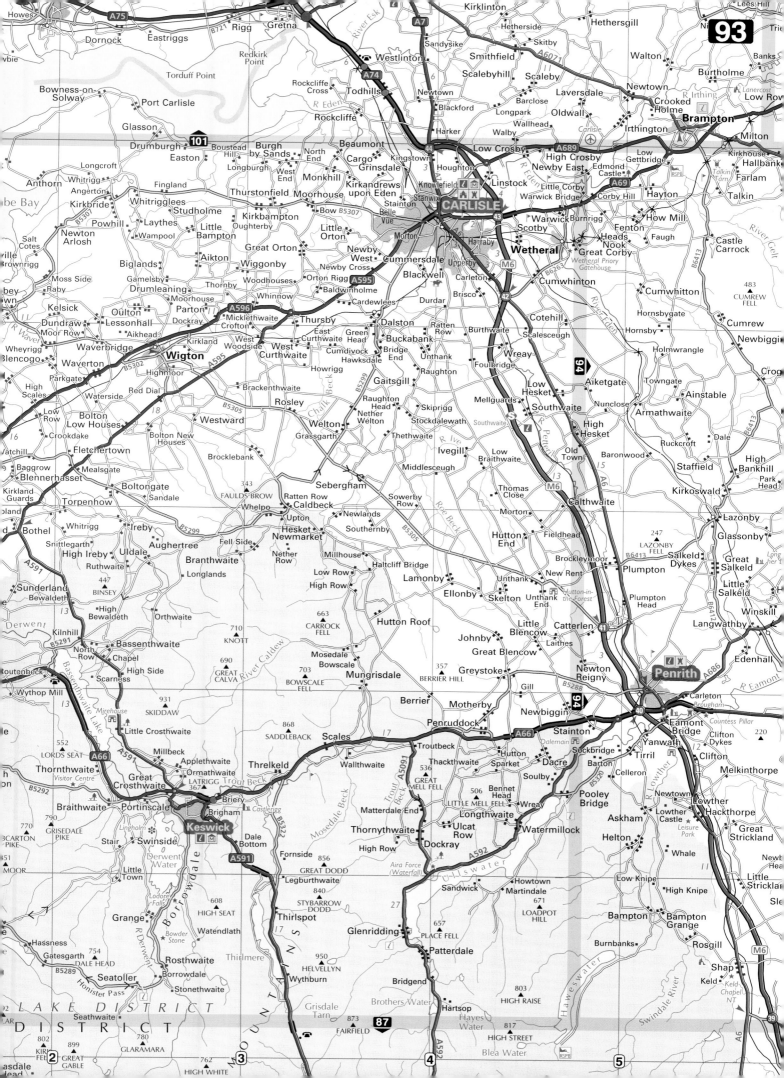

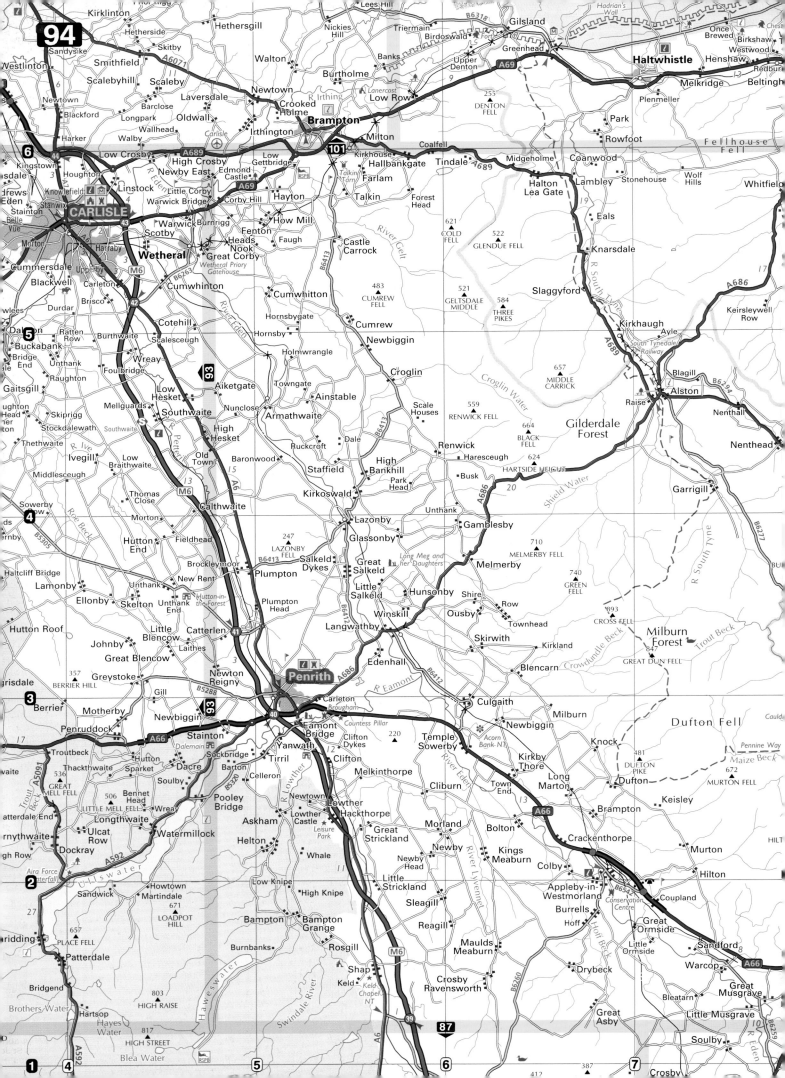

BERGEN
STAVANGER

GÖTEBORG
Summer Only

HAMBURG
Summer Only

AMSTERDAM

...AND

...m

0    1    2    3    4    5 miles

0  1  2  3  4  5  6  7 kilometres

...sington Colliery

...rpe

Peterlee

...len
Blackhall Colliery
Blackhall Rocks
Blackhall
...sleden
...Henry
...eraton    Hart
A179
High
Throston    Headland
Elwick    Historic
Quay
AA
Dalton
Piercy    HARTLEPOOL
Brierton    Hartlepool Bay

A19
A689    Greatham
Newton    Graythorpe    Tees Bay
Bewley    Hartlepool Power
Station Visitor
Centre
Billingham    Seal    Coatham
A1185    Sands    Warrenby    Redcar
Cowpen
Bewley    Teesport
Haverton Hill    Marske-by-
B1275    Port    A1042    the-Sea
B1046    Clarence    A1085
Toll    River Tees    Kirkleatham    Saltburn-by-the-Sea
A66    Old Hall    Yearby    Saltburn Smugglers
North    South Grangetown    New    New Brotton
Ormesby    Bank    Lackenby    Marske    Hummersea Scar
AA    Wilton    Upleatham    Brotton    Carlin    Skinningrove
Eston    How    Street    Boulby
MIDDLESBROUGH    Dunsdale    Skelton    Houses
A174    New    North    Kilton    Loftus    Staithes
Teesside Park    Normanby    Skelton    Skelton    Heritage Centre
Acklam    Tocketts    Liverton    Dalehouse
es    Ormesby Hall NT    B1269    Mines    Easington    Port Mulgrave
A172    Boosbeck    Lingdale    Kilton
A19    Marton    A171    Margrove    Thorpe    Liverton    Hinderwell
B1380    Park    Handale    Newton    Runswick
Stainton    5    6    Guisborough    Stanghow    Roxby    Mulgrave    Bay
Hemlington    Nunthorpe    Pinchinthorpe    90    7    Moorsholm    Borrowby    8    Kettleness    Göldsboro
Newton    Hutton Hall    Ellerby
B1266

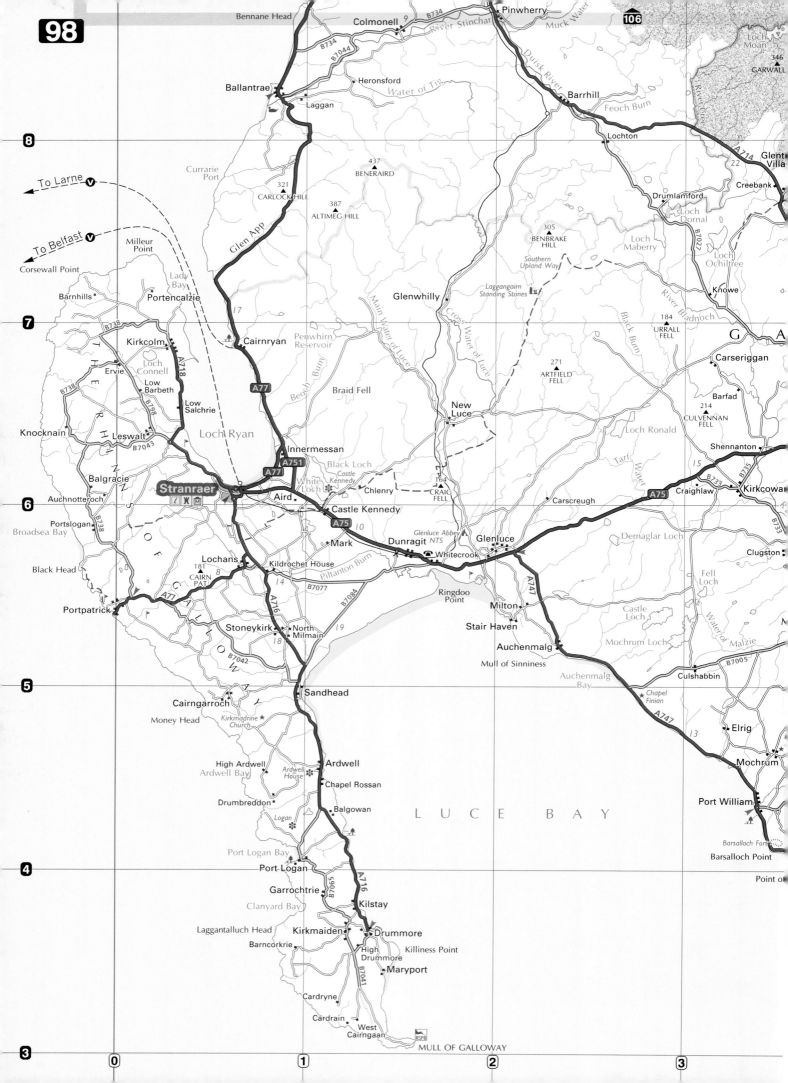

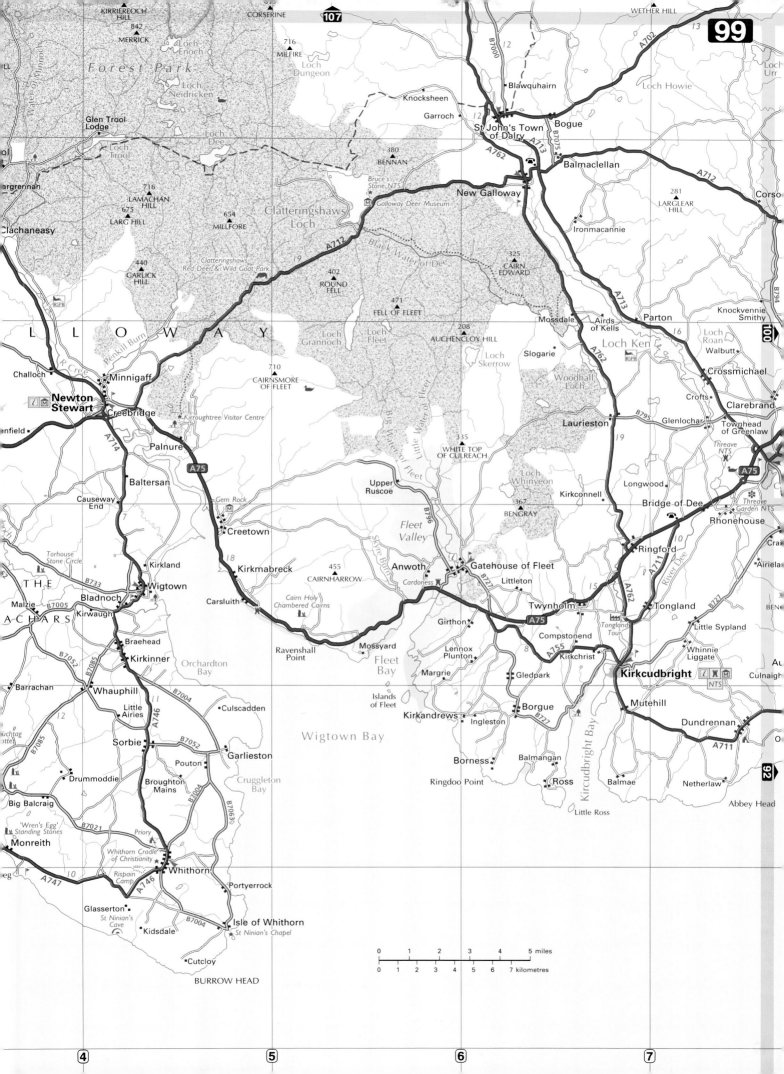

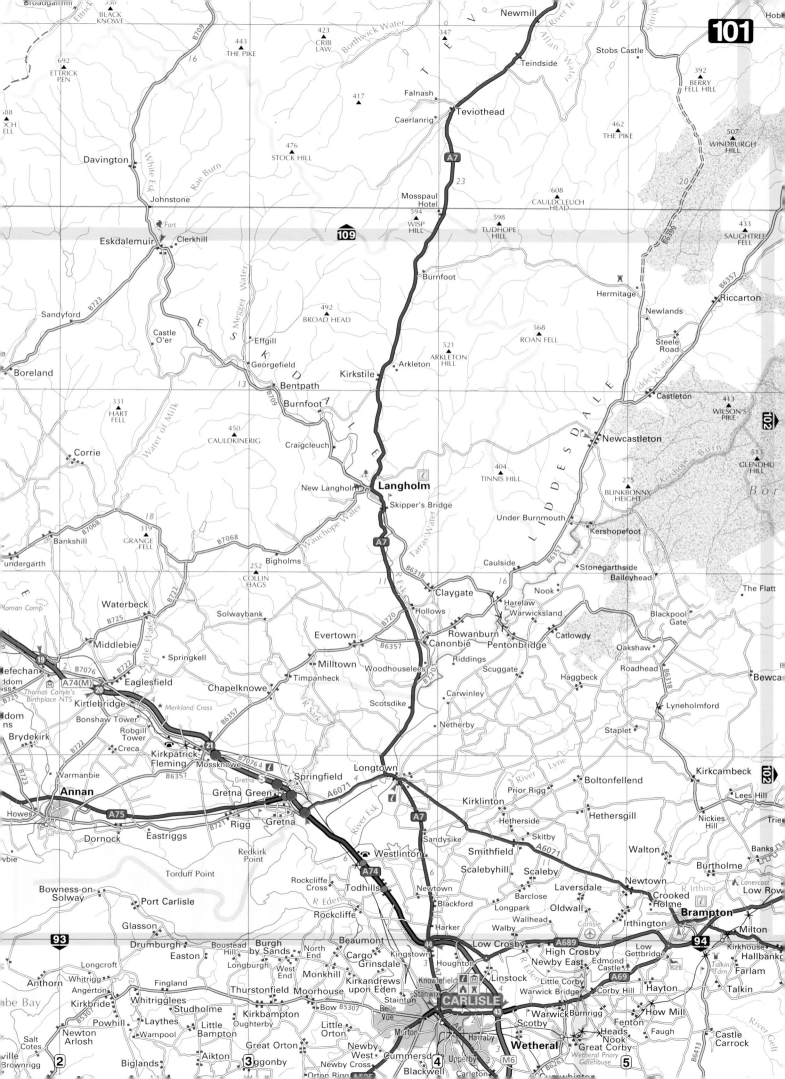

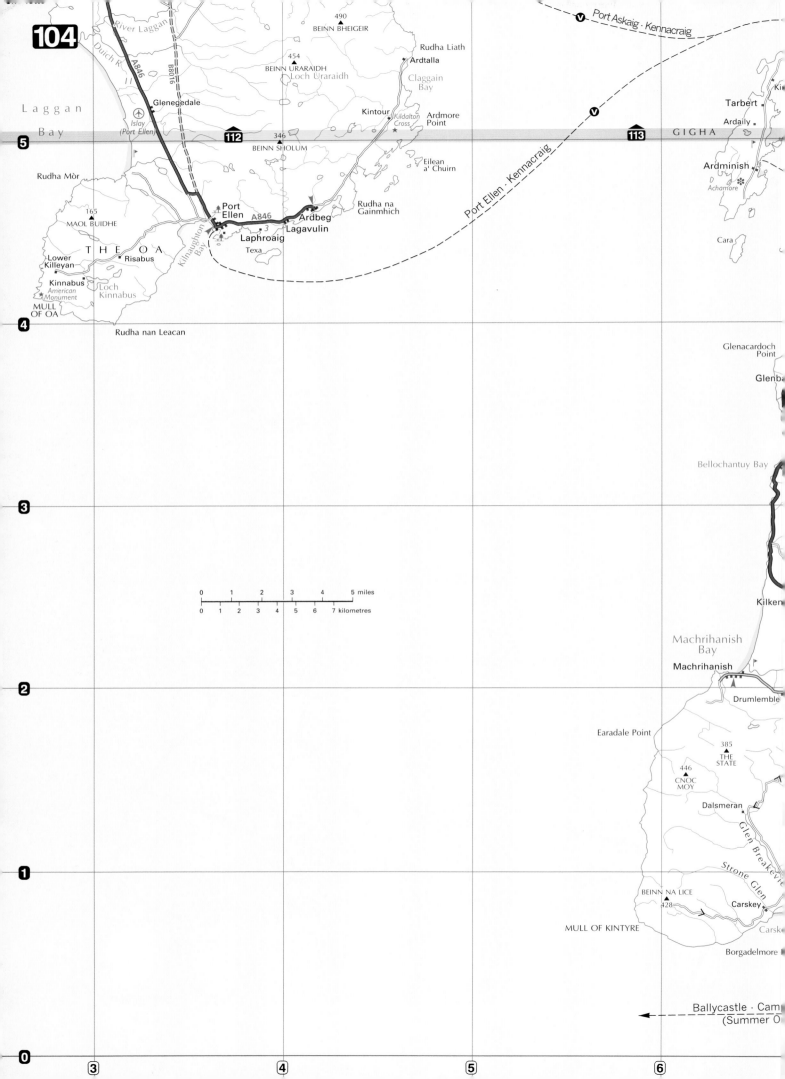

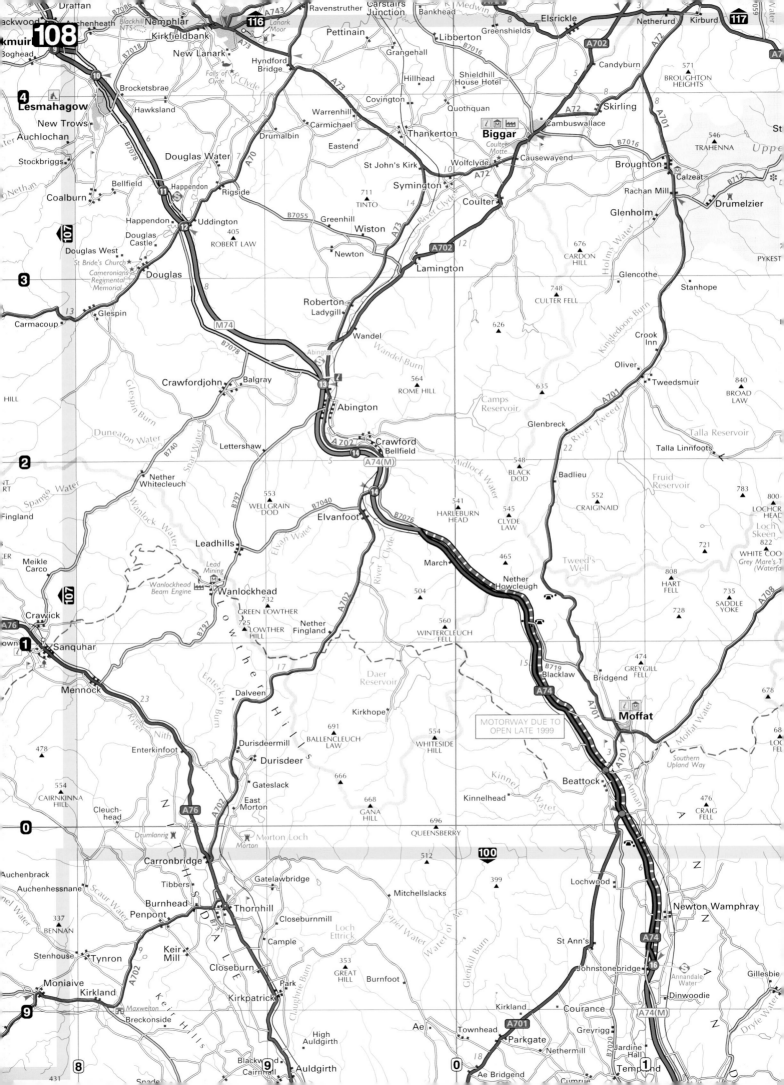

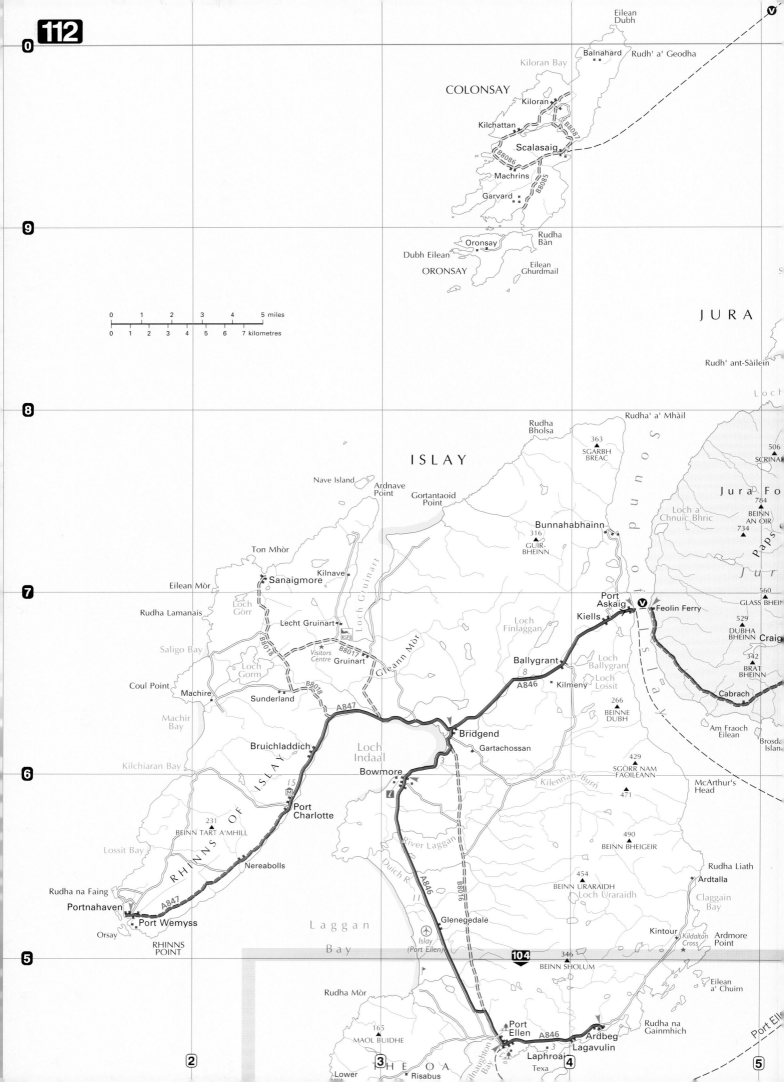

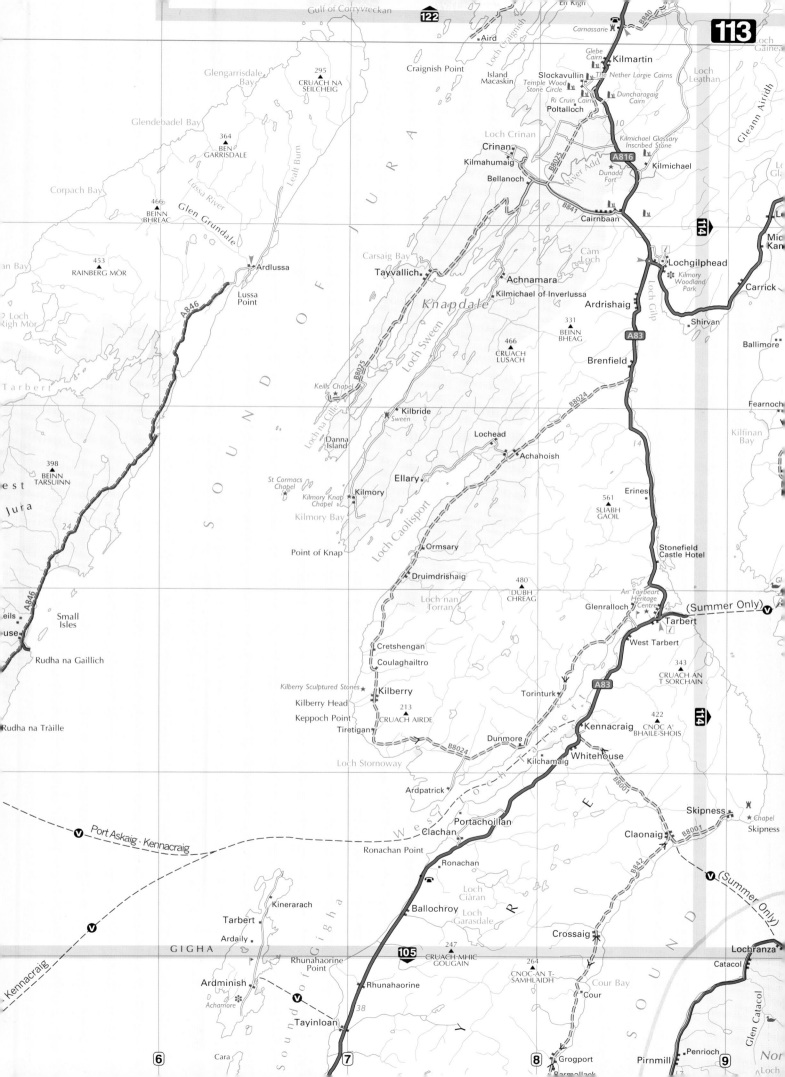

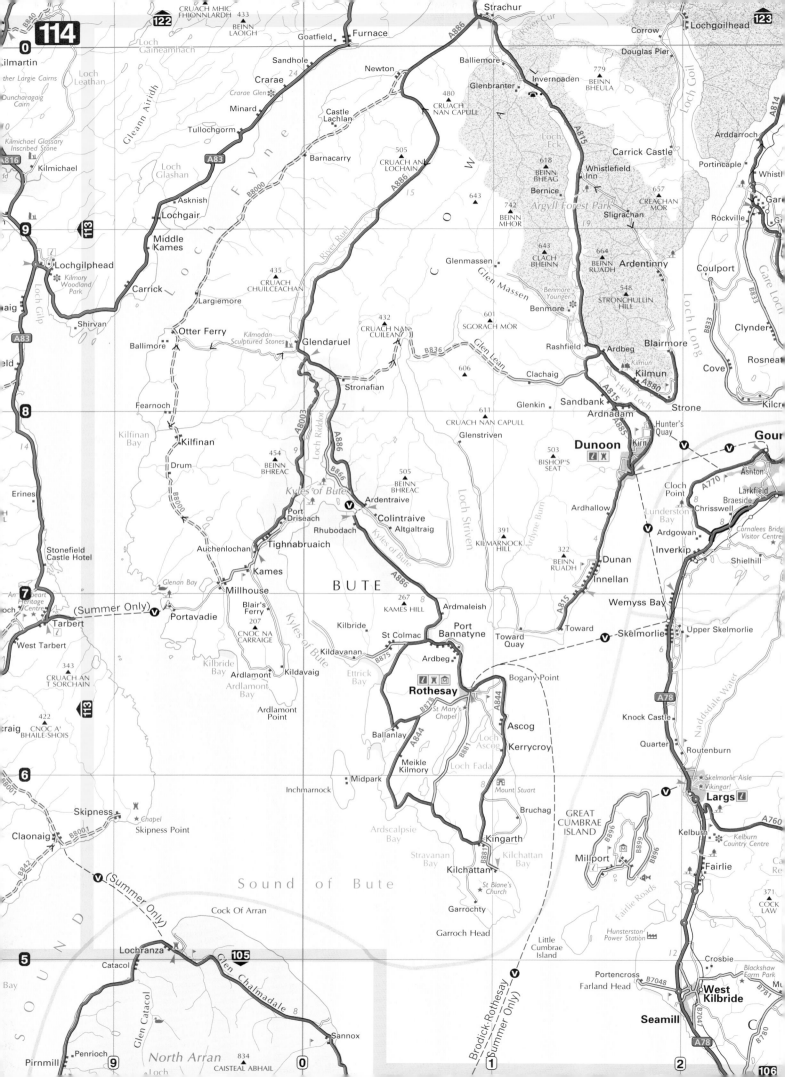

0  1  2  3  4  5 miles
0  1  2  3  4  5  6  7 kilometres

**Dunbar** ℹ

Broxburn
1650
Barns Ness
East Barns
A1
12
Skateraw
Chapel Point
Moonhill
Homestead
Torness Power Station
Thorntonloch
Innerwick
Crowhill
Dry Brook
Reed Point
Dunglass
Collegiate Church ★
Cove
Pease Bay
Siccar Point
Fast Castle Head
Cockburnspath
319
COCKLAW HILL
Oldhamstocks
A1107
196
BROWN RIG
ST ABB'S HEAD
Ecclaw
391
HEART LAW
Monynut Water
Grantshouse
St Abbs
Coldingham
Coldingham Bay
Southern Upland Way
Butterdean
21
Houndwood
B6438
A1107
22
Eyemouth ℹ 🏛
Eye Water
Quixwood
Heugh Head ☎
Cairncross
262
HORSELEY HILL
Abbey St Bathans
Edin's Hall Broch
Reston
Ayton
Burnmouth
Ellemford
14
B6438
Auchencrow
B6355
Whitchester
325
COCKBURN LAW
Marygold
Lamberton
Marshall Meadows Bay
Lintlaw
B6355
A6112
Preston
B6437
B6355
Primrosehill
Chirnside
Foulden
399
DIRRINGTON GREAT LAW
B6365
Cumledge
Church ★
Manderston
15
Chirnsidebridge
Edrom
Broadhaugh
Edington
Whiteadder Water
1333
Tithe Barn
A6105
North Northumberland Heritage Coast
A6105
**Berwick-upon-Tweed** ℹ 🏛
Duns
A6105
Allanton
Hutton
Barracks
Town Ramparts
Gavinton
Crumstane Farm Park
Blackadder
B6437
B6460
Paxton
Sunwick
B6461
Paxton
Tweedmouth
Polwarth
Whitsome
Hilton
Fishwick
Loanend
East Ord
Spittal
Huds Head
110
7
Nisbet Hill
Sinclair's Hill
13
Horndean
Hornliffe
Murton
Thornton
111
Scremerston
Fogo
A6112
A1167
Forgorig
B6437
B6461
Ladykirk
B6470
Norham
A698
A1
Cheswick
Charterhall
Swinton
Upsettlington
Shoreswood
West Allerdean
B6354
Ancroft
B6460
Simprim
Grindon
Felkington
Goswick
Greenlaw
B6460
B6461
11
A6112
B6525
Haggerston
7
8
Leitholm
10
37
9
Shellacres
0

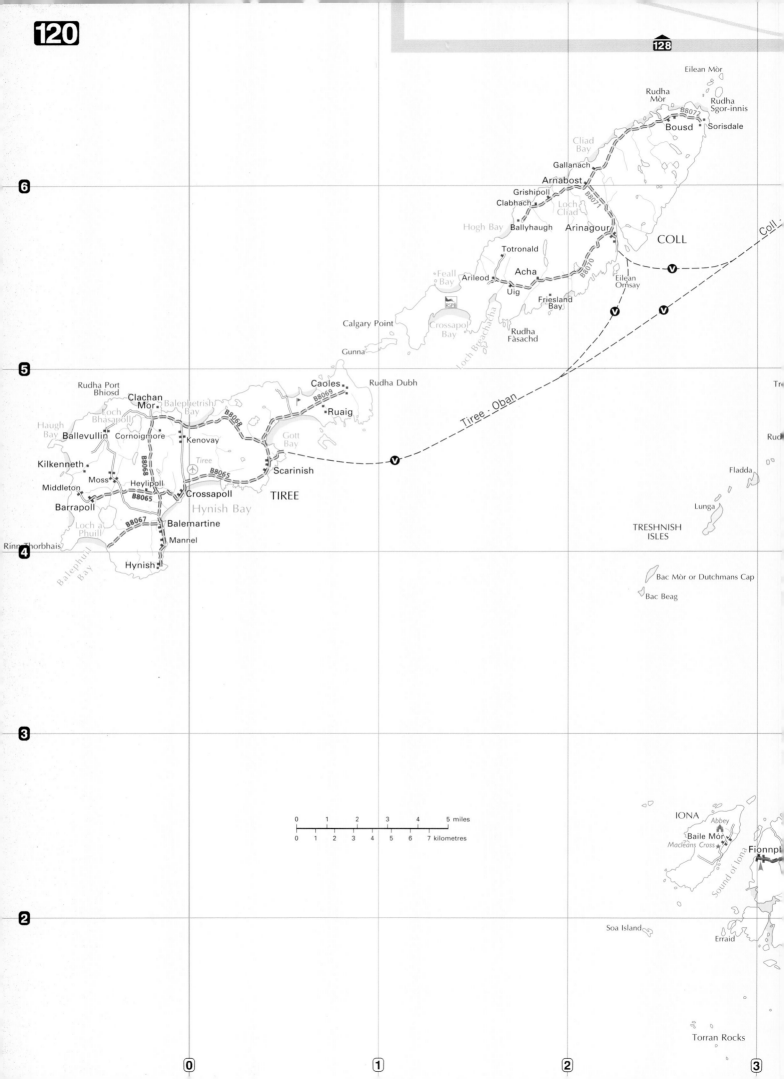

Eilean Mòr

Rudha Mòr

Rudha Sgor-innis

B8072

Bousd • Sorisdale

**6**

Cliad Bay

Gallanach

**Arnabost**

Grishipoll

Clabhach

B8071

Loch Cliad

Hogh Bay   Ballyhaugh   **Arinagour**

**COLL**

Coll -

Totronald

Acha

B8070

V

Arileod

Feall Bay

Uig

Eilean Ornsay

V

RSPB

Friesland Bay

Rudha Fàsachd

V

Calgary Point

Crossapol Bay

Loch Breachacha

Gunna

**5**

Rudha Dubh

Rudha Port Bhiosd

**Caoles**

Tre

Loch Bhasapoll

**Clachan Mòr**

Balephetrish Bay

B8069

**Ruaig**

B8068

Tiree - Oban

Haugh Bay

**Ballevullin**   Cornoigmore

B8068

Kenovay

Gott Bay

Fladda

Kilkenneth

Tiree

B8065

Rud

Moss

Heylipoll

**Scarinish**

Lunga

Middleton

B8068

**Crossapoll**

V

**Barrapoll**

B8065

**TIREE**

**TRESHNISH ISLES**

Loch a' Phuill

B8067

**Balemartine**

Hynish Bay

Rinn Thorbhais

Mannel

Bac Mòr or Dutchmans Cap

**4**

Balephuil Bay

**Hynish**

Bac Beag

**3**

**IONA**

Abbey

**Baile Mòr**

Macleans Cross ★

**Fionnph**

Sound of Iona

**2**

Soa Island

Erraid

Torran Rocks

0   1   2   3   4   5 miles

0   1   2   3   4   5   6   7 kilometres

**0**   **1**   **2**   **3**

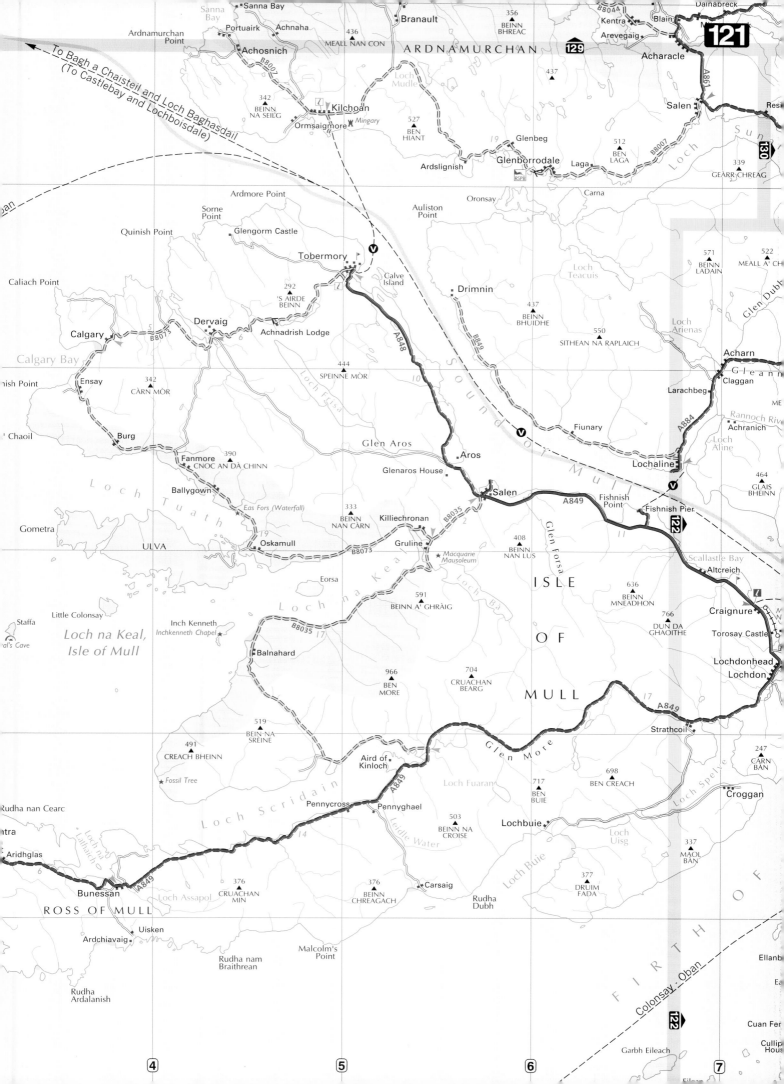

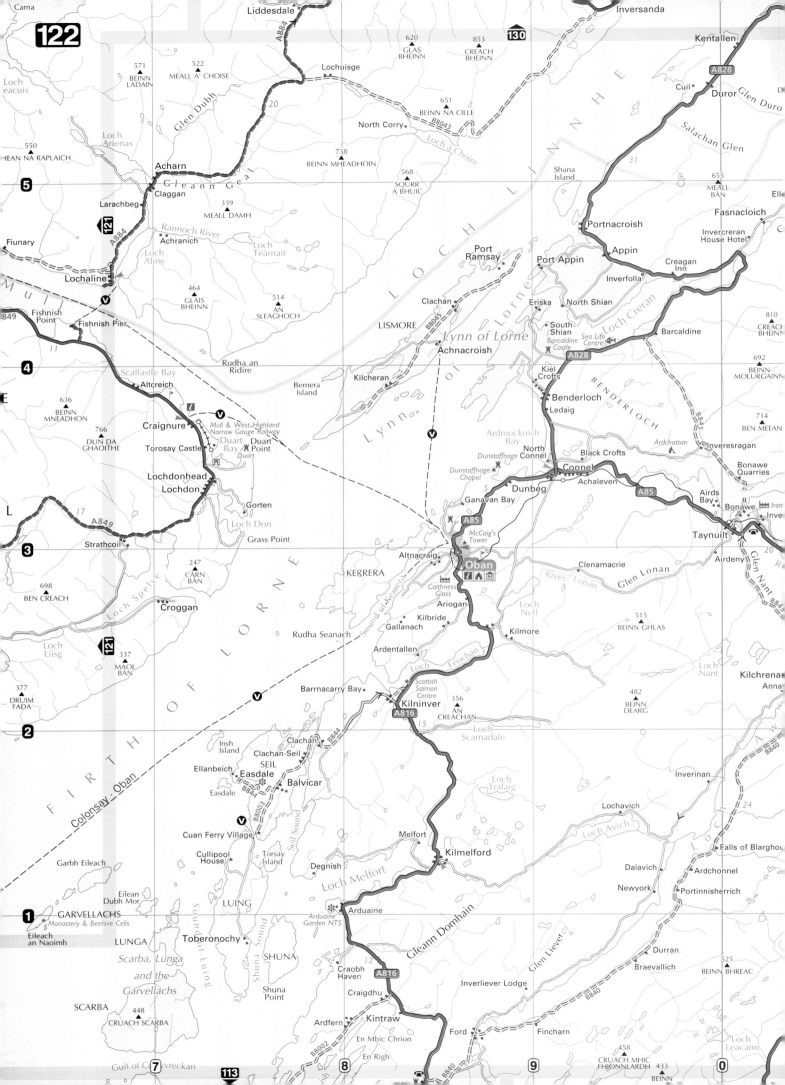

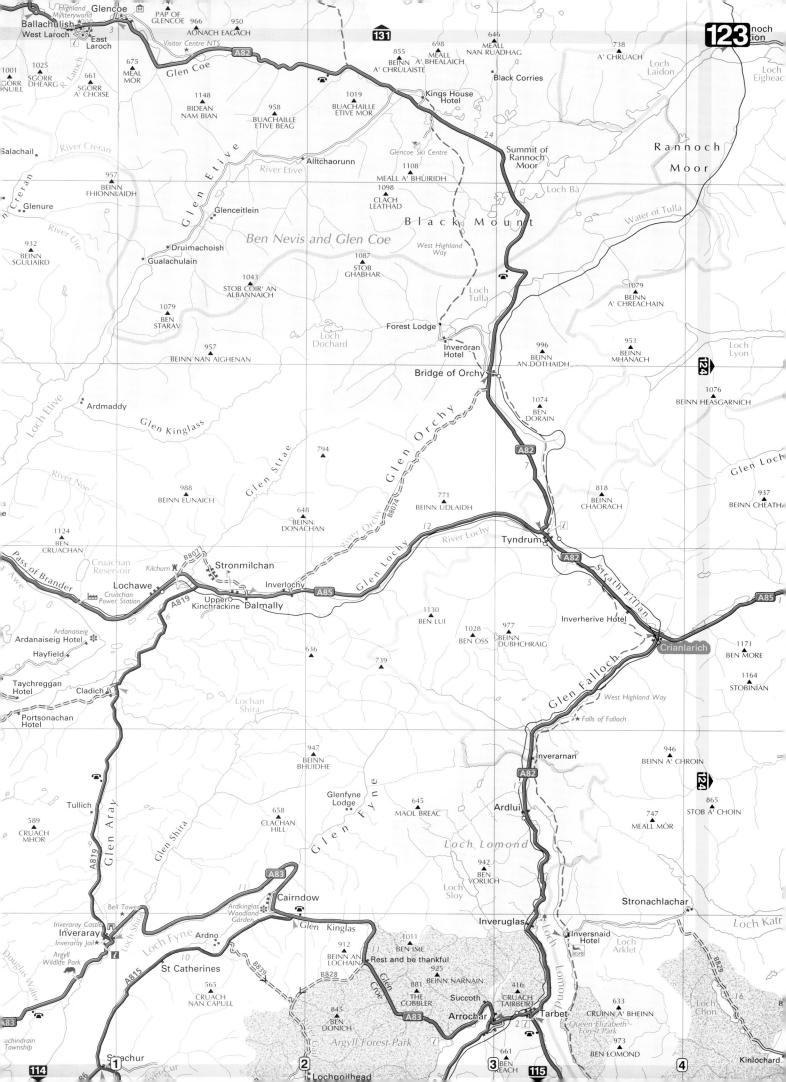

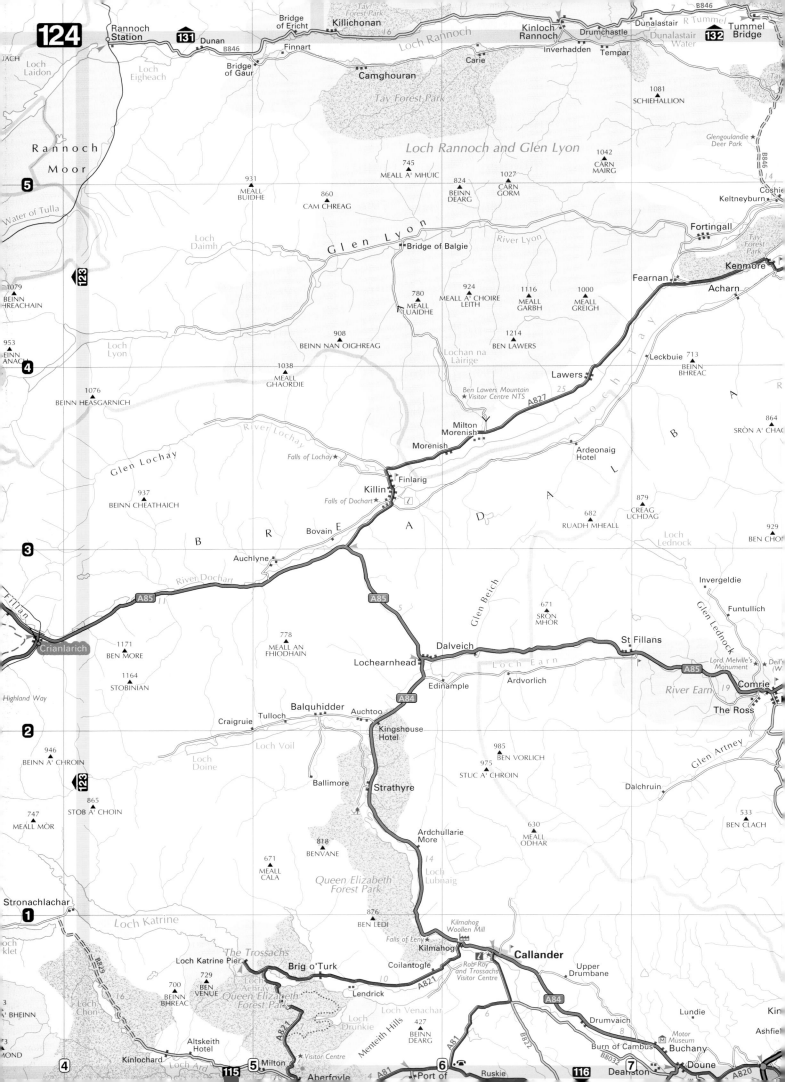

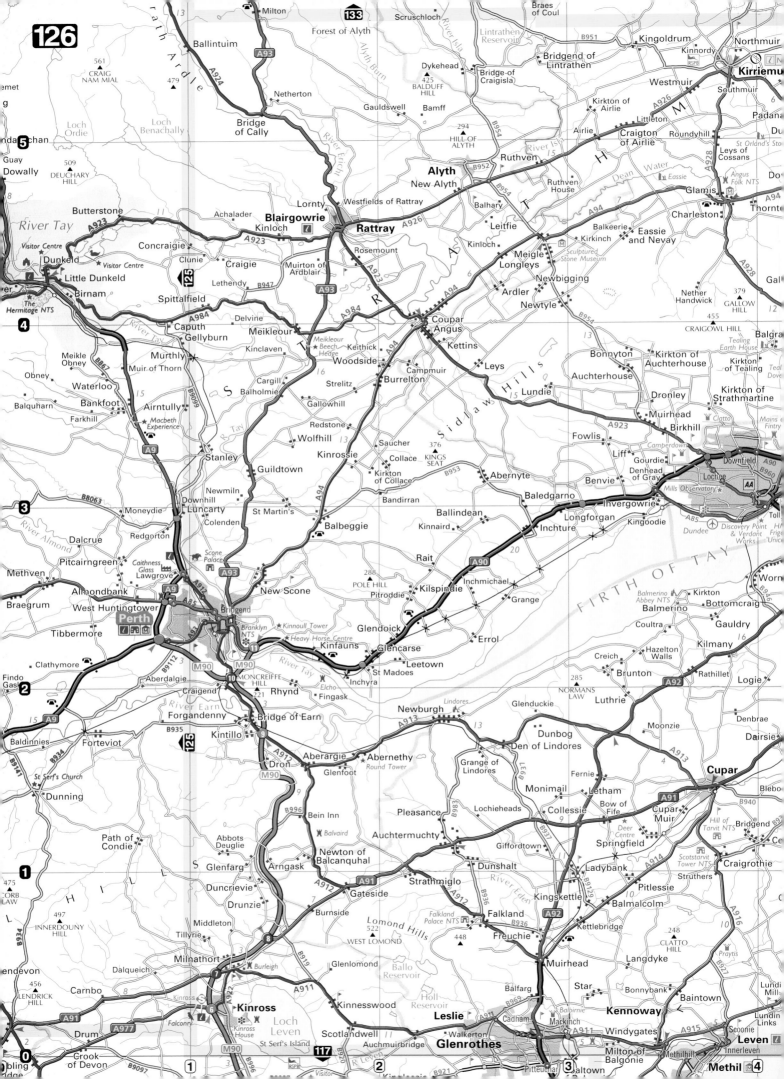

136

Loch Eynort

**The Cuillin Hills**

974
SGÙRR
A' GHEADAIDH

**Cuillin Hills**

434 ▲
AN CRUACHIN
Glenbrittle House

927
▲ BLAVEN
Loch na
Crèitheach

Bualintur

1009
▲ SGÙRR
ALASDAIR

Loch
Coruisk

894
▲ GARS
BHEINN

Camasuna

Kirkibo

225
▲
CEANN NA BEINNE

Rudh' an Dùnain

Soay Sound

139
▲
BEINN
BHREAC

Loch
Scavaig

344
▲
BEN
MEABOS

Mol-chlach

Elgol

G

SOAY

Rudh'
Aonghais

**2**

**← To Loch Baghasdail (Lochboisdale)**

Stratha
Poir

Ⓥ

C U I L L I N   S O U N D

**1**

CANNA

210
▲
CÀRN A' GHAILL

Rudha
Shamhnan Insir

Garrisdale Point

A'Chill

Canna
Harbour

Sanday

302
▲
MULLACH
MÒR

Sound of Canna

Rudha na Roinne

Oigh-sgeir

A Bhrideanach

Kinloch

Loch
Scresort

570
▲
ORVAL

**0**

**RUM**

810
▲
ASKIVAL

763
▲
SGÙRR NAN
GILLEAN

**The Small Isles**

Sound of Rum

Rudha nam
Meirleach

**9**

Bay of
Laig

Cleadale

299
▲ AN
CRUACHAN

Rudha an Fhasaidh

Laig

Sound of Eigg

**EIGG**

Kildonnan

393
▲
AN SGÙRR

Sandavore

Galmisdale

Eilean
Chathastail

MUCK

Eilean
nan Each

**8**

Pòrt Mòr

0   1   2   3   4   5 miles

0   1   2   3   4   5   6   7 kilometres

Sanna Point

Kilmory

Sanna
Bay

Sanna Bay

Brana

**7**

Achnaha

436
▲
MEALL NAN CON

ARI

Ardnamurchan
Point

Portuairk

121

120

Achosnich

B8007

Loch
Mudlo

**← To Bagh a Chais**
(To Casti

**2**      Eilean Mòr      **3**      **4**      **5**

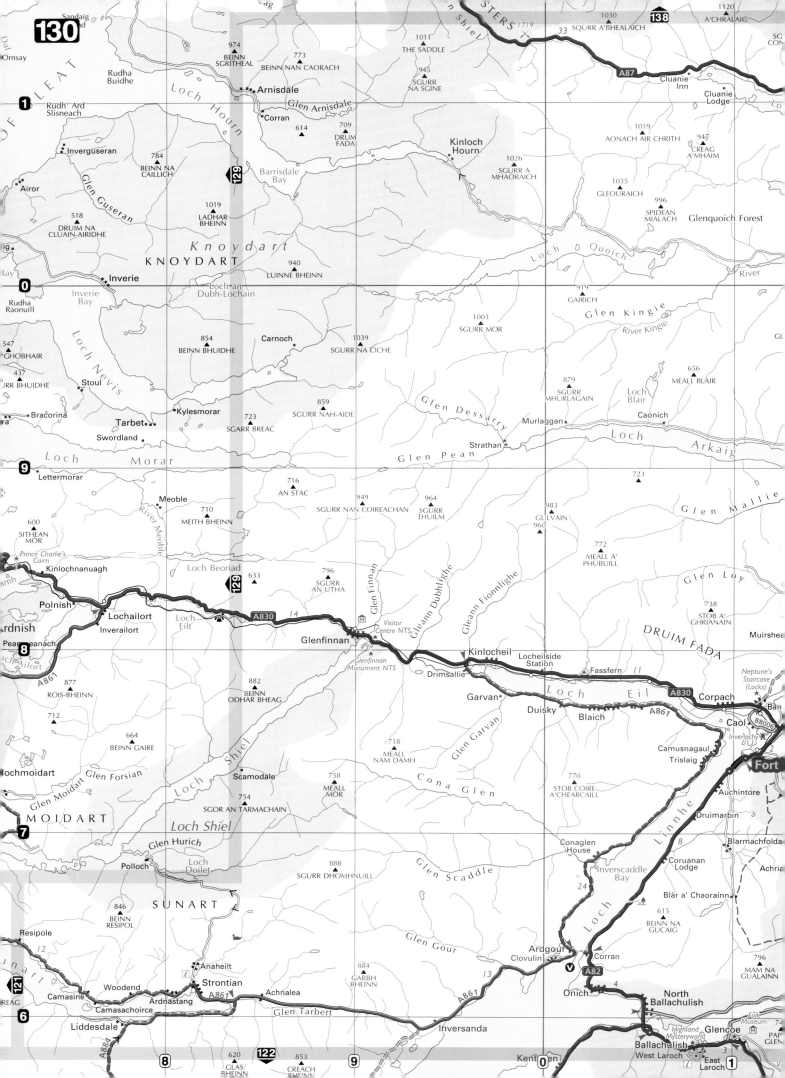

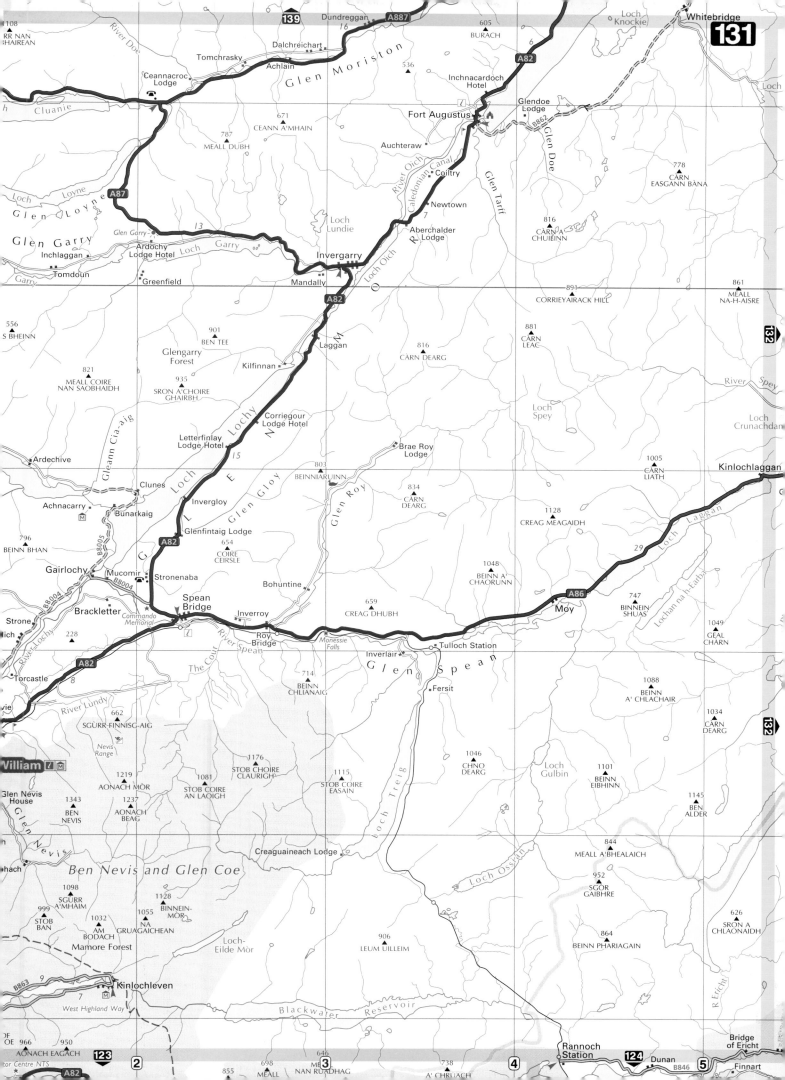

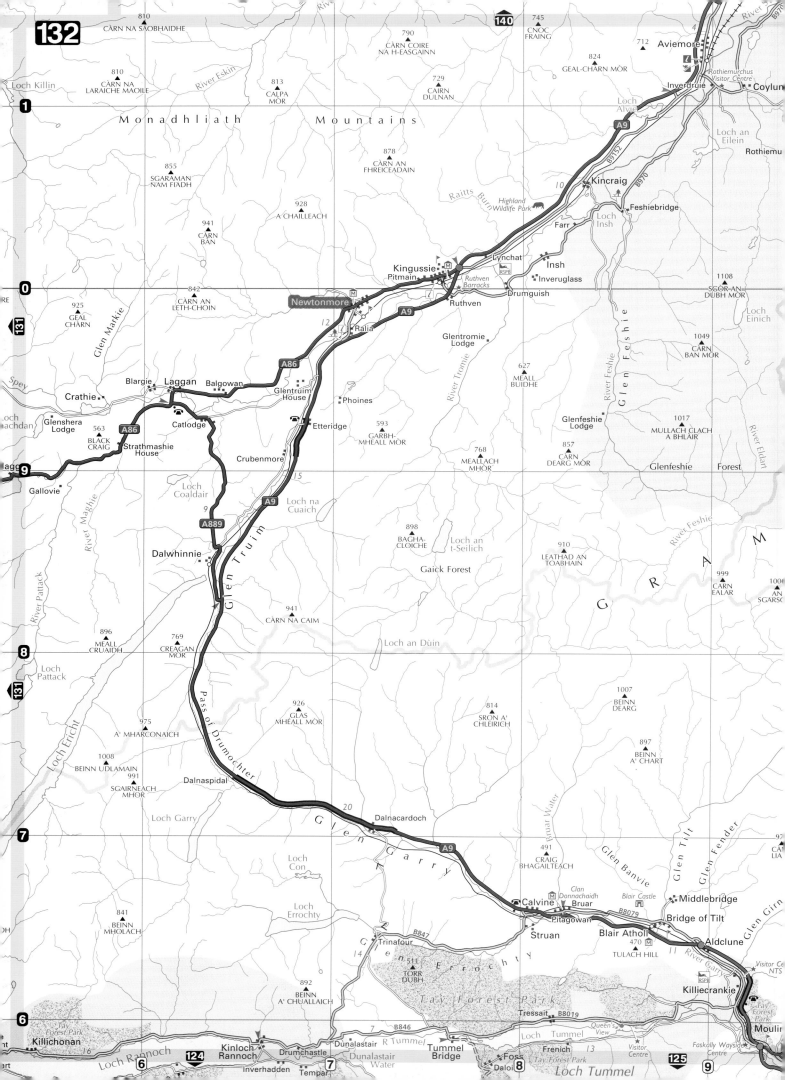

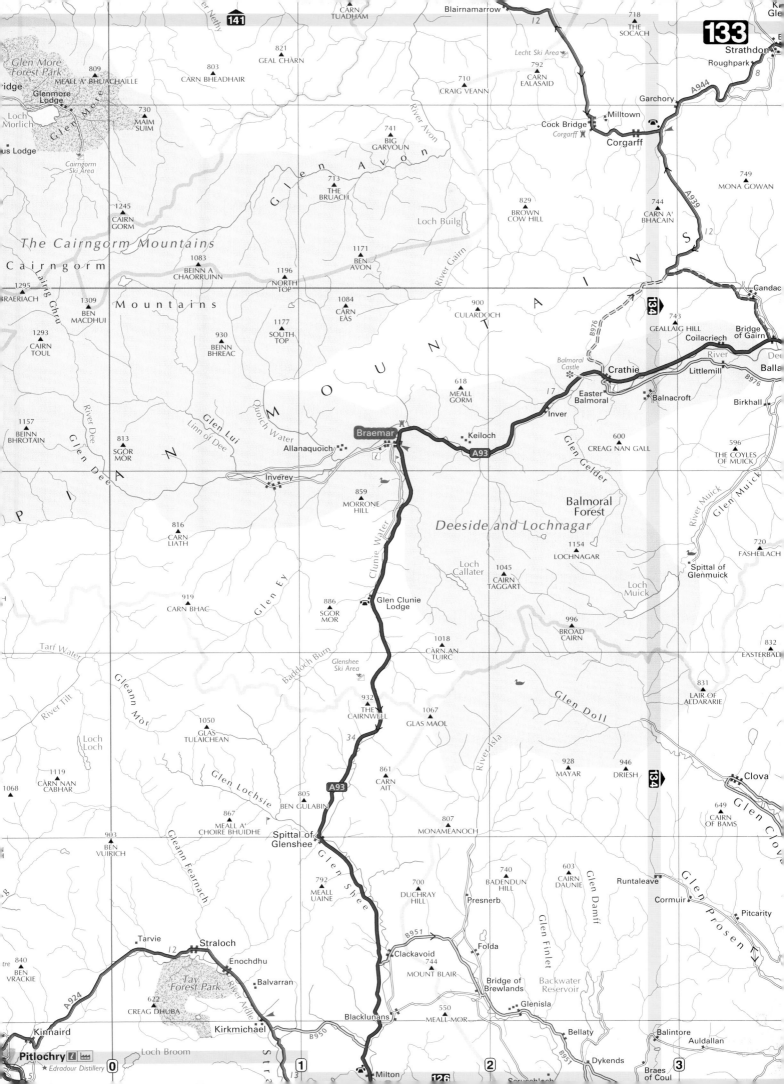

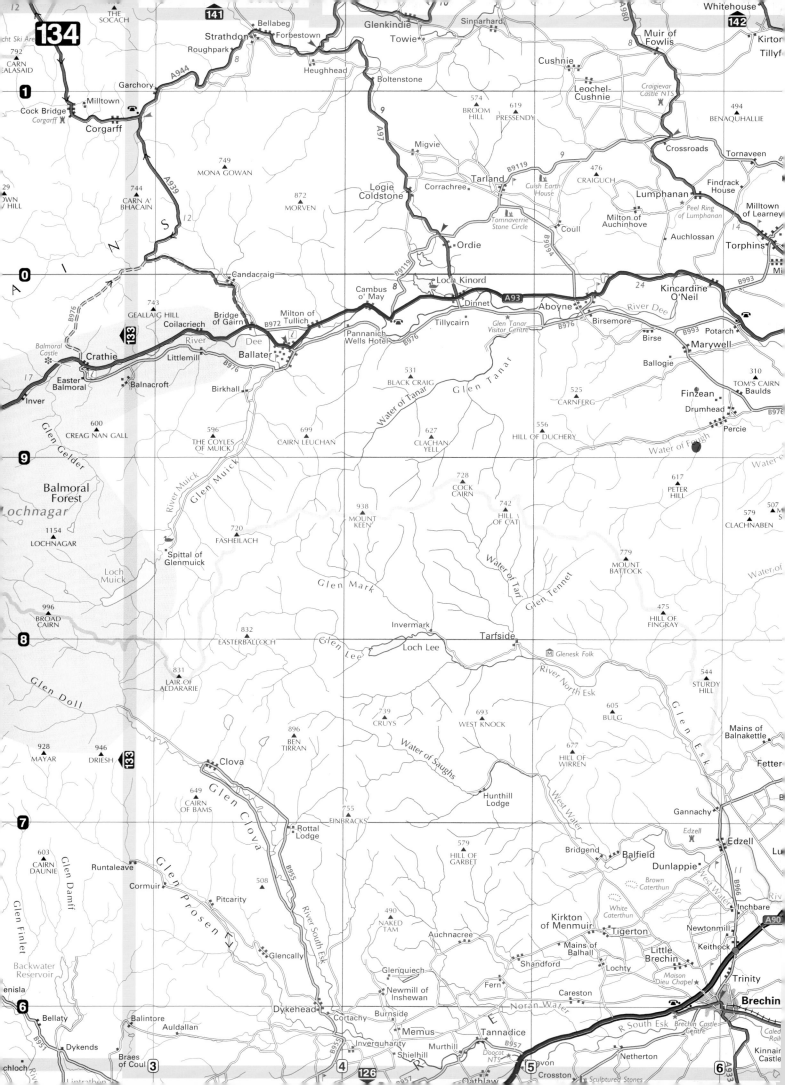

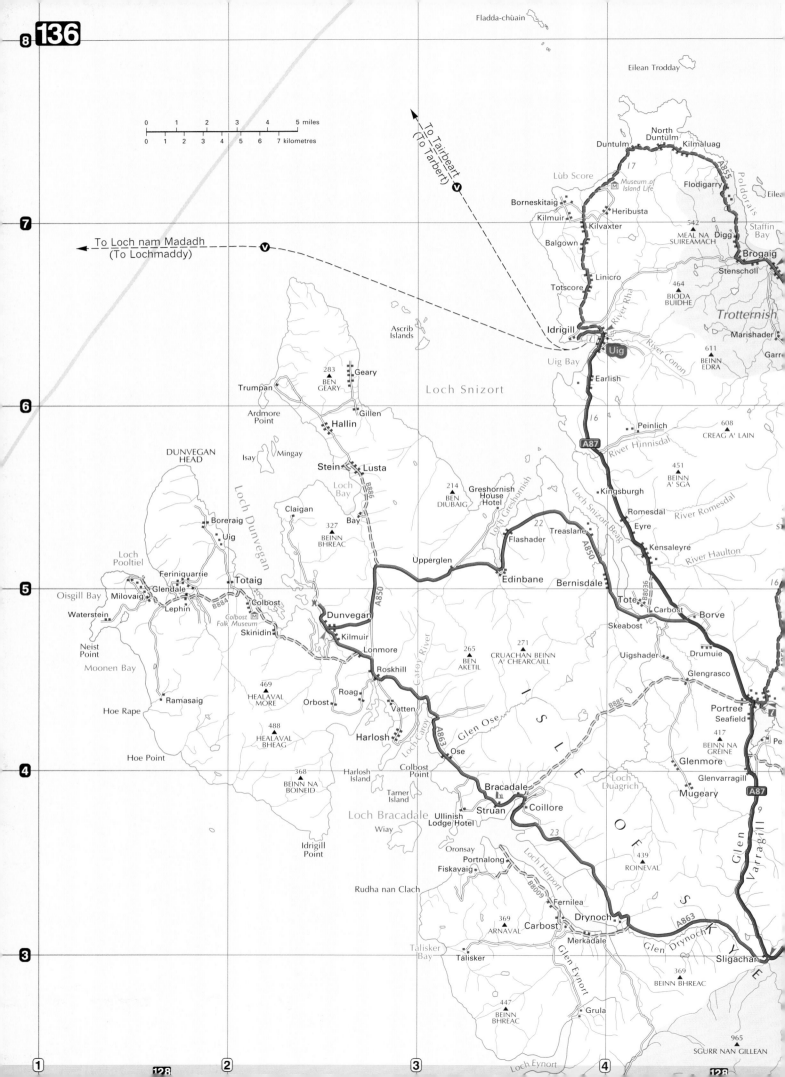

0 1 2 3 4 5 miles
0 1 2 3 4 5 6 7 kilometres

To Tairbeart
(To Tarbert)
V

To Loch nam Madadh
(To Lochmaddy)
V

Fladda-chùain

Eilean Trodday

North
Duntulm
Duntulm
Kilmaluag
Flodigarry
Eilea

Lùb Score
Museum of
Island Life
Borneskitaig
Heribusta
Kilmuir
Kilvaxter
542
MEAL NA
SUIREAMACH
Digg
Staffin
Bay
Balgown
Brogaig
Stenscholl

Linicro
464
BIODA
BUIDHE
Totscore
Trotternish

Idrigill
611
BEINN
EDRA
Marishader
Garr

Uig Bay
Uig
River Conon
River Rha

Earlish

Loch Snizort

16
Peinlich
608
CREAG A' LAIN

A87
River Hinnisdal

283
BEN
GEARY
Geary
451
BEINN
A' SGA

Trumpan
Gillen
Kingsburgh

Ardmore
Point
Hallin
Romesdal
River Romesdal
Eyre

DUNVEGAN
HEAD
Isay
Mingay
Stein
Lusta
214
BEN
DIUBAIG
Greshornish
House
Hotel
22
Treaslane
Kensaleyre
River Haulton

Loch
Bay
Flashader
Loch Snizort Beag

Claigan
Bay
Upperglen
A850
Edinbane
Bernisdale
16

Boreraig
327
BEINN
BHREAC
Loch Greshornish
Tote
B8036
Carbost
Borve

Loch
Pooltiel
Uig
Feriniquarrie
Glendale
Totaig
Skeabost
Drumuie

Oisgill Bay
Milovaig
Colbost
Dunvegan
Kilmuir
265
BEN
AKETIL
271
CRUACHAN BEINN
A' CHEARCAILL
Uigshader
Glengrasco

Waterstein
Lephin
Colbost
Folk Museum
Skinidin
Lonmore
Catoy River
B885
Portree
Seafield

Neist
Point
Roskhill
417
BEINN NA
GREINE
Pe

Moonen Bay
469
HEALAVAL
MORE
Roag
Orbost
Vatten
I S L E
Glengrasco
Glenmore

Ramasaig
Harlosh
488
HEALAVAL
BHEAG
Loch Catoy
A863
Ose
Glen Ose
Loch
Duagrich
Glenvarragill
Mugeary
A87

Hoe Rape
Hoe Point
368
BEINN NA
BOINEID
Harlosh
Island
Colbost
Point
Bracadale
439
ROINEVAL
9

Tarner
Island
Struan
Coillore
O F
Glen Varragill

Idrigill
Point
Loch Bracadale
Ullinish
Lodge Hotel
Wiay
23

Oronsay
Portnalong
Loch Harport

Fiskavaig
B8009
S
Rudha nan Clach
Fernilea
Drynoch
A863

369
ARNAVAL
Carbost
Merkadale
Glen Drynoch
Sligachan

Talisker
Bay
Talisker
447
BEINN
BHREAC
Glen Eynort
Grula
Y
E

965
SGURR NAN GILLEAN
Loch Eynort

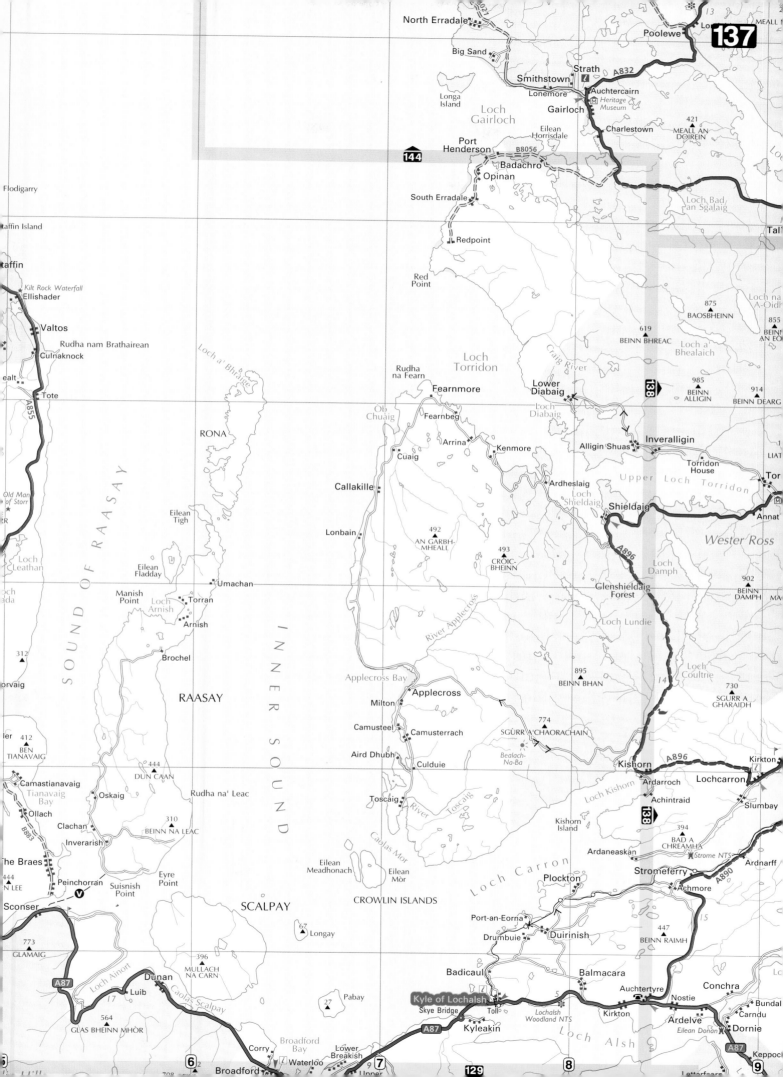

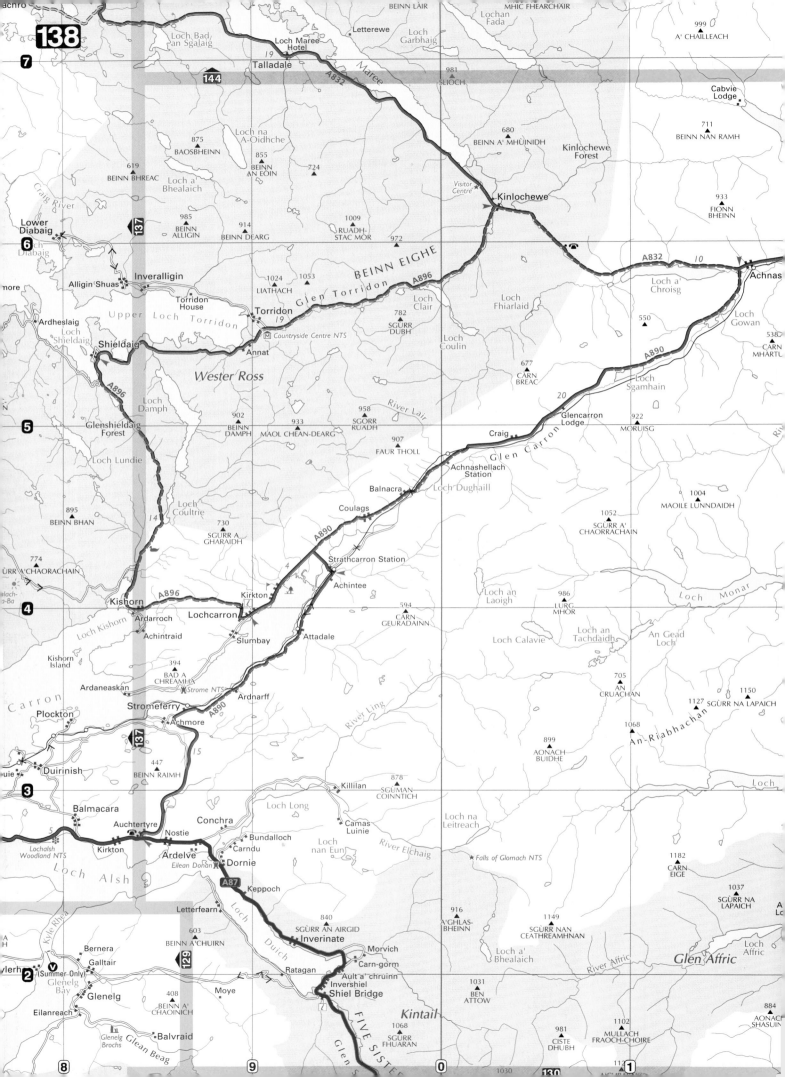

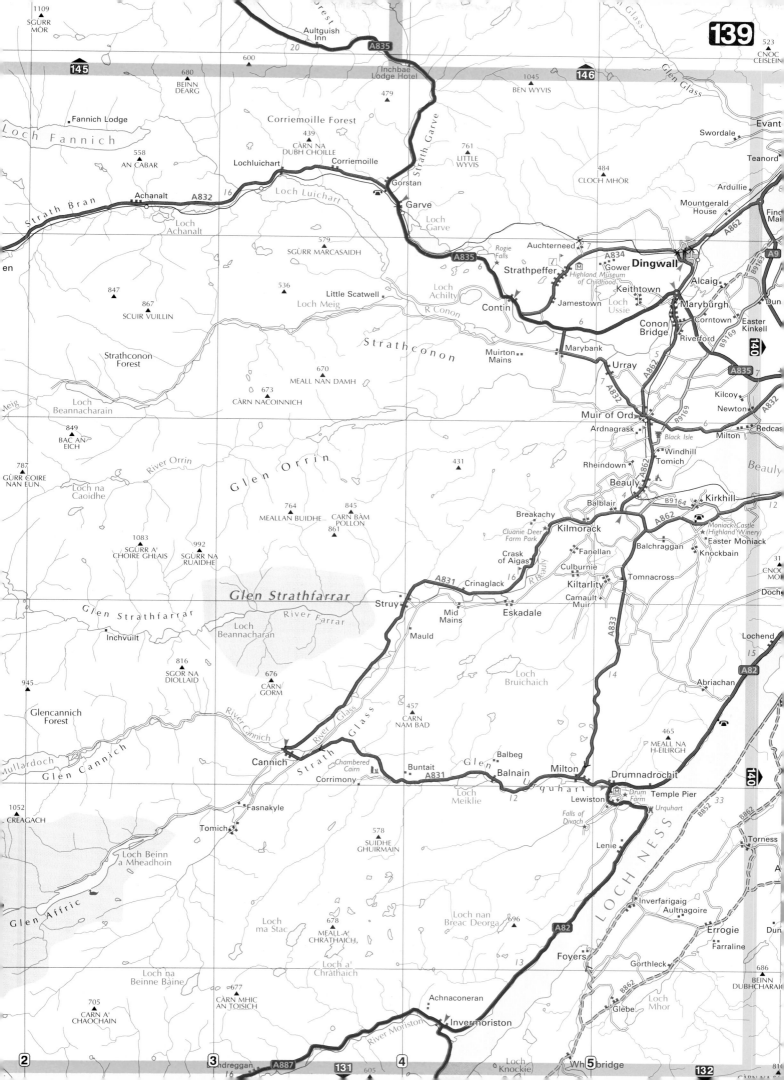

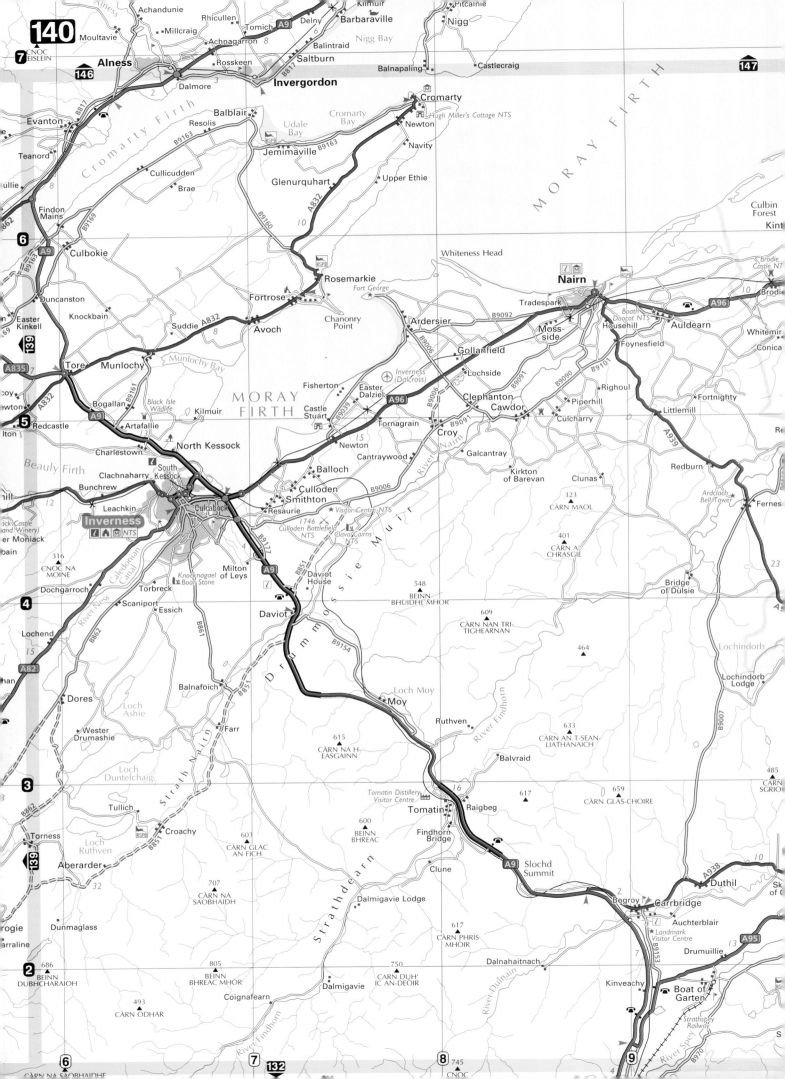

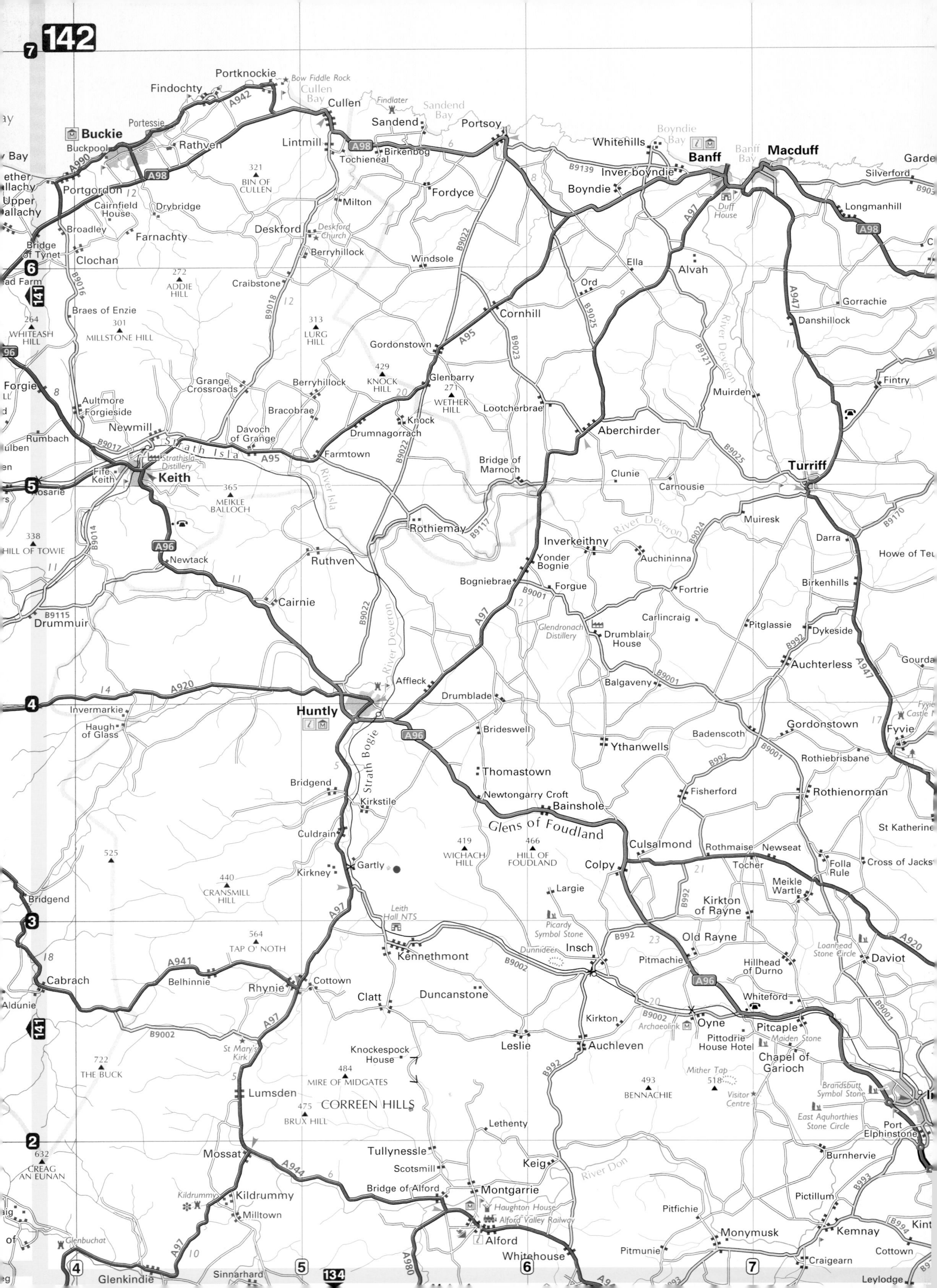

Portknockie
Findochty
Portessie
Buckie
Buckpool
Rathven
Lintmill
Cullen
Sandend
Portsoy
Whitehills
Boyndie Bay
Banff
Macduff
Garde
Silverford
Bow Fiddle Rock
Cullen Bay
Findlater
Sandend Bay
A942
A98
Birkenbog
Tochieneal
Fordyce
B9139
Inver-boyndie
Banff Bay
Duff House
A97
Longmanhill
A98
Portgordon
Cairnfield House
Drybridge
Milton
Boyndie
B9121
Gorrachie
Danshillock
A947
Broadley
Farnachty
Deskford
Deskford Church
Windsole
Ella
Alvah
Bridge of Tynet
Clochan
Berryhillock
Ord
River Deveron
Muirden
Fintry
A990
B9016
Addie Hill 272
Craibstone
321 BIN OF CULLEN
12
B9018
Cornhill
B9025
B9121
Whiteash Hill 264
Braes of Enzie
Millstone Hill 301
Grange Crossroads
Berryhillock
Knock Hill
Glenbarry
Wether Hill 271
Lootcherbrae
Aberchirder
Clunie
Carnousie
Turriff
Forgie
Aultmore
Forgieside
Newmill
Davoch of Grange
Knock
Drumnagorrach
B9022
A96
Rumbach
Strath Isla
Strathisla Distillery
A95
Farmtown
B9117
Muiresk
Darra
Howe of Teu
Fife Keith
Keith
River Isla
Bridge of Marnoch
B9024
Rosarie
Meikle Balloch 365
Rothiemay
Inverkeithny
Auchininna
Birkenhills
Hill of Towie 338
B9014
Newtack
Ruthven
Yonder Bognie
Forgue
Fortrie
Pitglassie
Dykeside
B9115
Drummuir
Cairnie
11
B9022
Bogniebrae
B9001
Carlincraig
Auchterless
Gourda
A97
Glendronach Distillery
Drumblair House
A947
Affleck
Balgaveny
B9001
Drumblair House
A920
Invermarkie
Haugh of Glass
Huntly
Drumblade
Badenscoth
Gordonstown
Fyvie Castle
Fyvie
Brideswell
B9997
Rothiebrisbane
Strath Bogie
A96
Ythanwells
B9001
Rothienorman
Bridgend
Kirkstile
Thomastown
Newtongarry Croft
Fisherford
St Katherine
Culdrain
Bainshole
Glens of Foudland
Culsalmond
Rothmaise
Newseat
525
Kirkney
440 CRANSMILL HILL
Gartly
Wichach Hill 419
Hill of Foudland 466
Colpy
Tocher
Folla Rule
Cross of Jacks
Bridgend
A97
Leith Hall NTS
Largie
B9992
Kirkton of Rayne
Meikle Wartle
564
TAP O' NOTH
Picardy Symbol Stone
Dunnideer
Old Rayne
Loanhead Stone Circle
Daviot
A920
Cabrach
Belhinnie
Rhynie
Cottown
Clatt
Duncanstone
Kennethmont
B9002
Insch
Pitmachie
Hillhead of Durno
A96
Whiteford
B9001
Aldunie
A941
St Mary's Kirk
B9002
Knockespock House
Leslie
Kirkton
Archaeolink
Oyne
Pitcaple
Chapel of Garioch
THE BUCK 722
484 MIRE OF MIDGATES
Auchleven
Pittodrie House Hotel
Maiden Stone
Brandsbutt Symbol Stone
Lumsden
475 BRUX HILL
CORREEN HILLS
Lethenty
BENNACHIE 493
Mither Tap 518
Visitor Centre
East Aquhorthies Stone Circle
Port Elphinstone
CREAG AN EUNAN 632
Mossat
A944
Tullynessle
Scotsmill
Keig
River Don
Burnhervie
Kildrummy
Milltown
Bridge of Alford
Montgarrie
Pitfichie
Monymusk
Pictillum
Kemnay
Kint
Glenbuchat
A97
Sinnarhard
A980
Alford
Alford Valley Railway
Haughton House
Whitehouse
Pitmunie
Craigearn
Cottown
Glenkindie
134
A9

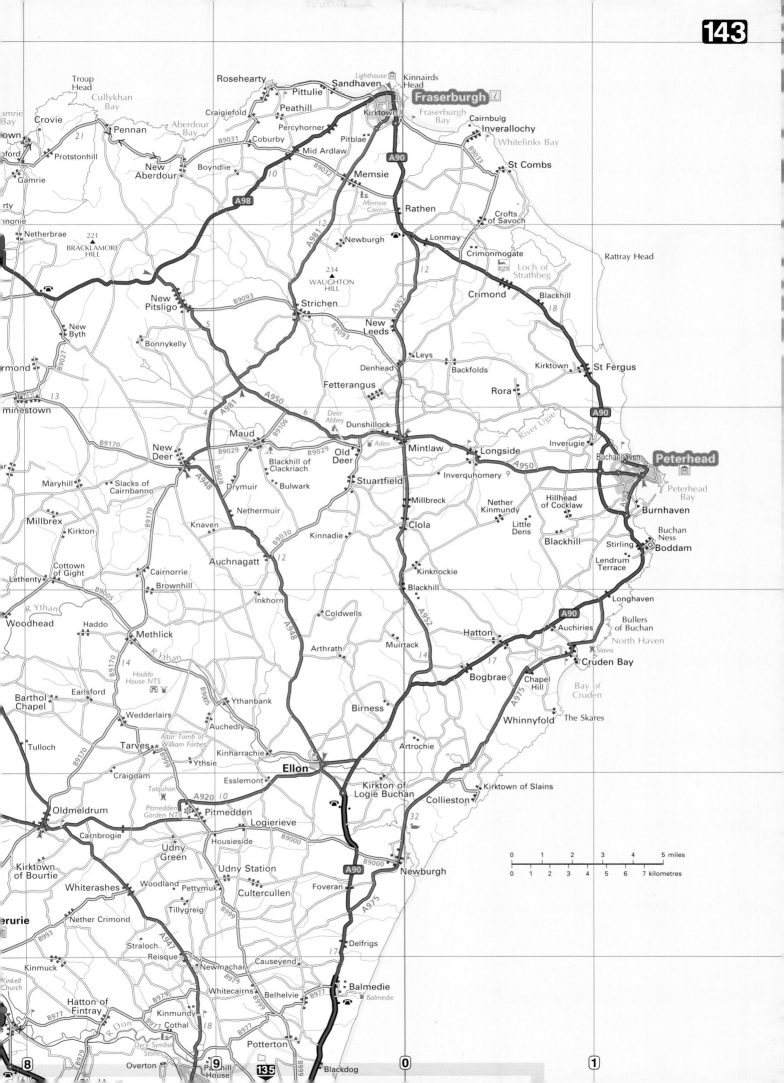

Troup Head
Cullykhan Bay
Aberdour Bay
Whitelinks Bay
Rattray Head
Fraserburgh Bay
Peterhead Bay
Bay of Cruden
North Haven

Rosehearty
Pittulie
Sandhaven
Kinnairds Head
Lighthouse
**Fraserburgh**
Craigiefold
Peathill
Percyhorner
Kirktown
Cairnbulg
Inverallochy
Crovie
Pennan
Coburby
Pitblae
St Combs
Protstonhill
Mid Ardlaw
Gamrie
New Aberdour
Boyndlie
Memsie
Rathen
Netherbrae
Newburgh
Lonmay
Crimonmogate
BRACKLAMORE HILL
221
WAUGHTON HILL
234
Memsie Cairn
Crimond
Blackhill
Loch of Strathbeg
New Pitsligo
Strichen
New Leeds
Bonnykelly
New Byth
Leys
Denhead
Backfolds
Kirktown
St Fergus
Fetterangus
Rora
Deer Abbey
Dunshillock
River Ugie
Maud
Aden
Mintlaw
Longside
Inverugie
New Deer
Old Deer
Bucharnhaven
**Peterhead**
Blackhill of Clackriach
Stuartfield
Inverquhomery
Maryhill
Drymuir
Bulwark
Millbreck
Nether Kinmundy
Hillhead of Cocklaw
Slacks of Cairnbanno
Kirkton
Nethermuir
Clola
Little Dens
Blackhill
Burnhaven
Millbrex
Knaven
Kinnadie
Buchan Ness
Boddam
Stirling
Cottown of Gight
Cairnorrie
Brownhill
Kinknockie
Lendrum Terrace
Lethenty
Inkhorn
Blackhill
Auchnagatt
Coldwells
Longhaven
Woodhead
Haddo
Bullers of Buchan
Haddo House NTS
Arthrath
Muirtack
Hatton
Auchiries
Slains
Cruden Bay
Methlick
Bogbrae
Chapel Hill
Whinnyfold
The Skares
Barthol Chapel
Earlsford
Wedderlairs
Ythanbank
Birness
Artrochie
Tulloch
Auchedly
Tarves
Kinharrachie
Ythsie
**Ellon**
Esslemont
Kirkton of Logie Buchan
Collieston
Kirktown of Slains
Craigdam
Tolquhon
Altar-Tomb of William Forbes
Oldmeldrum
Pitmedden Garden NTS
Pitmedden
Logierieve
Carnbrogie
Kirktown of Bourtie
Udny Green
Housieside
Udny Station
Whiterashes
Woodland
Pettymuk
Cultercullen
Foveran
Newburgh
Nether Crimond
Tillygreig
Straloch
Reisque
Delfrigs
Kinmuck
Newmachar
Causeyend
Kinkell Church
Hatton of Fintray
Whitecairns
Belhelvie
Balmedie
Balmedie
Kinmundy
Cothal
Potterton
Overton
Dyce Symbol Stones
Parkhill House
Blackdog

Roads: A90, A98, A981, A952, A950, A948, A920, A947, A975, A9000, B9031, B9032, B9033, B9027, B9093, B9106, B9029, B9028, B9030, B9170, B9005, B999, B979, B977, B993

Scale:
0 1 2 3 4 5 miles
0 1 2 3 4 5 6 7 kilometres

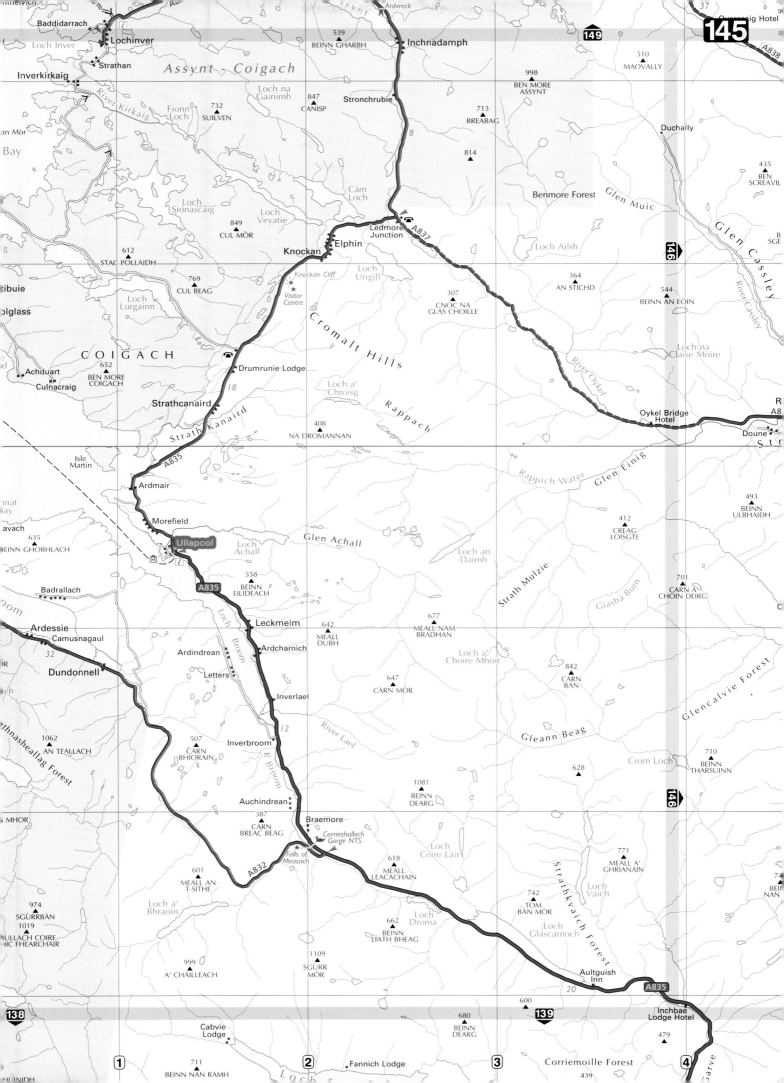

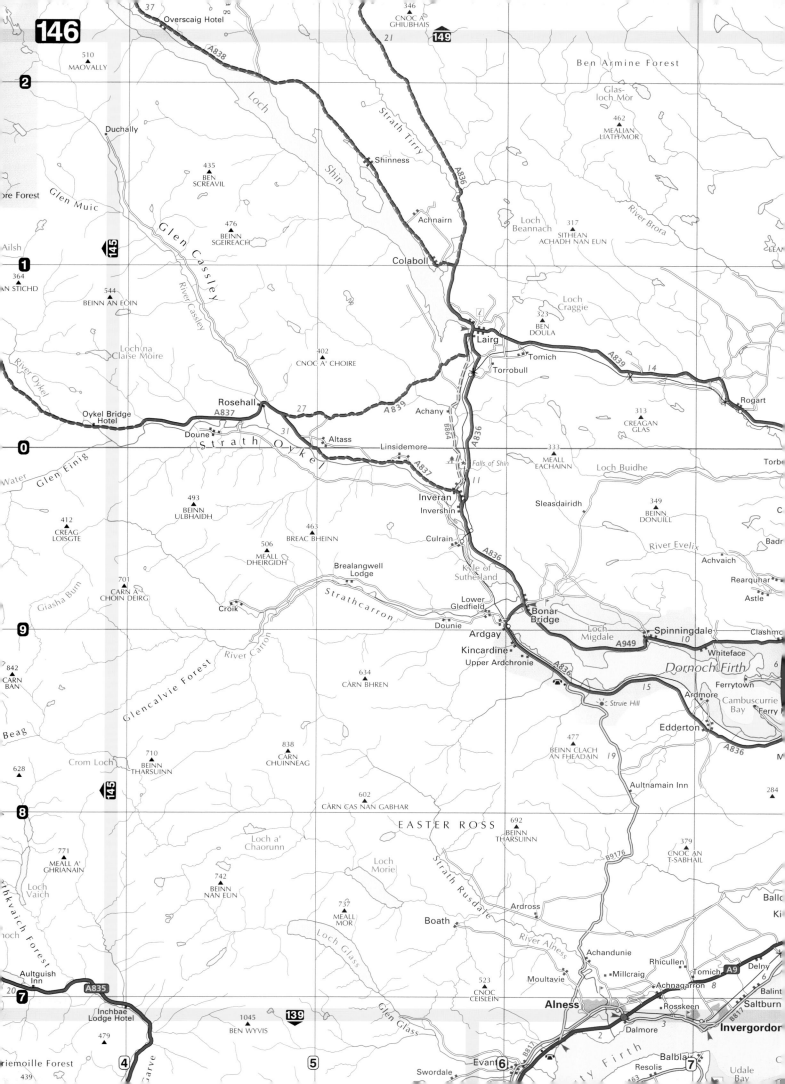

346
CNOC A'
GHIUBHAIS

Ben Armine Forest

21

37
Overscaig Hotel

**2**

510
MAOVALLY

Duchally

Glas-
loch Mòr

462
MEALLAN
LIATH MOR

Loch

435
BEN
SCREAVIL

Strath Tirry

Shin

Shinness

317
SITHEAN
ACHADH NAN EUN

Loch
Beannach

Achnairn

River Brora

**1**

Glen Muic

476
BEINN
SGEIREACH

Glen Cassley

River Cassley

Colaboll

LEA

Ailsh

ore Forest

N STICHD 364

Loch
Craggie

323
BEN
DOULA

544
BEINN AN EÒIN

Loch na
Claise Mòire

402
CNOC A' CHOIRE

Lairg

Tomich

A839

14

Torrobull

Rogart

**0**

River Oykel

Oykel Bridge
Hotel

Rosehall

A837

27

Achany

B864

A836

CREAGAN
GLAS 313

Doune

Strath Oykel

31

Altass

Linsidemore

A837

Falls of Shin

333
MEALL
EACHAINN

Loch Buidhe

Torbe

Water

Glen Einig

11

Inveran

Invershin

Sleasdairidh

349
BEINN
DONUILL

River Evelix

Achvaich

493
BEINN
ULBHAIDH

Culrain

A836

Rearquhar

412
CREAG
LOISGTE

463
BREAC BHEINN

Astle

506
MEALL
DHEIRGIDH

Brealangwell
Lodge

Kyle of
Sutherland

701
CARN A'
CHOIN DEIRG

Giasha Burn

Croik

Strathcarron

Lower
Gledfield

**9**

842
CARN
BAN

River Carron

Dounie

Bonar
Bridge

Loch
Migdale

A949

Spinningdale

10

Clashmo

Ardgay

Whiteface

Beag

628

Crom Loch

710
BEINN
THARSUINN

634
CÀRN BHREN

Kincardine

Upper Ardchronie

A836

*Dornoch Firth*

6

Glencalvie Forest

Ferrytown

Ardmore

15

Cambuscurrie
Bay

Ferry

838
CARN
CHUINNEAG

477
BEINN CLACH
AN FHEADAIN

19

Struie Hill

Edderton

A836

M

**8**

771
MEALL A'
GHRIANAIN

602
CÀRN CAS NAN GABHAR

EASTER ROSS

692
BEINN
THARSUINN

Aultnamain Inn

284

thkvaich
Forest

Loch
Vaich

742
BEINN
NAN EUN

Loch a'
Chaorunn

Loch
Morie

379
CNOC AN
T-SABHAIL

**145**

737
MEALL
MOR

B9176

Strath Rusdale

Ballo

Ki

och

7 Forest

Aultguish
Inn

A835

20

Boath

Ardross

River Alness

Achandunie

Rhicullen

Tomich

A9

Delny

6

Millcraig

Moultavie

Achnagarron

8

Balint

Inchbae
Lodge Hotel

**139**

523
CNOC
CEISLEIN

**Alness**

Rosskeen

Saltburn

B817

**4**

1045
BEN WYVIS

479

Glen Glass

Dalmore

**Invergordon**

riemoille Forest

439

Carve

**5**

**6**

Evan

Swordale

Balblair

7

Firth

Resolis

Udale
Bay

63

**149**

**7**

B817

CNOC NA
BREUN-CHOILLE
CREAG NAM FIADH

Cairns, Stone Row
& Stone Circles

CREAG
SCALABSDALE

Langwell
House

**147**

**150**

**151**

A9

Strath of Kildonan

Kildonan Lodge

17

Kildonan 416

BEINN
DUBHAIN

A897

401
CNOC NA
MAOILE

Strath Skinsdale

337
CNOC NA H-
INNSE MOIRE

River Helmsdale

Torrish

404
CREAG
THORARAIDH

Ord of Caithness

Navidale House Hotel

421
CNOC NAN CRÙBAG MÒR

Black Water

Glen Loth

624
BEINN
DHORAIN

591
BEINN NA
MÉILICH

Timespan

West
Helmsdale

East Helmsdale

Helmsdale

Gartymore

Portgower

3
OC
NACHD

Balnacoil
Lodge

Strath Brora

River Brora

Dalreavoch
Lodge

Loch
Brora

Lothmore

Lothbeg

A9

21

Loch
Horn

520
BEN-
HORN

Golspie Burn

378
CAGAR
FEOSAIG

Dalchalm

Brora

Doll

446
BEN LUNDIE

Backies

Rhives

Carn Liath

Dunrobin Castle

Golspie

busavie
Platform

Loch
Fleet

Skelbo

Skelbo Street

sh

7

Fourpenny

Embo

Birichin

B9168

Embo Street

Pitgrudy

Evelix

A949

3

A9

Camore

Dornoch

Cuthill

Dornoch Firth

Tarbat Ness

Innis Mhor

Brucefield

Wilkhaven

nt

Portmahomack

Inver

Rockfield

B9165

Arboll

Toulvaddie

Tain

rangie

Loch
Eye

Rhynie

B9165

Fearn

Balmuchy

Newfield

6

Hill of
Fearn

Tullich

Hilton of Cadboll Chapel

B9166

Arabella

Hilton

raggan

B9175

Shandwick

Balintore

ary

Ankerville

Shandwick Bay

Milton

Shandwick Bay

Kilmuir

Pitcalnie

Barbaraville

Nigg

Nigg Bay

Burghead
Well

Hopeman

aid

**140**

Castlecraig

**141**

Burghead

B9012

Cummingston

Balnapaling

B9013

Roseisle

Cromarty
Bay

Cromarty

gh Miller's Cottage NTS

**8**

Newton

**9**

**0**

Burghead Bay

College of
Roseisle

**1**

F I R T H

0   1   2   3   4   5 miles

0   1   2   3   4   5   6   7 kilometres

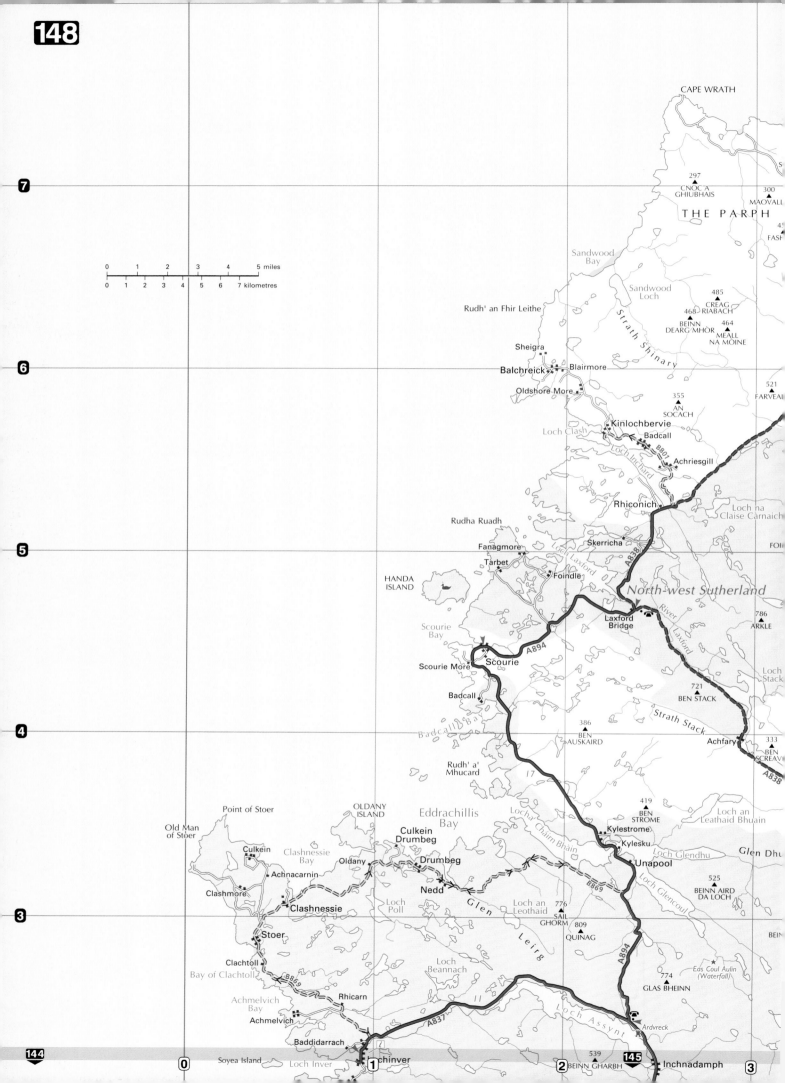

CAPE WRATH

297
CNOC A'
GHIUBHAIS

300
MAOVALL

THE PARPH

4
FASH

Sandwood
Bay

Sandwood
Loch

485
CREAG
RIABACH

Rudh' an Fhir Leithe

468
BEINN
DEARG MHÒR

464
MEALL
NA MÒINE

Sheigra

Balchreick    Blairmore

521
FARVEAL

Oldshore More

355
AN
SOCACH

Kinlochbervie
Badcall

B801
Achriesgill

Loch Clash

Loch Inchard

Rhiconich

Loch na
Claise Càrnaich

Rudha Ruadh

Skerricha

FOI

Fanagmore
Tarbet

Loch Laxford

A838

786
ARKLE

Foindle

North-west Sutherland

HANDA
ISLAND

River Laxford

Laxford
Bridge

Scourie
Bay

7

Loch
Stack

Scourie More    Scourie

A894

721
BEN STACK

Badcall

386
BEN
AUSKAIRD

Strath Stack

333
BEN
SCREAV

Rudh' a'
Mhucard

Badcall Bay

17

Achfary

A838

Point of Stoer

OLDANY
ISLAND

Eddrachillis
Bay

419
BEN
STROME

Loch an
Leathaid Bhuain

Old Man
of Stoer

Culkein
Drumbeg

Loch a' Chàirn Bhàin

Kylestrome

Culkein

Clashnessie
Bay

Oldany

Drumbeg

Kylesku

Loch Glendhu

Glen Dhu

Achnacarnin

Nedd

Unapool

525
BEINN AIRD
DA LOCH

Clashmore

Glen

Loch Poll

Loch an
Leothaid

776
SAIL
GHORM

809
QUINAG

Loch Glencoul

Clashnessie

Leirg

BEIN

Stoer

A894

Loch
Beannach

774
GLAS BHEINN

Eas Coul Aulin
(Waterfall)

Clachtoll

Bay of Clachtoll

B869

Rhicarn

Achmelvich
Bay

A837

Loch Assynt

Ardvreck

Achmelvich

Baddidarrach

0

Soyea Island    Loch Inver    chinver

539
BEINN GHARBH

Inchnadamph    3

2

0  1  2  3  4  5 miles

0  1  2  3  4  5  6  7 kilometres

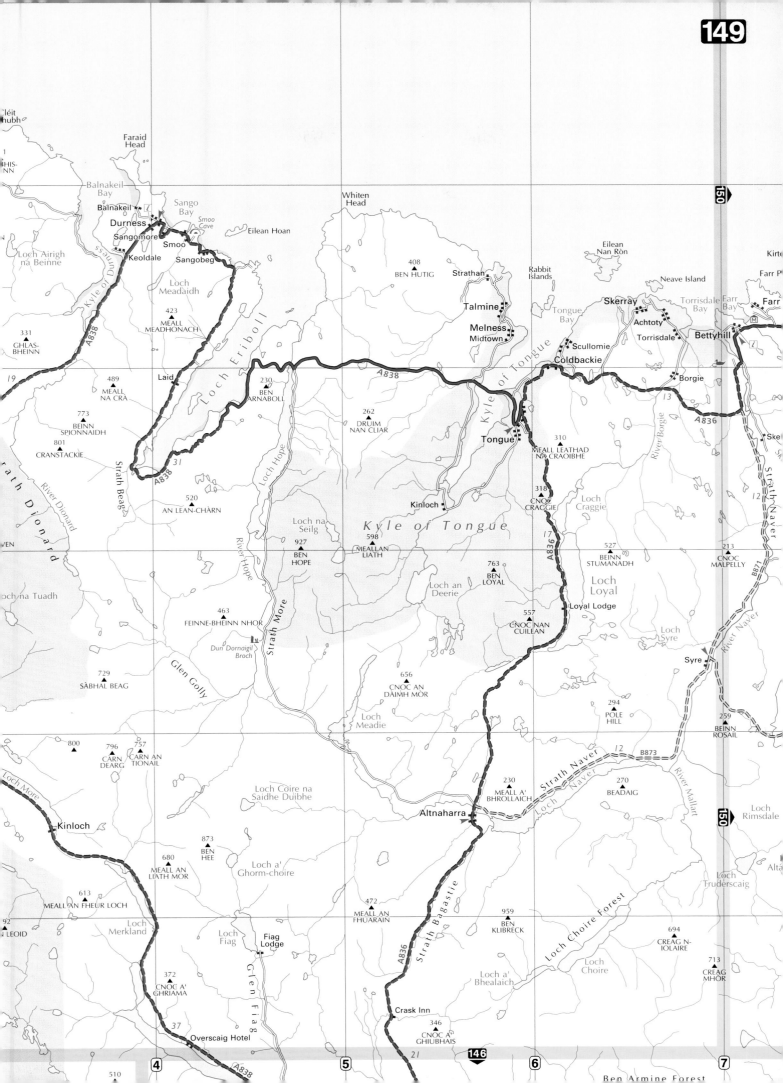

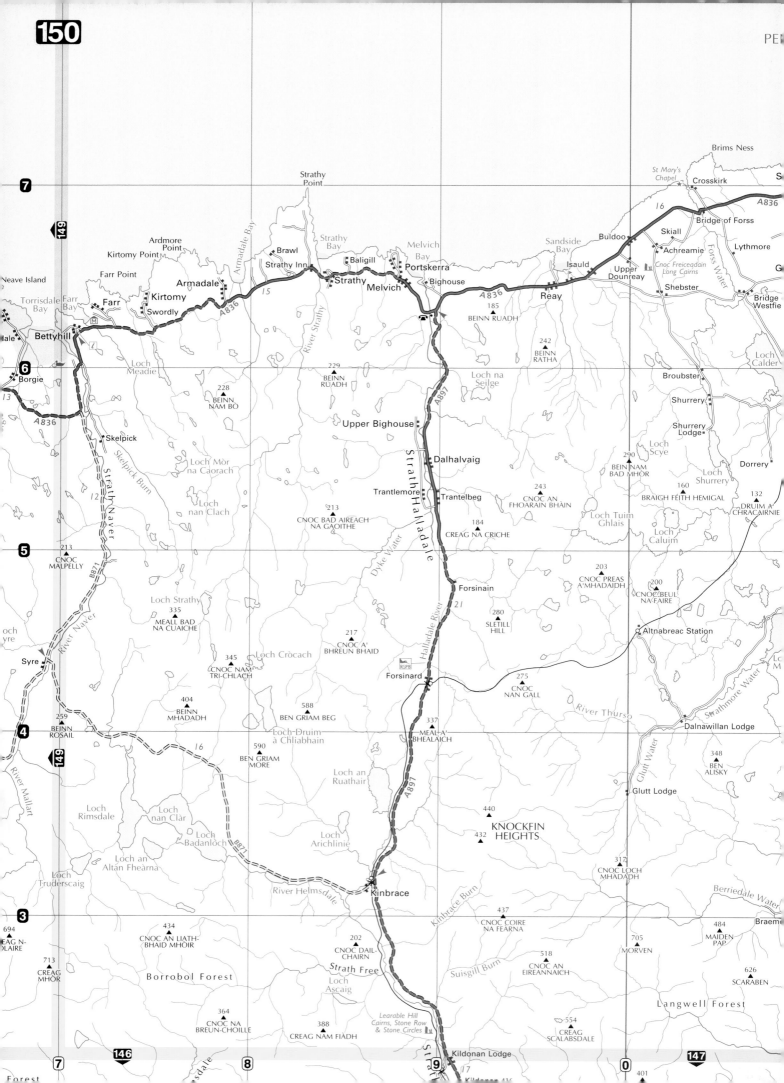

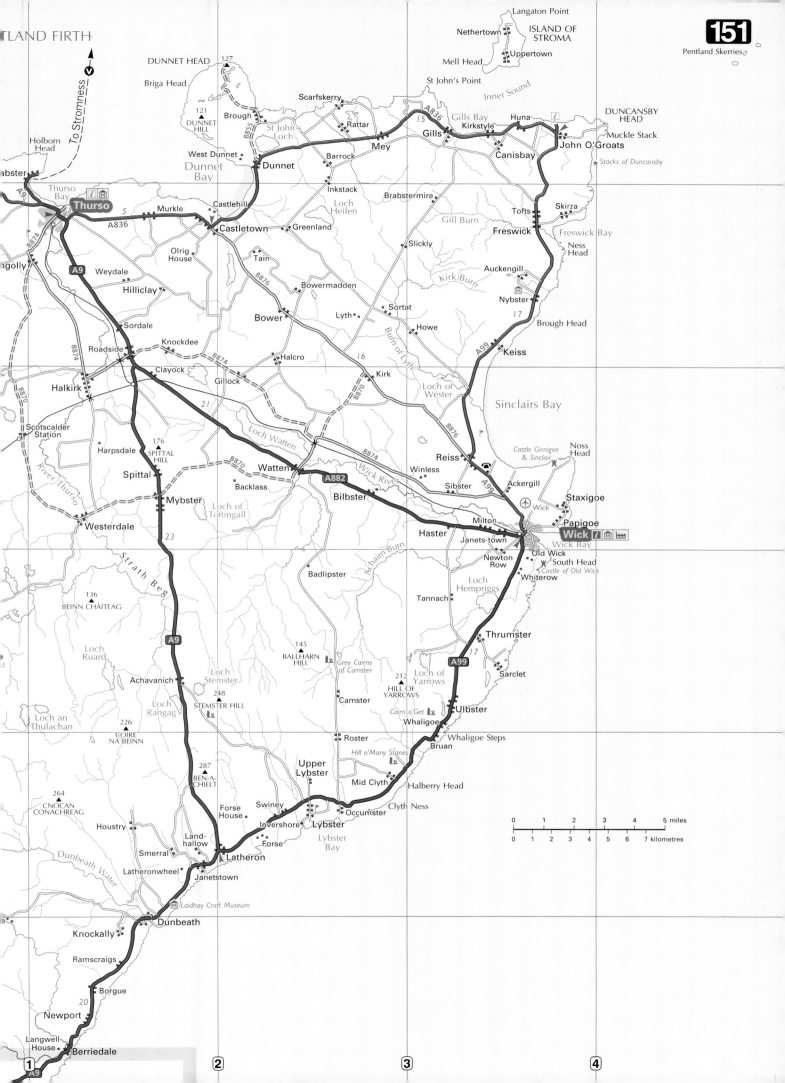

Western Isles

## WESTERN ISLES

The Western Isles, na h-Eileanan Siar, stretch for 130 miles along the edge of the Atlantic, fringed on the west by mile after mile of clean, sandy beaches. The islands have a distinctive culture and Gaelic is the first language of the majority of islanders. Roadside place name signs are in Gaelic. Although one island, Lewis (north) and Harris (south) are very different. Lewis is low-lying and covered with bleak peat moors, whereas Harris is rocky and mountainous, with fertile green 'machair' land to the west.

North Uist, Benbecula and South Uist offer beaches and low-lying 'machair' to the west, and mountains and moorland to the east, while Barra has a rocky, broken east coast and fine-sand bays on the west, rising to a summit at Heaval.

## Ferry Services

Lewis is linked by ferry to the mainland at Ullapool, with daily sailings (except Sunday). There are ferry services from Harris (Tairbeart) and North Uist (Loch nam Madadh) to Uig on Skye. Harris and North Uist are connected by a ferry service between An T-ob (Leverburgh) and Otternish. South Uist and Barra are served by ferry services from Oban, and a ferry service operates between South Uist and Barra. South Uist and North Uist are connected by causeways via Benbecula.

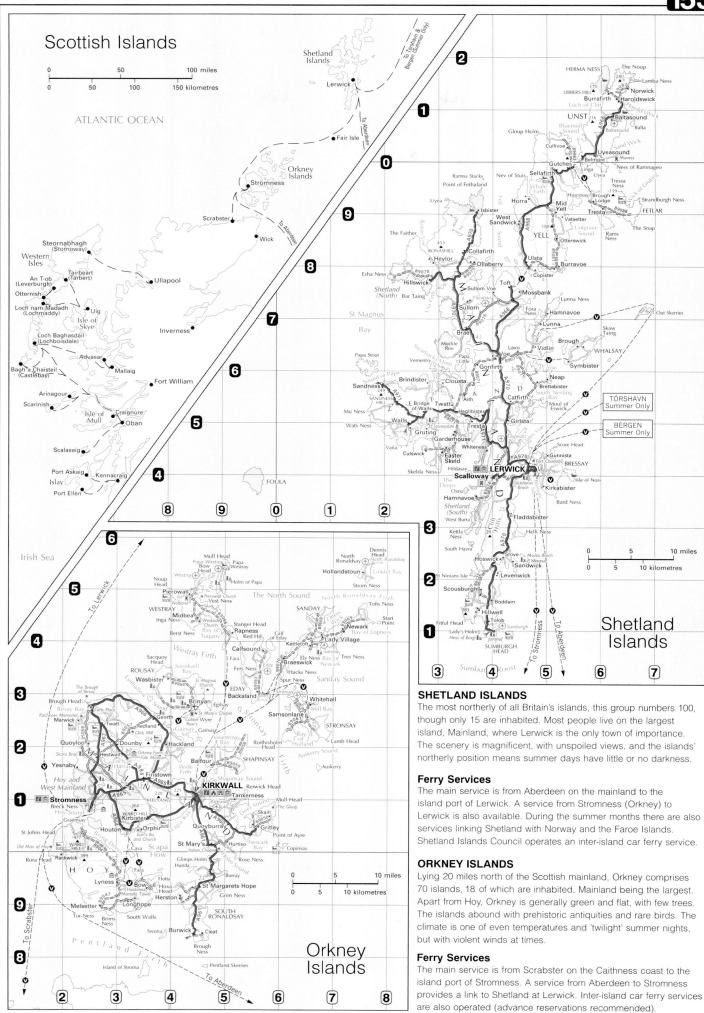

## Scottish Islands

## SHETLAND ISLANDS

The most northerly of all Britain's islands, this group numbers 100, though only 15 are inhabited. Most people live on the largest island, Mainland, where Lerwick is the only town of importance. The scenery is magnificent, with unspoiled views, and the islands' northerly position means summer days have little or no darkness.

### Ferry Services

The main service is from Aberdeen on the mainland to the island port of Lerwick. A service from Stromness (Orkney) to Lerwick is also available. During the summer months there are also services linking Shetland with Norway and the Faroe Islands. Shetland Islands Council operates an inter-island car ferry service.

## ORKNEY ISLANDS

Lying 20 miles north of the Scottish mainland, Orkney comprises 70 islands, 18 of which are inhabited, Mainland being the largest. Apart from Hoy, Orkney is generally green and flat, with few trees. The islands abound with prehistoric antiquities and rare birds. The climate is one of even temperatures and 'twilight' summer nights, but with violent winds at times.

### Ferry Services

The main service is from Scrabster on the Caithness coast to the island port of Stromness. A service from Aberdeen to Stromness provides a link to Shetland at Lerwick. Inter-island car ferry services are also operated (advance reservations recommended).

Shetland Islands

Orkney Islands

# Ireland

Abbeydorney B3
Abbeyfeale B3
Abbeyleix D3
Adamstown D3
Adare B3
Adrigole B2
Ahascragh C4
Ahoghill E6
Allihies A2
Anascaul A2
Annalong E5
Annestown D2
Antrim E6
Ardagh B3
Ardara C6
Ardcath E4
Ardee D5
Ardfert B3
Ardfinnan C3
Ardglass E5
Ardgroom A2
Arklow E3
Arless D3
Armagh D6
Armoy E7
Arthurstown D2
Arvagh D5
Ashbourne E4
Ashford E4
Askeaton B3
Athboy D5
Athea B3
Athenry C4
Athleague C4
Athlone C4
Athy D4
Augher D6
Aughnacloy D6
Aughrim E3
Avoca E3

Bagenalstown D3
(Muine Bheag)
Bailieborough D5
Balbriggan E4
Balla B5
Ballacolla D3
Ballaghaderreen C5
Ballina C3
Ballina B5
Ballinafad C5
Ballinagh D5
Ballinakill D3
Ballinalee C5
Ballinamallard D6
Ballinamore C5
Ballinascarty B2
Ballinasloe C4
Ballindine B5
Ballineen B2
Ballingarry C3
Ballingarry B3
Ballingeary B2
(Béal Atha an
Ghaorthaidh)
Ballinhassig C2
Ballinlough C5
Ballinrobe B5
Ballinspittle C2
Ballintober C5
Ballintra C6
Ballivor D4
Ballon D3
Ballybaun C4
Ballybay D5
Ballybofey C6
Ballycanew E3
Ballycarry E6
Ballycastle B6
Ballycastle E7
Ballyclare E6
Ballyconneely A4
Ballycotton C2
Ballycumber C4
Ballydehob B1
Ballydesmond B2
Ballyduff C2
Ballyduff B3
Ballyfarnan C5
Ballygalley E6
Ballygar C4
Ballygawley D6
Ballygowan E6
Ballyhaise D5
Ballyhale D3
Ballyhaunis C5
Ballyhean B5
Ballyheige B3
Ballyjamesduff D5
Ballykeeran C4
Ballylanders C3
Ballylongford B3
Ballylooby C3
Ballylynan D3
Ballymahon C4
Ballymakeery B2
Ballymena E6
Ballymoe C5
Ballymoney D7
Ballymore C4
Ballymore Eustace D4
Ballymote C5
Ballynahinch E6
Ballynure E6
Ballyporeen C3
Ballyragget D3
Ballyroan D4
Ballyronan D6
Ballysadare C5
Ballyshannon C6
Ballyvaughan B4
Ballywalter E6
Balrothery E4
Baltimore B1

Baltinglass D3
Banagher C4
Banbridge E6
Bandon B2
Bangor E6
Bangor Erris B5
Bansha C3
Banteer B2
Bantry B2
Beaufort B2
Belcoo C6
Belfast E6
Belgooly C2
Bellaghy D6
Belleek C6
Belmullet B6
(Béal an Mhuirhead)
Belturbet D5
Benburb D6
Bennett's Bridge D3
Beragh D6
Birr C4
Blacklion C6
Blackwater E3
Blarney C2
Blessington D4
Boherbue B2
Borris D3
Borris-in-Ossory C4
Borrisokane C4
Borrisoleigh C3
Boyle C5
Bracknagh D4
Bray E4
Bridgetown D2
Brittas D4
Broadford C3
Broadford B3
Broughshane E6
Bruff C3
Bruree C3
Bunclody D3
Buncrana D7
Bundoran C6
Bunmahon D2
Bunnahowen B6
Bunnyconnellan B5
Burnfort C2
Bushmills D7
Butler's Bridge D5
Buttevant C2

Cadamstown C4
Caherconlish C3
Caherdaniel A2
Cahersiveen A2
Cahir C3
Caledon D6
Callan C3
Caltra C4
Camp A3
Cappagh White C3
Cappamore C3
Cappoquin C2
Calinstown D5
Carlanstown D5
Carlow D3
Carndonagh D7
Carnew D3
Carnlough E7
Carracastle C5
Carrick C6
(An Charraig)
Carrickfergus E6
Carrickmacross D5
Carrickmore D6
Carrick-on-Shannon C5
Carrick-on-Suir D3
Carrigahorig C4
Carrigaline C2
Carrigallen D5
Carriganimmy B2
Carrigans D7
Carrigart C2
(Carraig Airt)
Carrigtohill C2
Carrowkeel D7
Carryduff E6
Cashel C3
Castlebar B5
Castlebellingham E5
Castleblayney D5
Castlebridge E3
Castlecomer D3
Castlederg D6
Castledermot D3
Castleisland B3
Castlemaine B2
Castlemartyr D2
Castleplunkett C5
Castlepollard D5
Castlerea C5
Castlerock D7
Castleshane D5
Castletown D4
Castletown
Bearhaven A2
Castletownroche C2
Castletownshend B1
Castlewellan E5
Causeway B3
Cavan D5
Celbridge D4
Charlestown C5
Charleville B3
(Rath Luirc)
Clady D6
Clane D4
Clara C4
Clarecastle B3
Claremorris B5
Clarinbridge B4
Clashmore C2
Claudy D7

Clifden A4
Cliffoney D6
Clogh D3
Cloghan C4
Clogheen C3
Clogher D6
Cloghamon B3
Clonakilty B2
Clonard E4
Clonaslee D4
Clonbulloge D4
Clonbur B5
(An Fhairche )
Clondalkin E4
Clondara C4
Clones D5
Clonmany D7
Clonmel C3
Clonmellon D5
Clonmore C3
Clonony C3
Clonoulty C3
Clonroche D3
Clontibret D5
Cloondara C5
Cloonlara C3
Clough E6
Cloughjordan C4
Cloyne C2
Coagh D6
Coalisland D6
Cobh C2
Coleraine D7
Collinstown D5
Collon D5
Colloney C5
Comber E6
Cong B5
Conna C2
Cookstown D6
Coole D5
Cooraclare B3
Cootehill D5
Cork C2
Cornamona B4
Corofin B4
Courtmacsherry B2
Courtown Harbour E3
Craigavon E6
Craughwell C4
Creeslough C7
Creggs C5
Croagh B3
Crolly (Croithli) C7
Crookedwood D4
Crookhaven B1
Crookstown B2
Croom B3
Crossakeel D5
Cross Barry B2
Crosshaven C2
Crossmaglen D5
Crossmolina B5
Crumlin E6
Crusheen B4
Culdaff D7
Culleybackey E6
Curracloe D3
Curraghboy C4
Curry C5
Cushendall E7

Daingean D4
Delvin D5
Derrygonnelly C6
Dervock E7
Dingle A2
(An Daingean)
Doagh E6
Donaghadee E6
Donaghmore C3
Donegal C6
Doneraile C2
Doon C4
Doonbeg B3
Douglas C2
Downpatrick E6
Dowra C5
Draperstown D6
Drimoleague B2
Dripsey B2
Drogheda E5
Dromahair C6
Dromcolliher B3
Dromod C5
Dromore E6
Dromore D6
Dromore West C6
Drum D5
Drumcliff C6
Drumconrath D5
Drumkeeran C5
Drumlish C5
Drumquin D6
Drumshanbo C5
Drumsna C5
Duagh B3
Dublin E4
Duleek E5
Dunboyne E4
Duncormick D2
Dundalk E5
Dunderrow C2
Dundrum E5
Dunfanaghy C7
Dungannon D6
Dungarvan C2
Dungarvan D3
Dungiven D7
Dungloe C7
(An Clochan Liath)
Dungourney C2
Dunkineely C6
Dun Laoghaire E4
Dunlavin D4
Dunleer E5

Dunloy E7
Dunmanway B2
Dunmore C5
Dunmore East D2
Dunmurry E6
Dunshaughlin D4
Durrow D4
Durrus B2
Dysart C4

Easky B6
Edenderry D4
Edgeworthstown D5
Eglinton D7
Elphin C5
Emyvale D6
Enfield D4
Ennis B3
Enniscorthy D3
Enniscrone B6
Enniskean B2
Enniskillen D6
Ennistymon B4
Eyrecourt C4

Farnaght C5
Farranfore B2
Feakle C4
Fenagh C5
Ferbane C4
Fermoy C2
Ferns D3
Fethard D2
Fethard C3
Finnea D5
Fintona D6
Fivemiletown D6
Fontstown D4
Foxford B5
Foynes B3
Freemount B3
Frenchpark C5
Freshford D3
Fuerty C5

Galbally C3
Galway B4
Garrison C6
Garristown E4
Garvagh D7
Geashill D4
Gilford E6
Glandore B1
Glanworth C2
Glaslough D6
Glassan C4
Glenamaddy C5
Glenarm E7
Glenavy E6
Glenbeigh A2
Glencolumbkille C6
(Gleann Cholm
Cille)
Glendalough E4
Glenealy E3
Glengarriff B2
Glenmore D3
Glenties C6
Glin B3
Glinsk B3
(Glinsce)
Golden C3
Goleen B1
Goresbridge D3
Gorey E3
Gort B4
Gortin D6
Gowran B3
Graiguenamanagh
D3
Granard C5
Grange C6
Greyabbey E6

Greystones E4
Gulladuff D6

Hacketstown D3
Headford B4
Herbertstown C3
Hillsborough E6
Hilltown E5
Holycross C3
Holywood E6
Howth E4

Inch A2
Inchigeelagh B2
Inishannon B2
Irvinestown D6

Johnstown C3

Kanturk B2
Keadue C5
Keady D5
Keel A5
Keenagh C5
Kells E6
Kells D5
Kenmare B2
Kesh C6
Kilbeggan D4
Kilberry D6
Kilbrittain B2
Kilcar C6
(Cill Charthaigh)
Kilcock D4
Kilcolgan B4
Kilconnell C4
Kilcoole E4
Kilcormac C4
Kilcullen D4
Kilcurry E5
Kildare D4
Kildavin D3
Kildorrery B4
Kilfenora B4
Kilgarvan B2
Kilkee B3
Kilkeel E5
Kilkelly C5
Kilkenny D3
Kilkieran B4
Kilkinlea B3
Kill D2
Killadysert B3
Killala B6
Killaloe C3
Killarney B2
Killashee C5
Killeigh D4
Killenaule C3
Killeshandra D6
Killimer B3
Killimor C4
Killiney E4
Killinick D2
Killorglin B2
Killough E5
Killucan D4
Killybegs C6
Killyleagh E6
Kilmacanoge E4
Kilmacrenan C7
Kilmacthomas D2
Kilmaganny D3
Kilmaine B5
Kilmallock C3
Kilmanagh D3
Kilmeadan D2
Kilmeage D4
Kilmeedy B3
Kilmichael B2
Kilmore Quay D2
Kilnaleck D5

Kilrea D7
Kilrush B3
Kilsheelan C3
Kiltealy D3
Kiltegan D3
Kiltimagh B5
Kiltoom C4
Kingscourt D5
Kinlough C6
Kinnegad D4
Kinnitty C4
Kinsale C2
Kinvarra B4
Kircubbin E6
Knock B5
Knockcroghery C4
Knocklofty C3
Knocktopher D3

Lahinch B4
Laragh E4
Larne E6
Lauragh A2
Laurencetown C4
Leap B2
Leenane B5
Leighlinbridge D3
Leitrim C5
Leixlip D4
Lemybrien C2
Letterfrack B5
Letterkenny D7
Lifford D7
Limavady D7
Limerick C3
Lisbellaw D6
Lisburn E6
Liscannor B4
Liscarroll B3
Lisdoonvarna B4
Lismore C3
Lisnaskea D6
Lisryan D5
Listowel B3
Loghill B3
Londonderry D7
Longford C5
Loughbrickland E6
Loughgall D6
Loughglinn C5
Loughrea C4
Louisburgh B5
Lucan D4
Lurgan E6
Lusk E4

Macroom B2
Maghera E5
Maghera D6
Magherafelt D6
Maguiresbridge D6
Malahide E4
Malin C6
Malin More C6
Mallow C2
Manorhamilton C6
Markethill D6
Maynooth D4
Mazetown E6
Middletown D6
Midleton C2
Milford C7
Millstreet B2
Milltown D2
Milltown Malbay B3
Mitchelstown C3
Moate C4
Mohill C5
Monaghan D5
Monasterevin D4
Moneygall C4
Moneymore D6
Monivea C4

Mooncoin D2
Moorfields E6
Mount Bellew C4
Mount Charles C6
Mountmellick D4
Mountrath D4
Mountshannon C4
Moville D7
Moy D6
Moynalty D5
Moyvore C4
Muckross B2
Muff D7
Mullinavat D3
Mullingar D4
Mulrany B5
Myshall D3

Naas D4
Naul E4
Navan D5
Neale B5
Nenagh C3
Newbliss D5
Newbridge D4
(Droichead Nua)
Newcastle E5
Newcastle West B3
Newinn C3
Newmarket B2
Newmarket-on-
Fergus B3
Newport B5
Newport B5
New Ross D3
Newry E5
Newtown D3
Newtownabbey E6
Newtownards E6
Newtownbutler D5
Newtownhamilton D5
Newtown-
mountkennedy E4
Newtownstewart D6
Newtown Forbes C5
Nobber D5

Oilgate D3
Oldcastle D5
Omagh D6
Omeath E5
Oola C3
Oranmore B4
Oughterard B4
Ovens C2

Pallas Grean C3
Parknasilla A2
Partry B5
Passage East D2
Passage West C2
Patrickswell C3
Paulstown D3
Pettigo C6
Plumbridge D6
Pomeroy D6
Portadown E6
Portaferry E6
Portarlington D4
Portavogie E6
Portglenone E6

Portlaoise D4
Portmarnock E4
Portrane E4
Portroe D7
Portrush D7
Portstewart D7
Portumna C4
Poulgorm Bridge B2
Poyntzpass E6

Raharney D4
Randalstown E6
Rasharkin E7
Rathangan D4
Rathcoole D4
Rathcormack C2
Rathdowney C3
Rathdrum E3
Rathfriland E5
Rathkeale B3
Rathmelton D7
Rathmolyon D4
Rathmore B2
Rathmullan D7
Rathnew E3
Rathowen D5
Rathvilly D3
Ratoath D4
Ray D7
Ring (An Rinn) C2
Ringaskiddy C2
Rockcorry D5
Roosky C5
Rosapenna C7
Rosbercon D3
Roscommon C5
Roscrea C4
Ross Carbery B1
Rosscor C6
Rosses Point C6
Rosslare Harbour D2
Rosslea D5
Rostrevor E5
Roundstone B4
Roundwood E4
Rush E4

St Johnstown D7
Saintfield E6
Sallins D4
Scarriff C4
Scartaglen B2
Scarva E6
Scramoge C5
Seskinore D6
Shanagarry C2
Shanagolden B3
Shannonbridge C4
Shercock D5
Shillelagh D3
Shinrone C4
Shrule B4
Silvermines C3
Sion Mills D6
Sixmilebridge B3
Skerries E4
Skibbereen B1
Slane D5
Sligo C6
Smithborough D5

Sneem A2
Spiddal B4
(An Spideal)
Stewartstown D6
Stonyford D3
Strabane D6
Stradbally D4
Stradone E3
Strandhill C6
Strangford E6
Stranorlar C6
Strokestown C5
Summerhill D4
Swanlinbar C5
Swatragh D6
Swinford B5
Swords E4

Taghmon D3
Tagoat D2
Tahilla A2
Tallaght E4
Tallow C2
Tallowbridge C2
Tandragee E6
Tang C4
Tarbert B3
Templemore C3
Templetouhy C3
Termonfeckin E5
Thomastown D3
Thurles C3
Timahoe D4
Timoleague B2
Tinahely D3
Tipperary C3
Tobercurry C5
Tobermore D6
Toomyvara C3
Toormore B1
Tralee B3
Tramore D2
Trim D4
Tuam B4
Tuamgraney C3
Tulla B3
Tullamore D4
Tullow D3
Tulsk C5
Turlough B5
Tyrellspass D4

Urlingford C3

Virginia D5

Warrenpoint E5
Waterford D2
Watergrasshill C2
Waterville A2
Westport B5
Wexford D3
Whitegate C2
Whitehead E6
Wicklow E4
Woodenbridge E3
Woodford C4

Youghal C2

**A** **B** **C**

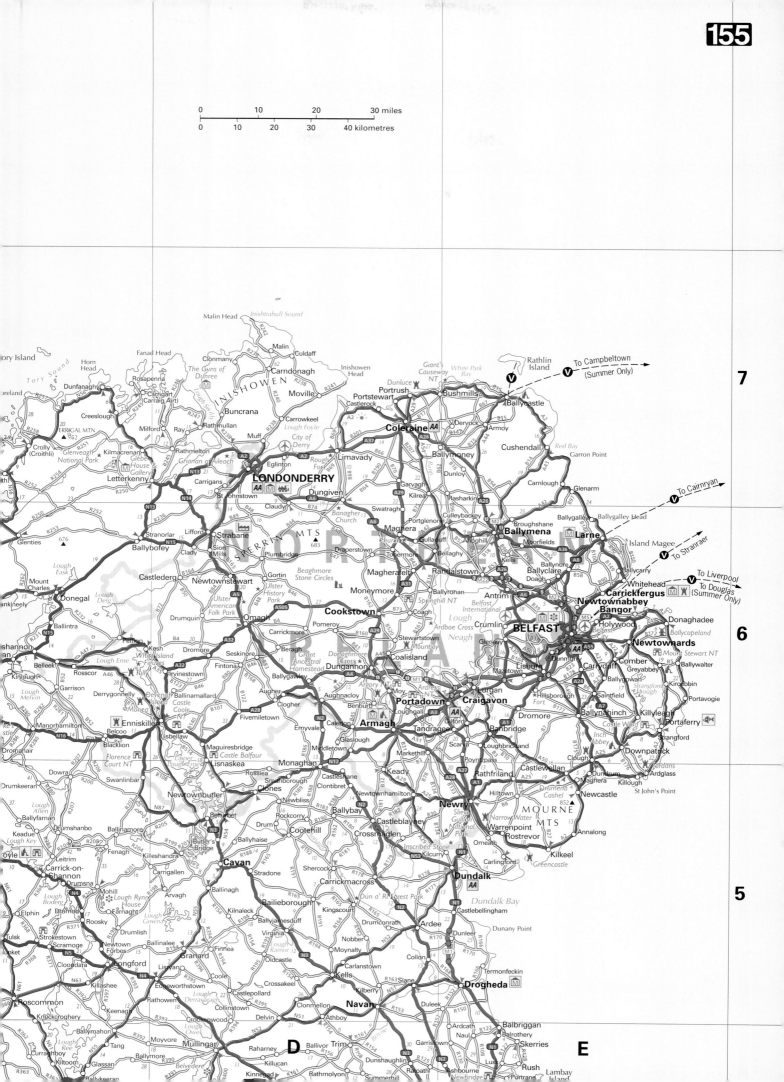

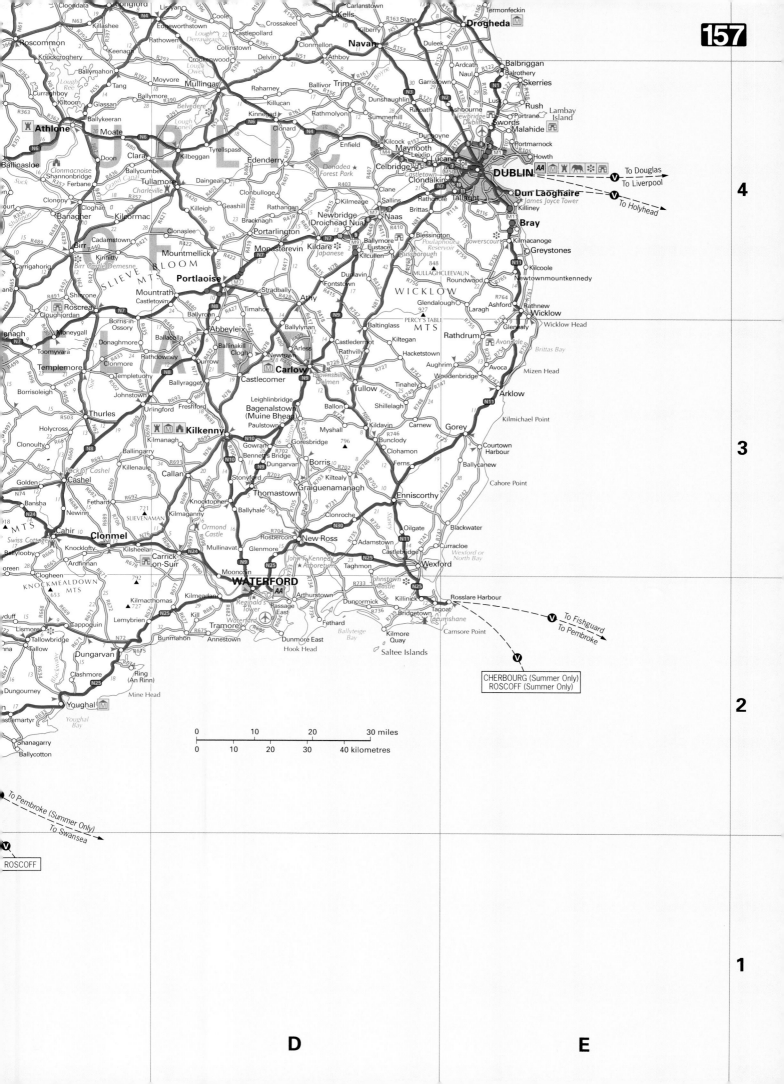

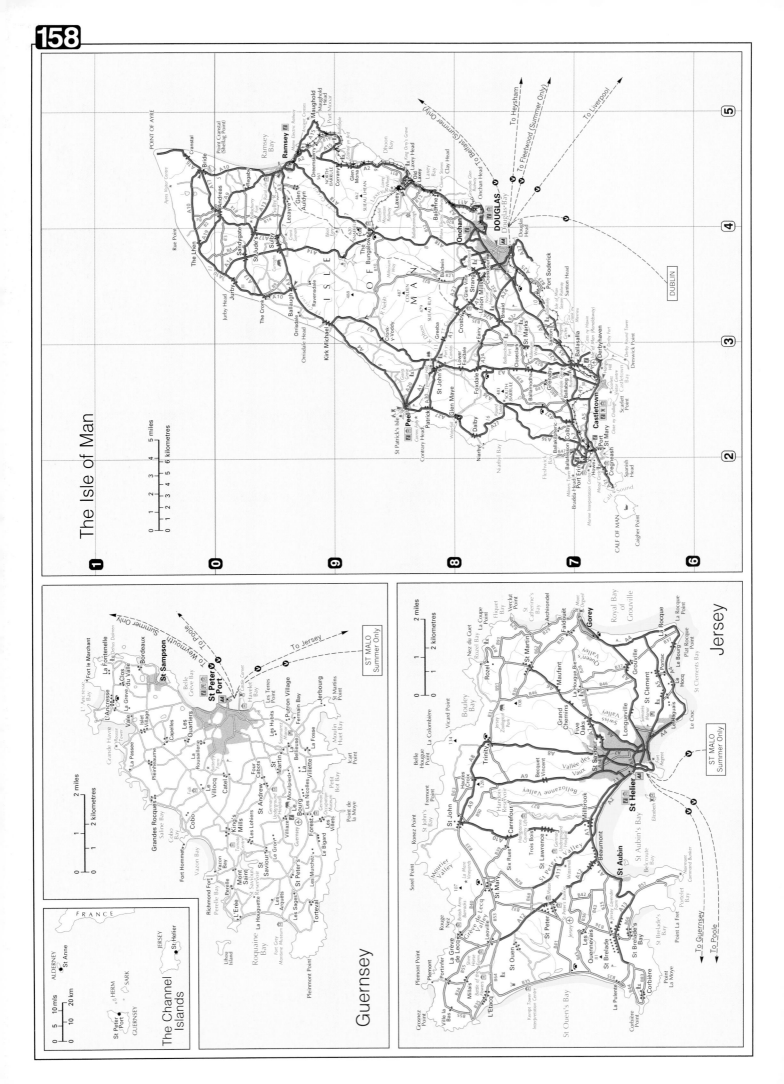

# The Isle of Man

0 1 2 3 4 5 miles
0 1 2 3 4 5 6 kilometres

# The Channel Islands

FRANCE

ALDERNEY
St Anne

HERM
SARK
GUERNSEY
St Peter Port

JERSEY
St Helier

0 5 10 mils
0 10 20 km

# Guernsey

0 1 2 miles
0 1 2 kilometres

# Jersey

0 1 2 miles
0 1 2 kilometres

# key to town plans

Refer also to page V, 'Using this atlas'

159

## Central London

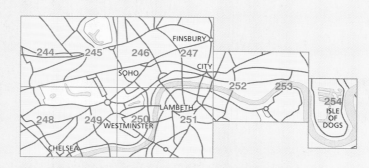

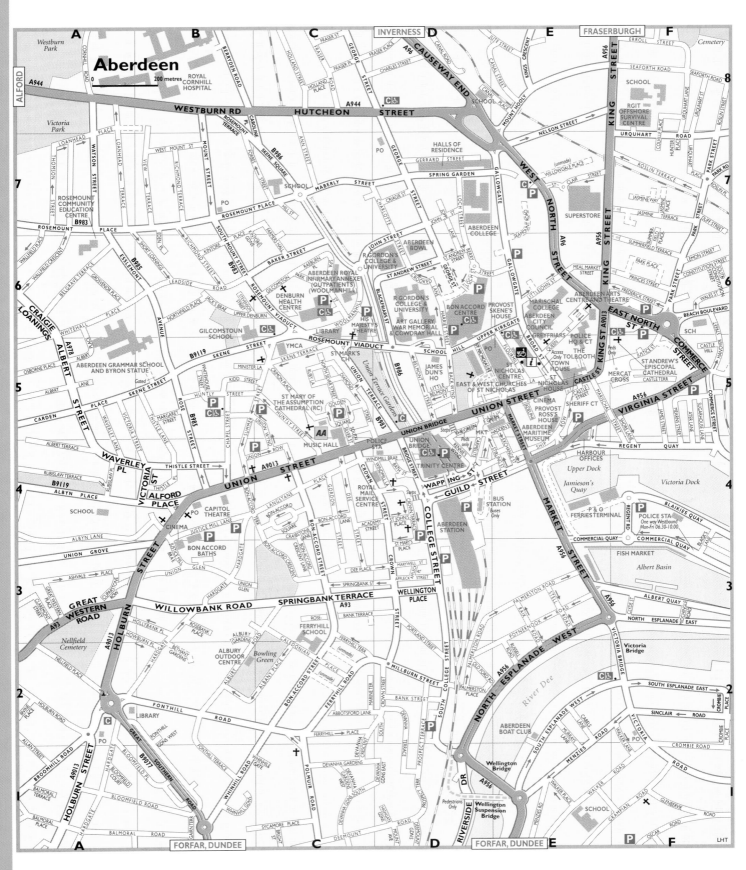

# Aberystwyth

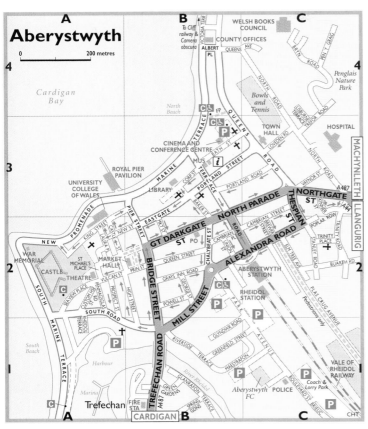

Aberystwyth is found on atlas page **43**,
grid reference **5881**

| | | | | | |
|---|---|---|---|---|---|
| Albert Place | B4 | Mill Street | B1-B2 | Trefechan Road | B1 |
| Baker Street | B3 | New Promenade | A2-B3 | Trefor Road | C3-C4 |
| Bath Steet | B3 | New Street | A2-B2 | Trinity Place | C2 |
| Boulevard St Brieuc | C1 | North Parade | B2-C3 | Trinity Road | C2-C3 |
| Brewer Street | C2 | North Road | C3-C4 | Union Street | B2 |
| Bridge Street | B1-B2 | Northgate Street | C3 | Vaynor Street | C3 |
| Bryn Road | C4 | Park Avenue | B2-C1 | Victoria Terrace | B4 |
| Buarth Road | C2 | Pen y Graig | C4 | Vulcan Street | A2 |
| Cambrian Place | B2 | Penmagsglas Road | A2 | | |
| Cambrian Street | C2-C3 | Pier Street | B2-B3 | | |
| Castle Street | A2 | Plas Crug Avenue | C1-C2 | | |
| Chalybeate Street | B2 | Poplar Row | C2-C3 | | |
| Corporation Street | B3 | Portland Road | B3-C3 | | |
| Custom House Street | A2 | Portland Street | B3-C3 | | |
| Eastgate | B2-B3 | Powell Street | B2 | | |
| Elmtree Avenue | C2 | Princess Street | B2 | | |
| George Street | B2 | Prospect Street | A2 | | |
| Glanrafon Terrace | B1 | Queen Street | B2 | | |
| Glyndwr Road | B1 | Queens Avenue | B4-C4 | | |
| Grays Inn Road | B2 | Queens Road | B4-C3 | | |
| Great Darkgate Street | B2 | Rheidol Terrace | A1 | | |
| Green Gardens | B1 | Riverside Terrace | B1 | | |
| Greenfield Street | B1-C1 | St Michael's Place | A2 | | |
| High Street | A2-B3 | Sea View Place | A2 | | |
| King Street | A2-A3 | Skinner Street | C3 | | |
| Laura Place | A2 | South Marine Terrace | A1-A2 | | |
| Lisburne Terrace | C3-C4 | South Road | A2-B1 | | |
| Loveden Road | C3 | Spring Gardens | B1 | | |
| Maesyrafon | B1-C1 | Stanley Road | C2 | | |
| Marine Terrace | B4-B3 | Terrace Road | B3-C2 | | |
| Market Street | B2 | Thespian Street | C2-C3 | | |

# Aberdeen

Aberdeen is found on atlas page **135**,
grid reference **9306**

**AA shop**
19–20 Golden Square, Aberdeen AB9 1JN    C5

| | | | | | |
|---|---|---|---|---|---|
| Abbotsford Lane | C2-D2 | Bon-Accord Crescent | C4-C3 | Crooked Lane | D6 |
| Academy Street | C4-D4 | Bon-Accord Crescent Lane | C3-C4 | Crown Street | C4-D4-D3-D2 |
| Adelphi | E5 | Bon-Accord Lane | C4 | Crown Terrace | D4 |
| Affleck Place | D3 | Bon-Accord Square | C4 | Cuparstone Row | A3 |
| Affleck Street | D3 | Bon-Accord Street | C2-C3-C4 | Deemount Gardens | D1 |
| Albany Place | B2-C2 | Bon-Accord Terrace | B4-C4 | Deemount Road | C1-D1 |
| Albert Lane | A5 | Bridge Street | D4 | Dee Place | C3-D3 |
| Albert Quay | F3-E3 | Bright Street | C1 | Dee Street | C4-C3 |
| Albert Place | A5-A6 | Broad Street | E5-E6 | Devanha Crescent | C1-C2-D1 |
| Albert Street | A4-A5 | Broomhill Road | A1-A2 | Devanha Gardens | C1-D1 |
| Albert Terrace | A4-A5 | Cabels Lane | E2 | Devanha Gardens East | D1 |
| Albury Gardens | B2-B3 | Caledonian Place | C3-C2 | Devanha Gardens South | C1 |
| Albury Road | B2-C3 | Canal Place | D8-E8 | Devanha Gardens West | C1 |
| Albyn Lane | A4-B4 | Canal Road | D8 | Devanha Terrace | D1-D2 |
| Albyn Place | A4 | Canal Street | D8-E8 | Diamond Street | C5 |
| Alford Place | B4 | Carden Place | A5 | Duff Street | F6-F7 |
| Allan Street | A1-A2 | Carmelite Street | D4-D5 | East North Street | E6-F6 |
| Ann Street | C7-C8 | Caroline Place | B8-C7 | Eden Place | B6-B7 |
| Ashvale Place | A3 | Castle Street | E5 | Erroll Street | E8 |
| Ater Lane | F4-F5 | Castle Hill | F5 | Esslemont Avenue | A6-B6-B5 |
| Back Wynd | D5 | Castle Terrace | F5 | Exchange Street | E5-E4 |
| Baker Street | C6 | Causewayend | D8 | Farmers Hall | C7-C6 |
| Balmoral Place | A1 | Chapel Street | B5-B4 | Ferryhill Place | C2 |
| Balmoral Road | A1-B1 | Charles Street | C8-D8 | Ferryhill Road | C2-D2 |
| Balmoral Terrace | A1 | Charlotte Street | D7-D6 | Ferryhill Terrace | C3-C2 |
| Bank Street | D2 | Claremont Street | A3 | Flourmill Lane | E5-E6 |
| Bath Street | D4 | Clyde Street | F3 | Fonthill Gardens West | B2 |
| Beach Boulevard | F6 | College Street | D4-D3 | Fonthill Road | A2-B2-C2 |
| Belgrave Terrace | A6 | Colville Place | F7-F8 | Fonthill Terrace | B1-B2 |
| Belmont Street | D5 | Commerce Street | F4-F5 | Forbes Street | B7-C7 |
| Berry Street | D6-E6 | Commercial Quay | E3-F3 | Fraser Place | C8-D8 |
| Berryden Road | B8 | Constitution Street | F6 | Fraser Road | C8 |
| Bethany Gardens | B2 | Cornhill Road | A8 | Fraser Street | C8 |
| Blackfriars Street | D5-D6 | Craibstone Lane | C3-C4 | Frederick Street | F6 |
| Black's Lane | F3-F4 | Craigie Loanings | A6 | Gairn Terrace | B1 |
| Blaikies Quay | F4 | Craigie Street | D7 | Gallowgate | E7-E6 |
| Bloomfield Court | A1 | Crimon Place | C5 | George Street | C8-D8-D7-D6 |
| Bloomfield Place | A2-A1-B1 | Crombie Place | F2 | Gerrard Street | D7 |
| Bloomfield Road | A1-B1 | Crombie Road | F1 | Gilcomston Park | C6 |

| | | | | | |
|---|---|---|---|---|---|
| Glenbervie Road | F1 | Hanover Street | F6-F5 | North Silver Street | C5 | Spa Street | C6 |
| Golden Square | C5 | Hardgate | A1-A2-B2-B3-B4 | Northfield Place | B6 | Spring Garden | D7 |
| Gordon Street | C4-C3 | Harriet Street | D5-D6 | Old Ford Road | D2 | Springbank Street | C3-D3 |
| Grampian Road | E1-F1 | Highgate Gardens | D1 | Osborne Place | A5 | Springbank Terrace | C3-D3 |
| Great Southern Road | A2-B1 | Hill Street | C7 | Oscar Road | F1 | Stell Road | E3 |
| Great Western Place | A3 | Holburn Road | A2 | Palmerston Place | D2 | Stevenson Street | B6 |
| Great Western Road | A2-A3 | Holburn Street | A1-A2-A3-B3-B4 | Palmerston Road | D2-D3-E3 | Stirling Street | D4-E4 |
| Grosvenor Place | A6 | Holland Place | C8 | Park Place | F6 | Sugar House Lane | F4-F5 |
| Guild Street | D4-E4 | Holland Street | C8 | Park Road | F7 | Summerfield Place | F6-F7 |
| Hadden Street | E5 | Hollybank Place | A3-B3 | Park Street | F6-F7 | Summerfield Terrace | F6 |
| | | Howburn Place | A3-B3-B2 | Polmuir Road | C1-C2 | Summer Street | B4-B5-C5 |
| | | Hunter Place | F7 | Portland Street | D3-D2 | Sycamore Place | B1-C1 |
| | | Huntly Street | B5-C5-C4 | Poynernook Road | D2-E2-E3 | The Green | D4-D5 |
| | | Hutcheon Street | C8-D8 | Princes Street | F6 | Thistle Lane | B5-B4 |
| | | Irvine Place | A2 | Prospect Terrace | D1-D2 | Thistle Place | B4 |
| | | Jack's Brae | B6 | Queen Street | E5-E6 | Thistle Street | B4 |
| | | James Street | F5-F4 | Raeburn Place | C6 | Thomson Street | A7 |
| | | Jasmine Place | F7 | Raik Road | E3-E2 | Union Bridge | D4-D5 |
| | | Jasmine Terrace | F7 | Regent Road | F4 | Union Glen | B3 |
| | | Jasmine Way | F7 | Regent Quay | E4-F4 | Union Grove | A3-B3 |
| | | John Street | C6-D6-D7 | Rennies Wynd | D4 | Union Row | B4-C4 |
| | | Jopp's Lane | D7-D6 | Richmond Street | B6-B7 | Union Street | B4-C4-D5-E5 |
| | | Justice Street | F5 | Richmond Terrace | B7 | Union Terrace | C5-D5 |
| | | Justice Mill Brae | B3-B4 | Riverside Drive | D1 | Union Wynd | B5-C5-C4 |
| | | Justice Mill Lane | B4 | Rose Street | B5-B4 | Upper Denburn | B6-C6 |
| | | Jute Street | D8-E8 | Rosebank Place | B3 | Upper Kirkgate | D5-D6-E6 |
| | | Kidd Street | B5-C5 | Rosebank Terrace | C3-D3 | Urquhart Lane | F7-F8 |
| | | King Street | E5-E6-F7-F8 | Rosemount Place | A7-B7-C7 | Urquhart Place | F7 |
| | | Kings Crescent | E8 | Rosemount Terrace | B8-B7 | Urquhart Road | F7 |
| | | Kintore Gardens | B7-B6-C6 | Rosemount Viaduct | B6-C5-D5 | Urquhart Street | F8-F7 |
| | | Kintore Place | B6-B7-C7 | Roslin Place | F7 | Victoria Bridge | F3-F2 |
| | | Langstane Place | C4 | Roslin Street | F8 | Victoria Road | F2-F1 |
| | | Leadside Road | B6 | Roslin Terrace | F7 | Victoria Street | A5-B4 |
| | | Lemon Street | F6 | Rubislaw Place | A4 | View Terrace | B7-B8 |
| | | Little Belmont Street | D5 | Rubislaw Terrace | A4 | Virginia Street | E5-F5 |
| | | Little John Street | E6 | Ruby Lane | C5 | Wales Street | F6 |
| | | Loanhead Place | A7-A8 | Russell Road | E2 | Walker Lane | F1-F2 |
| | | Loanhead Terrace | A7-A8 | St Andrew Street | D6 | Walker Place | E1 |
| | | Loch Street | D6 | St Clair Street | E7 | Walker Road | E1-F1 |
| | | Maberly Street | C7-D7 | St John's Place | D4 | Wallfield Crescent | A6-A7 |
| | | Marischal Street | E5-F5-F4 | St Mary's Place | D3 | Wallfield Place | A6-A7 |
| | | Market Street | E5-E4-E3 | St Nicholas Street | D5-E5 | Wapping Street | D4 |
| | | Margaret Street | B5 | School Hill | D5 | Watson Street | A7-A8 |
| | | Marine Terrace | C2 | Seaforth Road | F8 | Waverley Lane | A5-A4 |
| | | Marywell Street | D3 | Seamount Road | E6-E7 | Waverley Place | A4-B4 |
| | | Meal Market Street | E6 | Ship Row | E4-E5 | Wellington Place | D3 |
| | | Mearns Street | F5-F4 | Shore Lane | F4-F5 | West Mount Street | B7 |
| | | Menzies Road | E1-E2-F2 | Short Loanings | A7-B6 | West North Street | E7-E6 |
| | | Midchingle Road | F3 | Sinclair Road | F2 | Westburn Road | A8-B8 |
| | | Millburn Street | D2 | Skene Square | B7-C7 | Whinhill Gardens | B1 |
| | | Minister Lane | B5-C5 | Skene Street | A5-B5-C5 | Whinhill Gate | B1-C1 |
| | | Mount Avenue | D1 | Skene Terrace | C5 | Whinhill Road | B1-C2 |
| | | Mount Hooly | E8 | South College Street | D3-D2-D1 | Whitehall Place | A5-A6-B6 |
| | | Mount Street | B7-B8 | South Constitution Street | F6 | Whitehouse Street | B5 |
| | | Murrays Lane | E1-E2 | South Crown Street | D2 | Willowbank Road | A3-B3 |
| | | Nellfield Street | A2 | South Esplanade East | E1-E2-F2 | Willowdale Place | E7 |
| | | Nelson Street | E7-E8 | South Esplanade West | E1-E2-F2 | Windmill Brae | C4-D4 |
| | | North Esplanade East | F3 | South Mount Street | B7-B6 | Windmill Lane | D4 |
| | | North Esplanade West | D1-E3 | South Silver Street | C4-C5 | Woolmanhill | C6 |

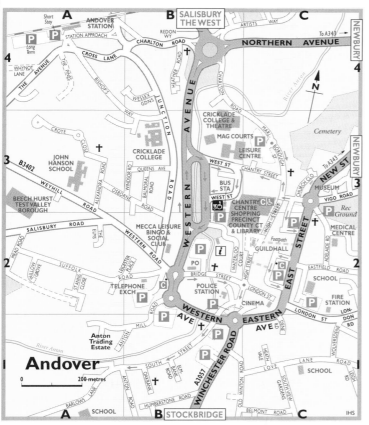

# Andover

Andover is found on atlas page **23**, grid reference **3645**

| | | | |
|---|---|---|---|
| Adelaide Road | C2-C3 | The Elms | A2 |
| Alexandra Road | A3 | The Pines | A4 |
| Anton Mill Road | A1-B1-B2 | Vigo Road | C3 |
| Anton Road | B1 | Waterloo Court | B2 |
| Artists Way | B4-C4 | Wessex Gardens | B4 |
| Balmoral Road | B3 | Western Avenue | B1-B2-B3 |
| Barlows Lane | A1 | Western Road | A2-B2 |
| Belmont Road | B1-C1 | West Street | B2-B3 |
| Bishop's Way | A4-B4-B3 | Weyhill Road | A3 |
| Bridge Street | B2 | Whynot Lane | A4 |
| Chantry Street | B3-C3 | Winchester Road | B1 |
| Charlton Road | B4-B3-C3 | Windsor Road | B3 |
| Church Close | C3 | Willow Grove | A2 |
| Cross Lane | A4 | Wolversdene Road | C1 |
| Croye Close | A3 | | |
| Dene Road | C1 | | |
| Eastfield Road | C2 | | |
| East Street | C2-C3 | | |
| Eastern Avenue | C1-C2 | | |
| Elmbank Road | B1 | | |
| Heath Vale | C1 | | |
| Heather Drive | B4 | | |
| High Street | B2-C2-C3 | | |
| Humberstone Road | B1 | | |
| Junction Road | B2-B3-B4 | | |
| Leicester Place | B2 | | |
| Leigh Road | C1 | | |
| London Road | C1 | | |
| London Street | C1 | | |
| Love Lane | C1-C2 | | |
| Marlborough Street | C3 | | |
| Mead Road | A2 | | |
| New Street | C3 | | |
| Northern Avenue | B4-C4 | | |
| Oak Bank Road | B1 | | |
| Old Winton Road | B1-C1 | | |
| Osborne Road | A3-B3 | | |
| Queens Avenue | B3 | | |
| Redon Way | B4 | | |
| St Anns Close | A2 | | |
| Salisbury Road | A2 | | |
| South Street | B1-B2 | | |
| Southview Gardens | C1 | | |
| Station Approach | A4 | | |
| Suffolk Road | A2-B2 | | |
| The Avenue | A4 | | |

162

# Basingstoke

Basingstoke is found on atlas page **24**, grid reference **6352**

**AA shop**
21–23 Wote Street, Basingstoke RG21 1NE  B2

| | | | |
|---|---|---|---|
| Alencon Link | B3-B4-C3 | New Street | B2 |
| Basing View | C4 | Norn Hill | C4 |
| Beaconsfield Road | B1 | Old Reading Road | C4 |
| Blair Road | A1 | Penrith Road | A2 |
| Bounty Rise | A1 | Provident Way | B4 |
| Bounty Road | A1-B1 | Rayleigh Road | A3 |
| Bramblys Close | A2 | Ringway South | A1-B1-C1 |
| Bramblys Drive | A2 | Rochford Road | A3 |
| Budds Close | A2 | St Mary's Court | C3 |
| Bunnian Place | B4 | Sarum Hill | A2-B2 |
| Burgess Road | A4-B4 | Seal Road | B1-B2 |
| Chapel Hill | A4-B4 | Southend Road | A3 |
| Chequers Road | B2-C3 | Solbys Road | A3 |
| Chester Place | A2 | Soper Grove | B4 |
| Church Square | A2-B2 | Southern Road | B2 |
| Church Street | B2 | Timberlake Road | B3-C3 |
| Churchill Way | A3-B3 | Victoria Street | B2 |
| Churchill Way East | C3 | Vyne Road | B4 |
| Cliddesden Road | B1 | White Hart Lane | C2 |
| Council Road | B1 | Winchcombe Road | A2 |
| Cross Street | B2 | Winchester Road | A1-A2-B2 |
| Crossborough Hill | C1-C2 | Winchester Street | B2 |
| Culver Road | A1 | Worting Road | A3 |
| Devonshire Place | A1-A2 | Wote Street | B2 |
| Eastfield Avenue | C2-C3 | | |
| Eastrop Lane | C2-C3 | | |
| Eastrop Way | C3 | | |
| Elbow Corner | B3 | | |
| Essex Road | A3 | | |
| Fairfields Road | B1 | | |
| Flaxfield Road | A3-B2 | | |
| Frances Road | A2 | | |
| Frescade Crescent | A1 | | |
| Goat Lane | C3 | | |
| Hackwood Road | C1-C2 | | |
| Hamelyn Road | A2 | | |
| Hawkfield Lane | A1 | | |
| Jubilee Road | B1 | | |
| London Road | C2 | | |
| London Street | B2 | | |
| Longcroft Close | A2 | | |
| Mortimer Lane | A3 | | |
| New Road | B2-C2-C3 | | |

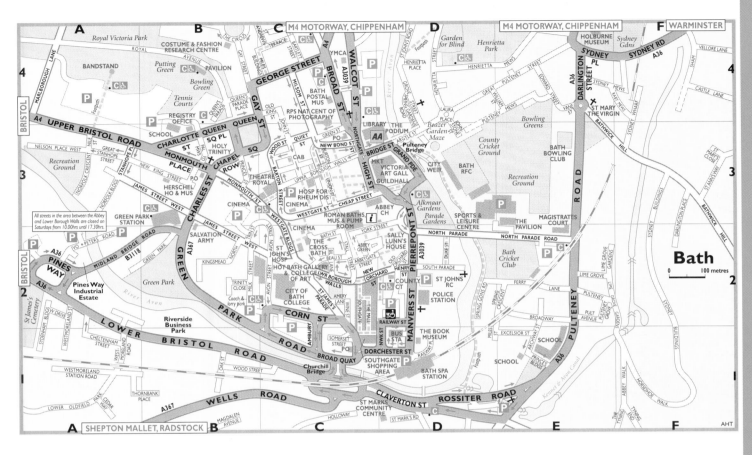

# Bath

Bath is found on atlas page **22**,
grid reference **7464**

**AA shop**
13 Northgate Street, Bath BA1 5AS          D3

| | | | | | | | |
|---|---|---|---|---|---|---|---|
| Abbey Walk | F1 | Green Street | C3 | Northgate Street | C3 | Sydenham Buildings | A1-A2 |
| Abbeygate Street | C2 | Grove Street | D3-D4 | Oak Street | B1 | Sydney Buildings | F1-F2-F3 |
| Ambury | C1-C2 | Henrietta Mews | D4-E4 | Old King Street | C4 | Sydney Mews | E4-F4 |
| Amery Lane | C2 | Henrietta Street | D4 | Old Orchard Street | D2 | Sydney Place | E4-F4 |
| Archway Street | E1-E2 | Henry Street | D2 | Palace Mews Yard | B3 | Sydney Road | F4 |
| Argyle Street | D3 | High Street | C3 | Pierrepont Street | D2-D3 | Sydney Wharf | F3-F4 |
| Avon Street | C2-C3 | Holloway | C1 | Pines Way | A2 | The Circus | B4 |
| Bartlett Street | C4 | Horseshoe Walk | F1 | Prince's Buildings | E1 | The Mall | C1-C2 |
| Barton Street | C3 | Ivo Peters Road | A2 | Princes Street | B3 | The Tyning | F1 |
| Bath Street | C2 | James Street West | A3-B3-B2-C2 | Pulteney Avenue | E2 | Thornbank Place | A1-B1 |
| Bathwick Hill | E4-E3-F3-F2 | John Street | C3-C4 | Pulteney Gardens | E2-F1-F2 | Trinity Street | B2 |
| Beau Street | C2 | Johnstone Street | D3 | Pulteney Mews | D3-D4-E4 | Tyning End | F1 |
| Bilbury Lane | C2 | Kingsmead North | B2 | Pulteney Road | E1-E2-E3-E4 | Union Street | C3 |
| Bridge Street | C3-D3 | Laura Place | D3-D4 | Pultney Grove | E2 | Upper Borough Walls | C3 |
| Broad Quay | C1 | Lime Grove | E2-F2 | Queen Square | B3-B4-C3-C4 | Upper Bristol Road | A4-A3-B3 |
| Broad Street | C3-C4 | Lime Grove Gardens | F2-E2 | Queen Square Place | B3 | Vane Street | E4 |
| Broadway | E2 | Lower Borough Walls | C2 | Queen's Parade | B4 | Vellore Lane | F4 |
| Burton Street | C3 | Lower Bristol Road | A2-A1-B1-C1 | Queen's Parade Place | B4 | Walcot Street | C3-C4 |
| Cedar Way | A1 | Lower Oldfield Park | A1 | Quiet Street | C3 | Wells Road | B1-C1 |
| Chapel Row | B3 | Magdalen Avenue | B1 | Raby Mews | F4 | Westgate Buildings | C2-C3 |
| Charles Street | B2-B3 | Manvers Street | D1-D2 | Railway Place | D1 | Westgate Street | C3 |
| Charlotte Street | B3 | Marlborough Lane | A4 | Railway Street | D2 | Westmoreland Drive | A2 |
| Cheap Street | C3-D2 | Midland Bridge Road | A2-B2 | Rossiter Road | D1-E1 | Westmoreland Road | A1 |
| Cheltenham Street | A1 | Mile's Buildings | C4 | Royal Avenue | A4-B4 | Westmoreland Station Road | A1 |
| Claverton Street | C1-D1 | Miles Street | E1 | St Andrew's Terrace | C4 | Westmoreland Street | A1-A2 |
| Corn Street | C2 | Milk Street | B2 | St Ann's Way | F3 | William Street | D4-E4 |
| Darlington Place | F2-F3 | Milsom Street | C4-C3 | St James's Parade | C1-C2 | Wine Street | C2 |
| Darlington Street | E4 | Monmouth Place | B3 | St John's Road | D4 | Wood Street | B1-C1 |
| Dorchester Street | C1-D1 | Monmouth Street | B3-C2 | St Mark's Road | D1 | Wood Street | C3 |
| Duke Street | D2 | Nelson Place West | A3 | St Mary's Close | F3 | York Street | C2-D2 |
| Edward Street | E4 | New Bond Street | C3 | Sham Castle Lane | F4 | | |
| Excelsior Street | E2 | New King Street | A3-B3 | Somerset Street | C1 | | |
| Ferry Lane | E2 | New Orchard Street | C2-D2 | South Parade | D2 | | |
| Gay Street | B4-C4-C3 | Newark Street | D1 | Southgate | C1-C2 | | |
| George Street | B4-C4 | Nile Street | A3 | Spring Crescent | E2 | | |
| Great Pulteney Street | D4-E4 | Norfolk Buildings | A3 | Spring Gardens Road | D2 | | |
| Great Stanhope Street | A3 | Norfolk Crescent | A3 | Spring Gardens Road | D3-D4 | | |
| Green Park | A2-B2 | North Parade | D2 | Stall Street | C2 | | |
| Green Park Road | B2-B1-C1 | North Parade Road | E2 | Stanhope Place | A3 | | |

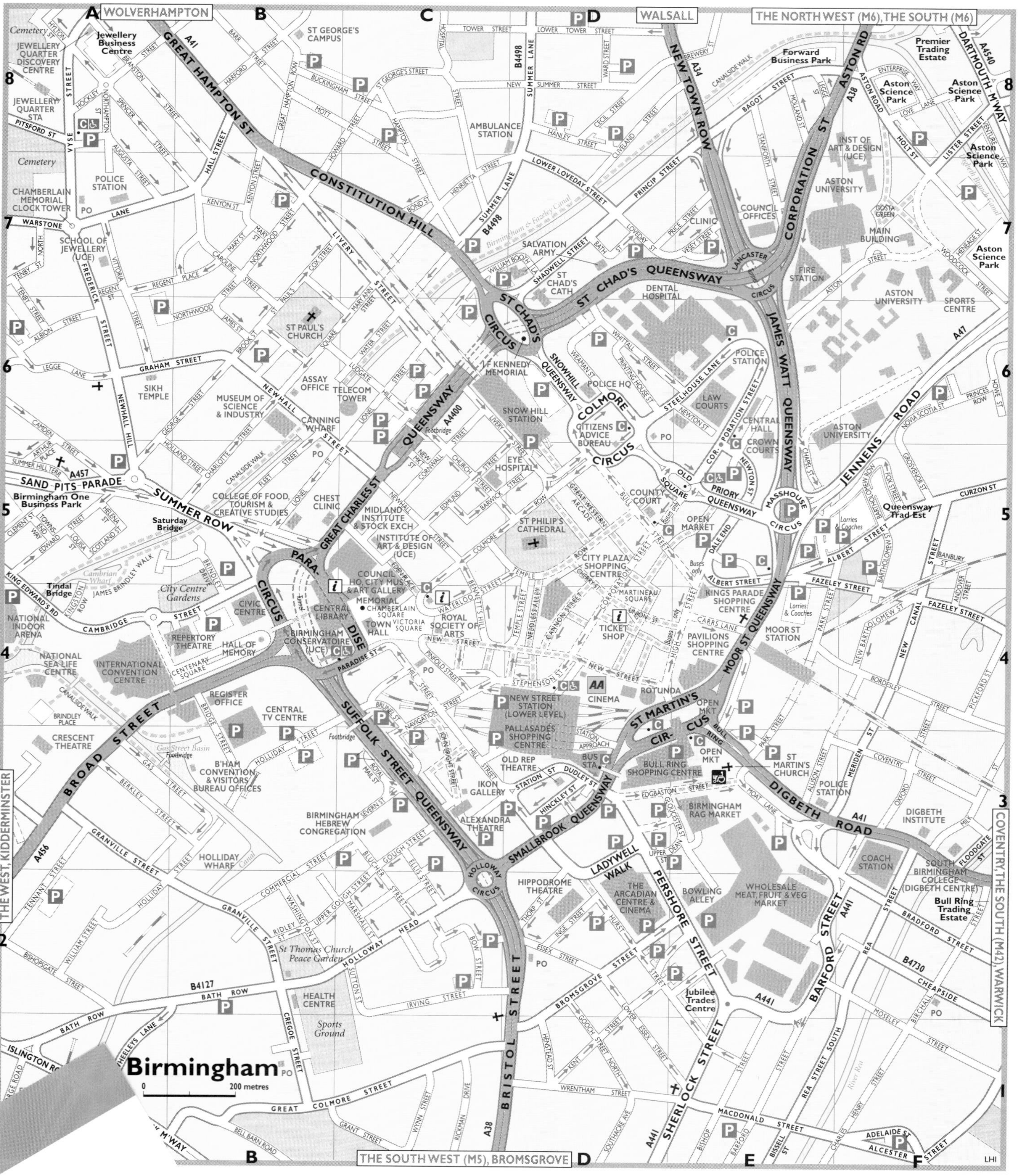

164

Birmingham

A WOLVERHAMPTON B C P D WALSALL THE NORTH WEST (M6), THE SOUTH (M6)

**Labels (left to right, top to bottom):**

Cemetery
JEWELLERY QUARTER DISCOVERY CENTRE
Jewellery Business Centre
ST GEORGE'S CAMPUS
TOWER STREET
LOWER TOWER STREET
BREWERY
Forward Business Park
Premier Trading Estate
DARTMOUTH M WAY
ASTON RD
A41
GREAT HAMPTON ST
B4498
NEW TOWN ROW
A34
A38
ASTON ROAD
Aston Science Park
A5440
CANALSIDE WALK
JEWELLERY QUARTER STA
PITSFORD ST
CONSTITUTION HILL
SUMMER LANE
AMBULANCE STATION
LOWER LOVEDAY STREET
PRINCIP STREET
BAGOT STREET
INST OF ART & DESIGN (UCE)
Aston University
Aston Science Park
Cemetery
CHAMBERLAIN MEMORIAL CLOCK TOWER
POLICE STATION
PO
WARSTONE
SCHOOL OF JEWELLERY (UCE)
SALVATION ARMY
SHADWELL STREET
ST CHAD'S CATH
ST CHAD'S QUEENSWAY
COUNCIL OFFICES
CLINIC
PRICE STREET
CORPORATION ST
FIRE STATION
COSTA GREEN
MAIN BUILDING
Aston Science Park
ST PAUL'S CHURCH
ST CHAD'S CIRCUS
SNOWHILL QUEENSWAY
DENTAL HOSPITAL
POLICE HQ
LAW COURTS
COLMORE CIRCUS
JAMES WATT QUEENSWAY
CROWN COURTS
CENTRAL HALL
Aston University
SPORTS CENTRE
A47
SIKH TEMPLE
MUSEUM OF SCIENCE & INDUSTRY
ASSAY OFFICE
TELECOM TOWER
JF KENNEDY MEMORIAL
SNOW HILL STATION
CITIZENS ADVICE BUREAU
OLD SQUARE
PRIORY QUEENSWAY
JENNENS ROAD
PRINCES ROW
HOCKLEY
CANNING WHARF
EYE HOSPITAL
COUNTY COURT
OPEN MARKET
MASSHOUSE CIRCUS
Queensway Trad Est
CURZON ST
SAND PITS PARADE
A457
SUMMER ROW
COLLEGE OF FOOD, TOURISM & CREATIVE STUDIES
CHEST CLINIC
MIDLAND INSTITUTE & STOCK EXCH
INSTITUTE OF ART & DESIGN (UCE)
ST PHILIP'S CATHEDRAL
CITY PLAZA SHOPPING CENTRE
DALE END
MARTINEAU SQUARE
KINGS PARADE SHOPPING CENTRE
FAZELEY STREET
Birmingham One Business Park
Saturday Bridge
GREAT CHARLES ST QUEENSWAY
PARADISE CIRCUS
COUNCIL HQ, CITY MUSEUM & ART GALLERY
Central Library
CHAMBERLAIN SQUARE
TOWN HALL
ROYAL SOCIETY OF ARTS
WATERLOO ST
TICKET SHOP
PAVILIONS SHOPPING CENTRE
MOOR STREET
MOOR ST QUEENSWAY
Tindal Bridge
Cambrian Wharf
James Brindley Walk
CIVIC CENTRE
REPERTORY THEATRE
HALL OF MEMORY
Birmingham Conservatoire (UCE)
VICTORIA SQUARE
NEW STREET
NEW STREET STATION (LOWER LEVEL)
PALLASADES SHOPPING CENTRE
CINEMA
ROTUNDA
ST MARTIN'S CIRCUS
OPEN MKT
ST MARTIN'S CHURCH
POLICE STATION
DIGBETH INSTITUTE
National Indoor Arena
CAMBRIDGE STREET
INTERNATIONAL CONVENTION CENTRE
REGISTER OFFICE
CENTRAL TV CENTRE
OLD REP THEATRE
BUS STA
BULL RING SHOPPING CENTRE
DIGBETH ROAD
A41
SOUTH BIRMINGHAM COLLEGE (DIGBETH CENTRE)
National Sea Life Centre
BROAD STREET
CRESCENT THEATRE
Gas Street Basin
Footbridge
B'HAM CONVENTION & VISITORS BUREAU OFFICES
IKON GALLERY
ALEXANDRA THEATRE
SUFFOLK STREET QUEENSWAY
SMALLBROOK QUEENSWAY
PERSHORE STREET
Birmingham Rag Market
COACH STATION
Bull Ring Trading Estate
A456
HOLLIDAY WHARF
BIRMINGHAM HEBREW CONGREGATION
HOLLOWAY CIRCUS
HIPPODROME THEATRE
THE ARCADIAN CENTRE & CINEMA
LADYWELL WALK
WHOLESALE MEAT, FRUIT & VEG MARKET
BARFORD STREET
A441
B4730
GRANVILLE STREET
HOLLOWAY HEAD
BRISTOL STREET
BOWLING ALLEY
CHEAPSIDE
B4127
BATH ROW
ST THOMAS CHURCH PEACE GARDEN
HEALTH CENTRE
Sports Ground
Jubilee Trades Centre
A441
SHERLOCK STREET
MACDONALD STREET
River Rea
A38
BIRMINGHAM
0 — 200 metres
A441
M WAY
BELL BARN ROAD
GREAT COLMORE STREET
ADELAIDE ST
ALCESTER STREET

B THE SOUTH WEST (M5), BROMSGROVE D E F
THE WEST, KIDDERMINSTER
COVENTRY, THE SOUTH (M42), WARWICK

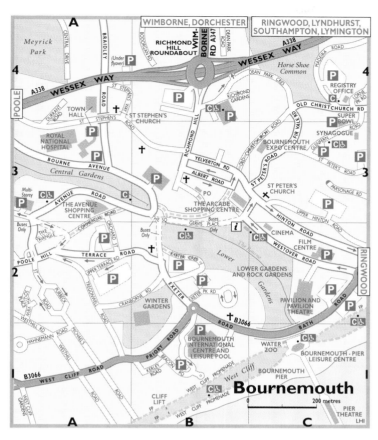

# Bournemouth

Bournemouth is found on atlas page 12, grid reference **0809**

| | |
|---|---|
| Albert Road | B3 |
| Avenue Road | A3-B3 |
| Bath Road | C1-C2 |
| Beacon Road | B1 |
| Bodorgan Road | B4 |
| Bourne Avenue | A3-B3 |
| Braidley Road | A3-A4 |
| Central Drive | A4 |
| Commercial Road | A2-A3 |
| Cranborne Road | A2-B2 |
| Dean Park Crescent | B4-C4 |
| Dean Park Road | B4 |
| Durrant Road | A4 |
| Exeter Crescent | B2 |
| Exeter Park Road | B2 |
| Exeter Road | B1-B2 |
| Fir Vale Road | C3-C4 |
| Gervis Place | B2-B3 |
| Glenfern Road | C3 |
| Hahnemann Road | A1 |
| Hinton Road | C2-C3 |
| Kerley Road | B1 |
| Lorne Park Road | C4 |
| Madeira Road | C4 |
| Old Christchurch Road | B3-C3-C4 |
| Orchard Street | A2-A3 |
| Parsonage Road | C3 |
| Poole Hill | A2 |
| Priory Road | B1-B2 |
| Purbeck Road | A2 |
| Richmond Gardens | B4 |
| Richmond Hill | B3-B4 |
| St Michael's Road | A2-A1-B1 |
| St Peter's Road | C3 |
| St Stephen's Road | A3-A4-B3 |
| St Stephen's Way | A4 |
| South View Place | A2 |
| Terrace Road | A2-B2 |
| The Square | B3 |
| The Triangle | A2 |
| Tregonwell Road | A1-A2 |
| Upper Hinton Road | C2-C3 |
| Upper Terrace Road | A2 |
| Wessex Way | A4-B4-C4 |
| West Cliff Gardens | A1 |
| West Cliff Road | A1 |
| Westhill Road | A1-A2 |
| Westover Road | C2 |
| Wimborne Road | B4 |
| Yelverton Road | B3 |

165

# Birmingham

Birmingham is found on atlas page **61**, grid reference **0786**

**AA shop**
134 New Street, Birmingham B2 4NP     D4

| | | | |
|---|---|---|---|
| Adelaide Street | F1 | Brook Street | B6 |
| Albert Street | E5-F5 | Brunel Street | C4 |
| Albion Street | A6 | Buckingham Street | B8-C8 |
| Alcester Street | F1 | Bull Ring | E3-E4 |
| Allison Street | E3-F4 | Bull Street | D5-E5 |
| Andover Street | F4-F5 | Cambridge Street | A4-B4 |
| Arthur Place | A5 | Camden Street | A6-A5 |
| Aston Road | F8 | Canalside Walk | B3-A3-A4-A5-B5 |
| Aston Street | E6-E7 | Cannon Street | D4 |
| Augusta Street | A7-A8 | Caroline Street | B7-B6 |
| Bagot Street | E8 | Carrs Lane | E4 |
| Banbury Street | F5 | Cecil Street | D8 |
| Barford Street | E1-E2-F2 | Centenary Square | B4 |
| Barr Street | B8 | Chamberlain Square | C4 |
| Bartholomew Row | F5 | Chapel Street | E5 |
| Bartholomew Street | F4-F5 | Charles Henry Street | E1-F1 |
| Barwick Street | C5-D5 | Charlotte Street | B5-B6 |
| Bath Row | A1-A2-B2 | Cheapside | F2 |
| Bath Street | D7 | Cherry Street | D4-D5 |
| Bell Barn Road | B1 | Church Street | C5-D5 |
| Bennett's Hill | C4-C5 | Clement Street | A5 |
| Berkley Street | A3-B3 | Cliveland Street | D7-D8-E8 |
| Birchall Street | F1-F2 | Colmore Circus | D5-D6 |
| Bishop Street | E1 | Colmore Row | C5-D5 |
| Bishopsgate Street | A2 | Commercial Street | B2-B3-C3 |
| Bissell Street | E1 | Constitution Hill | B7-C7 |
| Blucher Street | C3-C2 | Cornwall Street | C5-C6 |
| Bond Street | C7 | Corporation Street | D4-E5-E8 |
| Bordesley Street | E4-F4 | Coventry Street | F3 |
| Bow Street | C2 | Cox Street | B7 |
| Bradford Street | F2 | Cregoe Street | B1-B2 |
| Branston Street | A8-B8 | Curzon Street | F5 |
| Brewery Street | E8 | Dale End | E5 |
| Bridge Street | B3-B4 | Dartmouth Middleway | F8 |
| Brindley Drive | B4-B5 | Digbeth Road | E3-F3 |
| Brindley Place | A4 | Dudley Street | D3 |
| Bristol Street | D1-D2-C2 | Eden Place | C5-C4 |
| Broad Street | A3-A4-B4 | Edgbaston Street | D3-E3 |
| Bromsgrove Street | D1-D2-E2 | Edmund Street | C5 |

| | | | |
|---|---|---|---|
| Edward Street | A5 | Irving Street | C2 |
| Ellis Street | C2-C3 | Islington Row Middleway | A1 |
| Enterprise Way | F8 | James Brindley Walk | A4-A5-B5 |
| Essex Street | D2 | James Street | B6 |
| Fazeley Street | E5-F4 | James Watt Queensway | E5-E6 |
| Fleet Street | B5-B6 | Jennens Road | E5-F5-F6 |
| Floodgate Street | F3 | John Bright Street | C3 |
| Fox Street | F5 | Kent Street | D1-D2 |
| Frederick Street | A7-A6 | Kenyon Street | B7 |
| Gas Street | A3-B3 | King Edwards Road | A5-A4 |
| George Road | A1 | Kingston Row | A4 |
| George Street | A5-A6-B6 | Ladywell Walk | D2-D3 |
| Gloucester Street | E3 | Lancaster Circus | E7 |
| Gooch Street North | D1-D2 | Lee Bank Middleway | A1-B1 |
| Gosta Green | F7 | Legge Lane | A6 |
| Gough Street | C3 | Legge Street | E8 |
| Graham Street | A6-B6 | Lionel Street | B5-C6-C7 |
| Grant Street | B1-C1 | Lister Street | F7-F8 |
| Granville Street | A3-B2 | Livery Street | B7-C7-C6-D5 |
| Great Charles Street | B5-C5 | Louisa Street | A5 |
| Queensway | | Love Lane | F8 |
| Great Colmore Street | B1-C1 | Loveday Street | D7 |
| Great Hampton Row | B8 | Lower Essex Street | D2-D1-E1 |
| Great Hampton Street | A8-B8 | Lower Loveday Street | D7 |
| Great Western Arcade | D5 | Lower Tower Street | D8 |
| Grosvenor Street | F5 | Ludgate Hill | B6-C6 |
| Hall Street | B7-B8 | Macdonald Street | E1 |
| Hampton Street | C7-C8 | Marshall Street | C2 |
| Hanley Street | D8 | Martineau Square | C4 |
| Harford Street | B8 | Mary Ann Street | C6-C7 |
| Helena Street | A5 | Mary Street | B7 |
| Heneage Street | F7 | Masshouse Circus | E5 |
| Henrietta Street | C7 | Meriden Street | F3 |
| Henstead Street | D1 | Milk Street | F2 |
| High Street | D4-E4 | Moat Lane | E3 |
| Hill Street | C3-C4-D3 | Molland Street | E8 |
| Hinckley Street | D3 | Moor Street Queensway | E4-E5 |
| Hockley Street | A8-B8 | Moseley Street | F1-F2 |
| Holland Street | A5-B5 | Mott Street | B8-C8-C7 |
| Holliday Street | A2-B3-C4 | Navigation Street | C3-C4 |
| Holloway Circus | C2-C3 | Needless Alley | D4 |
| Holloway Head | B2-C2 | New Bartholomew Street | F4 |
| Holt Street | F7-F8 | New Canal Street | F4-F5 |
| Hospital Street | C7-C8 | New Market Street | C5 |
| Howard Street | B7-B8-C8 | New Street | C4-D4 |
| Howe Street | F6 | New Summer Street | C8-D8 |
| Hurst Street | D2-E2-E1 | New Town Row | E7-E8 |
| Hylton Street | A8 | Newhall Hill | A5-A6 |
| Inge Street | D2 | Newhall Street | B6-C5 |

| | | | |
|---|---|---|---|
| Newton Street | E5-E6 | Temple Row | C5-D5 |
| Northampton Street | A8-A7 | Temple Street | D4-D5 |
| Northwood Street | B6-B7 | Tenby Street | A6-A7 |
| Nova Scotia Street | F6 | Tenby Street North | A7 |
| Old Square | D5-E5 | Tennant Street | A2-A3 |
| Oxford Street | F3-F4 | Thorp Street | D2 |
| Paradise Circus | B5-B4 | Tower Street | C8-D8 |
| Paradise Street | B4-C4 | Townsend Way | A5 |
| Park Street | E3-E4-E5 | Union Street | D4-E4 |
| Pershore Street | D3-D2-E2 | Upper Dean Street | D3-E3 |
| Pickford Street | F4 | Upper Gough Street | B2-C2 |
| Pinfold Street | C4 | Vesey Street | E7 |
| Pitsford Street | A8 | Victoria Square | C4 |
| Price Street | D7-E7 | Vittoria Street | A6-A7 |
| Princes Row | F6 | Vyse Street | A7-A8 |
| Princip Street | D7-E8 | Ward Street | D8 |
| Printing House Street | D6 | Warstone Lane | A7-B7 |
| Priory Queensway | E5 | Washington Street | B2 |
| Rea Street | F2-F3 | Water Street | C6 |
| Rea Street South | E1-F1-F2 | Waterloo Street | C4-D5 |
| Regent Place | A7-B7 | Weaman Street | D6 |
| Regent Street | A7 | Wheeleys Lane | A1-B2 |
| Rickman Drive | C1 | Wheeleys Road | A1 |
| Ridley Street | B2 | Whittall Street | D6-E6 |
| Royal Mail Street | C3 | William Booth Lane | C7-D7 |
| St Chad's Circus | C6-D6-D7 | William Street | A2 |
| St Chad's Queensway | D6-D7-E7 | Woodcock Street | F7 |
| St George's Street | C8 | Wrentham Street | D1-E1 |
| St Martin's Circus | D3-D4-E4-E3 | Wynn Street | C1 |
| St Paul's Square | B6-C6-B7 | |
| Sand Pits Parade | A5 | |
| Scotland Street | A5 | |
| Severn Street | C3 | |
| Shadwell Street | D7 | |
| Sherlock Street | D1-E1-E2 | |
| Smallbrook Queensway | D3 | |
| Snowhill Queensway | D6 | |
| Southacre Avenue | D1 | |
| Spencer Street | B7-A7-A8 | |
| Staniforth Street | E8-E7 | |
| Station Approach | D3 | |
| Station Street | D3 | |
| Steelhouse Lane | D6-E6 | |
| Stephenson Street | D4 | |
| Suffolk Street Queensway | B4-C3 | |
| Summer Hill Terrace | A5 | |
| Summer Lane | C7-D7-D8 | |
| Summer Row | A5-B5 | |
| Sutton Street | C2 | |

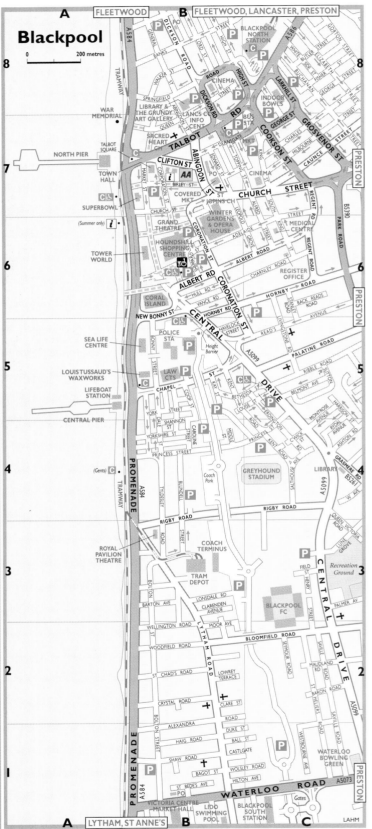

# Blackpool

Blackpool is found on atlas page **80**,
grid reference **3036**

## AA shop
13 Clifton Street, Blackpool FY1 1JD                    B7

| | | | |
|---|---|---|---|
| Abingdon Street | B7-B8 | St Chad's Road | B2 |
| Adelaide Street | B6-C7 | St Heliers Road | C1-C2 |
| Albert Road | B6-C6 | Salthouse Avenue | C4 |
| Alexandra Road | B1-B2 | Saville Road | C1-C2 |
| Alfred Street | C6-C7 | Seymour Road | C2 |
| Ashton Road | C4 | Shannon Street | B4-B5 |
| Back Reads Road | C6 | Shaw Road | B1 |
| Bagot Street | B1 | Sheppard Street | B6 |
| Ball Street | B1-C1 | South King Street | C6-C7 |
| Banks Street | B8 | Springfield Road | B8 |
| Baron Road | C2 | Stanley Road | C5-C6 |
| Barton Avenue | B3 | Sutton Place | C5 |
| Belmont Avenue | C5 | Talbot Road | B7-C8 |
| Bethesda Street | B5-C5 | Topping Street | B7-C7 |
| Birley Street | B7 | Tyldesley Road | B3-B4 |
| Bloomfield Road | B2-C3 | Vance Road | B6 |
| Blundell Street | B3-B4 | Walker Street | B8 |
| Bolton Street | B1-B3 | Waterloo Road | B1-C1 |
| Bonny Street | B5 | Wellington Road | B2-B3 |
| Buchanan Street | C7-C8 | Westbourne Avenue | C1 |
| Butler Street | C8 | Whiteside Street | C8 |
| Caroline Street | B4 | Wolsey Road | B1-C1 |
| Castlegate | B1-C1 | Woodfield Road | B2 |
| Caunce Street | C7 | York Street | B5 |
| Central Drive | B6-C1 | Yorkshire Street | B4 |
| Chadwick Street | C4 | | |
| Chapel Street | B5 | | |
| Charles Street | C7-C8 | | |
| Charnley Road | B6-C6 | | |
| Church Street | B7-C8 | | |
| Clarendon Road | B2 | | |
| Clare Street | B2 | | |
| Clifton Street | B7 | | |
| Cocker Street | B8 | | |
| Cookson Street | C7-C8 | | |
| Coop Street | B5 | | |
| Coronation Street | B7-C5 | | |
| Corporation Street | B7 | | |
| Crystal Road | B2 | | |
| Dale Street | B4-B5 | | |
| Deansgate | B7-C8 | | |
| Dickson Road | B7-B8 | | |
| Duke Street | B1 | | |
| Edward Street | B7 | | |
| Elizabeth Street | C8 | | |
| Erdington Road | C4-C5 | | |
| Field Street | C3 | | |
| Fisher Street | C8 | | |
| General Street | B8 | | |
| George Street | C7-C8 | | |
| Gorton Street | C8 | | |
| Grasmere Road | C4 | | |
| Haig Road | B1 | | |
| Harrison Street | C4-C5 | | |
| Havelock Street | B5 | | |
| Henry Street | C2-C3 | | |
| High Street | B8-C8 | | |
| Hilton Avenue | B1-C1 | | |
| Hornby Road | B6-C6 | | |
| Hull Street | B6 | | |
| Kay Street | B5 | | |
| Kent Road | B5-C4 | | |
| Keswick Road | C4 | | |
| King Street | C7 | | |
| Larkhill Street | C8 | | |
| Leamington Road | C7 | | |
| Leopold Grove | B7-C6 | | |
| Livingstone Road | C5-C6 | | |
| Lonsdale Road | B3 | | |
| Lord Street | B8 | | |
| Louise Street | B5-C5 | | |
| Lowrey Terrace | B2 | | |
| Lune Grove | C3 | | |
| Lytham Road | B1-B3 | | |
| Market Street | B7 | | |
| Maudland Road | C2 | | |
| Middle Street | B4 | | |
| Milbourne Street | C7-C8 | | |
| Montrose Avenue | C4-C5 | | |
| Moor Avenue | B2 | | |
| New Bonny Street | B6 | | |
| North Promenade | B6-B8 | | |
| Palatine Road | C5 | | |
| Palmer Avenue | C3 | | |
| Park Road | C5-C7 | | |
| Peter Street | C7 | | |
| Princess Street | B4-C5 | | |
| Promenade | A1-B6 | | |
| Queen Street | B7-B8 | | |
| Queen Victoria Road | C4 | | |
| Read's Avenue | B5-C6 | | |
| Regent Road | C6-C7 | | |
| Ribble Road | C5 | | |
| Rigby Road | B3-C4 | | |
| Rydal Avenue | C4-C5 | | |
| St Bede's Avenue | B1 | | |

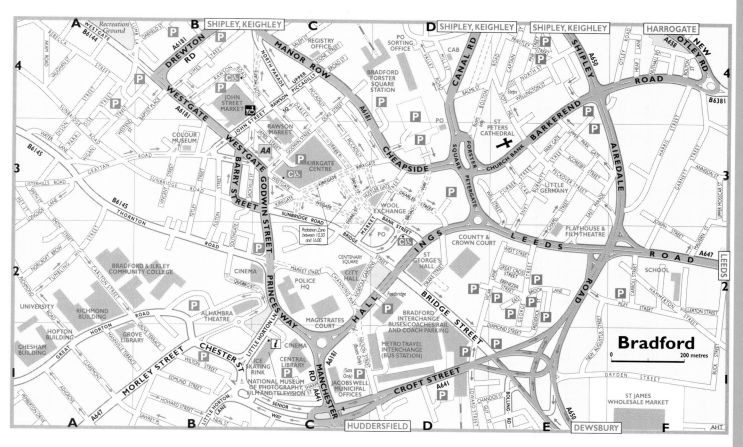

# Bradford

Bradford is found on atlas page **82**,
grid reference 163**2**

**AA shop**
101 Godwin Street, Bradford BD1 3PP    C3

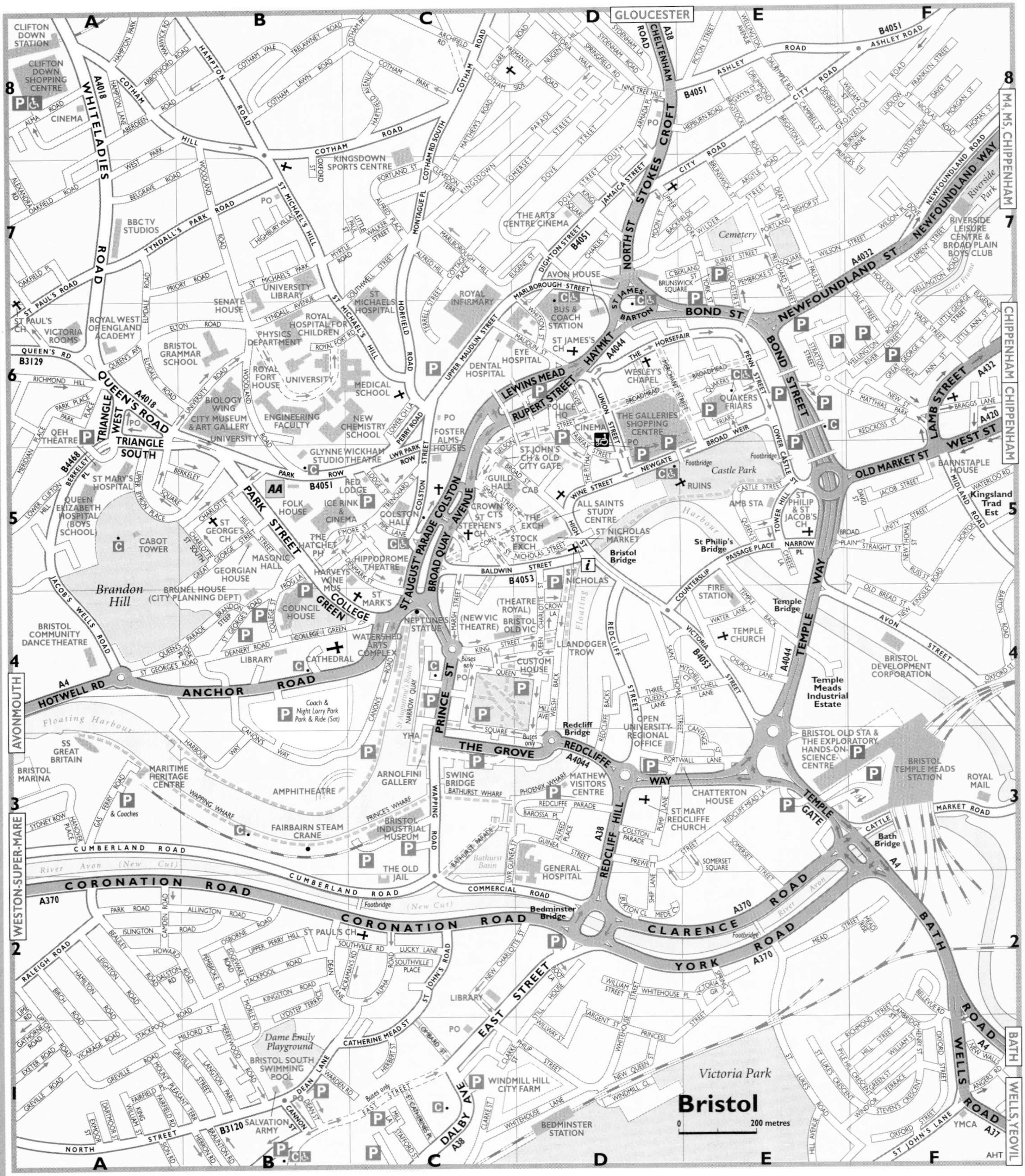

GLOUCESTER

**Bristol**

0          200 metres

CLIFTON DOWN STATION
CLIFTON DOWN SHOPPING CENTRE
CINEMA
WHITELADIES ROAD
A4018
BBC TV STUDIOS
KINGSDOWN SPORTS CENTRE
THE ARTS CENTRE CINEMA
Cemetery
RIVERSIDE LEISURE CENTRE & BROAD PLAIN BOYS CLUB
Riverside Park
River Frome
M4, M5, CHIPPENHAM
NEWFOUNDLAND WAY
A4032
NEWFOUNDLAND STREET
St PAUL'S CH
VICTORIA ROOMS
B3129
QUEEN'S RD
ROYAL WEST OF ENGLAND ACADEMY
BRISTOL GRAMMAR SCHOOL
SENATE HOUSE
UNIVERSITY LIBRARY
St MICHAELS HOSPITAL
ROYAL HOSPITAL FOR CHILDREN
ROYAL INFIRMARY
AVON HOUSE
MARLBOROUGH STREET
BUS & COACH STATION
St JAMES BARTON
BOND ST
BOND STREET
CHIPPENHAM
A432
A420
WEST ST
LAMB STREET
BRAGG'S LANE
Triangle West
A4018
QUEEN'S ROAD
TRIANGLE SOUTH
QEH THEATRE
St MARY'S HOSPITAL
QUEEN ELIZABETH HOSPITAL (BOYS) SCHOOL
ROYAL FORT HOUSE
UNIVERSITY
BIOLOGY WING
CITY MUSEUM & ART GALLERY
ENGINEERING FACULTY
NEW CHEMISTRY SCHOOL
GLYNNE WICKHAM STUDIO THEATRE
PARK ROW
LWR PARK ROW
PERRY ROAD
FOSTER ALMSHOUSES
PO
DENTAL HOSPITAL
EYE HOSPITAL
St JAMES CH
LEWINS MEAD
RUPERT STREET
POLICE HQ
WESLEY'S CHAPEL
QUAKERS FRIARS
THE GALLERIES SHOPPING CENTRE
HAYMKT
HORSEFAIR
St PHILIP & St JACOB'S CH
OLD MARKET ST
BARNSTAPLE HOUSE
KINGSLAND TRAD EST
BRISTOL COMMUNITY DANCE THEATRE
B4468
BERKELEY PL
AA
B4051
FOLK HOUSE
RED LODGE
ICE RINK & CINEMA
St GEORGE'S CH
MASONIC HALL
GEORGIAN HOUSE
HARVEY'S WINE MUS
HIPPODROME THEATRE
COLSTON HALL
GOLSTON AVENUE
BROAD QUAY
St AUGUST PARADE
COLSTON
St STEPHEN'S CH
THE EXCH
STOCK EXCH
NICHOLAS STREET
BALDWIN ST
B4053
CROWN CTS
GUILD HALL
CAB
ST JOHN'S CH & OLD CITY GATE
NEWGATE
WINE STREET
UNION STREET
CINEMA
BROAD WEIR
LOWER CASTLE ST
Footbridge
CASTLE STREET
RUINS
Castle Park
AMB STA
TOWER HILL
NARROW PLAIN
St NICHOLAS MARKET
All SAINTS STUDY CENTRE
St NICHOLAS
Bristol Bridge
St Philip's Bridge
FIRE STATION
COUNTERSLIP
Temple Bridge
TEMPLE STREET
TEMPLE CHURCH
Temple Meads Industrial Estate
BRISTOL DEVELOPMENT CORPORATION
CABOT TOWER
Brandon Hill
BRUNEL HOUSE (CITY PLANNING DEPT)
COUNCIL HOUSE
COLLEGE GREEN
St MARK'S CH
CATHEDRAL
WATERSHED ARTS COMPLEX
NEPTUNE'S STATUE
PRINCE ST
(NEW VIC THEATRE)
BRISTOL OLD VIC
(THEATRE ROYAL)
LLANDOGER TROW
CUSTOM HOUSE
QUEEN SQUARE
REDCLIFF
THREE QUEEN'S LANE
OPEN UNIVERSITY REGIONAL OFFICE
HOTWELL RD
A4
ANCHOR ROAD
Coach & Night Lorry Park
Park & Ride (Sat)
Floating Harbour
SS GREAT BRITAIN
BRISTOL MARINA
MARITIME HERITAGE CENTRE
WAPPING WHARF
AMPHITHEATRE
ARNOLFINI GALLERY
SWING BRIDGE
BATHURST WHARF
YHA
THE GROVE
REDCLIFF BRIDGE
A4044
WAY
MATHEW VISITORS CENTRE
St MARY REDCLIFFE CHURCH
CHATTERTON HOUSE
REDCLIFF HILL
TEMPLE GATE
BRISTOL OLD STA & THE EXPLORATORY, HANDS-ON-SCIENCE CENTRE
BRISTOL TEMPLE MEADS STATION
ROYAL MAIL
& Coaches
PRINCES WHARF
BRISTOL INDUSTRIAL MUSEUM
FAIRBAIRN STEAM CRANE
THE OLD JAIL
Bathurst Basin
GENERAL HOSPITAL
A38
REDCLIFF PARADE
GUINEA STREET
SOMERSET SQUARE
Bath Bridge
A4
MARKET ROAD
CATTLE MARKET
River Avon (New Cut)
CUMBERLAND ROAD
COMMERCIAL ROAD
CORONATION ROAD
A370
WESTON-SUPER-MARE
Bedminster Bridge
CLARENCE ROAD
A370
YORK ROAD
A370
Footbridge
BATH ROAD
A4
WELLS ROAD
A37
BATH
WELLS, YEOVIL
RALEIGH ROAD
St PAUL'S CH
LUCKY LANE
SOUTHVILLE RD
LIBRARY
PO
EAST STREET
Dame Emily Playground
BRISTOL SOUTH SWIMMING POOL
CATHERINE MEAD ST
WINDMILL HILL CITY FARM
Victoria Park
BEDMINSTER STATION
B3120
SALVATION ARMY
DALBY AVE
A38
YMCA
St JOHN'S LANE
AHT

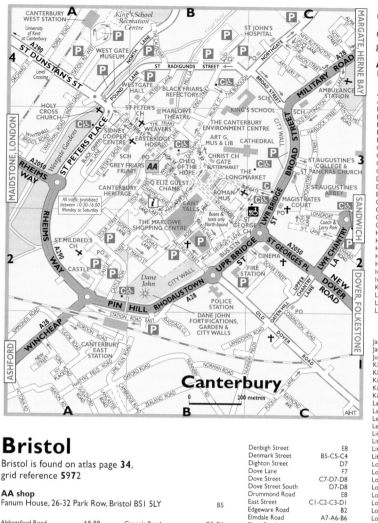

Canterbury

# Canterbury

Canterbury is found on atlas page **29**,
grid reference 1457

**AA shop**
13 Best Lane, Canterbury CT1 2JB                  B3

| | | | | | | |
|---|---|---|---|---|---|
| Alma Street | C4 | Linden Grove | A3-A4 | Rheims Way | A2-A3 |
| Artillery Street | C4 | Longport | C2 | Rhodaus Close | B1 |
| Beer Cart Lane | C2-B3 | Love Lane | C2 | Rhodaus Town | B2 |
| Best Lane | B3 | Lower Bridge Street | C2-C3 | Roper Road | A4 |
| Black Griffin Lane | A3 | Lower Chantry Lane | C2 | Rose Lane | B2-B3 |
| Broad Street | C3 | Martyrs Field Road | A1 | St Dunstan's Street | A4 |
| Burgate | B3-C3 | Mill Lane | B4 | St George's Lane | B2-C2 |
| Cambridge Road | A1-B1 | Military Road | C4 | St Georges Place | C2 |
| Cassington Road | C1-C2 | Monastery Street | C3 | St Georges Street | B2-B3 |
| Castle Row | A2 | New Dover Road | C2 | St John's Lane | B2 |
| Castle Street | A2-B2 | New Ruttington Lane | C4 | St Margaret's Street | B2-B3 |
| Dover Street | C2 | New Street | A1 | St Mary's Street | A2-B2 |
| Duck Lane | B4 | Norman Road | B1-C1 | St Peter's Grove | A3-B3 |
| Edward Road | C2 | North Holmes Road | C3-C4 | St Peters Lane | B3-B4 |
| Gordon Road | A1 | North Lane | A4-B4 | St Peters Place | A3 |
| Gravel Walk | B2 | Northgate | C4 | St Peters Street | A3-B3 |
| Guildford Road | A1 | Notley Street | C4 | St Radigunds Street | B4 |
| Guildhall Street | B3 | Nunnery Fields | B1-C1 | Simmonds Road | A1-A2 |
| Havelock Street | C3-C4 | Nunnery Road | B1 | Station Road East | A2-A1-B1 |
| Hawks Lane | B3 | Oaten Hill | C1-C2 | Station Road West | A4 |
| Heath Road | A1 | Old Dover Road | B2-C2-C1 | Stour Street | A2-B2 |
| High Street | B3 | Old Ruttington Lane | C3-C4 | Sun Street | B3 |
| Hospital Lane | A2-B2 | Orchard Street | A4 | The Borough | B4-C4 |
| Ivy Lane | C2 | Oxford Road | A1-B1 | The Causeway | B4 |
| Ivy Place | A1 | Palace Street | B3-B4 | The Friars | B3 |
| King Street | B3-B4 | Pin Hill | A2-B2 | Tudor Road | A1 |
| Lancaster Road | A1 | Pound Lane | A4-B4 | Union Place | C4 |
| Lansdown Road | B1-C1 | Puckle Lane | C1 | Union Street | C4 |
| Lime Kiln Road | A1-B1 | Raymond Avenue | C1 | Upper Bridge Street | B2-C2 |
| | | | | Upper Chantry Lane | C2 |
| | | | | Victoria Road | A1 |
| | | | | Watling Street | B2 |
| | | | | White Horse Lane | B3 |
| | | | | Whitehall Road | A3 |
| | | | | Whitehall Bridge Road | A3 |
| | | | | Wincheap | A1-A2 |
| | | | | York Road | A1 |
| | | | | Zealand Road | B1 |

169

# Bristol

Bristol is found on atlas page **34**,
grid reference 5972

**AA shop**
Fanum House, 26-32 Park Row, Bristol BS1 5LY       B5

| | | | | | | |
|---|---|---|---|---|---|
| Abbotsford Road | A8-B8 | Canon's Road | C3-C4 | Denbigh Street | E8 |
| Aberdeen Road | A8-B8 | Canon's Way | B3-B4 | Denmark Street | B5-C5-C4 |
| Acraman's Road | B2-C2 | Canynge Street | E3-E4 | Dighton Street | D7 |
| Alexandra Road | A7 | Castle Street | E5 | Dove Lane | F7 |
| Alfred Hill | C7 | Catherine Mead Street | B1-C1 | Dove Street | C7-D7-D8 |
| Alfred Place | C7 | Cattle Market Road | F3 | Dove Street South | D7-D8 |
| Alfred Road | D3 | Charles Street | D7 | Drummond Road | E8 |
| Allington Road | B1-B2 | Charlotte Street | B5 | East Street | C1-C2-C3-D1 |
| Alma Road | A8 | Charlotte Street South | B5 | Edgeware Road | B2 |
| Alpha Road | C2 | Cheese Lane | E5 | Elmdale Road | A7-A6-B6 |
| Anchor Road | A4-B4-C4 | Cheltenham Road | D8 | Elton Road | A6-B6 |
| Angers Road | F1 | Church Lane | E4 | Eugene Street | C7-D7 |
| Archfield Road | C8 | City Road | D7-E7-E8-F8 | Eugene Street | F6-F7 |
| Argyle Road | E7-E8 | Clare Road | C8-D8 | Exeter Road | A1 |
| Armada Place | D8 | Clarence Road | D2-E2-E3 | Exmoor Street | A1 |
| Ashley Road | E8-F8 | Clarke Street | D1 | Fairfax Street | D5-D6 |
| Avon Street | E4-F4 | Clement Street | F7 | Fairfield Place | A1 |
| Backfields | D7-E7 | Clevedon Terrace | C7 | Fairfield Road | A1 |
| Baldwin Street | C5-D5 | College Green | B4-C4-B5 | Franklyn Street | F8 |
| Barossa Place | D3 | College Street | B4 | Fremantle Road | C8-D8 |
| Barton Road | F4-F5 | Colston Avenue | C5 | Frog Lane | B5 |
| Bath Road | F1-F2 | Colston Parade | D3 | Frogmore Street | B5-C5 |
| Bathurst Parade | C3 | Colston Street | C5-C6 | Gas Ferry Road | A3 |
| Beauley Road | A2 | Commercial Road | C2-D2 | Gathorpe Road | A1 |
| Belgrave Road | A7-B7 | Corn Street | C5 | Gloucester Street | E7-E6 |
| Bellevue Road | F2 | Coronation Road | A2-B2-C2-D2 | Great Ann Street | F6 |
| Berkeley Place | A5 | Cotham Hill | A8-B8 | Great George Street | B5 |
| Berkeley Square | A5-B5 | Cotham Lawn Road | B8-C8 | Great George Street | F6 |
| Birch Road | A1-A2 | Cotham Park | C8 | Green Street | F1 |
| Bishop Street | E7 | Cotham Road | B8-C8 | Greville Road | A1 |
| Bond Street | D6-E6-E5 | Cotham Road South | C7-C8 | Greville Road | A1-B1 |
| Boot Lane | D2 | Cotham Side | D8 | Grosvenor Road | E8-F8 |
| Bragg's Lane | F6 | Cotham Vale | B8 | Guinea Street | D2-D3 |
| Brandon Steep | B4 | Cottage Place | C7 | Gwyn Street | E8 |
| Braunton Road | B1 | Countership | D4-E4-E5 | Halston Drive | F7-F8 |
| Brighton Street | E8 | Crow Lane | D4 | Hamilton Road | A1-A2 |
| Brigstocke Road | E7-E8 | Cumberland Road | A3-B3-B2-C2 | Hampton Lane | A8 |
| Broadmead | D6-E6 | Cumberland Street | D7-E7 | Hampton Park | A8 |
| Broad Plain | E5-F5 | Dalby Avenue | C1 | Hampton Road | B8 |
| Broad Quay | C4-C5 | Dale Street | F6-F7 | Hanover Place | A3 |
| Broad Street | C5-D5 | Dalston Road | E8 | Harbour Way | A3-B3 |
| Broad Weir | E5-E6 | Dalrymple Road | E8 | Hartfield Avenue | A8 |
| Brunswick Street | E8 | Dartmoor Street | A1 | Haymarket | D6 |
| Burnell Drive | E8-F8 | Davey Street | F8 | Hebron Road | B1 |
| Burton Close | D2 | David Street | F5 | Henry Street | F1 |
| Cambridge Street | F1 | Deanery Road | B4 | Hepburn Road | D8-E8 |
| Camden Road | A2 | Dean Lane | B2 | Herbert Street | C1 |
| Campbell Street | E8 | Dean Street | B1 | Highbury Villas | B7 |
| Cannon Street | B1 | Dean Street | E7 | High Street | D5 |
| | | | | Hill Avenue | E1 |
| | | | | Hill Street | B5 |
| | | | | Hill Street | F1 |
| | | | | Horfield Road | C6-C7 |
| | | | | Horton Street | F5 |
| | | | | Hotwell Road | A3-A4 |
| | | | | Houlton Street | F6-F7 |
| | | | | Howard Road | A2-B2 |
| | | | | Islington Road | A2-B2 |
| | | | | Jacob Street | F5 |

| | | | | | | |
|---|---|---|---|---|---|
| Jacob's Wells Road | A4-A5 | Oxford Street | F4 | Spring Street | E2 |
| Jamaica Street | D7 | Park Place | A6 | Stackpool Road | A1-B2 |
| Jubilee Street | F5 | Park Road | A2 | Stafford Street | C1 |
| Kingsdown Parade | C7-C8-D8 | Park Row | B5-C5 | Steven's Crescent | F1 |
| Kings Square | D7 | Park Street | B5 | Stillhouse Lane | D1-D2 |
| King Street | C4-D4 | Passage Place | E5 | Stokes Croft | D7-D8 |
| Kingston Road | B2 | Pembroke Road | B2 | Straight Street | F5 |
| King William Street | A1 | Pembroke Street | E7 | Stratton Street | E6 |
| Lamb Street | F5-F6 | Penn Street | E6 | Surrey Street | E7 |
| Langton Park | B1 | Perry Road | C6 | Sydenham Lane | D8 |
| Leighton Road | A1-A2 | Philip Street | C1-D1 | Sydenham Road | D8 |
| Lewins Mead | C6-D6 | Picton Street | E8 | Sydney Row | A3 |
| Lime Road | A2 | Pipe Lane | C5 | Temple Back | E4-E5 |
| Little Ann Street | F6 | Portland Square | E7 | Temple Gate | E3 |
| Little George Street | F6-F7 | Portland Street | C7 | Temple Way | E4-E5 |
| Little Paul Street | C7 | Portwall Lane | D3-E3 | Terrell Street | C6-C7 |
| Lodge Street | C5 | Prewett Street | D3-E3 | The Grove | C3-D3 |
| Lombard Street | C1 | Prince Street | C3-C4 | The Horsefair | D6-E6 |
| Lower Castle Street | E5-E6 | Princess Street | D1-E1-E2 | The Pithay | D5 |
| Lower Church Lane | C6 | Princes Street | E8-F7 | Thomas Street | F8 |
| Lower Clifton Hill | A5 | Priory Road | A7-B7 | Three Queens Lane | D4 |
| Lower Guinea Street | C2-C3 | Pritchard Street | E7-E6 | Tower Hill | E5 |
| Lower Maudlin Street | C6-D6 | Pump Lane | D3 | Trelawney Road | B8-C8 |
| Lower Park Row | C5 | Pyle Hill Crescent | E1-F1 | Trenchard Street | C5 |
| Lucky Lane | C2 | Quakers Friars | E6 | Triangle South | A6 |
| Ludlow Close | F8 | Queen Charlotte Street | D4-D5 | Triangle West | A6 |
| Lydstep Terrace | B2 | Queen's Avenue | A6 | Tyndall Avenue | B6-B7 |
| Marlborough Hill | C7 | Queen's Parade | A4-B4 | Tyndall's Park Road | A7-B7 |
| Marlborough Street | C6-D7 | Queen's Road | A6-B6-B5 | Union Street | D5-D6 |
| Marsh Street | C4-C5 | Queen Square | C3-C4-D4-D3 | Unity Street | F5 |
| Mead Rise | F2 | Queen Street | E5 | University Road | A6-B6 |
| Mead Street | E2-F2 | Raleigh Road | A2 | Upper Byron Place | A5 |
| Mede Close | D2 | Redcliff Backs | D3-D4 | Upper Maudlin Street | C6 |
| Merchant Street | D6-E6 | Redcliffe Parade | D3 | Upper Perry Hill | B2 |
| Meridian Place | A5-A6 | Redcliffe Way | D3-D4 | Upper York Street | D7-E7 |
| Merryvood Road | B1-B2 | Redcliff Hill | D2-D3 | Upton Road | A1-A2 |
| Midland Road | F5 | Redcliff Mead Lane | E3 | Vicarage Road | A1 |
| Milford Street | A1-B1 | Redcross Street | D3-D4 | Victoria Grove | E2 |
| Mill Avenue | D4 | Redcross Street | F6 | Victoria Street | D5-D4-E4-E3 |
| Mill Lane | C1 | Richmond Hill | A6 | Victoria Walk | D8 |
| Mitchell Court | E4 | Richmond Terrace | E1-F1 | Wade Street | F6 |
| Mitchell Lane | E4 | River Street | F6 | Walker Street | C7 |
| Montague Place | C7 | Royal Fort Road | B6-C6 | Wapping Road | C3 |
| Moon Street | D7 | Rupert Street | D6 | Warden Road | C1-D1 |
| Morgan Street | F8 | Russ Street | F5 | Warwick Road | A8 |
| Morley Road | B1-B2 | St Augustine's Parade | C4-C5 | Water Lane | E4 |
| Mount Pleasant Terrace | A1-B1 | St Catherines Place | C1 | Waterloo Road | F5 |
| Murray Street | C1 | St George's Road | A4-B4 | Wellington Avenue | E8 |
| Myrtle Road | B7-C7 | St James' Barton | D6-D7 | Wellington Road | E6-F6-F7 |
| Narrow Place | E5 | St John's Lane | F1 | Wells Road | F1 |
| Narrow Quay | C3-C4 | St John's Road | C2 | Welsh Back | D4-D5 |
| Nelson Street | C5-D6 | St Luke's Crescent | E1-F1 | West Park | A7-A8 |
| New Charlotte Street | C2-D2 | St Luke's Road | E1-F1-F2 | West Street | F5-F6 |
| Newfoundland Road | F7-F8 | St Matthew's Road | C7-C8 | Whitehouse Lane | C1-D1 |
| Newfoundland Street | E6-E7-F7 | St Matthias Park | E6-F6 | Whitehouse Place | D2-E2 |
| Newfoundland Way | F7-F8 | St Michael's Hill | B7-B6-C6 | Whitehouse Street | D1-D2 |
| Newgate | D5 | St Michael's Park | B7 | Whiteladies Road | A6-A7-A8 |
| New Kingsley Road | F4-F5 | St Nicholas Road | F8 | Whitson Street | D6 |
| New Queen Street | D1 | St Nicholas Street | C5-D5 | Wilder Street | D7-E7 |
| New Street | F6 | St Paul's Road | A6-A7 | William Street | D2 |
| New Thomas Street | F5 | St Paul's Street | E7 | William Street | E8-F8 |
| New Walls | F1 | St Thomas Street | D3-D4 | William Street | F1 |
| Nine Tree Hill | D8 | Sargent Street | D1-D2 | Willway Street | D1 |
| North Street | A1-B1 | Ship Lane | D2-D3 | Wilson Place | F7 |
| North Street | D7 | Silver Street | D6 | Wilson Street | E7-F7 |
| Nugent Hill | D8 | Sion Road | A1 | Windmill Close | D1 |
| Oakfield Place | A7 | Small Street | C5-D5 | Windsor Terrace | E1-F1 |
| Oakfield Road | A7 | Somerset Square | E2-E3 | Wine Street | D5 |
| Old Bread Street | F4-F5 | Somerset Street | E3 | Woodland Road | B5-B6-B7-B8 |
| Old Market Street | F5 | Southville Place | C2 | York Place | B4 |
| Osborne Road | B2 | Southville Road | B2-C2 | York Road | D2-E2-F2 |
| Oxford Street | F1 | Southwell Street | C7 | York Street | E6-E7 |
| Oxford Street | B7 | Springfield Road | D8 | | |

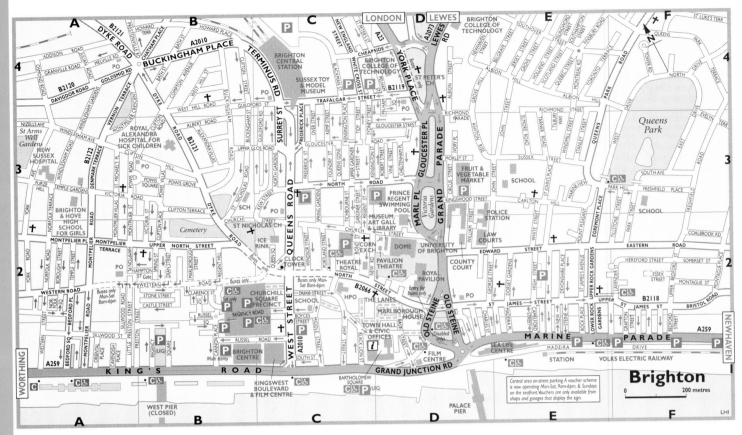

170

# Brighton

Brighton is found on atlas page **15**,
grid reference **3104**

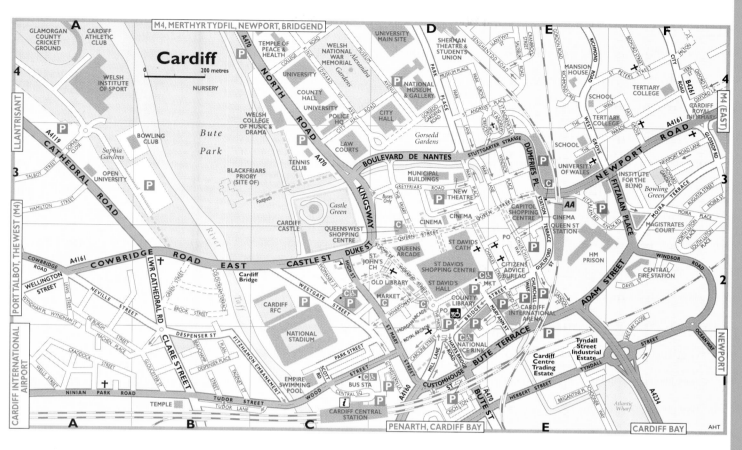

# Cardiff

Cardiff is found on atlas page **33**,
grid reference 1876

**AA shop**
Fanum House, 140 Queen Street, Cardiff CF1 1YF          E3

| | | | | | | |
|---|---|---|---|---|---|---|
| Adam Street | E2-F2 | Glossop Road | F3 | Park Lane | D4-D3-E3 | Wood Street | C1-D1 |
| Augusta Street | F3 | Gloucester Street | B1 | Park Place | D4-D3 | Working Street | D2 |
| Bedford Street | F4 | Gordon Road | E4 | Park Street | C1-D1 | Womanby Street | C2 |
| Beauchamp Street | B1 | Gorsedd Gardens Road | D4 | Plantagenet Street | B1-B2 | Wyndham Place | A2 |
| Boulevard de Nantes | C3-D3 | Great Western Lane | D1 | Queen Street | D2-D3-E3 | Wyndham Street | A2-A1 |
| Bridge Street | D1-D2-E2 | Green Street | B2 | Richmond Crescent | E4 | | |
| Brigantine Place | E1 | Greyfriars Road | D3 | Richmond Road | E4 | | |
| Brook Street | B2 | Guildford Street | E2 | Royal Arcade | D1-D2 | | |
| Bute Street | D1-E1 | Hamilton Street | A3 | St Andrew's Crescent | D3-E4 | | |
| Bute Terrace | D1-E1 | Hayes Bridge Road | D1 | St Andrew's Lane | E3-E4 | | |
| Caroline Street | D1 | Herbert Street | E1 | St Andrew's Place | D4-E4 | | |
| Castle Street | C2 | High Street | C2 | St John Street | D2 | | |
| Cathedral Road | A4-A3-B2 | Howard Gardens | F3 | St Marys Street | D1-D2 | | |
| Central Square | C1 | King Edward VII Avenue | C3-D3 | St Peters Street | E4-F4 | | |
| Charles Street | D3-D2-E2 | Kingsway | C3-D3 | Salisbury Road | E4 | | |
| Churchill Way | E2-E3 | Knox Road | E3-F3 | Sandon Street | E2 | | |
| City Hall Road | C3-C4-D4 | Lewis Street | A2 | Schooner Way | E1 | | |
| City Road | F4 | Llantwit Street | D4-E4 | Scott Road | C1 | | |
| Clare Street | B1 | Lower Cathedral Road | B2 | Senghenydd Road | D4-E4 | | |
| Coldstream Terrace | B2 | Machen Place | A1-B1 | Sophia Close | A3 | | |
| College Road | C4 | Mary Ann Street | E1-E2 | South Luton Place | F2-F3 | | |
| Cowbridge Road | A2 | Mill Lane | D1 | Station Terrace | E2-E3 | | |
| Cowbridge Road East | A2-B2-C2 | Milton Street | F4 | Stuttgarter Strasse | D3-E3 | | |
| Craddock Street | A1-B1 | Morgan Arcade | D1-D2 | The Friary | D3 | | |
| Cranbrook Street | E4 | Moira Place | F3 | The Hayes | D1-D2 | | |
| Crichton Street | D1 | Moira Street | F3 | The Parade | E3-F3-F4 | | |
| Customhouse Street | D1 | Moira Terrace | F2-F3 | The Walk | E3-E4-F4 | | |
| David Street | E2 | Museum Avenue | C4-D4 | Talbot Street | A3 | | |
| Davis Street | F2 | Museum Place | D4 | Tudor Lane | B1-C1 | | |
| De Burgh Street | A1-A2-B1 | Neville Street | A2-B2 | Tudor Street | B1-C1 | | |
| Despenser Place | B1 | Newport Road | E3-F3-F4 | Tyndall Street | E1-F1 | | |
| Despenser Street | B2 | Newport Road Lane | F3 | Vere Street | F4 | | |
| Duke Street | C2-D2 | Ninian Park Road | A1-B1 | Wellington Street | A2 | | |
| Dumfries Place | E3 | North Luton Place | F2-F3 | Wells Street | A1 | | |
| East Bay Close | F1-F2 | North Road | B4-C4-C3 | Westgate Street | C2-D1 | | |
| East Grove | F3 | Ocean Way | F1 | West Grove | E4-E3 | | |
| Fitzalan Place | F2-F3 | Oxford Lane | F4 | Wharton Street | D2 | | |
| Fitzalan Road | E3 | Oxford Street | F4 | Windsor Place | E3 | | |
| Fitzhamon Embankment | B1-C1 | Park Grove | D4 | Windsor Road | F2 | | |

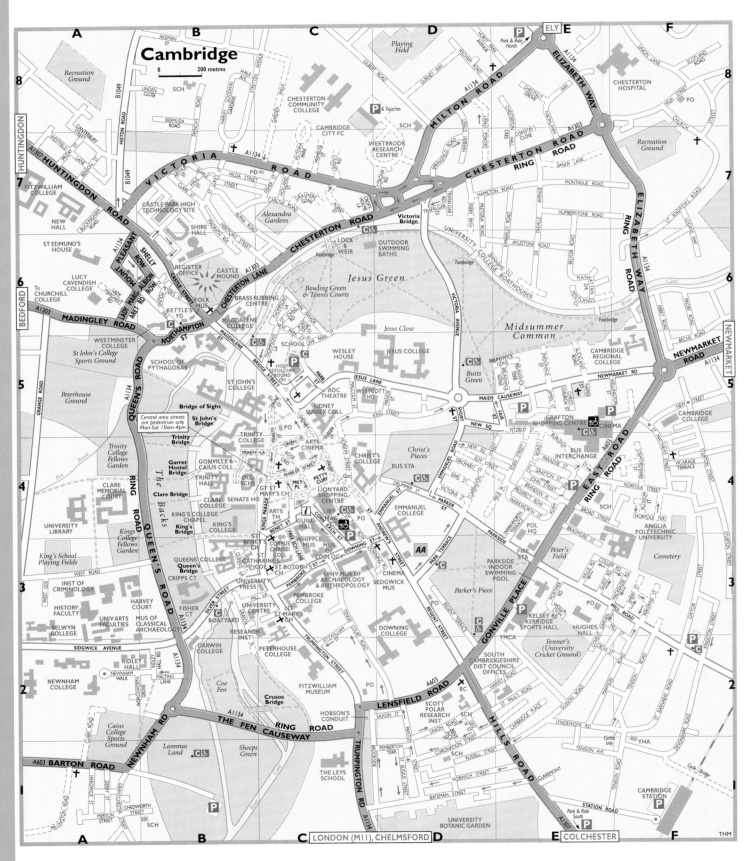

# Cambridge

0    200 metres

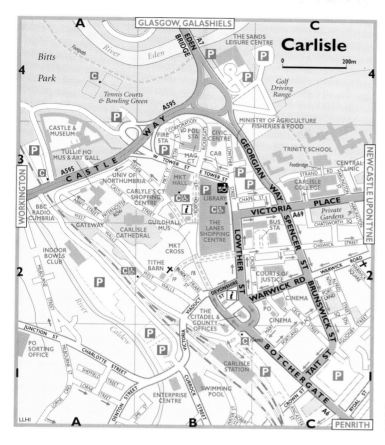

# Carlisle

Carlisle is found on atlas page **93**,
grid reference **3956**

| | |
|---|---|
| Abbey Street | A3 |
| Aglionby Street | C1-C2 |
| Alfred Street North | C2 |
| Alfred Street South | C2 |
| Blackfriars Street | B2 |
| Botchergate | B1-C1 |
| Brunswick Street | C1-C2 |
| Castle Street | A3-B3-B2 |
| Castle Way | A3-B3-B4 |
| Cecil Street | C1-C2 |
| Chapel Street | B3-C3 |
| Charlotte Street | A1-B1 |
| Chatsworth Square | C3 |
| Chiswick Street | C2 |
| Corporation Road | B3-B4 |
| Crosby Street | B2-C2 |
| Crown Street | C1 |
| Currock Street | B1 |
| Denton Street | A1-B1 |
| Devonshire Street | B2 |
| East Tower Street | B3 |
| Eden Bridge | B4 |
| Fisher Street | A3-B3 |
| Georgian Way | B3-C3 |
| Harlington Place | C2-C3 |
| Harlington Street | C3 |
| Junction Street | A1 |
| Lancaster Street | C1 |
| Lime Street | A1-B1 |
| Lorne Crescent | A1 |
| Lorne Street | A1 |
| Lowther Street | B2-B3 |
| Market Street | B3 |
| Mary Street | C1-C2 |
| Milbourne Street | A1-A2 |
| Paternoster Row | A3 |
| Peter Street | B3 |
| Portland Place | C1-C2 |
| Portland Square | C2 |
| Rickergate | B3 |
| Robert Street | B1 |
| Rydal Street | C1 |
| Scotch Street | B3 |
| Sheffield Street | A1 |
| Spencer Street | C2-C3 |
| Strand Road | C3 |

| | |
|---|---|
| Tait Street | C1 |
| Victoria Place | B3-C3 |
| Victoria Viaduct | B1-B2 |
| Warwick Road | B2-C2 |
| Warwick Square | C2 |
| Water Street | B1 |
| West Tower Street | B3 |
| West Walls | A3-A2-B2 |

173

# Cambridge

Cambridge is found on atlas page **53**,
grid reference **4558**

**AA shop**
Janus House, 46–48 St Andrew's Street, Cambridge CB2 3BH   D3

| | | | | | | | | |
|---|---|---|---|---|---|---|---|---|
| Abbey Road | F5-F6 | Christchurch Street | E5 | Gonville Place | D2-D3-E3 | Linden Close | A8-B8 | Paradise Street | E4 | Searle Street | B7-C7 |
| Adam and Eve Street | E4 | Church Street | F7-F8 | Grafton Street | E4 | Logans Way | F6-F7 | Park Parade | C6 | Shelly Row | A6-B6 |
| Akeman Street | B8 | City Road | E4 | Grange Road | A3-A4-A5-A6 | Lower Park Street | C5-C6 | Park Street | C5 | Short Street | D5 |
| Albert Street | C7 | Clare Road | A1-A2 | Granta Place | B2-B3 | Lyndewode Road | E2 | Park Terrace | D3-D4 | Sidgewick Avenue | A2-B2 |
| Albion Row | B6 | Clare Street | B7 | Grantchester Street | A1 | Madingley Road | A6-B6-B5 | Parker Street | D4 | Silver Street | B3-C3 |
| Alpha Road | B7-B6-C6 | Claremont | E1 | Grasmere Gardens | C7 | Magdalene Street | B5-B6 | Parkside | E3-D3-D4 | Springfield Road | D7 |
| Arthur Street | B7 | Clarendon Street | D4-E4 | Green Street | C4-C5 | Magrath Avenue | B7-B6 | Parsonage Street | E5 | Staffordshire Street | F4 |
| Ascham Road | D8 | Collier Road | E3-F3 | Green's Road | C7 | Maids Causeway | D5-E5 | Pemberton Terrace | C1-D1 | Station Road | E1-F1 |
| Auckland Road | E5 | Corn Exchange Street | C3-C4 | Gresham Road | E2 | Malcolm Street | C5 | Pembroke Street | C3 | Stretten Avenue | B7-B8-C8 |
| Aylestone Road | D6-E6 | Corona Road | D7 | Guest Road | E3 | Magdalene Street | B2 | Pentlands Close | E6 | Sturton Street | F3-F4-F5 |
| Banhams Close | D6-E6 | Coronation Street | D1-D2 | Gurney Way | D8 | Malting Lane | B2 | Perowne Street | F3 | Sussex Street | C4-C5 |
| Barton Road | A1 | Covent Garden | E2-E3 | Gwydir Street | F2-F3 | Manhattan Drive | E6 | Portugal Street | C6 | Sydney Street | C4-C5 |
| Bateman Street | C1-D1-E1 | Cross Street | E2-F2 | Hale Avenue | B8 | Manor Street | D5 | Pound Hill | B6 | Tenison Avenue | E1 |
| Beche Road | F5-F6 | De Freville Avenue | E6-E7 | Hale Street | B7 | Market Place | C4 | Pretoria Road | D6-D7 | Tenison Road | E1-F1-E2-F2 |
| Belvoir Road | E6-E7 | Derby Street | A1 | Hamilton Road | D7-E7 | Market Street | C4 | Primrose Street | C7 | Tennis Court Road | C3-C2-D2 |
| Benet Street | C4 | Devonshire Road | F1-F2 | Hardwick Street | A1 | Mawson Road | E2-F2-F3 | Priory Road | F5-F6 | The Fen Causeway | B2-C2 |
| Benson Street | A7 | Downing Place | C3-D3 | Harvey Goodwin Gardens | B7-B8 | Melbourne Place | D4-E4 | Priory Street | A7 | Thomson's Lane | C5-C6 |
| Bermuda Road | B8 | Downing Street | C3-D3 | Harvey Road | D2-E2 | Merton Street | A1 | Prospect Row | E4 | Trafalgar Road | D7 |
| Blossom Street | F4 | Drummer Street | D4 | Hawthorn Way | E7-E8 | Mill Lane | B3-C3 | Queen's Lane | B3 | Trafalgar Street | D7 |
| Bradmore Street | E3-E4 | Earl Street | D4 | Herbert Street | D7-D8 | Mill Road | F2-F3-E3 | Queens Road | B2-B4-A4-B5 | Trinity Lane | B4-C4 |
| Brandon Place | E4 | East Road | E3-E4-F4-F5 | Hertford Street | B7-B6-C6 | Mill Street | E3-F3-F2 | Regent Street | D2-D3 | Trinity Street | C4-C5 |
| Brentwick Street | D1-D2 | Eden Street | E4 | High Street | F8 | Millington Road | A1 | Regent Terrace | D2-D3 | Trumpington Street | C2-C3 |
| Bridge Street | B5-C5 | Elizabeth Way | E8-E7-F7-F6-F5 | Hilda Street | B7-C7 | Milton Road | D7-D8-E8 | Ridley Hall Road | B2 | Trumpington Road | C1-C2 |
| Broad Street | E4-F4 | Elm Street | D4-E4 | Hills Road | E1-D2 | Montague Road | E7-F7 | Rose Crescent | C4 | Union Lane | F8 |
| Brookside | C1-C2 | Emery Street | F3 | Histon Road | A7-A8 | Mortimer Road | E3 | Russell Street | D1-E1 | Union Road | D2 |
| Brunswick Gardens | E5 | Emmanuel Road | D4-D5 | Hobson Street | C4-C5 | Mount Pleasant | A6 | St Andrew's Street | D3-D4-C4 | Vicarage Terrace | F4 |
| Brunswick Terrace | E5 | Emmanuel Street | D4 | Holland Street | C7 | Napier Street | E5 | St Andrews Road | F6-F7 | Victoria Avenue | D5-D6-D7 |
| Buckingham Road | A7 | Fair Street | E5 | Humberstone Road | E7-F7 | New Park Street | C5-C6 | St Barnabas Road | F2 | Victoria Park | C7-C8 |
| Burleigh Street | E4-E5 | Ferry Path | D6-D7 | Huntington Road | A7 | New Square | D5-D4 | St Eligius Street | D1 | Victoria Road | A7-B7-C7-D7 |
| Cambridge Place | E2 | Fisher Street | C7 | Hurst Park Avenue | D8-E8 | New Street | F5 | St John's Road | C6 | Victoria Street | D4 |
| Canterbury Street | A7-A8 | Fitzroy Street | E5 | James Street | E5 | Newmarket Road | E5-F5 | St John's Street | C5 | Warkworth Street | E4 |
| Carlyle Road | B7-C7 | Fitzwilliam Street | C2-C3 | Jesus Lane | C5-D5 | Newnham Road | A1-B1-B2 | St Luke's Street | B7 | Warkworth Terrrace | E3-E4 |
| Castle Street | B6 | Free School Lane | C3-C4 | John Street | E4 | Newnham Walk | A2-B2 | St Matthews Street | F4-F5 | Wellington Street | E5-F5 |
| Chantry Close | E7 | French Road | B7-B8 | Kimberley Road | E6-E7 | Norfolk Street | E4-F4 | St Paul's Road | D2-E2 | West Gardens | A3 |
| Chedworth Street | A1-B1 | Garden Walk | C7-C8 | King Street | D5-E5 | Norfolk Terrace | F4 | St Peter's Street | B6 | West Road | A3-B3 |
| Chesterton Hall Crescent | E7-E8 | George IV Street | D2 | Kings Parade | C4 | Northampton Street | B5-B6 | St Tibbs Row | C3-C4 | Westfield Lane | A7 |
| Chesterton Lane | B6-C6 | George Street | D7-D8 | Kingston Street | F2-F3 | Norwich Street | D1-E1 | Sandy Lane | E7 | Willis Road | E3 |
| Chesterton Road | E7-D7-C7-C6 | Gilbert Road | C8-D8 | Lady Margaret Road | A6 | Orchard Street | D4-E4 | Saxon Street | C2-D2 | Wollaston Road | E3 |
| Chestnut Grove | E8 | Glisson Road | E1-E2 | Lenfield Road | C2-D2 | Panton Street | D1-D2 | Scotland Road | F8 | Wordsworth Grove | A2 |

# Chester

Chester is found on atlas page **71**,
grid reference **4066**

**AA shop**
63–65 Foregate Street, Chester CH1 1YZ                     D3

| | | | | | | |
|---|---|---|---|---|---|---|
| Abbey Square | C3 | Garden Lane | B4-C4 | Queens Avenue | E3-E4 | Watergate Street | B2-C2 |
| Abbey Street | C3 | George Street | C4 | Queens Drive | E1 | Weaver Street | C2 |
| Albion Street | C1-D1 | Gladstone Avenue | A4 | Queens Park Road | D1-E1 | West Lorne Street | B4 |
| Anne's Way | E1 | Gloucester Street | D4 | Queens Road | E4 | Westminster Road | F4 |
| Bath Street | E2-E3 | Gorse Stacks | C4-D4-D3 | Raymond Street | B4 | Wetherby Close | A4 |
| Beaconsfield Street | E3-F4 | Granville Street | A4-B4 | Russell Street | E3 | Whipcord Lane | A4-B4-B3 |
| Bedward Road | B3 | Grey Friars | B2-C2 | St Anne Street | D4 | York Street | D3 |
| Black Friars | B1-C2 | Grosvenor Park Road | E2-E3 | St George's Crescent | E1 | | |
| Boughton | E3-F3 | Grosvenor Street | C1-C2 | St John Street | D2 | | |
| Bridge Street | C2 | Haydock Close | A4 | St Johns Road | E1 | | |
| Brook Street | D4-E4 | Henry Place | D4 | St Martins Way | B2-B3-B4-C4 | | |
| Bunce Street | C1 | Hoole Lane | F3 | St Oswalds Way | C4-D4-D3-E3 | | |
| Cambrian Road | B4 | Hoole Way | D4 | St Werburgh Street | C2-C3 | | |
| Canal Side | D3-E3 | Hunter Street | B3-C3 | Seaville Street | E3 | | |
| Canal Street | B3-B4-C4 | Kempton Close | A4 | Sedgefield Road | A4 | | |
| Castle Drive | C1 | King Street | B3-C3 | Seller Street | E3 | | |
| Castle Street | C1 | Leadworks Lane | E3 | Shipgate Street | C1 | | |
| Catherine Street | A3-A4-B4 | Lightfoot Street | F4 | Sibell Street | E4 | | |
| Charles Street | D4 | Little St John Street | D2 | Souters Lane | D1-D2 | | |
| Chichester Street | B4-C4 | Lorne Street | B4-C4 | South Crescent Road | E1 | | |
| City Road | E3-E4 | Louise Street | B4 | South View Road | A3-B3 | | |
| City Walls Road | B2-B3 | Love Street | D2-D3 | Stanley Place | B2 | | |
| Commonhall Street | C2 | Lower Bridge Street | C1-C2 | Stanley Street | B2 | | |
| Crewe Street | E4 | Lower Park Road | E1 | Station Road | E4 | | |
| Cross Street | F3-F4 | Lyon Street | D4 | Steam Mill Street | E3 | | |
| Cuppin Street | C1-C2 | Mason Street | C4 | Steele Street | D1 | | |
| Curzon Park North | A1 | Milton Street | D3-D4 | Stuart Place | D4 | | |
| Dee Hills Park | E3-F3 | New Crane Street | B2 | The Groves | D2-E2 | | |
| Dee Lane | E2-E3 | Newgate Street | D2 | Tower Road | A3-B3 | | |
| Delamere Street | C4 | Nicholas Street | C1-C2 | Trafford Street | D4 | | |
| Duke Street | C1-D1 | Nicholas Street Mews | B2 | Union Street | D2-E2 | | |
| Eastgate Street | C2-D2 | Northgate Street | C2-C3 | Upper Northgate Street | C4 | | |
| Edinburgh Way | E1 | Nun's Road | B2-B1-C1 | Vernon Road | A3-A4-B4 | | |
| Egerton Street | D4-E4-E3 | Orchard Street | B4 | Vicars Lane | D2 | | |
| Elizabeth Crescent | E1-F1 | Park Street | D1-D2 | Victoria Crescent | D1-E1 | | |
| Epsom Court | A4 | Pepper Street | C2-D2 | Victoria Road | C4 | | |
| Forest Street | D2-E2 | Phillip Street | F4 | Volunteer Street | D2 | | |
| Francis Street | D4-E4 | Princes Avenue | E3-E4 | Walls Avenue | B2-B3 | | |
| Frodsham Street | D2-D3 | Queen Street | D3 | Water Tower Street | B3-C3 | | |

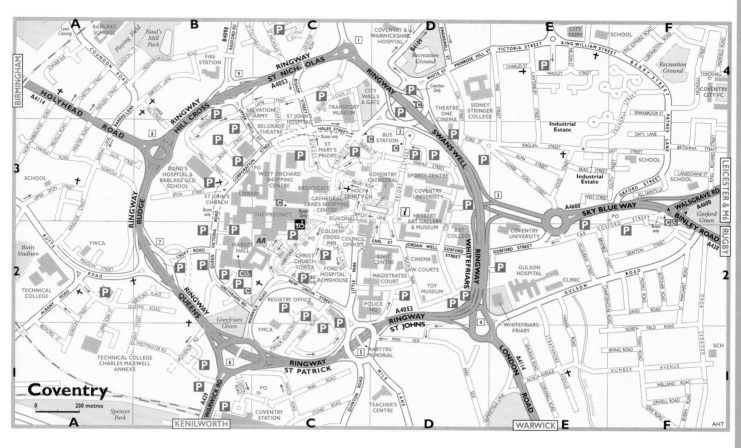

# Coventry

Coventry is found on atlas page **61**,
grid reference **3378**

**AA shop**
39–40 Hertford Street, Coventry CV1 1LF                    C2

| | | | | | | |
|---|---|---|---|---|---|---|
| Abbotts Lane | B4 | Gloucester Street | A3-B3 | Nicholls Street | F4 | Spon Street | B3 |
| Acacia Avenue | E1 | Gordon Street | A1-A2 | Norfolk Street | A3-B3 | Stanier Avenue | A4 |
| Albany Road | A1-A2 | Gosford Street | D2-E2 | Northfield Road | E1-F2 | Stoney Road | C1 |
| Alma Street | E3 | Grafton Street | F2 | Northumberland Road | A3-A4 | Stoney Stanton Road | D4 |
| Barras Lane | A3-B4 | Greyfriars Road | B2 | Orwell Road | F1 | Strathmore Avenue | E1-E2 |
| Bayley Lane | C3-D3 | Grosvenor Road | B1 | Oxford Street | F3 | Swanswell Street | D4 |
| Bedford Street | A1-A2 | Gulson Road | E2-F2 | Park Road | C1 | Terry Road | F1 |
| Berry Street | F4 | Hales Street | C3 | Park Side | D1 | Thackhall Street | F4 |
| Binley Road | F2-F3 | Harper Road | E1-E2 | Paynes Lane | F3-F4 | Tower Street | C4 |
| Bishop Street | C3-C4 | Hartford Place | B2 | Primrose Hill Street | D4 | Trinity Street | C3 |
| Bond Street | B3 | Hertford Street | C2 | Priory Row | C3-D3 | Upper Hill Street | B3-B4 |
| Botoner Road | F2 | High Street | C2-C3 | Priory Street | D2-D3 | Upper Spon Street | A3 |
| Bramble Street | E2-F2 | Highfield Road | F4 | Quarryfield Lane | D1-E1 | Upper Well Street | B4-C3 |
| Britannia Street | F3 | Hill Street | B3 | Queen Victoria Road | B2-B3 | Upper York Street | A1-A2 |
| Burges | C3 | Holyhead Road | A4-B3 | Queens Road | A2-B2 | Vauxhall Street | E3-F4 |
| Butts Road | A3-B2 | Hood Street | E3 | Quinton Road | C1 | Vecqueray Street | E2 |
| Canterbury Street | E3-E4 | Humber Avenue | E1-F1 | Radford Road | B4 | Victoria Street | E4 |
| Charles Street | E4 | Irving Road | E1-F1 | Raglan Street | E3 | Vine Street | E3-E4 |
| Chapel Street | C3-C4 | Jordan Well | D2 | Read Street | E3 | Walsgrave Road | F3 |
| Charterhouse Road | E1-E2 | King Edward Road | F4 | Regent Street | A1-B2 | Warwick Road | B1-C2 |
| Chester Street | A4 | King Richard Street | F3-F4 | Ringway Hillcross | B3-B4 | Waveley Road | A3 |
| Cook Street | C4 | King William Street | E4-F4 | Ringway Queens | B1-B2 | Welland Road | F1 |
| Cornwall Road | E1 | Lamb Street | B3-C4 | Ringway Rudge | B2-B3 | West Street | E3 |
| Coronation Road | F4 | Lansdowne Street | F3 | Ringway St Johns | D1-D2 | Westminster Road | B1 |
| Corporation Street | B3-C3 | Leicester Row | C4 | Ringway St Nicholas | C4 | White Street | D4 |
| Coundon Road | A4-B4 | Little Park | C2 | Ringway St Patrick | C1 | Windsor Street | A2-A3 |
| Coundon Street | A4-B4 | London Road | D1-E1 | Ringway Swanswell | C4-D3 | Yardley Street | E4 |
| Cox Street | D2-D4 | Lower Ford Street | E3 | Ringway Whitefriars | D2-D3 | | |
| Croft Road | B2 | Manor Road | B1-C1 | St Columba's Close | B4-C4 | | |
| David Road | F1 | Meadow Street | A2 | St Georges Road | F1-F2 | | |
| Days Lane | F3 | Melville Road | A3-A4 | St Margaret Road | F2 | | |
| Earl Street | C2-D2 | Meriden Street | A4 | St Nicholas Street | C4 | | |
| East Street | E3-F3 | Middleborough Road | A4-B4 | Salt Lane | C2 | | |
| Eaton Road | B1 | Mile Lane | C1-D1 | Seagrave Road | E1 | | |
| Fairfax Street | C3-D3 | Minster Road | A3-A4 | Severn Road | F1 | | |
| Far Gosford Street | E2-F3 | Monks Road | F2 | Silver Street | C4 | | |
| Ford Street | D3 | Much Park | D2 | Sky Blue Way | E3-F3 | | |
| Friars Road | C1-C2 | Nelson Street | E4 | South Street | E3-F3 | | |
| | | New Union Street | C2 | Sparkbrook Street | F4 | | |

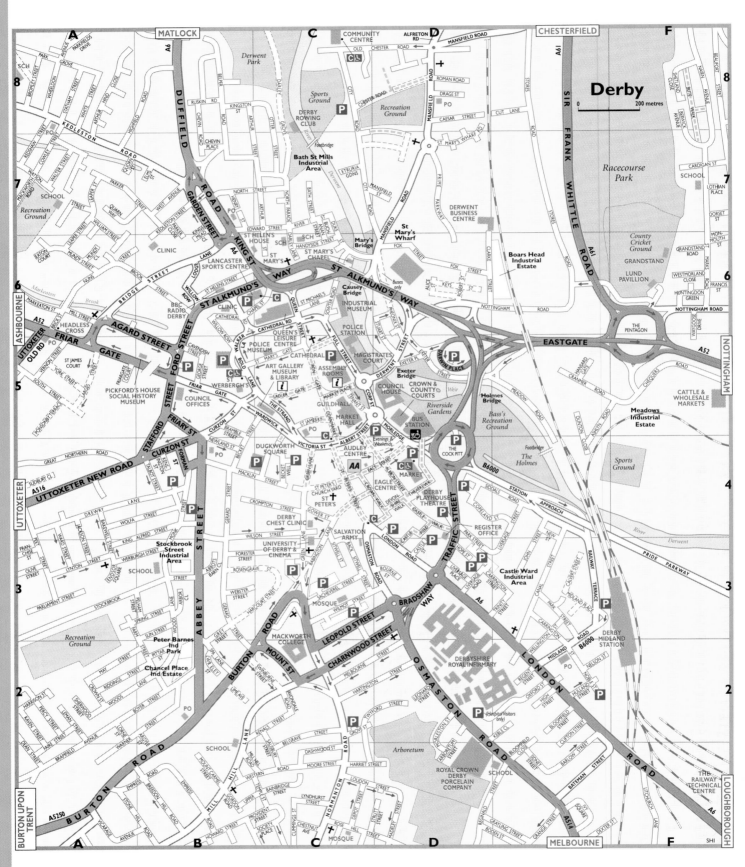

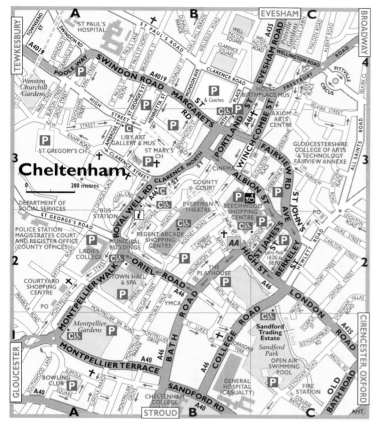

# Cheltenham

Cheltenham is found on atlas page **35**,
grid reference **9422**

**AA shop**
90 High Street, Cheltenham GL50 1EG — B2

| | | | | | | |
|---|---|---|---|---|---|---|
| Albert Place | C4 | Hewlett Road | C2 | Priory Street | C2 |
| Albert Road | C4 | High Street | A3-A4-B3-C2 | Promenade | B2-B3 |
| Albion Street | B3-C3 | Imperial Square | A2-B2 | Regent Street | B2-B3 |
| All Saints Road | C3-C4 | Keynsham Road | C1 | Rodney Road | B2 |
| Ambrose Street | A3 | Keynshambury Road | C1 | Royal Crescent | A3 |
| Argyll Road | C1 | King Street | A4 | Royal Well Road | A2-B3 |
| Bath Parade | B2 | Knapp Road | A3 | St George's Place | A2-A3 |
| Bath Road | B1-B2 | Leighton Road | C2 | St George's Road | A2-A3 |
| Bath Street | B2 | London Road | C1-C2 | St George's Street | A3-B4 |
| Bayshill Road | A2 | Malden Road | C4 | St John's Avenue | C2-C3 |
| Bennington Street | B3 | Marle Hill Parade | B4 | St Luke's Road | B1 |
| Berkeley Street | C2 | Monson Avenue | B4 | St Margarets Road | B3-B4 |
| Brunswick Street | B4 | Montpellier Drive | B1 | St Paul's Lane | A4-B4 |
| Burton Street | A3-A4 | Montpellier Grove | A1-B1 | St Paul's Road | A4-B4 |
| Cambray Place | B2 | Montpellier Parade | A1-B1 | St Paul's Street South | A4 |
| Carlton Street | C2 | Montpellier Spa Road | A1-A2 | Sandford Road | B1 |
| Clarence Road | B4 | Montpellier Street | A1-A2 | Selkirk Close | C4 |
| Clarence Square | B4 | Montpellier Terrace | A1-B1 | Selkirk Street | C3-C4 |
| Clarence Street | A3-B3 | Montpellier Walk | A1-A2 | Sherborne Place | C3 |
| College Baths Road | B4 | New Street | A3 | Sherborne Street | C3-C4 |
| College Road | B1-C2 | North Place | B3-B4 | Southwood Lane | A1 |
| Corpus Street | C1 | North Street | B3 | Suffolk Parade | A1 |
| Devonshire Street | A3-A4 | Old Bath Road | C1 | Suffolk Square | A1 |
| Duke Street | C2 | Oriel Road | A2-B2 | Swindon Road | A4-B4 |
| Dunalley Parade | B4 | Orrisdale Terrace | B1 | Swindon Street | A4 |
| Dunalley Street | B4 | Oxford Street | C2 | Townsend Street | A4 |
| Evesham Road | C4 | Parabola Road | A1-A2 | Trafalgar Street | B2 |
| Fairview Road | B3-C3 | Park Street | A4 | Victoria Place | C3 |
| Gloucester Place | C3 | Pitville Circus | C4 | Victoria Walk | B1-B2 |
| Granville Street | A4 | Pitville Lawn | C4 | Wellesley Road | B4 |
| Great Norwood Street | A1 | Poole Way | A4 | Wellington Road | C4 |
| Grosvenor Street | C2 | Portland Street | B3-B4 | Wellington Square | B4 |
| Grove Street | A3-A4 | Prestbury Road | C4 | Wellington Street | B2 |
| Henrietta Street | B3-B4 | Priory Place | C2 | Winchcombe Street | B3-C3-C4 |

**177**

# Derby

Derby is found on atlas page **62**,
grid reference **3536**

**AA shop**
22 East Street, Derby DE1 2AF — C4

| | | | | | | |
|---|---|---|---|---|---|---|
| Abbey Street | B2-B3-B4 | Brook Street | A6-B6 | Dean Street | A2-A1 |
| Abbots Barn Close | B3 | Buchanan Street | C6-C7 | Depot Street | C1 |
| Agard Street | A6-B6-B5 | Burton Road | A1-B1-B2-C2-C3 | Derwent Street | D5-D6 |
| Albert Street | C4-C5-D5 | Bute Walk | F8-F7 | Devonshire Walk | D4 |
| Albion Street | D4 | Caesar Street | D8 | Dexter Street | E1-F1 |
| Alfreton Road | D8 | Calvert Street | E3 | Dorset Street | F7 |
| Alice Street | D6 | Canal Street | E3-E4 | Drage Street | D8 |
| Arbor Close | B3 | Cardigan Street | F7 | Drewry Lane | A4-B4 |
| Arboretum Street | D1-D2 | Carrington Street | D3-E3 | Duke Street | C7-C6 |
| Argyle Street | B2 | Castle Field | D3-D4 | Duffield Road | B8-B7 |
| Arthur Hind Close | A7-A8 | Castle Street | D3 | Dunton Close | E5-E4 |
| Arthur Street | B8-C8-C7-C6 | Castle Walk | D3 | Eastgate | E5 |
| Ashlyn Road | E4-E5-F5 | Cathedral Road | B6-C6 | East Street | C4-D4 |
| Avondale Road | C2 | Cavendish Street | D4 | Eaton Court | A6 |
| Babington Lane | C3-C4 | Chancel Street | B2 | Edward Street | B7-C7 |
| Back Sitwell Street | C3 | Chapel Street | C6 | Elms Street | B7 |
| Bainbridge Street | C1 | Charnwood Street | C2-D2-D3 | Empress Road | A1-B1 |
| Bakewell Street | A4-A3 | Chester Road | C8-D8 | Endsor Square | A3 |
| Barlow Street | E1-E2 | Chequers Road | F5 | Etruria Gardens | C7 |
| Bateman Street | E1 | Chestnut Avenue | C1 | Exeter Place | D5 |
| Bath Street | C7 | Chevin Place | B7 | Exeter Street | D5 |
| Beaufort Street | F8-F7 | Chevin Road | B8-B7 | Faire Street | A1-A2 |
| Becket Street | B4-B5-C5 | City Road | C8-C7-D7-D6 | Farm Street | A3-B3-B2 |
| Becket Well | C4 | Clarke Street | D6-E6 | Ford Street | B5-B6 |
| Belgrave Street | C1-C2 | Clifton Street | E1-E2 | Forester Street | B3-C3 |
| Belper Road | B8-B7 | Copeland Street | D4-E4 | Forman Street | B4 |
| Berwick Avenue | F8-F7 | Corn Market | C5 | Fox Street | D6 |
| Bloomfield Close | E1 | Corporation Street | D5 | Franchise Street | A3 |
| Bloomfield Street | E2 | Cowley Street | A7-A8 | Francis Street | F6 |
| Boden Street | D1-E1 | Cranmer Road | E5-F5 | Friar Gate | A6-A5-B5 |
| Bold Lane | B5-C5 | Crompton Street | B4-C4 | Friargate Court | A1-A2 |
| Bourne Street | D3 | Crown Street | A2 | Friary Street | B5 |
| Boyer Street | A2-B2 | Crown Walk | C4-D4 | Full Street | C6-C5 |
| Bradshaw Way | D3 | Cummings Street | C1 | Garden Street | B6-B7 |
| Bramble Street | C3 | Curzon Street | B4-B5 | George Street | B5 |
| Bramfield Avenue | A1-A2 | Cut Lane | E8 | Gerard Street | B2-B3-B4 |
| Breedon Hill Road | B1 | Darley Grove | C8-C7 | Gordon Road | B1 |
| Brick Street | A6 | Darley Lane | C6-C7 | Gower Street | C4 |
| Bridge Street | A5-A6-B6 | Darwin Place | D5 | Grandstand Road | A6 |
| Bromley Street | A8 | Dashwood Street | C1 | Grange Street | E1 |
| | | | | Grayling Street | D1-E1 |
| | | | | Great Northern Road | A4 |
| | | | | Green Lane | C3-C4 |
| | | | | Grey Street | B3 |
| | | | | Grove Street | C2-D2 |
| | | | | Handyside Street | C6 |
| | | | | Hansard Gate | E5 |
| | | | | Harcourt Street | B3-C3 |
| | | | | Harriet Street | C1-D1 |
| | | | | Harrison Street | A2 |

| | | | | | |
|---|---|---|---|---|---|
| Hartington Street | C2-D2 | Mount Carmel Street | B1 | Salisbury Street | C1-C2 |
| Henry Street | B7 | Mundy Close | A6 | Sherwood Street | A2 |
| Highfield Road | A7-A8-B8 | Mundy Street | A6 | Shetland Close | F8 |
| High Street | E2 | Nairn Avenue | F7-F8 | Siddals Road | D4-E4 |
| Hope Street | D3 | Nelson Street | E2 | Sidney Street | E1 |
| Howard Street | B1 | New Street | E4 | Sir Frank Whittle Road | F6-E6-E8 |
| Hulland Street | E2 | Newland Street | B4 | Sitwell Street | C3 |
| Huntingdon Green | F6 | Noble Street | E2 | Society Place | C1 |
| Iron Gate | C5 | Normanton Road | C1-C2-C3 | South Street | A5 |
| Ivy Square | E1 | North Parade | C7 | Sowter Road | C6 |
| Jackson Street | A3-A4 | North Street | B3 | Spa Lane | B2 |
| John Street | E3-E4 | Nottingham Road | D6-E6-F6 | Spring Street | B3 |
| Keble Close | C1 | Nuns Street | A6 | Stafford Street | B4-B5 |
| Kedleston Road | A8-A7-B7 | Old Chester Road | C8-D8 | Statham Street | A8 |
| Kedleston Street | B7 | Olive Street | A3 | Station Approach | D4-E4 |
| Kensington Street | B4 | Osmaston Road | E1-C4 | Stockbrook Street | A2-A3-B3 |
| Keys Street | D5 | Otter Street | C7-C8 | Stone Hill Road | A1-B1 |
| King Alfred Street | A3-B3-B4 | Oxford Street | E2 | Stores Road | E6-E7-E8 |
| Kings Mead Close | B6 | Parker Close | B6-B7 | Strutt Street | D1 |
| Kingston Street | B8-C8 | Parker Street | A7-B7 | Stuart Street | D5-D6 |
| King Street | B6-C6 | Parkfields Drive | A8 | Sudbury Close | A4 |
| Kirk Street | D8 | Park Grove | A8 | Sun Street | B3 |
| Larges Street | A5 | Park Street | D4-D3-E3 | Swinburne Street | C2 |
| Leaper Street | A6-A7 | Parliament Street | A3 | Talbot Street | B4 |
| Leman Street | A2 | Peet Street | A3-A4 | Temple Street | C1 |
| Leonard Street | B3 | Pelham Street | B3 | Tenant Street | C5 |
| Leopold Street | C2-C3-D3 | Percy Street | A2 | Theatre Walk | D4 |
| Lime Avenue | B2-C2 | Phoenix Street | D6 | The Cock Pitt | D4 |
| Litchurch Lane | F1 | Pittar Street | B2 | The Pentagon | F5-F6 |
| Liversage Place | D3 | Ponsonby Terrace | A5 | The Strand | C5 |
| Liversage Road | D3 | Pride Parkway | E4-F3 | Traffic Street | D3-D4 |
| Liversage Street | E3-E4 | Prime Parkway | D7 | Trinity Street | E3 |
| Lodge Lane | B6 | Provident Street | C1 | Twyford Street | C2-D2 |
| London Road | D4-D3-E3-E2-F2-F1 | Quarn Way | A7 | Upper Bainbridge Street | B1-C1 |
| Lorne Street | A2 | Quorn Street | A7 | Uttoxeter New Road | A4-B4 |
| Lothian Place | F7 | Queen Street | C5-C6 | Uttoxeter Old Road | A5 |
| Loudon Street | C1-D1 | Railway Terrace | E3-E4 | Vicarage Avenue | A1-B1 |
| Lower Eley Street | B2 | Raven Street | A1-A2 | Victoria Street | C4 |
| Lyndhurst Street | C1 | Redshaw Street | A7-A8 | Vernon Street | A5 |
| Lynton Street | A3 | Regent Street | E2 | Walter Street | A7 |
| Macklin Street | B4-C4 | Reginald Street | D1-E1 | Ward Street | A3-A4 |
| Mackworth Road | A7 | Renals Street | B2-C2 | Warner Street | A1-A2-B2 |
| Madeley Street | D1 | Riddings Street | A2 | Wardwick | B5-C5-C4 |
| Mansfield Road | D6-D7-D8-E8 | River Street | C7 | Watson Street | A7 |
| Mansfield Street | C7-D7 | Robert Street | D6 | Waygoose Drive | F5-F6 |
| May Street | A2 | Roman Road | D8 | Webster Street | B3-C3 |
| Markeaton Street | A6 | Rose Hill Street | C1-D1 | Wellington Street | E2-E3 |
| Market Place | C5 | Rosengrave Street | B3-C3 | Werburgh Street | A3-B3 |
| Meadow Road | E5 | Ruskin Road | B8 | West Avenue | B7 |
| Melbourne Street | C2-D2 | Sacheverel Street | C3 | Western Road | B1-C1 |
| Midland Place | E1 | Sadler Gate | C5 | Westmorland Close | F6 |
| Midland Road | E2-E3 | St Alkmund's Way | B6-D5 | Wheeldon Avenue | A8 |
| Mill Hill Lane | B1-B2-C2 | St Helens Street | B6 | White Street | A8 |
| Mill Hill Road | B1-C1 | St James Court | A5 | William Street | A6-A7 |
| Mill Street | A6 | St James Street | C5 | Willow Row | B5-B6 |
| Monk Street | B3-B4 | St Marks Road | F6-F7 | Wilmot Street | C3-D3 |
| Monmouth Street | F6 | St Mary's Gate | B5-C5 | Wilson Street | B3-B4-C4 |
| Moore Street | C1 | St Mary's Wharf Road | D7-D8 | Wolfa Street | A4-B4 |
| Morledge | D4-D5 | St Michael's Lane | C6 | Woods Lane | A2-B2-B3 |
| Morleston Street | D1-D2 | St Peter's Church Yard | C4 | Wood Street | D6 |
| Mount Street | C2 | St Peter's Street | C4 | York Street | A5 |

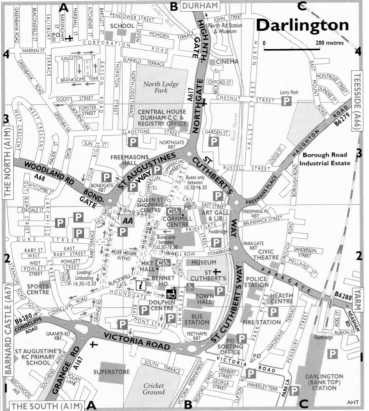

# Darlington

Darlington is found on atlas page **89**,
grid reference **28**14

**AA shop**
47 Skinnergate, Darlington DL3 7NR                     A2

| | | | | | | |
|---|---|---|---|---|---|---|
| Adelaide Street | C1 | High Row | B2 | Thornton Street | A3-A4 |
| Albion Street | C1 | Houndgate | A2-B2 | Tubwell Row | B2 |
| Barningham Street | A4 | John Street | B4-C4 | Valley Street North | C3-C4 |
| Bartlett Street | A4 | Kingston Street | A4 | Victoria Embankment | B1 |
| Beaconsfield Street | A4 | Kitchener Street | A4 | Victoria Road | A1-B1-C1 |
| Beaumont Street | B1-B2 | Larchfield Street | A2-A3 | Warren Street | A4 |
| Beck Street | B4 | Lodge Street | C3 | Waverley Terrace | C1 |
| Bedford Street | B1 | Marshall Street | A4 | West Crescent | A3-A4 |
| Beechwood Avenue | A1 | Maude Street | A3 | West Powlett Street | A2 |
| Blackwell Gate | A2-B2 | Melland Street | C2 | Wilkes Street | B4 |
| Bondgate | A3-A2-B2 | Montrose Street | C4 | Woodland Road | A3 |
| Borough Road | C2-C3 | Mowden Terrace | B4 | Wycombe Street | A3 |
| Branksome Terrace | A4 | Neasham Road | C1 | | |
| Brunswick Street | B2-C2 | North Lodge Terrace | B3-B4 | | |
| Chestnut Street | B4-C4 | Northgate | B2-B3-B4 | | |
| Church Row | B2 | Outram Street | A2-A3 | | |
| Clifton Road | B1-C1 | Oxford Street | B4 | | |
| Commercial Street | B2-B3 | Park Lane | C1 | | |
| Coniscliffe Road | A1-A2 | Park Place | C1-C2 | | |
| Corporation Road | A4-B4 | Parkgate | C2 | | |
| Crown Street | B2-B3 | Pendower Street | A4-B4 | | |
| Dodd's Street | A4 | Pensbury Street | C1-C2 | | |
| Duke Street | A2 | Polam lane | A1 | | |
| Dundee Street | C4 | Post House Wynd | A2-B2 | | |
| Easson Road | A3-A4 | Powlett Street | A2 | | |
| East Mount Road | C3-C4 | Prebend Row | B2 | | |
| East Raby Street | A2 | Priestgate | B2 | | |
| East Street | B2-B3 | Primrose Street | A2 | | |
| Elmfield Terrace | A4-B4 | Raby Street West | A2 | | |
| Eskdale Street | A2 | Raby Terrace | A2 | | |
| Feethams | B1-B2 | Russell Street | B3-C3 | | |
| Forster Street | A3 | Salisbury Terrace | A4 | | |
| Four Riggs | A3 | Salt Yard | A2 | | |
| Freemans Place | C3 | Sanderson Street | C2 | | |
| Garden Street | B3 | Selbourne Terrace | A3-A4 | | |
| George Street | B1 | Skinnergate | A2 | | |
| Gladstone Street | A3-B3 | South Terrace | B1 | | |
| Grange Road | A1-A2 | Southend Avenue | A1 | | |
| Greenbank Road | A3-A4 | St Augustines Way | A3-B3 | | |
| Hargreave Terrace | C1-C2 | St Cuthbert's Way | B1-B2-B3 | | |
| Haughton Road | C3-C4 | Stanhope Road South | A1-A2 | | |
| Herbert Street | B1 | Stonebridge | B2 | | |
| High Northgate | B4 | Sun Street | A3 | | |

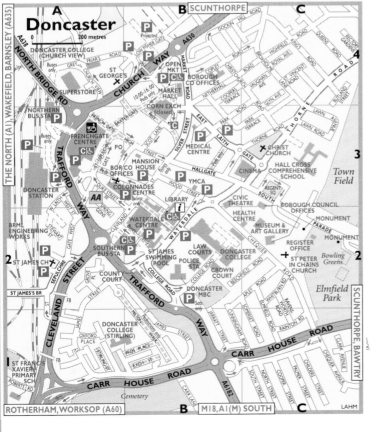

# Doncaster

Doncaster is found on atlas page **83**,
grid reference **570**3

**AA shop**
34 Duke Street, Doncaster DN1 3EA                     A3

| | | | |
|---|---|---|---|
| Apley Road | B2-C2 | Park Road | B3-C3-C4 |
| Baxter Gate | A3-B3 | Park Terrace | B3-C3 |
| Beechfield Road | B2-C2 | Prospect Place | B1 |
| Broxholme Lane | C4 | Queens Road | C4 |
| Carr House Road | A1-B1-C1 | Rainton Road | C1 |
| Carr Lane | B1 | Ravensworth Road | C1-C2 |
| Chequer Avenue | C1 | Rectory Gardens | C4 |
| Chequer Road | B2-C2-C1 | Regent Square | C3 |
| Childers Street | C1 | Roberts Road | A1 |
| Christchurch Road | B4-C4-C3 | Royal Avenue | C4 |
| Church View | A4 | Rutland Street | C4 |
| Church Way | A4-B4 | St James's Bridge | A2 |
| Clark Avenue | C1 | St James Street | A1-A2-B2-B1 |
| Cleveland Street | A1-A2-B3 | St Sepulchre Gate | A3 |
| College Road | B2 | St Sepulchre Gate West | A1-A2 |
| Cooper Street | C1 | St Vincent Road | C4 |
| Coopers Terrace | B4 | Scot Lane | B3 |
| Copley Road | B4-C4 | Silver Street | B3 |
| Cunningham Road | B1-C1 | Somerset Road | C1-C2 |
| Dockin Hill Road | B4-C4 | South Parade | C3-C2 |
| Duke Street | A3-B3 | South Street | C1 |
| East Laith Gate | B3-C3 | Spring Gardens | A3-A2 |
| Elmfield Road | C2-C1 | Stewart Street | A2 |
| Exchange Street | B1 | Stirling Street | A1 |
| French Gate | A3 | Thorne Road | C3-C2 |
| Glyn Avenue | C4 | Trafford Way | A3-A2-B2-B1 |
| Grey Friar's Road | A4-B4 | Vaughan Avenue | C4 |
| Grove Place | A2 | Waterdale | B2-B3 |
| Hallgate | B3 | West Laith | A2-A3 |
| High Street | A3-B3 | West Street | A2-A3 |
| Highfield Road | C4 | Whitburn Road | C2 |
| Jarratt Street | B1 | Wood Street | B3 |
| King's Road | C4 | | |
| Lawn Avenue | C3 | | |
| Lawn Road | C3 | | |
| Low Fisher Gate | B4 | | |
| Market Road | B4 | | |
| Milton Walk | A2-B2-B1 | | |
| Netherhall Road | B4-C4 | | |
| North Bridge Road | A4 | | |
| North Street | C1 | | |
| Oxford Place | A1 | | |
| Palmer Street | C1 | | |

178

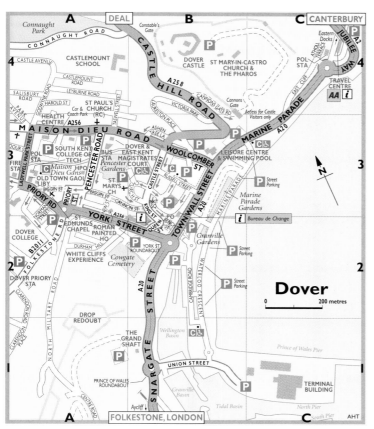

# Dover

Dover is found on atlas page **29**, grid reference **3241**

**AA Port shop**
Eastern Docks Terminal, Dover CT16 1JA          C4

| | | | | |
|---|---|---|---|---|
| Ashen Tree Lane | B3 | Waterloo Crescent | B2-B1 |
| Atholl Terrace | C4 | Woolcomber Street | B3 |
| Biggin Street | A3 | York Street | A3-B3 |
| Cambridge Road | B2 | | |
| Cannon Street | A3-B3 | | |
| Cannons Gate Road | B4 | | |
| Castle Avenue | A4 | | |
| Castle Hill Road | B4-B3 | | |
| Castle Street | B3 | | |
| Castlemount Road | A4 | | |
| Centre Road | A1 | | |
| Church Street | B3 | | |
| Clarendon Place | A1 | | |
| Clarendon Road | A2-A1 | | |
| Connaught Road | A4 | | |
| Dour Street | A3 | | |
| Durham Hill | A2 | | |
| East Cliff | C4 | | |
| Folkestone Road | A2 | | |
| Godwyne Road | A3-A4 | | |
| Harold Street | A3 | | |
| Jubilee Way | C4 | | |
| King Street | B3 | | |
| Ladywell Park Street | A3 | | |
| Laureston Place | B4-B3 | | |
| Leyburne Road | A4 | | |
| Maison Dieu Road | A3-B3 | | |
| Marine Parade | B2-B3-C4 | | |
| New Street | A3 | | |
| Norman Street | A3 | | |
| North Military Road | A1-A2 | | |
| Park Avenue | A4-A3 | | |
| Pencester Road | A3 | | |
| Priory Road | A3 | | |
| Priory Street | A3 | | |
| Queen Street | B2 | | |
| Russell Street | B3 | | |
| Salisbury Road | A4 | | |
| Snargate Street | B1-B2 | | |
| Taswell Street | A3-A4 | | |
| Townwall Street | B2-B3 | | |
| Union Street | B1 | | |
| Victoria Park | B4 | | |

# Dundee

Dundee is found on atlas page **126**, grid reference **4030**

**AA shop**
124 Overgate, Dundee DD1 1DX          B3

| | | | | |
|---|---|---|---|---|
| Bank Street | B3 | Union Street | B2 |
| Barrack Street | A3-B3 | Victoria Road | B4-C4 |
| Bell Street | A4-B4 | Ward Road | A3 |
| Blackscroft | C4 | West Bell Street | A3-A4 |
| Brown Street | A3 | West Marketgait | A2-A3-A4 |
| Camperdown Street | C3 | Westport | A2 |
| Castle Street | B3-C3 | Whitehall Crescent | B2 |
| Chrichton Street | B2-B3 | Whitehall Street | B2 |
| City Square | B3 | Willison Street | A3-B3 |
| Commercial Street | B3-C3 | | |
| Constable Street | C4 | | |
| Constitution Road | A3-A4 | | |
| Court House Square | A3 | | |
| Cowgate | B4-C4 | | |
| Cross Lane | A2 | | |
| Dens Street | C4 | | |
| Dock Street | C3 | | |
| Dudhope Street | A4-B4 | | |
| East Marketgait | C3-C4 | | |
| Euclid Crescent | B3-B4 | | |
| Exchange Street | C3 | | |
| Gellatly Street | C3 | | |
| Hawkhill | A3 | | |
| Hilltown | B4 | | |
| King Street | C4 | | |
| Laurel Bank | A4 | | |
| Lindsay Street | A3 | | |
| Mary Anne Lane | C3-C4 | | |
| Meadowside | A3-B3-B4 | | |
| Murraygate | B3-B4 | | |
| Nethergate | A2 | | |
| Nethergate High Street | A2-B2-B3 | | |
| North Marketgait | A4-B4-C4 | | |
| Panmure Street | B4 | | |
| Reform Street | B3 | | |
| Riverside Drive | A1-B1 | | |
| Seagate | B3-C3-C4 | | |
| South Marketgait | B2-C2-C3 | | |
| South Tay Street | A2 | | |
| South Ward Road | A3 | | |
| St Andrew's Street | C4 | | |
| St Roque's Lane | C4 | | |
| Trades Lane | C3-C4 | | |

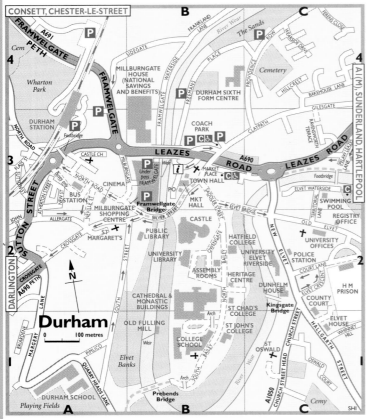

# Durham

Durham is found on atlas page **96**,
grid reference **274**2

| | | | |
|---|---|---|---|
| Allergate | A2 | Sutton Street | A3 |
| Atherton Street | A2-A3 | Territorial Lane | C2-C3 |
| Bakehouse Lane | C4 | Wearside Drive | C4 |
| Briardene | A1 | Whinney Hill | C1 |
| Castle Church | A3 | | |
| Church Street | C1 | | |
| Church Street Head | C1 | | |
| Claypath | B3-C3 | | |
| Court Lane | C2 | | |
| Crossgate | A2 | | |
| Elvet Bridge | B3-C3-C2 | | |
| Elvet Crescent | C2 | | |
| Elvet Waterside | C3 | | |
| Ferens Close | C4 | | |
| Flass Street | A3 | | |
| Framwelgate | A3-A4 | | |
| Framwelgate Peth | A4 | | |
| Framwelgate Waterside | B3-B4 | | |
| Frankland Lane | B4 | | |
| Freemans Place | B3-B4-C4 | | |
| Gilesgate | C3-C4 | | |
| Halgarth Street | C1 | | |
| Hilcrest | C4 | | |
| John Street | A2 | | |
| Leazes Road | B3-C3 | | |
| Margery Lane | A1-A2 | | |
| Milburngate | A3-B3 | | |
| Neville Street | A2-A3 | | |
| New Elvet | C2-C3 | | |
| New Street | A3 | | |
| North Bailey | B1-B2 | | |
| North Road | A3 | | |
| Old Elvet | C2 | | |
| Oswald Court | C1 | | |
| Owengate | B2 | | |
| Pelaw Leazes Lane | C3 | | |
| Pimlico | A1 | | |
| Providence Row | C3-C4 | | |
| Quarry Heads Lane | A1 | | |
| Ravensworth Terrace | C3 | | |
| Saddler Street | B2-B3 | | |
| Sidegate | A4-B4 | | |
| Silver Street | B2-B3 | | |
| South Bailey | B1 | | |
| South Street | A1-A2-B2 | | |
| Sutton Street | A2-A3 | | |

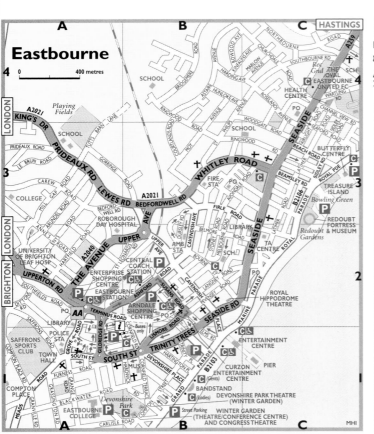

# Eastbourne

Eastbourne is found on atlas page **16**,
grid reference **61**99

**AA shop**
2 Terminus Building, Upperton Road, Eastbourne BN21 1BE    A2

| | | | |
|---|---|---|---|
| Arundel Road | A2-A3 | Kinfauns Avenue | B4-C4 |
| Ashford Road | A2-B2 | King's Drive | A3-A4 |
| Astaire Avenue | B4 | Langney Road | B2 |
| Avondale Road | B3-C3 | Latimer Road | C2-C3-C4 |
| Beach Road | C3 | Le Brun Road | A3 |
| Beamsley Road | C3 | Lewes Road | A3-B3 |
| Bedfordwell Road | A3-B3 | Lismore Road | B1-B2 |
| Belmore Road | B2-C2 | Marine Parade | B1-B2-C2 |
| Blackwater Road | A1-B1 | Marlow Avenue | C4 |
| Bourne Street | B2 | Meads Road | A1 |
| Bowood Avenue | B4 | Melbourne Road | B2-B3 |
| Bridgemere Road | B4 | Mill Gap Road | A3 |
| Carew Road | A3 | Moy Avenue | B3-B4 |
| Carlisle Road | A1-B1 | Northbourne Road | C4 |
| Cavendish Avenue | B2-B3 | Pevensey Road | B2 |
| Cavendish Place | B1-B2 | Prideaux Road | A3 |
| Channel View Road | C3-C4 | Ringwood Road | B4-B3-C3 |
| Churchdale Road | B4-C4 | Roselands Avenue | C3-C4 |
| Compton Place Road | A1 | Royal Parade | C2-C3 |
| Compton Street | B1 | Saffrons Road | A1-A2 |
| Cornfield Road | B1-B2 | Seaford Road | C3 |
| Cornfield Terrace | B1 | Seaside | C2-C3-C4 |
| Courtlands Road | B3-B4 | Seaside Road | B2 |
| Devonshire Place | B1 | Sidley Road | C3 |
| Dittons Road | A2 | South Street | A1-B1 |
| Dursley Road | B2-B3 | Southbourne Road | C4 |
| Elms Road | B1 | Southfields Road | A2 |
| Enys Road | A2-A3 | St Anne's Road | A2-A3 |
| Fairlight Road | C3-C4 | St Leonards Road | A2-B2 |
| Firle Road | B3-C3 | St Philips Avenue | B3-B4-C4 |
| Furness Road | A1 | Susans Road | B2 |
| Gildredge Road | A1-A2 | Sydney Road | B2-B3 |
| Gorringe Road | A3-B3 | Terminus Road | A2-B2 |
| Grand Parade | B1 | The Avenue | A2 |
| Grange Road | A1 | Trinity Place | B1 |
| Granville Road | A1 | Trinity Trees | B1 |
| Grassington Road | A1 | Tutts Barn Lane | A3-A4-B4 |
| Grove Road | A1-A2 | Upper Avenue | A2-B2-B3 |
| Harding Avenue | B4-C4 | Upperton Road | A2 |
| Hardwick Road | B1 | Wartling Road | C4 |
| Hartfield Road | A2-A3 | Whitley Road | B3-C3 |
| Hartington Place | B1 | Woodgate Road | B4-C4-C3 |
| Hunloke Avenue | B4 | | |

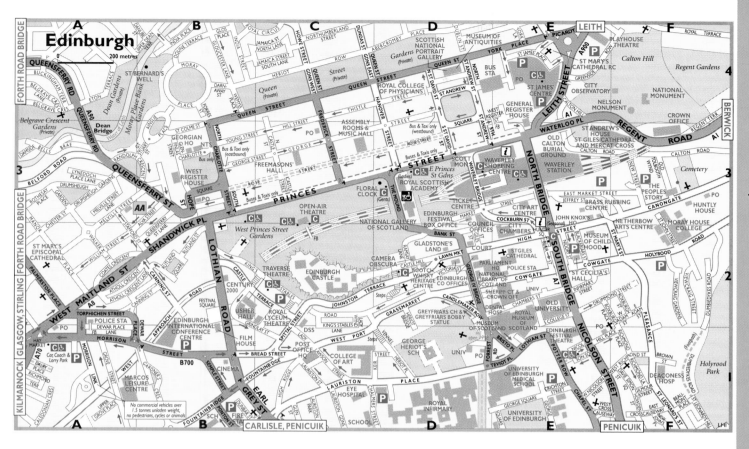

# Edinburgh

Edinburgh is found on atlas page 117,
grid reference 2573

**AA shop**
Fanum House, 18–22 Melville Street, Edinburgh EH3 7PD    A3

| | | | | | | |
|---|---|---|---|---|---|---|
| Abercromby Place | C4-D4 | Davie Street | F1 | High Street | D2-E2-E3 | North Bridge | E3-E2 | St Leonard's Hill | F1 |
| Ainslie Place | B3-B4 | Dewar Place | A1-A2 | Hill Place | E1-F1 | North Castle Street | C3-C4 | St Leonards Street | F1 |
| Alva Street | A2-B3 | Dewar Place Lane | A1 | Hill Street | C3-C4 | North Charlotte Street | B3 | St Mary's Street | F2-E3 |
| Atholl Crescent | A2-B2 | Doune Terrace | B4 | Holyrood Road | F2-F3 | North David Street | D4 | Semple Street | B1 |
| Atholl Crescent Lane | A2-B2 | Drummond Street | E2-F2 | Hope Street | B3 | North St Andrew Street | D4 | Shandwick Place | B2-B3 |
| Bank Street | D2 | Drumsheugh Gardens | A3 | Howden Street | F1 | Northumberland Street | C4 | Simon Square | F1 |
| Beaumont Place | F1 | Dublin Street | D4 | Howe Street | C4 | Old Tolbooth Wynd | F3 | South Bridge | E2 |
| Belford Road | A3 | Dumbiedykes Road | F1-F2 | India Place | B4 | Palmerston Place | A2 | South Charlotte Street | B3 |
| Belgrave Crescent | A4 | Dunbar Street | B1 | India Street | B4 | Picardy Place | E4 | South College Street | E2 |
| Belgrave Crescent Lane | A4 | Dundas Street | C4 | Infirmary Street | E2 | Pleasance | F1-F2 | South David Street | D3-D4 |
| Bells Brae | A3 | Earl Grey Street | B1-C1 | Jamaica Street North Lane | B4-C4 | Ponton Street | B1 | South St Andrew Street | D3-D4 |
| Blackfriars Street | E2 | East Adam Street | F2 | Jamaica Street South Lane | B4-C4 | Potter Row | E1 | Spittal Street | C1-C2 |
| Blair Street | E2 | East Cross Causeway | E1 | Jeffrey Street | E3 | Princes Street | B3-C3-D3-E3 | Stafford Street | A3-A2-B2 |
| Bread Street | B1-C1 | East Market Street | E3-F3 | Johnston Terrace | C2-D2 | Queen Street | B3-B4-C4-D4 | Teviot Place | E1 |
| Bristo Place | E1 | Eton Terrace | A4 | Keir Street | C1-D1 | Queen Street Gardens East | C4 | The Mound | D2-D3 |
| Brown Street | F1 | Forres Street | B4 | King's Stables Road | B2-C2-D2 | Queen Street Gardens West | C4 | Thistle Street | C4-D4 |
| Buckingham Terrace | A4 | Forrest Road | D1 | King's Stables Lane | C2-D2 | Queensferry Road | A3-A4 | Torphichen Street | A2 |
| Caledonian Crescent | A1 | Fountainbridge | B1-C1 | Lady Lawson Street | C1 | Queensferry Street | A3-B3 | Upper Dean Terrace | A4-B4 |
| Calton Hill | E4 | Frederick Street | C3-C4 | Lady Wynd | C2 | Queensferry Street Lane | B2-B3 | Upper Grove Place | A1 |
| Calton Road | E4-E3-F3 | Gardner's Crescent | B1 | Lauriston Gardens | C1 | Ramsay Lane | D2 | Vennel | D1 |
| Candlemaker Row | D2 | George IV Bridge | D2 | Lauriston Park | C1 | Randolph Crescent | A3-B3 | Victoria Street | D2 |
| Canning Street | A2-B2 | George Square | E1 | Lauriston Place | C1-D1 | Regent Road | E4-F4-F3 | Viewcraig Gardens | F2 |
| Canongate | F3 | George Street | B3-C3-D3-D4 | Lauriston Street | C1 | Regent Terrace | F4 | Viewcraig Street | F2 |
| Castle Hill | D2 | Gilmour Street | F1 | Lawn Market | D2 | Richmond Lane | F1 | Walker Street | A2-A3 |
| Castle Street | C3 | Glen Street | C1 | Leith Street | E3-E4 | Richmond Place | F1 | Waterloo Place | E3-E4-F4 |
| Castle Terrace | B2-C2 | Glenfinlas Street | B3 | Lothian Road | B2-B1 | Richmond Terrace | A1 | Waverley Bridge | D3 |
| Chalmers Street | C1-D1 | Gloucester Lane | B4 | Lothian Street | E1 | Rose Street | B3-C3 | Wemyss Place | B4 |
| Chambers Street | D2-E2 | Gloucester Place | B4 | Lynedoch Place Lane | A3 | Rothesay Place | A3 | West Adam Street | F2 |
| Chapel Street | E1-F1 | Grassmarket | D2 | Manor Place | A2-A3 | Roxburgh Place | E2-F2 | West Approach Road | A1-B1-B2 |
| Charlotte Square | B3 | Great Stuart Street | A3-B3 | Market Street | D2-D3-E3 | Roxburgh Street | F2 | West Cross Causeway | E1-F1 |
| Chester Street | A2-A3 | Greenside Row | E4-F4 | Melville Street | A2-A3 | Royal Circus | B4-C4 | West Maitland Street | A1-A2 |
| Clarendon Crescent | A4 | Grindlay Street | B2-B1-C1 | Melville Street Lane | A3 | Royal Terrace | F4 | West Nicolson Street | E1 |
| Coates Crescent | A2-B2 | Grove Street | A1 | Moray Place | B4 | Rutland Square | B2 | West Port | C1-D2 |
| Cowgate | D2-E2-F2 | Hanover Street | C4-D4-D3 | Morrison Link | A1 | Rutland Street | B2 | West Register Street | D4-E4 |
| Cockburn Street | D3-E3-E2 | Haymarket | A1 | Morrison Street | A1-B1 | St Andrew Square | D3-D4 | West Richmond Street | E1-F1 |
| Crichton Street | E1 | Heriot Bridge | D1-D2 | New Street | F3 | St Colme Street | B3 | William Street | A2 |
| Dalry Place | A1 | Heriot Place | D1 | Nicolson Square | E1 | St Giles Street | D2 | York Lane | E4 |
| Damside | A3 | Heriot Row | B4-C4 | Nicolson Street | E1-E2 | St James Place | E4 | York Place | D4-E4 |
| Darnaway Street | B4 | High Riggs | C1 | Niddry Street | E2 | St John Street | F2-F3 | Young Street | B3-C3 |

182

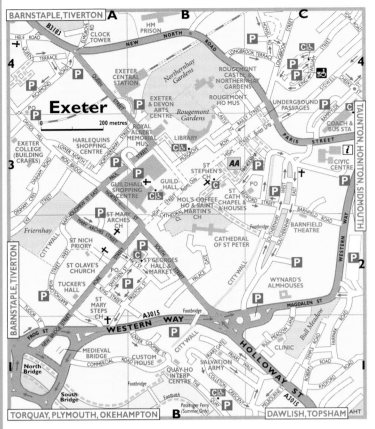

# Exeter

Exeter is found on atlas page **9**,
grid reference **9292**

**AA shop**
1–5 Princesshay, Bedford Street, Exeter EX1 1NQ — B3

| | | | |
|---|---|---|---|
| Bailey Street | B3-C3-C4 | Paul Street | A3-B3 |
| Bampfylde Street | C3-C4 | Preston Street | A2-B2 |
| Barnfield Road | C2-C3 | Princesshay | B3-C3 |
| Bartholomew Street East | A2-A3 | Queen Street | A4-B3 |
| Bartholomew Street West | A2 | Queen's Terrace | A4 |
| Bedford Street | B3-C3 | Radford Road | C1 |
| Bull Meadow Lane | C1-C2 | Richmond Road | A4 |
| Castle Street | B3-B4 | Roberts Road | C1 |
| Cathedral Close | B2-B3 | St Davids Hill | A3-A4 |
| Cheek Street | C4 | Sidwell Street | C3-C4 |
| Colleton Crescent | B1-C1 | Smythen Street | A2-B2 |
| Commercial Road | A1-B1 | South Street | B2 |
| Dinham Crescent | A2-A3 | Southernhay East | C2-C3 |
| Dinham Road | A3 | Southernhay West | C2-C3 |
| Elmgrove Road | A4 | Temple Road | C1 |
| Exe Street | A2-A3 | The Quay | B1 |
| Fairpark Road | C1-C2 | Tudor Street | A1-A2 |
| Fore Street | A2-B2 | Western Way | A1-B1 |
| Friars Gate | B1 | Western Way | C2-C3 |
| Friars Walk | B1-C1 | York Road | C4 |
| Frog Street | A1 | | |
| Hele Road | A4 | | |
| High Street | B2-B3-C3 | | |
| Holloway Street | B1-C1 | | |
| Howell Road | C4 | | |
| Iron Bridge | A3 | | |
| King Street | A2-B2 | | |
| King William Street | C4 | | |
| Longbrook Street | C4 | | |
| Longbrook Terrace | B4-C4 | | |
| Lower Coombe Street | B1 | | |
| Lower North Street | A3 | | |
| Magdalen Street | C2 | | |
| Market Street | A2-B2 | | |
| Mary Arches Street | A2 | | |
| Melbourne Street | C1 | | |
| Musgrove Row | B3 | | |
| New Bridge Street | A1-A2 | | |
| New North Road | A4-B4 | | |
| North Street | A3-B3-B2 | | |
| Northernhay Street | A3-B3 | | |
| Palace Gate | B2 | | |
| Paris Street | C3-C4 | | |

# Gloucester

Gloucester is found on atlas page **35**,
grid reference **8318**

**AA shop**
51 Westgate Street, Gloucester GL1 2NW — A3

| | | | |
|---|---|---|---|
| Albion Street | A1 | St Mary's Street | A4 |
| Alvin Street | C3-C4 | St Michael's Square | B1 |
| Archdeacon Street | A3-A4 | St Oswald's Road | A4 |
| Arthur Street | C1 | Skinner Street | B4 |
| Barbican Road | A2 | Southgate Street | A1-B2 |
| Barton Street | C1 | Station Approach | C2 |
| Bearland | A3 | Station Road | C2 |
| Belgrave Road | C1 | The Oxbode | B2-B3 |
| Berkeley Street | A3 | Trier Way | C1 |
| Blackdog Way | B4-C3 | Wellington Street | B1-C1 |
| Brunswick Road | A1-B2 | Westgate Street | A3-B3 |
| Brunswick Square | A1 | Worcester Street | B3-B4 |
| Bruton Way | C1-C3 | | |
| Bull Lane | A2-A3 | | |
| Catherine Street | B4 | | |
| Clare Street | A4 | | |
| Clarence Street | B2-C2 | | |
| College Street | A3 | | |
| Commercial Street | A2 | | |
| Cromwell Street | B1 | | |
| Eastgate Street | B2-C1 | | |
| Gouda Way | A4-B4 | | |
| Great Western Road | C3 | | |
| Greyfriars | A2-B1 | | |
| Hampden Way | B2-C1 | | |
| Hare Lane | B3 | | |
| Ladybellgate | A2 | | |
| London Road | C3 | | |
| Longsmith Street | A2-A3 | | |
| Market Parade | B2-C3 | | |
| Mount Street | A4 | | |
| Nettleton Road | C1-C2 | | |
| Northgate Street | B3 | | |
| Oxford Street | C3-C4 | | |
| Park Road | B1 | | |
| Park Street | B3-B4 | | |
| Parliament Street | A1-B1 | | |
| Pitt Street | A4-B3 | | |
| Priory Road | A4 | | |
| Quay Street | A3 | | |
| Russell Street | B2-C2 | | |
| St Aldate Street | B3 | | |
| St John's Lane | B3 | | |

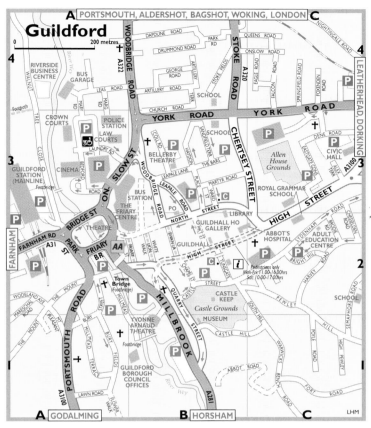

# Guildford

Guildford is found on atlas page **25**,
grid reference **9949**

**AA shop**
22 Friary Street, Guildford GU1 4EH      A2

| | | | |
|---|---|---|---|
| Abbot Road | B1-C1 | Millmead | A2-B1 |
| Alex Terrace | C3 | Millmead Terrace | A1 |
| Artillery Road | B4 | Mount Pleasant | A1-A2 |
| Artillery Terrace | B4 | Nightingale Road | C4 |
| Bedford Road | A3 | North Street | A2-B3 |
| Bridge Street | A2-A3 | Onslow Road | B4-C4 |
| Bright Hill | C2 | Onslow Street | A3-B4 |
| Brodie Road | C2 | Park Road | B4 |
| Bury Fields | A1 | Park Street | A2 |
| Bury Street | A1-A2 | Pewley Hill | B2-C1 |
| Castle Hill | B1-C1 | Portsmouth Road | A1-A2 |
| Castle Street | B2-C2 | Poyle Road | C1 |
| Chapel Street | B2 | Quarry Street | A2-B1 |
| Chertsey Street | B3-C2 | Queens Road | B4-C4 |
| Chesselden Road | C2-C3 | Sandfield Terrace | B3 |
| Church Road | B3-B4 | Semaphore Road | C1-C2 |
| College Road | B3 | South Hill | B2-C1 |
| Dapdune Road | B4 | Springfield Road | C4 |
| Dene Road | C3 | Stoke Fields | B4 |
| Drummond Road | B4 | Stoke Road | B4 |
| Eagle Road | C4 | Swan Lane | B2 |
| Eastgate Gardens | C3 | Sydenham Road | C2-C3 |
| Falcon Road | C4 | The Bars | B3 |
| Farnham Road | A2 | The Mount | A1-A2 |
| Flower Walk | A1 | Tunsgate | B2 |
| Foxenden Road | C4 | Walnut Tree Close | A2-A4 |
| Friary Bridge | A2 | Ward Street | B3 |
| Friary Street | A2-B2 | Whitelion Walk | B2 |
| George Road | B4 | Wodeland Ave | A2 |
| Harvey Road | C2 | Woodbridge Road | B2-B3-B4-A4 |
| Haydon Place | B3 | York Road | B3-C4 |
| High Pewley | C1 | | |
| High Street | B2-C3 | | |
| Laundry Road | A3 | | |
| Lawn Road | A1 | | |
| Leapale Lane | B3 | | |
| Leapale Road | B3 | | |
| Leas Road | A4 | | |
| Margaret Road | A3-A4 | | |
| Market Street | B2 | | |
| Martyr Road | B3 | | |
| Mary Road | A3-A4 | | |
| Millbrook | A2-B1 | | |

**183**

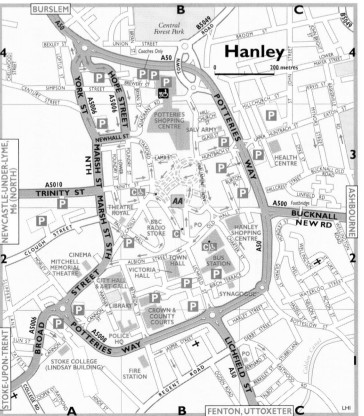

# Hanley

Hanley is found on atlas page **72**,
grid reference **8847**

**AA shop**
32–38 Stafford Street, Hanley ST1 1JP      B2

| | | | |
|---|---|---|---|
| Albion Street | B2 | Lower Foundry Street | A3 |
| Baskerville Road | C3-C4 | Lower Mayer Street | C4 |
| Berkeley Street | C1 | Marsh Street North | A3 |
| Bernard Street | C1 | Marsh Street South | A2-A3 |
| Bethesda Street | B1-B2 | Mayer Street | B4-C4 |
| Bexley Street | A4 | Morley Street | A2 |
| Birch Terrace | B2-C2 | Mynors Street | C3-C4 |
| Botteslow Street | C1 | Nelson Place | C1-C2 |
| Brewery Street | B4 | Newhall Street | A3-B3 |
| Broad Street | A1-A2 | Ogden Road | B1 |
| Broom Street | B4-C4 | Old Hall Street | B2-C2 |
| Bryan Street | B4 | Pall Mall | A2-B2-B3 |
| Bucknall New Road | C2 | Parliament Row | B3 |
| Bucknall Old Road | C3 | Piccadilly | A2-B2 |
| Burton Place | B3-C3 | Picton Street | C1-C2 |
| Cannon Street | A1-A2 | Potteries Way | A1-B1-C2-B4 |
| Century Street | A3-A4 | Quadrant Road | B3-B4 |
| Charter Street | B2-C2 | Raymond Street | A1 |
| Chellwood Street | A4 | Regent Road | B1 |
| Clough Street | A2 | St John Street | C3-C4 |
| College Road | A1 | St Luke Street | C2 |
| Cooper Street | A1 | Simpson Street | A4 |
| Derby Street | C1 | Slippery Lane | A1-A2 |
| Eastwood Road | C1 | Stafford Street | B3 |
| Eaton Street | C3 | Stubbs Lane | C1 |
| Foundry Street | B3 | Sun Street | A1 |
| Gilman Street | C2 | Talbot Street | C1 |
| Glass Street | B3 | Town Road | B4 |
| Harley Street | B1-C1-C2 | Trinity Street | A3-B3 |
| Hassell Street | C1-C2 | Union Street | A4-B4 |
| Hillchurch Street | B3-C4 | Upper Huntbach Street | C3 |
| Hillcrest Street | C3 | Waterloo Street | C2 |
| Hinde Street | A1 | Well Street | C2 |
| Hope Street | A4-B3-B4 | Wellington Road | C2 |
| Hordley Street | C2 | Wellington Street | C2 |
| Huntbach Street | B3-C3 | Yates Street | A1 |
| Jasper Street | B1 | York Street | A3-A4 |
| Jervis Street | C4 | | |
| John Bright Street | C4 | | |
| Lamb Street | B3 | | |
| Lichfield Street | B1-B2-C1 | | |
| Linfield Road | C3 | | |
| Loftus Street | A4 | | |

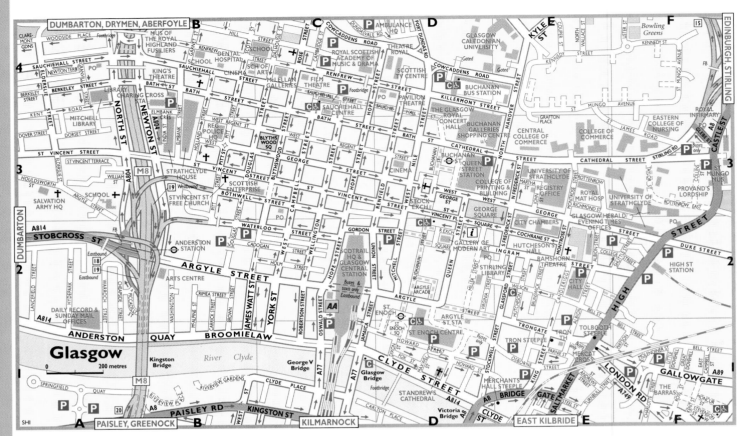

# Glasgow

Glasgow is found on atlas page 115,
grid reference 5865

**AA shop**
269 Argyle Street, Glasgow G2 8DW                     C2

| | | | | | | | |
|---|---|---|---|---|---|---|---|
| Albion Street | E1-E2 | Elmbank Crescent | B4 | Maxwell Street | D1 | Scott Street | B4-C4 |
| Anderston Quay | A1-B1 | Elmbank Street | B3-B4 | Mc Alpine Street | B1-B2 | Shuttle Street | F2 |
| Argyle Arcade | D2 | Fox Street | D1 | Miller Street | D2 | South Frederick Street | E2-E3 |
| Argyle Street | B2-C2-D2 | Gallowgate | F1 | Mitchell Street | D2-D3 | Springfield Quay | A1 |
| Bath Street | A4-B4-C4-C3-D3 | Garret Street | B4 | Molendiner Street | F1 | Steel Street | E1 |
| Bell Street | E2-F1 | George Square | D2-D3-E2-E3 | Moncur Street | F1 | Stevenson Street West | F1 |
| Berkeley Place | A4 | George Street | D3-E3-E2-F2 | Montrose Street | E2-E3 | Stirling Road | F3 |
| Berkeley Street | A4-B4 | Glassford Street | E2 | Newton Street | B2-B3-B4 | Stockwell Street | D1-E1 |
| Blythswood Street | B2-B4 | Glebe Street | F3 | North Frederick Street | E3 | Taylor Street | F3 |
| Bothwell Street | A3-C3 | Gordon Street | C2-D2 | North Hanover Street | E3-E4 | Trongate | E1-E2 |
| Bridgegate | D1-E1 | Grafton Place | E3-E4 | North Street | A2-A4 | Turnbull Street | E1 |
| Broomielaw | B1-C1 | Granville Street | A4 | North Wallace Street | E4 | Union Street | C2-D2 |
| Brown Street | B1-B2 | Great Doverhill | F1 | Osborne Street | D1-E1 | Victoria Bridge | D1 |
| Brunswick Street | E2 | High Street | F2-F3 | Oswald Street | C1-C2 | Vincent Place | D2-D3 |
| Buchanan Street | D2-D3 | Hill Street | B4-C4 | Paisley Road | A1-B1 | Virginia Street | D2 |
| Cadogan Street | B2-C2 | Holdsworth Street | A3 | Parnie Street | E1 | Warroch Street | A1-A2 |
| Cambridge Street | C4 | Holland Street | B3-B4 | Piccadilly Street | A2 | Washington Street | B1-B2 |
| Candleriggs | E1-E2 | Holm Street | B2-C2 | Pitt Street | B3-B4 | Waterloo Street | B2-C2 |
| Carlton Place | C1-D1 | Hope Street | C2-C3-C4-D4 | Port Dundas Road | D4 | Watson Street | F1 |
| Carrick Street | B1-B2 | Howard Street | C1-D1 | Queen Street | D2-D3 | Wellington Street | C2-C3-C4 |
| Castle Street | F3-F4 | Hutcheson Street | E2 | Renfield Street | D3-D4 | West Campbell Street | C2-C3-C4 |
| Cathedral Street | D3-F3 | Hydepark Street | A2 | Renfrew Street | B4-C4-D4 | West George Street | B3-C3-D3 |
| Charlotte Street | F1 | India Street | B3-B4 | Richmond Street | E3 | West Nile Street | D3-D4 |
| Cheapside Street | A1-A2 | Ingram Street | D2-E2 | Riverview Gardens | B1 | West Regent Street | B4-B3-C3-D3 |
| Clyde Place | B1 | Jamaica Street | C1-C2 | Riverview Place | B1 | West Street | B1 |
| Clyde Street | C1-D1 | James Watt Street | B1-B2 | Robertson Street | C1-C2 | William Street | A3 |
| Cochrane Street | E2 | John Street | E2-E3 | Rose Street | C4 | Wilson Street | D2-E2 |
| College Street | E2-F2 | Kennedy Street | E4-F4 | Ross Street | F1 | Woodside Place | A4 |
| Collins Street | F3 | Kent Road | A4 | Rottenrow | E3 | York Street | C1-C2 |
| Couper Street | E4 | Kent Street | F1 | Rottenrow East | F3 | | |
| Cowcaddens Road | C4-D4-E4 | Killermont Street | D4-E4 | Royal Exchange Square | D2 | | |
| Crimea Street | B2 | King Street | E1 | St Andrews Street | E1 | | |
| Dixon Street | D1 | Kingston Street | B1-C1 | St Enoch Square | D1 | | |
| Dorset Street | A3 | Kyle Street | E4 | St James Road | E4-E3-F3 | | |
| Douglas Street | B2-B3-C3-C4 | Lancefield Street | A2 | St Mungo Avenue | E4-F4 | | |
| Dover Street | A3 | Lister Street | F4 | St Vincent Street | A3-B3-C3-D3 | | |
| Duke Street | F2 | Little Doverhill | F1 | St Vincent Terrace | A3 | | |
| East Campbell Street | F1 | London Road | E1-F1 | Saltmarket | E1 | | |
| Elderslie Street | A3-A4 | Martha Street | E3 | Sauchiehall Street | A4-B4-C4 | | |

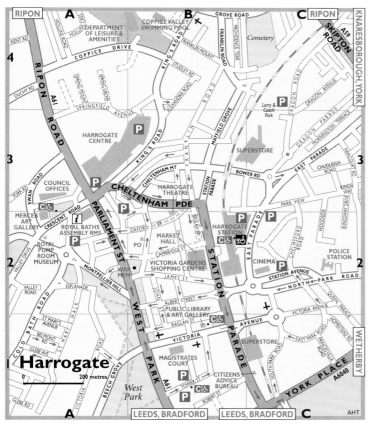

# Harrogate

Harrogate is found on atlas page **82**,
grid reference **3054**

| | | | |
|---|---|---|---|
| Albert Street | B2 | Raglan Street | B1-B2 |
| Alexandra Road | B3-B4 | Ripon Road | A3-A4 |
| Beech Grove | A1-B1 | Robert Street | B1 |
| Belmont Road | A1 | St Mary's Avenue | A1 |
| Beulah Street | B2-B3 | St Mary's Walk | A1-A2 |
| Bower Road | B3-C3 | Skipton Road | C4 |
| Cambridge Street | B2 | South Park Road | C1 |
| Chelmsford Road | C2-C3 | Spring Grove | A4 |
| Cheltenham Mount | B3 | Spring Mount | A4 |
| Cheltenham Parade | A3-B3 | Springfield Avenue | A3-A4-B3-B4 |
| Chudleigh Road | C3 | Station Avenue | C2 |
| Cold Bath Road | A1-A2 | Station Parade | B3-B2-B1-C1 |
| Coppice Drive | A4-B4 | Studley Road | B4 |
| Crescent Road | A2-A3 | Swan Road | A2-A3 |
| Dragon Avenue | C3-C4 | Tower Street | B1 |
| Dragon Parade | C3-C4 | Valley Drive | A2 |
| Dragon Road | C3-C4 | Valley Road | A2 |
| Duchy Road | A4 | Victoria Avenue | B1-C1-C2 |
| East Parade | C2-C3 | Victoria Road | A1-A2 |
| East Park Road | C1-C2 | West Park | B2-B1 |
| Esplanade | A2 | Woodside | C2-C3 |
| Franklin Mount | B4 | York Place | B1-C2 |
| Franklin Road | B3-B4 | York Road | A3 |
| Glebe Avenue | A1 | | |
| Glebe Road | A1 | | |
| Grove Road | B4-C4 | | |
| Harcourt Road | C3 | | |
| Hollins Crescent | A4 | | |
| Hollins Road | A4 | | |
| Homestead Road | C1 | | |
| James Street | B2 | | |
| John Street | B1-B2 | | |
| Kent Road | A4 | | |
| King's Road | A3-B3-B4 | | |
| Kings Way | C3 | | |
| Kingsway Drive | C2-C3 | | |
| Mayfield Grove | B3-B4 | | |
| Montpellier Hill | A2 | | |
| Mornington Terrace | C3-C4 | | |
| North Park Road | C2 | | |
| Oxford Street | A2-B2 | | |
| Park View | B3-C3 | | |
| Parliament Street | A2-A3 | | |
| Princes Villa Road | C1 | | |
| Providence Terrace | B4 | | |
| Queen Parade | C1-C2 | | |

185

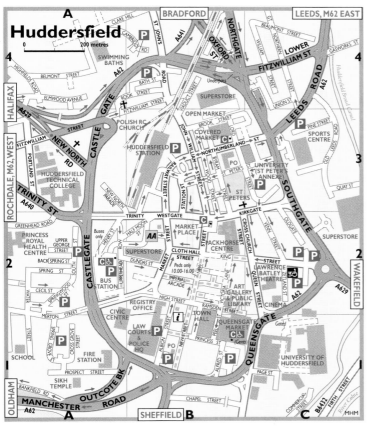

# Huddersfield

Huddersfield is found on atlas page **82**,
grid reference **1416**

**AA shop**
7 Cherry Tree Centre, Market Street, Huddersfield HD1 2ET   B2

| | | | |
|---|---|---|---|
| Albion Street | B1-B2 | Old Leeds Road | C3-C4 |
| Alfred Street | B1 | Oldgate | C2-C3 |
| Back Spring Street | A2 | Outcote Bank | A1-B1 |
| Bankfield Road | A1 | Oxford Street | B4 |
| Bath Street | B4 | Page Street | C1 |
| Beaumont Street | C4 | Peel Street | B1-B2 |
| Belmont Street | A4 | Pine Street | C3 |
| Brook Street | B3 | Portland Street | A3 |
| Byram Street | B3 | Princess Street | B1 |
| Castlegate | B1-A2-B4 | Prospect Street | A1 |
| Cecil Street | A2 | Quay Street | C3 |
| Chapel Street | B1 | Queen Street | C2 |
| Claremont Street | A4 | Queensgate | B1-C2 |
| Cloth Hall Street | B2 | Railway Street | B3 |
| Commercial Street | C1 | Ramsden Street | B2-C2 |
| Cross Church Street | C2 | Rook Street | A4-B4 |
| Cross Grove Street | A1 | St John's Road | B4 |
| Dundas Street | B2 | St Peter's Street | B3-C3 |
| Elmwood Avenue | A4 | South Street | A1-A2 |
| Firth Street | C1 | Southgate | B4-C2 |
| Fitzwilliam Street | A3-B4 | Spring Grove Street | A1 |
| Gasworks Street | C4 | Spring Street | A2 |
| Great Northern Street | C4 | Springwood Street | A2 |
| Greenhead Road | A2 | Station Street | B3 |
| Half Moon Street | B2 | Trinity Street | A3 |
| Henry Street | A2 | Trinity Westgate | A2-B2 |
| High Street | B2 | Union Street | C4 |
| Highfields Road | A4 | Upper George Street | A2 |
| Imperial Arcade | B2 | Upperhead Row | A2 |
| John William Street | B3 | Venn Street | C2-C3 |
| King Street | B2-C2 | Viaduct Street | B4 |
| Kirkgate | B2-C3 | Victoria Lane | B2 |
| Leeds Road | C3-C4 | Water Street | A2-A1 |
| Lord Street | B3-C3 | William Street | A3 |
| Lower Fitzwilliam Street | C4 | Wood Street | B3 |
| Manchester Road | A1-B1 | Zetland Street | C2 |
| Market Street | A2-B2 | | |
| Merton Street | A1-A2 | | |
| New North Parade | A3-B3 | | |
| New North Road | A3-A4 | | |
| New Street | B1-B2 | | |
| Northgate | B4-C4 | | |
| Northumberland Street | B3-C3 | | |

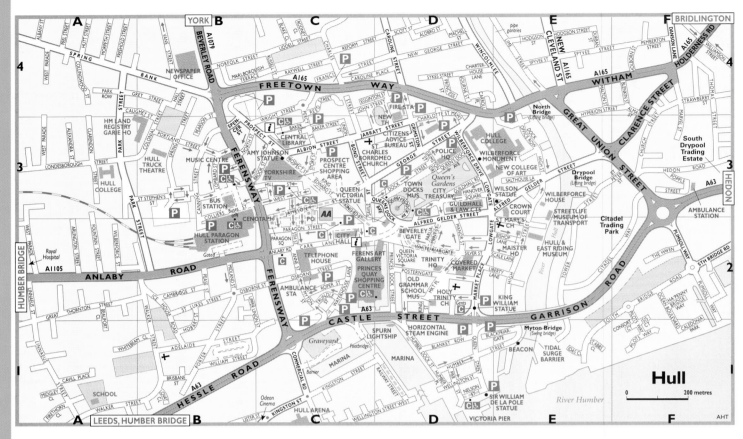

186

# Hull

Hull is found on atlas page **85**,
grid reference **0829**

**AA shop**
28 Paragon Street, Hull HU1 3NE                    C2

| | | | | | | | | |
|---|---|---|---|---|---|---|---|---|
| Adelaide Street | B1 | Collingwood Street | A4 | Idas Close | E1 | Pease Street | B2 | Strawberry Street | F4 |
| Albion Street | C3 | Colonial Street | B3-B4 | Isis Court | F1-F2 | Peel Street | A4 | Sykes Street | D4 |
| Aldbro Street | D4 | Commercial Road | C1 | Jameson Street | C3 | Pemberton Street | F4 | The Haven | F2 |
| Alexandra Street | A3 | Consort Court | F1 | Jarratt Street | C3-D3 | Percy Street | C3-C4 | Thomas Street | F3-F4 |
| Alfred Gelder Street | D2-D3-E3 | Dock Office Row | E3 | John Street | C4-D4 | Pier Street | D1 | Tower Street | E1-E3 |
| Alma Street | F4 | Dock Street | C3-D3 | King Edward Street | C2-C3 | Pilots Way | F1-F2 | Trundle Street | C2 |
| Anlaby Road | A2-B2-C2 | Durban Street | E4 | King Street | D2 | Plimsoll Way | F2 | Union Street | C3 |
| Anne Street | C2 | Egginton Street | C4-D4 | Kingston Street | C1-D1 | Popple Street | F3 | Upper Union Street | B2-C1 |
| Arlington Street | A2-A3 | Ferensway | B4-C1 | Liberty Lane | D2-E2 | Porter Street | B1-B2 | Vane Street | B4 |
| Baker Street | C3 | Firethorn Close | A1 | Liddell Street | C4 | Portland Street | B3 | Walker Street | A1-B2 |
| Beaufort Close | A1-A2 | Fountain Street | A2-A3 | Lime Street | E4 | Posterngate | D2 | Waterhouse Lane | C2 |
| Beverley Road | B4 | Francis Street | C4-D4 | Linnaeus Street | A1-A2 | Princes Dock Street | D2 | Wellington Street | D1 |
| Bishop Lane | E2 | Freehold Street | A4 | Lister Street | B1-C1 | Princess Street | D4 | Wellington Street West | C1-D2 |
| Blackfriargate | D1-E1 | Freetown Way | B4-E4 | Lombard Street | B3 | Prospect Street | B4-C3 | West Parade | A2-A3-A4 |
| Blake Close | C4 | Garrison Road | D1-F2 | Londesborough Street | A3-B3 | Queen Street | D1 | West Street | C3 |
| Blanket Row | D1 | George Street | C3-D4 | Lovat Close | B1 | Queen's Dock Avenue | D2-D3 | Whitebeam Close | A1-B1 |
| Blenkin Street | F4 | Great Thornton Street | A1-B2 | Lowgate | D3 | Railway Street | D1 | Whitefriargate | D2 |
| Bond Street | C3 | Great Union Street | E4-F3 | Malton Street | E4 | Raywell Street | C4 | Wilberforce Drive | D3-D4 |
| Bourne Street | D4 | Grey Street | A4-B4 | Manor Street | D2 | Reed Street | C4 | Wilberforce Street | A2 |
| Brisbane Street | B1 | Grimston Drive | D3 | Market Place | D2 | Reform Street | C4-D4 | William Street | B1 |
| Brook Street | B3-C3 | Grimston Street | D3 | Marlborough Terrace | B4-C4 | Rodney Close | C4 | Williamson Street | F4 |
| Caledonia Park | F1-F2 | Guildhall Road | D3 | Marvel Street | F3-F4 | Roper Street | C2 | Wincolmlee | D4-E4 |
| Cambridge Street | A2 | Ha'penny Bridge Way | F2 | Midgley Close | A1 | Russell Street | C4 | Witham | E4-F4 |
| Canning Street | B2-B3 | Hall Street | B4 | Midland Street | B2 | St Abbs Close | E1 | Wright Street | B3-C4 |
| Caroline Place | C4-D4 | Hanover Square | D3 | Mill Street | C3 | St Lukes Street | B2 | | |
| Caroline Street | D4 | Hedon Road | F3 | Morpeth Street | A4 | St Peter Street | E3-F3 | | |
| Carr Lane | C2 | Hessle Road | B1-C1 | Myton Street | C2 | St Stephen's Street | A2-B2 | | |
| Carroll Place | D4 | High Street | E2-E3 | Nelson Street | D1 | Salthouse Lane | E3 | | |
| Castle Street | C1-D1 | Hobart Street | B1-B2 | New George Street | D4 | Savile Street | C3 | | |
| Caughey Street | A4-B4 | Hodgson Street | E4 | Norfolk Street | B4-C4 | Scale Lane | D2-E2 | | |
| Cavill Place | A1 | Holborn Street | F4 | North Street | B3 | Scoff Street | D4 | | |
| Charles Street | C3-C4 | Holderness Street | F4 | Ocean Boulevard | F1-F2 | Silver Street | D3 | | |
| Charlotte Street Mews | D3-D4 | Humber Dock Street | D1 | Osborne Street | B2-C2 | South Bridge Road | E1-F2 | | |
| Charterhouse Lane | D4 | Humber Place | D1 | Paragon Square | C2-C3 | South Street | C2 | | |
| Church Street | F3-F4 | Humber Street | D1-E1 | Paragon Street | C3 | Spencer Street | B3 | | |
| Citadel Way | E2-F3 | Hutt Street | A4 | Park Row | A4 | Spring Bank | A4-B4 | | |
| Clarence Street | E4-F4 | Hyperion Street | E4-F4 | Park Street | A4-B2 | Spring Street | B3-B4 | | |
| Clarendon Street | A3 | Ice House Road | B1-B2 | Parliament Street | D2 | Spyvee Street | E4-F4 | | |
| Colliers Street | B3 | | | Pearson Street | B3-B4 | Story Street | C3 | | |

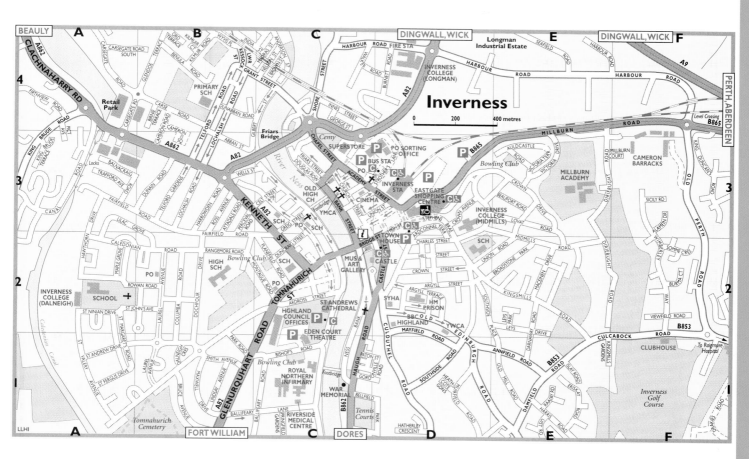

# Inverness

Inverness is found on atlas page **140**,
grid reference **6645**

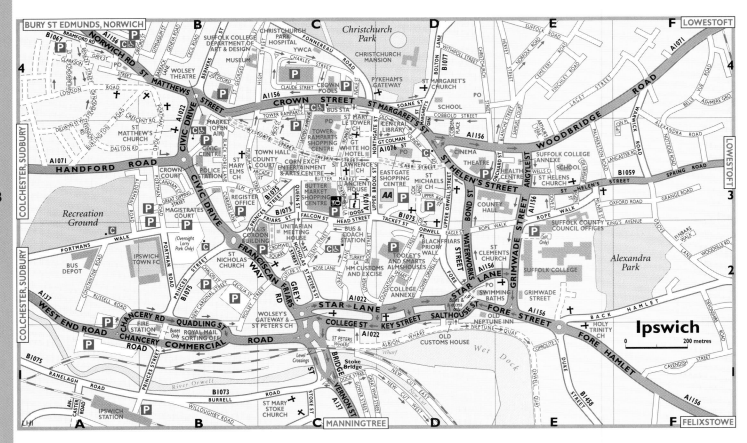

# Ipswich

Ipswich is found on atlas page **54**,
grid reference 1614

**AA shop**
Upper Brook Street, Ipswich IP4 1DU                    D3

| | | | | | | |
|---|---|---|---|---|---|
| Albion Wharf | C1-D1 | Coprolite Street | A2 | Key Street | E3-F3 | St Margaret's Street | D4 |
| Aldermans Road | A2-A3 | Cox Lane | E1 | King's Avenue | C1-D2 | St Matthews Street | C4-D3 |
| Alexandra Road | F3-F4 | Crescent Road | D3 | Lacey Street | E2-F3 | St Nicholas Street | B4 |
| Ancaster Road | A1 | Cromwell Square | A4 | Lancaster Road | E3-F4 | St Peter's Street | C2 |
| Arcade Street | B3-C3 | Crown Street | C2 | Lloyds Avenue | E3-F3 | St Peters Wharf | C2 |
| Argyle Street | E3 | Curriers Lane | B4-C4 | London Road | C3-C4 | St Stephen's Lane | C1 |
| Arthur's Terrace | E3 | Cutler Street | B2-B3 | Lower Brook Street | A4-B4 | Salthouse Street | C3 |
| Ashmere Grove | F4 | Dalton Road | C2 | Lower Orwell Street | C2-C3 | Samuel Court | D2 |
| Back Hamlet | E2-F2 | Devonshire Road | A3-B3 | Milner Street | D2 | Silent Street | E3-E4 |
| Barrack Lane | B4 | Dillwyn Street West | A2 | Museum Street | E2-E3 | Smart Street | C2 |
| Bedford Street | B4 | Dock Street | A3-A4 | Neale Street | C3-C4 | Soane Street | D2 |
| Bellevue Road | F3-F4 | Dogs Head Street | C1 | Neptune Quay | C4 | Spring Road | D4 |
| Benezet Street | A4 | Dove Street | C3 | New Cardinal Street | D1-E1 | Star Lane | F3 |
| Berners Street | B4 | Duke Street | E3 | New Cut East | B2 | Stevenson Road | C2-E2 |
| Black Horse Lane | B3 | Eagle Street | E1 | New Cut West | C1-D1 | Stoke Street | A3-A4 |
| Blanche Street | E3-E4 | Elm Street | D2 | Norfolk Road | C1-D1 | Suffolk Road | C1 |
| Bolton Lane | D4 | Falcon Street | B3-C3 | Northgate Street | E4 | Tacket Street | E4 |
| Bond Street | D2-D3 | Finbars Walk | C3 | Norwich Road | C3-D4 | Tavern Street | D2-D3 |
| Bramford Road | A4 | Finchley Road | F2 | Nottidge Road | A4-B4 | Tower Ramparts | C3 |
| Bridge Street | C1 | Fonnereau Road | E4 | Old Foundry Road | F3 | Tower Street | B4-C4 |
| Burlington Road | A3-B4 | Fore Hamlet | C4 | Orchard Street | D4-D3 | Turret Lane | C3-C4 |
| Burrell Road | B1-C1 | Fore Street | E1-F1 | Orford Street | D3-E3 | Upper Bar Street | C2 |
| Butter Market | C3 | Foundation Street | D2-E1 | Orwell Place | A4-B4 | Upper Brook Street | D3 |
| Canham Street | B3 | Franciscan Way | D2 | Orwell Quay | D2 | Upper Orwell Street | C3 |
| Carr Street | D3 | Friars Street | B2-C2 | Oxford Road | E1 | Upton Place | D2-D3 |
| Cavendish Street | F1 | Gaye Street | C3 | Palmerston Road | E3-F3 | Vernon Street | F3-F4 |
| Cecil Road | B4 | Geneva Road | A4 | Portman Road | E3 | Warwick Road | C1 |
| Cecilia Street | B2 | Gower Street | B4 | Portmans Walk | B2-B4 | Waterworks Street | F3-F4 |
| Cemetery Road | E4 | Grange Road | C1 | Princes Street | A2-B2 | Wells Close | D2 |
| Chalon Street | B2 | Great Colman Street | F3 | Quadling Street | A1-C3 | West End Road | E3 |
| Chancery Road | B1-A1-A2-B2 | Great Gipping Street | D3 | Queen Street | B1-B2 | Westgate Street | A1-A2 |
| Charles Street | C4 | Great Whip Street | B3 | Ranelagh Road | C3 | Wilberforce Street | B4-C3 |
| Christchurch Street | D3-D4 | Grey Friars Road | C1-D1 | Regent Street | A1 | Willoughby Road | A4 |
| Civic Drive | B2-B4 | Grimwade Street | C2 | Rope Walk | E3 | Withipoll Street | B1 |
| Clarkson Street | A4-B4 | Grove Lane | E2-E3 | Rose Lane | D2-E3 | Wolsey Street | D4 |
| Claude Street | C4 | Gymnasium Street | F2-F3 | Russell Road | C2 | Woodbridge Road | B1-C2 |
| Cobbold Street | D4 | Handford Road | B4 | St Georges Street | A2 | Woodville Road | D3-F4 |
| Cobden Place | D3 | Harvey Street | A3-B3 | St Helen's Street | B4 | | F2 |
| College Street | C1-C2 | High Street | E4 | St Margaret's Green | D3-F3 | | |
| Commercial Road | B1-C1 | Jefferies Road | B4-C4 | | | | |
| Constantine Road | | | | | | | |

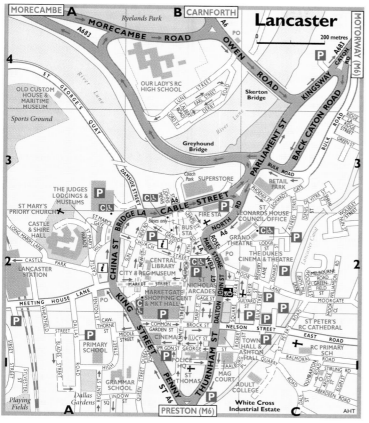

# Lancaster

Lancaster is found on atlas page **87**,
grid reference **4761**

| | | | | | | |
|---|---|---|---|---|---|
| Aalborg Place | B1-C1 | Kingsway | C4 | Sun Street | B2 |
| Aberdeen Road | C1 | Lindow Square | A1 | Sylvester Street | A1 |
| Albert Road | B3-B4 | Lindow Street | A1-A2 | Thurnham Street | B1 |
| Alfred Street | C2-C3 | Lodge Street | C2 | Wheatfield Street | A1-A2 |
| Argyle Street | C1 | Long Marsh Lane | A2 | Williamson Road | C2 |
| Back Caton Road | C3-C4 | Lord Street | B3 | Wolseley Street | C2-C3 |
| Balmoral Road | C1 | Lucy Street | B1 | Woodville Street | C2 |
| Bath Mill Lane | C2 | Lune Street | B3-B4 | | |
| Blades Street | A1 | Market Street | A2-B2 | | |
| Brewery Lane | C2 | Mary Street | B1-B2 | | |
| Bridge Lane | A2-B2 | Meeting House Lane | A2 | | |
| Brock Street | B1 | Melbourne Road | C2 | | |
| Bryer Street | C2 | Middle Street | A1-B1 | | |
| Bulk Road | C3-C4 | Moor Close | C1-C2 | | |
| Bulk Street | C1-C2 | Moor Lane | B2-C2 | | |
| Cable Street | B2-B3 | Moorgate | C2 | | |
| Castle Hill | A2 | Morecambe Road | A4-B4 | | |
| Castle Park | A2 | Nelson Street | B1-C1 | | |
| Caton Road | C4 | New Road | B2 | | |
| Cawthorne Street | A1 | New Street | B2 | | |
| Chapel Street | B2 | North Road | B2-B3 | | |
| Cheapside | B2 | Nun Street | B2 | | |
| China Street | A2 | Owen Road | B4-C4 | | |
| Church Street | B2 | Parliament Street | C3-C4 | | |
| Common Garden Street | B1 | Penny Street | B1-B2 | | |
| Dale Street | C1 | Phoenix Street | C3 | | |
| Dallas Road | A1-A2 | Quarry Road | C1 | | |
| Dalton Square | B1-B2 | Queen Square | B1 | | |
| Damside Street | A3-B3-B2 | Queen Street | B1 | | |
| De Vitre Street | C3 | Regent Street | A1 | | |
| Denis Street | C2-C3 | Ridge Lane | C4 | | |
| Derby Road | B3-B4 | Ridge Street | C3 | | |
| Dumbarton Road | C1 | Robert Street | B1 | | |
| Earl Street | B4 | Rosemary Lane | B2 | | |
| East Road | C1 | St George's Quay | A3-A4 | | |
| Edward Street | C2 | St Johns Mews | B3 | | |
| Elgin Street | C1 | St Leonard's Gate | B2-C2-C3 | | |
| Fenton Street | A1-A2 | St Mary's Gate | A2 | | |
| Friar Street | B2 | St Mary's Parade | A2 | | |
| Gage Street | B2 | St Peter's Road | C1-C2 | | |
| George Street | B1 | Shaw Street | C3 | | |
| Great John Street | B2 | Sibsey Street | A1 | | |
| Green Street | C3 | Spring Garden Street | B1 | | |
| Greenfield Street | C2 | Stirling Road | C1 | | |
| High Street | A1 | Stonewell | B2 | | |
| King Street | A2-B2-B1 | Sulyard Street | B2-C2 | | |

# Llandudno

Llandudno is found on atlas page **69**,
grid reference **7882**

| | | | |
|---|---|---|---|
| Abbey Road | A3-C4 | Hill Terrace | B4-C4 |
| Albert Street | B2-C3 | Howard Road | C2 |
| Anglesey Road | A3-A4 | Hywell Place | C2 |
| Argyll Road | C2 | King's Avenue | B2 |
| Arvon Avenue | B3-B4 | King's Road | B1-B2 |
| Augusta Street | C2-C3 | Knowles Road | B1-B2 |
| Bodafon Street | C3 | Lees Road | B2 |
| Bodnant Road | C1 | Lloyd Street | B3-C3 |
| Brookes Street | B3-C3 | Lloyd Street West | A2 |
| Bryniau Road | A2-B1 | Llwynon Road | A4-B4 |
| Builder Street | C2 | Madoc Street | B3-C3 |
| Builder Street West | B1-C2 | Maelgwn Road | B3 |
| Cae Mawr | B1 | Maesdu Road | B1-C1 |
| Caroline Road | B3-C3 | Mostyn Street | B3-C3 |
| Chapel Street | B3 | Mowbray Road | B1 |
| Charlton Street | C3 | Norman Road | C2 |
| Church Close | A2 | North Parade | C4 |
| Church Walks | A3-B4 | Oxford Road | C2 |
| Clement Avenue | B3 | Plas Road | B4 |
| Clifton Road | B3 | Rectory Lane | B3-B4 |
| Clonnel Street | C3 | St Andrew's Avenue | B2-B3 |
| Conwy Road | C2-C3 | St Andrew's Place | B3 |
| Council Street West | C2 | St David's Road | B2-B3 |
| Cwlach Road | B3-B4 | St George's Place | C3 |
| Cwm Road | C1-C2 | St Mary's Road | B3-C2 |
| Dale Road | A2 | St Seirol's Road | B2-B3 |
| Deganwy Avenue | B3 | Somerset Street | C3 |
| Denness Place | B2 | South Parade | B4-C3 |
| Dinas Road | B2 | The Oval | A2-B3 |
| Dyffryn Road | B1-B2 | The Parade | C3 |
| Eryl Place | B2 | Thorpe Street | C2 |
| Ffordd Dewi | C1 | Trevor Street | C3 |
| Ffordd Dulyn | B1-B2 | Trinity Avenue | B1-C3 |
| Ffordd Dwyfor | C1 | Trinity Crescent | A1-B1 |
| Ffordd Elisabeth | C1 | Trinity Square | C3 |
| Ffordd Gwynedd | C1 | Tudno Street | B4 |
| Ffordd Penrhyn | C1-C2 | Ty-Gwyn Road | B4 |
| Ffordd yr Orsedd | C1 | Ty Isa Road | C3-C4 |
| Ffordd Ysbyty | B1-C1 | Tyn-y-Coed Road | A4 |
| Garage Street | C2-C3 | Upper Mostyn Street | B4 |
| Gloddaeth Avenue | A2-B3 | Vaughan Street | C2-C3 |
| Gloddaeth Street | B3 | West Parade | A2-A3 |
| Great Ormes Road | A1-A3 | Winllan Avenue | A2-B2 |
| Haulfre Gardens | A3 | York Road | B3 |
| Herkomer Crescent | A1-A2 | | |
| Herkomer Road | A2 | | |

189

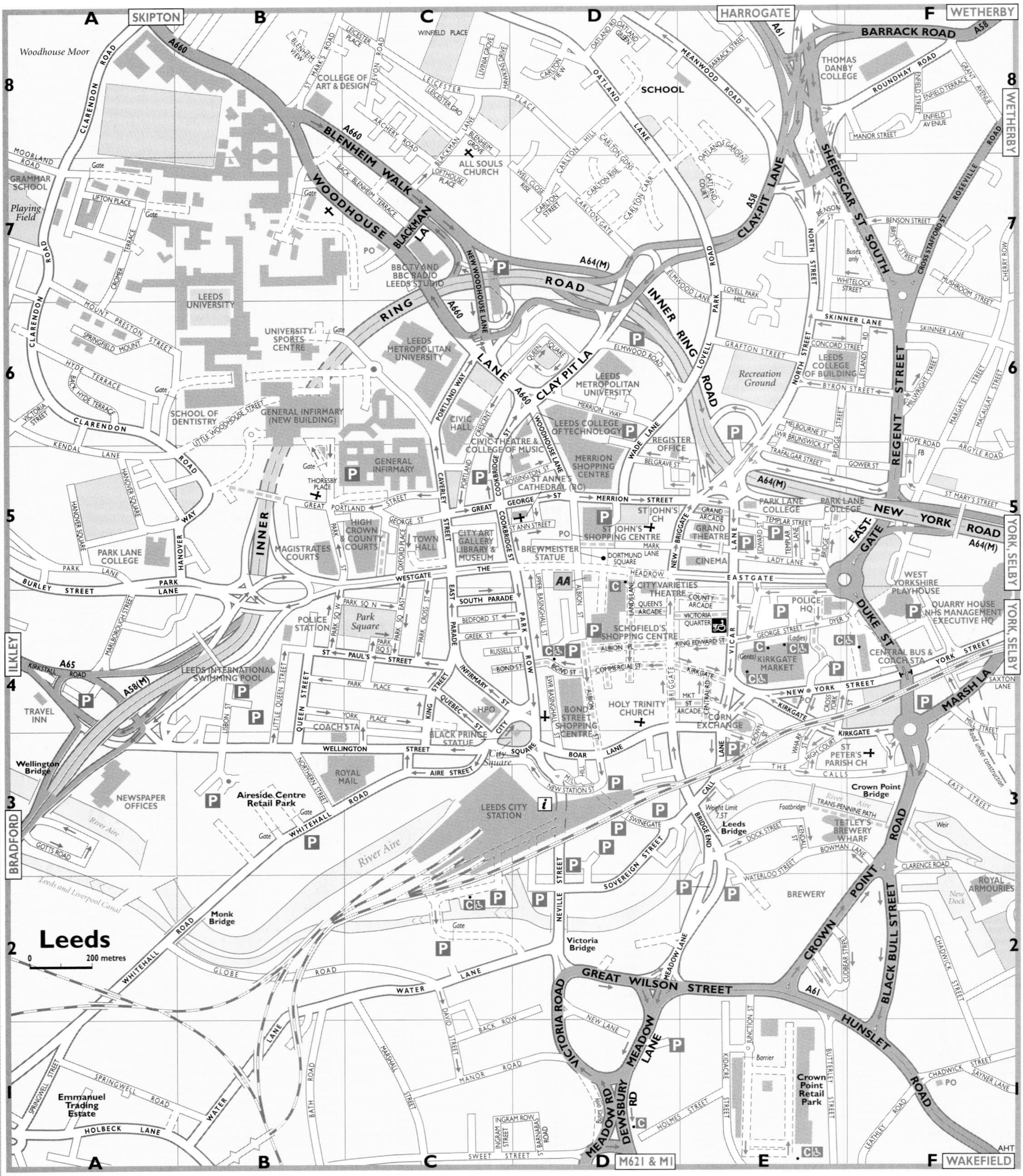

190

# Leeds

SKIPTON · HARROGATE · WETHERBY · BARRACK ROAD · WETHERBY

Woodhouse Moor

CLARENDON ROAD · MOORLAND ROAD · GRAMMAR SCHOOL · Playing Field

COLLEGE OF ART & DESIGN · LEICESTER PLACE · WINFIELD PLACE · Leicester Grove · BLENHEIM VIEW · ARCHERY ROAD

THOMAS DANBY COLLEGE · ROUNDHAY ROAD · SCHOOL · OATLAND LANE · MEANWOOD ROAD · OATLAND ROAD

BLENHEIM WALK · WOODHOUSE · BLACKMAN LA · ALL SOULS CHURCH · LOFTHOUSE PLACE · NEW WOODHOUSE LANE

BBC TV AND BBC RADIO LEEDS STUDIO · A660 · RING ROAD · A64(M)

SHEEPSCAR ST SOUTH · CLAY PIT LANE · A58 · INNER RING ROAD · NORTH STREET · BENSON STREET · SKINNER LANE · REGENT STREET

LEEDS UNIVERSITY · LEEDS METROPOLITAN UNIVERSITY · UNIVERSITY SPORTS CENTRE · WOODHOUSE LANE · CLAY PIT LA

LEEDS COLLEGE OF BUILDING · LEEDS COLLEGE OF TECHNOLOGY · Recreation Ground · CONCORD STREET · BYRON STREET

SCHOOL OF DENTISTRY · GENERAL INFIRMARY (NEW BUILDING) · CIVIC HALL · MERRION WAY · REGISTER OFFICE · MELBOURNE ST

CLARENDON · HYDE TERRACE · SPRINGFIELD MOUNT · CIVIC THEATRE & COLLEGE OF MUSIC · MERRION SHOPPING CENTRE · GRAFTON STREET · TRAFALGAR STREET · GOWER ST

HANOVER SQUARE · PARK LANE COLLEGE · GENERAL INFIRMARY · THORESBY PLACE · ST ANNE'S CATHEDRAL (RC) · MERRION STREET · A64(M) · PARK LANE COLLEGE · NEW YORK ROAD

HIGH CROWN & COUNTY COURTS · GEORGE ST · ST JOHN'S CH · ST JOHN'S SHOPPING CENTRE · GRAND ARCADE · GRAND THEATRE · TEMPLAR STREET

MAGISTRATES COURTS · TOWN HALL · CITY ART GALLERY LIBRARY & MUSEUM · BREWMEISTER STATUE · CINEMA · LADY LANE · WEST YORKSHIRE PLAYHOUSE

POLICE STATION · Park Square · WESTGATE · SOUTH PARADE · CITY VARIETIES THEATRE · COUNTY ARCADE · VICTORIA QUARTER · POLICE HQ · QUARRY HOUSE NHS MANAGEMENT EXECUTIVE HQ

PAUL'S STREET · PARK PLACE · QUEEN'S ARCADE · SCHOFIELD'S SHOPPING CENTRE · ALBION · COMMERCIAL ST · KIRKGATE MARKET · CENTRAL BUS & COACH STA

LEEDS INTERNATIONAL SWIMMING POOL · KIRKSTALL · A65 · ILKLEY · A58(M) · TRAVEL INN · INFIRMARY ST · HPO · BOND ST · HOLY TRINITY CHURCH · CORN EXCHANGE · ST PETER'S PARISH CH · MARSH LA · YORK, SELBY · A64(M)

BLACK PRINCE STATUE · COACH STA · WELLINGTON STREET · AIRE STREET · CITY SQUARE · BOND STREET SHOPPING CENTRE · BOAR LANE · CROWN POINT BRIDGE

Wellington Bridge · NEWSPAPER OFFICES · Aireside Centre Retail Park · WHITEHALL · ROYAL MAIL · LEEDS CITY STATION · LEEDS BRIDGE · TETLEY'S BREWERY WHARF · ROYAL ARMOURIES

River Aire · Leeds and Liverpool Canal · GOTTS ROAD · Monk Bridge · SWINEGATE · SOVEREIGN STREET · BRIDGE END · BREWERY · New Dock · Weir

Leeds
0        200 metres

WHITEHALL ROAD · GLOBE ROAD · WATER LANE · DAVID STREET · Victoria Bridge · MEADOW LANE · GREAT WILSON STREET · CROWN POINT ROAD · A61 · HUNSLET ROAD

EMMANUEL TRADING ESTATE · SPRINGWELL ROAD · HOLBECK LANE · BATH ROAD · MARSHALL STREET · MANOR ROAD · VICTORIA ROAD · DEWSBURY RD · MEADOW RD · INGRAM ROW · Crown Point Retail Park · SAYNER LANE

HOLBECK · SWEET STREET · M621 & M1 · WAKEFIELD

BRADFORD · River Aire

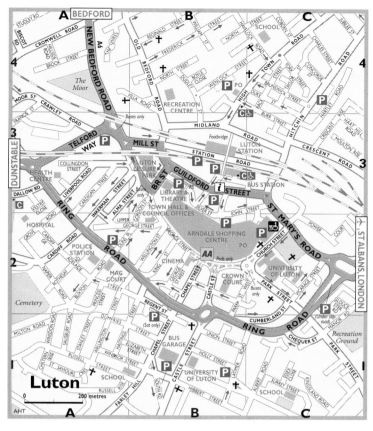

# Luton

Luton is found on atlas page **38**,
grid reference **0921**

**AA shop**
45 George Street, Luton LU1 2AQ　　　　　　B2

| | | | | | |
|---|---|---|---|---|---|
| Adelaide Street | A2-B2 | Gordon Street | B2-B3 | Silver Street | B3 |
| Albert Road | B1-C1 | Grove Road | A2-A3 | South Road | B1 |
| Alma Street | A2-B3 | Guildford Street | B3-C3 | Stanley Street | A1-A2 |
| Back Street | C4 | Hart Hill Drive | C3 | Station Road | B3-C3 |
| Biscot Road | A4 | Hartley Road | C3-C4 | Strathmore Avenue | C1 |
| Boyle Close | B4 | Hastings Street | A1-B2 | Studley Road | A4 |
| Bridge Street | B3 | Havelock Road | B4-C4 | Surrey Street | C1 |
| Brook Street | A4 | Hibbert Street | B1 | Tavistock Street | B1 |
| Brunswick Street | C4 | High Town Road | B3-C4 | Taylor Street | C4 |
| Burr Street | C3-C4 | Hillside Road | A4 | Telford Way | A3 |
| Buxton Road | A2 | Hitchin Road | C3-C4 | The Shires | A4 |
| Cardiff Grove | A2 | Holly Street | B1 | Union Street | B1 |
| Cardiff Road | A2 | Inkerman Street | A2-A3 | Upper George Street | A2-B2 |
| Cardigan Street | A3 | John Street | B2-C3 | Vestry Close | A3 |
| Castle Street | B1-B2 | Jubilee Street | C4 | Vicarage Street | C2 |
| Chapel Street | B1-B2 | King Street | B2 | Villa Road | A4-B4 |
| Charles Street | C4 | Kingsland Road | C1 | Wellington Street | A1-B2 |
| Chequer Street | C1 | Latimer Road | B1-C1 | Wenlock Street | B4-C4 |
| Chiltern Rise | A1 | Liverpool Road | A3 | William Street | B4 |
| Church Street | B2-C2 | Manor Road | C1-C2 | Windsor Street | A1-B1 |
| Cobden Street | C4 | Meyrick Avenue | A2 | Winsdon Road | A1-A2 |
| Collingdon Street | A3 | Midland Road | D3-C3 | York Street | C4 |
| Concorde Street | C4 | Mill Street | B3 | | |
| Crawley Green Road | C2 | Milton Road | A1 | | |
| Crawley Road | A3-A4 | Moor Street | A4 | | |
| Crescent Rise | C3-C4 | Moulton Rise | C3 | | |
| Crescent Road | C3 | Napier Road | A2 | | |
| Cromwell Road | A4 | New Bedford Street | A4-B3 | | |
| Cumberland Street | C1-C2 | New Town Street | B1-C1 | | |
| Dallow Road | A3 | North Street | B4-C4 | | |
| Dudley Street | B3-B4 | Old Bedford Road | A4-B3 | | |
| Duke Street | C3-C4 | Park Street | C1-C2 | | |
| Dumfries Street | A2-B1 | Park Street West | B2-C2 | | |
| Duns Place | A2-B2 | Power Court | C2 | | |
| Dunstable Road | A4-C2 | Princess Street | A2 | | |
| Elizabeth Street | A1-B1 | Regent Street | B1-B2 | | |
| Essex Close | C1 | Reginald Street | B4 | | |
| Farley Hill | A1-B1 | Rothesay Road | A2 | | |
| Francis Street | A3-A4 | Russell Rise | A1 | | |
| Frederick Street | B4 | Russell Street | A1-B1 | | |
| George Street | B2 | St Mary's Road | C2-C3 | | |
| George Street West | B2 | St Saviours Crescent | A1 | | |
| Gloucester Road | C2 | Salisbury Road | A1-A2 | | |

# Leeds

Leeds is found on atlas page **82**,
grid reference **2932**

**AA shop**
95 The Headrow, Leeds LS1 6LU　　　　　　D5

| | | | | | | | | | |
|---|---|---|---|---|---|---|---|---|---|
| Aire Street | C3 | Chadwick Street | F1-F2 | Grant Avenue | F8 | Lovell Park Road | D6-E6-E7 | Park Cross Street | C4-C5 | The Headrow | C5-D5 |
| Albion Place | D4 | Cherry Row | F6-F7 | Great George Street | C5-D5 | Lower Basinghall Street | D3-D4 | Park Lane | A5-B5 | Thoresby Place | B5 |
| Albion Street | D3-D5 | City Square | C3-C4-D3-D4 | Great Portland Street | B5-C5 | Lower Brunswick Street | E5-E6 | Park Place | B4-C4 | Trafalgar Street | E5 |
| Archery Road | C8 | Clarence Road | F3 | Great Wilson Street | D2-E2 | Macaulay Street | F5-F6 | Park Row | D4 | Upper Basinghall Street | D4-D5 |
| Argyle Road | F5 | Clarendon Road | A8-A7-A6-B5 | Greek Street | C4-D4 | Manor Road | C1-D1 | Park Square East | C4 | Vicar Lane | E4-E5 |
| Back Blenheim Terrace | B7-C7 | Clay-Pit Lane | D6-D7-E7 | Hawkins Drive | C8 | Manor Street | F8 | Park Square North | B4-C4 | Victoria Quarter | D4-E4 |
| Back Hyde Terrace | A6 | Commercial Street | D4 | Hanover Square | A5 | Margate Street | F5-F6 | Park Square South | C4 | Victoria Road | D1-D2 |
| Back Row | C1-D2 | Concord Street | E6-F6 | Hanover Way | B5 | Mark Lane | D5 | Park Square West | B4 | Victoria Street | A6 |
| Barrack Road | F8 | Cookridge Street | C5-C6 | High Court | E3 | Market Street Arcade | D4-E4 | Park Street | B5 | Wade Lane | D5-D6 |
| Barrack Street | F8 | County Arcade | D4-E4 | Holbeck Lane | A1 | Marlborough Street | A4 | Portland Crescent | C5-C6 | Water Lane | B1-B2-C2-D2 |
| Bath Road | B1-B2 | Cromer Terrace | A6-A7 | Holmes Street | D1-E1 | Marsh Lane | F4 | Portland Way | C6 | Waterloo Street | E2-E3 |
| Bedford Street | C4 | Cross Stamford Street | F6-F7 | Hope Road | F5 | Marshall Street | B1-B2 | Quebec Street | C3-C4 | Well Close Rise | D7 |
| Belgrave Street | D5-E5 | Cross York Street | E4 | Hunslet Road | E2-F1 | Meadow Lane | C1-C2 | Queen's Arcade | D4 | Wellington Street | A3-B3-C3 |
| Benson Street | F7 | Crown Point Road | E2-F2-F3 | Hyde Terrace | A6 | Meadow Road | D1 | Queen Square | D6 | Westgate | C5 |
| Black Bull Street | F1-F2 | Crown Street | E3 | Infirmary Street | C4 | Meanwood Road | D8-E8 | Queen Street | B3-B4 | Wharf Street | E3 |
| Blackman Lane | C7 | Cudbear Street | E2 | Ingram Row | C1-D1 | Melbourne Street | E6 | Regent Street | F5-F6 | Whitehall Road | A1-C3 |
| Blenheim Grove | C8 | David Street | C1-C2 | Ingram Street | C1 | Merrion Street | D5-E5 | Roseville Road | F7-F8 | Whitelock Street | E7-F7 |
| Blenheim View | B8-C8 | Devon Road | C8 | Inner Ring Road | B5-E5 | Merrion Way | D6 | Rossington Street | C5-D5 | Winfield Place | C8 |
| Blenheim Walk | B8-D7 | Dewsbury Road | D1 | Junction Street | E1-E2 | Mill Hill | D3 | Roundhay Road | E8-F8 | Woodhouse Lane | A8-D5 |
| Boar Lane | D3 | Dock Street | E3 | Kelso Road | A7 | Mill Street | F3-F4 | Russell Street | C4-D4 | York Place | B4-C4 |
| Bond Street | C4-D4 | Dortmund Square | D5 | Kendal Lane | A5-A6 | Millwright Street | F6 | St Ann Street | D5 | York Street | F4 |
| Bowman Lane | E3-F3 | Duke Street | F4 | Kendall Street | E3 | Moorland Road | A7 | St Barnabas Road | D1 | | |
| Bridge End | D3 | Dyer Street | E4-F4 | Kidacre Street | E1 | Mount Preston Street | A6-A7 | St Mark's Road | B8 | | |
| Bridge Street | E5-E6 | East Parade | C4-C5 | King Edward Street | D4-E4 | Mushroom Street | F6-F7 | St Mary's Road | F5 | | |
| Briggate | D3-D4 | East Street | F3 | King Street | C3-C4 | Neville Street | D2-D3 | St Paul's Street | B4-C4 | | |
| Bristol Street | F7 | Eastgate | F5 | Kirkgate | E4-E3-F3 | New Briggate | D5-E5 | Saxton Lane | F4 | | |
| Burley Street | A4-A5 | Edward Street | E5 | Kirkstall Road | A4 | New Lane | D1-D2 | Sayner Lane | F1 | | |
| Butterley Street | E1 | Elmwood Lane | D7-E7 | Lands Lane | D4 | New Station Street | D3 | Sheepscar Street South | E7-F7 | | |
| Byron Street | E6-F6 | Elmwood Road | D6 | Leathley Road | F1 | New Woodhouse Lane | C6-C7 | Skinner Lane | E6-F6 | | |
| Call Lane | E3 | Enfield Avenue | F8 | Leicester Grove | C8 | New York Road | E5-F5 | South Parade | C4 | | |
| Carlton Carr | D7 | Enfield Terrace | F8 | Leicester Place | C8-D8 | New York Street | E4-F4 | Sovereign Street | D2-D3 | | |
| Carlton Gate | D7 | Enfield Street | F8 | Leylands Road | F6 | North Street | E6-E7 | Springfield Mount | A6 | | |
| Carlton Gardens | D7-D8 | George Street | C5 | Lifton Place | A7 | Northern Street | B3 | Springwell Road | A1-B1 | | |
| Carlton Hill | D7-D8 | George Street | E4 | Lisbon Street | B3-B4 | Oatland Court | E7 | Springwell Street | A1 | | |
| Carlton Rise | D7 | Globe Road | A2-B2-C2 | Little Queen Street | B3-B4 | Oatland Drive | D8 | Sweet Street | C1-D1 | | |
| Carlton Street | D7 | Gotts Road | A3 | Little Woodhouse Street | B5-B6 | Oatland Lane | D7-D8 | Swinegate | D3 | | |
| Carlton View | D8 | Gower Street | E5-F5 | Livinia Grove | C8 | Oatland Road | D8 | Templar Lane | E5 | | |
| Caverley Street | C5-C6 | Grafton Street | E6 | Lofthouse Place | C7 | Oatlands Gardens | E7-E8 | Templar Street | E5 | | |
| Central Road | E4 | Grand Arcade | E5 | Lovell Park Hill | E6-E7 | Oxford Place | C5 | The Calls | E3-F3 | | |

191

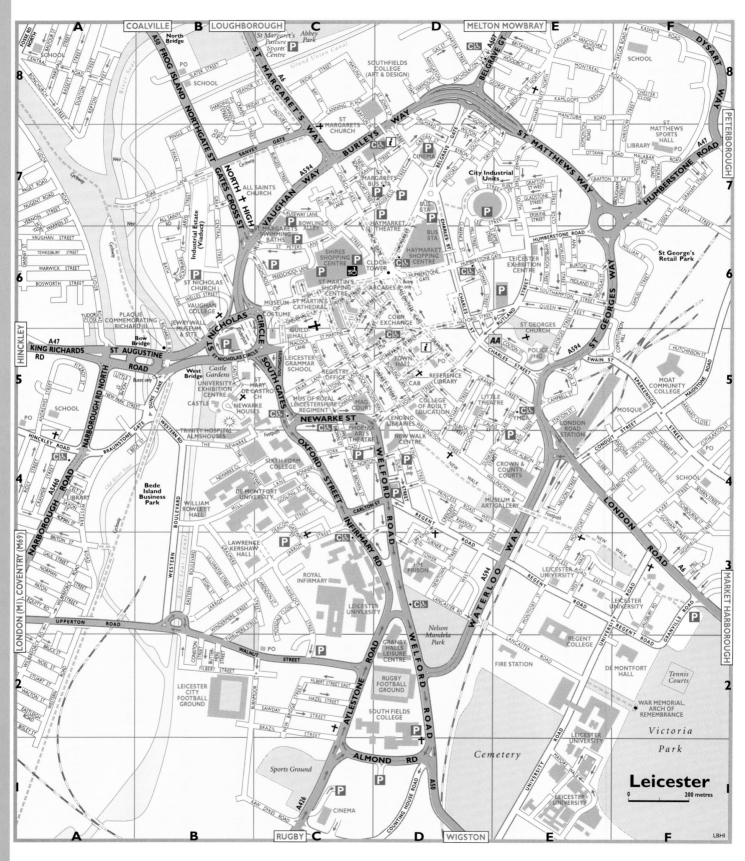

Leicester

0          200 metres

# Maidstone

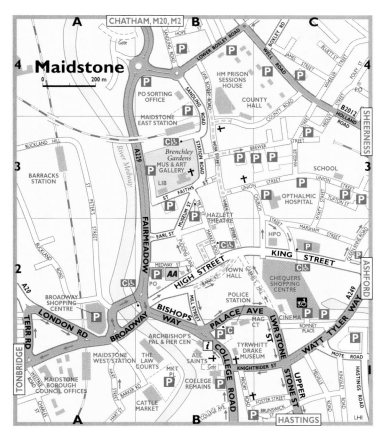

Maidstone is found on atlas page **28**,
grid reference **7555**

**AA shop**

26-27 High Street, Maidstone ME14 1JF      B2

| | | | |
|---|---|---|---|
| Bank Street | B2 | Lower Stone Street | C1-C2 |
| Barker Road | A1-B1 | Market Buildings | B2 |
| Barker Street | A2 | Market Street | B3 |
| Bishops Way | B1-B2 | Marsham Street | C2 |
| Bluett Street | C4 | Medway Street | B2 |
| Boxley Road | C4 | Melville Road | C1 |
| Brewer Street | B3-C3 | Mill Street | B1-B2 |
| Broadway | A1-B2 | Mote Road | C1 |
| Brunswick Street | C1 | Museum Street | B2-B3 |
| Buckland Hill | A3 | Palace Avenue | B1-C2 |
| Buckland Road | A2-A3 | Priory Road | B1 |
| Charles Street | A1 | Pudding Lane | B2 |
| Church Street | C2-C3 | Queen Anne Road | C2 |
| College Avenue | B1 | Romney Place | C1 |
| College Road | B1 | St Faiths Street | B3 |
| County Road | B3-C4 | St Peter's Street | A2-A3 |
| Earl Street | B2 | Sandling Road | B3-B4 |
| Fairmeadow | B2-B4 | Station Road | B3 |
| Foley Street | C4 | Terrace Road | A1-A2 |
| Foster Street | B1-C1 | Tufton Street | C3 |
| Gabriel's Hill | B2-C2 | Union Street | B3-C3 |
| Hart Street | A1 | Upper Stone Street | C1 |
| Hastings Road | C1 | Watt Tyler Way | C1-C2 |
| Hedley Street | C3-C4 | Week Street | B2-B3 |
| High Street | B2 | Well Road | C4 |
| Holland Road | C3-C4 | Westree Road | A1 |
| Hope Street | B4 | Wheeler Street | C3-C4 |
| James Street | C4 | Wyatt Street | C2-C3 |
| Kingsley Road | C1 | | |
| King Street | C3-C4 | | |
| Knightrider Street | B1-C1 | | |
| London Road | A1-A2 | | |
| Lower Boxley Road | B4 | | |

# Leicester

Leicester is found on atlas page **62**,
grid reference **5804**

**AA shop**

132 Charles Street, Leicester LE1 1NA      E5

| | | | | | |
|---|---|---|---|---|---|
| Abbey Street | D7 | Calais Hill | E4-E5 | Dysart Way | F7-F8 |
| Albion Street | D4-D5 | Calais Street | D5-E5 | East Bond Street | C6-C7 |
| All Saints Road | B6-B7 | Calgary Road | E8 | East Street | E4-E5 |
| Almond Road | C1-D1 | Campbell Street | E5 | Eastern Boulevard | B2-B4 |
| Andrewes Street | A4-A5 | Cank Street | C5-D6 | Eastleigh Road | A2 |
| Ann Street | E6 | Canning Place | C8-D8 | Edmonton Road | E7-E8 |
| Archdeacon Lane | D8 | Carlton Street | C4-D4 | Equity Road | A3 |
| Aylestone Road | C1-D3 | Castle Street | B5-C5 | Erskine Street | E7 |
| Balfour Street | A8 | Causeway Lane | C7 | Filbert Street | B2-C2 |
| Barnard Close | F5 | Celt Street | A4 | Filbert Street East | C2 |
| Bassett Street | A8 | Central Road | A4 | Fitzroy Street | A5 |
| Bath Lane | B5-B6 | Chancery Street | C5 | Fleet Street | E7 |
| Bay Street | C8 | Charles Street | D7-D6-D5-E5 | Fox Street | E5 |
| Bede Street | A4-B4 | Charlton Street | C4-D4 | Freeschool Lane | C6 |
| Bedford Street North | E8 | Charter Street | D8 | Friar Lane | C5 |
| Bedford Street South | D7 | Chatham Street | D4-D5 | Friday Street | B8-C8 |
| Belgrave Gate | D7-D8-E8 | Chester Close | F8 | Frog Island | B8 |
| Bell Lane | F6-F7 | Christow Street | F8 | Gallowtree Gate | D6 |
| Belvoir Street | D5 | Church Gate | C7-C6-D6 | Garden Street | D7 |
| Bisley Street | A1-A2 | Clarence Street | D6-D7 | Gas Street | D8 |
| Blackfriars Street | B6 | Clarendon Street | C3 | Gateway Street | C4-C3 |
| Bonchurch Street | A7-A8 | Clyde Street | E7 | Gaul Street | A3 |
| Bonners Lane | C4 | College Street | F4 | George Street | D8-E8 |
| Bosworth Street | A6 | Colton Street | E5 | Gladstone Street | E7 |
| Bowling Green Street | D5 | Conduit Street | E4-F5 | Glebe Street | E4-F4 |
| Braunstone Gate | A4-B5 | Coniston Street | B2 | Gosling Street | C4 |
| Brazil Street | B2-C1 | Constitution Hill | E5-F5-F6 | Gotham Street | F3-F4 |
| Britannia Street | E8 | Cranmer Street | A4 | Gower Street | D8-E7 |
| Briton Street | A3 | Crescent Street | D4 | Grafton Place | C7-C8 |
| Brougham Street | F7 | Cuthlaxton Street | F4-F5 | Grafton Street East | E7-F7 |
| Bruce Street | A2 | Dannet Street | A6 | Grafton Street West | E7 |
| Brunswick Street | F7 | Deacon Street | C3-C4 | Graham Street | F7 |
| Burgess Street | C7 | De Montfort Street | E2-E3-E4 | Granby Street | D5-E5 |
| Burleys Way | C7-D8 | Dover Street | D4-D5 | Grange Lane | C4 |
| Burnmoor Street | B1-C2 | Dryden Street | D7-E7 | Grasmere Street | B2-B3-C2 |
| Burton Street | E6 | Duke Street | D4 | Gravel Street | C7-D7 |
| Butt Close Lane | C7 | Dunkirk Street | D4-E4 | Great Central Street | B6-B7 |
| Buttermere Street | B2 | Duns Lane | B5 | Greyfriars | C5 |
| Byron Street | D7 | Dunton Street | A8 | Guildhall Lane | C6 |

| | | | | | |
|---|---|---|---|---|---|
| Halford Street | D6-E6 | Newarke Street | C5 | Slater Street | B8 |
| Harding Street | B8 | Newbridge Street | C1-C2 | Soar Lane | A7-B7 |
| Havelock Street | C2-C3 | New Park Street | A5-B5 | South Albion Street | E4 |
| Haymarket | D6-D7 | New Road | C7 | Southampton Street | E6 |
| Hazel Street | C2 | New Street | C5 | Southgates | C5 |
| Heanor Street | B8-C8 | Newtown Street | D3 | Sparkenhoe Street | F4-F5 |
| High Cross Street | C6-B6-B7 | New Walk | D4-E4-E3-F3 | Station Street | E5 |
| Highfield Street | F3-F4 | Nicholas Street | E6 | Stuart Street | A2 |
| High Street | C6-D6 | Noel Street | A2 | Sussex Street | F6-F7 |
| Hinckley Road | A4-A5 | Northgate Street | B7-B8 | Swain Street | E5-F5 |
| Hobart Street | F4 | Norman Street | A3 | Swan Street | B7 |
| Hoby Street | A6-A7 | Norton Street | C4-D4 | The Newarke | B4-C4 |
| Horsefair Street | C5-D5 | Nugent Street | A7 | Taylor Road | F8 |
| Hotel Street | C5 | Old Mill Lane | B7 | Tewkesbury Street | A6 |
| Humberstone Gate | D6-E6 | Orchard Street | D7-D8 | The Gateway | B4-C4 |
| Humberstone Road | E6-F7 | Ottawa Road | E7-F7 | Thames Street | D8 |
| Hutchinson Street | F5 | Oxford Street | C4 | Thirlmere Street | B2-B3 |
| Infirmary Road | C4-D3 | Paget Road | A7 | Tichbourne Street | F4 |
| Jarrom Street | B3-C3-C4 | Pasture Lane | C7-C8 | Tower Street | D3 |
| Jarvis Street | B6-B7 | Paton Street | A3 | Tudor Close | A5 |
| Johnson Street | B8 | Peacock Lane | C5 | Tudor Road | A5-A6-A7 |
| Kamloops Crescent | E8 | Pingle Street | B7 | Turner Street | D3 |
| Kashmir Road | F8-F7 | Pocklingtons Walk | C5-D5 | Ullswater Street | B3 |
| Kent Street | F6-F7 | Prebend Street | E4-F4 | University Road | E1-E2-F3 |
| King Richards Road | A5 | Princess Road East | E3-F3 | Upper King Street | D3 |
| King Street | D4-D5 | Princess Road West | D4-F4 | Upperton Road | A2-B2 |
| Latimer Street | D3-E3-E2 | Queen Street | E6 | Vancouver Road | E8 |
| Lee Street | D7-E7 | Raw Dykes Road | B1-C1 | Vaughan Way | C6-C7 |
| Lincoln Street | F4-F5 | Rawson Street | D4 | Vaughan Street | A6 |
| Little Holme Street | A5 | Regent Road | D4-D3-E3-F3 | Vernon Street | A7 |
| London Road | E4-F3 | Repton Street | A7-A8 | Walnut Street | B2-C2 |
| Lower Brown Street | C4 | Richard III Road | B5-B6 | Walton Street | A2 |
| Madras Road | F7 | Ridley Street | A4 | Warren Street | A6-A7 |
| Maidstone Road | F5-F6 | Roman Street | A4 | Warwick Street | A6 |
| Malabar Road | F7 | Rutland Street | D5-E6 | Waterloo Way | D2-D3-E3-E4 |
| Manitoba Road | E8-F8 | Rydal Street | B3 | Watling Street | C8 |
| Mansfield Street | D7 | St Augustine Road | A5-B5 | Welford Road | D1-D2-D3-D4 |
| Market Place | C5-D6 | St George Street | E5-E6 | Welles Street | B6 |
| Market Place South | C5-C6 | St Georges Way | F5-F5-F6 | Wellington Street | D5-D4-E4 |
| Market Street | D5 | St James Street | E6 | Western Boulevard | B3-B4-B5 |
| Marshall Street | A8 | St John Street | D8 | Western Road | A1-A2-A3-A4-B4 |
| Mayors Walk | E1 | St Margaret's Way | B8-C8-C7 | West Street | D2-D3-E4 |
| Midland Street | E6 | St Martins | C5 | West Walk | E3 |
| Mill Hill Lane | F3 | St Matthews Way | E7 | Wharf Street North | E7-E8 |
| Mill Lane | B4-C4 | St Nicholas Circle | B6-B7-B5-C5 | Wharf Street South | E6-E7 |
| Mill Street | D6-D7 | St Peters Lane | C6 | Wilberforce Road | A1-A2 |
| Millstone Lane | C5 | Salisbury Road | F3 | William Street | F6 |
| Morledge Street | E6 | Samuel Street | F6 | Wilton Street | D7 |
| Montreal Road | E8-F8 | Sanvey Gate | B7-C7 | Wimbledon Street | E6 |
| Mossdale Close | C2-C3 | Sawday Street | C4 | Windermere Street | B3 |
| Narborough Road | A3-A4 | Saxby Street | F4 | Woodboy Street | E8 |
| Narborough Road North | A4-A5 | Saxon Street | A4 | Yeoman Street | D6 |
| Navigation Street | D8 | Severn Street | F4 | York Road | C4 |
| Nelson Street | E4 | Short Street | C7 | | |
| Newarke Close | B4 | Silver Street | C6 | | |

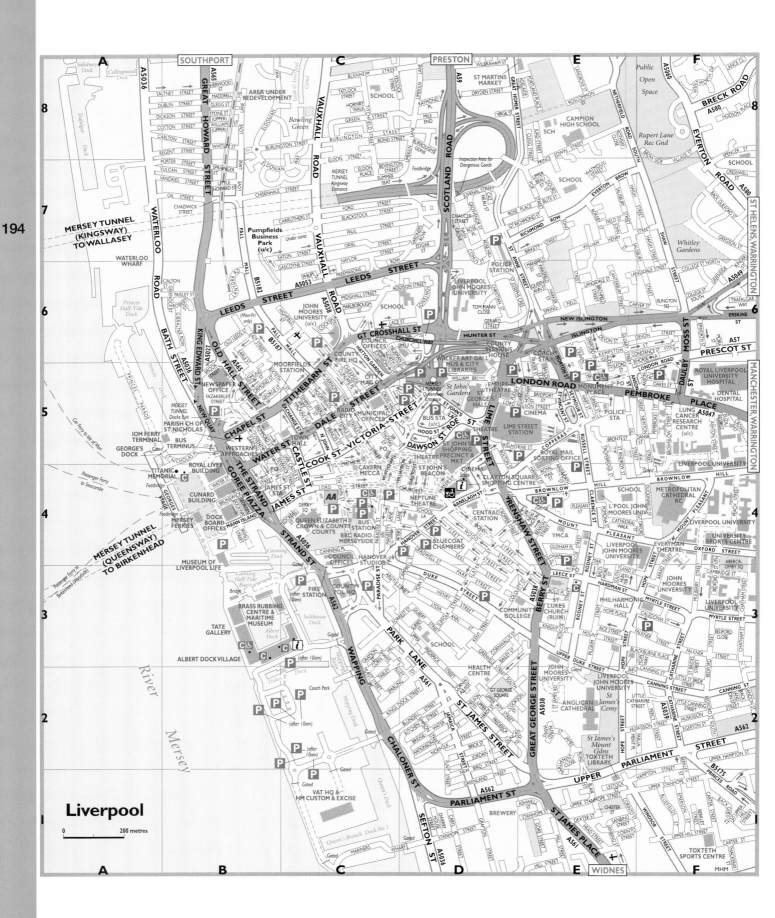

Liverpool

0        200 metres

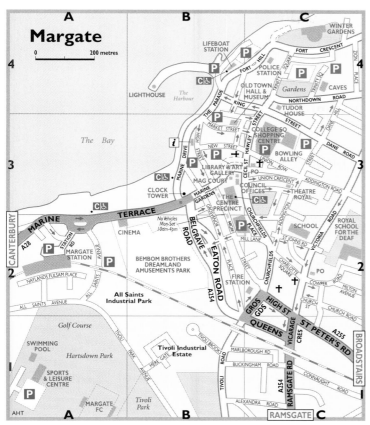

# Margate

Margate is found on atlas page **29**, grid reference **3571**

| | | | | | |
|---|---|---|---|---|---|
| Addington Road | C3 | Fort Crescent | C4 | New Street | B3 |
| Addington Street | C2-C3 | Fort Hill | B4-C4 | Northdown Road | C4 |
| Alexandra Road | B1-C1 | Fulsam Place | A2 | Queens Avenue | C1 |
| All Saints Avenue | A2 | Grosvenor Gardens | C2 | Ramsgate Road | C1 |
| Belgrave Road | B2 | Grosvenor Place | B2-B3 | St Johns Road | C2 |
| Buckingham Road | B1-C1 | Hawley Street | C3-C4 | St Peter's Road | C1 |
| Cecil Street | C3 | High Street | B3-B2-C2 | Station Road | A2 |
| Charlotte Square | C2 | King Street | B4-C4-C3 | The Parade | B4 |
| Churchfields | C2 | Marine Drive | B3 | Tivoli Brooks | B1 |
| Churchfields Place | C2-C3 | Marine Gardens | B3 | Tivoli Park Avenue | A2-A1-B1 |
| Church Road | C2-C1 | Marine Terrace | A2-A3-B3 | Tivoli Road | B1 |
| Church Street | C2 | Market Street | B3-C3 | Trinity Square | C4 |
| Connaught Road | C1 | Marlborough Road | B1-C1 | Union Crescent | C3 |
| Cowper Road | C2 | Mere Gate | B1 | Union Row | C3 |
| Dane Hill | C3-C4 | Mill Lane | B2-C2 | Vicarage Crescent | C1 |
| Dane Road | C3 | Milton Avenue | C2 | Victoria Road | C2-C3 |
| Eaton Road | B1-B2 | Naylands | A2 | Zion Place | C4 |

**195**

# Liverpool

Liverpool is found on atlas page **78**, grid reference **3490**

**AA shop**
Lord Street, Derby Square, Liverpool L2 1UF    C4

| | | | | | |
|---|---|---|---|---|---|
| Addison Street | C6-D6 | Brunswick Street | B4 | Covent Garden | B5 |
| Adelaide Place | E8 | Burlington Street | B8-D8 | Craven Street | E5-E6 |
| Ainsworth Street | E4-E5 | Burroughs Gardens | D8 | Cresswell Street | F7 |
| Alfred Mews | E2 | Bute Street | E7 | Cross Hall Street | C5-D5 |
| Anson Place | F5 | Caledonia Street | F3 | Crown Street | F5 |
| Anson Street | E5 | Calton Street | B6 | Cunliffe Place | C5 |
| Argyle Street | C3-D3 | Cambridge Street | F3 | Dale Street | C5-D5 |
| Arrad Street | F3-F4 | Campbell Street | D3-D4 | Dansie Street | E5-F5 |
| Ashton Street | F4-F5 | Canning Place | C4 | Daulby Street | F5 |
| Ashwell Street | E1 | Canning Street | E2-F2 | Dawson Street | D5 |
| Audley Street | E5-E6 | Canterbury Street | E6 | Devon Street | E6-F6 |
| Back Canning Street | F2-F3 | Carlton Street | A8-B8 | Dexter Street | E1 |
| Back Gibson Street | F1 | Carpenters Row | C3 | Dickson Street | A8-B8 |
| Back Guildford Street | F7 | Carruthers Street | B7-C7 | Douro Street | E7 |
| Back Sandon Street | F2 | Carter Street | F1 | Dryden Street | D8 |
| Bailey Street | D2-E3 | Carver Street | E6-F6 | Dublin Street | A8-B8 |
| Baltimore Street | E3-E4 | Caryl Street | D1 | Duckinfield Street | F4 |
| Bath Street | A6-B5 | Castle Street | C4-C5 | Duke Street | C3-E3 |
| Bayhorse Lane | E5-F6 | Catharine Street | F2-F3 | Dwerry House Street | D1 |
| Beckwith Street | C3 | Cathedral Walk | E4 | Earle Street | B5-B6 |
| Bedford Close | F3 | Cazneau Street | D7 | East Street | B6 |
| Bedford Street North | F3-F4 | Chadwick Street | B7 | Eaton Street | B7-C7 |
| Bedford Street South | F2-F3 | Chaloner Street | C2-D1 | Eberle Street | C5 |
| Benson Street | E4 | Chapel Street | B5 | Edgar Street | D7 |
| Berkley Street | F1-F2 | Chatham Street | F3 | Edmund Street | B5 |
| Berry Street | E3 | Chaucer Street | D7 | Egerton Street | F2 |
| Bevington Street | C7-D7 | Cheapside | C5-C6 | Eldon Place | C7 |
| Birchfield Street | E6 | Chester Street | E1 | Eldon Street | C7-C8 |
| Birkett Street | E7 | Chisenhale Street | B7-C7 | Eldonian Way | B8-C8 |
| Bixteth Street | B5-C5 | Christian Street | D6 | Elizabeth Street | F5 |
| Blackburne Place | E3-F3 | Church Street | C4-D4 | Emerson Street | F1 |
| Blackstock Street | C7-D7 | Churchill Way | C6-D6 | Epworth Street | F6 |
| Blair Street | E1 | Clarence Street | E4 | Erskine Street | F6 |
| Blenheim Street | C8-D8 | Clegg Street | E7-E8 | Everton Road | F7-F8 |
| Bluefields Street | F1 | Cockspur Street | C6 | Everton Row | E7 |
| Blundell Street | C2-D2 | College Street North | F6 | Exchange Street East | C5 |
| Bold Place | E3 | College Street South | F6 | Falkner Street | E3-F3 |
| Bold Street | D4-E3 | Colquitt Street | D3-E3 | Fazakerley Street | B5 |
| Bolton Street | D4-D5 | Comus Street | D6-D7 | Fenwick Street | B5-C4 |
| Bond Street | C8-D8 | Constance Street | E6-F6 | Finch Place | F6 |
| Breck Road | F8 | Cook Street | C4-C5 | Fleet Street | D3-D4 |
| Brick Street | D2 | Cookson Street | D2-E2 | Flint Street | D1-D2 |
| Bridgewater Street | D2 | Cooper Street | D4-E4 | Fontenoy Street | D6 |
| Bridport Street | E5 | Copperas Hill | D4-E5 | Ford Street | C7-D7 |
| Bronte Street | E5 | Corinto Street | E1-F1 | Forrest Street | C3-D3 |
| Brook Street | B5 | Corn Hill | C3 | Fox Street | D8-E7 |
| Brow Side | F7-F8 | Cornwall Street | D2 | Fraser Street | E5-E6 |
| Brownlow Hill | D4-F4 | Corwallis Street | D3-E3 | Freemasons Row | C6-D7 |
| Brownlow Street | F4-F5 | Cotton Street | A8-B8 | Gardners Row | B7-C6 |
| | | | | Gascoyne Street | B7-C6 |
| | | | | George Street | B5 |
| | | | | George's Dockway | B4 |
| | | | | Gerard Street | D6 |
| | | | | Gibralter Row | B6 |
| | | | | Gilbert Street | D3 |
| | | | | Gildart Street | E5-E6 |
| | | | | Gill Street | E5-F4 |
| | | | | Glegg Street | B8 |
| | | | | Gore Street | E1 |
| | | | | Goree Piazza | C4-C5 |
| | | | | Gradwell Street | D3-D4 |

| | | | | | |
|---|---|---|---|---|---|
| Grafton Street | D1 | Matthews Street | C4-C5 | St James Place | E1 |
| Grayson Street | C3 | Midghall Street | C6 | St James Road | E1-E2 |
| Great Crosshall Street | C6-D6 | Mile End | D8 | St James Street | D2-E2 |
| Great George Street | E1-E3 | Mill Street | E1 | St John's Lane | D5 |
| Great Homer Street | D7-D8 | Moira Street | F6 | St Josephs Crescent | D6-E6 |
| Great Howard Street | B6-B8 | Monument Place | E5 | St Nicholas Place | B5 |
| Great Newton Street | F4-F5 | Moorfields | C5 | St Thomas Street | C5-D5 |
| Great Orford Street | F4 | Moss Street | F6 | St Vincent Street | E5 |
| Greek Street | E5 | Mount Pleasant | F4 | Salisbury Street | E7-F6 |
| Green Street | C8-D8 | Mount Pleasant Street | E4-F4 | Saltney Street | A8-B8 |
| Greenland Street | D1-E2 | Mount Street | E3 | Sanbino Street | E1 |
| Greenock Street | B6 | Mulberry Street | F3-F4 | Sandon Street | F2-F3 |
| Greenside | F6 | Myrtle Street | F3 | School Lane | C4-D4 |
| Gregson Street | F7 | Nash Grove | D7 | Scotland Road | D6-D8 |
| Grenville Street South | D3-E2 | Naylor Street | C6-D7 | Seel Street | D4-E3 |
| Grosvenor Street | D7 | Nelson Street | D2 | Sefton Street | D1 |
| Hackins Hey | C5 | Netherfield Road South | E8-F7 | Seymour Street | E5 |
| Haigh Street | E7-F6 | New Bird Street | D1-D2 | Shaw Street | F6-F7 |
| Hampton Street | E1-F2 | New Islington | E6-F6 | Shaws Alley | C3-D2 |
| Hanover Street | C3-D4 | New Quay | B5 | Sherwood Street | B8 |
| Hardman Street | E3 | Newington | E4 | Simpson Street | D2 |
| Harker Street | E6 | Norfolk Street | D2 | Skelthorne Street | D5-E5 |
| Hart Street | E5 | North John Street | C5 | Slater Street | D3-D4 |
| Hatton Garden | C5-C6 | Norton Street | E5-E6 | Soho Street | E7 |
| Hawke Street | E4-E5 | Oakes Street | F5 | South Hunter Street | E3 |
| Head Street | E1 | Oil Street | A7-B7 | South John Street | C4-C5 |
| Henry Street | D3 | Old Hall Street | B5-B6 | Sparling Street | C2-D2-D3 |
| Highfield Street | B6-c6 | Old Leeds Street | B6 | Spencer Street | F8 |
| Hill Street | E1 | Oldham Place | E4 | Spranger Street | B7 |
| Hodson Place | F8 | Oldham Street | E4 | Springfield | E6-E7 |
| Hood Street | D5 | Oriel Street | C7-D7 | Stafford Street | E5-E6 |
| Hope Place | E3 | Ormond Street | B5 | Stanhope Street | D1-E1 |
| Hope Street | E2-F4 | Oxford Street | F4 | Stanley Street | C4-C5 |
| Hopeway | F3 | Paisley Street | B6 | Stone Street | B8 |
| Hornby Walk | C8 | Pall Mall | B7-C5 | Strand Street | B4-C4 |
| Hotham Street | E5 | Paradise Street | C3-C4 | Suffolk Street | D3 |
| Hunter Street | D6 | Park Lane | C3-D2 | Summer Seat | C7-D7 |
| Hurst Street | C2-C3 | Parker Street | D4 | Tabley Street | C2-D3 |
| Huskisson Street | E2-F2 | Parliament Close | E1-D2 | Tarleton Street | D4-D5 |
| Ilford Street | E5 | Parliament Place | F2 | Tatlock Street | C8 |
| Iliad Street | E8 | Parliament Street | D1-E1 | Tempest Hey | C5 |
| Irwell Street | B4 | Parr Street | D3 | Temple Street | C5 |
| Islington | E6 | Paul Street | C7-D7 | Thackeray Street | F1 |
| Islington Square | F6 | Peach Street | F4 | The Strand | B4-B5 |
| Jamaica Street | D1-D2 | Pembroke Place | E5-F5 | Titchfield Street | C7-C8 |
| James Street | B4-C4 | Pembroke Street | F5 | Tithebarn Street | C5-C6 |
| John Street | E7 | Percy Street | F2 | Tom Mann Close | D6 |
| Johnson Street | C5-C6 | Peter's Lane | C4-D4 | Trafalgar Way | F6 |
| Jordan Street | D2 | Philips Street | C6 | Trowbridge Street | E4-E5 |
| Juvenal Street | D7 | Pilgrim Street | E3 | Upper Beau Street | E7 |
| Kempson Street | E6-F6 | Pitt Street | D2-D3 | Upper Duke Street | E2-E3 |
| Kent Street | D3 | Pleasant Street | E4 | Upper Frederick Street | C3-D2-E2 |
| Kinder Street | F6-F7 | Pomonia Street | E4 | Upper Hampton Street | F2 |
| King Edward Street | B5-B6 | Porter Street | A7-B7 | Upper Hill Street | F1 |
| Kings Dock Street | C2-D2 | Portland Place | E8 | Upper Parliament Street | E1-F2 |
| Kitchen Street | D2 | Pownhall Street | C3 | Upper Richmond Street | D7-E7 |
| Knight Street | E3 | Prescot Street | F6 | Upper Stanhope Street | E1-F1 |
| Lace Street | C6-D6 | Prince Edwin Street | E7-E8 | Upper Stone Street | B8 |
| Lance Close | E8 | Princes Parade | A5-A6 | Upper William Street | B8 |
| Langrove Street | E8 | Princes Road | F1-F2 | Vandries Street | A7-B7 |
| Langsdale Street | E6-F6 | Princes Street | C5 | Vauxhall Road | C6-C8 |
| Lanyork Road | B6 | Pudsey Street | D5-E5 | Vernon Street | C5 |
| Leece Street | E3 | Queen Ann Street | E6 | Vescock Street | C8-D8 |
| Leeds Street | B6-D6 | Ranelagh Street | D4 | Victoria Street | C5-D5 |
| Lestock Street | E1 | Raymond Place | D8 | Village Street | F7-F8 |
| Lime Street | D4-D6 | Redcross Street | B4-C4 | Virgil Street | D8 |
| Limekiln Lane | D7-D8 | Regent Street | A8-B8 | Vulcan Street | A7-B7 |
| Little Canning Street | F2 | Renshaw Street | D4-E4 | Wakefield Street | E6 |
| Little Catharine Street | F2 | Rice Street | E3 | Wapping | C2-C3 |
| Little Howard Street | B7 | Richmond Row | D7-E7 | Water Street | B4-B5-C5 |
| Little St Brides Street | F2 | Roberts Street | B6 | Waterloo Road | A6-A8 |
| London Road | D5-E5-F5-F6 | Rodney Street | E3-E4 | Watkinson Street | D2 |
| Lord Nelson Street | D5-E5 | Roe Street | D5 | Watmough Street | E7 |
| Lord Street | C4 | Rokeby Street | E7 | Webster Street | C6-D6 |
| Love Lane | B7-B8 | Roscoe Street | E3-E4 | Wentworth Road | F8 |
| Lower Castle Street | C4-C5 | Roscommon Street | E8 | Whitechapel | C4-D5 |
| Lydia Ann Street | D3 | Rose Hill | D6-D7 | Whitley Street | B8 |
| Maddrell Street | B8 | Rose Place | D7-E7 | Wilbraham Street | D8 |
| Manesty's Lane | C4 | Royal Mail Street | E4-E5 | Wilde Street | E5 |
| Mann Island | B4 | Rumford Street | B5 | William Brown Street | D5 |
| Mansfield Street | E6-E7 | Russell Street | E4-E5 | Williamson Street | C4-D5 |
| Mariners Wharf | C1-D1 | St Andrew Street | E4-E5 | Windsor Street | E1-F1 |
| Marlborough Street | C6 | St Ann Street | D7-E6 | Wood Street | D3-D4 |
| Maryland Street | E4-E3-F3 | St Brides Street | F2-F3 | York Street | D3 |

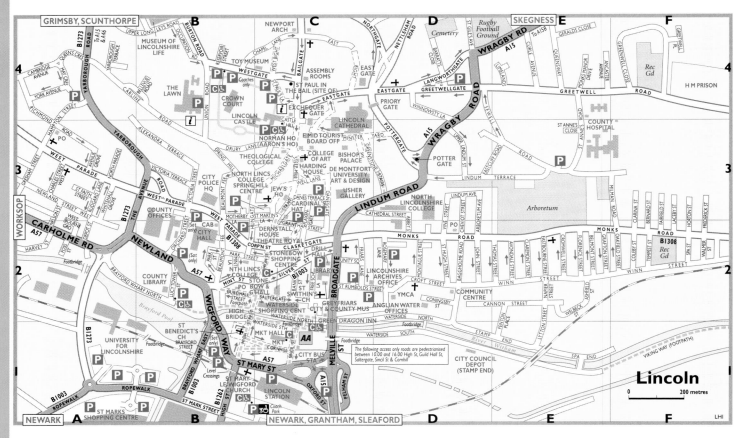

# Lincoln

Lincoln is found on atlas page **76**,
grid reference **9771**

**AA shop**
33 Sincil Street, Lincoln LN5 7ET                    C1

| | | | | | | | | | |
|---|---|---|---|---|---|---|---|---|---|
| Abbey Street | D2-D3 | Danes Terrace | C3 | Lytton Street | E1-E2 | St Mark Street | B1 | Yarborough Road | A4-B3 |
| Alexandra Terrace | A4-B3 | Danesgate | C2-C3 | May Crescent | A4 | St Martin's Lane | C3 | Yarborough Terrace | A4 |
| Arboretum Avenue | D2-D3 | Depot Street | A2-A3 | Melville Street | D1 | St Mary Street | B1-C1 | York Avenue | A4 |
| Ancaster Way | E4 | Drury Lane | B3-C3 | Michaelgate | C3 | St Pauls Lane | C4 | | |
| Ashfield Street | E2 | Eastbourne Street | E2 | Milman Road | F2-F3 | St Rumbolds Street | C2-D2 | | |
| Ashlin Grove | A3 | East Bight | C4 | Minster Yard | C3-D3 | Saltergate | B2 | | |
| Avondale Street | E2 | Eastcliff Road | D3-E3 | Mint Lane | B2 | Sewell Road | D4-F3 | | |
| Baggholme Road | D2 | Eastgate | C4-D4 | Mint Street | B2 | Silver Street | C2 | | |
| Bailgate | C4 | Fairfield Street | F2-F3 | Monks Manor Drive | E4 | Sincil Street | C1 | | |
| Bank Street | C2 | Fenton Place | E1-E2 | Monks Road | C2-F2 | Spa End | E1-F1 | | |
| Barratts Close | D4 | Flaxengate | C2-C3 | Montague Street | D2 | Spa Street | F2 | | |
| Beaumont Fee | B2-B3 | Florence Street | E2 | Motherby Lane | B3 | Spring Hill | B3 | | |
| Bellevue Road | B4 | Foss Street | A2 | Napier Street | E2 | Stamp End | D1-E1 | | |
| Belmont Street | E2 | Frederick Street | F2-F3 | Nelson Street | A2-A3 | Steep Hill | C3 | | |
| Bernard Street | F2-F3 | Free School Lane | C2 | Nettleham Road | D4 | Tempest Street | F2 | | |
| Brayford Street | B1 | Friars Lane | C2 | Newland | A2-B2 | The Avenue | A2-B3 | | |
| Brayford Wharf East | B1-B2 | Geralds Close | E4 | Newland Street West | A2-A3 | The Strait | C3 | | |
| Brayford Wharf North | A2-B2 | Grafton Street | E2 | Northgate | C4-D4 | Thomas Street | E2 | | |
| Broadgate | C2-C3 | Grantham Street | C2 | North Parade | A3 | Union Road | B3-B4 | | |
| Burton Road | B4 | Greenstone Stairs | C3-D3 | Oakfield Street | F2 | Unity Square | C2 | | |
| Cambridge Avenue | A4 | Greenwell Close | F4 | Occupation Road | B4 | Upper Lindum Street | D3 | | |
| Cannon Street | D2-E2 | Greetwell Place | F4 | Orchard Street | B2-B3 | Upper Long Leys Road | A4-B4 | | |
| Carholme Road | A2-A3 | Greetwell Road | D4-F4 | Oxford Street | C1 | Victoria Street | B3 | | |
| Carline Road | A4-B3 | Greetwellgate | D4 | Park Street | B2-C2 | Victoria Terrace | B3 | | |
| Castle Hill | C3-C4 | Gresham Street | A3 | Pelham Bridge | C1 | Vine Street | D2-D3 | | |
| Cathedral Street | C3-D3 | Guildhall Street | B2 | Pelham Street | C1 | Walmer Street | F2 | | |
| Chapel Lane | B4-C4 | Hampton Street | A3-A4 | Pottergate | D3 | Waterside North | C2-D2 | | |
| Charles Street West | A3 | Harvey Street | A2 | Queens Crescent | A4 | Waterside South | C1-E1 | | |
| Cheviot Street | D2-D3 | High Street | B1-C3 | Queensway | E4 | Welbeck Street | E2 | | |
| Claremont Street | E2 | Horton Street | F2-F3 | Reservoir Street | B4 | Well Lane | C3 | | |
| Clarina Street | F2-F3 | Hungate | B2-B3 | Richmond Road | A4-A3 | West Bight | C4 | | |
| Clasketgate | C2 | John Street | D2 | Ropewalk | A1-B1 | West Parade | A3-B2 | | |
| Coleby Street | F2 | Laceby Street | F2-F3 | Rosemary Lane | D2 | Westbourne Grove | A2-A3 | | |
| Coningsby Street | D2 | Langworthgate | D4 | Rudgard Lane | A3 | Westgate | B4-C4 | | |
| Cornhill | C1 | Limelands | E3 | St Anne's Close | E3 | Whitehall Grove | A3 | | |
| Corporation Street | B2-C2 | Lindum Terrace | D3-E3 | St Anne's Road | E3-E4 | Wigford Way | B1-B2 | | |
| Croft Street | D2 | Lindum Avenue | D3 | St Faith Street | A3 | Winn Street | D2-F2 | | |
| Curle Avenue | E4 | Lindum Road | C2-D3 | St Giles Avenue | D4 | Winnowsty Lane | D3-D4 | | |
| Cromwell Street | E2 | Lucy Tower Street | B2 | St Hugh Street | D2 | Wragby Road | D3-E4 | | |

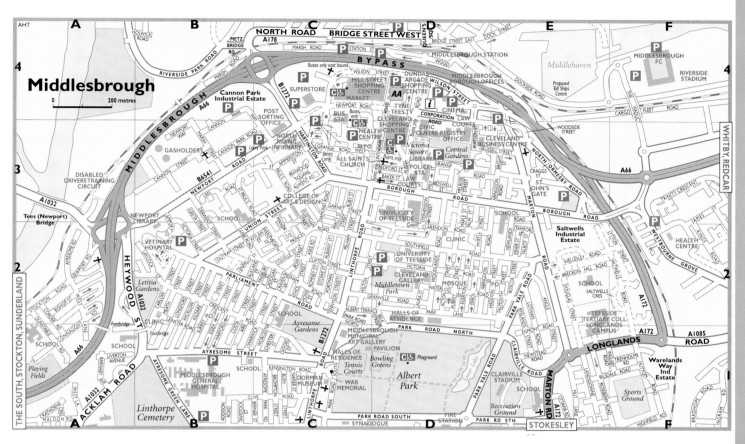

# Middlesbrough

Middlesbrough is found on atlas page **97**, grid reference **4919**

**AA shop**
17 Corporation Road, Middlesbrough TS1 1LS       D4

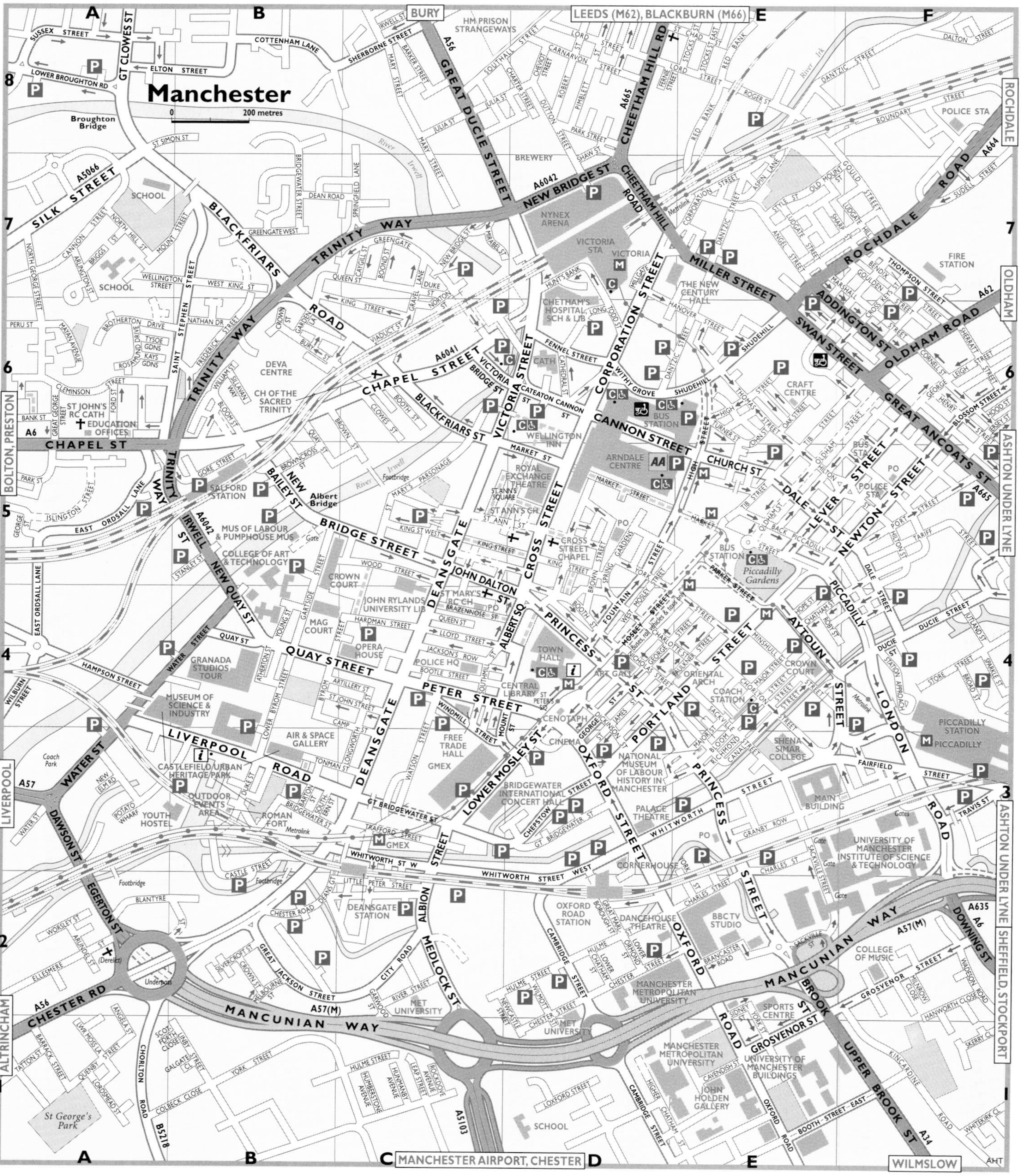

# Manchester

198

0    200 metres

**BURY** — **LEEDS (M62), BLACKBURN (M66)** — **ROCHDALE** — **OLDHAM** — **ASHTON UNDER LYNE** — **ASHTON UNDER LYNE | SHEFFIELD, STOCKPORT** — **WILMSLOW** — **MANCHESTER AIRPORT, CHESTER** — **ALTRINCHAM** — **LIVERPOOL** — **BOLTON, PRESTON**

Grid references: A B C D E F (top and bottom), 8 7 6 5 4 3 2 1 (sides)

Selected labels:

SUSSEX STREET, GT CLOWES ST, LOWER BROUGHTON RD, ELTON STREET, COTTENHAM LANE, SHERBORNE STREET, IRWELL STREET, GREAT DUCIE STREET, HM PRISON STRANGEWAYS, CHEETHAM HILL RD, DANTZIC STREET, ROCHDALE ROAD, POLICE STA, A664, OLDHAM, A62

Broughton Bridge, SILK STREET, A5066, SCHOOL, BLACKFRIARS ROAD, TRINITY WAY, River Irwell, NEW BRIDGE ST, NYNEX ARENA, VICTORIA STA, CHEETHAM HILL, MILLER STREET, THE NEW CENTURY HALL, SWAN STREET, GREAT ANCOATS STREET, FIRE STATION, CRAFT CENTRE

DEVA CENTRE, CHAPEL STREET, A6041, VICTORIA ST, CH OF THE SACRED TRINITY, ST JOHN'S RC CATH, EDUCATION OFFICES, CHAPEL ST, A6, BLACKFRIARS ST, CATEATON CANNON, CATH, CHETHAM'S HOSPITAL SCH & LIB, CORPORATION STREET, HANOVER, SHUDEHILL, CANNON STREET, ARNDALE CENTRE, CHURCH ST, DALE ST, LEVER ST, NEWTON STREET, A665, POLICE STA

SALFORD STATION, NEW BAILEY ST, Albert Bridge, MUS OF LABOUR & PUMPHOUSE MUS, COLLEGE OF ART & TECHNOLOGY, BRIDGE STREET, DEANSGATE, JOHN DALTON ST, ROYAL EXCHANGE THEATRE, ST ANN'S SQUARE, ST ANN'S CH, CROSS STREET CHAPEL, MARKET ST, PICCADILLY GARDENS, BUS STATION, PICCADILLY

CROWN COURT, JOHN RYLANDS UNIVERSITY LIB, ST MARY'S RC CH, QUAY ST, OPERA HOUSE, MAG COURT, POLICE HQ, BOOTLE STREET, ALBERT SQ, TOWN HALL, ART GALL, ORIENTAL ARCH, COACH STATION, CROWN COURT

GRANADA STUDIOS TOUR, WATER ST, QUAY STREET, MUSEUM OF SCIENCE & INDUSTRY, LIVERPOOL ROAD, PETER STREET, CENTRAL LIBRARY, CENOTAPH, FREE TRADE HALL, CINEMA, GMEX, NATIONAL MUSEUM OF LABOUR HISTORY IN MANCHESTER, SHENA SIMAR COLLEGE, PICCADILLY STATION, PICCADILLY, FAIRFIELD

Coach Park, A57, WATER ST, AIR & SPACE GALLERY, CASTLEFIELD URBAN HERITAGE PARK, OUTDOOR EVENTS AREA, ROMAN FORT, YOUTH HOSTEL, GT BRIDGEWATER ST, LOWER MOSLEY ST, OXFORD STREET, BRIDGEWATER INTERNATIONAL CONCERT HALL, PORTLAND STREET, PRINCESS STREET, WHITWORTH STREET, PALACE THEATRE, MAIN BUILDING, LONDON ROAD, TRAVIS ST, A6

DAWSON ST, EGERTON ST, Footbridge, BLANTYRE, WHITWORTH ST W, WHITWORTH STREET WEST, CHESTER ROAD, DEANSGATE STATION, ALBION, OXFORD ROAD STATION, DANCEHOUSE THEATRE, CORNERHOUSE, CHARLES STREET, UNIVERSITY OF MANCHESTER INSTITUTE OF SCIENCE & TECHNOLOGY, BBC TV STUDIO, MANCUNIAN WAY, A57(M), A635, DOWNING STREET

CHESTER RD, A56, MANCUNIAN WAY, A57(M), GREAT JACKSON STREET, CITY ROAD, MEDLOCK ST, MET UNIVERSITY, CAMBRIDGE STREET, OXFORD ROAD, MANCHESTER METROPOLITAN UNIVERSITY, HULME STREET, COLLEGE OF MUSIC, GROSVENOR ST, UNIVERSITY OF MANCHESTER BUILDINGS, SPORTS CENTRE, BROOK STREET, UPPER BROOK ST, A34

St George's Park, B5218, HULME STREET, JOHN HOLDEN GALLERY, SCHOOL, A5103

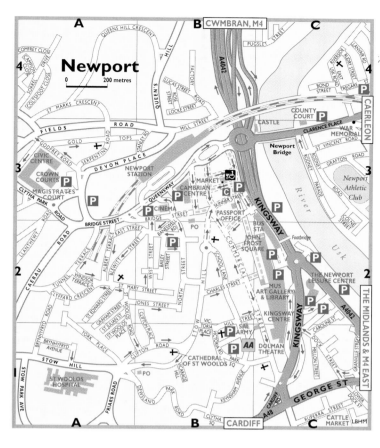

# Newport

Newport is found on atlas page **34**, grid reference **3188**

## AA shop
133 Commercial Street, Newport NP9 1LY      C1

| | | | | | |
|---|---|---|---|---|---|
| Albert Terrace | A2 | Fields Road | A3-B3 | Rudry Street | C4 |
| Bailey Street | B2 | Friars Road | A1 | Ruperra Street | C1 |
| Baneswell Road | B2-B3 | George Street | C1 | St Edward Street | A2 |
| Blewitt Street | A2-B2 | Godfrey Road | A3 | St Julian Street | A1-A2 |
| Bond Street | C4 | Gold Tops | A3-B3 | St Marks Crescent | A3-A4 |
| Bridge Street | A2-A3-B2-B3 | Grafton Road | C3 | St Mary Street | A2-B2 |
| Brynhyfryd Avenue | A1 | Graham Street | A1-A2 | St Vincent Road | C3 |
| Brynhyfryd Road | A1-A2 | Granville Street | C1 | St Woolos Place | A1-A2 |
| Caerau Road | A2 | Hill Street | B1-B2-C2 | St Woolos Road | A2-A1-B1 |
| Campion Close | A4 | Jones Street | A2-B2 | School Lane | B2 |
| Cardiff Road | C1 | Keynsham Avenue | B1 | Serpentine Road | A3 |
| Caroline Street | C1-C2 | Kingsway | C1-C2-C3-B3 | Skinner Street | B3 |
| Charles Street | B2 | Llanthewy Road | A2-A3 | Sorrel Drive | A4 |
| Clarence Place | C3-C4 | Llanvair Road | C4 | Stanlet Road | B3 |
| Clifton Place | B2-B1 | Locke Street | B4 | Stow Hill | A1-B1-B2 |
| Clifton Road | A1-B1 | Lower Dock Street | C1 | Stow Park Avenue | A1 |
| Clyffard Crescent | A2 | Lucas Street | B4 | Tregare Street | C4 |
| Clytha Park Road | A3 | Mellon Street | C1 | Tunnel Terrace | A2 |
| Clytha Square | B1 | Mill Street | B3-B4 | Vicarage Hill | B1 |
| Colne Street | C3-C2 | North Street | B2 | Victoria Place | B1 |
| Coltsfoot Close | A4 | Park Square | B1 | Victoria Road | B1 |
| Comfrey Close | A4 | Pugsley Street | B4-C4 | West Street | B2 |
| Commercial Street | B2-C2-C1 | Queen's Hill | B3-B4 | Windsor Terrace | A2 |
| Devon Place | A3-B3 | Queens Hill Crescent | A4-B4 | York Place | A1-A2 |
| Dewsland Park Road | A1-B1 | Queensway | A3-B3 | | |
| Dock Street | C1 | Riverside | C4 | | |
| East Street | A2-B2 | Rodney Parade | C3 | | |
| East Usk Road | C4 | Rodney Road | C3 | | |
| Factory Road | B4 | Rose Street | B4 | | |

# Manchester

Manchester is found on atlas page **79**, grid reference **8497**

## AA shop
St Ann's House, St Ann's Place, Manchester M2 7LP      D5

| | | | | | | | |
|---|---|---|---|---|---|---|---|
| Addington Street | E7-F6 | Brown Street | D4-D5 | Crown Street | B6 | | |
| Albert Square | C4-D4 | Browncross Street | B5 | Dale Street | E5-F5-F4 | | |
| Albion Street | C2-C3 | Bury Street | B6-C6 | Dalton Street | F8 | | |
| Angel Street | E6 | Byrom Street | B4-C4 | Dantzic Street | D6-F8 | | |
| Angela Street | A1-A2 | Cambridge Street | D1-D2 | Dawson Street | A3 | | |
| Arlington Street | A7 | Camp Street | B4-C4-C3 | Dean Road | B7-C7 | | |
| Artillery Street | B4-C4 | Canal Street | E3-E4 | Deans Gate | B2 | | |
| Arundel Street | A2 | Cannon Street | A7 | Deansgate | C3-C4-C5 | | |
| Aspin Lane | E7 | Cannon Street | D6-E5 | Dickinson Street | D3-D4 | | |
| Atherton Street | B4 | Carnarvon Street | D8 | Downing Street | F2 | | |
| Aytoun Street | E4 | Castle Street | B2-B3 | Duke Street | B3 | | |
| Back Piccadilly | E5 | Cateaton Street | D6 | Duke Street | C7 | | |
| Bank Street | A6 | Cathedral Street | D6 | Ducie Street | F4 | | |
| Barker Street | C8 | Cavendish Street | E1 | Dutton Street | D7-D8 | | |
| Barrack Street | A1 | Caygill Street | C7 | East Ordsall Lane | A4-A5 | | |
| Barton Street | B3 | Chapel Street | A5-B6-C6 | Egerton Street | A2 | | |
| Bendix Street | F6-F7 | Charles Street | E2-E3 | Ellesmere Street | A2 | | |
| Blackfriars Road | A7-B7-B6-C6 | Charlotte Street | D4-E4 | Elton Street | A8-B8 | | |
| Blackfriars Street | C6 | Charter Street | C8-D8 | Fairfield Street | F3 | | |
| Blantyre Street | A2-B2 | Chatham Street | E4 | Faulkner Street | D4-E4 | | |
| Bloom Street | B6 | Chepstow Street | D3 | Fennel Street | D6 | | |
| Bloom Street | E3-E4 | Chester Road | B2 | Fernie Street | D8 | | |
| Blossom Street | F6 | Chester Road | A1-A2 | Ford Street | A6 | | |
| Boond Street | C7 | Chester Street | D1-D2-E2 | Fountain Street | D4-D5 | | |
| Booth Street | C6 | Cheetham Hill Road | D7-D8 | Frederick Street | B6 | | |
| Booth Street | D4 | Cheviot Street | D8 | Galgate Close | B1 | | |
| Booth Street East | E1-F1 | Chorlton Road | A1-A2 | Garden Lane | B6 | | |
| Bootle Street | C4 | Chorlton Street | E3-E4 | Gartside Street | B4-B5 | | |
| Boundary Street | E8-F8 | Church Street | E5 | Garwood Street | C2-C1 | | |
| Brancaster Road | E2 | City Road | C2 | George Leigh Street | F6 | | |
| Brazennose Street | C4 | Cleminson Street | A6 | George Street | A5 | | |
| Bridge Street | B5-C5 | Clowes Street | C6 | George Street | D3-D4-E4 | | |
| Bridgewater Street | B3 | Colbeck Close | A1-B1 | Gore Street | B5 | | |
| Bridgewater Street | B7-B8 | Cornell Street | F6 | Gould Street | E8-F7 | | |
| Briggs Street | A7 | Corporation Street | D6-D7-E7 | Goulden Street | F6-F7 | | |
| Broad Street | F4 | Cottenham Lane | B8 | Granby Row | E3 | | |
| Brook Street | E2 | Cross Keys Street | F6-F7 | Gravel Lane | C6-C7 | | |
| Brotherton Drive | A6 | Cross Street | D5 | Great Ancoats Street | F5-F6 | | |
| Brown Street | B6-C6-C5 | Crown Street | B2 | Great Bridgewater Street | C3-D3 | | |

| | | | | | |
|---|---|---|---|---|---|
| Great Clowes Street | A8 | King Street West | C5 | St Ann Street | C5-D5 |
| Great Ducie Street | C8-C7-D7 | Leap Street | C1 | St Ann's Square | C5-D5 |
| Great George Street | A6 | Lever Street | E5-F5-F6 | St Chad Street | D8-E8 |
| Great Jackson Street | B2-C2 | Linby Street | B1 | St James Street | D3-D4 |
| Great Marlborough Street | D2 | Little Peter Street | C2 | St John Street | B4-C4 |
| Greengate West | B7 | Liverpool Road | A4-A3-B4 | St Mary's Parsonage | C5 |
| Greengate | C7 | Lloyd Street | C4 | St Peter's Square | D4 |
| Grosvenor Street | E1-F2 | London Road | F3-F4 | St Simon Street | A8-B8 |
| Hampson Street | A4 | Long Millgate | D6-D7 | St Stephen Street | A6-B6 |
| Hanover Street | D7-E6 | Longworth Street | C3-C4 | Scotforth Close | A1-B1 |
| Hanworth Close | F2 | Lord Street | D8-E8 | Sharp Street | E7-F7 |
| Hardman Street | C4 | Lordsmead Street | A1 | Shaw Street | D7-D8 |
| Henry Street | F5-F6 | Lower Broughton Road | A8 | Sherborne Street | B8-C8 |
| High Street | E5-E6 | Lower Byrom Street | B3-B4 | Sherratt Street | F6 |
| Higher Chatham Street | D1-E1 | Lower Chatham Street | D2 | Shudehill | D6-E6 |
| Hilton Street | E5-F5 | Lower Mosley Street | C3-D3 | Sidney Street | E2 |
| Hood Street | F6 | Lower Moss Lane | A1 | Silk Street | A7 |
| Hope Street | E4 | Lower Ormond Street | D2 | Sillavan Way | B6 |
| Hulme Street | C1 | Loxford Street | D1 | Silvercroft Street | B2 |
| Hulme Street | C2-D2 | Ludgate Hill | E7-F7 | Skerry Close | F1 |
| Humberstone Avenue | C1 | Ludgate Street | E7 | Southall Street | C8-D8 |
| Hunmanby Avenue | C1 | Major Street | E3-E4 | Southern Street | B3 |
| Hunt's Bank | D7 | Mancunian Way | B2-F2 | Southmill Street | C4 |
| Irwell Street | C8 | Market Street | D5-E5 | Sparkle Street | F4 |
| Islington Street | A5 | Marshall Street | E7-F7-F6 | Spring Gardens | D4-D5 |
| Jackson's Row | C4 | Mary Street | C7-C8 | Springfield Lane | C7-C8 |
| Jersey Street | F5-F6 | Mayan Avenue | A6 | Stanley Street | B5 |
| John Dalton Street | C5-D4 | Medlock Street | C2 | Station Approach | F4 |
| John Street | E6 | Melbourne Street | B2 | Stocks Street | E8 |
| Julia Street | C8-D8 | Miller Street | E7 | Stocks Street East | E8 |
| Jutland Street | F4 | Milnrow Close | F2 | Store Street | F4 |
| Kays Gardens | A6 | Minshull Street | E4 | Style Street | E7 |
| Kincardine Road | F1-F2 | Mirabel Street | C7 | Sudell Street | F7-F8 |
| King Street | B6-C6 | Mosley Street | D4 | Sussex Street | A8 |
| King Street | C5-D5 | Mount Street | A7-B7 | Swan Street | E6-F6 |
| | | Nathan Drive | B6 | Tariff Street | F5 |
| | | New Bailey Street | B5 | Tatton Street | A1 |
| | | New Bridge Street | C7-D7 | Thomas Street | E6 |
| | | New Elm Road | A3 | Thompson Street | F6-F7 |
| | | New Quay Street | B4-B5 | Tib Street | E5-E6-F6 |
| | | Newcastle Street | D1-D2 | Todd Street | D6 |
| | | Newton Street | E5-F5 | Tonman Street | B3-C3 |
| | | Nicholas Street | D4 | Trafford Street | C3 |
| | | North George Street | A6-A7 | Travis Street | F3 |
| | | North Hill Street | A7 | Trinity Way | B5-B6-B7-C7 |
| | | Norton Street | C6-C7 | Turner Street | E6 |
| | | Oak Street | E6 | Tysoe Gardens | A6 |
| | | Old Mount Street | E7 | Upper Brook Street | E1-F1 |
| | | Oldham Road | F6-F7 | Viaduct Street | C6 |
| | | Oldham Street | E5-E6-F6 | Victoria Bridge Street | C6 |
| | | Oxford Street | D3-D2-E2 | Victoria Street | C6-D6 |
| | | Park Street | A5 | Wadeson Road | F2 |
| | | Park Street | D8 | Water Street | A3-A4-B4 |
| | | Parker Street | E4-E5 | Watson Street | C3-C4 |
| | | Peru Street | A6 | Wellington Street | A7-B7 |
| | | Peter Street | C4-D4 | West King Street | B7 |
| | | Piccadilly | E5-F4 | West Mosley Street | D4-D5 |
| | | Pimblett Street | D8 | Whitekirk Close | F1 |
| | | Port Street | F5 | Whitworth Street | D3-E3 |
| | | Portland Street | D3-D4-E4 | Whitworth Street West | C3-D3 |
| | | Potato Wharf | A3 | Wilburn Street | A4 |
| | | Princess Street | D4-E3-E2 | William Street | B6 |
| | | Quay Street | B4-C4 | Wilmott Street | D1-D2 |
| | | Quay Street | B5-B6 | Windmill Street | C3-C4 |
| | | Queen Street | C4 | Withy Grove | D6 |
| | | Queen Street | B7-C7 | Wood Street | C5 |
| | | Quenby Street | A1 | Worsley Street | A2 |
| | | Red Bank | E7-E8 | York Street | B1 |
| | | Richmond Street | E3-E4 | York Street | E2-E3 |
| | | River Street | C2 | York Street | D5-E4 |
| | | Robert Street | D8 | York Street | E1-E2 |
| | | Roby Street | E4 | Young Street | B4 |
| | | Rochdale Road | E7-F7-F8 | | |
| | | Rockdove Avenue | C1 | | |
| | | Roger Street | E8 | | |
| | | Rosamund Drive | A6 | | |
| | | Sackville Street | E2-E3-E4 | | |

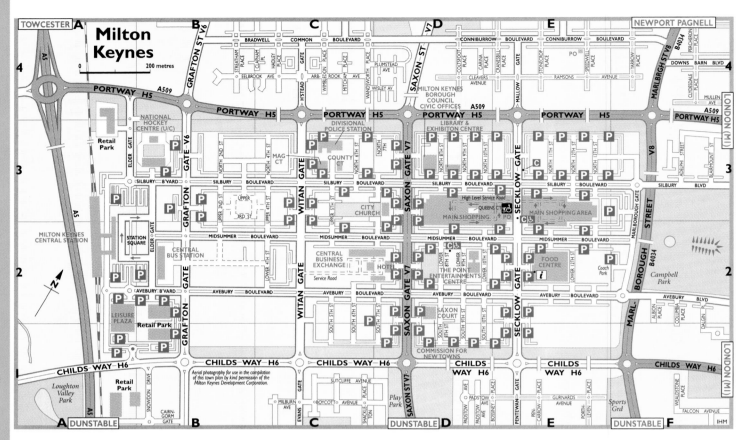

200

# Milton Keynes

Milton Keynes is found on atlas page **38**,
grid reference **8537**

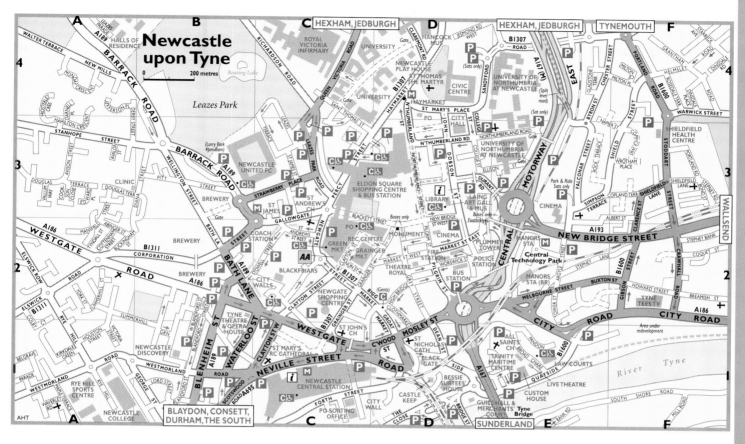

# Newcastle upon Tyne

Newcastle upon Tyne is found on atlas page **103**,
grid reference **2464**

### AA shop

33–35 Whitecross Way, Eldon Centre, Newcastle upon Tyne NE1 7YN    C2

| | | | | | | | |
|---|---|---|---|---|---|---|---|
| Abinger Street | A2 | Derby Street | D1 | Milton Close | E2 | Stoddart Street | F2 |
| Albert Street | E2-E3-F3 | Diana Street | A3-A4 | Milton Place | F1 | Stowell Street | E2-F2 |
| Argyle Street | E2 | Dinsdale Place | B2-A3-B3 | Monday Crescent | F4 | Strawberry Place | F3 |
| Avalon Street | A3 | Dinsdale Road | F4 | Mosley Street | E4-F4 | Summerhill Green | F2-F3-F4 |
| Avison Street | A3 | Douglas Terrace | F4 | Napier Street | A4 | Summerhill Street | B2-C2 |
| Bank Road | E1 | Durant Road | A3 | Neville Street | D1-D2 | The Close | B3-C3 |
| Barrack Road | B3-B4-A4 | Edward Place | D3-E3 | New Bridge Street | E4-E3-F3 | Tower Street | A2-A1-B1 |
| Bath Lane | B2-C2 | Ellison Street | A3 | New Bridge Street West | C1 | Tyndall Street | A2 |
| Belgrave Parade | A1 | Elswick Road | D3-E3 | New Mills | E3-E2-F2-F3 | Vallum Way | D1 |
| Bigg Market | C2-D2 | Elswick Row | A2 | Newgate Street | D2-D3 | Victoria Street | E2 |
| Blackett Street | C3-C2-D2-D3 | Falconar Street | A2 | Northumberland Road | A4 | Walter Terrace | B2 |
| Blandford Street | B1-B2 | Forth Street | E3 | Northumberland Street | C2-C3 | Warwick Street | A3 |
| Blenheim Street | B1-B2 | Frosterley Crescent | C1-D1 | Nun Street | D3-E3 | Waterloo Street | A1 |
| Bond Street | F3 | Gallowgate | A3-A4 | Pandon | D3-D4 | Waverley Road | A4 |
| Breamish Street | F2 | George Street | C2-C3 | Percy Street | C2 | Wellington Street | F4 |
| Bridge Street | D1 | Gibson Street | A1-B1 | Pilgrim Street | E1 | West Blandford Street | B1-C1-C2 |
| Broad Chare | E1 | Gladstone Terrace | F2 | Pitt Street | C3 | Westgate Road | A1 |
| Buckingham Street | A2-C2 | Grainger Street | E4 | Portland Road | D2 | Westmorland Road | B3 |
| Buxton Street | E2-F2 | Grantham Road | C1-C2-D2 | Quayside | B3 | Worswick Street | B1-B2 |
| Byron Street | E4 | Grey Street | D2 | Queen Victoria Road | F4-F3 | Wrotham Place | A2-B2-C2-C1-D1 |
| Central Motorway East | D2-E4 | Groat Market | D2 | Richardson Road | E1 | York Street | A1-B1 |
| Chester Street | E4-F4 | Hamilton Crescent | D1-D2 | Rock Terrace | C4 | | D2 |
| City Road | E2-E1-F2 | Haymarket | A3-A4 | Rosedale Terrace | B4-C4 | | F3 |
| Claremont Road | D4 | Helmsley Road | D3-D4 | Rye Hill | E3 | | A2 |
| Clayton Street | C2 | High Bridge | F4 | St Andrews Street | F4 | | |
| Clayton Street West | C1 | Houston Street | D2 | St James Street | A1-A2 | | |
| Clarence Street | F2-F3 | Howard Street | A1 | St Mary's Place | C2 | | |
| Clothmarket | D1-D2 | Jefferson Place | F2 | St Thomas Street | C3 | | |
| Colby Court | A1-A2 | Jesmond Road West | A4 | Sandyford Road | D4 | | |
| College Street | D3-D4 | John Dobson Street | D4 | Scotswood Road | C3-C4 | | |
| Collingwood Street | D1 | Kirkdale Green | D2-D3-D4 | Shield Street | D4-E4 | | |
| Cookson Close | A3 | Leazes Park Road | A1 | Shieldfield Lane | B1 | | |
| Copland Terrace | F3 | Leazes Terrace | C3-C4 | Side | E3-F3-F4 | | |
| Coppice Way | F3 | Lord Street | C3-C4 | Simpson Terrace | F3 | | |
| Coquet Street | F2 | Mansfield Street | B1 | South Shore Road | D1 | | |
| Corporation Street | A2-B2-C2 | Maple Terrace | B2-B3 | Stanhope Street | E3 | | |
| Cottenham Street | B2 | Market Street East | A1 | Starbeck Avenue | E1-F1 | | |
| Crawhall Street | F2 | Market Street West | D2 | Stepney Bank | A3-B3 | | |
| Darnell Place | A3-A4 | Melbourne Street | D2 | Stepney Lane | F4 | | |
| Dean Street | | Mill Road | | Stepney Road | | | |

# Newquay

Newquay is found on atlas page **4**,
grid reference **8161**

202

| | | | | | | |
|---|---|---|---|---|---|
| Agar Road | B2 | Linden Crescent | B1 | Trevena Terrace | A3 |
| Albany Road | C3 | Listry Road | A2-B2 | Ulalia Road | C3 |
| Alma Place | A3 | Manor Road | A3 | Vivian Close | B2 |
| Anthony Road | A1-B1 | Marcus Hill | B2-B3 | Wesley Yard | A3 |
| Bank Street | A3-B3 | Mayfield Crescent | B2 | | |
| Beach Road | A3 | Mayfield Road | B2 | | |
| Beachfield Avenue | A3 | Mellanurane Lane | B1-C1 | | |
| Beacon Road | A4 | Mitchell Avenue | B2-B3 | | |
| Belmont Place | A4 | Mount Wise | A3 | | |
| Berry Hill | B2-B3 | Mount Wise Cottages | A2-B2 | | |
| Bracken Terrace | B2 | Narrowcliff | C3-C4 | | |
| Broad Street | A3 | North Quay Hill | A4 | | |
| Chapel Hill | A3 | Oakleigh Terrace | B2 | | |
| Cheviot Road | B1 | Old Barn Court | A1 | | |
| Chichester Crescent | C1 | Pargolla Road | B3-C2 | | |
| Chynance Drive | A1-A2 | Pengannel Close | A1 | | |
| Chyverton Close | A1 | Quarry Park Road | C2 | | |
| Clevedon Road | A2 | Rawley Lane | B1 | | |
| Clifden Close | B2 | Reeds Way | A2 | | |
| Cliff Road | B3-C3 | Robartes Road | C2 | | |
| Colvreath Road | C3 | St George's Road | A2-A3 | | |
| Crantock Street | A3 | St John's Road | A2-A3 | | |
| Dane Road | A4 | St Michael's Road | A2-B2 | | |
| East Street | B3 | St Thomas Road | B2-C2 | | |
| Edgcumbe Avenue | C2-C3 | Seymour Avenue | B3 | | |
| Edgcumbe Gardens | C3 | Springfield Road | B3 | | |
| Eliot Gardens | C3 | Station Parade | C3 | | |
| Ennors Road | A2 | Sydney Road | A3 | | |
| Estuary View | A1 | The Crescent | A3 | | |
| Fairview Terrace | B2-B3 | Toby Way | A4 | | |
| Fernhill Road | A3 | Tolcarne Road | C3 | | |
| Fore Street | A3-A4 | Tor Road | B3 | | |
| Gannel Link Road | A2-A1-B1 | Tower Road | A3-A4 | | |
| Goonvrea Close | C1 | Trebarwith Crescent | B3 | | |
| Gover Lane | A3 | Tredour Road | B1 | | |
| Gresham Close | C1 | Treforda Road | C1 | | |
| Grosvenor Avenue | B2-B3 | Tregunnel Hill | A1-A2 | | |
| Hawkins Road | B1 | Trelawney Road | B2 | | |
| Headleigh Road | B2 | Treloggan Road | C1 | | |
| Holywell Road | C2 | Trembath Crescent | A1-B1 | | |
| Island Crescent | B3 | Trenance Avenue | B2-C2 | | |
| Jubilee Street | A3 | Trenance Lane | B1-B2 | | |
| Kew Close | C1 | Trenance Road | B2-C2 | | |
| King Edward Crescent | A4 | Trenarth Road | B2 | | |
| King Street | A3 | Treninnick Hill | C1 | | |
| Lanhenvor Avenue | B2 | Trethewey Way | A1 | | |
| Linden Avenue | B1-B2 | Trevemper Road | B1-C1 | | |

# Northampton

Northampton is found on atlas page **49**,
grid reference **7560**

**AA shop**
67 Abington Street, Northampton NN1 2BH                    C3

| | | | | | | |
|---|---|---|---|---|---|
| Abington Square | C3 | Georges Street | A4 | Swan Street | B1-B2 |
| Abington Street | B2-B3-C3 | Gold Street | A2 | The Drapery | A2-B2 |
| Albion Place | B1-B2 | Grafton Street | A4 | The Riding | B2-C2 |
| Alcombe Road | C4 | Great Russell Street | C4 | Tower Street | A3 |
| Alexandra Road | C2-C3 | Greyfriars | A3-B3-C3 | Upper Bath Street | A3 |
| Althorp Street | A3 | Guildhall Road | B1-B2 | Upper Mounts | B3-B4 |
| Angel Street | B2 | Hazelwood Road | C2 | Upper Priory Street | A4 |
| Arundel Street | A4 | Herbert Street | A3 | Victoria Gardens | B1 |
| Ash Street | B4 | Horsemarket | A2-A3 | Victoria Promenade | B1-C1 |
| Bailiff Street | B4 | Horseshoe Street | A1-A2 | Victoria Street | B3-B4 |
| Barrack Road | A4-B4 | Hunter Street | C4 | Wellington Street | B3-C3 |
| Bath Street | A3 | King Street | A2 | William Street | B4 |
| Bedford Road | C1 | Kingswell | A2 | York Road | C2-C3 |
| Bidders Close | B1 | Ladys Lane | A3-B3-C3 | | |
| Billing Road | C2 | Lower Harding Street | A4 | | |
| Bradshaw Street | A2-A3 | Lower Mounts | C3 | | |
| Bridge Street | A1-A2 | Lower Priory Street | A4 | | |
| Broad Street | A3-A4 | Margaret Street | B4 | | |
| Campbell Street | A4-B4 | Market Square | B2 | | |
| Castillian Street | B2 | Mayor Hold | A3 | | |
| Castle Street | A3 | Mercer's Row | B2 | | |
| Cattlemarket Road | C4 | Newland | B3 | | |
| Charles Street | B4-C4 | Oak Street | B4 | | |
| Cheyne Walk | C1-C2 | Overstone Road | C3-C4 | | |
| Church Lane | A3-B3-B4 | Pike Lane | A2-A3 | | |
| Clare Street | C4 | Quorn Way | A4 | | |
| Cloutsham Street | C4 | Regent Street | A4 | | |
| College Street | A2 | Robert Street | B4 | | |
| Commercial Street | A1 | St Andrew's Street | A3-A4 | | |
| Connaught Street | B4 | St Giles Square | A3 | | |
| Cranstoun Street | B4-C4 | St Giles Street | B2-C2 | | |
| Craven Street | B4-C4 | St Giles Terrace | C2-C3 | | |
| Crispin Street | A3 | St James Street | A1 | | |
| Deal Street | B4 | St John's Street | B1 | | |
| Derngate | C1-C2-B2 | St Katherine's Street | A2 | | |
| Duke Street | B4-C4 | St Mary's Street | A2 | | |
| Dunster Street | C3-C4 | St Michael's Road | C3 | | |
| Earl Street | B3-C4 | St Peter's Way | A1 | | |
| Elm Street | B4 | Sheep Street | A3-A4 | | |
| Fetter Street | B1-B2 | Silver Street | A3 | | |
| Foundry Street | A1 | Somerset Street | C4 | | |
| Gas Street | A1 | Spencer Parade | C2 | | |
| George Row | B2 | Spring Gardens | C2 | | |

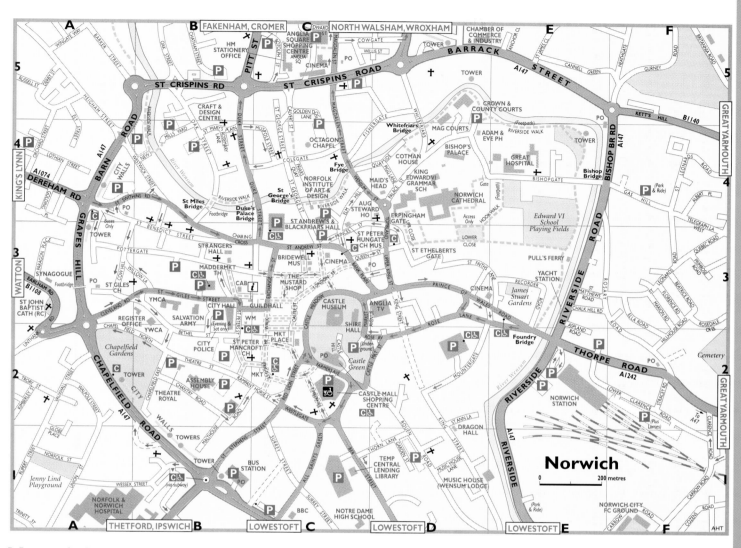

# Norwich

Norwich is found on atlas page **67**,
grid reference **2308**

### AA shop
Fanum House, 126 Thorpe Road, Norwich NR1 1RL

| | | | | | | | | | | |
|---|---|---|---|---|---|---|---|---|---|---|
| Albert Place | F4 | Chapelfield Road | A2-B2-B1 | Grapes Hill | A3-A4 | Prince of Wales Road | F3 | St Matthews Road | F3-F4 | Wingate Way | C5-D5 |
| All Saints Green | C1 | Charing Cross | B3 | Gurney Road | F5 | Princes Street | D3-E3 | St Peters Street | B4 | | A3-B3 |
| Anchor Close | E5 | Chatham Street | B5 | Heathgate | F5 | Quayside | C3 | St Stephens Street | E3 | | A5 |
| Aspland Road | E2-E3 | Clarence Road | F1-F2 | Heigham Street | A4-A5 | Quebec Road | C4-D4 | St Swithins Road | B2-B3 | | |
| Bank Plain | C3-D3 | Cleveland Road | A3-B3 | Hillhouse Road | F2-F3 | Queen Street | F3 | Stracey Road | B1-C1-C2 | | |
| Barker Street | A5 | Colegate | B4-C4 | Kett's Hill | F4-F5 | Rampant Horse Street | C3-D3 | Surrey Street | A4-B4-B3 | | |
| Barn Road | A4-A5 | Cow Hill | A3 | Kimberley Street | A2 | Recorder Road | B2-C2 | Telegraph Lane West | F2 | | |
| Barrack Street | D5-E5 | Cowgate | C5-D5 | King Street | D3-D2-D1-E1 | Red Lion Street | E3 | The Walk | C1-C2 | | |
| Beatrice Road | F3 | Cozens Road | F1 | London Street | C3 | Riverside | C2 | Theatre Street | F3-F4 | | |
| Bethel Street | B2-B3 | Derby Street | A5 | Lothian Street | A4 | Riverside Road | E1-E2 | Thorn Lane | C2-C3 | | |
| Bishop Road | E4-F4 | Dereham Road | A4 | Lower Clarence Road | E2-F2-F1 | Rosary Road | E2-E3-E4 | Thorpe Road | B2 | | |
| Bishopgate | E4 | Duke Street | B5-B4-C4-C3 | Magdalen Street | C4-C5 | Rose Avenue | E4-E3-F3-F2 | Timberhill | C1-D1 | | |
| Botolph Street | C5 | Earlham Road | A3 | Malthouse Road | B1-B2 | Rose Lane | C2-D2 | Tombland | E2-F2 | | |
| Brigg Street | C2 | Edward Street | C5 | Marion Road | F3 | Rosedale Crescent | D2-D3-E3-E2 | Trinity Street | C2 | | |
| Britannia Road | F5 | Ella Road | F2-F3 | Market Avenue | C2-C3 | Rosemary Lane | F3 | Trory Street | D3-D4 | | |
| Calvert Street | C4-C5 | Elm Hill | C3-C4 | Mountergate | D2 | Rouen Road | B4 | Union Street | A1 | | |
| Cannell Green | E5-F5 | Ely Street | A4-A5 | Music House Lane | D1 | Rupert Street | C2-D2-D1 | Unthank Road | A2 | | |
| Carrow Road | F1 | Exchange Street | C3 | Muspole Street | B4-C4 | Russell Street | A1-A2 | Upper King Street | A1 | | |
| Castle Hill | C2 | Farmers Avenue | C2 | New Mills Yard | B4 | St Andrew Street | A5 | Vauxhall Street | A2-A3 | | |
| Castle Meadow | C2-C3 | Fishergate | C4-D5 | Norfolk Street | A1 | St Ann Lane | C3 | Walpole Street | D3 | | |
| Castle Street | C3 | Florence Road | F3 | Oak Street | B4-B5 | St Benedict Street | D2 | Wensum Street | A2 | | |
| Cattle Market Street | C2-D2 | Friars Quay | C4 | Orchard Street | A4-A5 | St Crispins Road | A4-B3 | Wessex Street | A2 | | |
| Chalk Hill Road | E3 | Garden Street | D1 | Palace Street | D4 | St Faiths Lane | B5-C5-D5 | Westlegate | C4-D4 | | |
| Chantry Road | B2 | Gas Hill | F4 | Paragon Place | A3 | St George Street | D3-E3 | Westwick Street | A1-B1 | | |
| Chapel Field North | A2-B2 | Globe Place | A1-A2 | Pigg Lane | D4 | St Giles Close | C3-C4-C5 | Whitefriars | C2 | | |
| Chapelfield East | B2 | Golden Dog Lane | C5 | Pitt Street | B5-C5 | St James Close | F3 | Willis Street | A4-B4 | | |
| | | Golding Place | A3-A4 | Pottergate | A3-B3 | St Leonards Road | E5 | Willow Lane | D4-D5 | | |
| | | | | Primrose Road | | St Mary's Plain | | | | | |

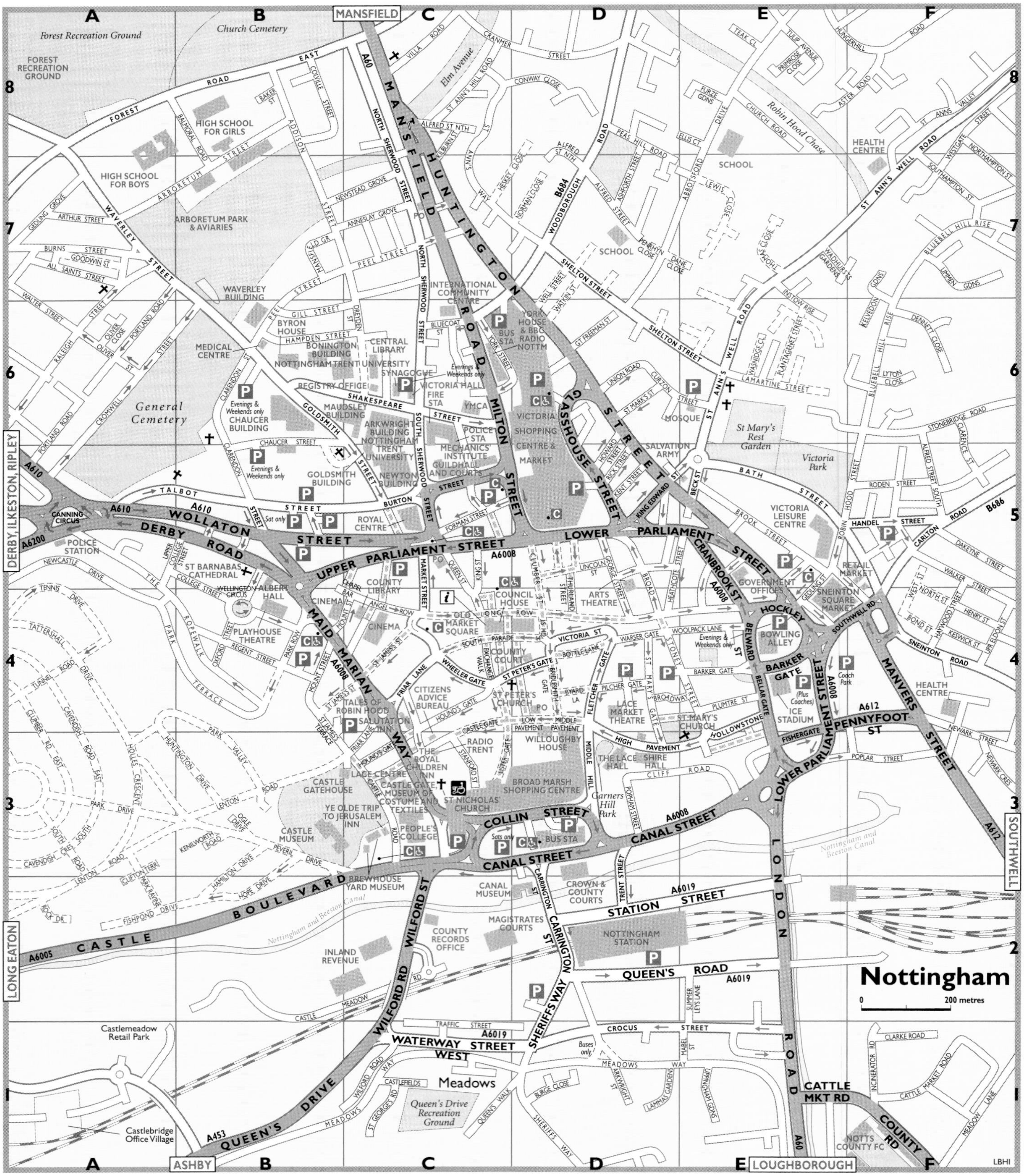

204

# Nottingham

MANSFIELD

ASHBY

LOUGHBOROUGH

DERBY, ILKESTON, RIPLEY

LONG EATON

SOUTHWELL

0    200 metres

Forest Recreation Ground

FOREST RECREATION GROUND

Church Cemetery

FOREST ROAD

EAST

Arboretum

ARBORETUM PARK & AVIARIES

HIGH SCHOOL FOR BOYS

HIGH SCHOOL FOR GIRLS

WAVERLEY STREET

WAVERLEY BUILDING

MEDICAL CENTRE

General Cemetery

BURNS STREET

GOODWIN ST

ALL SAINTS STREET

WALTER STREET

RALEIGH STREET

CROMWELL

PORTLAND ROAD

GILL STREET

BYRON HOUSE

HAMPDEN STREET

BONINGTON BUILDING

NOTTINGHAM TRENT UNIVERSITY

CENTRAL LIBRARY

REGISTRY OFFICE

SHAKESPEARE STREET

MAUDSLEY BUILDING

ARKWRIGHT BUILDING

CHAUCER BUILDING

CHAUCER STREET

GOLDSMITH BUILDING

GOLDSMITH STREET

NEWTON BUILDING

BURTON

ROYAL CENTRE

CANNING CIRCUS

POLICE STATION

WOLLATON STREET

DERBY ROAD

TALBOT STREET

UPPER PARLIAMENT STREET

LOWER PARLIAMENT STREET

ST BARNABAS CATHEDRAL

WELLINGTON ALBERT HALL

WELLINGTON CIRCUS

CINEMA

PLAYHOUSE THEATRE

REGENT STREET

MAID MARIAN WAY

COUNTY LIBRARY

OLD MARKET SQUARE

COUNCIL HOUSE

LONG ROW

PARADE

COUNTY COURT

WHEELER GATE

FRIAR LANE

ST PETER'S GATE

CITIZENS ADVICE BUREAU

TALES OF ROBIN HOOD

SALUTATION INN

THE ROYAL CHILDREN INN

LACE CENTRE

CASTLE GATEHOUSE

YE OLDE TRIP TO JERUSALEM INN

CASTLE MUSEUM

CASTLE GATE MUSEUM OF COSTUME AND TEXTILES

PEOPLE'S COLLEGE

BREWHOUSE YARD MUSEUM

CASTLE BOULEVARD

WILFORD RD

WILFORD STREET

COUNTY RECORDS OFFICE

INLAND REVENUE

MAGISTRATES COURTS

CANAL MUSEUM

CANAL STREET

COLLIN STREET

BUS STA

CROWN & COUNTY COURTS

STATION STREET

NOTTINGHAM STATION

QUEEN'S ROAD

SHERIFFS WAY

CARRINGTON ST

WATERWAY STREET WEST

Meadows

Queen's Drive Recreation Ground

QUEEN'S DRIVE

Castlemeadow Retail Park

Castlebridge Office Village

ST NICHOLAS' CHURCH

ST PETER'S CHURCH

ST MARY'S CHURCH

LACE MARKET THEATRE

THE LACE HALL

SHIRE HALL

WILLOUGHBY HOUSE

BROAD MARSH SHOPPING CENTRE

Garners Hill Park

HIGH PAVEMENT

LOW PAVEMENT

MIDDLE PAVEMENT

HOCKLEY

BARKER GATE

BOWLING ALLEY

ICE STADIUM

Coach Park

PENNYFOOT ST

PARLIAMENT STREET

MANVERS STREET

LONDON ROAD

COUNTY RD

CATTLE MKT RD

NOTTS COUNTY FC

HUNTINGDON STREET

MANSFIELD ROAD

NORTH SHERWOOD STREET

SOUTH SHERWOOD STREET

PEEL STREET

INTERNATIONAL COMMUNITY CENTRE

VICTORIA HALL

YMCA

POLICE STA

MECHANICS' INSTITUTE

GUILDHALL AND COURTS

MILTON STREET

VICTORIA SHOPPING CENTRE & MARKET

BUS STA

YORK HOUSE & BBC RADIO NOTTM

GLASSHOUSE STREET

ST ANN'S WELL ROAD

SALVATION ARMY

Mosque

St Mary's Rest Garden

Victoria Park

VICTORIA LEISURE CENTRE

SHELTON STREET

ALFRED STREET

SCHOOL

WOODBOROUGH ROAD

Robin Hood Chase

CHURCH ROAD

HEALTH CENTRE

SCHOOL

GOVERNMENT OFFICES

RETAIL MARKET

SNEINTON SQUARE MARKET

SOUTHWELL RD

SNEINTON ROAD

CARLTON ROAD

HEALTH CENTRE

ARTS THEATRE

BROAD ST

CRANBROOK ST

BELWARD

CANAL STREET

A60

A453

A6005

A610

A6008

A612

A6019

B684

B686

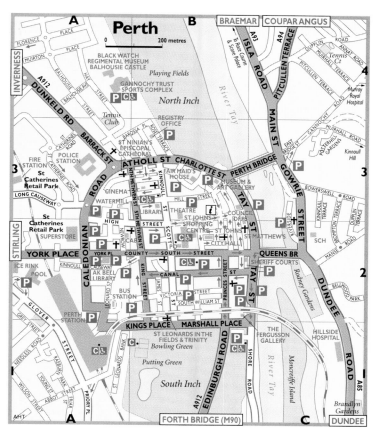

# Perth

Perth is found on atlas page **126**,
grid reference **1123**

| | | | | | |
|---|---|---|---|---|---|
| Abbot Street | A1 | Kings Place | A1-B1 | Tay Street | B1-B3 |
| Annat Road | C4 | Kinnoull Causeway | A2 | Victoria Street | B2 |
| Atholl Street | A3-B3 | Kinnoull Street | B3 | Wilson Street | A1 |
| Balhousie Avenue | A1 | Kinnoull Terrace | C2-C3 | York Place | A2 |
| Balhousie Street | A3-A4 | Leonard Street | A2 | Young Street | A1 |
| Barossa Place | A3-B3 | Long Causeway | A3 | | |
| Barrack Street | A3 | Main Street | C3-C4 | | |
| Bellwood Park | C2 | Manse Road | C2 | | |
| Bowerswell Road | C3 | Marshall Place | B1 | | |
| Brompton Terrace | C2-C3 | Mill Street | B3 | | |
| Caledonian Road | A2-A3 | Muirhall Road | C3 | | |
| Canal Street | B2 | Muirhall Terrace | C4 | | |
| Charlotte Street | B3 | Muirton Place | A4 | | |
| County South Street | A2-B2 | Needless Road | A1 | | |
| Dundee Road | C1-C2 | Newrow | A2 | | |
| Dunkeld Street | A3-A4 | North Methven Street | A3-B3 | | |
| Dupplin Road | C4 | Perth Bridge | B3-C3 | | |
| Dupplin Terrace | C2-C3 | Pitcullen Terrace | C4 | | |
| East Bridge Street | C3 | Potterhill Gardens | C3 | | |
| Edinburgh Road | B1 | Princes Street | B2 | | |
| Florence Place | A4 | Priory Place | A1 | | |
| Friar Street | A1 | Queen's Bridge | C2 | | |
| Gannochy Road | C3-C4 | Raeburn Park | A1 | | |
| Glover Street | A1-A2 | Riverside | C2-C3 | | |
| Gowrie Street | C2-C3 | Rose Terrace | B3 | | |
| Grey Street | A1-A2 | St Catherines Road | A3 | | |
| Hay Street | A3-A4 | St Leonards Bank | A1 | | |
| High Street | A2-B2 | Scott Street | B2 | | |
| Isla Road | B4-C4 | Shore Road | B1 | | |
| James Street | B2 | South Methven Street | B2-B3 | | |
| King Street | B2 | South William Street | B2 | | |

# Nottingham

Nottingham is found on atlas page **62**,
grid reference **5739**

**AA shop**
484 Derby Road, Nottingham NG7 2GT

| | | | | | | | | | |
|---|---|---|---|---|---|---|---|---|---|
| Abbotsford Drive | D6-D7-E7-E8 | Cattle Market Road | E1-F1 | George Street | D4-D5 | London Road | E1-E2-E3 | Plantagenet Street | E6 | Talbot Street | A5-B5 |
| Addison Street | B8-B7-C7 | Cavendish Crescent South | A3 | Gill Street | B6-C6 | Long Row | C4-D4 | Plumptre Street | E4 | Tattershall Drive | A4 |
| Alfred Street North | C8-D8-D7 | Cavendish Road East | A3-A4 | Glasshouse Street | D5-D6 | Low Pavement | D4 | Popham Street | D3 | Teak Close | E8 |
| Alfred Street | D7 | Chapel Bar | B4-C4 | Goldsmith Street | B6-C6-C5 | Lower Parliament Street | D5-E5-E3 | Poplar Street | E3-F3 | Tennis Drive | A4-A5 |
| Alfred Street South | F5-F6 | Chaucer Street | B5-B6 | Goodwin Street | A7 | Lyton Close | F6 | Portland Road | A5-A6-A7 | The Ropewalk | A5-A4-B4 |
| All Saints Street | A7 | Church Road | E8 | Great Freeman Street | D6 | Mabel Street | E1 | Primrose Close | E8 | Thomas Close | E7 |
| Angel Row | C4 | Clarence Street | F5-F6 | Hamilton Drive | B2-B3 | Maid Marian Way | B4-C4-C3 | Queen Street | C4-C5 | Thurland Street | D4-D5 |
| Annesley Grove | B7-C7 | Clarendon Street | B5-B6 | Hampden Street | B6-C6 | Mansfield Grove | B7 | Queen's Drive | B1-C1 | Traffic Street | C1-D1 |
| Arboretum Street | A7-B7-B8 | Clarke Road | F1 | Handel Street | F5 | Mansfield Road | C6-C7-C8 | Queen's Road | D2-E2 | Trent Street | D2-D3 |
| Arkwright Street | D1 | Cliff Road | D3-E3 | Haywood Street | F4-F5 | Manvers Street | F3-F4 | Queen's Walk | C1-D1 | Tulip Avenue | E8 |
| Arthur Street | A7 | Clifton Terrace | A2-A3 | Heathcote Street | D4-D5-E5 | Market Street | C4-C5 | Raleigh Street | A6-A7 | Tunnel Road | A4 |
| Ashforth Street | D7-D8 | Clumber Road East | A3-A4 | Henry Street | F4 | Meadow Lane | F1 | Regent Street | B4 | Union Road | D6 |
| Aster Road | E8-F8 | Clumber Street | D4-D5 | Heskey Close | C7-D7-D8 | Meadows Way | B1-C1-D1-E1 | Rick Street | D5 | Upper College Street | A4-A5 |
| Baker Street | B8 | College Street | A5-B5-B4 | High Pavement | D4-D3-E3 | Middle Hill | D3 | Robin Hood Street | E5-F5-F6 | Upper Eldon Street | F4 |
| Balmoral Road | A8-B8-B7 | Collin Street | C3-D3 | Hockley | E4 | Middle Pavement | D4 | Rock Drive | A2 | Upper Parliament Street | B5-C5 |
| Barker Gate | E4 | Colville Street | B8 | Holles Crescent | A3 | Mount Street | B4-C4 | Roden Street | F5 | Uppingham Gardens | E1 |
| Bath Street | E5 | Conway Close | C8-D8 | Hollowstone | E3-E4 | Newark Crescent | F3 | St Ann's Hill Road | C8 | Victoria Street | D4 |
| Beck Street | E5 | County Road | F1 | Hope Drive | B2-B3 | Newark Street | F3-F4 | St Ann's Valley | F7-F8 | Villa Road | C8 |
| Bellar Gate | E4 | Cranbrook Street | E4-E5 | Hound's Gate | C3-C4 | Newcastle Drive | A4-A5 | St Ann's Way | C7-C8 | Wadhursts Gardens | E7-F7 |
| Belward Street | E4 | Cranmer Street | C8-D8 | Howard Street | D5-D6 | Newstead Grove | B7-C7 | St Ann's Well Road | E6-E7-F7-F8 | Walker Street | F4-F5 |
| Bluebell Hill Rise | F6-F7 | Crocus Street | D1-E1 | Hungerhill Road | E8-F8 | Norman Close | D7 | St George's Road | C1 | Walter Street | A6-A7 |
| Bluecoat Street | C6 | Cromwell Street | A5-A6-B6 | Huntington Drive | A4-A3-B3 | North Sherwood Street | C8-C6 | St James Street | B4-C4 | Warser Gate | D4 |
| Bond Street | F4 | Curzon Street | D6-E6 | Huntington Street | C7-D6-D5-E5 | North Street | F4 | St James's Terrace | B3-B4 | Wasnidge Close | E6 |
| Bottle Lane | D4 | Dakeyne Street | F5 | Incinerator Road | F1 | Northampton Street | F7-F8 | St Mark's Street | D6 | Waterway Street West | C1-D1 |
| Bridlesmith Gate | D4 | Dane Close | D7-E7 | Instow Rise | E6-E7 | Ogle Drive | B3 | St Mary's Gate | D3-D4 | Watkin Street | D6-D7 |
| Broad Stoney Street | D5-D4-E4 | Dennett Close | F6 | Kelvedon Gardens | F6-F7 | Oliver Close | A6 | St Peter's Gate | C4-D4 | Waverley Street | A8-A7-B7-B6 |
| Broadway | D4-E4 | Derby Road | A5-B5 | Kenilworth Road | B3 | Oliver Street | A6 | Shakespeare Street | B6-C6 | Well Street | D6-D7 |
| Brook Street | E5 | Dreyden Street | C6 | Kent Street | D5 | Oxford Street | B4 | Shelton Street | D7-D6-E6 | West Street | F4-F5 |
| Burge Close | D1 | Ellis Court | E8 | Keswick Street | F4 | Park Drive | A3 | Sheriffs Way | D1-D2 | Westgate Street | F7-F8 |
| Burns Street | A7 | Exchange Walk | C4 | Kilburn Street | C7-C8 | Park Ravine | A2 | Sneinton Road | F4 | Wheeler Gate | C4 |
| Byard Lane | D4 | Fishergate | E3-E4 | King Edward Street | D5-E5 | Park Row | B4 | South Parade | C4-D4 | Wilford Road | C1-C2 |
| Canal Street | C3-D3-E3 | Fishpond Drive | A2-B2 | King Street | C4-C5 | Park Terrace | A4-B4 | South Road | A3 | Wilford Street | C2-C3 |
| Carlton Road | F5 | Fletcher Gate | D4 | Lamartine Street | E6 | Park Valley | A4-B4-B3 | South Sherwood Street | C5-C6 | Wollaton Street | A5-B5-C5 |
| Carrington Street | D2-D3 | Forest Road East | A7-A8-B8-C8 | Lammas Gardens | D1 | Peas Hill Road | D7-D8 | Southampton Street | F7 | Woodborough Road | D7-D8 |
| Castle Boulevard | A2-B2 | Forman Street | C5 | Lenton Road | A2-A3-B3 | Peel Street | B6-B7-C7 | Southwell Road | E4-F4 | Woolpack Lane | D4-E4 |
| Castle Meadow Road | B2-C2 | Friar Lane | C3-C4 | Lewis Close | E7 | Pennyfoot Street | E4-F4 | Stanford Street | C3 | York Street | C6 |
| Castle Road | C3 | Furze Gardens | E8 | Limmen Gardens | F7 | Penrhyn Close | D7 | Station Street | D2-E2 | | |
| Castlefields | C1 | Gedling Grove | A7 | Lincoln Street | D5 | Peveril Drive | B3 | Stonebridge Road | E6-F6 | | |
| Castlegate | C3-C4 | Gedling Street | E4-E5 | Lister Gate | C3 | Pilcher Gate | D4 | Summer Leys Lane | E2 | | |

205

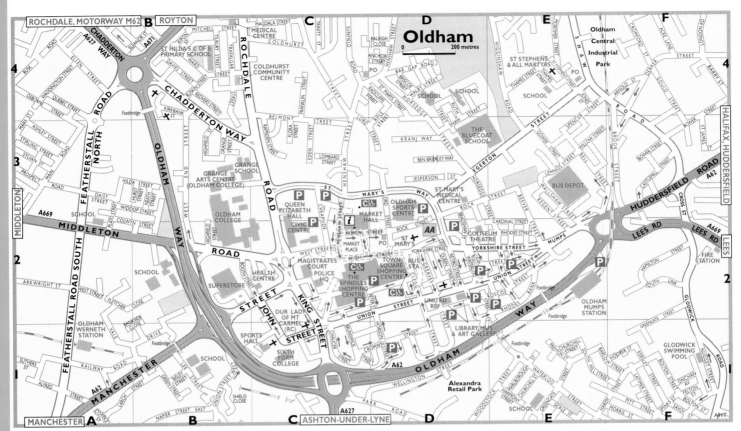

# Oldham

Oldham is found on atlas page **79**,
grid reference **9204**

**AA shop**
37 Yorkshire Street, Oldham OL1 3RZ                     D2

| | | | | | | | | | |
|---|---|---|---|---|---|---|---|---|---|
| Acre Lane | F4 | Davies Street | B4 | Kranj Way | D3 | Retiro Street | D2 | West End Street | B2-B3-B4 |
| Albion Street | C2-D2 | Derker Street | F4 | Larch Street | A1-B1 | Rhodes Bank | E2 | West Street | A2 |
| Alfred Street | A1 | Eden Street | C3 | Latimer Street | F1 | Rhodes Street | E2 | West Street | C2 |
| Anchor Street | C4-D4 | Egerton Street | D3-E3-E4 | Lee Street | B1 | Rifle Street | D3-D4 | Widdop Street | A3-B3 |
| Arkwright Street | A2 | Eleanor Street | A4-B4 | Lees Road | F2 | Ripon Street | B4 | Willow Street | E3 |
| Arnold Street | F4 | Ellen Street | A4 | Lemnos Street | E3 | Rochdale Road | B4-B3-C3-C2 | Woodstock Street | D1-E1 |
| Ashley Street | A3-A4 | Featherstall North Road | A3-A4 | Lombard Street | C3 | Rock Street | D2-D3-E3 | Yorkshire Street | D2-E2 |
| Bankside Close | A1-B1-B2 | Featherstall Road South | A1-A2 | London Road | F4 | Roscoe Street | D2-D3 | | |
| Bar Gap Road | D4 | Felton Street | F1 | Lord Street | C4-D3-D2 | Ruskin Street | B4 | | |
| Barlow Street | E1-F1 | Fletcher Close | A2-B2 | Magdala Street | B4-C4 | Ruth Street | D3-D4 | | |
| Barry Street | F4 | Flora Street | C3 | Main Road | A3 | St James Street | F3 | | |
| Beever Street | E2-E3 | Franklin Street | C3 | Malby Street | D4 | St Mary's Way | C3-D3 | | |
| Bell Street | E3 | George Street | C3 | Manchester Street | A1-B1-B2-C2 | St Marys Street | D4 | | |
| Belmont Street | C3-C4 | Glodwick Road | F1-F2 | Marlborough Street | E1 | St Stephen's Street | E4 | | |
| Ben Brierley Way | D3 | Gould Street | F3-F4 | Mars Street | A3-A4 | Savoy Street | F1 | | |
| Bisley Street | B1 | Gower Street | E3 | Middleton Road | A3-A2-B2-C2 | Shaw Road | E4-F4-F3 | | |
| Bolton Street | F1 | Grange Street | B3 | Mitchell Street | B4 | Shaw Street | D3-D4 | | |
| Booth Street | B2-C2 | Greaves Street | D2-D1 | Morris Street | E1-F1 | Shield Close | B1 | | |
| Bow Street | D2-E2 | Green Street | B1 | Mortimer Street | E4 | Sickle Street | E1 | | |
| Bower Street | F3-F4 | Greengate Street | E1-F1-F2 | Mumps | E2 | South Link | F2 | | |
| Bradshaw Street | D2-D3 | Hamilton Street | F2 | Neath Street | B3 | Southill Street | E1-F1 | | |
| Briscoe Street | D4 | Hardy Street | E1-F1 | Nugget Street | F1 | Spencer Street | E3-E4 | | |
| Brook Street | F3-F4 | Harmony Street | E1 | Oldham Way | B4-B1-D1-E2 | Spinks Street | F1 | | |
| Brunswick Street | C1-D1 | Henshaw Street | C2-C3-C4-D4 | Onchan Avenue | F1 | Stirling Street | A3 | | |
| Busk Road | A4 | Higginshaw Road | D4-E4-E3 | Osborne Street | A3-A4 | Sunfield Road | C4 | | |
| Cardinal Street | E2 | High Street | C2-D2 | Park Road | C1-D1 | Suthers Street | A1 | | |
| Castlemill Street | F3 | Highfield Street | B2-B3 | Peter Street | C2-D2 | Sylvan Street | A3 | | |
| Chadderton Way | A4-B4-B3 | Hilda Street | A3-B3 | Pitt Street | E1-F1 | Thames Street | E4 | | |
| Chaucer Street | C1 | Hobson Street | D2-D1 | Plato Street | A2-A3 | Tilbury Street | B4 | | |
| Cheapside Street | C2-C3 | Hooper Street | E1-F1 | Preston Street | E1 | Trafalgar Street | B3-B4 | | |
| Churchill Street | E1 | Horsedge Street | D4-D3-E2 | Prospect Road | A3 | Trinity Street | C4 | | |
| Clegg Street | D2-D1 | Huddersfield Road | F3 | Quebec Street | A4 | Union Street | C1-C2-D2-E2 | | |
| Coldhurst Street | B4-C4 | Hurst Street | A3-B3 | Queen Street | D2 | Union Street West | B1 | | |
| Colwyn Street | A3-A2-B2 | Jesperson Street | D3 | Radcliffe Street | C4-D4 | Vale Drive | A2-A1-B1 | | |
| Coppice Street | A1 | John Street | C2-C1 | Railway Road | A1-B1 | Waddington Street | A4 | | |
| Cromford Street | F4 | Jones Street | E4 | Raleigh Close | C4-D4 | Wallshaw Street | E2-E3 | | |
| Cromwell Street | C1-D1 | Kersley Street | F1 | Ramsden Street | C3 | Ward Street | B4 | | |
| Cross Street | F2-F3 | King Street | C2-C1 | Redvers Street | B4 | Waterloo Street | D2-E1 | | |
| Daisy Street | A3 | Kirkbank Street | B4 | Regent Street | E2-E3 | Wellington Street | C1-D1-D2 | | |

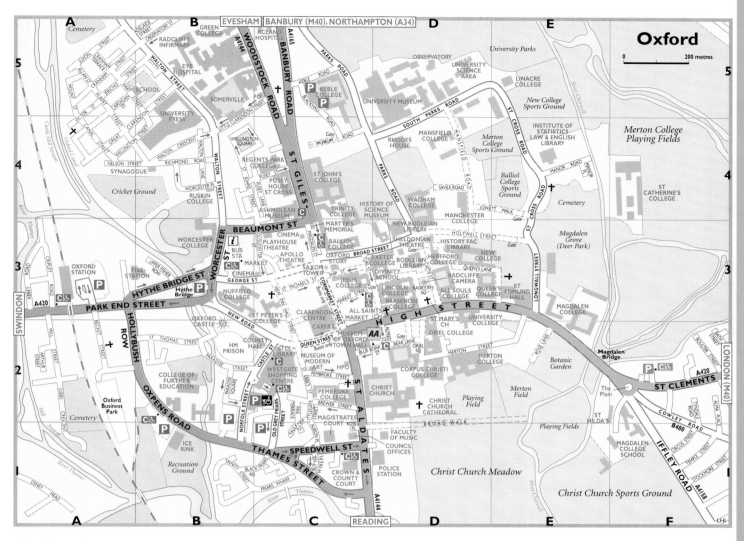

# Oxford

Oxford is found on atlas page **37**,
grid reference **5106**

## AA shop
133–134 High Street, Oxford OX1 4DN                C2

| | | | | | | | | |
|---|---|---|---|---|---|---|---|---|
| Abbey Road | A3 | Cowley Road | F1-F2 | Market Street | C3 | Rose Place | C1 | Worcester Place | B4 |
| Adelaide Street | B5 | Cranham Street | A5-B5 | Merton Street | D2-E2 | St Aldates | C1-C2 | Worcester Street | B3 |
| Albert Street | A4-A5 | Cranham Terrace | A5 | Mill Street | A2-A3 | St Clements | F2 | | |
| Albion Place | C1 | Cripley Road | A3 | Mount Street | A5 | St Cross Road | E3-E4-E5 | | |
| Alfred Street | D2 | Faulkner Street | C1-C2 | Museum Road | C4 | St Ebbe's Street | C2 | | |
| Allam Street | A5 | Friars Wharf | C1 | Nelson Street | A4-B4 | St Giles | C4 | | |
| Alma Place | F1-F2 | George Street | B3-C3 | New Inn Hall Street | C2-C3 | St Johns Street | B4-C4 | | |
| Arthur Street | A2 | Gibbs Crescent | A1-A2 | New Road | B3-B2-C2 | St Michael's Street | C3 | | |
| Banbury Road | C4-C5 | Gloucester Street | C3 | Norfolk Street | B1-B2 | St Thomas Street | B2 | | |
| Bath Street | F2 | Great Clarendon Street | A4-B4-B5 | Observatory Street | B5 | Savile Road | D4 | | |
| Bear Lane | D2 | Hart Street | A5-B5 | Old Grey Friars Street | C1-C2 | Ship Street | C3 | | |
| Beaumont Street | B3-C3 | High Street | C2-D3-E3-E2 | Oriel Square | D2 | South Parks Road | D4-D5 | | |
| Becket Street | A2-A3 | Hollybush Row | A3-A2-B2 | Osney Mead | A1 | Speedwell Street | C1 | | |
| Black Friars Road | B1-C1 | Holywell Street | D3-E3 | Oxpens Road | B1-B2 | Stockmore Street | F1 | | |
| Blackhall Road | C4-C5 | Hythe Bridge Street | A3-B3 | Paradise Square | B2 | Temple Street | F1 | | |
| Blue Boar Street | C2-D2 | Iffley Road | F1-F2 | Paradise Street | B2 | Thames Street | B1-C1 | | |
| Boulter Street | F2 | Jericho Street | A5-B5 | Park End Street | A3-B3 | Trinity Street | B1 | | |
| Brewer Street | C2 | Jowett Walk | D4-E4 | Parks Road | C5-C4-D4-D3 | Turl Street | C3-D3 | | |
| Broad Street | C3-D3 | Juxon Street | A5 | Pembroke Street | C2 | Tyndale Road | F2 | | |
| Broad Walk | C1-D1-D2-E2 | Keble Road | C5 | Pike Terrace | C2 | Upper Fisher Row | B3 | | |
| Butterwyke Place | C1 | Little Clarendon Street | B4-B5-C5 | Pusey Lane | C4 | Victor Street | A4-A5 | | |
| Canal Street | A4 | Littlegate Street | C2 | Pusey Street | C4 | Walton Crescent | B4 | | |
| Cardigan Street | A5 | Longwall Street | E3 | Queen Street | C2 | Walton Lane | B4 | | |
| Castle Street | C2 | Magdalen Street | C3 | Queen's Lane | D3-E3 | Walton Street | A5-B5-B4-B3 | | |
| Catte Street | D3 | Manor Place | E4 | Radcliffe Square | D3 | Wellington Square | B4-C4 | | |
| Circus Street | F1 | Manor Road | E4 | Richmond Road | B4 | Wellington Street | A4-B4 | | |
| Cornmarket Street | C2-C3 | Mansfield Road | D4-D5 | Rose Lane | E2 | Woodstock Road | B5-C5-C4 | | |

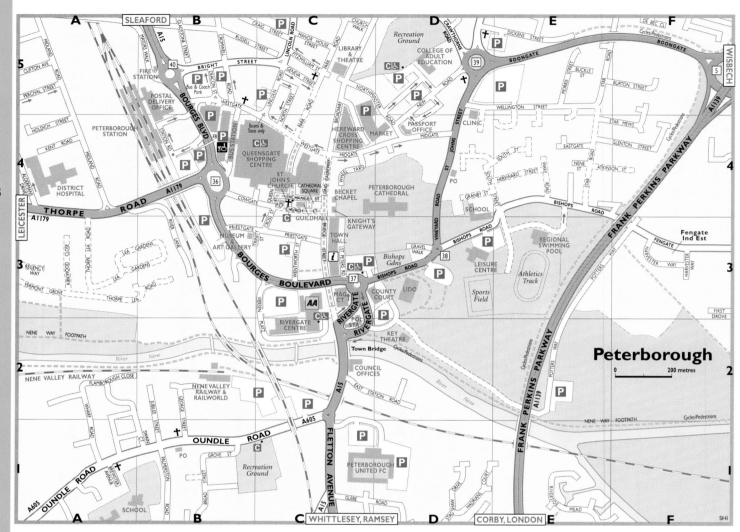

# Peterborough

Peterborough is found on atlas page **64**,
grid reference **1998**

**AA shop**
Unit 16 Rivergate Centre, Peterborough PE1 1EL     C3

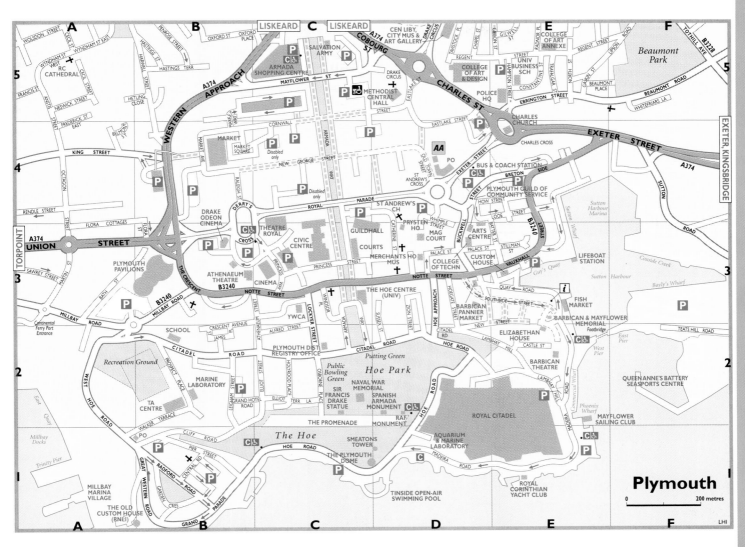

# Plymouth

Plymouth is found on atlas page **6**,
grid reference **4754**

**AA shop**
10 Old Town Street, Plymouth PL1 1DE                 D4

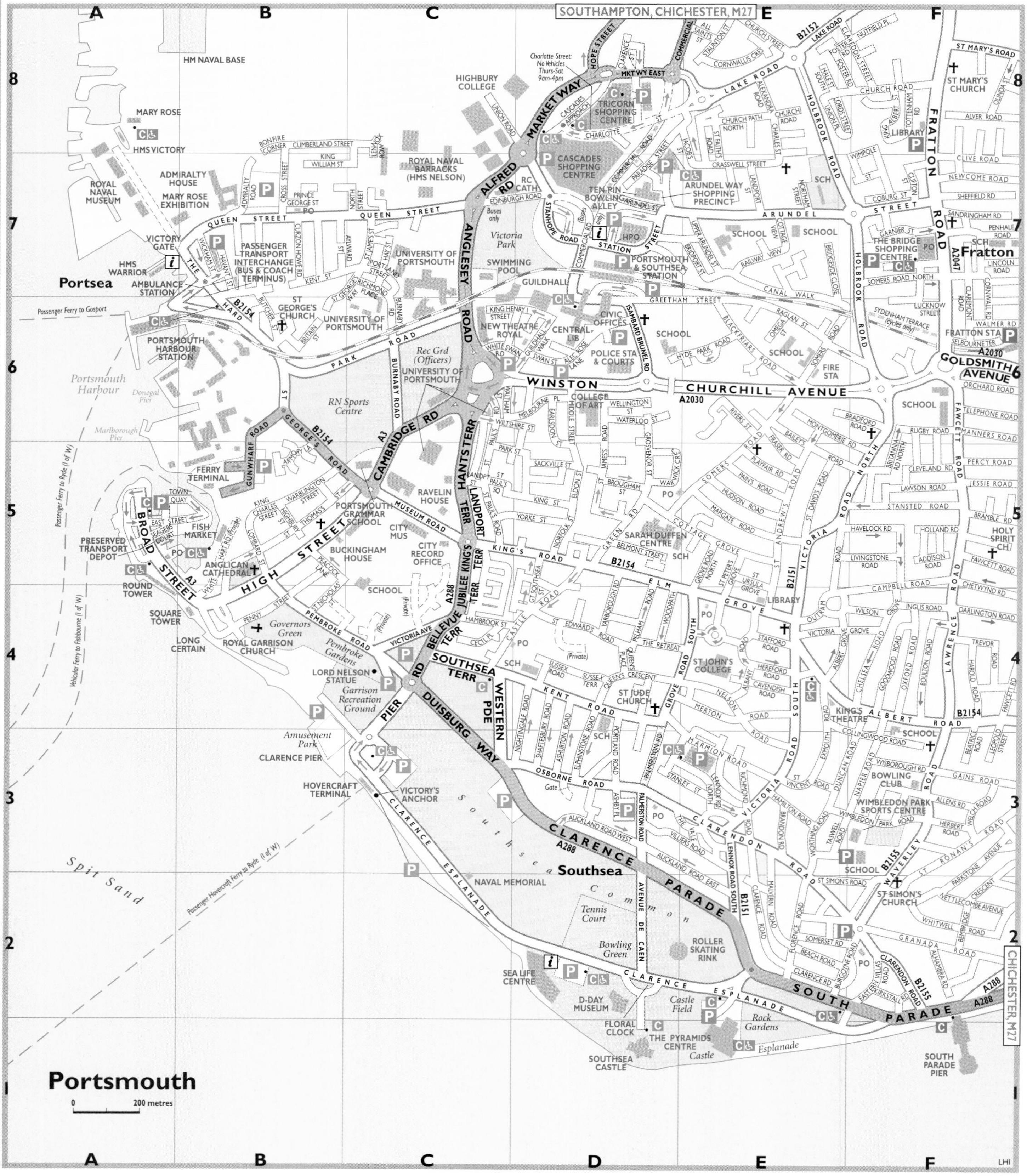

210

**Portsmouth**

0    200 metres

A  B  C  SOUTHAMPTON, CHICHESTER, M27  E  F

**Portsea**

**Southsea**

**Fratton**

GOLDSMITH AVENUE

CHICHESTER, M27

HM NAVAL BASE

MARY ROSE
HMS VICTORY
ROYAL NAVAL MUSEUM
ADMIRALTY HOUSE
MARY ROSE EXHIBITION
VICTORY GATE
HMS WARRIOR
AMBULANCE STATION
PORTSMOUTH HARBOUR STATION

Portsmouth Harbour
Donegal Pier
Marlborough Pier

Passenger Ferry to Gosport
Helicopter Ferry to Ryde (I of W)
Passenger Hovercraft Ferry to Ryde (I of W)

PRESERVED TRANSPORT DEPOT
ROUND TOWER
SQUARE TOWER
LONG CERTAIN
TOWN QUAY
EAST STREET
FISH MARKET
PO
ANGLICAN CATHEDRAL
BROAD STREET
HIGH STREET

Spit Sand

Governors Green
ROYAL GARRISON CHURCH
Pembroke Gardens
LORD NELSON STATUE
Garrison Recreation Ground
Amusement Park
CLARENCE PIER
HOVERCRAFT TERMINAL
VICTORY'S ANCHOR

BONFIRE CORNER
CUMBERLAND STREET
KING WILLIAM ST
PRINCE GEORGE ST
CROSS STREET
QUEEN STREET
QUEEN STREET
ST GEORGE'S CHURCH
PASSENGER TRANSPORT INTERCHANGE (BUS & COACH TERMINUS)
UNIVERSITY OF PORTSMOUTH
UNIVERSITY OF PORTSMOUTH
RN Sports Centre
FERRY TERMINAL
GUNWHARF ROAD
GEORGE'S ROAD
CAMBRIDGE RD
B2154
PORTSMOUTH GRAMMAR SCHOOL
KING CHARLES STREET
WARBLINGTON STREET
ST THOMAS ST
PENNY ST
RAVELIN HOUSE
MUSEUM ROAD
CITY MUS
CITY RECORD OFFICE
Buckingham House
SCHOOL
PEMBROKE ROAD
VICTORIA AVE
PIER RD
BELLEVUE TERR
SOUTHSEA TERR
WESTERN PDE
DUISBURG WAY
Southsea

HIGHBURY COLLEGE
ROYAL NAVAL BARRACKS (HMS NELSON)
UNION ROAD
LENNOX ROAD
ALFRED RD
RC CATH
EDINBURGH ROAD
ANGLESEY ROAD
PARK ROAD
BURNABY ROAD
Victoria Park
SWIMMING POOL
GUILDHALL
HANTS TERR
LANDPORT
KING'S TERR
JUBILEE TERR
A288
KING'S ROAD
B2154

Charlotte Street: No Vehicles Thurs-Sat 9am-4pm
HOPE STREET
MARKET WAY
MKT WY EAST
CASCADES APPROACH
TRICORN SHOPPING CENTRE
CHARLOTTE
CASCADES SHOPPING CENTRE
TEN-PIN BOWLING ALLEY
ARUNDEL WAY SHOPPING PRECINCT
STANHOPE ROAD
STATION
i
HPO
PORTSMOUTH & SOUTHSEA STATION
KING HENRY ST
NEW THEATRE ROYAL
CENTRAL LIB
CIVIC OFFICES
POLICE STA & COURTS
WINSTON CHURCHILL AVENUE
A2030
COLLEGE OF ART
WELLINGTON ST
WATERLOO ST
GROSVENOR ST
SACKVILLE ST
KING ST
YORKE ST
ST PAUL'S RD
WILTSHIRE ST
PARK ROAD
EARLSDON ST
GREEN
ELM GROVE
SARAH DUFFEN CENTRE
BELMONT ST
STAFFORD ROAD
ST JOHN'S COLLEGE
CASTLE ROAD
ST JUDE'S CHURCH
GROVE ROAD
NELSON ROAD
MERTON ROAD
MARMION ROAD
OSBORNE ROAD
CLARENCE PARADE
A288
NAVAL MEMORIAL
Common
Tennis Court
Bowling Green
SEA LIFE CENTRE
D-DAY MUSEUM
FLORAL CLOCK
THE PYRAMIDS CENTRE
SOUTHSEA CASTLE
Castle
Castle Field
Rock Gardens
ROLLER SKATING RINK
CLARENCE ESPLANADE
SOUTH PARADE
SOUTH PARADE PIER
AVENUE DE CAEN

COMMERCIAL ROAD
B2152
LAKE ROAD
NUTFIELD RD
CHURCH STREET
CORNWALLIS CRES
HOLBROOK ROAD
CHURCH PATH NORTH
CHURCH ROAD
CRASSWELL STREET
ARUNDEL
SCHOOL
SCHOOL
THE BRIDGE SHOPPING CENTRE
RAILWAY VIEW
CANAL WALK
GREETHAM STREET
BLACKFRIARS RD
RAGLAN ST
FIRE STA
HYDE PARK ROAD
VICTORIA ROAD NORTH
ST PETER'S GROVE
SOMERS ROAD
VICTORIA ROAD SOUTH
GROVE ROAD SOUTH
THE RETREAT
CLARENDON ROAD
B2151
B2154
CAMPBELL ROAD
OUTRAM ROAD
WILSON GROVE
VICTORIA GROVE
ALBERT ROAD
FLORENCE ROAD
PALMERSTON ROAD
AUCKLAND ROAD WEST
AUCKLAND ROAD EAST
VILLIERS ROAD
LENNOX ROAD SOUTH
HAMPSHIRE TERR
BEACH ROAD
GRANADA ROAD
SOMERSET RD
CLARENCE RD

ST MARY'S ROAD
ST MARY'S CHURCH
ALVER ROAD
CLIVE ROAD
NEWCOME ROAD
SHEFFIELD RD
COBURG ST
FRATTON ROAD
A2047
LINCOLN ROAD
PENHALE RD
SANDRINGHAM RD
FRATTON STA
SELBOURNE TER
GOLDSMITH AVENUE
ORCHARD ROAD
SCHOOL
TELEPHONE ROAD
RUGBY ROAD
MANNERS ROAD
CLEVELAND ROAD
PERCY ROAD
JESSIE ROAD
STANSTED RD
BRAMBLE RD
HOLY SPIRIT CH
FAWCETT ROAD
CHETWYND RD
DARLINGTON ROAD
HAVELOCK RD
HOLLAND RD
LIVINGSTONE ROAD
ADDISON ROAD
TREVOR ROAD
KING'S THEATRE
LAWRENCE ROAD
HAROLD ROAD
B2154
COLLINGWOOD ROAD
WAVERLEY ROAD
BOWLING CLUB
WISBOROUGH RD
GAINS ROAD
WIMBLEDON PARK SPORTS CENTRE
HERBERT ROAD
WELCH ROAD
ST SIMON'S CHURCH
ST RONAN'S RD
PARKSTONE AVENUE
KETTLECOMBE AVENUE
WHITWELL RD
SOUTH PARADE
B2155

LHI

# Ramsgate

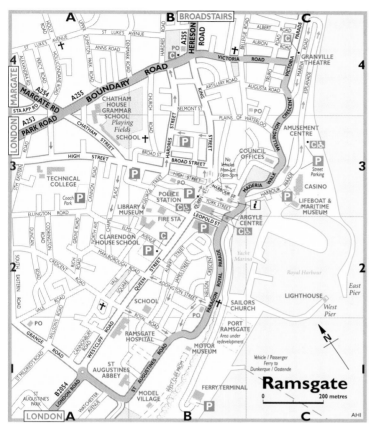

Ramsgate is found on atlas page **29**,
grid reference **3865**

| | | | |
|---|---|---|---|
| Addington Street | B2 | James Street | B2 |
| Albert Road | C4 | King Street | B3-B4 |
| Albert Street | B2 | Leopold Street | B2-B3 |
| Albion Road | B4-C4 | London Road | A1 |
| Alexandra Road | A4 | Madeira Walk | B3-C3 |
| Anns Road | A4 | Margate Road | A4 |
| Artillery Road | B4 | Marina Road | C4 |
| Augusta Road | B4-C4 | Marlborough Road | A2-B2 |
| Bellevue Road | B4 | Nelson Crescent | B2 |
| Belmont Street | B4 | North Avenue | A2 |
| Boundary Road | A4-B4 | Paragon Royal Parade | B1-B2 |
| Broad Street | B3 | Park Road | A3 |
| Cannonbury Road | A1 | Percy Road | A4 |
| Canon Road | A3 | Plains of Waterloo | B3-C3 |
| Chapel Place | A2-A3 | Queen Street | A2-B2-B3 |
| Chatham Street | A3 | Richmond Road | A2 |
| Church Road | B3-B4 | Royal Road | A2-B2-B1 |
| Codrington Road | A2 | St Augustine's Park | A1 |
| Crescent Road | A2 | St Augustines Road | A1-B1 |
| Denmark Road | A4-B4 | St Luke's Avenue | A4-B4 |
| Duncan Road | A2 | St Mildred's Road | A1 |
| Ellington Road | A2-A3 | South Eastern Road | A2-A3 |
| Elms Avenue | A2-B2 | Station Approach Road | A4 |
| Esplanade | C3-C4 | Truro Road | C4 |
| George Street | B3 | Upper Dumpton Park Road | A4 |
| Grange Road | A1 | Vale Road | A1-A2 |
| Grove Road | A2 | Vale Square | A2-B2 |
| Harbour Parade | B3-C3 | Victoria Parade | C4 |
| Harbour Street | B3 | Victoria Road | B4-C4 |
| Hardres Road | B4 | Watchester Avenue | A1 |
| Hardres Street | B3-B4 | Wellington Crescent | C3-C4 |
| Hereson Road | B4 | West Cliff Promenade | B1 |
| High Street | A3-B3 | Westcliff Road | A1-A2 |
| Hollicondane Road | A4 | Willson's Road | A1-A2 |
| Holly Road | A4 | York Street | B3 |

211

# Portsmouth

Portsmouth is found on atlas page **13**,
grid reference **6400**

**AA shop**
12 London Road, Portsmouth PO1 1NL

| | | | | | |
|---|---|---|---|---|---|
| Addison Road | F5 | Burgoyne Road | E2-F2 | Duisburg Way | C3-C4 |
| Admiralty Road | B7 | Burnaby Road | C6 | Duncan Road | E3-F3 |
| Albany Road | E4 | Butcher Street | B6-B7 | Earlsdon Street | D6 |
| Albert Grove | E4-E5 | Cambridge Road | C5-C6 | East Street | A5-B5 |
| Albert Road | E4-F4 | Campbell Road | F5 | Eastern Villas Road | F2 |
| Alec Rose Lane | D6 | Canal Walk | E7 | Edinburgh Road | C7-D7 |
| Alexandra Road | E8 | Cascades Approach | D8 | Eldon Street | D5 |
| Alfred Road | C7-D7 | Castle Road | C4-D4-D5 | Elm Grove | D5-E4 |
| Alhambra Road | F2 | Cavendish Road | E4 | Elphinstone Road | D3-D4 |
| All Saints Street | E8 | Cecil Place | C4 | Exmouth Road | E3-E4 |
| Allens Road | F3 | Charles Street | E7-E8 | Fawcett Road | F5-F6 |
| Alver Road | F8 | Charlotte Street | D8-E8 | Florence Road | E2 |
| Anglesey Road | C6-C7 | Chelsea Road | F4 | Foster Road | E8-F8 |
| Armory Lane | B5 | Chetwynd Road | F4-F5 | Fraser Road | E5-E6 |
| Arundel Street | D7-E7-F7 | Church Path North | E8 | Fratton Road | F6-F7-F8 |
| Ashby Place | D3 | Church Road | E8-F8 | Gains Road | F3 |
| Ashurton Road | D3-D4 | Church Street | E8 | Garnier Street | F7 |
| Auckland Road East | D3-E3-E2 | Claredon Street | F8 | Goldsmith Avenue | F6 |
| Auckland Road West | D3 | Claremont Road | F6-F7 | Goodwood Road | F4 |
| Avenue De Caen | D2 | Clarence Esplanade | C3-F1 | Granada Road | F2 |
| Aylward Street | B7-C7 | Clarence Parade | D3-E2 | Great Southsea Street | D4-D5 |
| Bailey's Road | E6-E5-F5 | Clarence Road | E2-E3 | Green Road | D5 |
| Beach Road | E2 | Clarence Street | D8 | Greetham Street | D7-E7 |
| Beatrice Road | F3-F4 | Clarendon Road | D3-E3-E2-F2 | Grosvenor Street | D5-D6 |
| Bellevue Terrace | C4 | Cleveland Road | F5 | Grove Road North | E5 |
| Belmont Street | D5 | Clifton Street | F7 | Grove Road South | D4-E4 |
| Bembridge Crescent | F2-F3 | Clive Road | F7-F8 | Guildhall Walk | D6 |
| Blackfriars Road | E6 | Coburg Street | F7 | Gunwharf Road | B5-B6 |
| Bonfire Corner | B8 | Collingwood Road | E4-F4-F3 | Hale Street South | E8 |
| Boulton Road | F4 | Commercial Road | D7-D8-E8 | Hambrook Street | C4-D4 |
| Bradford Road | E6-F6 | Cornwall Road | F6-F7 | Hamilton Road | E3 |
| Bramble Road | F5 | Cornwallis Crescent | E8 | Hampshire Terrace | C5-C6 |
| Brandon Road | E3 | Cottage Grove | D5-E5 | Harold Road | F4 |
| Bridgeside Close | E7 | Cottage View | E7 | Havant Street | B7 |
| Bridport Street | E7 | Crasswell Street | E7 | Havelock Road | F5 |
| Britain Street | B6 | Cross Street | B7-B8 | Hay Street | C7 |
| Britannia Road North | F5-F6 | Cumberland Street | B8-C8 | Herbert Road | F3 |
| Broad Street | A5-B5-B4 | Curzon Howe Road | B7 | Hereford Road | E4 |
| Brougham Street | D5 | Darlington Road | F4 | High Street | B4-B5-C5 |
| | | | | Highbury Street | B5 |
| | | | | Holbrook Road | F6-F7-E7-E8 |
| | | | | Holland Road | F5 |
| | | | | Hope Street | D8 |
| | | | | Hudson Road | E5 |
| | | | | Hyde Park Road | D6-E6 |
| | | | | Inglis Road | F4 |
| | | | | Isambard Brunel Road | D6 |
| | | | | Jacob's Street | E8 |
| | | | | Jessie Road | F5 |

| | | | | | |
|---|---|---|---|---|---|
| Jubilee Terrace | C4-C5 | Pain's Road | E5 | Somerset Road | E2-F2 |
| Kent Road | D4 | Palmerston Road | D3-D4 | South Parade | E2-F2 |
| Kent Street | B7-C7 | Paradise Street | D7-D8-E8 | Southsea Terrace | C4 |
| King Albert Street | F8 | Park Road | B6-C6 | Stafford Road | E4 |
| King Charles Street | B5 | Park Street | C5-D5 | Stanhope Road | D7 |
| King Henry 1 Street | C6-D6 | Parkstone Avenue | F2-F3 | Stanley Street | D3-E3 |
| King Street | D5 | Peacock Lane | B5 | Stansted Road | F5 |
| King William Street | B7-C7 | Pelham Road | D4-D5 | Station Street | D7 |
| King's Road | C5-D5 | Pembroke Road | B4-C4 | Staunton Street | E8 |
| King's Terrace | C5 | Penhale Road | F7 | Sussex Road | D4 |
| Kirkstall Road | F2 | Penny Street | B4-B5 | Sussex Terrace | D4 |
| Lake Road | E8 | Percy Road | F5 | Swan Street | D6 |
| Landport Street | C5 | Pier Road | C4 | Sydenham Terrace | F6 |
| Landport Street | E7 | Playfair Road | E5 | Taswell Road | E3-F3 |
| Landport Terrace | C5 | Portland Road | D3-D4 | Telephone Road | F6 |
| Lawrence Road | F4-F5 | Portland Street | C7 | The Hard | B6-B7 |
| Lawson Road | F5 | Prince George Street | B7 | The Retreat | D4-D5 |
| Lennox Road North | E3 | Queen Street | B7-C7 | The Vale | E3 |
| Lennox Road South | E2-E3 | Queen's Crescent | D4 | Tottenham Road | F8 |
| Lennox Row | C8 | Queen's Place | D4 | Town Quay | A5-B5 |
| Leopold Street | F3-F4 | Raglan Street | E6 | Trevor Road | F4 |
| Lincoln Road | F7 | Railway View | E7 | Union Place | E8 |
| Livingstone Road | F5 | Richmond Place | C7 | Union Road | C8-D8 |
| Lombard Street | B5 | Richmond Road | E3 | Upper Arundel Street | E7 |
| Lords Street | E8-F8 | Rivers Street | E6 | Victoria Avenue | C4 |
| Lucknow Street | F6 | Rugby Road | F6 | Victoria Grove | E4-F4 |
| Malvern Road | E2-E3 | Sackville Street | D5 | Victoria Road North | E4-F6 |
| Manners Road | F6 | St Andrew's Road | E4-E5-E6 | Victoria Road South | E3-E4 |
| Margate Road | E5 | St David's Road | E5 | Villiers Road | D3-E3 |
| Market Way | D8 | St Edward's Road | D4 | Walmer Road | F6 |
| Market Way East | D8 | St Faith's Road | E7-E8 | Waltham Street | C6-D6 |
| Marmion Road | E3-E4 | St George's Road | B6-B5-C5 | Warblington Street | B5 |
| Melbourne Place | D6 | St George's Way | B6-B7 | Warwick Crescent | D5-E5 |
| Merton Road | E4 | St James's Road | D5-D6 | Waterloo Street | D6 |
| Middle Street | D5-D6 | St Jame's Street | C7 | Waverley Road | F2-F3-F4 |
| Montgomerie Road | E6-F6 | St Mary's Road | F8 | Welch Road | F3 |
| Museum Road | C5 | St Nicholas' Street | B4-C5 | Wellington Street | D6 |
| Napier Road | F3-F4 | St Paul's Road | C5-C6 | Western Parade | C3-C4 |
| Nelson Road | E3-E4 | St Paul's Square | C5 | White Hart Road | B4-B5 |
| Nettlecombe Avenue | F2 | St Peter's Grove | E4-E5 | White Swan Road | C6-D6 |
| Newcome Road | F7 | St Ronan's Road | F2-F3 | Whitwell Road | F2 |
| Nightingale Road | D3-D4 | St Simon's Road | E2-F2 | Wickham Street | B7 |
| Norfolk Street | D5 | St Thomas's Street | B5-C5 | Wilson Grove | F4 |
| North Street | B7-C7 | St Ursula Grove | E5 | Wiltshire Street | C6-D6 |
| Northam Street | E7 | St Vincent Road | E3 | Wimbledon Park Road | E3-F3 |
| Nutfield Place | F8 | Sandringham Road | F7 | Wimpole Street | F7-F8 |
| Olinda Street | F8 | Seagers Court | A5 | Winston Churchill Avenue | D6-E6 |
| Omega Street | E6 | Selbourne Terrace | F6 | Wisborough Road | F3 |
| Orchard Road | F6 | Shaftesbury Road | D3-D4 | Woodpath | D4 |
| Osborne Road | D3 | Sheffield Road | F7 | Worthing Road | E3 |
| Outram Road | E4-E5 | Somers Road | E5-E6 | Yarborough Road | D4-D5 |
| Oxford Road | F4 | Somers Road North | F7 | Yorke Street | C5-D5 |

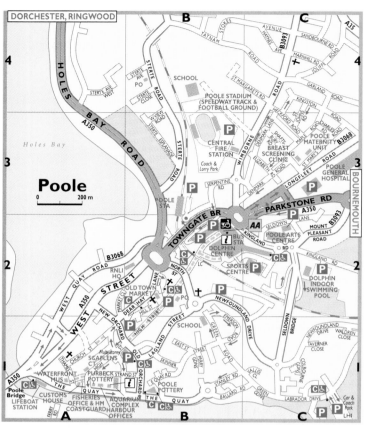

# Poole

Poole is found on atlas page 11,
grid reference **0090**

**AA shop**
10 Falkland Square, Poole BH15 1ER                    B2

| | | | |
|---|---|---|---|
| Ballard Road | B1-C1 | Shaftsbury Road | C3 |
| Charles Road | C3 | Skinner Street | B1 |
| Church Street | A1 | Stanley Road | B1 |
| Colbourne Gardens | C1 | Sterte Avenue | B4 |
| Dear Hay Lane | B2 | Sterte Avenue West | A4 |
| Denman Lane | C3 | Sterte Close | B4 |
| Denman Road | C3 | Sterte Esplanade | B3 |
| East Quay Road | B1 | Sterte Road | B4-B3 |
| East Street | B1 | Stokes Avenue | B4-C4 |
| Elizabeth Road | C3 | Strand Street | A1-B1 |
| Emerson Road | B2-B1 | Tatnam Road | B4-C4 |
| Ferry Road | A1 | Taverner Close | C1 |
| Garland Road | C4 | Thames Street | A1 |
| Green Gardens | C1 | The Quay | A1-B1 |
| Green Road | B1 | Towngate Bridge | B2-B3 |
| Haynes Avenue | C4 | Vallis Close | C1 |
| Heckford Road | C3-C4 | Waldren Close | C1 |
| High Street | A1-B1-B2 | West Quay Road | A1-A2-B2 |
| Hill Street | B2 | West Street | A1-A2-B2 |
| Holes Bay Road | A4-B3-B2 | West View Road | B3-B4 |
| Jolliffe Road | C4 | Wimborne Road | B3-C3-C4 |
| Kingland Road | C2 | | |
| Kingston Road | C3-C4 | | |
| Labrador Drive | C1 | | |
| Lagland Street | B1-B2 | | |
| Longfleet Road | C3 | | |
| Maple Road | C3-C4 | | |
| Market Close | A2 | | |
| Marnhill Road | C4 | | |
| Mount Pleasant Road | C2 | | |
| New Orchard | A2-A1 | | |
| Newfoundland Drive | C1 | | |
| North Street | B2 | | |
| Old Orchard | B1 | | |
| Parkstone Road | C3 | | |
| Perry Gardens | B1 | | |
| St Johns Road | C3-C4 | | |
| St Margarets Road | B4-C4 | | |
| St Mary's Road | C3 | | |
| Sandbourne Road | C4 | | |
| Seldown Bridge | C1-C2 | | |
| Seldown Lane | C2 | | |
| Serpentine Road | B3 | | |

# Preston

Preston is found on atlas page **80**,
grid reference **5329**

**AA shop**
3-4 Cheapside, Preston PR1 2AP                    B2

| | | | | | |
|---|---|---|---|---|---|
| Adelphi Street | A3-A4 | Ladywell Street | A2 | Walker Street | A3-B3 |
| Appleby Street | B4 | Lancaster Road | B4-B3-C3-C2 | Warwick Street | A4-B3 |
| Ashmoor Street | A4 | Laurel Street | C1-C2 | West Market Street | B3 |
| Avenham Lane | C1 | Lawson Street | B3-B4 | Winckley Square | B1 |
| Avenham Road | B1-C1 | Lord Street | C2 | Winckley Street | B1 |
| Avenham Street | C1-C2 | Lune Street | B2 | | |
| Bairstow Street | B1 | Main Spritweild | C1-C2 | | |
| Berwick Road | C1 | Manchester Road | C2 | | |
| Birley Street | B2 | Market Street | B2 | | |
| Bolton's Court | C1-C2 | Marsh Lane | A2-A3 | | |
| Butler Street | A1 | Maudland Road | A3 | | |
| Cannon Street | B1-B2 | Meadow Street | C3-C4 | | |
| Carlisle Street | C3 | Melling Street | B4 | | |
| Chaddock Street | B1 | Moor Lane | A3-A4 | | |
| Chapel Street | B1 | Mount Street | B1 | | |
| Charlotte Street | C1 | Noor Street | C4 | | |
| Christian Road | A1 | North Road | B4-C4-C3 | | |
| Church Row | C2 | North Street | B3 | | |
| Church Street | B2-C2 | Oak Street | C1 | | |
| Constable Street | C4 | Old Vicarage | C3 | | |
| Corporation Street | A1-A2-A3 | Orchard Street | B2 | | |
| Craggs Row | B4 | Ormskirk Road | C3 | | |
| Cross Street | B1 | Oxford Street | C1 | | |
| Crown Street | B4 | Pole Street | C2-C3 | | |
| Derby Street | C2 | Pump Street | C3 | | |
| Edward Street | A3 | Ringway | B2-B3-C3 | | |
| Elizabeth Street | B3 | Rose Street | C2 | | |
| Fishergate | A1-B1 | Saint Ignatius Square | C3-C4 | | |
| Fleet Street | A2-B2 | St Paul's Road | C3-C4 | | |
| Fox Street | B1-B2 | St Paul's Square | C3 | | |
| Friargate | A3-B2 | St Peter's Square | A3-A4 | | |
| Fylde Road | A3-A4 | St Peter's Street | A4 | | |
| Fylde Street | A3 | St Wilfred Street | A2 | | |
| Garden Street | B1 | Sedgwick Street | C4 | | |
| Glover Street | C1 | Shepherd Street | C1-C2 | | |
| Glovers Court | B1-B2 | Snow Hill | B3 | | |
| Great George Street | B4-C4 | Stanleyfield Road | B4 | | |
| Great Shaw Street | A3-B3 | Stoney Gate | C1-C2 | | |
| Guildhall Street | B1-B2 | Syke Street | C1 | | |
| Harrington Street | A4 | Theatre Street | A1 | | |
| Heatley Street | A2 | Tithebarn Street | C2-C3 | | |
| Hope Street | A3 | Turner Street | C2 | | |
| Kent Street | C4 | Victoria Street | A4 | | |

212

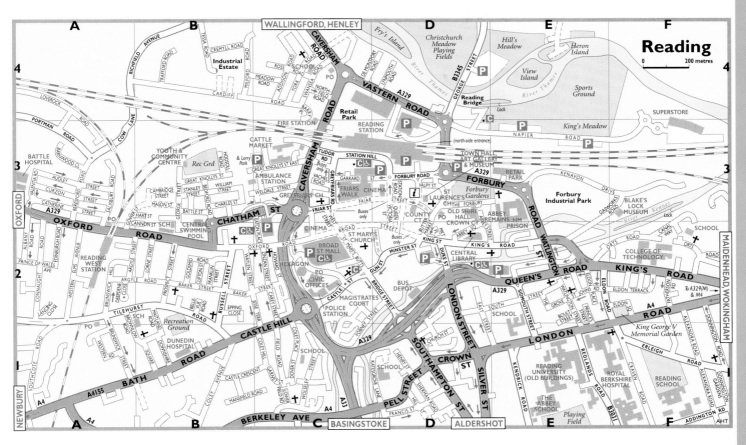

# Reading

Reading is found on atlas page **24**,
grid reference **7173**

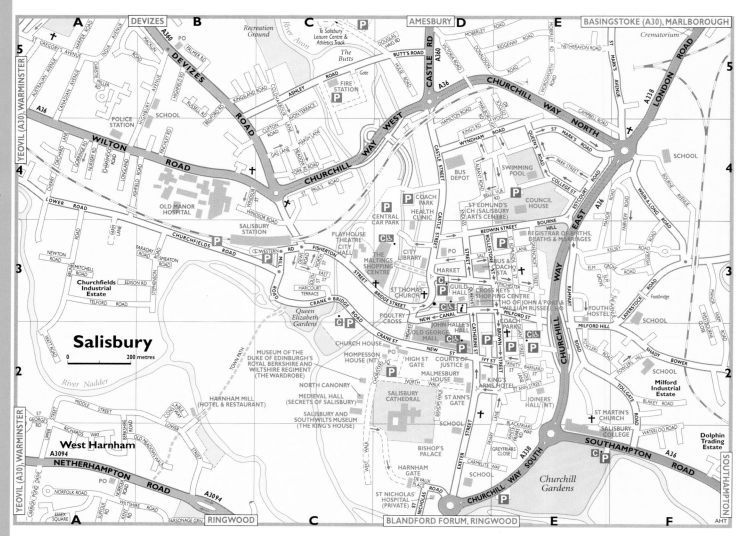

214

# Salisbury

Salisbury is found on atlas page **23**,
grid reference 1429

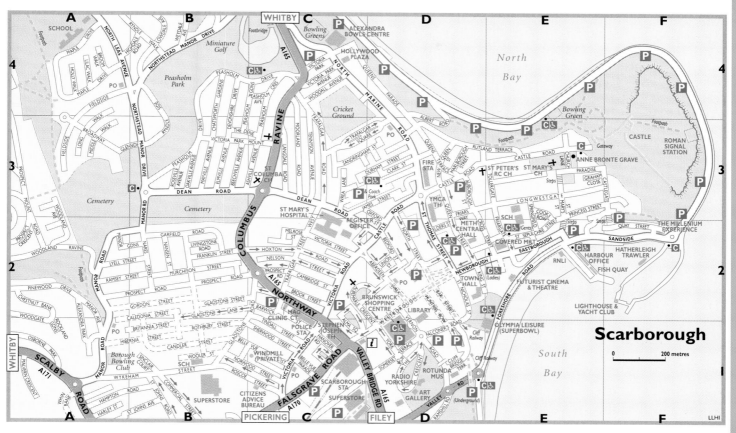

# Scarborough

Scarborough is found on atlas page **91**,
grid reference **0488**

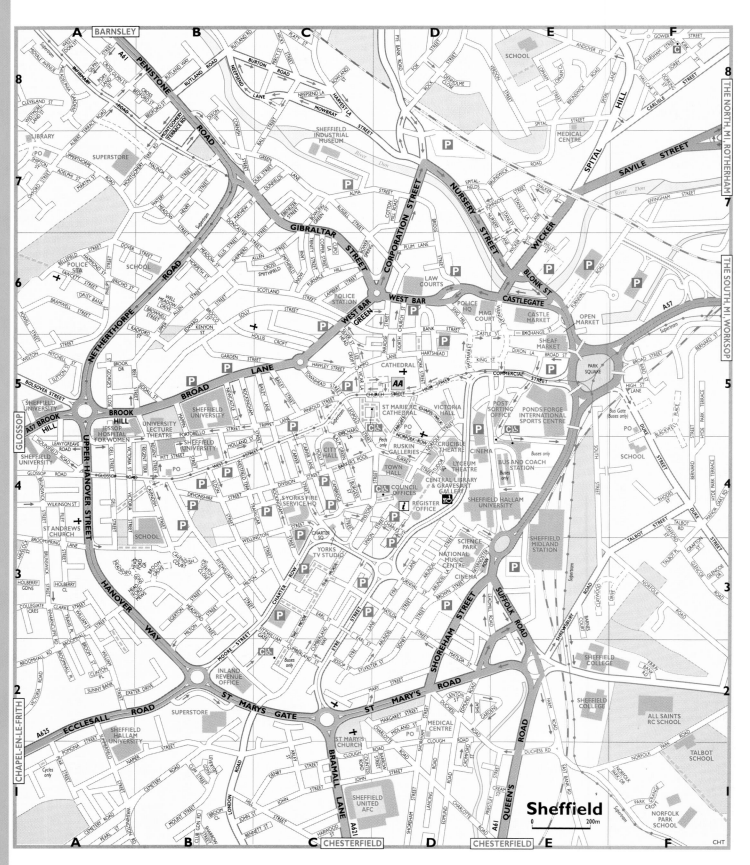

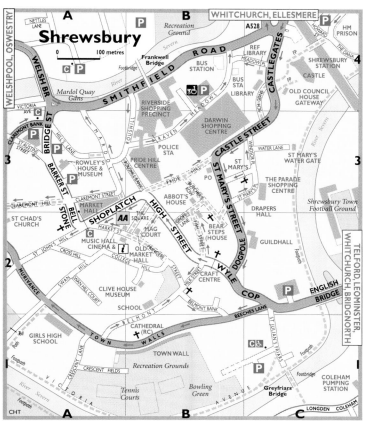

# Shrewsbury

Shrewsbury is found on atlas page **59**, grid reference **4912**

**AA shop**
8 Market Street, Shrewsbury SY1 1LE                    A2

| | | | | | | |
|---|---|---|---|---|---|---|
| Barker Street | A3 | Fish Street | B2-B3 | St John's Hill | A2 |
| Beeches Lane | B1-C2 | Grope Lane | B2-B3 | St Julian's Friars | C1-C2 |
| Belmont | A1-B2 | High Street | B2-B3 | St Mary's Place | B3-C3 |
| Belmont Bank | B2 | Hill's Lane | A3 | St Mary's Street | B2-B3 |
| Bellstone | A2-A3 | Howard Street | C4 | School Gardens | C3-C4 |
| Bridge Street | A3 | Longden Coleham | C1 | Shoplatch | A2-B3 |
| Butcher's Row | B3 | Mardol | A3-A4 | Smithfield Road | A4-C4 |
| Castle Street | B3-C3 | Market Street | A2 | Swan Hill | A2 |
| Castlegates | C4 | Meadow Place | B4-C4 | Swan Hill Court | A2 |
| Claremont Bank | A3 | Milk Street | B2 | The Dana | C4 |
| Claremont Hill | A3 | Murivance | A2 | The Square | B2-B3 |
| Claremont Street | A3 | Nettles Lane | A4 | Town Walls | A2-B1 |
| College Hill | A2-B2 | Pride Hill | B3 | Victoria Avenue | A4 |
| Crescent Fields | A1-B1 | Princess Street | B2 | Water Lane | C3 |
| Crescent Lane | A1 | Raven Meadows | B3-B4 | Welsh Bridge | A4 |
| Cross Hill | A2 | Roushill | A3-B4 | Windsor Place | C3 |
| Dogpole | B2 | Roushill Bank | B3 | Wyle Cop | B2-C2 |
| English Bridge | C2 | St Austins Street | A3 | | |

# Sheffield

Sheffield is found on atlas page **74**, grid reference **3587**

**AA shop**
5 St James' Row, Sheffield, South Yorks S1 1AY                    D5

| | | | | | | |
|---|---|---|---|---|---|---|
| Adelphi Street | A7 | Broomhall Place | A2 | Countess Road | C1 |
| Albert Terrace Road | A7-A8 | Broomhall Road | A2 | Cream Street | E1 |
| Allen Street | B6-C6 | Broomhall Street | A2-A3 | Cromford Street | D1 |
| Alma Street | C7-D7 | Broomspring Lane | A3-A4 | Cross Bedford Street | A8-B8 |
| Andover Street | E8 | Brown Street | D3 | Cross Gilpin Street | A8 |
| Arley Street | C1 | Brownell Street | B6 | Cross Smithfield | B6-C6 |
| Arundel Lane | D3 | Brunswick Road | E7-E8-F8 | Cumberland Street | C2 |
| Arundel Street | C2-D2-D3-D4 | Brunswick Street | A3-A4 | Cumberland Way | C2-C3 |
| Bailey Lane | C5 | Burgess Street | C4 | Cupo Lane | C6 |
| Bailey Street | C5 | Burton Road | B8-C8 | Daisy Bank | A6 |
| Ball Street | C7-C8 | Cambridge Street | C4 | Denby Street | C1 |
| Balm Green | C4-C5 | Campo Lane | C5-D5 | Denholme Close | D8 |
| Bank Street | D6 | Carlisle Street | F7-F8 | Devonshire Street | B4 |
| Bard Street | F5 | Carver Lane | C4 | Division Street | C4 |
| Barker's Pool | C4 | Carver Street | C4 | Dixon Lane | E5 |
| Barnes Court | E3 | Castle Street | D6-E6 | Dixon Street | B8 |
| Barrow Street | D1 | Castlegate | E6 | Doncaster Street | B7-B6-C6 |
| Bedford Street | B8 | Cavendish Court | B3 | Dorking Street | F8 |
| Beet Street | A5-B5 | Cavendish Street | B3-B4 | Dover Street | A6-B6 |
| Bellefield Street | A6 | Cemetery Road | A1-B1 | Duchess Road | D2-D1-E1 |
| Bennett Street | B1-C1 | Chapel Walk | D5 | Duke Street | F3-F4-F5 |
| Bernard Street | F4-F5-F6 | Charles Street | D4 | Dun Street | B7-C7 |
| Blackwell Place | C5 | Charlotte Road | C2-D2-D1-E1 | Dunfields | C7 |
| Blonk Street | E6 | Charter Row | C3 | Earl Street | C3-C2-D2 |
| Bolsover Street | A5 | Charter Square | C3-C4 | Earsham Street | F8 |
| Bower Spring | C6 | Church Street | C5-D5 | East Bank Road | E1 |
| Bowling Green Street | C7 | Clarke Street | A3 | Ebenezer Street | C7 |
| Bramall Lane | C1-C2 | Claywood Drive | E3-F3 | Ecclesall Road | A1-A2-B2 |
| Bramwell Street | A6 | Cleveland Street | A8 | Edmund Road | D1-D2 |
| Bridge Street | D6-D7 | Cliff Street | B1 | Edward Street | B5-B6 |
| Broad Lane | B5-C5 | Clinton Place | A2 | Effingham Street | F7 |
| Broad Street | E5 | Clough Road | C1-D1-D2 | Egerton Close | B3 |
| Broad Street | F5 | Club Garden Road | B1 | Egerton Street | B3 |
| Brocco Street | B6 | Collegiate Crescent | A3 | Eldon Street | B3-B4 |
| Brook Drive | A5 | Commercial Street | D5-E5 | Ellis Street | B6 |
| Brook Hill | A5 | Copper Street | C6 | Exchange Street | E6 |
| Broom Close | B1 | Cornish Street | B7-B8 | Exeter Drive | A2-B2 |
| Broom Grove | B3 | Corporation Street | D6-D7 | Eyre Lane | C2-C3-D3 |
| Broom Street | A2 | Cotton Mill Road | D7 | Eyre Street | C2-C3-D3 |

| | | | | | | |
|---|---|---|---|---|---|---|
| Garden Street | B5-C5 | Midvale Avenue | A8 | Silver Street Head | C5-C6 |
| Gell Street | A3-A4-A5 | Milton Street | B2-B3-C3 | Smithfield | C6 |
| Gibraltar Street | C6-C7 | Mitchell Street | A5 | Snig Hill | D6 |
| Gilpin Street | A8 | Montgomery Terrace Road | A7-B8 | Snow Lane | C6 |
| Glencoe Drive | F3 | Moore Street | B2-B3-C3 | Solly Street | B5-B6-C6 |
| Glencoe Road | F3 | Morpeth Street | B6 | Sorby Street | F8 |
| Glossop Road | A4-B4 | Mount Street | B1 | South Street | E3-E4-E5 |
| Gower Street | F8 | Mowbray Street | C8-C7-D7 | Spital Hill | E7-E8-F8 |
| Grafton Street | F3 | Napier Street | A1-B1 | Spital Lane | E8-F8 |
| Green Lane | B7-C7 | Neepsend Lane | B8-C8 | Spital Street | E8 |
| Hallcar Street | F8 | Netherthorpe Road | A5-A6-B6-B7 | Spitalfields | D7 |
| Hammond Street | A6 | Newcastle Street | B5 | St George's Close | A5 |
| Hanover Way | A3-B3-B2 | Norfolk Park Drive | F1 | St Mary's Road | C2-D2-E2 |
| Hartshead | D5 | Norfolk Park Road | E1-F1-F2 | St Marys Gate | B2-C2 |
| Harvest Lane | C8 | Norfolk Road | F2-F3 | St Philip's Street | A6 |
| Harwood Street | C1 | Norfolk Row | D4-D5 | Stafford Street | F3-F4 |
| Havelock Street | A3 | Norfolk Street | D4-D5 | Stanley Lane | E7 |
| Hawley Street | C5 | North Church Street | D5-D6 | Stanley Street | E6-E7 |
| Haymarket | D5 | Nursery Lane | D7-E7-E6 | Suffolk Road | E2-E3 |
| Headford Gardens | A3-B3 | Nursery Street | D7-D6-E6 | Summerfield Street | A1-A2 |
| Headford Grove | A3-B3 | Orchard Lane | C5 | Sunny Bank | A2 |
| Headford Mews | A3-B3 | Oxford Street | A7 | Surrey Street | D4 |
| Headford Street | B3 | Paradise Street | D5-D6 | Sutton Street | A5 |
| Henry Street | B7 | Park Grange Croft | F1 | Sylvester Street | C2-D2 |
| Hicks Street | C8 | Park Square | E5-F5 | Talbot Place | F3 |
| High Street | D5 | Paternoster Row | D3 | Talbot Road | F4 |
| High Street Lane | F5 | Pear Street | A1 | Talbot Street | F3-F4 |
| Hill Street | B1-C1 | Pearl Street | A1 | The Moor | C2-C3 |
| Holberry Close | A3 | Penistone Road | A8-B8-B7 | Townhead Street | C5 |
| Holberry Gardens | A3 | Percy Street | C8 | Trafalgar Street | B4-C4-C3 |
| Holland Street | B4 | Philadelphia Gardens | A8 | Travis Place | A3 |
| Hollis Croft | B6-C5 | Pinfold Street | C5 | Trinity Street | C6 |
| Holly Street | C4-C5 | Pinstone Street | C3-C4-D4 | Trippet Lane | C5 |
| Hounsfield Road | A4 | Pitt Street | B4 | Tudor Square | D4 |
| Hyde Park Terrace | F4-F5 | Platt Street | C8 | Union Street | C3-D4 |
| Infirmary Road | A8-B8-B7 | Plum Lane | D6 | Upper Allen Street | B5-B6 |
| Jericho Street | A6 | Pomona Street | A1-A2 | Upper Hanover Street | A3-A4-A5 |
| Jessop Street | C2 | Portland Street | A8 | Upperthorpe Road | A7 |
| John Street | B1-C1-D1 | Portobello Street | B4-B5 | Verdon Street | D8-E8 |
| Johnson Street | D7-E7 | Powell Street | A5-A6 | Vicar Lane | C5 |
| King Street | D5-E5 | Priestley Street | D1-E1 | Victoria Road | A2 |
| Kirk Street | F8 | Pye Bank Road | D8 | Victoria Street | A3-A4 |
| Lambert Street | C6 | Queen's Road | E1-E2 | Waingate | E6 |
| Lancing Road | D1 | Radford Street | A6-B6 | Walker Street | E7 |
| Leadmill Road | D3-E3 | Regent Street | B4 | Washington Road | A1-B1 |
| Leavygreave Road | A4 | Regent Terrace | B4 | Watery Street | B7 |
| Lee Croft | C5 | Rhodes Street | F4 | Well Meadow Drive | B6 |
| Lenton Street | D2 | Rock Street | D8 | Wellington Street | B3-C4 |
| Leopold Street | C4-C5 | Rockingham Street | B5-C5-C4-C3 | West Bar | D6 |
| Leverton Gardens | B1 | Rowland Street | C8 | West Bar Green | C6 |
| London Road | B1-B2 | Russell Street | C7 | West Don Street | A8 |
| Lopham Close | E8 | Rutland Road | B8 | West Street | B4-C4 |
| Lopham Street | E8 | Rutland Way | B8 | Westfield Terrace | B4 |
| Malinda Street | B7 | Savile Street | E7-F7 | Westmoreland Street | A8 |
| Manor Oaks Road | F4 | Scotland Street | B6-C6 | Weston Street | A5-A6 |
| Mappin Street | B4-B5 | Sharrow Street | B1 | Wharncliffe Road | A2-A3 |
| Margaret Street | D2 | Sheaf Gardens | D2-E2 | Wicker | E6-E7 |
| Martin Street | A7 | Shepherd Street | B6-C6-C7 | Wicker Lane | E6-E7 |
| Mary Street | C2-D2 | Shipton Street | A7 | Wilkinson Street | A4 |
| Mathew Street | B5 | Shoreham Street | D1-D2-D3 | Willey Street | E6 |
| Matilda Street | C3-D3-D2 | Shrewsbury Road | E2-E3 | William Street | A2-A3 |
| Meadow Street | B6-B7 | Siddall Street | B5 | York Street | D5 |
| Midland Street | D2 | Sidney Street | D2-D3 | | |

217

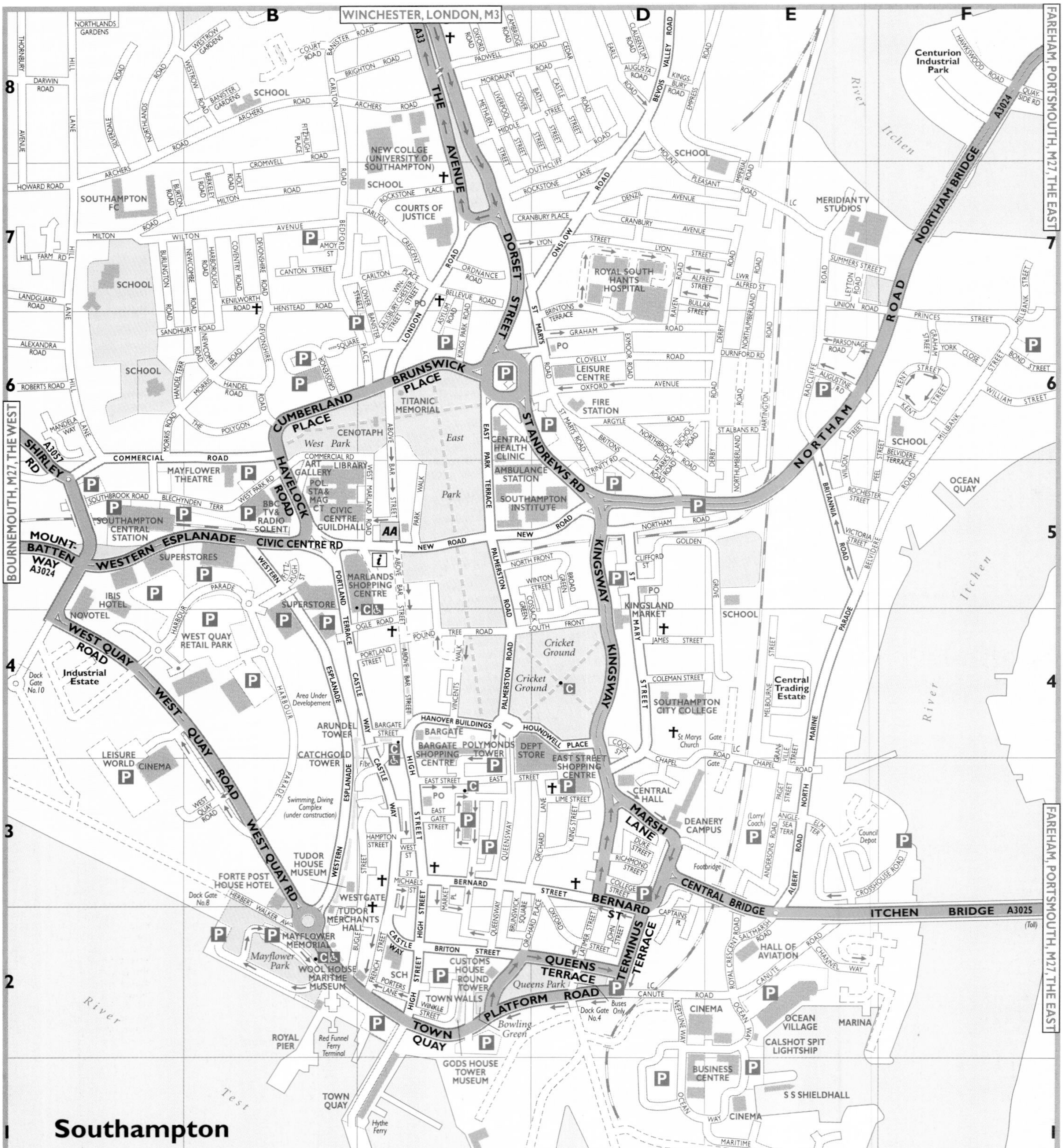

218

# Southampton

WINCHESTER, LONDON, M3

FAREHAM, PORTSMOUTH, M27, THE EAST

BOURNEMOUTH, M27, THE WEST

FAREHAM, PORTSMOUTH, M27, THE EAST

0    400 metres

Map labels include:

NORTHLANDS GARDENS, THORNBURY, HILL LANE, DARWIN ROAD, HOWARD ROAD, ALEXANDRA ROAD, ROBERTS ROAD, LANDGUARD ROAD, HILL FARM RD, SCHOOL, SOUTHAMPTON FC, MILTON ROAD, WILTON AVENUE, COVENTRY ROAD, BURLINGTON ROAD, NEWCOMBE ROAD, HARBOROUGH ROAD, DEVONSHIRE ROAD, CROMWELL ROAD, BERKELEY ROAD, HOLT ROAD, CARLTON ROAD, ARCHERS ROAD, BANISTER GARDENS, WESTROW GARDENS, COURT ROAD, BRIGHTON ROAD, FITZHUGH PLACE

NEW COLLEGE (UNIVERSITY OF SOUTHAMPTON), SCHOOL, COURTS OF JUSTICE, THE AVENUE

OXFORD, PADWELL, MORDAUNT, LIVERPOOL, METHUEN, MIDDLE, DOVER, BATH, CASTLE, SOUTHCLIFF, ROCKSTONE, DENZIL, CRANBURY PLACE, CRANBURY AVENUE, BEVOIS, VALLEY ROAD, KINGSBURY ROAD, EMPRESS, CAUSTON, EARL, AUGUSTA ROAD, PLEASANT, IMPERIAL

CENTURION INDUSTRIAL PARK, River Itchen, NORTHAM BRIDGE, A3024, MERIDIAN TV STUDIOS

ROYAL SOUTH HANTS HOSPITAL, ALFRED STREET, LWR ALFRED ST, BULLAR STREET, UNION ROAD, RAVEN ROAD, DERBY ROAD, DURNFORD RD, NORTHUMBERLAND ROAD, HARTINGTON, BRITANNIA

CUMBERLAND PLACE, BRUNSWICK PLACE, CENOTAPH, TITANIC MEMORIAL, HAVELOCK ROAD, MAYFLOWER THEATRE, COMMERCIAL RD ART GALLERY, POL STA & MAG CT, LIBRARY, CIVIC CENTRE GUILDHALL, BBC TV & RADIO SOLENT, West Park, East Park, STANDREWS RD, CENTRAL HEALTH CLINIC, AMBULANCE STATION, SOUTHAMPTON INSTITUTE, FIRE STATION, CLOVELLY LEISURE CENTRE, ST ALBANS RD, ST MARYS ROAD

SOUTHAMPTON CENTRAL STATION, WESTERN ESPLANADE, CIVIC CENTRE RD, MOUNTBATTEN WAY A3024, SHIRLEY RD A3057, SUPERSTORES, IBIS HOTEL, NOVOTEL, WEST QUAY ROAD, WEST QUAY RETAIL PARK, Industrial Estate, Dock Gate No.10, Area Under Development, HARBOUR PARADE, MARLANDS SHOPPING CENTRE, PORTLAND TERRACE, KINGSWAY, ST MARY, KINGSLAND MARKET, NEW ROAD, PALMERSTON, NORTH FRONT, WINTON STREET, BROAD STREET, POUND TREE ROAD, Cricket Ground, SOUTHAMPTON CITY COLLEGE, CENTRAL TRADING ESTATE, COLEMAN STREET, JAMES STREET, MELBOURNE, MARINE PARADE, GROVE STREET

LEISURE WORLD, CINEMA, ARUNDEL TOWER, CATCHGOLD TOWER, Swimming, Diving Complex (under construction), CASTLE WAY, HIGH STREET, BARGATE, HANOVER BUILDINGS, BARGATE SHOPPING CENTRE, POLYMONDS TOWER, DEPT STORE, EAST STREET SHOPPING CENTRE, EAST STREET, CENTRAL HALL, DEANERY CAMPUS, St Marys Church, CHAPEL, MARSH LANE, CENTRAL BRIDGE, ITCHEN BRIDGE A3025 (Toll)

TUDOR HOUSE MUSEUM, FORTE POST HOUSE HOTEL, Dock Gate No.8, WESTGATE, TUDOR MERCHANTS HALL, MAYFLOWER MEMORIAL, Mayflower Park, WOOL HOUSE MARITIME MUSEUM, ROYAL PIER, Red Funnel Ferry Terminal, TOWN QUAY, CUSTOMS HOUSE, ROUND TOWER, TOWN WALLS, Queens Park, Bowling Green, GODS HOUSE TOWER MUSEUM, QUEENS TERRACE, TERMINUS TERRACE, PLATFORM ROAD, Dock Gate No.4, Buses Only, HALL OF AVIATION, OCEAN VILLAGE, MARINA, CALSHOT SPIT LIGHTSHIP, BUSINESS CENTRE, S S SHIELDHALL, CINEMA, OCEAN QUAY, OCEANOGRAPHY CENTRE, MARITIME WALK

River Test, Hythe Ferry

CHT

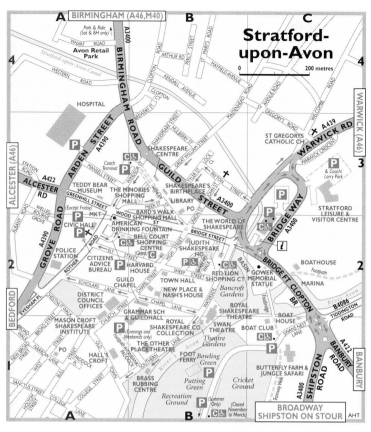

# Stratford-upon-Avon

Stratford-upon-Avon is found on atlas page **48**,
grid reference **2055**

| | | | |
|---|---|---|---|
| Albany Road | A2-A3 | Percy Street | B4 |
| Alcester Road | A3 | Rother Street | A2-A3 |
| Arden Street | A3 | Rowley Crescent | C4 |
| Arthur Road | B4 | St Gregory's Road | C4-C3 |
| Avenue Road | C4 | St Mary's Road | B4 |
| Avonbank Paddock | B1 | Sanctus Street | A1 |
| Banbury Road | C1 | Scholars Lane | A2-B2 |
| Birmingham Road | A4-B3 | Shakespeare Street | B3-B4 |
| Brewery Street | B3-B4 | Sheep Street | B2 |
| Bridge Foot | C2 | Shipston Road | C1 |
| Bridge Street | B2 | Shreeves Walk | B2 |
| Bridge Way | C2-C3 | Southern Lane | A1-B1 |
| Broad Street | A1-A2 | Station Road | A3 |
| Broad Walk | A1 | Swans Nest Lane | C1 |
| Bull Street | A1 | Tiddington Road | C1-C2 |
| Chapel Lane | B2 | Tyler Street | B3 |
| Chapel Street | B2 | Union Street | B2-B3 |
| Chestnut Walk | A1-A2 | Warwick Road | C3 |
| Church Street | A1-A2-B2 | Waterside | B2 |
| Clopton Bridge | C2 | Welcombe Road | C3-C4 |
| Clopton Court | B4 | Wellesbourne Grove | A2-A3 |
| Clopton Road | B4 | Western Road | A4 |
| College Lane | A1 | West Street | A1 |
| College Street | A1 | Wharf Road | A4 |
| Ely Street | A2-B2 | Windsor Street | A3-B3 |
| Evesham Place | A2 | Wood Street | A3-B2 |
| Great William Street | B3 | | |
| Greenhill Street | A3 | | |
| Grove Road | A2-A3 | | |
| Guild Street | B3 | | |
| Henley Street | B2-B3 | | |
| High Street | B2 | | |
| Holtom Street | A1 | | |
| John Street | B3 | | |
| Kendall Avenue | B4 | | |
| Lock Close | B3 | | |
| Maidenhead Road | B3-B4-C4 | | |
| Mansell Street | A3 | | |
| Mayfield Avenue | B4 | | |
| Meer Street | A3-B3 | | |
| Mulberry Street | B3 | | |
| Narrow Lane | A1 | | |
| New Broad Street | A1 | | |
| Old Town | A1 | | |
| Paddock Place | A1 | | |
| Payton Street | B3-C3 | | |

# Southampton

Southampton is found on atlas page **13**,
grid reference **4112**

**AA shop**
126 Above Bar Street, Southampton SO9 1GY     C5

| | | | | | | | | | |
|---|---|---|---|---|---|---|---|---|---|
| Above Bar Street | C4-C5-C6 | Canute Road | D2-E2 | Elm Terrace | E3 | Latimer Street | D2 | Oxford Avenue | D6-E6 |
| Albert Road North | E3 | Captains Place | D2 | Empress Road | D8-E8 | Leyton Road | E7 | Oxford Road | C8 |
| Alexandra Road | A6 | Carlton Crescent | B7-C7 | Exmoor Road | D6 | Lime Street | D3 | Oxford Street | D2-D3 |
| Alfred Street | D7-E7 | Carlton Place | B7-C7 | Fitzhugh Place | B8 | Liverpool Street | C7-C8 | Padwell Road | C8-D8 |
| Amoy Street | B7 | Carlton Road | B7-B8 | Fitzhugh Street | B5 | London Road | C6-C7 | Paget Street | E3 |
| Andersons Road | E3 | Castle Street | D8 | French Street | C2 | Lower Alfred Street | E7 | Palmerston Road | C4-C5 |
| Anglesea Terrace | E3 | Castle Way | B4-C4-C3-D2 | Golden Grove | D5-E5-E4 | Lower Banister Street | C6-C7 | Park Walk | C5 |
| Archers Road | A7-A8-B8-C8 | Cedar Road | D8 | Graham Road | D6-E6 | Lyon Street | C7-D7-E7 | Parsonage Road | E6 |
| Argyle Road | D6-E6 | Central Bridge | D3-E3-E2 | Graham Street | F6 | Mandela Way | A6 | Peel Street | E5-F6 |
| Asylum Road | C6-C7 | Channel Way | E2 | Granville Street | E3-E4 | Marine Parade | E3-E4-E5 | Platform Road | C2-D2 |
| Augusta Road | D8 | Chapel Road | D3-D4-E4-E3 | Grosvenor Square | B6 | Maritime Walk | E1 | Porters Lane | C2 |
| Augustine Road | E6 | Civic Centre Road | B5-C5 | Hampton Street | C3 | Market Place | C3 | Portland Street | C4 |
| Banister Gardens | B8 | Clausentum Road | D8 | Handel Road | B6 | Marsh Lane | D3 | Portland Terrace | B4-B5 |
| Banister Road | B8-C8 | Clifford Street | D5 | Handel Terrace | A6-B6 | Melbourne Street | E4 | Pound Tree Road | C4 |
| Bargate Street | C4 | Clovelly Road | D6-E6 | Hanover Buildings | C4 | Methuen Street | C7-C8 | Princes Street | F6 |
| Bath Street | F6 | Coleman Street | D4-E4 | Harborough Road | B7 | Middle Street | C8-D8 | Quayside Road | F8 |
| Bedford Place | B7-B6-C6 | College Street | D3 | Harbour Parade | A4-B5-B4-B3 | Millbank Street | F6-F7 | Queens Terrace | D2 |
| Bellevue Road | C7 | Commercial Road | A5-A6-B6-C6 | Hartington Road | E5-E6-E7 | Milton Road | A7-B7 | Queensway | C2-C3 |
| Belvidere Road | E5-F5 | Cook Street | D4 | Havelock Road | B5-B6 | Mordaunt Road | C8-D8 | Radcliffe Road | E6-E7 |
| Belvidere Terrace | F6 | Cossack Green | C5-D4 | Hawkswood Road | F8 | Morris Road | A6-B6 | Raven Road | D6-D7 |
| Berkeley Road | B7 | Court Road | B8 | Henstead Road | B7 | Mount Pleasant Road | D8-D7-E7 | Richmond Street | D3 |
| Bernard Street | C3-D3 | Coventry Road | B7 | Herbert Walker Avenue | B2-B3 | Mountbatten Way | A5 | Roberts Road | A6 |
| Bevois Valley Road | D8 | Cranbury Avenue | D7-E7 | High Street | C2-C3-C4 | Neptune Way | D2 | Rochester Street | E5-F5 |
| Blechynden Terrace | A5-B5 | Cranbury Place | C7-D7 | Hill Farm Road | A7 | New Road | C5-D5 | Rockstone Lane | C7-D7 |
| Bond Street | F6 | Cromwell Road | B7-B8 | Hill Lane | A6-A7-A8 | Newcombe Road | B6-B7 | Rockstone Place | C7 |
| Brighton Road | B8-C8 | Crosshouse Road | E3-F3 | Holt Road | B7 | Nichols Road | D6 | Royal Crescent Road | E2 |
| Brintons Terrace | D6-D7 | Cumberland Place | B6-C6 | Houndwell Place | C4-D4 | North Front | C5-D5 | Salisbury Street | C6-C7 |
| Britannia Road | E5-E6 | Darwin Road | A8 | Howard Road | A7 | Northam Bridge | F7-F8 | Saltmarsh Road | E2 |
| Briton Street | C2 | Denzil Avenue | D7-E7 | Imperial Road | E7-E8 | Northam Road | D5-E5-E6-F7 | Sandhurst Road | A6-B6 |
| Britons Road | D5-D6 | Derby Road | E5-E6-E7 | Itchen Bridge | E2-F2 | Northbrook Road | D5-D6 | Shirley Road | A5-A6 |
| Broad Green | D5 | Devonshire Road | B6-B7 | James Street | D4-E4 | Northlands Gardens | A8 | Silverdale Road | A8 |
| Brunswick Place | C6 | Dorset Street | C6-C7 | John Street | D2 | Northlands Road | A8 | South Front | C4-D4 |
| Brunswick Square | C2-C3 | Dover Street | C8-D8 | Kenilworth Road | B7 | Northumberland Road | E5-E6-E7 | Southbrook Road | A5 |
| Bugle Street | B2-C2-C3 | Duke Street | D3 | Kent Street | F6 | Ocean Way | D1-E1-E2 | Southcliff Road | C7-D7-D8 |
| Bullar Street | D7-E7 | Durnford Road | E6 | King Street | D3 | Ogle Road | B4-C4 | St Albans Road | E6 |
| Burlington Road | A6-A7 | Earls Road | D8 | Kings Park Road | C6-C8 | Onslow Road | D7 | St Andrews Road | C6-D6-D5 |
| Burton Road | A7 | East Gate Street | C3 | Kingsbury Road | D7 | Orchard Lane | D3 | St Marks Road | D5-D6 |
| Cambridge Road | C8 | East Park Terrace | C5-C6 | Kingsway | D4-D5 | Orchard Place | C2-D2-D3 | St Mary Street | D3-D4-D5 |
| Canton Street | B7 | East Street | C3-D3 | Landguard Road | A7 | Ordnance Road | C7 | St Marys Road | D5-D6-D7 |

| | |
|---|---|
| St Michaels Street | C3 |
| Summers Street | E7-F7 |
| Terminus Terrace | D2 |
| The Avenue | C7-C8 |
| The Polygon | B6 |
| Thornbury Avenue | A7-A8 |
| Town Quay | C2 |
| Trinity Road | D5-D6 |
| Union Road | E7-F7 |
| Victoria Street | E5 |
| Vincents Walk | C4 |
| West Marland Road | C5 |
| West Park Road | B5 |
| West Quay Road | A4-B4-B3 |
| West Street | C3 |
| Western Esplanade | A5-B5-B4-B3 |
| Westrow Gardens | B8 |
| Westrow Road | A8-B8 |
| William Street | F6 |
| Wilson Street | E5-E6 |
| Wilton Avenue | A7-B7 |
| Winchester Street | C7 |
| Winkle Street | C2 |
| Winton Street | C5-D5 |
| York Close | F6 |

219

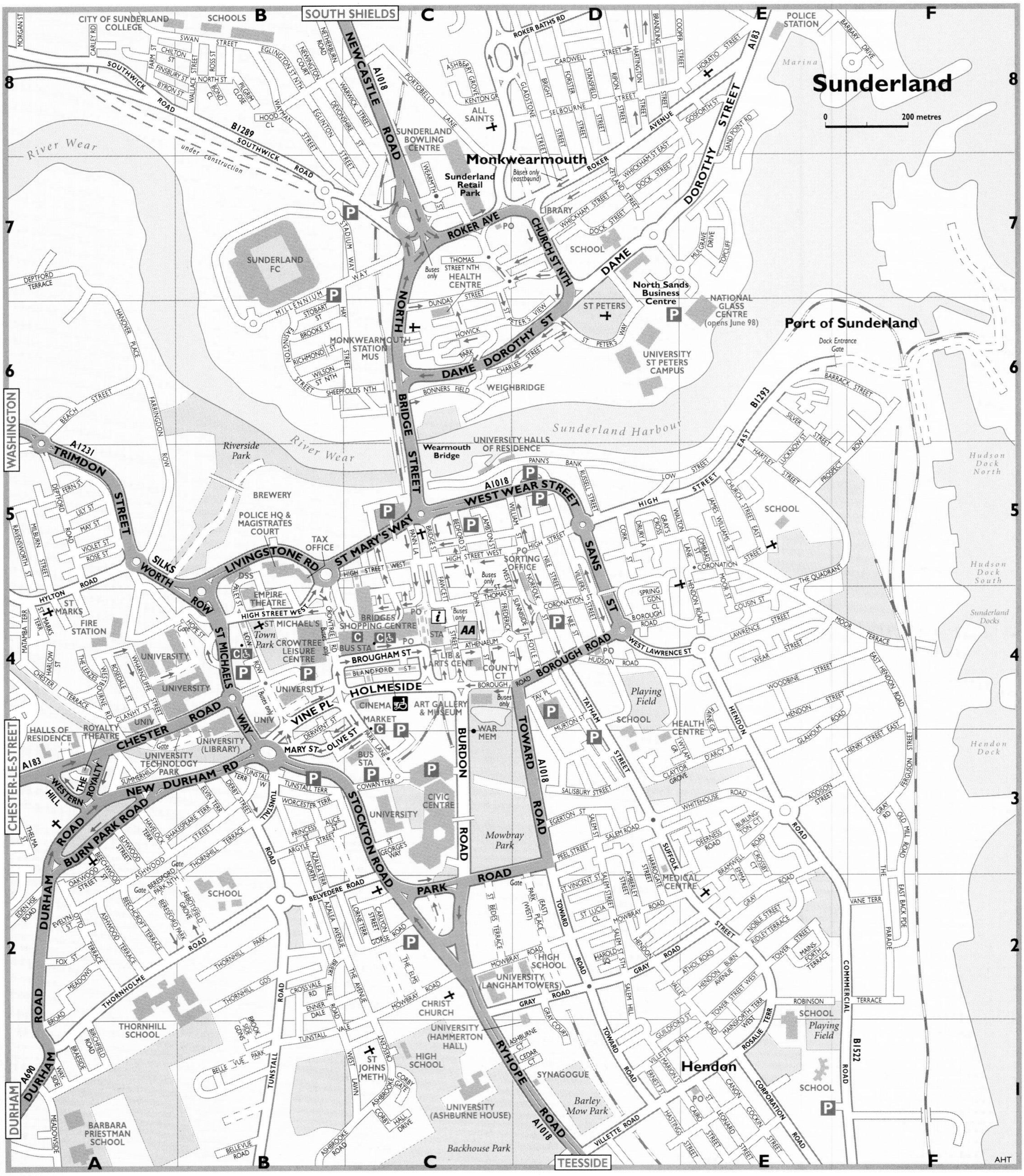

# Sunderland

SOUTH SHIELDS

POLICE STATION

Marina

0    200 metres

CITY OF SUNDERLAND COLLEGE

SCHOOLS

ROKER BATHS RD

Monkwearmouth

Sunderland Bowling Centre

Sunderland Retail Park

SUNDERLAND FC

ROKER AVE

CHURCH ST NTH

DAME DOROTHY STREET

LIBRARY

SCHOOL

THOMAS STREET NTH HEALTH CENTRE

St Peters

North Sands Business Centre

NATIONAL GLASS CENTRE (opens June 98)

Port of Sunderland

Monkwearmouth Station Mus

DAME DOROTHY ST

UNIVERSITY ST PETERS CAMPUS

WEIGHBRIDGE

BONNERS FIELD

WASHINGTON

River Wear

Riverside Park

BRIDGE STREET

Sunderland Harbour

Wearmouth Bridge

UNIVERSITY HALLS OF RESIDENCE

TRIMDON STREET

A1231

BREWERY

POLICE HQ & MAGISTRATES COURT

TAX OFFICE

WEST WEAR STREET

High Street

EAST

Hudson Dock North

SILKSWORTH ROW

LIVINGSTONE RD

ST MARY'S WAY

SORTING OFFICE

SANS ST

SCHOOL

Hudson Dock South

EMPIRE THEATRE

HIGH STREET WEST

BRIDGES SHOPPING CENTRE

BROUGHAM ST

BOROUGH ROAD

WEST LAWRENCE ST

Sunderland Docks

FIRE STATION

ST MICHAELS WAY

CROWTREE LEISURE CENTRE

BLANDFORD ST

ARTS CENT

COUNTY CT

UNIVERSITY

HOLMESIDE

VINE PL

CINEMA

ART GALLERY & MUSEUM

WAR MEM

TOWARD ROAD

HEALTH CENTRE

Playing Field

Hendon Dock

CHESTER ROAD

UNIVERSITY (LIBRARY)

MARKET

BUS STA

MARY ST

OLIVE ST

BURDON RD

HALLS OF RESIDENCE

ROYALTY THEATRE

UNIVERSITY TECHNOLOGY PARK

NEW DURHAM RD

STOCKTON ROAD

UNIVERSITY

CIVIC CENTRE

PARK ROAD

BURN PARK ROAD

DURHAM ROAD

A690

CHESTER-LE-STREET

Mowbray Park

RYHOPE ROAD

A1018

BELVEDERE ROAD

Hendon

THORNHILL SCHOOL

CHRIST CHURCH

UNIVERSITY (LANGHAM TOWERS)

HIGH SCHOOL

SYNAGOGUE

SCHOOL

BARBARA PRIESTMAN SCHOOL

ST JOHNS (METH)

UNIVERSITY (HAMMERTON HALL)

UNIVERSITY (ASHBURNE HOUSE)

Barley Mow Park

Backhouse Park

B1522

COMMERCIAL ROAD

A     B     C     D     E     F

TEESSIDE

AHT

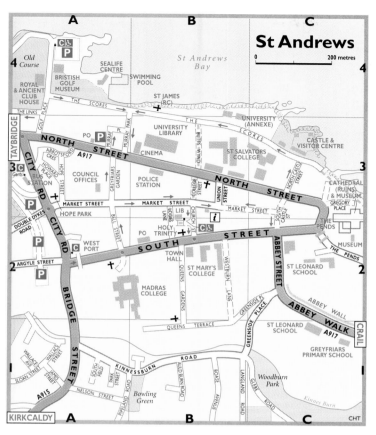

## St Andrews

St Andrews is found on atlas page 127,
grid reference 5116

## Sunderland

Sunderland is found on atlas page 96,
grid reference NZ3957

**AA shop**
49 Fawett Street, Sunderland SR1 1RR     C4

222

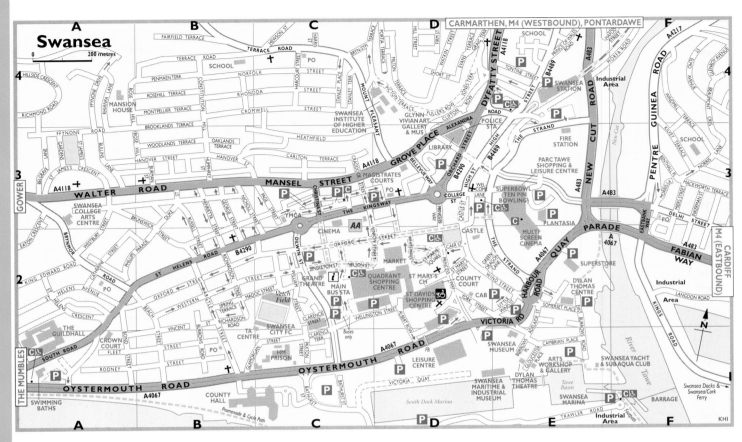

# Swansea

Swansea is found on atlas page **32**,
grid reference **6592**

## AA shop
20 Union Street, Swansea SA1 3EH       C3

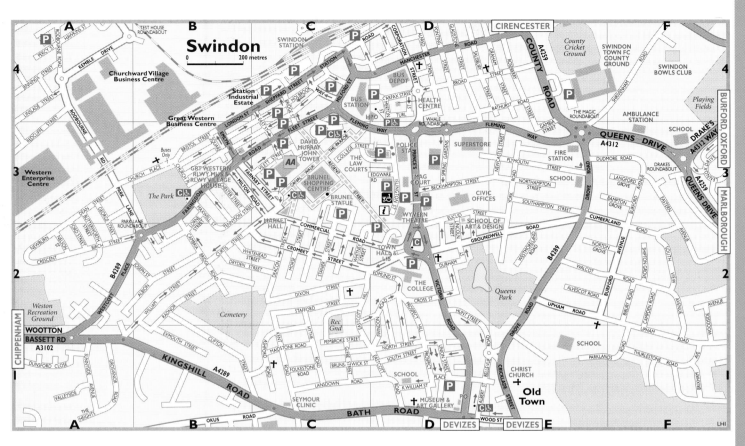

# Swindon

Swindon is found on atlas page **36**,
grid reference **1484**

**AA shop**
22 Canal Walk, Brunel Shopping Centre, Swindon SN1 1LD    C3

| | | | | | | | |
|---|---|---|---|---|---|---|---|
| Albert Street | D1 | Dryden Street | B2-C2 | Lennox Drive | F3 | Spring Gardens | D3 |
| Albion Street | B2 | Dudmore Road | E3-F3 | Linslade Street | A4 | Stafford Street | C2 |
| Alfred Street | D4 | Dunsford Close | A1 | London Street | B3-B4 | Stanier Street | C2 |
| Alvescot Road | E2 | Durham Street | D2 | Lorne Street | B2-B3 | Station Road | C4 |
| Ashford Road | C1 | East Street | C3-C4 | Maidstone Road | C1 | Sunnyside Avenue | A1 |
| Bampton Grove | E3-F3 | Eastcott Hill | C1-C2 | Manchester Road | C4-D4 | Swindon Road | D1-D2 |
| Bath Road | C1-D1 | Eastcott Road | D1 | Maxwell Street | B3 | Tennyson Street | B2-B3 |
| Bathurst Road | D4-E4 | Eastern Avenue | F2-F3 | Merton Street | D4 | The Heights | A1 |
| Beckhampton Street | D3 | Edgware Road | D3 | Milford Street | C4 | The Parade | C3 |
| Bellevue Road | D1 | Edmund Street | D2 | Milton Road | B3-C3 | Thurlestone Road | F1 |
| Bibury Road | F2 | Emlyn Square | B3 | Morse Street | C2 | Turl Street | D4 |
| Birch Street | A2 | Euclid Street | D3 | Nelson Street | A2 | Union Street | D1 |
| Bridge Street | C4 | Exmouth Street | B1-B2 | Newburn Crescent | A2 | Upham Road | E2-F1 |
| Bristol Street | B3 | Farnsby Street | B3-C3 | Newcastle Street | E3 | Valleyside | A1 |
| Brixham Avenue | F1 | Faringdon Road | B2-B3-C3 | North Street | D1 | Victoria Road | D1-D2 |
| Broad Street | D4-E4 | Fleet Street | C3-C4 | Northampton Street | E3 | Vilett Street | C3 |
| Brunswick Street | C1 | Fleming Way | C3-D3-E3 | Norton Grove | E2 | Walcot Road | E2-F2 |
| Burford Avenue | F3 | Folkestone Road | C1 | Okus Road | B1-C1 | Westcott Place | A2 |
| Butterworth Street | A2-A3 | Ford Street | A2 | Park Lane | A3 | Westmoreland Road | E2 |
| Cambria Bridge Road | B2-B3 | Gambia Street | E3 | Parklands Road | E1-F1 | Whitehead Street | B2-C2 |
| Campden Road | F2 | George Street | A2-A3 | Pembroke Street | C1 | Whitney Street | C2 |
| Canal Walk | C3 | Gladstone Street | D4 | Percy Street | A4 | William Street | B2 |
| Carfax Street | D4 | Glebe Street | C1 | Plymouth Street | D3-E3 | Wood Street | D1-E1 |
| Chester Street | B3 | Graham Street | E4 | Ponting Street | D4 | Woodside Avenue | F1-F2 |
| Church Place | B3 | Grosvenor Road | A1 | Princes Street | D3 | Wootton Bassett Road | A1 |
| Clifton Street | B1-B2 | Groundwell Road | D4-E4 | Prospect Hill | D1-D2 | York Road | E2-E3 |
| College Street | C3-D3 | Hawkins Street | A4 | Prospect Place | D1 | | |
| Commercial Road | C2-C3 | Holbrook Way | C4 | Queens Drive | E3-F3 | | |
| Corporation Street | D4 | Hunt Street | D2 | Radnor Street | B2 | | |
| County Road | E4 | Hythe Road | C1-C2 | Redcliffe Street | A3-A4 | | |
| Cricklade Street | E1 | Islington Street | D3 | Regent Street | C3 | | |
| Crombey Street | C2 | Jennings Street | A4 | Rodbourne Road | A3-A4 | | |
| Cross Street | D2 | Joseph Street | B2 | Roseberry Street | E4 | | |
| Cumberland Road | E3-F2 | Kemble Drive | A4 | Sheppard Street | C4 | | |
| Curtis Street | B2-C3 | Kent Road | C1 | Shipton Grove | F2 | | |
| Deacon Street | C2 | Kingshill Road | B1 | Shrivenham Road | E4-F4 | | |
| Dean Street | A3 | King William Street | D1 | South Street | D1 | | |
| Dixon Street | C2 | Langford Grove | F3 | South View Avenue | F2 | | |
| Drove Road | E2-E3 | Lansdown Road | C1 | Southampton Street | E3 | | |

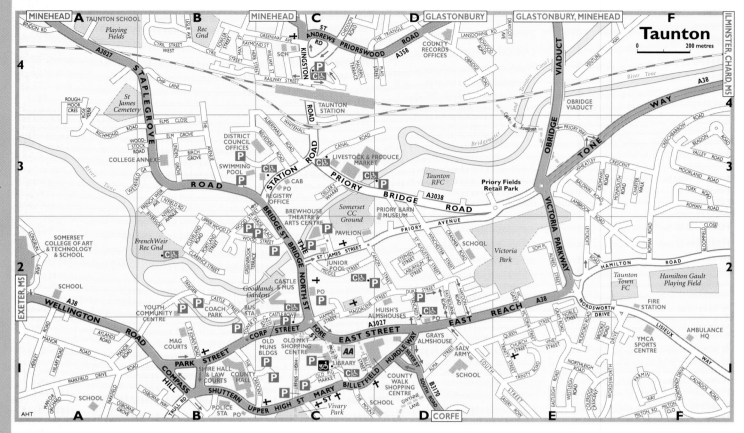

# Taunton

Taunton is found on atlas page **20**,
grid reference **2224**

**AA shop**
6 Cheapside, Taunton TA1 3BR                    C1

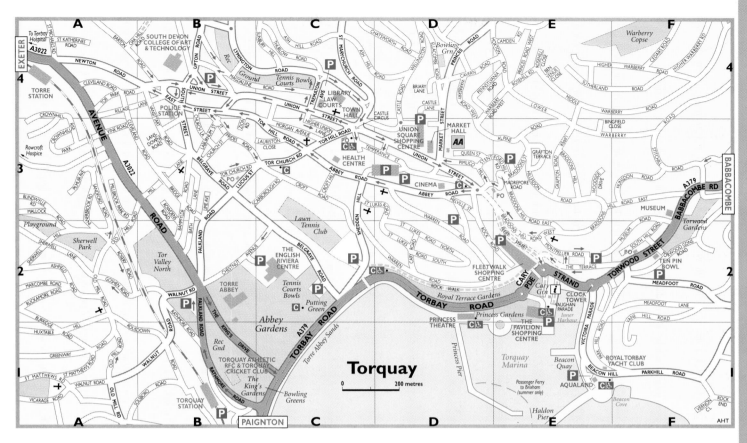

# Torquay

Torquay is found on atlas page **7**,
grid reference **9164**

**AA shop**
8 Market Street, Torquay TQ1 3AQ         D3

| | | | | | |
|---|---|---|---|---|---|
| Abbey Road | C3-D3 | Ellacombe Road | D4 | Parkhill Road | F1 | Temperance Street | C3-D3 |
| Alpine Road | D3-E3 | Falkland Road | B1-B3 | Pennsylvania Road | D4-E4 | The King's Drive | B2-C1 |
| Ash Hill Road | C4-D4 | Fleet Street | E2-E3 | Pilmuir Avenue | A3 | The Terrace | E2-F2 |
| Ashfield Road | A2 | Goshen Road | A2-B2 | Pimlico Hill | D3 | Thurlow Road | C4 |
| Avenue Road | A4-B2 | Grafton Road | E3 | Princes Road | D4 | Tor Church Road | B3-C3 |
| Babbacombe Road | F2-F3 | Grafton Terrace | E3 | Princes Road West | E4 | Tor Hill Road | B4-C3 |
| Bampfylde Road | B2-B3 | Greenway Road | A1 | Queen Street | D3 | Tor Park Road | A4 |
| Barton Road | A4-B4 | Higher Union Lane | C3 | Rathmore Road | B1-B2 | Torbay Road | C1-E2 |
| Bath Lane | B2-B3 | Higher Warberry Road | E4-F4 | Rillage Lane | A4-B4 | Torwood Close | F2 |
| Beacon Hill | E1-F1 | Hillesdon Road | E3 | Rock End | F1 | Torwood Gardens Road | F2 |
| Belgrave Road | B3-C2 | Hoxton Road | E4 | Rock Road | D3-E2 | Torwood Street | E2-F2 |
| Ben Venue Close | E4 | Hunsdon Road | F3 | Rosery Road | A2 | Trematon Avenue | C4 |
| Bingfield Close | E3 | Huxtable Hill | A1-A2 | Rooklands Avenue | A4 | Union Street | B4-D3 |
| Blindwylle Road | A3 | Innerbrook Road | A2-A3 | Rosehill Road | E4 | Upper Braddons Hill | E3-E4 |
| Braddons Hill Road | D3-E3-E2 | Laburnum Street | B3 | Rosehill Close | E4 | Upton Road | B4 |
| Braddons Hill Road East | E2-E3-F3 | Lansdowne Road | B3 | Rousdown Road | A1-B1 | Vane Hill Road | F1-F2 |
| Braddons Hill Road West | D3-E2 | Lauriston Close | C3 | Rowdens Road | B2-B3 | Vansittart Road | B3-B4 |
| Braddons Street | E3 | Lime Avenue | B3 | Ruckamore Road | A2 | Vaughan Parade | E2 |
| Briary Lane | D4 | Lower Warberry Road | E4-F4 | St Efrides Road | B4-C3 | Vernon Close | F1 |
| Bridge Road | B3 | Lucius Street | B3 | St Katherines Road | A4 | Vicarage Road | A1 |
| Burridge Road | A1-A2 | Lymington Road | B4-C4 | St Lukes Road | C3-D3 | Victoria Parade | E1-E2 |
| Camden Road | E4 | Madrepore Road | D3 | St Lukes Road North | D2 | Vine Road | A3 |
| Cary Parade | E2 | Magdalene Road | B4-C4 | St Lukes Road South | D2 | Walnut Road | A1-B2 |
| Cary Road | D2 | Mallock Road | A2-A3 | St Marychurch Road | C4 | Warberry Road West | D4-E4 |
| Castle Circus | C3 | Marcombe Road | A2 | St Matthews Road | A1 | Warren Road | C2-D2-D3 |
| Castle Lane | D4 | Market Street | D3-D4 | St Michaels Road | A4 | Wellington Road | D4 |
| Castle Road | D3-D4 | Meadfoot Lane | F2 | Sandford Road | A2-A3 | Woodside Drive | E3 |
| Cavern Road | D4-E4 | Meadfoot Road | F2 | Scarborough Road | B3-C3 | Zion Road | B3-B4 |
| Cedars Road | F4 | Melville Street | D3 | Shedden Hill | C2-C3 | | |
| Chatsworth Road | C4-D4 | Middle Warberry Road | E4-F4 | Sherwell Hill | A2 | | |
| Chestnut Avenue | B2-C2 | Mill Lane | B3 | Sherwell Lane | A2 | | |
| Church Lane | B3-B4 | Millbrook Park Road | A3 | Solsboro Road | A1-B1 | | |
| Church Street | B3 | Montpellier Road | E2 | South Hill Road | F2-F3 | | |
| Cleveland Road | A4-B3 | Morgan Avenue | C3 | South Street | B3-B4 | | |
| Croft Hill | C3 | Museum Road | E2-F2 | Stentiford Hill Road | D3-E3 | | |
| Croft Road | C2-C3 | Newton Road | A4 | Stitchill Road | F3-F4 | | |
| Crownhill Park | A3 | Oak Hill Road | A4-B4 | Strand | E2 | | |
| Crownhill Rise | A3-A4 | Old Mill Road | A1-A3 | Sunbury Hill | C4 | | |
| East Street | B4 | Park Hill Road | E1-F2 | Sutherland Road | E4-F4 | | |

226

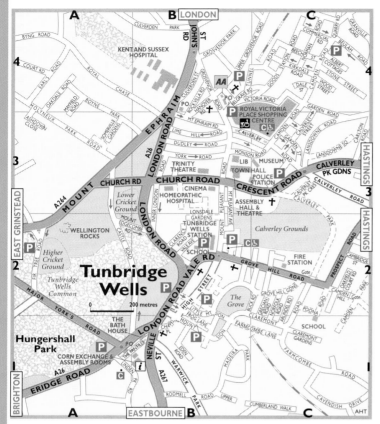

# Tunbridge Wells

Tunbridge Wells is found on atlas page **16**,
grid reference **5839**

**AA shop**
2 Upper Grosvenor Road, Tunbridge Wells TN1 2EN    B4

| | | | | | | |
|---|---|---|---|---|---|
| Albert Cottages | C4 | Granville Road | C4 | Tunnel Road | B4-C4 |
| Arundel Road | C1-C2 | Grecian Road | C2 | Upper Cumberland Walk | B1-C1 |
| Ashdown Close | A3-A4 | Grosvenor Park | B4 | Upper Grosvenor Road | B4-C4 |
| Beech Street | C4 | Grosvenor Road | B3-B4 | Vale Avenue | B2 |
| Belgrave Road | B4-C4 | Grove Hill Gardens | C2 | Vale Road | B2 |
| Beulah Road | C4 | Grove Hill Road | B2-C2 | Victoria Road | B4-C4 |
| Boyne Park | A4-A3-B3 | Hanover Road | B3-B4 | Warwick Park | B1 |
| Buck Road | B2-C2 | High Street | B2 | Wood Street | C4 |
| Byng Road | A4 | Inner London Road | B2-B3 | York Road | B3 |
| Calverley Park | C2-C3 | Kirkdale Road | C4 | | |
| Calverley Park Crescent | C3 | Lansdowne Road | C3 | | |
| Calverley Park Gardens | C3 | Lansdowne Square | C3 | | |
| Calverley Road | B3-C3 | Lime Hill Road | B3 | | |
| Calverley Street | C3-C4 | Linden Park Road | A1-B1 | | |
| Cambridge Street | C2 | Little Mount Sion | B1-B2 | | |
| Camden Hill | C2 | London Road | A1-B1-B2-B3 | | |
| Camden Park | C1-C2 | Lonsdale Gardens | B2 | | |
| Camden Road | C3-C4 | Madeira Park | B1 | | |
| Carlton Road | C3 | Major York's Road | A1-A2 | | |
| Castle Road | A3-A2-B2-B1 | Mayfield Road | A3-A4 | | |
| Cavendish Drive | C1 | Molyneux Park Road | A3-A4 | | |
| Chapel Place | B1 | Monson Road | B3-C3 | | |
| Church Road | A3-B3 | Mount Edgecombe Road | A2-B2 | | |
| Claremont Gardens | C1 | Mount Ephraim | A2-A3-B3-B4 | | |
| Claremont Road | C1-C2 | Mount Ephraim Road | B3 | | |
| Clarence Road | B2 | Mount Pleasant Avenue | B2-B3 | | |
| Commercial Road | C4 | Mount Pleasant Road | B2-B3 | | |
| Court Road | A4 | Mount Sion | B1 | | |
| Crescent Road | B3-C3 | Neville Street | B1 | | |
| Culverden Park | A4-B4 | Norfolk Road | C1-C2 | | |
| Culverden Street | B4 | Norman Road | C4 | | |
| Dale Street | C4 | Oakdale Road | A4 | | |
| Dudley Road | B3 | Oakfield Court Road | C2 | | |
| Earl's Road | A4 | Poona Road | C2 | | |
| Eden Road | B1 | Prospect Road | C2 | | |
| Eridge Road | A1 | Quarry Road | C4 | | |
| Farmcombe Lane | B1-C1 | Rock Villa Road | B3-B4 | | |
| Farmcombe Road | C1 | Rodmell Road | B1 | | |
| Fir Tree Road | A2 | Royal Chase | A4-B4-B3 | | |
| Frog Lane | B1-B2 | Somerville Gardens | A3 | | |
| Garden Road | C3-C4 | St John's Road | B4 | | |
| Garden Street | C3 | Stone Street | C4 | | |
| Goods Station Road | C4 | The Pantiles | A1-B1 | | |

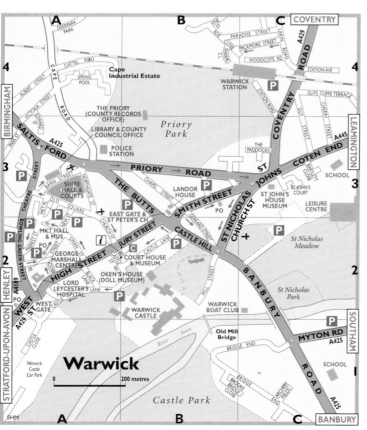

# Warwick

Warwick is found on atlas page **48**,
grid reference **2865**

| | | | |
|---|---|---|---|
| Albert Street | A4 | Smith Street | B2-C3 |
| Archery Fields | C1 | Spring Pool | A4 |
| Banbury Road | B2-C1 | Station Avenue | C4 |
| Barn Street | A3 | Station Road | C4 |
| Bartlett Close | C3 | Swan Street | A2 |
| Black Lane | A2 | The Butts | A3-B2 |
| Bowling Green Street | A2 | The Paddocks | C3 |
| Bridge Brooke Close | B1-C1 | Theatre Street | A3 |
| Bridge End | B1-C1 | Victoria Street | A3-A4 |
| Brook Street | A2 | Vine Street | B4 |
| Cape Road | A3-A4 | West Street | A1-A2 |
| Castle Close | A1 | Woodcote Road | C4 |
| Castle Hill | B2 | | |
| Castle Lane | A2-B2 | | |
| Castle Street | A2-B2 | | |
| Cattel Road | A4 | | |
| Chapel Street | B3 | | |
| Cherry Street | C3-C4 | | |
| Church Street | A2 | | |
| Coten End | C3 | | |
| Coventry Road | C3-C4 | | |
| Deerpark Park | A4 | | |
| Edward Street | A3-A4 | | |
| Gerrard Street | B2-B3 | | |
| Guy Street | C3-C4 | | |
| Guys Cliffe Terrace | C4 | | |
| High Street | A2 | | |
| Jury Street | A2-B2 | | |
| Lakin Road | C4 | | |
| Market Place | A3 | | |
| Market Street | A2 | | |
| Mill Street | B2 | | |
| Myton Road | C1 | | |
| New Street | A2-A3 | | |
| Northgate Street | A3 | | |
| Old Square | A3 | | |
| Packmore Street | B4-C4 | | |
| Paradise Street | B4-C4 | | |
| Park Street | A3 | | |
| Priory Road | A3-C3 | | |
| Roe Close | B4 | | |
| St John's Court | C3 | | |
| St Johns | C3 | | |
| St Nicholas Church Street | B2-C3 | | |
| Saltisford | A3-A4 | | |
| Sharpe Close | B4 | | |

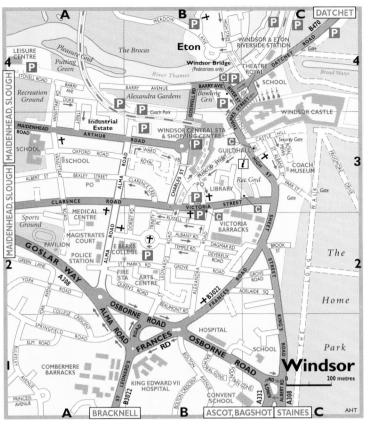

# Windsor

Windsor is found on atlas page **26**,
grid reference **9576**

| | | | |
|---|---|---|---|
| Adelaide Square | B2-C2 | Russell Street | B2 |
| Albany Road | B2 | St Albans Street | C3 |
| Albert Road | C1 | St Leonard's Road | A1-B1-B2-B3 |
| Albert Street | A3 | St Mark's Road | A2-B2 |
| Alexandra Road | B1-B2-B3 | Sheet Street | C2-C3 |
| Alma Road | B1-B2-B3 | Springfield Road | A1-A2 |
| Arthur Road | A3-B3 | Stovell Road | A4 |
| Balmoral Gardens | B1 | Temple Road | B2 |
| Barry Avenue | A4-B4 | Thames Street | B3-C4 |
| Beaumont Road | B2 | The Long Walk | C1-C2-C3 |
| Bexley Street | A3 | Trinity Place | B2-B3 |
| Bolton Avenue | B1 | Vansittart Road | A2-A3-A4 |
| Bolton Crescent | B1 | Victoria Street | B3-C3 |
| Brook Street | C2 | Ward Royal | B3 |
| Bulkeley Avenue | A1 | York Avenue | A1-A2 |
| Castle Hill | C3 | York Road | A2 |
| Charles Street | B3 | | |
| Clarence Crescent | B3 | | |
| Clarence Road | A3-B3 | | |
| College Crescent | A1-A2 | | |
| Dagmar Road | B2 | | |
| Datchet Road | C4 | | |
| Devereux Road | B2 | | |
| Dorset Road | B2-B3 | | |
| Duke Street | A3-A4 | | |
| Elm Road | A1 | | |
| Fountain Gardens | B1-C1 | | |
| Frances Road | B1-B2-C2 | | |
| Frogmore Drive | C3 | | |
| Goslar Way | A2 | | |
| Goswell Road | B3-B4 | | |
| Green Lane | A2 | | |
| Grove Road | B2-C2 | | |
| High Street (Eton) | B4 | | |
| High Street (Windsor) | C3 | | |
| King's Road | C1-C2 | | |
| Maidenhead Road | A3 | | |
| Meadow Lane | A4-B4 | | |
| Osborne Road | A2-B2-B1-C1 | | |
| Oxford Road | A3 | | |
| Park Street | C3 | | |
| Peascod Street | B3 | | |
| Princess Avenue | A1 | | |
| Queen's Road | A2-B2 | | |
| River Street | B4 | | |
| Royal Mews | C3 | | |

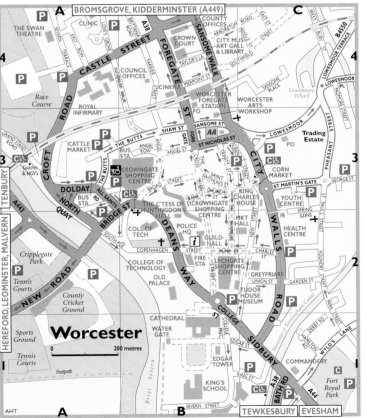

# Worcester

Worcester is found on atlas page **47**,
grid reference **8554**

**AA shop**
Unit 5 Haswell House, St Nicholas Street, Worcester WR1 1UW   B3

| | | | |
|---|---|---|---|
| All Saints Road | A3 | Padmore Street | C3-C4 |
| Angel Place | B3 | Park Street | C1-C2 |
| Angel Row | B3 | Pheasant Street | C3-C4 |
| Angel Street | B3 | Pierpoint Street | B4 |
| Arboretum Road | B4-C4 | Pump Street | B2-C2 |
| Bank Street | B3 | Queen Street | B3-C3 |
| Bath Road | C1 | Sansome Place | B4-C4 |
| Bridge Street | A2-B3 | Sansome Street | B3 |
| Brittania Road | B4 | Sansome Walk | B4 |
| Broad Street | B3 | Severn Street | B1 |
| Castle Street | A4-B4 | Severn Terrace | A4 |
| Charles Street | C2 | Shaw Street | B3 |
| Church Street | B3 | Sidbury | C1 |
| City Walls Road | C1-C2-C3 | South Parade | A2-B2 |
| College Precinct | B1 | Southfield Street | B4-C4 |
| College Street | B1-B2 | Spring Gardens | C2-C3 |
| Copenhagen Street | B2 | St Martin's Gate | C3 |
| Croft Road | A3-A4 | St Nicholas Street | B3 |
| Deans Way | B2-B3 | St Paul's Street | C2-C3 |
| Derby Road | C1 | St Swithun's Street | B3 |
| Dolday | A3 | Taylor's Lane | B4 |
| East Street | C4 | The Butts | A3-B3 |
| Easy Row | A4 | The Cross | B3 |
| Edgar Street | B1-C1 | The Shambles | B2-B3 |
| Farrier Street | B3-B4 | Trinity Street | B3 |
| Foregate | B3 | Union Street | C2 |
| Foregate Street | B3-B4 | Westbury Street | C4 |
| Foundry Street | C2 | Wyld's Lane | C1 |
| Garden Street | C2 | | |
| George Street | C3 | | |
| Grand Stand Road | A3 | | |
| Hamilton Road | C1 | | |
| High Street | B2-B3 | | |
| Infirmary Walk | A4-B4-B3 | | |
| King Street | B1-C1 | | |
| Love's Grove | A4 | | |
| Lowesmoor | C3-C4 | | |
| Lowesmoor Place | C4 | | |
| Lowesmoor Terrace | C4 | | |
| Middle Street | C4 | | |
| New Road | A2 | | |
| New Street | C2-C3 | | |
| North Quay | A2-A3 | | |

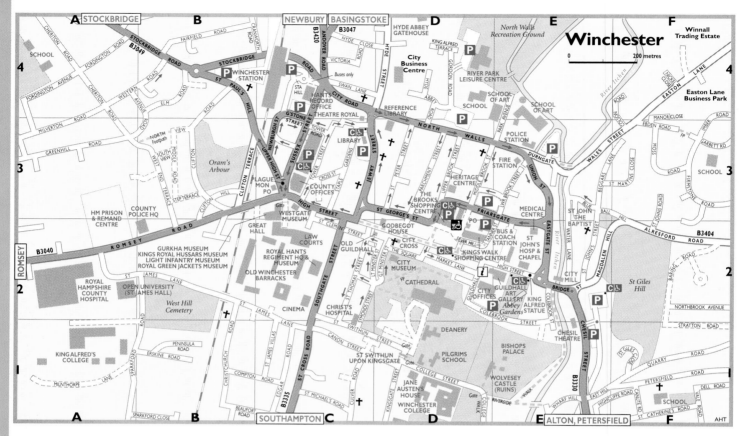

# Winchester

Winchester is found on atlas page **24**,
grid reference **4829**

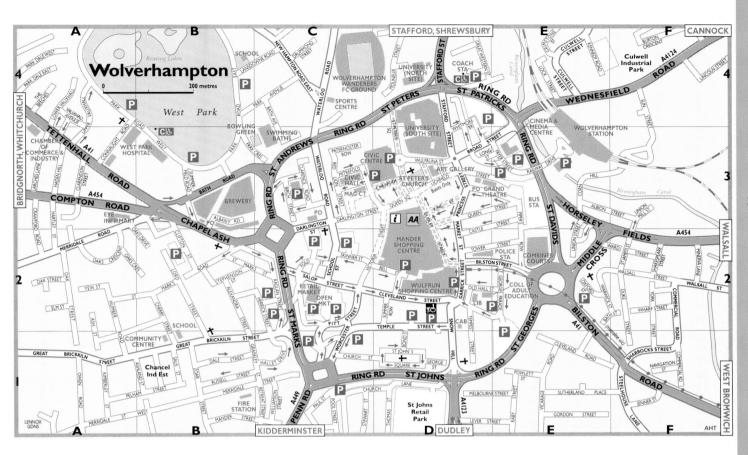

# Wolverhampton

Wolverhampton is found on atlas page **60**,
grid reference **91 98**

**AA shop**
19 The Gallery, Mander Centre, Wolverhampton WV1 3NG    D3

| | | | | | | | |
|---|---|---|---|---|---|---|---|
| Albany Road | B3 | Fryer Street | E3 | Molineux Street | D4 | St Georges Parade | E2 | Whitmore Street | D3-D4 |
| Albion Street | E3-F3 | Garrick Street | D2 | Navigation Street | F1 | St James's Street | F2 | Williamson Street | C1 |
| Alexandra Street | B1-B2 | George Street | D1 | New Hampton Road East | C4 | St John's Road | D1 | Worcester Street | C1-C2 |
| Ash Street | A1-A2 | Gordon Street | E1 | Oak Street | A1-A2 | St Mark's Road | A2-B2 | Wulfruna Street | D3 |
| Ashland Street | B1 | Gramstone Street | E4 | Oaks Crescent | A2-B2 | St Marks Street | B2-C2 | Yew Street | A2 |
| Bath Avenue | C3-C4 | Greasely Street | B1-C1 | Oaks Drive | A3-A2-B2 | St Peter's Square | D3-D4 | York Street | F1-F2 |
| Bath Road | B3-C3 | Great Brick Kiln Street | A1-B1-C1 | Old Hall Street | D2-E2 | Salisbury Street | B1 | Zoar Street | B1 |
| Bath Street | E2-F2 | Great Western Street | D4 | Owen Road | A1 | Salop Street | C2 | | |
| Bell Street | D2 | Haden Hill | A3 | Oxford Street | E2 | School Street | C2 | | |
| Bilston Road | E2-E1-F1 | Hallet Drive | C1 | Park Avenue | B4-C4 | Sharrocks Street | F1 | | |
| Bilston Street | D2-E2 | Hartley Street | A2-A3 | Park Crescent | B3-C3 | Shakespeare Street | F2 | | |
| Birch Street | C3 | Herbert Street | D4 | Park Dale East | A4 | Skinner Street | C2 | | |
| Bond Street | D1 | Herrick Street | C1-C2-B2 | Park Dale West | A4 | Snow Hill | D1-D2 | | |
| Broad Street | D3-E3 | Horseley Fields | E3-E2-F2 | Park Road East | B3-B4 | Stafford Street | D3-D4 | | |
| Burton Crescent | F4 | Humber Road | A1-A2 | Park Road West | B3-B4-A4 | Steelhouse Lane | F1 | | |
| Castle Street | D2-D3-C3 | Jenner Street | F1 | Paternoster Row | C3 | Stephenson Street | B2 | | |
| Chapel Ash | B3-B2 | Kennedy Road | E4 | Paul Street | C1 | Stewart Street | C1 | | |
| Cheapside | D3 | Kimberley Street | A1 | Pelham Street | A1-B1 | Summer Row | D2 | | |
| Cherry Street | B1-B2 | King Street | D3 | Penn Road | C1 | Summerfield Road | B3 | | |
| Church Lane | C1-D1 | Laburnum Street | A1-B2 | Piper's Row | E2-E3 | Sun Street | F3-F4 | | |
| Church Street | C1-D1 | Lansdowne Road | B4-C4 | Pitt Street | C2 | Sutherland Place | E1-F1 | | |
| Clarence Road | C3 | Larches Lane | A3 | Pool Street | C1 | Tempest Street | D1-D2 | | |
| Clarendon Street | A3 | Lennox Gardens | A1 | Powlett Street | E1 | Temple Street | D1-D2-C1-C2 | | |
| Cleveland Road | E1-F1 | Lever Street | D1-E1 | Princess Street | D3 | Tettenhall Road | A4-A3-B3 | | |
| Cleveland Street | C2-D2 | Lichfield Street | D3-E3 | Queen Street | D3-E3 | The Beeches | A4 | | |
| Clifton Street | B2-B3 | Lincoln Street | F4 | Queen Square | D3 | Thomas Street | D1 | | |
| Commercial Road | F1-F2 | Lock Street | E4 | Raby Street | E1 | Tower Street | D2-E2 | | |
| Compton Road | A3-B3 | Long Street | D3-E3 | Raglan Street | C2 | Union Mill Street | F3 | | |
| Connaught Road | A3-A4 | Lord Street | B1-B2 | Railway Drive | E3 | Union Street | E2-E3 | | |
| Corn Hill | E3-F3 | Lower Vauxhall | A4 | Red Lion Street | C3 | Upper Vauxhall Avenue | A3-A4 | | |
| Crawford Road | A2-A3 | Mander Street | B1-C1 | Retreat Street | C1 | Vauxhall Avenue | A4 | | |
| Culwell Street | E4 | Market Street | D2-D3 | Ring Road St Andrews | C3 | Vicarage Road | E1 | | |
| Dale Street | B1 | Melbourne Street | D1-E1 | Ring Road St Davids | E2-E3 | Victoria Street | C2-D2-D3 | | |
| Darlington Square | C2-C3-D3 | Merridale Road | A2-A3-B3 | Ring Road St Georges | D1-E1-E2 | Walsall Street | E2-F2 | | |
| Drummond Street | C4 | Merridale Street | B1-C1 | Ring Road St Johns | C1-D1 | Ward Street | E2-F2 | | |
| Dudley Street | D2-D3 | Merridale Street West | A1-B1 | Ring Road St Marks | C1-C2 | Warwick Street | E2-F2 | | |
| Duke Street | F1-F2 | Middle Cross | E2 | Ring Road St Patricks | D4-E4 | Waterloo Road | C3-C4 | | |
| Elm Street | A2 | Minerva Lane | F2 | Ring Road St Peters | C3-C4-D4 | Wednesfield Road | E4-F4 | | |
| Fold Street | C2 | Mitrefold | C3 | Russell Street | B1 | Wharf Street | F2 | | |

# York

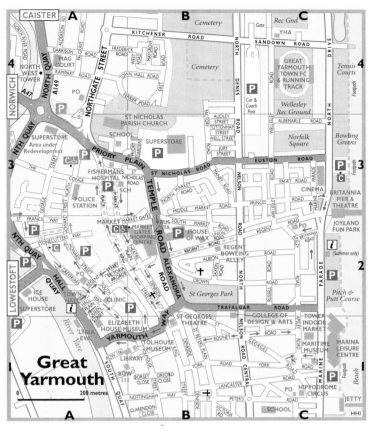

# Great Yarmouth

Great Yarmouth is found on atlas page **67**,
grid reference **5207**

| | | | | | | |
|---|---|---|---|---|---|
| Albemarle Road | C3 | Maygrove Road | B4 | South Market Road | B2 |
| Albion Road | B2-C2 | Middle Market Road | B3 | South Quay | A1 |
| Alderson Road | A4 | Nelson Road Central | B2-B1-C1 | Stonecutters Way | A2 |
| Alexandra Road | B2 | Nelson Road North | B2-B3 | Temple Road | B2-B3 |
| Apsley Road | C1-C2 | North Denes Road | B3-B4 | The Conge | A3 |
| Audley Street | B3 | North Drive | C3-C4 | Theatre Plain | A2-B2 |
| Britannia Road | C2 | North Market Road | B3 | Tolhouse Street | B1 |
| Clarendon Close | B1 | North Quay | A2-A3-A4 | Tottenham Street | B3 |
| Crown Road | B2-C2 | North River Road | A4 | Town Wall Road | A4-B4 |
| Deneside | B1-B2 | Northgate Street | A3-A4 | Trafalgar Road | B2-C2 |
| Dorset Close | B1 | Nottingham Way | A1-B1 | Union Road | B2 |
| East Road | B4 | Orford Close | B1 | Victoria Arcade | A2-B2 |
| Euston Road | C3 | Paget Road | C3 | Victoria Road | B1 |
| Factory Road | B3-B4 | Palgrave Road | A4 | Well Street | B3 |
| Ferrier Road | A4-B4 | Princes Road | C3 | Wellesley Road | C2-C3-C4 |
| Frederick Road | A4-B4 | Priory Gardens | B3 | West Road | B4 |
| Garrison Road | A4 | Priory Plain | A3-B3 | Yarmouth Way | A1-B1-B2 |
| George Street | A3 | Queen Street | A1-A2 | York Road | B1-C1 |
| Greyfriars Way | A1-A2 | Rampart Road | A4 | | |
| Hall Plain | A2 | Regent Road | B2-C2 | | |
| Hall Quay | A2 | Regent Street | A2 | | |
| Howard Street North | A2-A3 | Rodney Road | B1-C1 | | |
| Howard Street South | A2 | Row 106 | A1 | | |
| Jury Street | B3 | Russell Road | C2 | | |
| King Street | A2-B2-B1 | St Francis Way | A2 | | |
| Kitchener Road | A4-B4 | St Georges Road | B2-B1-C1 | | |
| Lancaster Road | B1-C1 | St Nicholas Road | A3-B3 | | |
| Manby Road | B3 | St Peter's Road | B1-C1 | | |
| Marine Parade | C1-C2-C3 | St Peters Plain | B1 | | |
| Market Gates | A2-B2 | Sandown Road | B4-C4 | | |
| Market Place | A2-A3 | Saxon Road | B2 | | |

**231**

# York

York is found on atlas page **83**,
grid reference **6051**

**AA shop**
6 Church Street, York YO1 2BG    D5

| | | | |
|---|---|---|---|
| Abbey Street | A8 | Cinder Lane | A4 |
| Agar Street | E6 | Claremont Terrace | C6-C7 |
| Albermarle Road | A2-A1-B1 | Clarence Street | C6-C7-D7 |
| Aldwark | D5-E5 | Clementhorpe | C2-D2 |
| Alne Terrace | F2 | Clifford Street | D3-D4 |
| Amber Street | E8 | Clifton Bootham | A8-A7-B7-B6-C6 |
| Anne Street | D1 | Clifton Dale | A8 |
| Apollo Street | F2 | Colliergate | D4-D5 |
| Avenue Road | A8-B8 | Compton Street | A7-A8 |
| Avenue Terrace | A8 | Coney Street | C4 |
| Baile Hill Terrace | C2-C3-D3 | Coppergate | D4 |
| Bar Lane | B3 | Cromwell Road | C3-D3 |
| Barbican Road | E2-F2-F3 | Cygnet Street | C2 |
| Belle Vue Street | F2 | Dale Street | B2-B3 |
| Belle Vue Terrace | F2 | Dalton Terrace | A2 |
| Bewlay Street | C1-D1 | Davygate | C5-D5 |
| Bishopgate Street | C2-D2-D3 | Deangate | D5 |
| Bishophill Junior | C3 | Dennison Street | E7 |
| Bishophill Senior | C3 | Dewsbury Terrace | B3-C3 |
| Bishopthorpe Road | C1-C2 | Diamond Street | E8 |
| Blake Street | C5 | Dodsworth Avenue | E8-F8-F7 |
| Blossom Street | B2-B3 | Driffield Terrace | A1-A2 |
| Bluebridge Lane | E2 | Dudley Street | E7 |
| Bootham Crescent | B7-C8 | Duncombe Place | C5 |
| Bootham Row | C6 | Dundas Street | E4-E5 |
| Bootham Terrace | B6 | East Mount Street | B2 |
| Bridge Street | C4 | Edgeware Road | F1 |
| Brook Street | D7 | Eldon Terrace | D8-E8 |
| Brownlow Street | D7-E7-E8 | Elvington Terrace | F3 |
| Buckingham Street | C3 | Emerald Street | E7-E8 |
| Burton Stone Lane | B7-B8 | Escrick Street | E2 |
| Cambridge Street | A2-A3 | Faber Street | F6 |
| Carl Street | D2 | Fairfax Street | C3 |
| Carmelite Street | E4 | Farndale Street | E1 |
| Castlegate | D4 | Fawcett Street | E2-E3 |
| Cemetery Road | E1-E2 | Feasegate | D4 |
| Charlton Street | C1 | Fenwick Street | C1-D1 |
| Cherry Street | D2 | Fetter Lane | C3-C4 |
| Church Street | D5 | Fewster Way | E2 |

| | | | |
|---|---|---|---|
| Fifth Avenue | F6 | Lawrence Street | F3 |
| Fishergate | E2-E3 | Layerthorpe | E5-E6-F6 |
| Foss Bank | E5-E6 | Leadmill Lane | E3 |
| Foss Islands Road | E5-F5-F4-F3 | Leake Street | F3 |
| Fossgate | D4 | Leeman Road | A5-B5-B4 |
| Frederic Street | B5 | Lendal | C5 |
| Fulford Road | E1-E2 | Levisham Street | E1 |
| Garden Place | E4 | Little Hallfield Road | F5 |
| Garden Street | D7 | Long Close Lane | E3-F3 |
| George Hudson Street | C4 | Longfield Terrace | B5-B6 |
| George Street | E3-E4 | Lord Mayor's Walk | C6-D6 |
| Gillygate | C6 | Lower Ebor Street | D2 |
| Glen Avenue | F6 | Lower Eldon Street | D7-D8 |
| Goodramgate | D5-D6 | Lower Priory Street | C3 |
| Gordon Street | F2 | Lowpetergate | D5 |
| Grange Street | E1 | Lowther Street | D7-E7 |
| Grangegarth | E1 | Lowther Terrace | A3 |
| Grape Lane | D5 | Lumley Road | B8 |
| Greencliffe Drive | A7 | Maida Grove | E1 |
| Grosvenor Road | B8-C8 | Mansfield Street | E5 |
| Grosvenor Terrace | B6-B7-C7-C8 | March Street | D7 |
| Grove View | A7 | Margaret Street | E3 |
| Hallfield Road | F5-F6 | Market Street | D4 |
| Hampden Street | C3 | Markham Crescent | D8-D7 |
| Hartoft Street | E1 | Markham Street | D8 |
| Hawthorne Grove | F6 | Marlborough Grove | E2 |
| Hawthorne Street | F6 | Marygate | B5-B6-C6 |
| Haxby Street | D7-D8 | Melbourne Street | E2 |
| Heslington Road | F2 | Micklegate | B3-B4-C4 |
| Heworth Green | E6-E7-F7 | Mill Lane | F7 |
| High Ousegate | D4 | Mill Mount Lane | A2-B2 |
| Highpetergate | C5-C6 | Millfield Road | C1-C2 |
| Holgate Road | A2-A3-B3 | Minster Yard | C5-D5 |
| Hope Street | E3 | Monkgate | D6-E6 |
| Horsman Avenue | E2-F2 | Moss Street | B3-B2-C2 |
| Howard Street | E1 | Mountvale | A1 |
| Hudson Street | C8 | Museum Street | C5 |
| Hungate | E4 | Navigation Road | E4-F3 |
| Huntington Road | E7-E8 | Nelson Street | D8-E8 |
| Hyrst Grove | F7 | Neville Street | D8 |
| Irwin Avenue | F7-F8 | Neville Terrace | D8-E8 |
| Jackson Street | D7-E7 | New Street | C4-C5 |
| James Street | F3-F4 | New Walk Terrace | E1 |
| Jewbury | E5 | Newborough Street | C8 |
| Kensal Rise | E1 | Newton Terrace | C2-C3 |
| Kent Street | E2 | Norfolk Street | C1-D1 |
| Kings Staithe | C4-D4-D3 | North Parade | B6 |
| Knavesmire Road | A1 | North Street | C4 |
| Kyme Street | C3 | Nunmill Street | C1-C2 |

| | | | |
|---|---|---|---|
| Nunnery Lane | B3-C3-C2 | Shipton Road | A8 |
| Nunthorpe Avenue | B1-B2 | Shipton Street | B8-C8 |
| Nunthorpe Crescent | C1 | Skeldergate | C4-C3-D3 |
| Nunthorpe Grove | C1 | South Parade | B2-B3 |
| Nunthorpe Road | C2 | Southlands Road | C1 |
| Palmer Lane | E4 | Spen Lane | D5-E5 |
| Paragon Street | E3-F3 | Spurriergate | D4 |
| Park Crescent | E7 | Stanley Street | D8 |
| Park Grove | E7-E8 | Station Avenue | B4 |
| Park Street | B2 | Station Rise | B4 |
| Parliament Street | D4 | Station Road | B4-C4-C5 |
| Pavement | D4 | Stonegate | C5-D5 |
| Peasholme Green | E5 | Swann Street | C2-C3 |
| Penley's Grove Street | D7-E7-E6 | Swinegate | D5 |
| Percy's Lane | E4 | Sycamore Place | B6 |
| Peter's Way | A7-B8 | Sycamore Terrace | B5-B6 |
| Piccadilly | D4-E3 | Tanner Row | C4 |
| Portland Street | C6 | Telford Terrace | B1 |
| Pottery Lane | F8 | The Avenue | A7 |
| Prices Lane | C2 | The Crescent | B3 |
| Priory Street | B3-C3 | The Mount | A1-A2-B2 |
| Queen Anne's Road | B6-B7 | The Shambles | D4-D5 |
| Queen Street | B3 | The Stonebow | E4-E5 |
| Railway Terrace | A3 | Thorpe Street | C1-C2 |
| Redeness Street | F5-F6 | Toft Green | B4 |
| Richardson Street | C1-D1 | Tower Street | D3-E3 |
| Rosslyn Street | A7 | Townend Street | D7 |
| Rougier Street | C4 | Trent Holme Drive | A1 |
| Russel Street | C1-C2 | Trinity Lane | C4-C3 |
| St Andrewgate | D5 | Union Terrace | C7-D7 |
| St Anns Court | E2-F2 | Upper Price Road | B2-C2 |
| St Aubyns Place | A1 | Victor Street | C3 |
| St Benedict Road | C2-C3 | Vine Street | C2-D2 |
| St Denys Road | E3-E4 | Walmgate | D4-E4-E3-F3 |
| St James Mount | A1 | Walpole Street | D8-E8 |
| St John's Street | D6-D7 | Water End | A8 |
| St Leonard's | C5-C6 | Water Lane | A8 |
| St Lukes Grove | B8 | Watson Street | A3 |
| St Mary's | B6 | Wellington Row | C4 |
| St Maurice's Road | D6-D5-E5 | Wellington Street | F2-F3 |
| St Olaves Road | B7-B8 | Wentworth Road | B1-B2 |
| St Pauls Terrace | A3 | Westminster Drive | A7 |
| St Peter's Grove | B7 | Wigginton Road | C8-D8-D7 |
| St Saviourgate | D4-D5 | Willis Street | F2-F3 |
| Sandringham Street | E1 | Winterscale Street | E2 |
| Scarborough Terrace | C8 | Wolsley Street | F2 |
| Scarcroft Hill | B1-B2 | | |
| Scarcroft Road | A2-B2-C2 | | |
| Scott Street | C1-C2 | | |

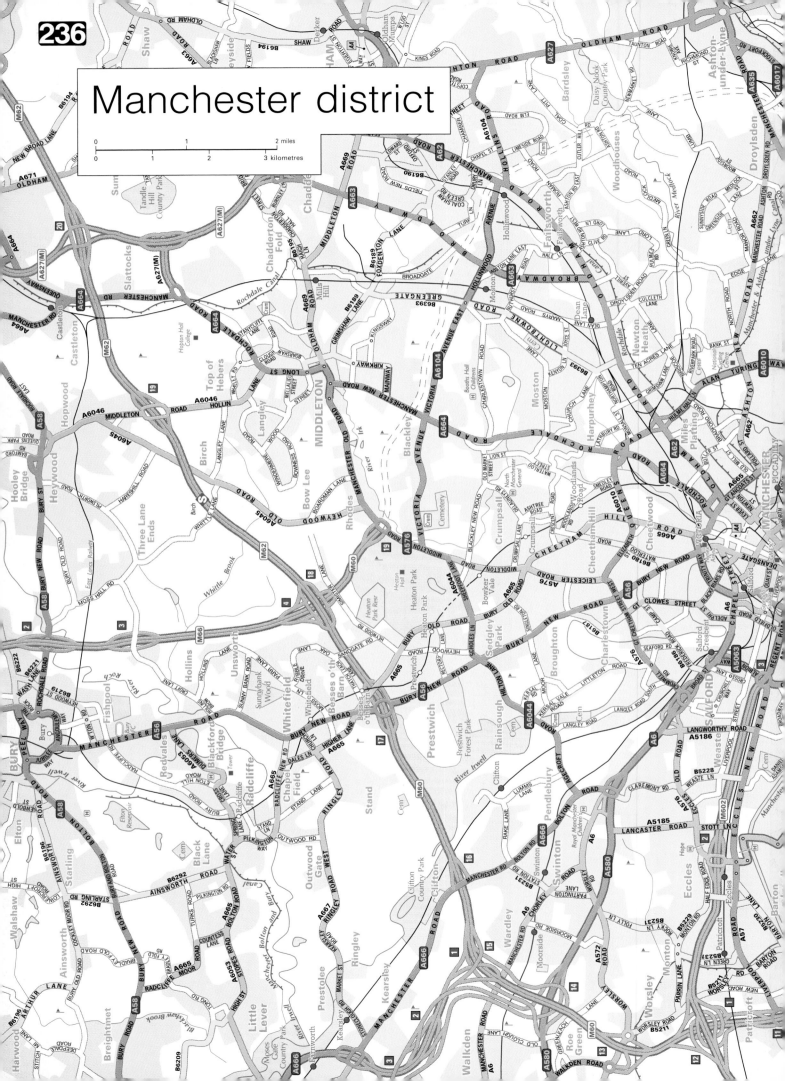

# Manchester district

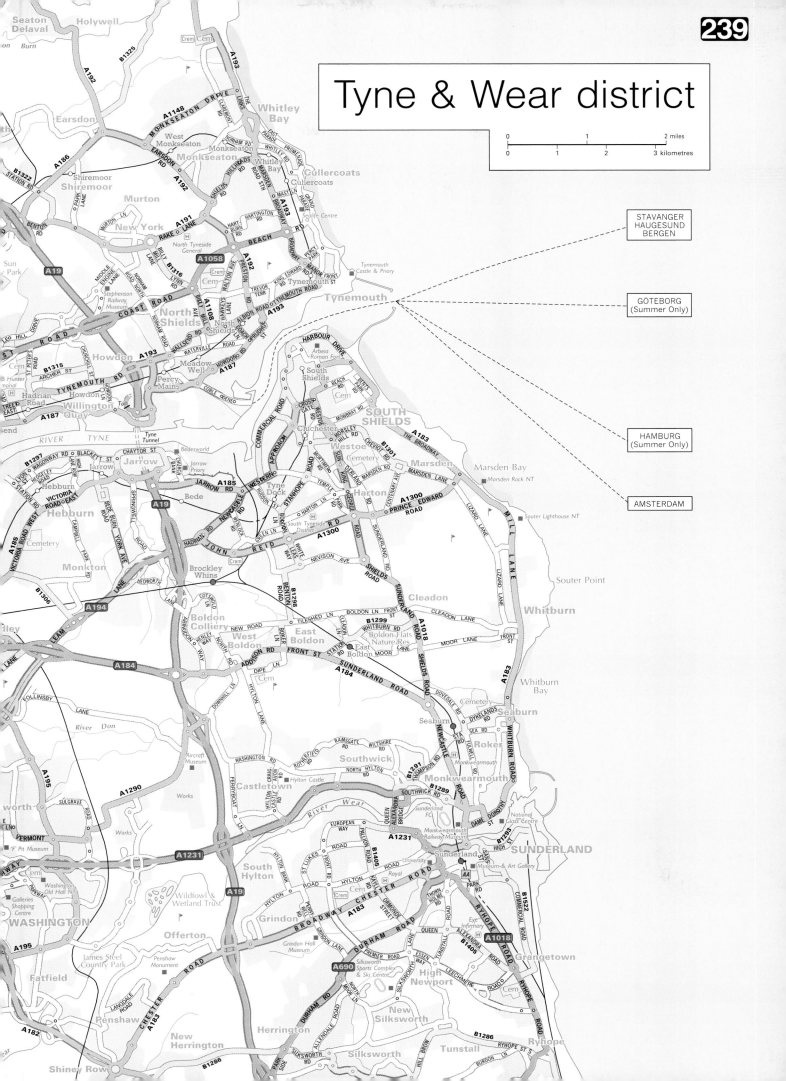

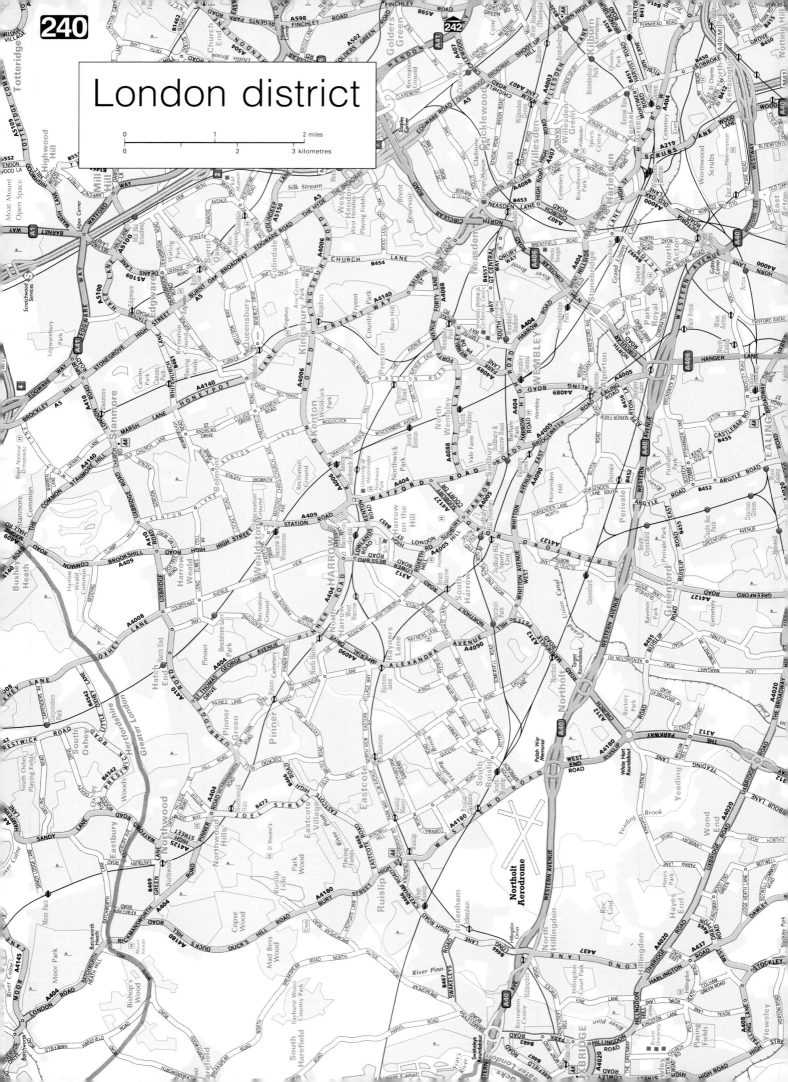

# London district

0       1       2 miles

0       2       3 kilometres

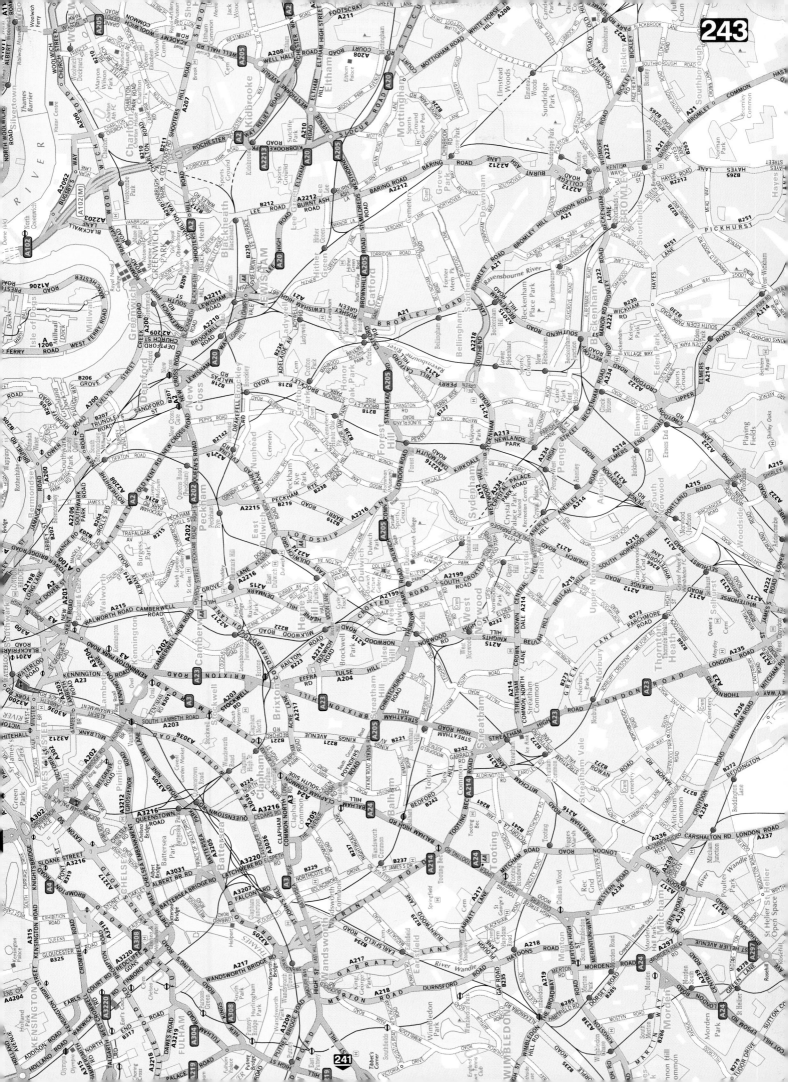

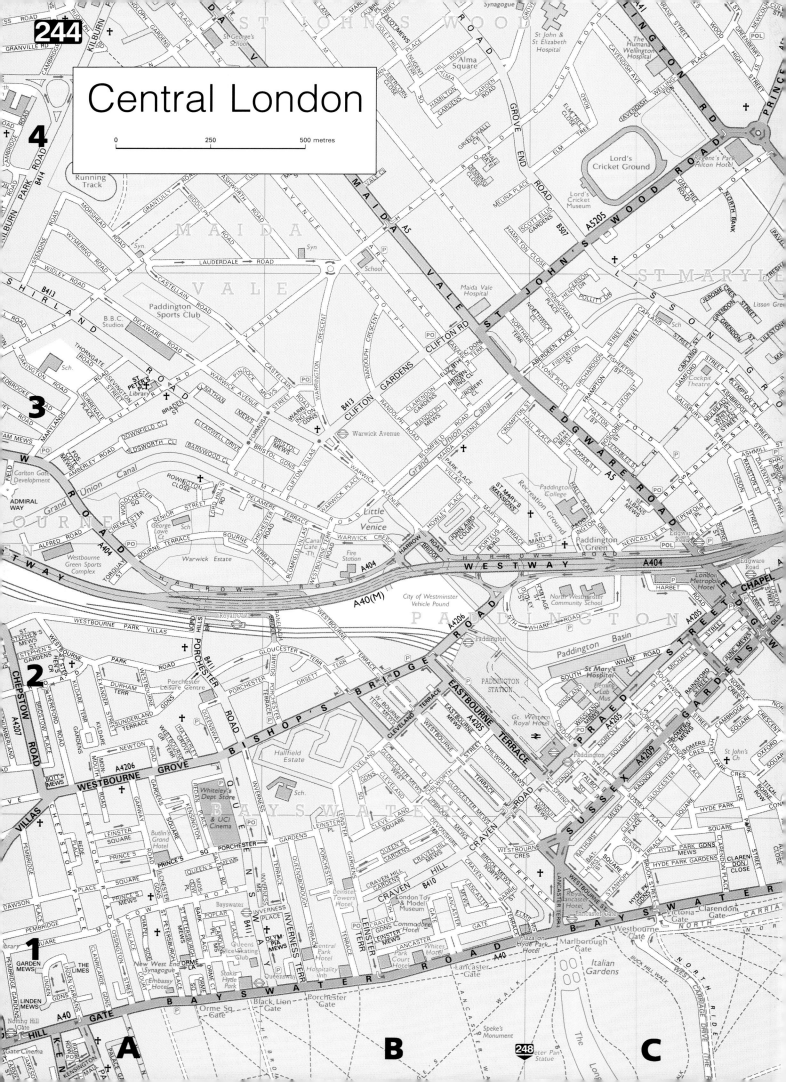

# Central London street index

In the index the street names are listed in alphabetical order and written in full, but may be abbreviated on the map. Postal codes are listed where information is available. Each entry is followed by its map page number in bold type, and an arbitrary letter and grid reference number. For example, for Exhibition Road SW7 **248** C3, turn to page 248. The letter 'C' refers to the grid square located at the bottom of the page; the figure '3' refers to the grid square located at the left-hand side of the page. Exhibition Road is found within the intersecting square. SW7 is the postcode. A proportion of street names and their references are also followed by the name of another street in italics. These entries do not appear on the map due to insufficient space but can be located adjacent to the name of the road in italics.

## A


Abbey Orchard Street *SW1* **250** B3
Abbey Street *SE1* **252** A1
Abbots Gardens *W8* **248** A3
*St Mary's Place*
Abbots Lane *SE1* **252** A2
Abbots Walk *W8* **248** A3
*St Mary's Place*
Abbotshade Road *SE16* **253** E2
Abchurch Lane *EC4* **247** F1
Abercorn Close *NW8* **244** B4
Abercorn Place *NW8* **244** B4
Aberdeen Place *NW8* **244** C3
Aberdour Street *SE1* **251** F2
Abingdon Road *W8* **248** A3
Abingdon Street *SW1* **250** B3
Abingdon Villas *W8* **248** A3
Achilles Way *W1* **249** E4
Ackroyd Drive *E3* **253** F4
Acorn Walk *SE16* **253** F2
Acton Street *WC1* **246** C4
Adam And Eve Court *W1* **245** E1
*Oxford Street*
Adam And Eve Mews *W8* **248** A3
Adam Street *WC2* **246** B1
Adam's Row *W1* **245** E1
Adams Place *E14* **254** A4
Addington Street *SE1* **250** C3
Addle Hill *EC4* **247** E1
Addle Street *EC2* **247** E2
Adelaide Street *WC2* **246** B1
*William IV Street*
Adelina Grove *E1* **252** D4
Adeline Place *WC1* **246** B2
Adelphi Terrace *WC2* **246** B1
*Adams Street*
Adler Street *E1* **252** B4
Admiral Place *SE16* **253** E2
Admiral Way *W9* **244** A3
Admirals Way *E14* **254** A3
Adpar Street *W2* **244** C3
Adrian Mews *SW10* **248** A1
Agar Street *WC2* **246** B1
Agatha Close *E1* **252** C2
Agdon Street *EC1* **247** D3
Agnes Street *E14* **253** F4
Ainstey Street *SE16* **253** D1
*Brunel Road*
Air Street *W1* **246** A1
Alaska Street *SE1* **250** C4
Albany Mews *SE5* **251** E1
Albany Road *SE5* **251** E1
Albany Street *NW1* **245** F4
Albatross Way *SE16* **253** D1
Albemarle Street *W1* **245** F1
Albemarle Way *EC1* **246** C3
*Clerkenwell Road*
Albert Court *SW7* **248** C3
Albert Embankment *SE1* **250** B1
Albert Gardens *E1* **253** D3
Albert Hall Mansions *SW7* **248** C3
Albert Mews *W8* **248** B3
Albert Place *W8* **248** B3
Alberta Street *SE17* **251** D1
Albion Close *W2* **245** D1
Albion Mews *W2* **245** D1
Albion Place *EC1* **247** D3
Albion Street *SE16* **253** D1
Albion Street *W2* **245** D1
Albion Way *EC1* **247** E2
Albion Yard *E1* **252** C4
Aldburgh Mews *W1* **245** E2
*Marylebone Lane*
Aldenham Street *NW1* **246** A4
Aldermanbury *EC2* **247** E2
Aldermanbury Square *EC2* **247** E2
*Aldermanbury*
Alderney Street *SW1* **249** F2
Aldersgate Street *EC1* **247** E3
Aldford Street *W1* **245** E1
Aldgate *EC3* **252** A3
Aldgate High Street *EC3* **252** A3
Aldsworth Close *W9* **244** A3
Aldwych *WC2* **246** C1
Alexander Place *SW7* **248** C2
Alexander Square *SW3* **248** C2
Alexander Street *W2* **244** A2
Alford Place *N1* **247** E4
Alfred Mews *W1* **246** A3
Alfred Place *WC1* **246** A3
Alfred Road *W2* **244** A2
Alice Street *SE1* **251** F3
Alie Street *E1* **252** B3
All Hallows Lane *EC4* **247** F1
All Soul's Place *W1* **245** F2
*Langham Street*
Allen Street *W8* **248** A3
Allington Street *SW1* **249** F3
Allsop Place *NW1* **245** D3
Alma Square *NW8* **244** B4
Alpha Grove *E14* **254** A3
Alpha Place *SW3* **249** D1
Alsace Road *SE17* **251** F1
Alscot Road *SE1* **252** B1
Alvey Street *SE17* **251** F2
Ambassador Square *E14* **254** B2
Ambergate Street *SE17* **251** D1
Amberley Road *W9* **244** A3
Ambrosden Avenue *SW1* **250** A3
Amelia Street *SE17* **251** E2
Amen Corner *EC4* **247** D2
Amen Court *EC4* **247** D2
America Square *EC3* **252** A3
America Street *SE1* **251** E4
Amoy Place *E14* **253** F3
Ampton Place *WC1* **246** C4
Ampton Street *WC1* **246** C4
Amsterdam Road *E14* **254** C2
Amwell Street *EC1* **246** C4
Anderson Street *SW3* **249** D2
Andrew Borde Street *WC2* **246** B2
*Charing Cross Road*
Angel Court *EC2* **247** F2
Angel Court *SW1* **250** A4
*King Street*
Angel Passage *EC4* **247** F1
Angel Place *SE1* **251** E4
Angel Street *EC1* **247** E2
Ann Moss Way *SE16* **253** D1
Ansdell Street *W8* **248** A3
Antill Terrace *E1* **253** D4
Apothecary Street *EC4* **247** D2
*New Bridge Street*
Apple Tree Yard *SW1* **246** A1
Appold Street *EC2* **247** F3
Aquinas Street *SE1* **251** D4
Arbour Square *E1* **253** D4
Archangel Street *SE16* **253** E1
Archer Street *W1* **246** A1
Arden Crescent *E14* **254** A2
Argent Street *SE1* **251** E4
*Loman Street*
Argyle Square *WC1* **246** B4
Argyle Street *WC1* **246** B4
Argyle Walk *WC1* **246** B4
Argyll Road *W8* **248** A3
Argyll Street *W1* **245** F2
Arlington Street *SW1* **249** F4
Arlington Way *EC1* **247** D4
Arne Street *WC2* **246** B2
Arneway Street *SW1* **250** A2
Arnhem Place *E14* **254** A2
Arnside Street *SE17* **251** E1
Arthur Street *EC4* **247** F1
Artichoke Hill *E1* **252** C3
Artillery Lane *E1* **252** A4
Artillery Passage *E1* **252** A4
*Artillery Lane*
Artillery Row *SW1* **250** A3
Artizan Street *E1* **252** A4
*Harrow Place*
Arundel Street *WC2* **246** C1
Ashbridge Street *NW8* **244** C3
Ashburn Gardens *SW7* **248** B2
Ashburn Mews *SW7* **248** B2
Ashburn Place *SW7* **248** B2
Ashby Street *EC1* **247** D4
Ashdown Walk *E14* **254** A2
Asher Drive *E1* **252** B3
Ashfield Street *E1* **252** C4
Ashland Place *W1* **244** E3
Ashley Place *SW1* **249** F3
Ashmill Street *NW1* **244** C3
Ashworth Road *W9* **244** A4
Aske Street *N1* **247** F4
Asolando Drive *SE17* **251** E2
*King & Queen Street*
Aspen Way *E14* **254** B4
Assam Street *E1* **252** B4
Assembly Passage *E1* **253** D4
Aste Street *E14* **254** B3
Astell Street *SW3* **249** D2
Aston Street *E14* **253** E4
Astwood Mews *SW7* **248** B2
Atherstone Mews *SW7* **248** B2
Atterbury Street *SW1* **250** B2
Attneave Street *WC1* **246** C4
Aubrey Place *NW8* **244** B4
Auckland Street *SE11* **250** C1
Augustus Street *NW1* **245** F4
Aulton Place *SE11* **251** D1
Austin Friars *EC2* **247** F2
Austin Friars Square *EC2* **247** F2
*Austin Friars*
Austral Street *SE11* **251** D2
Ave Maria Lane *EC4* **247** E2
Aveline Street *SE11* **250** C1
Avery Row *W1* **245** F1
Avis Square *E1* **253** E4
Avon Place *SE1* **251** E3
Avonmouth Street *SE1* **251** E3
Aybrook Street *W1* **245** E2
Aylesbury Road *SE17* **251** F1
Aylesbury Street *EC1* **247** D3
Aylesford Street *SW1* **250** A1
Aylward Street *E1* **253** D4
Ayres Street *SE1* **251** E4


## B


Babmaes Street *SW1* **250** A4
*Jermyn Street*
Bacchus Walk *N1* **247** F4
Bache's Street *N1* **247** F4
Back Church Lane *E1* **252** B4
Back Hill *EC1* **247** D3
Bacon Grove *SE1* **252** A1
Bainbridge Street *WC1* **246** B2
Baker Street *W1 & NW1* **245** D3
Baker's Mews *W1* **245** E2
Baker's Row *EC1* **247** F3
Baker's Yard *EC1* **247** D3
*Baker's Row*
Bakers Hall Court *EC3* **252** A3
*Harp Lane*
Balcombe Street *NW1* **245** D3
Balderton Street *W1* **245** E1
Baldwin Street *EC1* **247** F4
Baldwin's Gardens *EC1* **246** C3
Balfe Street *N1* **246** B4
Balfour Mews *W1* **245** E1
Balfour Place *W1* **245** E1
Balfour Street *SE17* **251** F2
Ballast Quay *SE10* **254** C1
Balneil Gate *SW1* **250** A1
Baltic Street East *EC1* **247** E3
Baltic Street West *EC1* **247** E3
Balvaird Place *SW1* **250** B2
Bancroft Road *E1* **250** C1
Bank End *SE1* **251** E4
Bankside *SE1* **251** E4
Bankside Jetty *SE1* **247** E1
Banner Street *EC1* **247** E3
Banyard Road *SE16* **252** C1
Barbon Close *WC1* **246** C3
Barge House Street *SE1* **247** D1
Bark Place *W2* **244** A1
Barkston Gardens *SW5* **248** A2
Barleycorn Way *E14* **253** F3
Barlow Place *W1* **245** F1
Barlow Street *SE17* **251** F2
Barnaby Place *SW7* **248** C2
Barnardo Street *E1* **253** D3
Barnby Street *NW1* **246** A4
Barnes Street *E14* **253** E4
Barnfield Place *E14* **254** A2
Barnham Street *SE1* **252** A2
Barnsdale Avenue *E14* **254** A2
Barnwood Close *W9* **244** A3
Baron's Place *SE1* **251** D3
Barque Mews *SE8* **254** A1
Barrett Street *W1* **245** E2
Barrie Street *W2* **244** B1
Barrow Hill Road *NW8* **244** C4
*St Johns Wood High Street*
Barter Street *WC1* **246** B2
Barth Lane *EC2* **247** F2
Bartholomew Close *EC1* **247** E2
Bartholomew Square *EC1* **247** E3
Bartholomew Street *SE1* **251** F2
Barton Street *SW1* **250** B3
Basil Street *SW3* **249** D3
Basinghall Avenue *EC2* **247** E2
Basinghall Street *EC2* **247** E2
Bastwick Street *EC1* **247** E3
Bate Street *E14* **253** F3
Bateman Street *W1* **246** A2
Bateman's Buildings *W1* **246** A2
Bath Court *EC1* **246** C3
*Warner Street*
Bath Place *N1* **247** F4
Bath Street *EC1* **247** E4
Bath Terrace *SE1* **251** E3
Bathurst Mews *W2* **244** C1
Bathurst Street *W2* **244** C1
Battle Bridge Lane *SE1* **251** F4
Batty Street *E1* **252** B4
Bayley Street *WC1* **246** A2
Baylis Road *SE1* **250** C3
Bayswater Road *W2* **244** A1
Baythorne Street *E3* **253** F4
Beaconsfield Road *SE17* **251** F1
Beak Street *W1* **246** A1
Bear Alley *EC4* **247** D2
*Farringdon Street*
Bear Gardens *SE1* **247** E1
Bear Lane *SE1* **251** D4
Bear Street *WC2* **246** B1
*Cranbourn Street*
Beatrice Place *W8* **248** A2
Beauchamp Place *SW3* **249** D3
Beauchamp Street *EC1* **247** D3
*Brooke Street*
Beaufort Gardens *SW3* **249** D3
Beaufort Street *SW3* **248** B1
Beaumont Mews *W1* **245** E2
Beaumont Place *W1* **246** A3
Beaumont Street *W1* **245** E3
Beccles Street *E14* **253** F3
Beckway Street *SE17* **251** F2
Bedale Street *SE1* **251** E3
*Borough High Street*
Bedford Avenue *WC1* **246** B2
Bedford Court *WC2* **246** B1
Bedford Gardens *W8* **248** A4
Bedford Place *WC1* **246** B3
Bedford Row *WC1* **246** C3
Bedford Square *WC1* **246** B2
Bedford Street *WC2* **246** B1
Bedford Way *WC1* **246** B3
Bedfordbury *WC2* **246** B1
Bedser Close *SE11* **250** C1
Beech Street *EC2* **247** E3
Beeston Place *SW1* **249** F3
Bekesbourne Street *E14* **245** E2
*Marylebone Lane*
Bekesbourne Street *E14* **253** E3
Belgrave Mews North *SW1* **249** E3
Belgrave Mews South *SW1* **249** E3
Belgrave Mews West *SW1* **249** E3
Belgrave Place *SW1* **249** E3
Belgrave Road *SW1* **249** F2
Belgrave Square *SW1* **249** E3
Belgrave Street *E1* **253** E3
Belgrove Street *WC1* **246** B4
Bell Lane *E1* **252** A4
Bell Street *NW1* **244** C3
Bell Yard *WC2* **246** C2
Belvedere Buildings *SE1* **251** E3
Belvedere Road *SE1* **250** C4
Ben Jonson Road *E1* **253** E4
Ben Smith Way *SE16* **252** C1
Benbow Street *SE8* **254** A1
Bendall Mews *W1* **245** D3
Bennet's Hill *EC4* **247** E1
*Castle Baynard Street*
Benson Quay *E1* **253** D3
Bentinck Mews *W1* **245** E2
*Marylebone Lane*
Bentinck Street *W1* **245** E2
Bere Street *E1* **253** E3
Bergen Square *SE16* **253** E1
Berkeley Gardens *W8* **248** A4
Berkeley Mews *W1* **245** D2
Berkeley Square *W1* **245** F1
Berkeley Street *W1* **245** F1
Bermondsey Square *SE1* **247** E2
*Long Lane*
Bermondsey Street *SE1* **252** A2
Bermondsey Wall East *SE16* **252** B1
Bermondsey Wall West *SE16* **252** B2
Bernard Street *WC1* **246** B3
Berners Mews *W1* **246** A2
Berners Street *W1* **246** A2
Berry Street *EC1* **247** E3
Berryfield Road *SE17* **251** E1
Berwick Street *W1* **246** A2
Bessborough Gardens *SW1* **250** B2
Bessborough Place *SW1* **250** A1
Bessborough Street *SW1* **250** A1
Betterton Street *WC2* **246** B2
Betts Street *E1* **252** C3
Bevenden Street *N1* **247** F4
Beverston Mews *W1* **245** D2
Bevin Close *SE16* **253** E2
Bevin Way *WC1* **246** C4
Bevington Street *SE16* **252** B1
Bevis Marks *EC3* **252** A4
Bewley Street *E1* **252** C3
Bickenhall Street *W1* **245** D3
Bidborough Street *WC1* **246** B4
Biddulph Road *W9* **244** A4
Bigland Street *E1* **252** C3
Billiter Square *EC3* **252** A3
*Fenchurch Avenue*
Billiter Street *EC3* **252** A3
Billson Street *E14* **254** C2
Bina Gardens *SW5* **248** B2
Bingham Place *W1* **245** E3
Binney Street *W1* **245** E1
Birchfield Street *E14* **253** E3
Birchin Lane *EC3* **247** F1
Bird Street *W1* **245** E2
Birdcage Walk *SW1* **250** A3
Birkenhead Street *WC1* **246** B4
Bishop's Court *EC4* **247** D2
*Old Bailey*
Bishop's Court *WC2* **246** C2
*Chancery Lane*
Bishop's Terrace *SE11* **251** D2
Bishops Bridge Road *W2* **244** B2
Bishopsgate *EC2* **247** F2
Bishopsgate Arcade *EC2* **252** A4
Bishopsgate Churchyard *EC2* **247** F2
Bittern Street *SE1* **251** E3
Black Prince Road *SE1 & SE11* **250** C2
Black Swan Yard *SE1* **252** A2
Blackall Street *EC2* **247** F3
Blackburne's Mews *W1* **245** E1
Blackfriars Bridge *EC4 & SE1* **247** D1
Blackfriars Lane *EC4* **247** D1
Blackfriars Passage *EC4* **247** D1
Blackfriars Road *SE1* **251** D4
Blacklands Terrace *SW3* **249** D2
Blackwall Tunnel *E14 & SE10* **254** C4
Blackwood Street *SE17* **251** F1
Blandford Square *NW1* **245** D3
Blandford Street *W1* **245** F2
Blasker Walk *E14* **254** A1
Bleeding Heart Yard *EC1* **247** D2
*Greville Street*
Blenheim Street *W1* **245** F1
*New Bond Street*
Bletchley Street *N1* **247** E4
Blithfield Street *W8* **248** A3
Blomfield Road *W9* **244** A3
Blomfield Street *EC2* **247** F2
Blomfield Villas *W2* **244** B2
Bloomburg Street *SW1* **249** F2
*Vauxhall Bridge Road*
Bloomfield Place *W1* **245** F1
*Bourdon Street*
Bloomfield Terrace *SW1* **249** E2
Bloomsbury Court *WC1* **246** B2
*High Holborn*
Bloomsbury Place *WC1* **246** B3
*Southampton Row*
Bloomsbury Square *WC1* **246** B2
Bloomsbury Street *WC1* **246** B2
Bloomsbury Way *WC1* **246** B2
Blount Street *E14* **253** E4
Blue Anchor Yard *E1* **252** B3
Blue Ball Yard *SW1* **250** A4
*St James's Street*
Blyth Close *E14* **254** C2
Bolsover Street *W1* **245** F3
Bolt Court *EC4* **247** D2
Bolton Gardens *SW5* **248** A2
Bolton Gardens Mews *SW10* **248** B1
Bolton Street *W1* **249** F4
Boltons Place *SW10* **248** B2
Bond Way *SW8* **250** B1
Bonding Yard Walk *SE16* **253** E1
Bonhill Street *EC2* **247** F3
Bonnington Square *SW8* **250** C1
Booker Close *E14* **253** F4
Boot Street *N1* **247** F4
Booth's Place *W1* **245** F2
*Wells Street*
Boreas Walk *N1* **247** E4
*Nelson Place*
Borough High Street *SE1* **251** E3
Borough Road *SE1* **251** E3
Borrett Close *SE17* **251** E1
Borthwick Street *SE8* **254** A1
Boscobel Place *SW1* **249** E2
Boscobel Street *NW8* **244** C3
Boss Street *SE1* **252** A2
Boston Place *NW1* **244** D3
Boswell Court *WC1* **246** B3
*Boswell Street*
Boswell Street *WC1* **246** B3
Botolph Lane *EC3* **247** F1
Bott's Mews *W2* **244** A2
Boulcott Street *E1* **253** E3
Boundary Lane *SE17* **251** E1
Boundary Road *SE1* **251** D4
Bourdon Street *W1* **245** F1
Bourlet Close *W1* **245** F2
Bourne Street *SW1* **249** E2
Bourne Terrace *W2* **244** A2
Bouverie Street *EC4* **247** D1
Bow Lane *EC4* **247** E1
Bow Street *WC2* **246** B2
Bowden Street *SE11* **251** D1
Bower Street *E1* **253** D3
Bowling Green Lane *EC1* **247** D3
Bowling Green Place *SE1* **251** F4
*Newcomen Street*
Bowling Green Street *SE11* **250** C1
Bowling Green Walk *N1* **247** F4
Boyd Street *E1* **252** B3
Boyfield Street *SE1* **251** D3
Boyle Street *W1* **245** F1
*Savile Row*
Boyson Road *SE17* **251** E1
Brackley Street *EC1* **247** E3
Brad Street *SE1* **251** D4
Braden Street *W9* **244** A3
Bradenham Close *SE17* **251** F1
Braganza Street *SE17* **251** D1
Braham Street *E1* **252** B3
Bramerton Street *SW3* **248** C1
Bramham Gardens *SW5* **248** A2
Branch Road *E14* **253** E3
Brandon Street *SE17* **251** E2
Brangton Road *SE11* **250** C1
Brass Tally Alley *SE16* **253** E1
Bray Crescent *SE16* **253** D2
Bray Place *SW3* **249** D2
Bread Street *EC4* **247** E1
Bream's Buildings *EC* **246** C2
Brechin Place *SW7* **248** B2
Breezer's Hill *E1* **252** C3
Bremner Road *SW7* **248** B3
Brendon Street *W1* **245** D2
Brenton Street *E14* **253** E4
Bressenden Place *SW1* **249** F3
Brettell Street *SE17* **251** F1
Brewer Street *W1* **246** A1
Brewers' Green *SW1* **250** A3
*Caxton Street*
Brewhouse Lane *E1* **252** C2
Brewhouse Walk *SE16* **253** E2
Brick Court *EC4* **246** C2
*Middle Temple Lane*
Brick Street *W1* **249** E4
Bride Lane *EC4* **247** D2
Bridewain Street *SE1* **252** B1
Bridewell Place *EC4* **247** D1
Bridford Mews *W1* **245** F3
Bridge House Quay *E14* **254** C4
Bridge Place *SW1* **249** F2
Bridge Street *SW1* **250** B3
Bridge Yard *SE1* **251** F4
Bridgeport Place *E1* **252** B2
*Kennet Street*
Bridgewater Square *EC2* **247** E3
*Beech Street*
Bridgewater Street *EC2* **247** E3
*Beech Street*
Bridgeway Street *NW1* **246** A2
Bridle Lane *W1* **246** A1
Bridstow Place *W2* **244** A2
Brightlingsea Place *E14* **253** F3
Brill Place *NW1* **246** A4
Briset Street *EC1* **247** D3
Bristol Gardens *W9* **244** A3
Bristol Mews *W9* **244** B3
Britannia Road *E14* **254** A2
Britannia Street *WC1* **246** C4
Britannia Walk *N1* **247** F4
Britten Street *SW3* **248** C1
Britton Street *EC1* **247** D3
Broad Court *WC2* **246** B2
Broad Sanctuary *SW1* **250** B3
Broad Walk *W2* **249** E4
Broadbent Street *W1* **245** F1
Broadley Street *NW8* **244** C4
Broadley Terrace *NW1* **245** D3
Broadstone Place *W1* **245** E2
Broadwall *SE1* **251** D4
Broadway *SW1* **250** A3
Broadwick Street *W1* **246** A1
Brockham Street *SE1* **251** E3
Brodlove Lane *E1* **253** D3
Bromley Street *E1* **253** E4
Brompton Place *SW3* **249** D3
Brompton Road *SW3* **249** D3
Brompton Square *SW3* **248** C3
Bronti Close *SE17* **251** E1
Brook Drive *SE11* **251** D2
Brook Gate *W1* **245** E1
Brook Mews North *W2* **244** B1

256

258

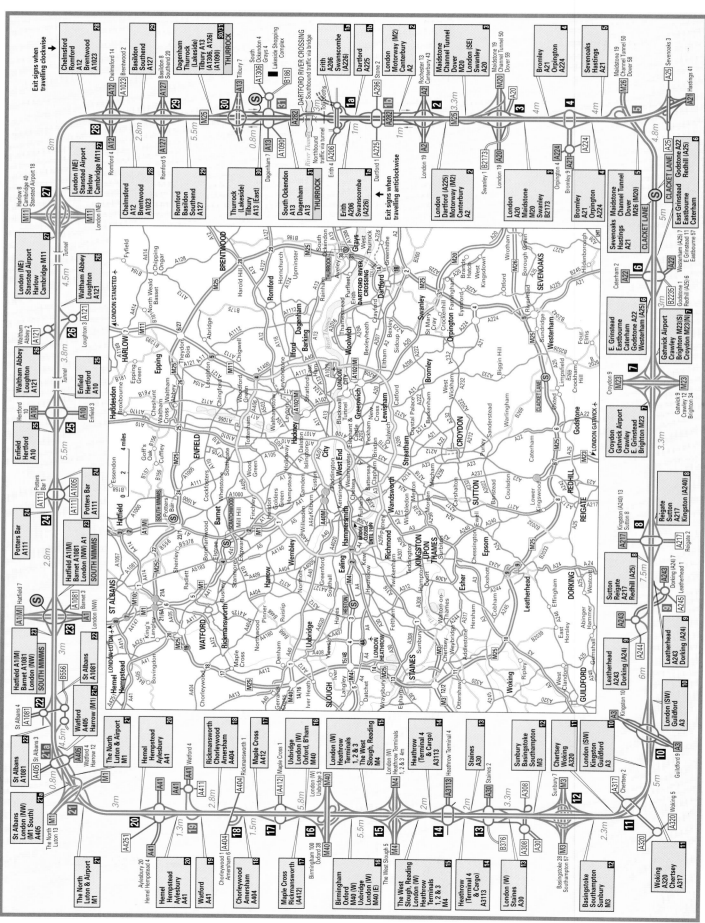

# the Channel Tunnel

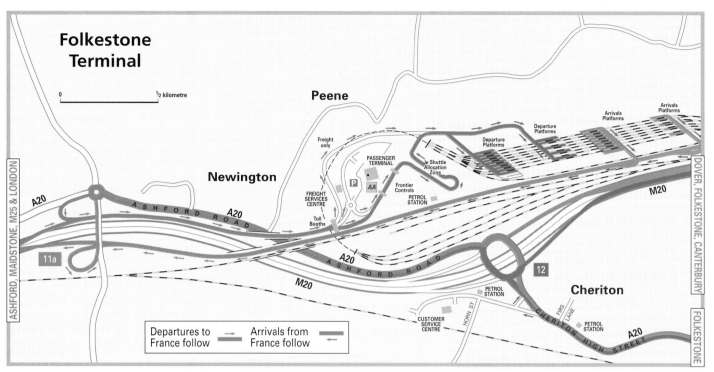

**Folkestone Terminal**

Peene

0 ½ kilometre

Newington

ASHFORD, MAIDSTONE, M25 & LONDON

A20

ASHFORD ROAD

A20

11a

M20

Freight only

PASSENGER TERMINAL

P

AA

FREIGHT SERVICES CENTRE

Frontier Controls

PETROL STATION

Toll Booths

A20

ASHFORD ROAD

le Shuttle Allocation Zone

Departure Platforms

Departure Platforms

Arrivals Platforms

Arrivals Platforms

M20

DOVER, FOLKESTONE, CANTERBURY

12

Cheriton

PETROL STATION

HORN ST

FIRS LANE

CHERITON HIGH STREET

PETROL STATION

A20

FOLKESTONE

CUSTOMER SERVICE CENTRE

| Departures to France follow → | Arrivals from France follow ← |
|---|---|

## Services to Europe

Eurotunnel Shuttle Service for cars, cars towing caravans and trailers, motorcycles, coaches and HGV vehicles, runs between terminals at Folkestone and Calais.

It takes just over one hour to travel from the M20 motorway in Kent, via the Channel Tunnel, to the A16 autoroute in France. The service runs 24 hours a day, 365 days of the year. Call Eurotunnel Call Centre (tel: 0990 353535) for the latest ticket and travel information.

Trains run at 15-minute intervals at peak times, with the journey in the tunnel from platform to platform taking just 35 minutes. Travellers pass through British and French frontier controls on departure, saving time on the other side of the Channel. Each terminal has tax-free and duty-free shops, bureaux de change, restaurants and a variety of shops. In Calais, the Cité de l'Europe contains numerous shops and restaurants, hotels and a hypermarket.

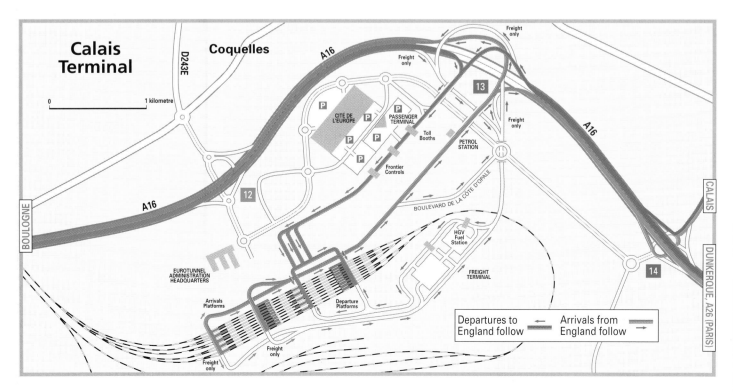

**Calais Terminal**

Coquelles

D243E

A16

Freight only

Freight only

Freight only

0 1 kilometre

P

CITÉ DE L'EUROPE

P

P

P

P

PASSENGER TERMINAL

Toll Booths

Frontier Controls

13

Freight only

PETROL STATION

A16

BOULOGNE

A16

12

BOULEVARD DE LA CÔTE D'OPALE

CALAIS

DUNKERQUE, A26 (PARIS)

14

EUROTUNNEL ADMINISTRATION HEADQUARTERS

Arrivals Platforms

Departure Platforms

HGV Fuel Station

FREIGHT TERMINAL

Freight only

Freight only

| Departures to England follow ← | Arrivals from England follow → |
|---|---|

# ports and airports

264

**London Heathrow Airport** – 16 miles west of London

**Telephone:** 0181 759 4321
**Parking:** short-stay, long-stay and business parking is available.
For charge details tel: 0800 844844 or 0345 405000
**Public Transport:** coach, bus, rail and London Underground.
There are several 4-star and 3-star hotels within easy reach of the airport.
Car hire facilities are available.

**London Gatwick Airport** – 35 miles south of London

**Telephone:** 01293 535353
**Parking:** short and long-stay parking is available at both the North and South terminals.
For charge details tel: 01293 502390 (short-stay) and either 0800 128128 or
0800 626671 (long-stay).
**Public Transport:** coach, bus and rail.
There are several 4-star and 3-star hotels within easy reach of the airport.
Car hire facilities are available.

**London Stansted Airport** – 36 miles north-east of London

**Telephone:** 01279 680500
**Parking:** short and long-stay open-air parking is available.
For charge details tel: 01279 681192
**Public Transport:** coach, bus and direct rail link to London on the 'Stansted Skytrain'.
There is one 4-star and one 3-star hotel within easy reach of the airport.
Car hire facilities are available.

**London Luton Airport**

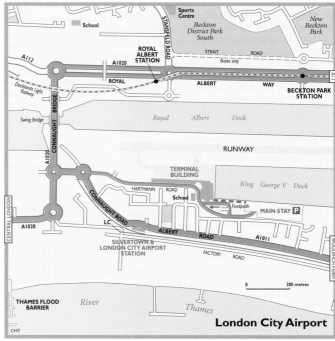

**London City Airport**

## London Luton Airport – 33 miles north of London

**Telephone:** 01582 405100
**Parking:** short and long-stay open-air parking is available.
**Public Transport:** coach, bus and rail.
There is one 2-star hotel at the airport and several 3-star hotels within easy reach of the airport.
Car hire facilities are available.

## London City Airport – 7 miles east of London

**Telephone:** 0171 646 0000
**Parking:** open-air parking is available.
For charge details tel: 0171 646 0088
**Public Transport:** shuttle-bus service into London. Easy access to the rail network and the London Underground.
There is a 4-star and 2-star hotel within easy reach of the airport.
Car hire facilities are available.

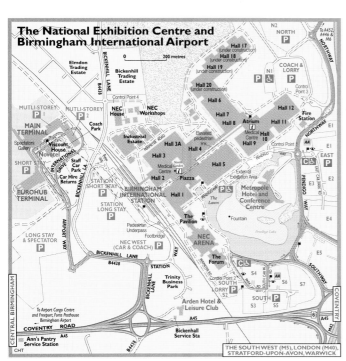

**The National Exhibition Centre and Birmingham International Airport**

**Manchester Airport**

## Birmingham International Airport – 8 miles east of Birmingham

**Telephone:** 0121 767 5511 (Main Terminal), 0121 767 7502 (Eurohub Terminal)
**Parking:** short and long-stay parking is available.
For charge details tel: 0121 767 7861
**Public Transport:** shuttle-bus service to Birmingham International railway station and the NEC.
There are several 3-star hotels within easy reach of the airport.
Car hire facilities are available.

## Manchester Airport – 10 miles south of Manchester

**Telephone:** 0161 489 3000
**Parking:** short and long-stay parking is available.
**Public Transport:** bus, coach and rail. Manchester airport railway station connects with the rail network.
There are several 4-star and 3-star hotels within easy reach of the airport.
Car hire facilities are available.

# major airports

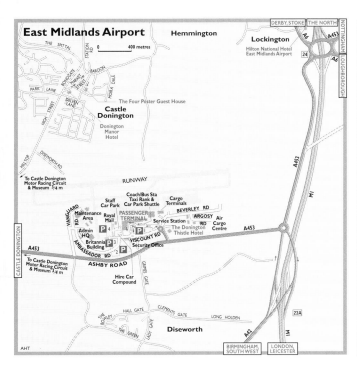

## East Midlands Airport – 15 miles south-west of Nottingham, next to the M1 at junctions 23A and 24

**Telephone:** 01332 852852
**Parking:** short and long-stay parking is available.
For charge details tel: 0800 128128
**Public Transport:** bus and coach services to major towns and cities in the East Midlands.
There is one 4-star and several 3-star hotels within easy reach of the airport.
Car hire facilities are available.

## Aberdeen Airport – 6 miles north-west of Aberdeen

**Telephone:** 01224 722331
**Parking:** open-air parking is available.
For charge details tel: 01224 722331 ext 5142
**Public Transport:** bus to central Aberdeen and Dyce Station.
There are several 4-star and 3-star hotels within easy reach of the airport.
Car hire facilities are available.

## Edinburgh Airport – 7 miles west of Edinburgh

**Telephone:** 0131 333 1000
**Parking:** open-air parking is available.
For charge details tel: 0131 344 3197
**Public Transport:** regular coach services operate between central Edinburgh and Glasgow.
There is one 4-star and several 3-star hotels within easy reach of the airport.
Car hire facilities are available.

## Glasgow Airport – 8 miles west of Glasgow

**Telephone:** 0141 887 1111
**Parking:** short and long-stay parking is available, mostly open-air.
For charge details tel: 0141 889 2751
**Public Transport:** regular coach services operate between central Glasgow and Edinburgh.
There are several 3-star hotels within easy reach of the airport.
Car hire facilities are available.

266

# major ports

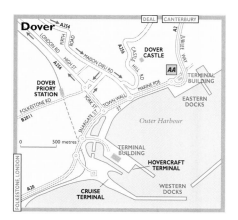

Pay-and-display parking is available at the Dover Eastern Docks and at the Hovercraft Terminal.
**For further information tel: 01304 240400**
Other long-stay parking facilities are available with a collection and delivery service.
**For charge details tel: 01304 201227**

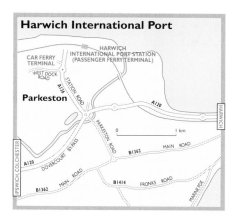

Open-air parking is available at the terminal.
**For charge details tel: 01255 242000**
Further parking is available 5 miles from Harwich International Port with a collection and delivery service.
**For charge details tel: 01255 870217**

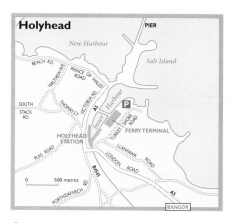

Open-air pay-and-display parking is available close to the Ferry Terminal.
**For charge details tel: 01407 762304 or 606782**

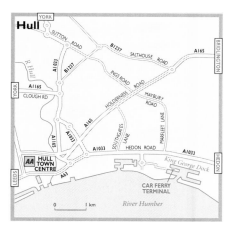

Free open-air parking is available at King George Dock (left at owners' risk).
**Tel: 01482 795141**
Undercover parking is also available.
**For charge details tel: 01482 781021**

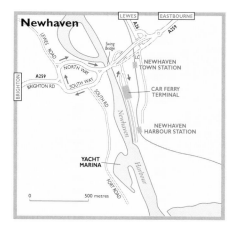

Open and limited parking is available within the harbour complex.
**For charge details tel: 01273 514131**

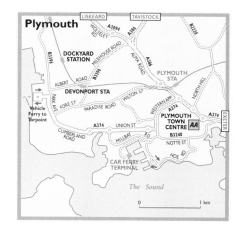

Free open-air parking is available outside the terminal building.
**Tel: 0990 360360 or 01752 252200**

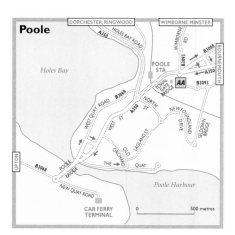

Open-air parking for 600 vehicles is available adjacent to the Ferry Terminal.
**For charge details tel: 01202 440220**

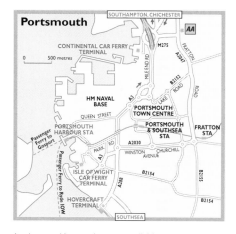

Lock-up parking services are available at Albert Johnson Quay.
**For charge details tel: 01705 751261**
Pay-and-display parking is available opposite the Hovercraft Terminal. Multi-storey parking is also available close to the Isle of Wight Passenger Ferry Terminal.
**For charge details tel: 01705 823153 or 812071**

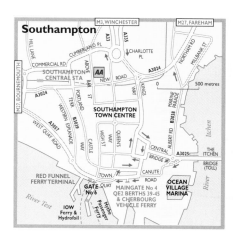

Covered or fenced compound parking for 1,600 vehicles is available within the Western Docks with a collection and delivery service.
**For charge details tel: 01703 228001/2/3**

# index to place names

Each place name entry in this index is identified by its County, County Borough or Council Area name. These are shown in *italics*.

A list of the abbreviated forms used is shown on the left.

To locate a place name in the atlas turn to the map page indicated in bold type in the index and use the 4-figure grid reference.

For example, **Hythe** *Kent* **29** 16**3**4 is found on page 29.

To pin-point our example the first bold figure '**1**' is found along the bottom edge of the page.

The following figure '6' indicates how many imaginary tenths to move east of the line '**1**'.

The next bold figure '**3**' is found up the left-hand side of the page.

The last figure '4' shows how many imaginary tenths to move north of the line '**3**'. You will locate Hythe where these two lines intersect.

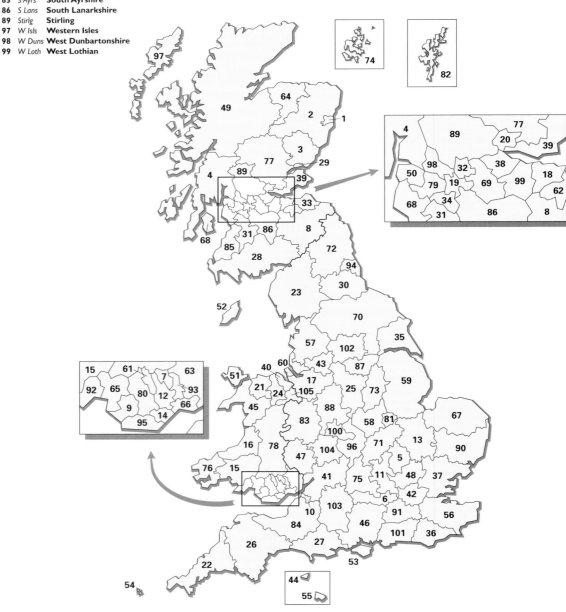

A'Chill Anlaby

269

# A


A'Chill Highld 128 2705
Ab Kettleby Leics 63 7223
Ab Lench Worcs 47 0151
Abbas Combe Somset 22 7022
Abberley Worcs 47 7567
Abberley Common Worcs 47 7467
Abberton Essex 41 0019
Abberton Worcs 47 9953
Abberwick Nthumb 111 1313
Abbess Roding Essex 40 5711
Abbey Devon 9 1410
Abbey Dore Herefd 46 3830
Abbey Green Staffs 72 9757
Abbey Hill Somset 10 2718
Abbey St Bathans Border 119 7661
Abbey Town Cumb 93 1750
Abbey Village Lancs 81 6422
Abbey Wood Gt Lon 27 4779
Abbeycwmhir Powys 45 0571
Abbeydale S York 74 3281
Abbeystead Lancs 81 5654
Abbot's Chair Derbys 74 0290
Abbot's Salford Warwks 48 0650
Abbotrule Border 110 6113
Abbots Bickington Devon 18 3813
Abbots Bromley Staffs 73 0724
Abbots Deuglie P & K 126 1111
Abbots Langley Herts 26 0901
Abbots Leigh Somset 34 5474
Abbots Morton Worcs 48 0255
Abbots Ripton Cambs 52 2377
Abbots Worthy Hants 24 4932
Abbotsbury Dorset 10 5785
Abbotsham Devon 18 4226
Abbotskerswell Devon 7 8568
Abbotsleigh Devon 7 8048
Abbotsley Cambs 52 2256
Abbotstone Hants 24 5634
Abbotswood Hants 23 3623
Abbott Street Dorset 11 9800
Abbotts Ann Hants 23 3243
Abcott Shrops 46 3978
Abdon Shrops 59 5786
Abenhall Gloucs 35 6717
Aber Gwynd 69 6572
Aber Clydach Powys 33 1021
Aber-arad Carmth 31 3140
Aber-banc Cerdgn 31 3541
Aber-giar Carmth 44 5040
Aber-Magwr Cerdgn 43 6673
Aber-meurig Cerdgn 44 5656
Aber-nant Rhondd 33 0103
Aberaeron Cerdgn 42 4562
Aberaman Rhondd 33 0100
Aberangell Gwynd 57 8410
Aberarder Highld 140 6225
Aberargie P & K 126 1615
Aberarth Cerdgn 42 4763
Aberavon Neath 32 7489
Aberbargoed Caerph 33 1500
Aberbeeg Blae G 33 2002
Abercairny P & K 125 9222
Abercanaid Myr Td 33 0503
Abercarn Caerph 33 2194
Abercastle Pembks 30 8533
Abercegir Powys 57 8001
Aberchalder Lodge Highld 131 3403
Aberchirder Abers 142 6252
Abercoed Cerdgn 44 6757
Abercraf Powys 33 8212
Abercregan Neath 33 8496
Abercwmboi Rhondd 33 0299
Abercych Pembks 31 2441
Abercynon Rhondd 33 0794
Aberdalgie P & K 125 0720
Aberdare Rhondd 33 0002
Aberdaron Gwynd 56 1726
Aberdeen Aber C 135 9306
Aberdesach Gwynd 68 4251
Aberdour Fife 117 1985
Aberdulais Neath 32 7799
Aberdyfi Gwynd 43 6196
Aberedw Powys 45 0847
Abereiddy Pembks 30 7931
Abererch Gwynd 56 3936
Aberfan Myr Td 33 0700
Aberfeldy P & K 125 8549
Aberffraw IOA 68 3569
Aberffrwd Cerdgn 43 6878
Aberford W York 83 4337
Aberfoyle Stirlg 115 5200
Abergarw Brdgnd 33 9184
Abergarwed Neath 33 8102
Abergavenny Mons 34 2914
Abergele Conwy 70 9477
Abergorlech Carmth 44 5833
Abergwesyn Powys 45 8552
Abergwili Carmth 31 4320
Abergwydol Powys 57 7903
Abergwynfi Neath 33 8995
Abergynolwyn Gwynd 57 6806
Aberhafesp Powys 58 0792
Aberhosan Powys 43 8197
Aberkenfig Brdgnd 33 8984
Aberlady E Loth 118 4679
Aberlemno Angus 127 5255
Aberllefenni Powys 57 7609
Aberllynfi Powys 45 1737
Aberlour Moray 141 2642
Abermorddu Flints 71 3056
Abermule Powys 58 1694
Abernant Carmth 31 3323
Abernethy P & K 126 1816
Abernyte P & K 126 2531
Aberporth Cerdgn 42 2651
Abersoch Gwynd 56 3127
Abersychan Torfn 34 2603
Aberthin V Glam 33 0074
Abertillery Blae G 33 2104
Abertridwr Caerph 33 1289
Abertridwr Powys 58 0319
Abertysswg Caerph 33 1305
Aberuthven P & K 125 9615
Aberyscir Powys 45 9929
Aberystwyth Cerdgn 43 5881
Abingdon Oxon 37 4997
Abinger Surrey 14 1145
Abinger Hammer Surrey 14 0947
Abington Nhants 50 7861
Abington S Lans 108 9323
Abington Pigotts Cambs 39 3044
Ablington Gloucs 36 1007
Ablington Wilts 23 1546
Abney Derbys 74 1980
Above Church Staffs 73 0150
Aboyne Abers 134 5298
Abram Gt Man 78 6001
Abriachan Highld 139 5535
Abridge Essex 27 4696
Abson Gloucs 35 7074
Abthorpe Nhants 49 6446
Aby Lincs 77 4078
Acaster Malbis N York 83 5845
Acaster Selby N York 83 5741
Accott Devon 19 6432
Accrington Lancs 81 7628
Acha Ag & B 120 1854
Acha Mor W Isls 152 3029
Achahoish Ag & B 113 7877
Achalader P & K 126 1245
Achaleven Ag & B 122 9233
Achanalt Highld 139 2661
Achandunie Highld 146 6472
Achany Highld 146 5602
Acharacle Highld 121 6767
Acharn Highld 122 7050
Acharn P & K 124 7543
Achavanich Highld 151 1842
Achduart Highld 145 0403
Achfary Highld 148 2939
Achiltibuie Highld 144 0208
Achinhoan Ag & B 105 7516
Achintee Highld 138 9441
Achintraid Highld 138 8438
Achlain Highld 131 2812
Achmelvich Highld 148 0524
Achmore Highld 138 8533
Achmore W Isls 152 3029
Achnacarnin Highld 148 0432
Achnacarry Highld 131 1787
Achnacloich Highld 129 5908
Achnaconeran Highld 139 4118
Achnacroish Ag & B 122 8541
Achnadrish Lodge Ag & B 121 4652
Achnafauld P & K 125 8736
Achnagarron Highld 146 6870
Achnaha Highld 128 4668
Achnahaird Highld 144 0013
Achnairn Highld 146 5512
Achnalea Highld 130 8561
Achnamara Ag & B 113 7887
Achnasheen Highld 138 1658
Achnashellach Station Highld 138 0048
Achnastank Moray 141 2733
Achosnich Highld 121 4467
Achranich Highld 122 7047
Achreamie Highld 150 0166
Achriabhach Highld 131 1468
Achriesgill Highld 148 2554
Achtoty Highld 149 6762
Achurch Nhants 51 0283
Achvaich Highld 146 7194
Ackergill Highld 151 3553
Acklam N York 97 4817
Acklam N York 90 7861
Ackleton Shrops 60 7698
Acklington Nthumb 103 2301
Ackton W York 83 4121
Ackworth Moor Top W York 83 4316
Acle Norfk 67 4010
Acock's Green W Mids 61 1283
Acol Kent 29 3067
Acomb N York 83 5651
Acomb Nthumb 102 9366
Acombe Somset 9 1914
Aconbury Herefd 46 5133
Acre Lancs 81 7924
Acrefair Wrexhm 70 2743
Acresford Derbys 61 2913
Acton Ches 71 6352
Acton Dorset 11 9978
Acton Gt Lon 26 2080
Acton Shrops 59 3185
Acton Staffs 72 8241
Acton Suffk 54 8945
Acton Worcs 47 8467
Acton Beauchamp Herefd 47 6850
Acton Bridge Ches 71 5975
Acton Burnell Shrops 59 5302
Acton Green Herefd 47 6950
Acton Park Wrexhm 71 3451
Acton Pigott Shrops 59 5402
Acton Round Shrops 59 6395
Acton Scott Shrops 59 4589
Acton Trussell Staffs 72 9318
Acton Turville Gloucs 35 8080
Adbaston Staffs 72 7627
Adber Dorset 21 5920
Adbolton Notts 62 5938
Adderbury Oxon 49 4735
Adderley Shrops 72 6640
Adderstone Nthumb 111 1330
Addiewell W Loth 117 9962
Addingham W York 82 0749
Addington Bucks 49 7428
Addington Gt Lon 27 3664
Addington Kent 28 6559
Addiscombe Gt Lon 27 3366
Addlestone Surrey 26 0564
Addlestonemoor Surrey 26 0565
Addlethorpe Lincs 77 5468
Adeney Shrops 72 6918
Adeyfield Herts 38 0708
Adfa Powys 58 0601
Adforton Herefd 46 4071
Adisham Kent 29 2253
Adlestrop Gloucs 48 2426
Adlingfleet E R Yk 84 8421
Adlington Ches 79 9180
Adlington Lancs 81 6013
Admaston Shrops 59 6313
Admaston Staffs 73 0423
Admington Warwks 48 2045
Adsborough Somset 20 2729
Adscombe Somset 20 1837
Adstock Bucks 49 7329
Adstone Nhants 49 5951
Adswood Gt Man 79 8888
Adversane W Susx 14 0723
Advie Highld 141 1234
Adwalton W York 82 2328
Adwell Oxon 37 6999
Adwick Le Street S York 83 5308
Adwick upon Dearne S York 83 4701
Ae D & G 100 9889
Ae Bridgend D & G 100 0186
Affetside Gt Man 81 7513
Affleck Abers 142 5540
Affpuddle Dorset 11 8093
Affric Lodge Highld 138 1822
Afon-wen Flints 70 1371
Afton Devon 7 8462
Afton IOW 12 3486
Agglethorpe N York 89 0885
Aigburth Mersyd 78 3886
Aike E R Yk 84 0446
Aiketgate Cumb 94 4846
Aikhead Cumb 93 2349
Aikton Cumb 93 2753
Ailby Lincs 77 4376
Ailey Herefd 46 3348
Ailsworth Cambs 64 1198
Ainderby Quernhow N York 89 3480
Ainderby Steeple N York 89 3392
Aingers Green Essex 41 1120
Ainsdale Mersyd 80 3112
Ainsdale-on-Sea Mersyd 80 2912
Ainstable Cumb 94 5246
Ainsworth Gt Man 79 7610
Ainthorpe N York 90 7007
Aintree Mersyd 78 3898
Ainville W Loth 117 1063
Aird Ag & B 113 7600
Aird D & G 98 0960
Aird W Isls 152 5635
Aird a Mhulaidh W Isls 152 1810
Aird Asaig W Isls 152 1202
Aird Dhubh Highld 137 7040
Aird of Kinloch Ag & B 121 5228
Aird of Sleat Highld 129 5900
Aird Uig W Isls 152 0533
Airdeny Ag & B 122 9929
Airdrie N Lans 116 7565
Airdriehill N Lans 116 7867
Airds Bay Ag & B 122 9932
Airds of Kells D & G 99 6770
Airidh a bhruaich W Isls 152 2417
Airieland D & G 99 7556
Airlie Angus 126 3150
Airmyn E R Yk 84 7224
Airntully P & K 125 0935
Airor Highld 129 7205
Airth Falk 116 9087
Airton N York 88 9059
Aisby Lincs 76 8692
Aisby Lincs 64 0138
Aisgill Cumb 88 7797
Aish Devon 7 6960
Aish Devon 7 8458
Aisholt Somset 20 1935
Aiskew N York 89 2788
Aislaby Dur 89 4012
Aislaby N York 90 8608
Aislaby N York 90 7785
Aisthorpe Lincs 76 9480
Aith Shet 153 3455
Akeld Nthumb 111 9529
Akeley Bucks 49 7037
Akenham Suffk 54 1449
Albaston Devon 6 4270
Alberbury Shrops 59 3614
Albourne W Susx 15 2516
Albourne Green W Susx 15 2616
Albrighton Shrops 59 4918
Albrighton Shrops 60 8004
Alburgh Norfk 55 2687
Albury Herts 39 4324
Albury Oxon 37 6505
Albury Surrey 14 0447
Albury End Herts 39 4223
Albury Heath Surrey 14 0646
Alby Hill Norfk 67 1934
Alcaig Highld 139 5657
Alcaston Shrops 59 4587
Alcester Warwks 48 0857
Alcester Lane End W Mids 61 0780
Alciston E Susx 16 5005
Alcombe Wilts 35 8169
Alconbury Cambs 52 1875
Alconbury Weston Cambs 52 1777
Aldborough N York 89 4066
Aldborough Norfk 66 1834
Aldbourne Wilts 36 2676
Aldbrough E R Yk 85 2438
Aldbrough St John N York 89 2011
Aldbury Herts 38 9612
Aldcliffe Lancs 87 4660
Aldclune P & K 132 8964
Aldeburgh Suffk 55 4656
Aldeby Norfk 67 4493
Aldenham Herts 26 1498
Alder Moor Staffs 73 2226
Alderbury Wilts 23 1827
Aldercar Derbys 62 4447
Alderford Norfk 66 1218
Alderholt Dorset 12 1212
Alderley Gloucs 35 7690
Alderley Edge Ches 79 8478
Aldermans Green W Mids 61 3683
Aldermaston Berks 24 5965
Alderminster Warwks 48 2348
Aldershot Hants 25 8650
Alderton Gloucs 47 0033
Alderton Nhants 49 7446
Alderton Shrops 59 4924
Alderton Suffk 55 3441
Alderton Wilts 35 8482
Alderwasley Derbys 73 3053
Aldfield N York 89 2669
Aldford Ches 71 4159
Aldgate Rutlnd 63 9804
Aldham Essex 40 9126
Aldham Suffk 54 0545
Aldingbourne W Susx 14 9205
Aldingham Cumb 86 2870
Aldington Kent 29 0736
Aldington Worcs 48 0644
Aldington Corner Kent 29 0636
Aldivalloch Moray 141 3526
Aldochlay Ag & B 115 3591
Aldon Shrops 46 4379
Aldoth Cumb 92 1448
Aldreth Cambs 53 4473
Aldridge W Mids 61 0500
Aldringham Suffk 55 4461
Aldro N York 90 8162
Aldsworth Gloucs 36 1509
Aldsworth W Susx 14 7608
Aldunie Moray 141 3626
Aldwark Derbys 74 2257
Aldwark N York 89 4663
Aldwick W Susx 14 9198
Aldwincle Nhants 51 0081
Aldworth Berks 37 5579
Alexandria W Duns 115 3979
Aley Somset 20 1838
Alfardisworthy Devon 18 2911
Alfington Devon 9 1197
Alfold Surrey 14 0333
Alfold Bars W Susx 14 0333
Alfold Crossways Surrey 14 0335
Alford Abers 142 5715
Alford Lincs 77 4575
Alford Somset 21 6032
Alfreton Derbys 74 4155
Alfrick Worcs 47 7453
Alfrick Pound Worcs 47 7452
Alfriston E Susx 16 5103
Algarkirk Lincs 64 2935
Alhampton Somset 21 6234
Alkborough Lincs 84 8821
Alkerton Gloucs 35 7705
Alkerton Oxon 48 3743
Alkham Kent 29 2542
Alkington Shrops 71 5339
Alkmonton Derbys 73 1838
All Cannings Wilts 23 0661
All Saints South Elmham Suffk 55 3482
All Stretton Shrops 59 4595
Allaleigh Devon 7 8053
Allanaquoich Abers 133 1291
Allanbank N Lans 116 8458
Allanton Border 119 8654
Allanton N Lans 116 8457
Allanton S Lans 116 7454
Allaston Gloucs 35 6304
Allbrook Hants 13 4521
Allen End Warwks 61 1696
Allen's Green Herts 39 4516
Allendale Nthumb 95 8355
Allenheads Nthumb 95 8645
Allensford Dur 95 0750
Allensmore Herefd 46 4635
Allenton Derbys 62 3732
Aller Devon 19 7625
Aller Somset 21 4029
Allerby Cumb 92 0839
Allercombe Devon 9 0494
Allerford Somset 20 9046
Allerston N York 90 8782
Allerthorpe E R Yk 84 7847
Allerton Mersyd 78 3987
Allerton W York 82 1234
Allerton Bywater W York 83 4227
Allerton Mauleverer N York 89 4157
Allesley W Mids 61 3080
Allestree Derbys 62 3439
Allet Common Cnwll 3 7948
Allexton Leics 51 8100
Allgreave Ches 72 9767
Allhallows Kent 28 8377
Allhallows-on-Sea Kent 40 8478
Alligin Shuas Highld 137 8357
Allimore Green Staffs 72 8519
Allington Dorset 10 4693
Allington Kent 28 7557
Allington Lincs 63 8540
Allington Wilts 35 8975
Allington Wilts 23 0663
Allington Wilts 23 2039
Allithwaite Cumb 87 3876
Alloa Clacks 116 8892
Allonby Cumb 92 0842
Allostock Ches 79 7471
Alloway S Ayrs 106 3318
Allowenshay Somset 10 3913
Allscott Shrops 59 6113
Allscott Shrops 60 7396
Alltami Flints 70 2665
Alltchaorunn Highld 123 1951
Alltmawr Powys 45 0746
Alltwalis Carmth 31 4431
Alltwen Neath 32 7303
Alltyblaca Cerdgn 44 5245
Allweston Dorset 11 6614
Allwood Green Suffk 54 0472
Almeley Herefd 46 3351
Almeley Wooton Herefd 46 3352
Almer Dorset 11 9199
Almholme S York 83 5808
Almington Staffs 72 7034
Almodington W Susx 14 8297
Almondbank P & K 125 0625
Almondbury W York 82 1614
Almondsbury Gloucs 34 6084
Alne N York 90 4965
Alnesbourn Priory Suffk 55 1940
Alness Highld 146 6569
Alnham Nthumb 111 9810
Alnmouth Nthumb 111 2410
Alnwick Nthumb 111 1813
Alperton Gt Lon 26 1883
Alphamstone Essex 54 8735
Alpheton Suffk 54 8750
Alphington Devon 9 9190
Alpington Norfk 67 2901
Alport Derbys 74 2264
Alpraham Ches 71 5859
Alresford Essex 41 0621
Alrewas Staffs 61 1614
Alsager Ches 72 7955
Alsagers Bank Staffs 72 7948
Alsop en le Dale Derbys 73 1554
Alston Cumb 94 7146
Alston Devon 10 3002
Alston Sutton Somset 21 4151
Alstone Gloucs 47 9832
Alstone Somset 21 3146
Alstone Green Staffs 72 8518
Alstonefield Staffs 73 1355
Alswear Devon 19 7222
Alt Gt Man 79 9403
Altandhu Highld 144 9812
Altarnun Cnwll 5 2281
Altass Highld 146 5000
Altcreich Ag & B 122 6938
Altgaltraig Ag & B 114 0473
Altham Lancs 81 7732
Althorne Essex 40 9198
Althorpe Lincs 84 8309
Altnabreac Station Highld 150 0045
Altnacraig Ag & B 122 8429
Altnaharra Highld 149 5635
Altofts W York 83 3823
Alton Derbys 74 3664
Alton Hants 24 7139
Alton Staffs 73 0741
Alton Wilts 23 1546
Alton Barnes Wilts 23 1062
Alton Pancras Dorset 11 7002
Alton Priors Wilts 23 1162
Altrincham Gt Man 79 7687
Altskeith Hotel Stirlg 124 4602
Alva Clacks 116 8897
Alvah Abers 142 6760
Alvanley Ches 71 4974
Alvaston Derbys 62 3833
Alvechurch Worcs 60 0272
Alvecote Warwks 61 2404
Alvediston Wilts 22 9723
Alveley Shrops 60 7584
Alverdiscott Devon 19 5225
Alverstoke Hants 13 6098
Alverstone IOW 13 5785
Alverthorpe W York 82 3121
Alverton Notts 63 7942
Alves Moray 141 1362
Alvescot Oxon 36 2704
Alveston Gloucs 35 6388
Alveston Warwks 48 2356
Alvingham Lincs 77 3691
Alvington Gloucs 34 6000
Alwalton Cambs 64 1396
Alwinton Nthumb 110 9106
Alwoodley W York 82 2840
Alwoodley Gates W York 82 3140
Alyth P & K 126 2448
Amber Hill Lincs 76 2346
Amber Row Derbys 74 3856
Ambergate Derbys 74 3451
Amberley Gloucs 35 8501
Amberley W Susx 14 0213
Amberstone E Susx 16 5911
Amble Nthumb 103 2604
Amblecote W Mids 60 8985
Ambler Thorn W York 82 0929
Ambleside Cumb 87 3704
Ambleston Pembks 30 0025
Ambrosden Oxon 37 6019
Amcotts Lincs 84 8514
America Cambs 53 4378
Amersham Bucks 26 9597
Amersham on the Hill Bucks 26 9798
Amerton Staffs 73 9927
Amesbury Wilts 23 1541
Amhuinnsuidhe W Isls 152 0408
Amington Staffs 61 2304
Amisfield Town D & G 100 0082
Amlwch IOA 68 4492
Ammanford Carmth 32 6212
Amotherby N York 90 7473
Ampfield Hants 13 4023
Ampleforth N York 90 5878
Ampney Crucis Gloucs 36 0601
Ampney St Mary Gloucs 36 0802
Ampney St Peter Gloucs 36 0801
Amport Hants 23 3044
Ampthill Beds 38 0337
Ampton Suffk 54 8671
Amroth Pembks 31 1608
Amulree P & K 125 8936
Amwell Herts 39 1613
An T-ob W Isls 152 0286
Anaheilt Highld 130 8162
Ancaster Lincs 63 9843
Anchor Shrops 58 1785
Ancroft Nthumb 111 9945
Ancrum Border 110 6224
Ancton W Susx 14 9800
Anderby Lincs 77 5275
Andersea Somset 21 3333
Andersfield Somset 20 2434
Anderson Dorset 11 8897
Anderton Ches 79 6475
Anderton Cnwll 6 4351
Andover Hants 23 3645
Andoversford Gloucs 35 0219
Andreas IOM 158 4199
Anelog Gwynd 56 1527
Anerley Gt Lon 27 3369
Anfield Mersyd 78 3692
Angarrack Cnwll 2 5838
Angarrick Cnwll 3 7937
Angelbank Shrops 46 5776
Angersleigh Somset 20 1918
Angerton Cumb 93 2257
Angle Pembks 30 8603
Angmering W Susx 14 0604
Angram N York 88 8899
Angram N York 83 5248
Angrouse Cnwll 2 6619
Anick Nthumb 102 9465
Ankerville Highld 147 8174
Ankle Hill Leics 63 7518
Anlaby E R Yk 84 0328

Avoch
Bath Side
271

Avoch Highld 140 7055
Avon Dorset 12 1498
Avon Dassett Warwks 49 4150
Avonbridge Falk 116 9172
Avonmouth Bristl 34 5178
Avonwick Devon 7 7158
Awbridge Hants 12 3224
Awkley Gloucs 34 5985
Awliscombe Devon 9 1301
Awre Gloucs 35 7008
Awsworth Notts 62 4844
Axborough Worcs 60 8579
Axbridge Somset 21 4354
Axford Hants 24 6043
Axford Wilts 36 2370
Axminster Devon 10 2998
Axmouth Devon 10 2591
Axton Flints 70 1080
Aycliffe Dur 96 2822
Aydon Nthumb 103 0065
Aylburton Gloucs 34 6101
Ayle Cumb 94 7149
Aylesbeare Devon 9 0392
Aylesbury Bucks 38 8213
Aylesby Lincs 85 2007
Aylesford Kent 28 7359
Aylesham Kent 29 2452
Aylestone Leics 50 5700
Aylestone Park Leics 50 5800
Aylmerton Norfk 66 1839
Aylsham Norfk 67 1926
Aylton Gloucs 47 6537
Aylworth Gloucs 36 1021
Aymestrey Herefd 46 4265
Aynho Nhants 49 5133
Ayot Green Herts 39 2214
Ayot St Lawrence Herts 39 1916
Ayot St Peter Herts 39 2115
Ayr S Ayrs 106 3321
Aysgarth N York 88 0088
Ayshford Devon 9 0415
Ayside Cumb 87 3983
Ayston Rutlnd 51 8600
Aythorpe Roding Essex 40 5815
Ayton Border 119 9260
Azerley N York 89 2574

# B

Babbacombe Devon 7 9265
Babbington Notts 62 4943
Babbinswood Shrops 59 3329
Babbs Green Herts 39 3916
Babcary Somset 21 5628
Babel Carmth 44 8235
Babel Green Suffk 53 7348
Babell Flints 70 1573
Babeny Devon 7 6775
Babington Somset 22 7051
Bablock Hythe Oxon 36 4304
Babraham Cambs 53 5150
Babworth Notts 75 6880
Bachau IOA 68 4383
Bache Shrops 59 4681
Bacheldre Powys 58 2492
Bachelor's Bump E Susx 17 8412
Back o' th' Brook Staffs 73 0751
Back of Keppoch Highld 129 6587
Back Street Suffk 53 7458
Backaland Ork 153 5630
Backbarrow Cumb 87 3584
Backe Carmth 31 2615
Backfolds Abers 143 0252
Backford Ches 71 3971
Backford Cross Ches 71 3873
Backies Highld 147 8302
Backlass Highld 151 2053
Backwell Somset 21 4968
Backworth T & W 103 3072
Bacon's End W Mids 61 1888
Baconsthorpe Norfk 66 1236
Bacton Herefd 46 3732
Bacton Norfk 67 3433
Bacton Suffk 54 0567
Bacton Green Suffk 54 0365
Bacup Lancs 81 8622
Badachro Highld 137 7873
Badbury Wilts 36 1980
Badby Nhants 49 5658
Badcall Highld 148 1541
Badcall Highld 148 2455
Badcaul Highld 144 0291
Baddeley Edge Staffs 72 9150
Baddeley Green Staffs 72 9151
Baddesley Clinton Warwks 61 2072
Baddesley Ensor Warwks 61 2798
Baddidarrach Highld 145 0822
Baddinsgill Border 117 1254
Badenscoth Abers 142 6938
Badenyon Abers 141 3319
Badgall Cnwll 5 2486
Badgeney Cambs 65 4397
Badger Shrops 60 7699
Badger's Cross Cnwll 2 4833
Badgers Mount Kent 27 4962
Badgeworth Gloucs 35 9019
Badgworth Somset 21 3952
Badharlick Cnwll 5 2686
Badicaul Highld 137 7529
Badingham Suffk 55 3068
Badlesmere Kent 28 0153
Badlieu Border 108 0518
Badlipster Highld 151 2448
Badluachrach Highld 144 9994
Badninish Highld 147 7594
Badrallach Highld 145 0691
Badsey Worcs 48 0743
Badshot Lea Surrey 25 8648
Badsworth W York 83 4614
Badwell Ash Suffk 54 9868
Badwell Green Suffk 54 0169
Bag Enderby Lincs 77 3571
Bagber Dorset 11 7513
Bagby N York 89 4680
Bagendon Gloucs 35 0106
Bagginswood Shrops 60 6881
Baggrow Cumb 93 1741
Bagh a Chaisteil W Isls 152 6698
Bagham Kent 29 0753
Bagillt Flints 70 2175
Baginton Warwks 61 3474
Baglan Neath 32 7492
Bagley Shrops 59 4027
Bagley Somset 21 4645
Bagley W York 82 2235
Bagmore Hants 24 6544
Bagnall Staffs 72 9250
Bagnor Berks 24 4569
Bagot Shrops 46 5873
Bagshot Surrey 25 9063
Bagshot Wilts 23 3165
Bagstone Gloucs 35 6987
Bagthorpe Notts 75 4651
Bagworth Leics 62 4408
Bagwy Llydiart Herefd 46 4426
Baildon W York 82 1539
Baildon Green W York 82 1439
Baile a Mhanaich W Isls 152 7755
Baile Ailein W Isls 152 2920
Baile Mor Ag & B 120 2824
Bailey Green Hants 13 6627
Baileyhead Cumb 101 5179
Bailiff Bridge W York 82 1425
Baillieston C Glas 116 6764
Bailrigg Lancs 87 4858
Bainbridge N York 88 9390
Bainshole Abers 142 6035
Bainton Cambs 64 0906
Bainton E R Yk 84 9652
Bainton Oxon 49 5827
Baintown Fife 126 3503
Bairnkine Border 110 6515
Baker Street Essex 40 6381
Baker's End Herts 39 3917
Bakewell Derbys 74 2168
Bala Gwynd 58 9235
Balallan W Isls 152 2920
Balbeg Highld 139 4431
Balbeggie P & K 126 1629
Balblair Highld 139 5145
Balblair Highld 140 7066
Balby S York 75 5600
Balcary D & G 92 8149
Balchraggan Highld 139 5343
Balchreick Highld 148 1960
Balcombe W Susx 15 3130
Balcombe Lane W Susx 15 3132
Balcomie Links Fife 127 6209
Baldersby N York 89 3578
Baldersby St James N York 89 3676
Balderstone Gt Man 79 9010
Balderstone Lancs 81 6332
Balderton Notts 75 8151
Baldhu Cnwll 3 7743
Baldinnie Fife 127 4211
Baldinnies P & K 125 0216
Baldock Herts 39 2434
Baldovie Dund C 127 4533
Baldrine IOM 158 4281
Baldslow E Susx 17 8013
Baldwin IOM 158 3581
Baldwin's Gate Staffs 72 7939
Baldwin's Hill Surrey 15 3839
Baldwinholme Cumb 93 3351
Bale Norfk 66 0136
Baledgarno P & K 126 2730
Balemartine Ag & B 120 9841
Balerno C Edin 117 1666
Balfarg Fife 126 2803
Balfield Angus 134 5468
Balfour Ork 153 4716
Balfron Stirlg 115 5489
Balgaveny Abers 142 6540
Balgavies Angus 127 5451
Balgonar Fife 117 0293
Balgowan D & G 98 1142
Balgowan Highld 132 6494
Balgown Highld 136 3868
Balgracie D & G 98 9860
Balgray Angus 126 4038
Balgray S Lans 108 8824
Balham Gt Lon 27 2873
Balhary P & K 126 2646
Balholmie P & K 126 1436
Baligill Highld 150 8565
Balintore Angus 133 2859
Balintore Highld 147 8675
Balintraid Highld 146 7370
Balivanich W Isls 152 7755
Balk N York 89 4780
Balkeerie Angus 126 3244
Balkholme E R Yk 84 7828
Ball Shrops 59 3026
Ball Green Staffs 72 8952
Ball Haye Green Staffs 72 9856
Ball Hill Hants 24 4163
Ball's Green Gloucs 35 8699
Ballabeg IOM 158 2570
Ballachulish Highld 130 0858
Ballafesson IOM 158 2070
Ballakilpheric IOM 158 2271
Ballamodha IOM 158 2773
Ballanlay Ag & B 114 0462
Ballantrae S Ayrs 98 0882
Ballards Gore Essex 40 9092
Ballards Green Warwks 61 2791
Ballasalla IOM 158 2870
Ballater Abers 134 3695
Ballaugh IOM 158 3493
Ballchraggan Highld 147 7675
Ballencrieff E Loth 118 4878
Ballevullin Ag & B 120 9546
Ballidon Derbys 73 2054
Balliekine N Ayrs 105 8739
Balliemore Ag & B 114 1099
Balligmorrie S Ayrs 106 2290
Ballimore Ag & B 114 9283
Ballimore Stirlg 124 5317
Ballindalloch Moray 141 1636
Ballindean P & K 126 2529
Ballingdon Essex 54 8640
Ballinger Common Bucks 38 9103
Ballingham Herefd 46 5731
Ballingry Fife 117 1797
Ballinluig P & K 125 9752
Ballinshoe Angus 126 4153
Ballintuim P & K 126 1055
Balloch Highld 140 7247
Balloch N Lans 116 7374
Balloch P & K 125 8419
Balloch S Ayrs 106 3295
Balloch W Duns 115 3982
Ballochroy Ag & B 113 7352
Ballogie Abers 134 5795
Balls Cross W Susx 14 9826
Balls Green E Susx 16 4936
Ballygown Ag & B 121 4343
Ballygrant Ag & B 112 3966
Ballyhaugh Ag & B 120 1758
Ballymenoch Ag & B 115 3086
Ballymichael N Ayrs 105 9231
Balmacara Highld 137 8028
Balmaclellan D & G 99 6579
Balmae D & G 99 6844
Balmaha Stirlg 115 4290
Balmalcolm Fife 126 3208
Balmangan D & G 99 6445
Balmedie Abers 143 9618
Balmer Heath Shrops 59 4434
Balmerino Fife 126 3524
Balmerlawn Hants 12 3003
Balmore E Duns 115 5973
Balmuchy Highld 147 8678
Balmuir Angus 127 5648
Balmule Fife 117 2088
Balmullo Fife 127 4220
Balnacoil Lodge Highld 147 8011
Balnacra Highld 138 9846
Balnacroft Abers 133 2894
Balnafoich Highld 140 6835
Balnaguard P & K 125 9451
Balnahard Ag & B 121 4534
Balnahard Ag & B 112 4199
Balnain Highld 139 4430
Balnakeil Highld 149 3968
Balnapaling Highld 147 7969
Balne N York 83 5918
Balquharn P & K 125 0235
Balquhidder Stirlg 124 5320
Balsall Common W Mids 61 2376
Balsall Heath W Mids 61 0784
Balsall Street W Mids 61 2276
Balscote Oxon 48 3942
Balsham Cambs 53 5850
Baltasound Shet 153 6208
Balterley Staffs 72 7650
Balterley Green Staffs 72 7650
Balterley Heath Staffs 72 7450
Baltersan D & G 99 4261
Baltonsborough Somset 21 5434
Balvarran P & K 133 0761
Balvicar Ag & B 122 7616
Balvraid Highld 129 8416
Balvraid Highld 140 8231
Balwest Cnwll 2 5930
Bamber Bridge Lancs 81 5625
Bamber's Green Essex 40 5722
Bamburgh Nthumb 111 1734
Bamff P & K 126 2251
Bamford Derbys 74 2083
Bamford Gt Man 81 8612
Bampton Cumb 94 5118
Bampton Devon 20 9522
Bampton Oxon 36 3103
Bampton Grange Cumb 94 5218
Banavie Highld 130 1177
Banbury Oxon 49 4540
Banc-y-ffordd Carmth 31 4037
Bancffosfelem Carmth 32 4811
Banchory Abers 135 6995
Banchory-Devenick Abers 135 9002
Bancycapel Carmth 31 4214
Bancyfelin Carmth 31 3218
Bandirran P & K 126 2030
Bandrake Head Cumb 86 3187
Banff Abers 142 6863
Bangor Gwynd 69 5772
Bangor's Green Lancs 78 3709
Bangor-is-y-coed Wrexhm 71 3845
Bangors Cnwll 18 2099
Bangrove Suffk 54 9372
Banham Norfk 54 0687
Bank Hants 12 2807
Bank Ground Cumb 86 3196
Bank Newton N York 81 9053
Bank Street Worcs 47 6362
Bank Top Lancs 78 5207
Bank Top W York 82 1024
Bankend D & G 100 0268
Bankfoot P & K 125 0635
Bankglen E Ayrs 107 5912
Bankhead Aber C 135 9009
Bankhead S Lans 116 9844
Banknock Falk 116 7779
Banks Cumb 101 5664
Banks Lancs 80 3920
Banks Green Worcs 47 9967
Bankshill D & G 101 1982
Banningham Norfk 67 2129
Bannister Green Essex 40 6920
Bannockburn Stirlg 116 8190
Banstead Surrey 27 2559
Bantham Devon 7 6643
Banton N Lans 116 7480
Banwell Somset 21 3959
Bapchild Kent 28 9263
Bapton Wilts 22 9938
Bar Hill Cambs 52 3863
Barabhas W Isls 152 3649
Barassie S Ayrs 106 3232
Barbaraville Highld 146 7472
Barber Booth Derbys 74 1184
Barber Green Cumb 87 3982
Barbieston S Ayrs 107 4317
Barbon Cumb 87 6282
Barbridge Ches 71 6156
Barbrook Devon 19 7147
Barby Nhants 50 5470
Barcaldine Ag & B 122 9641
Barcheston Warwks 48 2639
Barclose Cumb 101 4462
Barcombe E Susx 15 4114
Barcombe Cross E Susx 15 4115
Barcroft W York 82 0437
Barden N York 89 1493
Barden Park Kent 16 5746
Bardfield End Green Essex 40 6231
Bardfield Saling Essex 40 6826
Bardney Lincs 76 1269
Bardon Leics 62 4412
Bardon Mill Nthumb 102 7764
Bardowie E Duns 115 5873
Bardown E Susx 16 6629
Bardrainney Inver 115 3373
Bardsea Cumb 86 3074
Bardsey W York 83 3643
Bardsley Gt Man 79 9201
Bardwell Suffk 54 9473
Bare Lancs 87 4564
Bareppa Cnwll 3 7729
Barewood Herefd 46 3856
Barfad D & G 98 3266
Barford Norfk 66 1107
Barford Warwks 48 2760
Barford St John Oxon 49 4433
Barford St Martin Wilts 23 0531
Barford St Michael Oxon 49 4332
Barfrestone Kent 29 2650
Bargate Derbys 62 3546
Bargeddie N Lans 116 6964
Bargoed Caerph 33 1599
Bargrennan D & G 98 3577
Barham Cambs 52 1375
Barham Kent 29 2050
Barham Suffk 54 1451
Barholm Lincs 64 0810
Barkby Leics 63 6309
Barkby Thorpe Leics 63 6309
Barkers Green Shrops 59 5228
Barkestone-le-Vale Leics 63 7734
Barkham Berks 25 7766
Barking Gt Lon 27 4484
Barking Suffk 54 0753
Barking Tye Suffk 54 0652
Barkingside Gt Lon 27 4489
Barkisland W York 82 0519
Barkla Shop Cnwll 3 7350
Barkston Lincs 63 9341
Barkston Ash N York 83 4936
Barkway Herts 39 3835
Barlanark C Glas 116 6664
Barlaston Staffs 72 8938
Barlavington W Susx 14 9716
Barlborough Derbys 75 4777
Barlby N York 83 6333
Barlestone Leics 62 4205
Barley Herts 39 4038
Barley Lancs 81 8240
Barley Hole S York 74 3697
Barleycroft End Herts 39 4327
Barleythorpe Rutlnd 63 8409
Barling Essex 40 9389
Barlings Lincs 76 0774
Barlochan D & G 92 8157
Barlow Derbys 74 3474
Barlow N York 83 6428
Barlow T & W 96 1561
Barmby Moor E R Yk 84 7748
Barmby on the Marsh E R Yk 83 6928
Barmer Norfk 66 8133
Barming Heath Kent 28 7255
Barmollack Ag & B 105 8043
Barmouth Gwynd 57 6116
Barmpton Dur 96 3118
Barmston E R Yk 91 1659
Barnaby Green Suffk 55 4780
Barnacarry Ag & B 114 0094
Barnack Cambs 64 0705
Barnacle Warwks 61 3884
Barnard Castle Dur 95 0516
Barnard Gate Oxon 36 4010
Barnardiston Suffk 53 7148
Barnbarroch D & G 92 8456
Barnburgh S York 83 4803
Barnby Suffk 55 4789
Barnby Dun S York 83 6109
Barnby in the Willows Notts 76 8552
Barnby Moor Notts 75 6684
Barncorkrie D & G 98 0935
Barnes Gt Lon 26 2276
Barnes Street Kent 16 6447
Barnet Gt Lon 26 2496
Barnet Gate Gt Lon 26 2195
Barnetby le Wold Lincs 84 0509
Barney Norfk 66 9932
Barnham Suffk 54 8779
Barnham W Susx 14 9503
Barnham Broom Norfk 66 0807
Barnhead Angus 135 6657
Barnhill Ches 71 4854
Barnhill Dund C 127 4731
Barnhill Moray 141 1457
Barnhills D & G 98 9871
Barningham Dur 89 0810
Barningham Suffk 54 9676
Barnoldby le Beck Lincs 85 2303
Barnoldswick Lancs 81 8746
Barns Green W Susx 14 1226
Barnsdale Bar N York 83 5014
Barnsley Gloucs 36 0704
Barnsley S York 83 3406
Barnsley Shrops 60 7592
Barnsole Kent 29 2756
Barnstaple Devon 19 5633
Barnston Essex 40 6419
Barnston Mersyd 78 2783
Barnstone Notts 63 7335
Barnt Green Worcs 60 0173
Barnton C Edin 117 1874
Barnton Ches 71 6375
Barnwell All Saints Nhants 51 0484
Barnwell St Andrew Nhants 51 0584
Barnwood Gloucs 35 8518
Baron's Cross Herefd 46 4758
Barons Wood Devon 8 7003
Baronwood Cumb 94 5143
Barr S Ayrs 106 2794
Barrachan D & G 99 3649
Barrapoll Ag & B 120 9442
Barras Cumb 88 8312
Barrasford Nthumb 102 9173
Barrets Green Ches 71 5859
Barrhead E Rens 115 4958
Barrhill S Ayrs 98 2382
Barrington Cambs 52 3849
Barrington Somset 10 3818
Barripper Cnwll 2 6338
Barrmill N Ayrs 115 3651
Barrnacarry Bay Ag & B 122 8122
Barrock Highld 151 2570
Barrow Gloucs 47 8824
Barrow Lancs 81 7338
Barrow Rutlnd 63 8815
Barrow Shrops 59 6500
Barrow Somset 22 7231
Barrow Suffk 53 7663
Barrow Bridge Gt Man 81 6811
Barrow Burn Nthumb 110 8610
Barrow Gurney Somset 21 5268
Barrow Haven Lincs 84 0622
Barrow Hill Derbys 74 4275
Barrow Island Cumb 86 1968
Barrow Nook Lancs 78 4402
Barrow Street Wilts 22 8330
Barrow upon Soar Leics 62 5717
Barrow upon Trent Derbys 62 3528
Barrow Vale Somset 21 6460
Barrow's Green Ches 78 5287
Barrow's Green Ches 72 6857
Barrow-in-Furness Cumb 86 2068
Barrow-upon-Humber Lincs 84 0620
Barroway Drove Norfk 65 5703
Barrowby Lincs 63 8736
Barrowden Rutlnd 51 9400
Barrowford Lancs 81 8539
Barry Angus 127 5334
Barry V Glam 20 1268
Barry Island V Glam 20 1166
Barsby Leics 63 6911
Barsham Suffk 55 3989
Barston W Mids 61 2078
Bartestree Herefd 46 5640
Barthol Chapel Abers 143 8133
Bartholomew Green Essex 40 7221
Barthomley Ches 72 7652
Bartley Hants 12 3012
Bartley Green W Mids 60 0081
Bartlow Cambs 53 5845
Barton Cambs 52 4055
Barton Ches 71 4454
Barton Cumb 94 4826
Barton Devon 7 9167
Barton Gloucs 48 0925
Barton Herefd 46 2957
Barton Lancs 78 3509
Barton Lancs 80 5137
Barton N York 89 2208
Barton Oxon 37 5507
Barton Warwks 48 1051
Barton Bendish Norfk 65 7105
Barton End Gloucs 35 8498
Barton Green Staffs 73 1717
Barton Hartshorn Bucks 49 6430
Barton Hill N York 90 7064
Barton in Fabis Notts 62 5132
Barton in the Beans Leics 62 3906
Barton Mills Suffk 53 7173
Barton Seagrave Nhants 51 8877
Barton St David Somset 21 5432
Barton Stacey Hants 24 4341
Barton Town Devon 19 6840
Barton Turf Norfk 67 3522
Barton upon Irwell Gt Man 79 7697
Barton Waterside Lincs 84 0222
Barton-le-Clay Beds 38 0830
Barton-le-Street N York 90 7274
Barton-le-Willows N York 90 7163
Barton-on-Sea Hants 12 2393
Barton-on-the-Heath Warwks 48 2532
Barton-under-Needwood Staffs 73 1818
Barton-upon-Humber Lincs 84 0221
Barugh S York 82 3108
Barugh Green S York 82 3107
Barvas W Isls 152 3649
Barway Cambs 53 5575
Barwell Leics 50 4496
Barwick Devon 8 5907
Barwick Herts 39 3819
Barwick Somset 10 5513
Barwick in Elmet W York 83 4037
Baschurch Shrops 59 4221
Bascote Warwks 48 4063
Bascote Heath Warwks 48 3962
Base Green Suffk 54 0163
Basford Green Staffs 72 9851
Bashall Eaves Lancs 81 6943
Bashall Town Lancs 81 7142
Bashley Hants 12 2496
Basildon Berks 37 6078
Basildon Essex 40 7189
Basingstoke Hants 24 6352
Baslow Derbys 74 2572
Bason Bridge Somset 21 3446
Bassaleg Newpt 34 2786
Bassendean Border 110 6245
Bassenthwaite Cumb 93 2332
Bassett Hants 13 4216
Bassingbourn Cambs 39 3343
Bassingfield Notts 62 6137
Bassingham Lincs 76 9060
Bassingthorpe Lincs 63 9628
Bassus Green Herts 39 3025
Basted Kent 27 6055
Baston Lincs 64 1113
Bastwick Norfk 67 4217
Batch Somset 21 3255
Batchworth Herts 26 0694
Batchworth Heath Herts 26 0792
Batcombe Dorset 10 6103
Batcombe Somset 22 6938
Bate Heath Ches 79 6879
Batford Herts 38 1415
Bath Somset 22 7464
Bath Side Essex 41 2532

Bathampton
Birdbrook
272


Bathampton Somset 22 7766
Bathealton Somset 20 0823
Batheaston Somset 22 7767
Bathford Somset 22 7866
Bathgate W Loth 117 9768
Bathley Notts 75 7759
Bathpool Cnwll 5 2874
Bathpool Somset 20 2526
Bathville W Loth 116 9367
Bathway Somset 21 5952
Batley W York 82 2224
Batsford Gloucs 48 1833
Batson Devon 7 7339
Batt's Corner Surrey 25 8140
Battersby N York 90 5907
Battersea Gt Lon 27 2776
Battisborough Cross Devon 6 5948
Battisford Suffk 54 0554
Battisford Tye Suffk 54 0354
Battle E Susx 17 7515
Battle Powys 45 0130
Battleborough Somset 21 3450
Battledown Gloucs 35 9621
Battledykes Angus 127 4555
Battlefield Shrops 59 5117
Battlesbridge Essex 40 7894
Battlesden Beds 38 9628
Battleton Somset 20 9127
Battlies Green Suffk 54 9064
Battramsley Cross Hants 12 3198
Battyeford W York 82 1920
Baughton Worcs 47 8841
Baughurst Hants 24 5860
Baulds Abers 134 6093
Baulking Oxon 36 3191
Baumber Lincs 76 2274
Baunton Gloucs 35 0104
Baveney Wood Shrops 60 6979
Baverstock Wilts 23 0332
Bawburgh Norfk 66 1508
Bawdeswell Norfk 66 0420
Bawdrip Somset 21 3439
Bawdsey Suffk 55 3440
Bawtry S York 75 6493
Baxenden Lancs 81 7726
Baxter's Green Suffk 53 7557
Baxterley Warwks 61 2896
Bay Highld 136 2654
Bay Horse Lancs 80 4952
Bayble W Isls 152 5231
Baybridge Hants 13 5223
Baybridge Nthumb 95 9550
Baycliff Cumb 86 2872
Baydon Wilts 36 2878
Bayford Herts 39 3108
Bayford Somset 22 7229
Bayhead W Isls 152 7468
Bayley's Hill Kent 27 5151
Baylham Suffk 54 1051
Baynard's Green Oxon 49 5429
Baysdale Abbey N York 90 6206
Baysham Herefd 46 5727
Bayston Hill Shrops 59 4808
Baythorne End Essex 53 7242
Bayton Worcs 60 6973
Bayton Common Worcs 60 7173
Bayworth Oxon 37 4901
Beach Gloucs 35 7071
Beachampton Bucks 49 7736
Beachamwell Norfk 65 7505
Beachborough Kent 29 1638
Beachley Gloucs 34 5591
Beacon Devon 9 1805
Beacon End Essex 40 9524
Beacon Hill E Susx 16 5030
Beacon Hill Kent 17 8232
Beacon Hill Notts 75 8153
Beacon Hill Surrey 14 8736
Beacon's Bottom Bucks 37 7895
Beaconsfield Bucks 26 9490
Beadlam N York 90 6584
Beadlow Beds 38 1038
Beadnell Nthumb 111 2229
Beaford Devon 19 5515
Beal N York 83 5325
Beal Nthumb 111 0642
Bealbury Cnwll 5 3766
Bealsmill Cnwll 5 3576
Beam Hill Staffs 73 2325
Beamhurst Staffs 73 0536
Beaminster Dorset 10 4701
Beamish Dur 96 2253
Beamsley N York 82 0752
Bean Kent 27 5872
Beanacre Wilts 22 9066
Beanley Nthumb 111 0818
Beardon Devon 5 5184
Beardwood Lancs 81 6629
Beare Devon 9 9901
Beare Green Surrey 15 1742
Bearley Warwks 48 1860
Bearley Cross Warwks 48 1761
Bearpark Dur 96 2343
Bearsden W Duns 115 5372
Bearsted Kent 28 8055
Bearstone Shrops 72 7239
Bearwood W Mids 60 0286
Beattock D & G 108 0802
Beauchamp Roding Essex 40 5809
Beauchief S York 74 3381
Beaudesert Warwks 48 1565
Beaufort Blae G 33 1611
Beaulieu Hants 12 3802
Beauly Highld 139 5246
Beaumaris IOA 69 6076
Beaumont Cumb 93 3459
Beaumont Essex 41 1624
Beaumont Jersey 158 0000
Beaumont Hill Dur 96 2918
Beausale Warwks 61 2470
Beauworth Hants 13 5726
Beaver Kent 28 0040
Beaver Green Kent 28 0041
Beaworthy Devon 18 4699
Beazley End Essex 40 7429
Bebington Mersyd 78 3383
Bebside Nthumb 103 2781
Beccles Suffk 55 4289
Becconsall Lancs 80 4523
Beck Foot Cumb 87 6196
Beck Hole N York 90 8202
Beck Row Suffk 53 6977
Beck Side Cumb 86 2382
Beck Side Cumb 87 3780
Beckbury Shrops 60 7601
Beckenham Gt Lon 27 3769
Beckering Lincs 76 1280
Beckermet Cumb 86 0106
Beckett End Norfk 65 7798
Beckfoot Cumb 92 0949
Beckfoot Cumb 86 1600
Beckfoot Cumb 86 1989
Beckford Worcs 47 9736
Beckhampton Wilts 23 0868
Beckingham Lincs 76 8753
Beckingham Notts 75 7789
Beckington Somset 22 8051
Beckjay Shrops 46 3977
Beckley E Susx 17 8523
Beckley Hants 12 2296
Beckley Oxon 37 5611
Becks W York 82 0345
Beckside Cumb 87 6187
Beckton Gt Lon 27 4381
Beckwithshaw N York 82 2653
Becontree Gt Lon 27 4786
Becquet Vincent Jersey 158 0000
Bedale N York 89 2688
Bedburn Dur 95 0931
Bedchester Dorset 11 8517
Beddau Rhondd 33 0585
Beddgelert Gwynd 69 5948
Beddingham E Susx 16 4407
Beddington Gt Lon 27 3065
Beddington Corner Gt Lon 27 2866
Bedfield Suffk 55 2166
Bedfield Little Green Suffk 55 2365
Bedford Beds 38 0449
Bedgebury Cross Kent 17 7134
Bedham W Susx 14 0122
Bedhampton Hants 13 7006
Bedingfield Suffk 54 1768
Bedingfield Green Suffk 54 1866
Bedingfield Street Suffk 54 1768
Bedlam N York 89 2661
Bedlam Lane Kent 28 8845
Bedlington Nthumb 103 2681
Bedlinog Myr Td 33 0901
Bedminster Bristl 34 5871
Bedminster Down Bristl 34 5770
Bedmond Herts 38 0903
Bednall Staffs 72 9517
Bedrule Border 110 6017
Bedstone Shrops 46 3676
Bedwas Caerph 33 1789
Bedwellty Caerph 33 1600
Bedworth Warwks 61 3687
Bedworth Woodlands Warwks 61 3487
Beeby Leics 63 6608
Beech Hants 24 6938
Beech Staffs 72 8538
Beech Hill Berks 24 6964
Beechingstoke Wilts 23 0859
Beedon Berks 37 4878
Beedon Hill Berks 37 4877
Beeford E R Yk 85 1253
Beeley Derbys 74 2667
Beelsby Lincs 85 2001
Beenham Berks 24 5868
Beenham's Heath Berks 25 8375
Beeny Cnwll 4 1192
Beer Devon 9 2289
Beer Somset 21 4031
Beer Hackett Dorset 10 6011
Beercrocombe Somset 21 3220
Beesands Devon 7 8140
Beesby Lincs 77 4680
Beeson Devon 7 8140
Beeston Beds 52 1648
Beeston Ches 71 5358
Beeston Norfk 66 9015
Beeston Notts 62 5236
Beeston W York 82 2830
Beeston Regis Norfk 66 1642
Beeswing D & G 100 8969
Beetham Cumb 87 4979
Beetham Somset 10 2712
Beetley Norfk 66 9718
Began Cardif 34 2283
Begbroke Oxon 37 4614
Begdale Cambs 65 4506
Begelly Pembks 31 1107
Beggar's Bush Powys 46 2664
Beggarington Hill W York 82 2724
Beguildy Powys 45 1979
Beighton Norfk 67 3808
Beighton S York 75 4483
Beighton Hill Derbys 73 2951
Bein Inn P & K 126 1513
Beith N Ayrs 115 3553
Bekesbourne Kent 29 1955
Bekesbourne Hill Kent 29 1856
Belaugh Norfk 67 2818
Belbroughton Worcs 60 9277
Belchalwell Dorset 11 7909
Belchalwell Street Dorset 11 7909
Belchamp Otten Essex 54 8041
Belchamp St Paul Essex 53 7942
Belchamp Walter Essex 54 8240
Belchford Lincs 77 2975
Belford Nthumb 111 1034
Belgrave Leics 62 5906
Belhaven E Loth 118 6678
Belhelvie Abers 143 9417
Belhinnie Abers 142 4627
Bell Bar Herts 39 2505
Bell Busk N York 81 9056
Bell End Worcs 60 9477
Bell Heath Worcs 60 9477
Bell Hill Hants 13 7324
Bell o' th'Hill Ches 71 5245
Bellabeg Abers 134 3513
Bellamore Herefd 46 3840
Bellanoch Ag & B 113 7992
Bellasize E R Yk 84 8227
Bellaty Angus 133 2359
Belle Vue Cumb 93 3756
Belle Vue W York 83 3419
Belleau Lincs 77 4078
Bellerby N York 89 1192
Bellever Devon 8 6577
Bellfield S Lans 108 8234
Bellfield S Lans 108 9620
Bellingdon Bucks 38 9405
Bellingham Nthumb 102 8383
Belloch Ag & B 105 6737
Bellochantuy Ag & B 104 6632
Bellows Cross Dorset 12 0613
Bells Cross Suffk 54 1552
Bells Yew Green E Susx 16 6135
Bellshill N Lans 116 7360
Bellshill Nthumb 111 1230
Bellside N Lans 116 8058
Bellsquarry W Loth 117 0465
Belluton Somset 21 6164
Belmesthorpe Rutlnd 64 0410
Belmont Gt Lon 27 2562
Belmont Lancs 81 6715
Belmont S Ayrs 106 3419
Belmont Shet 153 5600
Belnacraig Abers 141 3716
Belowda Cnwll 4 9661
Belper Derbys 62 3447
Belper Lane End Derbys 74 3349
Belph Derbys 75 5475
Belsay Nthumb 103 0978
Belses Border 110 5725
Belsford Devon 7 7659
Belsize Herts 26 0300
Belstead Suffk 54 1241
Belstone Devon 8 6293
Belthorn Lancs 81 7124
Beltinge Kent 29 1967
Beltingham Nthumb 102 7863
Beltoft Lincs 84 8006
Belton Leics 62 4420
Belton Lincs 84 7806
Belton Lincs 63 9339
Belton Norfk 67 4802
Belton Rutlnd 63 8101
Beltring Kent 28 6747
Belvedere Gt Lon 27 4978
Belvoir Leics 63 8133
Bembridge IOW 13 6488
Bemersley Green Staffs 72 8854
Bemerton Wilts 23 1230
Bempton E R Yk 91 1972
Ben Rhydding W York 82 1347
Benacre Suffk 55 5184
Benbuie D & G 107 7196
Benderloch Ag & B 122 9038
Benenden Kent 17 8033
Benfield D & G 99 3763
Benfieldside Dur 95 0952
Bengates Norfk 67 3027
Bengeworth Worcs 48 0443
Benhall Green Suffk 55 3961
Benhall Street Suffk 55 3561
Benholm Abers 135 8069
Beningbrough N York 90 5257
Benington Herts 39 2923
Benington Lincs 77 3946
Benington Sea End Lincs 65 4145
Benllech IOA 68 5182
Benmore Ag & B 114 1385
Bennacott Cnwll 5 2992
Bennan N Ayrs 105 9921
Bennet Head Cumb 93 4423
Bennetland E R Yk 84 8228
Bennett End Bucks 37 7897
Benniworth Lincs 76 2081
Benover Kent 28 7048
Benson Oxon 37 6291
Bentfield Green Essex 39 5025
Benthall Shrops 60 6602
Bentham Gloucs 35 9116
Benthoul Aber C 135 8003
Bentlawn Shrops 59 3301
Bentley E R Yk 84 0136
Bentley Hants 25 7844
Bentley S York 83 5605
Bentley Suffk 54 1138
Bentley Warwks 61 2895
Bentley Heath Herts 27 2599
Bentley Heath W Mids 61 1675
Benton Devon 19 6536
Bentpath D & G 101 3190
Bentwichen Devon 19 7333
Bentworth Hants 24 6640
Benvie Angus 126 3231
Benville Dorset 10 5303
Benwick Cambs 52 3490
Beoley Worcs 48 0669
Beoraidbeg Highld 129 6793
Bepton W Susx 14 8618
Berden Essex 39 4629
Bere Alston Devon 6 4466
Bere Ferrers Devon 6 4563
Bere Regis Dorset 11 8494
Berea Pembks 30 7930
Berepper Cnwll 2 6523
Bergh Apton Norfk 67 3001
Berhill Somset 21 4436
Berinsfield Oxon 37 5795
Berkeley Gloucs 35 6899
Berkeley Heath Gloucs 35 6999
Berkeley Road Gloucs 35 7200
Berkhamsted Herts 38 9907
Berkley Somset 22 8049
Berkswell W Mids 61 2479
Bermondsey Gt Lon 27 3479
Bernera Highld 129 8020
Bernice Ag & B 114 1391
Bernisdale Highld 136 4050
Berrick Prior Oxon 37 6294
Berrick Salome Oxon 37 6293
Berriedale Highld 147 1222
Berrier Cumb 93 3929
Berriew Powys 58 1801
Berrington Nthumb 111 0043
Berrington Shrops 59 5206
Berrington Worcs 46 5767
Berrington Green Worcs 46 5766
Berrow Somset 20 2951
Berrow Worcs 47 7934
Berrow Green Worcs 47 7458
Berry Brow W York 82 1314
Berry Cross Devon 18 4714
Berry Down Cross Devon 19 5743
Berry Hill Gloucs 34 5712
Berry Hill Pembks 30 0640
Berry Pomeroy Devon 7 8261
Berry's Green Gt Lon 27 4359
Berryhillock Moray 142 5054
Berryhillock Moray 142 5060
Berrynarbor Devon 19 5646
Bersham Wrexhm 71 3049
Berthengam Flints 70 1179
Berwick E Susx 16 5105
Berwick Bassett Wilts 36 0973
Berwick Hill Nthumb 103 1775
Berwick St James Wilts 23 0739
Berwick St John Wilts 22 9422
Berwick St Leonard Wilts 22 9233
Berwick-upon-Tweed Nthumb 119 9953
Bescaby Leics 63 8126
Bescar Cumb 80 3913
Besford Shrops 59 5525
Besford Worcs 47 9144
Besom Hill Gt Man 79 9508
Bessacarr S York 75 6100
Bessels Leigh Oxon 37 4501
Besses o' th' Barn Gt Man 79 8005
Bessingby E R Yk 91 1566
Bessingham Norfk 66 1636
Bestbeech Hill E Susx 16 6231
Besthorpe Norfk 66 0595
Besthorpe Notts 75 8264
Beswick E R Yk 84 0147
Betchcott Shrops 59 4398
Betchworth Surrey 26 2150
Bethania Cerdgn 43 5763
Bethania Gwynd 57 7044
Bethel Gwynd 68 5265
Bethel Gwynd 70 9839
Bethel IOA 68 3970
Bethel Powys 58 1021
Bethersden Kent 28 9240
Bethesda Gwynd 69 6266
Bethesda Pembks 31 0918
Bethlehem Carmth 44 6825
Bethnal Green Gt Lon 27 3482
Betley Staffs 72 7548
Betsham Kent 27 6071
Betteshanger Kent 29 3152
Bettiscombe Dorset 10 3900
Bettisfield Wrexhm 59 4635
Betton Shrops 72 6936
Betton Strange Shrops 59 5009
Bettws Newpt 34 2890
Bettws Bledrws Cerdgn 44 5952
Bettws Cedewain Powys 58 1296
Bettws Evan Cerdgn 42 3047
Bettws-Newydd Mons 34 3606
Bettyhill Highld 150 7061
Betws Brdgnd 33 9086
Betws Carmth 32 6311
Betws Garmon Gwynd 69 5357
Betws Gwerfil Goch Denbgs 70 0346
Betws-y-coed Conwy 69 7956
Betws-yn-Rhos Conwy 69 9073
Beulah Cerdgn 42 2846
Beulah Powys 45 9251
Bevendean E Susx 15 3306
Bevercotes Notts 75 6972
Beverley E R Yk 84 0339
Beverstone Gloucs 35 8694
Bevington Gloucs 35 6596
Bewaldeth Cumb 93 2034
Bewcastle Cumb 101 5674
Bewdley Worcs 60 7875
Bewerley N York 89 1565
Bewholme E R Yk 85 1649
Bewlbridge Kent 16 6834
Bexhill E Susx 17 7407
Bexley Gt Lon 27 4973
Bexleyheath Gt Lon 27 4875
Bexleyhill W Susx 14 9125
Bexon Kent 28 8959
Bexwell Norfk 65 6303
Beyton Suffk 54 9363
Beyton Green Suffk 54 9363
Bhaltos W Isls 152 0936
Bibstone Gloucs 35 6991
Bibury Gloucs 36 1106
Bicester Oxon 49 5823
Bickenhill W Mids 61 1882
Bicker Lincs 64 2237
Bicker Bar Lincs 64 2438
Bicker Gauntlet Lincs 64 2139
Bickershaw Gt Man 79 6201
Bickerstaffe Lancs 78 4404
Bickerton Ches 71 5052
Bickerton Devon 7 8139
Bickerton N York 83 4550
Bickerton Nthumb 103 9900
Bickford Staffs 60 8814
Bickington Devon 19 5332
Bickington Devon 7 8072
Bickleigh Devon 9 9407
Bickleigh Devon 6 5262
Bickleton Devon 19 5030
Bickley Ches 71 5348
Bickley Gt Lon 27 4268
Bickley N York 91 9191
Bickley Worcs 47 6371
Bickley Moss Ches 71 5448
Bicknacre Essex 40 7802
Bicknoller Somset 20 1139
Bicknor Kent 28 8658
Bickton Hants 12 1412
Bicton Herefd 46 4764
Bicton Shrops 59 4415
Bicton Shrops 59 2983
Bidborough Kent 16 5643
Bidden Hants 24 7049
Biddenden Kent 28 8538
Biddenden Green Kent 28 8842
Biddenham Beds 38 0250
Biddestone Wilts 35 8673
Biddisham Somset 21 3853
Biddlesden Bucks 49 6340
Biddlestone Nthumb 111 9508
Biddulph Staffs 72 8858
Biddulph Moor Staffs 72 9058
Bideford Devon 18 4526
Bidford-on-Avon Warwks 48 1052
Bidston Mersyd 78 2890
Bielby E R Yk 84 7843
Bieldside Aber C 135 8702
Bierley IOW 13 5078
Bierton Bucks 38 8415
Big Balcraig D & G 99 3843
Big Carlae D & G 107 6597
Big Sand Highld 144 7578
Bigbury Devon 7 6646
Bigbury-on-Sea Devon 7 6544
Bigby Lincs 84 0507
Biggar Cumb 86 1966
Biggar S Lans 108 0437
Biggin Derbys 73 2548
Biggin Derbys 74 1559
Biggin N York 83 5434
Biggin Hill Gt Lon 27 4159
Biggleswade Beds 39 1944
Bigholms D & G 101 3180
Bighouse Highld 150 8964
Bighton Hants 24 6134
Bigland Hall Cumb 87 3583
Biglands Cumb 93 2553
Bignor W Susx 14 9814
Bigrigg Cumb 92 0013
Bilborough Notts 62 5241
Bilbrook Somset 20 0341
Bilbrook Staffs 60 8703
Bilbrough N York 83 5346
Bilbster Highld 151 2853
Bildershaw Dur 96 2024
Bildeston Suffk 54 9949
Billacott Cnwll 5 2690
Billericay Essex 40 6794
Billesdon Leics 63 7202
Billesley Warwks 48 1456
Billingborough Lincs 64 1133
Billinge Mersyd 78 5200
Billingford Norfk 66 0120
Billingford Norfk 54 1678
Billingham Dur 97 4624
Billinghay Lincs 76 1554
Billingley S York 83 4304
Billingshurst W Susx 14 0825
Billingsley Shrops 60 7085
Billington Beds 38 9422
Billington Lancs 81 7235
Billington Staffs 72 8820
Billockby Norfk 67 4313
Billy Row Dur 96 1637
Bilsborrow Lancs 80 5139
Bilsby Lincs 77 4776
Bilsham W Susx 14 9702
Bilsington Kent 17 0434
Bilsthorpe Notts 75 6460
Bilsthorpe Moor Notts 75 6560
Bilston Mdloth 117 2664
Bilston W Mids 60 9596
Bilstone Leics 62 3605
Bilting Kent 28 0549
Bilton E R Yk 85 1632
Bilton N York 83 4749
Bilton N York 89 3157
Bilton Nthumb 111 2210
Bilton Warwks 50 4873
Bilton Banks Nthumb 111 2010
Binbrook Lincs 76 2093
Binchester Blocks Dur 96 2232
Bincombe Dorset 11 6884
Binegar Somset 21 6149
Bines Green W Susx 15 1817
Binfield Berks 25 8471
Binfield Heath Oxon 37 7477
Bingfield Nthumb 102 9772
Bingham Notts 63 7039
Bingham's Melcombe Dorset 11 7702
Bingley W York 82 1039
Bings Shrops 59 5318
Binham Norfk 66 9839
Binley Hants 24 4253
Binley W Mids 61 3778
Binnegar Dorset 11 8887
Binniehill Falk 116 8572
Binns Farm Moray 141 3164
Binscombe Surrey 25 9645
Binsey Oxon 37 4907
Binstead Hants 25 7740
Binstead IOW 13 5892
Binsted W Susx 14 9806
Binton Warwks 48 1454
Bintree Norfk 66 0123
Binweston Shrops 59 3004
Birch Essex 40 9419
Birch Gt Man 79 8507
Birch Close Dorset 11 8803
Birch Cross Staffs 73 1230
Birch Green Essex 40 9418
Birch Green Herts 39 2911
Birch Green Worcs 47 8645
Birch Heath Ches 71 5461
Birch Hill Ches 71 5173
Birch Vale Derbys 74 0286
Birch Wood Somset 9 2414
Bircham Newton Norfk 65 7733
Bircham Tofts Norfk 65 7732
Birchanger Essex 39 5122
Birchburn N Ayrs 105 9129
Birchencliffe W York 82 1218
Bircher Herefd 46 4765
Birchfield W Mids 61 0790
Birchgrove Cardif 33 1679
Birchgrove E Susx 15 4029
Birchgrove Swans 32 7098
Birchington Kent 29 3069
Birchley Heath Warwks 61 2894
Birchmoor Green Beds 38 9534
Birchover Derbys 74 2362
Birchwood Ches 79 6591
Birchyfield Herefd 47 6453
Bircotes Notts 75 6391
Bird End W Mids 60 0194
Bird Street Suffk 54 0052
Birdbrook Essex 53 7041

Birdforth Botesdale 273

Birdforth N York 90 4875
Birdham W Susx 14 8200
Birdingbury Warwks 50 4368
Birdlip Gloucs 35 9214
Birdoswald Cumb 102 6166
Birds Edge W York 82 2007
Birds Green Essex 40 5808
Birdsall N York 90 8165
Birdsgreen Shrops 60 7785
Birdsmoorgate Dorset 10 3900
Birdwell S York 83 3401
Birdwood Gloucs 35 7418
Birgham Border 110 7939
Birichin Highld 147 7592
Birkacre Lancs 81 5714
Birkby N York 89 3202
Birkdale Mersyd 80 3214
Birkenbog Abers 142 5365
Birkenhead Mersyd 78 3288
Birkenhills Abers 142 7445
Birkenshaw W York 82 2028
Birkhall Abers 134 3493
Birkhill Angus 126 3534
Birkhill D & G 109 2015
Birkholme Lincs 63 9623
Birkin N York 83 5326
Birks W York 82 2626
Birkshaw Nthumb 102 7765
Birley Herefd 46 4553
Birley Carr S York 74 3392
Birling Kent 28 6860
Birling Nthumb 111 2406
Birling Gap E Susx 16 5596
Birlingham Worcs 47 9343
Birmingham W Mids 61 0786
Birnam P & K 125 0341
Birness Abers 143 9933
Birse Abers 134 5697
Birsemore Abers 134 5297
Birstall Leics 62 5909
Birstall W York 82 2225
Birstwith N York 89 2359
Birthorpe Lincs 64 1033
Birtley Herefd 46 3669
Birtley Nthumb 102 8778
Birtley T & W 96 2756
Birts Street Worcs 47 7836
Bisbrooke Rutlnd 51 8899
Biscathorpe Lincs 76 2284
Biscovey Cnwll 3 0552
Bish Mill Devon 19 7425
Bisham Berks 26 8485
Bishampton Worcs 47 9951
Bishop Auckland Dur 96 2028
Bishop Burton E R Yk 84 9839
Bishop Middleham Dur 96 3231
Bishop Monkton N York 89 3266
Bishop Norton Lincs 76 9892
Bishop Sutton Somset 21 5859
Bishop Thornton N York 89 2563
Bishop Wilton E R Yk 84 7955
Bishop's Castle Shrops 59 3288
Bishop's Cleeve Gloucs 47 9627
Bishop's Frome Herefd 47 6648
Bishop's Green Essex 40 6217
Bishop's Green Hants 24 5063
Bishop's Itchington Warwks 48 3857
Bishop's Norton Gloucs 47 8424
Bishop's Nympton Devon 19 7523
Bishop's Offley Staffs 72 7729
Bishop's Stortford Herts 39 4821
Bishop's Sutton Hants 24 6032
Bishop's Tachbrook Warwks 48 3161
Bishop's Tawton Devon 19 5729
Bishop's Waltham Hants 13 5517
Bishop's Wood Staffs 60 8309
Bishop´s Caundle Dorset 11 6913
Bishopbridge Lincs 76 0391
Bishopbriggs E Duns 116 6070
Bishopmill Moray 141 2163
Bishops Cannings Wilts 23 0364
Bishops Gate Surrey 25 9871
Bishops Hull Somset 20 2024
Bishops Lydeard Somset 20 1729
Bishopsbourne Kent 29 1852
Bishopsteignton Devon 7 9073
Bishopstoke Hants 13 4619
Bishopston Swans 32 5789
Bishopstone Bucks 38 8010
Bishopstone E Susx 16 4701
Bishopstone Herefd 46 4143
Bishopstone Kent 26 2068
Bishopstone Wilts 23 0625
Bishopstone Wilts 36 2483
Bishopstrow Wilts 22 8943
Bishopswood Somset 10 2612
Bishopsworth Bristl 21 5768
Bishopthorpe N York 83 5947
Bishopton Dur 96 3621
Bishopton Rens 115 4371
Bishopton Warwks 48 1956
Bishton Newpt 34 3887
Bishton Staffs 73 0220
Bisley Gloucs 35 9005
Bisley Surrey 25 9559
Bisley Camp Surrey 25 9357
Bispham Lancs 80 3140
Bispham Green Lancs 80 4813
Bissoe Cnwll 3 7741
Bisterne Hants 12 1401
Bitchet Green Kent 27 5654
Bitchfield Lincs 63 9828
Bittadon Devon 19 5441
Bittaford Devon 7 6656
Bittering Norfk 66 9417
Bitterley Shrops 46 5677
Bitterne Hants 13 4513
Bitteswell Leics 50 5385
Bitton Gloucs 35 6869
Bix Oxon 37 7284
Blaby Leics 50 5697
Black Bourton Oxon 36 2804
Black Callerton T & W 103 1769
Black Car Norfk 66 0995
Black Corner W Susx 15 2939
Black Corries Highld 123 2956
Black Crofts Ag & B 122 9234
Black Cross Cnwll 4 9060
Black Dog Devon 19 8009
Black Heddon Nthumb 103 0775
Black Lane Gt Man 79 7708
Black Lane Ends Lancs 81 9243
Black Moor W York 82 2939
Black Notley Essex 40 7620
Black Pill Swans 32 6190
Black Street Suffk 55 5186
Black Tar Pembks 30 9909
Black Torrington Devon 18 4605
Blackadder Border 119 8452
Blackawton Devon 7 8051
Blackbank Warwks 61 3586
Blackbeck Cumb 86 0207
Blackborough Devon 9 0909
Blackborough End Norfk 65 6615
Blackboys E Susx 16 5220
Blackbrook Derbys 62 3347
Blackbrook Staffs 72 7638
Blackbrook Surrey 15 1846
Blackburn Abers 135 8212
Blackburn Lancs 81 6827
Blackburn S York 74 3992
Blackburn W Loth 117 9865
Blackcraig E Ayrs 107 6308
Blackden Heath Ches 79 7871
Blackdog Abers 135 9513
Blackdown Devon 5 5079
Blackdown Dorset 10 3903
Blackdyke Cumb 92 1452
Blackenall Heath W Mids 60 0002
Blacker S York 83 3309
Blacker Hill S York 83 3602
Blackfen Gt Lon 27 4674
Blackfield Hants 13 4402
Blackford Cumb 101 3961
Blackford P & K 125 8908
Blackford Somset 21 4147
Blackford Somset 21 6526
Blackford Bridge Gt Man 79 8007
Blackfordby Leics 62 3217
Blackgang IOW 13 4876
Blackhall C Edin 117 1975
Blackhall Dur 97 4638
Blackhall Colliery Dur 97 4539
Blackhaugh Border 109 4238
Blackheath Essex 40 0021
Blackheath Gt Lon 27 3876
Blackheath Suffk 55 4274
Blackheath Surrey 14 0346
Blackheath W Mids 60 9786
Blackhill Abers 143 0039
Blackhill Abers 143 0755
Blackhill Abers 143 0843
Blackhill Dur 95 0851
Blackhill of Clackriach Abers 143 9246
Blackhorse Devon 9 9893
Blackhorse Hill E Susx 17 7714
Blackjack Lincs 64 2639
Blackland Somset 19 8336
Blackland Wilts 22 0168
Blacklaw D & G 108 0408
Blackley Gt Man 79 8502
Blacklunans P & K 133 1460
Blackmarstone Herefd 46 5038
Blackmill Brdgnd 33 9386
Blackmoor Hants 14 7733
Blackmoor Somset 21 4661
Blackmoorfoot W York 82 0913
Blackmore Essex 40 6001
Blackmore End Essex 40 7430
Blackmore End Herts 39 1716
Blackness Falk 117 0579
Blacknest Berks 25 9568
Blacknest Hants 25 7941
Blacko Lancs 81 8541
Blackpool Devon 7 8547
Blackpool Devon 7 8174
Blackpool Lancs 80 3036
Blackpool Gate Cumb 101 5377
Blackridge W Loth 116 8967
Blackrock Cnwll 2 6534
Blackrock Mons 33 2112
Blackrock Mons 34 5188
Blackrod Gt Man 78 6110
Blacksboat Moray 141 1838
Blackshaw D & G 100 0465
Blackshaw Head W York 82 9527
Blacksmith's Green Suffk 54 1465
Blacksnape Lancs 81 7121
Blackstone W Susx 15 2316
Blackthorn Oxon 37 6219
Blackthorpe Suffk 54 9063
Blacktoft E R Yk 84 8324
Blacktop Aber C 135 8604
Blackwall Derbys 73 2549
Blackwater Cnwll 3 7346
Blackwater Hants 25 8459
Blackwater IOW 13 5086
Blackwater Somset 10 2615
Blackwaterfoot N Ayrs 105 9028
Blackwell Cumb 93 4053
Blackwell Derbys 74 1272
Blackwell Derbys 75 4458
Blackwell Dur 89 2713
Blackwell Warwks 48 2443
Blackwell Worcs 60 9972
Blackwellsend Green Gloucs 47 7825
Blackwood Caerph 33 1797
Blackwood D & G 100 9087
Blackwood S Lans 116 7844
Blackwood Hill Staffs 72 9255
Blacon Ches 71 3868
Bladbean Kent 29 1847
Bladnoch D & G 99 4254
Bladon Oxon 37 4514
Bladon Somset 21 4220
Blaen Dyryn Powys 45 9336
Blaen-y-Coed Carmth 31 3427
Blaen-y-cwm Blae G 33 1311
Blaen-y-cwm Rhondd 33 9298
Blaenannerch Cerdgn 42 2448
Blaenau Ffestiniog Gwynd 57 7045
Blaenavon Torfn 34 2508
Blaenffos Pembks 31 1937
Blaengarw Brdgnd 33 9092
Blaengeuffardd Cerdgn 43 6480
Blaengwrach Neath 33 8605
Blaengwynfi Neath 33 8996
Blaenllechau Rhondd 33 0097
Blaenpennal Cerdgn 43 6264
Blaenplwyf Cerdgn 43 5775
Blaenporth Cerdgn 42 2648
Blaenrhondda Rhondd 33 9299
Blaenwaun Carmth 31 2327
Blaenycwm Cerdgn 43 8275
Blagdon Devon 7 8561
Blagdon Somset 20 2118
Blagdon Somset 21 5059
Blagdon Hill Somset 9 2117
Blagill Cumb 94 7347
Blaguegate Lancs 78 4506
Blaich Highld 130 0376
Blain Highld 129 6769
Blaina Blae G 33 2008
Blair Atholl P & K 132 8665
Blair Drummond Stirlg 116 7399
Blair's Ferry Ag & B 114 9869
Blairgowrie P & K 126 1745
Blairingone P & K 117 9896
Blairlogie Stirlg 116 8396
Blairmore Ag & B 114 1983
Blairmore Highld 148 1959
Blairnamarrow Moray 141 2015
Blaisdon Gloucs 35 7017
Blake End Essex 40 7023
Blakebrook Worcs 60 8276
Blakedown Worcs 60 8878
Blakeley Lane Staffs 72 9746
Blakemere Ches 71 5571
Blakemere Herefd 46 3641
Blakemore Devon 7 7660
Blakeney Gloucs 35 6707
Blakeney Norfk 66 0243
Blakenhall Ches 72 7247
Blakenhall W Mids 60 9197
Blakeshall Worcs 60 8381
Blakesley Nhants 49 6250
Blanchland Nthumb 95 9650
Bland Hill N York 82 2053
Blandford Camp Dorset 11 9107
Blandford Forum Dorset 11 8806
Blandford St Mary Dorset 11 8805
Blanefield Stirlg 115 5479
Blankney Lincs 76 0660
Blantyre S Lans 116 6957
Blar a' Chaorainn Highld 130 1066
Blargie Highld 132 6094
Blarmachfoldach Highld 130 0969
Blashford Hants 12 1506
Blaston Leics 51 8095
Blatherwycke Nhants 51 9795
Blawith Cumb 86 2888
Blawquhairn D & G 99 6282
Blaxhall Suffk 55 3656
Blaxton S York 75 6700
Blaydon T & W 103 1863
Bleadney Somset 21 4845
Bleadon Somset 21 3456
Bleak Street Somset 22 7631
Blean Kent 29 1260
Bleasby Lincs 76 1384
Bleasby Notts 75 7149
Bleasdale Lancs 81 5745
Bleatarn Cumb 94 7313
Bleathwood Herefd 46 5570
Blebocraigs Fife 127 4214
Bleddfa Powys 45 2068
Bledington Gloucs 36 2422
Bledlow Bucks 37 7702
Bledlow Ridge Bucks 37 7997
Bleet Wilts 22 8958
Blegbie E Loth 118 4861
Blencarn Cumb 94 6331
Blencogo Cumb 93 1947
Blendworth Hants 13 7113
Blennerhasset Cumb 93 1741
Bletchingdon Oxon 37 5018
Bletchingley Surrey 27 3250
Bletchley Bucks 38 8633
Bletchley Shrops 59 6233
Bletherston Pembks 31 0721
Bletsoe Beds 51 0258
Blewbury Oxon 37 5385
Blickling Norfk 66 1728
Blidworth Notts 75 5956
Blidworth Bottoms Notts 75 5954
Blindburn Nthumb 110 8210
Blindcrake Cumb 92 1434
Blindley Heath Surrey 15 3645
Blisland Cnwll 4 1073
Bliss Gate Worcs 60 7472
Blissford Hants 12 1713
Blisworth Nhants 49 7253
Blithbury Staffs 73 0819
Blitterlees Cumb 92 1052
Blo Norton Norfk 54 0179
Blockley Gloucs 48 1634
Blofield Norfk 67 3309
Bloomfield Border 110 5824
Blore Staffs 72 7234
Blore Staffs 73 1349
Blounts Green Staffs 73 0732
Blowick Mersyd 80 3516
Bloxham Oxon 49 4336
Bloxholm Lincs 76 0653
Bloxwich W Mids 60 9902
Bloxworth Dorset 11 8894
Blubberhouses N York 82 1655
Blue Anchor Cnwll 4 9157
Blue Anchor Somset 20 0243
Blue Bell Hill Kent 28 7462
Blundellsands Mersyd 78 3099
Blundeston Suffk 67 5297
Blunham Beds 52 1551
Blunsdon St Andrew Wilts 36 1389
Bluntington Worcs 60 9074
Bluntisham Cambs 52 3674
Blunts Cnwll 5 3463
Blunts Green Warwks 48 1468
Blurton Staffs 72 8941
Blyborough Lincs 76 9394
Blyford Suffk 55 4276
Blymhill Staffs 60 8112
Blymhill Lawn Staffs 60 8211
Blyth Notts 75 6287
Blyth Nthumb 103 3181
Blyth Bridge Border 117 1345
Blythburgh Suffk 55 4475
Blythe Border 110 5849
Blythe Bridge Staffs 72 9541
Blythe End Warwks 61 2190
Blythe Marsh Staffs 72 9640
Blyton Lincs 76 8594
Bo'ness Falk 117 0081
Boar's Head Gt Man 78 5708
Boarhills Fife 127 5613
Boarhunt Hants 13 6008
Boarley Kent 28 7659
Boars Hill Oxon 37 4902
Boarsgreave Lancs 81 8420
Boarshead E Susx 16 5332
Boarstall Bucks 37 6214
Boasley Cross Devon 5 5093
Boat of Garten Highld 140 9319
Boath Highld 146 5774
Bobbing Kent 28 8865
Bobbington Staffs 60 8090
Bobbingworth Essex 39 5305
Bocaddon Cnwll 4 1858
Bochym Cnwll 2 6920
Bocking Essex 40 7623
Bocking Churchstreet Essex 40 7525
Bockleton Worcs 46 5961
Boconnoc Cnwll 4 1460
Boddam Abers 143 1342
Boddam Shet 153 3915
Boddington Gloucs 47 8925
Bodedern IOA 68 3380
Bodelwyddan Denbgs 70 0075
Bodenham Herefd 46 5350
Bodenham Wilts 23 1626
Bodenham Moor Herefd 46 5450
Bodewryd IOA 68 4090
Bodfari Denbgs 70 0970
Bodffordd IOA 68 4277
Bodfuan Gwynd 56 3237
Bodham Norfk 66 1240
Bodiam E Susx 17 7825
Bodicote Oxon 49 4538
Bodieve Cnwll 4 9973
Bodinnick Cnwll 3 1352
Bodle Street Green E Susx 16 6514
Bodmin Cnwll 4 0667
Bodney Norfk 66 8298
Bodorgan IOA 68 3867
Bodrean Cnwll 3 8448
Bodsham Green Kent 29 1045
Bodwen Cnwll 4 0360
Bodymoor Heath Warwks 61 1996
Bogallan Highld 140 6350
Bogbrae Abers 143 0335
Boghall Mdloth 117 2465
Boghall W Loth 117 9867
Boghead S Lans 107 7742
Boghead Farm Moray 141 3559
Bogmoor Moray 141 3563
Bogmuir Abers 135 6471
Bogniebrae Abers 142 5945
Bognor Regis W Susx 14 9399
Bogroy Highld 140 9022
Bogue D & G 99 6481
Bohetherick Devon 5 4167
Bohortha Cnwll 3 8532
Bohuntine Highld 131 2983
Bojewyan Cnwll 2 3934
Bokiddick Cnwll 4 0562
Bolam Dur 96 1922
Bolam Nthumb 103 1082
Bolberry Devon 7 6939
Bold Heath Mersyd 78 5389
Boldmere W Mids 61 1194
Boldon Colliery T & W 96 3462
Boldre Hants 12 3198
Boldron Dur 95 0314
Bole Notts 75 7987
Bole Hill Derbys 74 3374
Bolehill Derbys 73 2955
Bolenowe Cnwll 2 6738
Bolfracks P & K 125 8248
Bolham Devon 9 9515
Bolham Water Devon 9 1612
Bolingey Cnwll 3 7653
Bollington Ches 79 9377
Bollington Cross Ches 79 9277
Bollow Gloucs 35 7413
Bolney W Susx 15 2622
Bolnhurst Beds 51 0859
Bolshan Angus 127 6252
Bolsover Derbys 75 4770
Bolster Moor W York 82 0815
Bolsterstone S York 74 2696
Boltby N York 90 4886
Boltenstone Abers 134 4110
Bolter End Bucks 37 7992
Bolton Cumb 94 6323
Bolton E Loth 118 5070
Bolton E R Yk 84 7752
Bolton Gt Man 79 7108
Bolton Nthumb 111 1013
Bolton Abbey N York 82 0754
Bolton Bridge N York 82 0653
Bolton by Bowland Lancs 81 7849
Bolton Hall N York 88 0789
Bolton le Sands Lancs 87 4867
Bolton Low Houses Cumb 93 2344
Bolton New Houses Cumb 93 2444
Bolton Percy N York 83 5341
Bolton Town End Lancs 87 4867
Bolton Upon Dearne S York 83 4502
Bolton-on-Swale N York 89 2599
Boltonfellend Cumb 101 4768
Boltongate Cumb 93 2340
Bolventor Cnwll 4 1876
Bomarsund Nthumb 103 2684
Bomere Heath Shrops 59 4719
Bonar Bridge Highld 146 6191
Bonawe Ag & B 122 0131
Bonawe Quarries Ag & B 122 0033
Bonby Lincs 84 0015
Boncath Pembks 31 2038
Bonchester Bridge Border 110 5812
Bonchurch IOW 13 5778
Bond's Green Herefd 46 3554
Bondleigh Devon 8 6505
Bonds Lancs 80 4944
Bone Cnwll 2 4632
Bonehill Devon 8 7277
Bonehill Staffs 61 1902
Boney Hay Staffs 61 0410
Bonhill W Duns 115 3979
Boningale Shrops 60 8202
Bonjedward Border 110 6522
Bonkle N Lans 116 8457
Bonnington Angus 127 5739
Bonnington C Edin 117 1269
Bonnington Kent 17 0535
Bonnybank Fife 126 3503
Bonnybridge Falk 116 8279
Bonnykelly Abers 143 8653
Bonnyrigg Mdloth 117 3065
Bonnyton Angus 126 3338
Bonsall Derbys 74 2758
Bonshaw Tower D & G 101 2472
Bont Mons 34 3819
Bont-Dolgadfan Powys 57 8800
Bontddu Gwynd 57 6718
Bonthorpe Lincs 77 4872
Bontnewydd Cerdgn 43 6165
Bontnewydd Gwynd 68 4859
Bontuchel Denbgs 70 0857
Bonvilston V Glam 33 0673
Bonwm Denbgs 70 1042
Bonymaen Swans 32 6795
Boode Devon 19 5037
Boohay Devon 7 8952
Booker Bucks 37 8391
Booley Shrops 59 5625
Boon Border 110 5745
Boon Hill Staffs 72 8150
Boorley Green Hants 13 5014
Boosbeck N York 97 6617
Boose's Green Essex 40 8431
Boot Cnwll 5 2697
Boot Cumb 86 1700
Boot Street Suffk 55 2248
Booth E R Yk 84 7326
Booth W York 82 0427
Booth Green Ches 79 9280
Booth Town W York 82 0926
Boothby Graffoe Lincs 76 9859
Boothby Pagnell Lincs 63 9730
Boothstown Gt Man 79 7200
Boothville Nhants 50 7864
Bootle Cumb 86 1088
Bootle Mersyd 78 3495
Boots Green Ches 79 7572
Booze N York 88 0102
Boraston Shrops 46 6169
Bordeaux Guern 158 0000
Borden Kent 28 8862
Borden W Susx 14 8324
Border Cumb 92 1654
Bordley N York 88 9465
Bordon Hants 14 8035
Bordon Camp Hants 14 7936
Boreham Essex 40 7609
Boreham Wilts 22 8944
Boreham Street E Susx 16 6611
Borehamwood Herts 26 1996
Boreland D & G 100 1691
Boreraig Highld 136 1853
Boreston Devon 7 7653
Boreton Ches 59 5106
Borgh W Isls 152 4055
Borgh W Isls 152 6501
Borgie Highld 149 6759
Borgue D & G 99 6248
Borgue Highld 151 1326
Borley Essex 54 8443
Borley Green Essex 54 8442
Borley Green Suffk 54 9960
Borneskitaig Highld 136 3770
Borness D & G 99 6145
Borough Green Kent 27 6157
Boroughbridge N York 89 3966
Borras Head Wrexhm 71 3653
Borrowash Derbys 62 4234
Borrowby N York 97 7715
Borrowby N York 89 4289
Borrowdale Cumb 93 2514
Borrowstoun Falk 117 9980
Borstal Kent 28 7366
Borth Cerdgn 43 6090
Borth-y-Gest Gwynd 57 5637
Borthwick Mdloth 118 3659
Borthwickbrae Border 109 4113
Borthwickshiels Border 109 4315
Borve Highld 136 4448
Borve W Isls 152 4055
Borve W Isls 152 6501
Borve W Isls 152 0394
Borwick Lancs 87 5272
Borwick Lodge Cumb 87 3499
Borwick Rails Cumb 86 1879
Bosavern Cnwll 2 3730
Bosbury Herefd 47 6943
Boscarne Cnwll 4 0367
Boscastle Cnwll 4 0990
Boscombe Dorset 12 1191
Boscombe Wilts 23 2038
Boscoppa Cnwll 3 0353
Bosham W Susx 14 8003
Bosham Hoe W Susx 14 8102
Bosherston Pembks 30 9694
Boskednan Cnwll 2 4434
Boskennal Cnwll 2 4223
Bosley Ches 72 9165
Bosoughan Cnwll 4 8760
Bossall N York 90 7160
Bossiney Cnwll 4 0688
Bossingham Kent 29 1548
Bossington Somset 19 8947
Bostock Green Ches 79 6769
Boston Lincs 64 3343
Boston Spa W York 83 4245
Boswarthan Cnwll 2 4433
Boswinger Cnwll 3 9841
Botallack Cnwll 2 3732
Botany Bay Gt Lon 27 2999
Botcheston Leics 62 4804
Botesdale Suffk 54 0475

Brinklow Burnfoot


Brinklow Warwks 50 4379
Brinkworth Wilts 35 0184
Brinscall Lancs 81 6221
Brinscombe Somset 21 4251
Brinsea Somset 21 4461
Brinsley Notts 75 4548
Brinsop Herefd 46 4444
Brinsworth S York 74 4289
Brinton Norfk 66 0335
Brinyan Ork 153 4327
Brisco Cumb 93 4252
Brisley Norfk 66 9421
Brislington Bristl 35 6270
Brissenden Green Kent 28 9439
Bristol Bristl 34 5972
Briston Norfk 66 0632
Brisworthy Devon 6 5665
Britannia Lancs 81 8821
Britford Wilts 23 1627
Brithdir Caerph 33 1401
Brithdir Gwynd 57 7618
British Torfn 34 2503
British Legion Village Kent 28 7257
Briton Ferry Neath 32 7394
Britwell Salome Oxon 37 6792
Brixham Devon 7 9255
Brixton Devon 6 5552
Brixton Gt Lon 27 3175
Brixton Deverill Wilts 22 8638
Brixworth Nhants 50 7470
Brize Norton Oxon 36 2907
Broad Alley Worcs 47 8867
Broad Blunsdon Wilts 36 1491
Broad Campden Gloucs 48 1537
Broad Carr W York 82 0919
Broad Chalke Wilts 23 0325
Broad Clough Lancs 81 8623
Broad Ford Kent 28 7139
Broad Green Essex 40 8823
Broad Green Suffk 53 7859
Broad Green Worcs 47 7756
Broad Green Worcs 60 9970
Broad Haven Pembks 30 8613
Broad Hill Cambs 53 5976
Broad Hinton Wilts 36 1075
Broad Laying Hants 24 4362
Broad Marston Worcs 48 1446
Broad Meadow Staffs 72 8348
Broad Oak Cumb 86 1194
Broad Oak E Susx 17 8219
Broad Oak E Susx 16 6022
Broad Oak Hants 24 7551
Broad Oak Herefd 34 4821
Broad Oak Kent 29 1761
Broad Oak Mersyd 78 5395
Broad Road Suffk 55 2676
Broad Street E Susx 17 8616
Broad Street Essex 39 5516
Broad Street Kent 28 7672
Broad Street Kent 28 8356
Broad Street Wilts 23 1059
Broad Street Green Essex 40 8509
Broad Town Wilts 36 0977
Broad's Green Essex 40 6912
Broadbottom Gt Man 79 9993
Broadbridge W Susx 14 8105
Broadbridge Heath W Susx 15 1431
Broadclyst Devon 9 9897
Broadfield Inver 115 3373
Broadfield Pembks 31 1303
Broadford Highld 129 6423
Broadford Bridge W Susx 14 0921
Broadgairhill Border 109 2010
Broadgate Lincs 64 3610
Broadgrass Green Suffk 54 9663
Broadhaugh Border 119 8655
Broadheath Gt Man 79 7689
Broadheath Worcs 47 6665
Broadhembury Devon 9 1004
Broadhempston Devon 7 8066
Broadholme Notts 76 8874
Broadland Row E Susx 17 8319
Broadlay Carmth 31 3709
Broadley Essex 39 4207
Broadley Gt Man 81 8816
Broadley Moray 142 3961
Broadley Common Essex 39 4207
Broadmayne Dorset 11 7286
Broadmere Hants 24 6247
Broadmoor Gloucs 35 6415
Broadmoor Pembks 31 0906
Broadnymett Devon 8 7001
Broadoak Dorset 10 4396
Broadoak Gloucs 35 6912
Broadoak Wrexhm 71 3658
Broadstairs Kent 29 3967
Broadstone Dorset 11 0095
Broadstone Mons 34 5102
Broadstone Shrops 59 5489
Broadwas Worcs 47 7555
Broadwater Herts 39 2422
Broadwater W Susx 15 1404
Broadwaters Worcs 60 8477
Broadway Carmth 31 2910
Broadway Carmth 31 3808
Broadway Pembks 30 8713
Broadway Somset 10 3215
Broadway Suffk 55 3979
Broadway Worcs 48 0937
Broadwell Gloucs 34 5811
Broadwell Gloucs 48 2027
Broadwell Oxon 36 2504
Broadwell Warwks 50 4565
Broadwey Dorset 11 6683
Broadwindsor Dorset 10 4302
Broadwood Kelly Devon 8 6106
Broadwoodwidger Devon 5 4189
Brobury Herefd 46 3444
Brochel Highld 137 5846
Brock Lancs 80 5140
Brock's Green Hants 24 5061
Brockamin Worcs 47 7753
Brockbridge Hants 13 6118
Brockdish Norfk 55 2179
Brockencote Worcs 60 8873
Brockenhurst Hants 12 3002
Brocketsbrae S Lans 108 8239
Brockford Green Suffk 54 1265
Brockford Street Suffk 54 1167
Brockhall Nhants 49 6362
Brockham Surrey 15 1949
Brockhampton Gloucs 47 9326
Brockhampton Gloucs 36 0322
Brockhampton Hants 13 7106
Brockhampton Herefd 46 5931
Brockhampton Green Dorset 11 7106
Brockholes W York 82 1510
Brockhurst Derbys 74 3364
Brockhurst Warwks 50 4683
Brocklebank Cumb 93 3042
Brocklesby Lincs 85 1311
Brockley Somset 21 4666
Brockley Suffk 54 8371
Brockley Green Suffk 53 7247
Brockley Green Suffk 54 8254
Brockleymoor Cumb 94 4937
Brockmoor W Mids 60 9088
Brockscombe Devon 5 4695
Brockton Shrops 59 3104
Brockton Shrops 60 7103
Brockton Shrops 59 3285
Brockton Shrops 59 5794
Brockton Staffs 72 8131
Brockweir Gloucs 34 5401
Brockwood Park Hants 13 6226
Brockworth Gloucs 35 8916
Brocton Cnwll 4 0168
Brocton Staffs 72 9619
Brodick N Ayrs 105 0135
Brodie Moray 140 9757
Brodsworth S York 83 5007
Brogaig Highld 136 4767
Brogborough Beds 38 9638
Broken Cross Ches 79 6873
Broken Cross Ches 79 8973
Brokenborough Wilts 35 9189
Brokerswood Wilts 22 8352
Bromborough Mersyd 78 3582
Brome Suffk 54 1376
Brome Street Suffk 54 1576
Bromeswell Suffk 55 3050
Bromfield Cumb 93 1746
Bromfield Shrops 46 4876
Bromham Beds 38 0051
Bromham Wilts 22 9665
Bromley Gt Lon 27 4069
Bromley S York 74 3298
Bromley Shrops 60 7395
Bromley W Mids 60 9088
Bromley Common Gt Lon 27 4266
Bromley Cross Essex 41 0627
Bromlow Shrops 59 3201
Brompton Kent 28 7668
Brompton N York 89 3796
Brompton N York 91 9482
Brompton Shrops 59 5408
Brompton Ralph Somset 20 0832
Brompton Regis Somset 20 9531
Brompton-on-Swale N York 89 2199
Bromsash Herefd 47 6524
Bromsberrow Gloucs 47 7433
Bromsberrow Heath Gloucs 47 7333
Bromsgrove Worcs 60 9670
Bromstead Heath Staffs 72 7917
Bromyard Herefd 47 6554
Bromyard Downs Herefd 47 6655
Bronaber Gwynd 57 7131
Bronant Cerdgn 43 6467
Broncroft Shrops 59 5486
Brongest Cerdgn 42 3245
Bronington Wrexhm 71 4839
Bronllys Powys 45 1434
Bronwydd Carmth 31 4123
Bronydd Powys 45 2245
Bronygarth Shrops 58 2637
Brook Carmth 31 2609
Brook Hants 12 2714
Brook Hants 23 3429
Brook IOW 13 3983
Brook Kent 29 0644
Brook Surrey 14 9237
Brook Surrey 14 0546
Brook End Beds 51 0763
Brook End Beds 52 1547
Brook End Bucks 38 9244
Brook End Cambs 51 0773
Brook Hill Hants 12 2714
Brook House Denbgs 70 0765
Brook Street Essex 27 5793
Brook Street Kent 17 9333
Brook Street Suffk 54 8248
Brook Street W Susx 15 3026
Brooke Norfk 67 2899
Brooke Rutlnd 63 8405
Brookfield Rens 115 4164
Brookhampton Oxon 37 6098
Brookhampton Somset 21 6327
Brookhouse Lancs 87 5464
Brookhouse S York 75 5188
Brookhouse Green Ches 72 8161
Brookhouses Derbys 74 0388
Brookland Kent 17 9926
Brooklands Gt Man 79 7890
Brookmans Park Herts 39 2404
Brooks Powys 58 1499
Brooks End Kent 29 2967
Brooks Green W Susx 14 1224
Brooksby Leics 63 6715
Brookthorpe Gloucs 35 8312
Brookville Norfk 65 7396
Brookwood Surrey 25 9557
Broom Beds 39 1742
Broom Dur 96 2441
Broom S York 75 4491
Broom Warwks 48 0853
Broom Green Norfk 66 9823
Broom Hill Dorset 12 0302
Broom Hill Notts 62 5447
Broom Hill S York 83 4102
Broom Hill Worcs 60 9175
Broom Street Kent 28 0462
Broom's Green Gloucs 47 7132
Broome Norfk 67 3591
Broome Shrops 59 4080
Broome Worcs 60 9078
Broome Park Nthumb 111 1012
Broomedge Ches 79 7085
Broomer's Corner W Susx 14 1220
Broomershill W Susx 14 0619
Broomfield Essex 40 7010
Broomfield Kent 28 8452
Broomfield Kent 29 1966
Broomfield Somset 20 2232
Broomfields Shrops 59 4217
Broomfleet E R Yk 84 8727
Broomhall Surrey 25 9566
Broomhaugh Nthumb 103 0261
Broomhill Nthumb 103 2401
Broomhill Green Ches 71 6247
Broomley Nthumb 103 0360
Broomsthorpe Norfk 66 8428
Brora Highld 147 9103
Broseley Shrops 60 6701
Brotherhouse Bar Lincs 64 2614
Brotherlee Dur 95 9237
Brothertoft Lincs 77 2746
Brotherton N York 83 4825
Brotton N York 97 6819
Broubster Highld 150 0359
Brough Cumb 95 7914
Brough Derbys 74 1882
Brough E R Yk 84 9326
Brough Highld 151 2273
Brough Notts 76 8458
Brough Shet 153 5665
Brough Lodge Shet 153 5892
Brough Sowerby Cumb 95 7912
Broughall Shrops 71 5741
Broughton Border 108 1136
Broughton Bucks 38 8413
Broughton Bucks 38 8939
Broughton Cambs 52 2878
Broughton Flints 71 3363
Broughton Gt Man 79 8201
Broughton Hants 23 3033
Broughton Lancs 80 5234
Broughton Lincs 84 9608
Broughton N York 82 9451
Broughton N York 90 7673
Broughton Nhants 51 8375
Broughton Oxon 49 4138
Broughton Staffs 72 7634
Broughton V Glam 33 9270
Broughton Astley Leics 50 5292
Broughton Beck Cumb 86 2882
Broughton Gifford Wilts 22 8763
Broughton Green Worcs 47 9561
Broughton Hackett Worcs 47 9254
Broughton Mains D & G 99 4545
Broughton Mills Cumb 86 2290
Broughton Moor Cumb 92 0533
Broughton Poggs Oxon 36 2303
Broughton Tower Cumb 86 2187
Broughton-in-Furness Cumb 86 2187
Broughty Ferry Dund C 127 4630
Brow End Cumb 86 2674
Brow-of-the-Hill Norfk 65 6819
Brown Candover Hants 24 5739
Brown Edge Lancs 80 3614
Brown Edge Staffs 72 9053
Brown Heath Ches 71 4564
Brown Lees Staffs 72 8756
Brown Street Suffk 54 0663
Brown's Green W Mids 61 0591
Brownber Cumb 87 7005
Brownheath Shrops 59 4629
Brownhill Abers 143 8640
Brownhills Fife 127 5215
Brownhills W Mids 61 0405
Brownieside Nthumb 111 1623
Browninghill Green Hants 24 5859
Brownlow Heath Ches 72 8360
Brownrigg Cumb 92 0420
Brownrigg Cumb 92 1652
Browns Hill Gloucs 35 8802
Brownsham Devon 18 2826
Brownsover Warwks 50 5177
Brownston Devon 7 6952
Browston Green Norfk 67 4901
Broxa N York 91 9491
Broxbourne Herts 39 3606
Broxburn E Loth 119 6977
Broxburn W Loth 117 0872
Broxfield Nthumb 111 2016
Broxted Essex 40 5727
Broxton Ches 71 4754
Broxwood Herefd 46 3654
Broyle Side E Susx 16 4513
Bruan Highld 151 3139
Bruar P & K 132 8265
Brucefield Highld 147 9386
Bruchag Ag & B 114 1157
Bruera Ches 71 4360
Bruern Abbey Oxon 36 2620
Bruichladdich Ag & B 112 2661
Bruisyard Suffk 55 3266
Bruisyard Street Suffk 55 3365
Brumby Lincs 84 8909
Brund Staffs 74 1061
Brundall Norfk 67 3308
Brundish Suffk 55 2769
Brundish Street Suffk 55 2671
Brunnion Cnwll 2 5036
Brunslow Shrops 59 3684
Bruntcliffe W York 82 2526
Brunthwaite W York 82 0546
Bruntingthorpe Leics 50 6089
Brunton Fife 126 3220
Brunton Nthumb 111 2024
Brunton Wilts 23 2456
Brushford Somset 20 9225
Brushford Barton Devon 8 6707
Bruton Somset 22 6835
Bryan's Green Worcs 47 8868
Bryanston Dorset 11 8607
Bryant's Bottom Bucks 26 8599
Brydekirk D & G 101 1870
Brymbo Wrexhm 71 2953
Brympton Somset 10 5115
Bryn Ches 71 6072
Bryn Gt Man 78 5600
Bryn Neath 33 8192
Bryn Shrops 59 2985
Bryn Du IOA 68 3472
Bryn Gates Lancs 78 5901
Bryn Golau Rhondd 33 0088
Bryn Saith Marchog Denbgs 70 0750
Bryn-bwbach Gwynd 57 6236
Bryn-coch Neath 32 7499
Bryn-Eden Gwynd 57 7129
Bryn-Henllan Pembks 30 0139
Bryn-mawr Gwynd 56 2433
Bryn-newydd Denbgs 70 1842
Bryn-penarth Powys 58 1004
Bryn-y-bal Flints 70 2564
Bryn-y-Maen Conwy 69 8376
Bryn-yr-Eos Wrexhm 70 2840
Brynaman Carmth 32 7114
Brynberian Pembks 31 1035
Brynbryddan Neath 32 7792
Bryncae Rhondd 33 9982
Bryncethin Brdgnd 33 9183
Bryncir Gwynd 56 4844
Bryncroes Gwynd 56 2231
Bryncrug Gwynd 57 6103
Bryneglwys Denbgs 70 1447
Brynfields Wrexhm 71 3044
Brynford Flints 70 1774
Bryngwran IOA 68 3577
Bryngwyn Mons 34 3909
Bryngwyn Powys 45 1849
Brynhoffnant Cerdgn 42 3351
Bryning Lancs 80 4029
Brynithel Blae G 33 2101
Brynmawr Blae G 33 1911
Brynmenyn Brdgnd 33 9084
Brynmill Swans 32 6392
Brynna Rhondd 33 9883
Brynrefail Gwynd 69 5562
Brynrefail IOA 68 4886
Brynsadler Rhondd 33 0280
Brynsiencyn IOA 68 4867
Brynteg IOA 68 4982
Bualintur Highld 128 4020
Buarth-draw Flints 70 1779
Bubbenhall Warwks 61 3672
Bubwith E R Yk 84 7136
Buchanan Smithy Stirlg 115 4689
Buchanhaven Abers 143 1247
Buchanty P & K 125 9328
Buchany Stirlg 124 7102
Buchlyvie Stirlg 115 5793
Buck's Cross Devon 18 3522
Buck's Mills Devon 18 3523
Buckabank Cumb 93 3749
Buckden Cambs 52 1967
Buckden N York 88 9477
Buckenham Norfk 67 3505
Buckerell Devon 9 1200
Buckfast Devon 7 7467
Buckfastleigh Devon 7 7366
Buckhaven Fife 118 3598
Buckholm Border 109 4738
Buckholt Mons 34 5016
Buckhorn Weston Dorset 22 7524
Buckhurst Hill Essex 27 4194
Buckie Moray 142 4265
Buckingham Bucks 49 6933
Buckland Bucks 38 8812
Buckland Devon 7 6743
Buckland Gloucs 48 0835
Buckland Hants 12 3196
Buckland Herts 39 3533
Buckland Kent 29 3042
Buckland Oxon 36 3498
Buckland Surrey 26 2150
Buckland Brewer Devon 18 4220
Buckland Common Bucks 38 9207
Buckland Dinham Somset 22 7551
Buckland Filleigh Devon 18 4609
Buckland in the Moor Devon 7 7273
Buckland Monachorum Devon 6 4968
Buckland Newton Dorset 11 6805
Buckland Ripers Dorset 11 6582
Buckland St Mary Somset 10 2613
Buckland-Tout-Saints Devon 7 7645
Bucklebury Berks 24 5570
Bucklerheads Angus 127 4636
Bucklers Hard Hants 13 4000
Bucklesham Suffk 55 2441
Buckley Flints 70 2763
Buckley Green Warwks 48 1567
Buckley Mountain Flints 70 2765
Bucklow Hill Ches 79 7383
Buckminster Leics 63 8722
Bucknall Lincs 76 1668
Bucknall Staffs 72 9047
Bucknell Oxon 49 5625
Bucknell Shrops 46 3574
Buckpool Moray 142 4165
Bucks Green W Susx 14 0833
Bucks Hill Herts 26 0500
Bucks Horn Oak Hants 25 8041
Bucksburn Aber C 135 8909
Buckshead Cnwll 3 8346
Buckton E R Yk 91 1872
Buckton Herefd 46 3873
Buckton Nthumb 111 0838
Buckworth Cambs 52 1476
Budbrooke Warwks 48 2665
Budby Notts 75 6169
Budd's Titson Cnwll 18 2401
Buddileigh Staffs 72 7449
Buddon Angus 127 5232
Bude Cnwll 18 2105
Budge's Shop Cnwll 5 3259
Budlake Devon 9 9800
Budle Nthumb 111 1535
Budleigh Salterton Devon 9 0682
Budlett's Common E Susx 16 4723
Budock Water Cnwll 3 7831
Buerton Ches 72 6843
Bugbrooke Nhants 49 6757
Bugford Devon 7 8350
Buglawton Ches 72 8763
Bugle Cnwll 4 0158
Bugley Dorset 22 7824
Bugthorpe E R Yk 90 7757
Buildwas Shrops 59 6204
Builth Road Powys 45 0353
Builth Wells Powys 45 0350
Bulbourne Herts 38 9313
Bulbridge Wilts 23 0830
Bulby Lincs 64 0526
Buldoo Highld 150 0067
Bulford Wilts 23 1643
Bulford Barracks Wilts 23 1843
Bulkeley Ches 71 5354
Bulkington Warwks 61 3986
Bulkington Wilts 22 9458
Bulkworthy Devon 18 3914
Bull Bay IOA 68 4294
Bull's Green Herts 39 2717
Bull's Green Norfk 67 4194
Bullamore N York 89 3994
Bullbridge Derbys 74 3552
Bullbrook Berks 25 8869
Bullen's Green Herts 39 2105
Bulley Gloucs 35 7619
Bullgill Cumb 92 0938
Bullinghope Herefd 46 5136
Bullington Hants 24 4541
Bullington Lincs 76 0877
Bullington End Bucks 38 8145
Bullockstone Kent 29 1665
Bulmer Essex 54 8440
Bulmer N York 90 6967
Bulmer Tye Essex 54 8438
Bulphan Essex 40 6385
Bulstone Devon 9 1789
Bulstrode Herts 26 0302
Bulstrode Park Bucks 26 9888
Bulverhythe E Susx 17 7708
Bulwark Abers 143 9345
Bulwell Notts 62 5343
Bulwick Nhants 51 9694
Bumble's Green Essex 39 4005
Bunacaimb Highld 129 6588
Bunarkaig Highld 131 1887
Bunbury Ches 71 5657
Bunbury Heath Ches 71 5558
Bunchrew Highld 140 6246
Buncton W Susx 15 1413
Bundalloch Highld 138 8927
Bunessan Ag & B 121 3821
Bungay Suffk 55 3389
Bunker's Hill Lincs 77 2653
Bunnahabhainn Ag & B 112 4173
Bunny Notts 62 5829
Buntait Highld 139 4030
Buntingford Herts 39 3629
Bunwell Norfk 66 1292
Bunwell Street Norfk 66 1193
Bupton Derbys 73 2237
Burbage Derbys 74 0472
Burbage Leics 50 4492
Burbage Wilts 23 2261
Burcher Herefd 46 3360
Burchett's Green Berks 26 8481
Burchett's Green E Susx 16 6631
Burcombe Wilts 23 0730
Burcot Oxon 37 5695
Burcot Worcs 60 9871
Burcote Shrops 60 7495
Burcott Bucks 38 8415
Burcott Bucks 38 8823
Burdale N York 90 8762
Bures Suffk 54 9034
Burford Oxon 36 2512
Burford Shrops 46 5868
Burg Ag & B 121 3845
Burgates Hants 14 7728
Burge End Herts 38 1432
Burgess Hill W Susx 15 3218
Burgh Suffk 55 2351
Burgh by Sands Cumb 93 3259
Burgh Castle Norfk 67 4805
Burgh Heath Surrey 26 2457
Burgh Hill E Susx 17 7226
Burgh le Marsh Lincs 77 5065
Burgh next Aylsham Norfk 67 2125
Burgh on Bain Lincs 76 2186
Burgh St Margaret Norfk 67 4413
Burgh St Peter Norfk 67 4693
Burghclere Hants 24 4761
Burghead Moray 141 1168
Burghfield Berks 24 6668
Burghfield Common Berks 24 6566
Burghill Herefd 46 4844
Burghwallis S York 83 5311
Burham Kent 28 7262
Buriton Hants 13 7419
Burland Ches 71 6153
Burlawn Cnwll 4 9970
Burleigh Berks 25 9169
Burleigh Gloucs 35 8601
Burlescombe Devon 9 0716
Burleston Dorset 11 7794
Burlestone Devon 7 8248
Burley Hants 12 2102
Burley Rutlnd 63 8810
Burley Shrops 59 4881
Burley Gate Herefd 46 5947
Burley in Wharfedale W York 82 1646
Burley Lawn Hants 12 2103
Burley Street Hants 12 2004
Burley Wood Head W York 82 1544
Burleydam Ches 71 6042
Burlingham Green Norfk 67 3610
Burlingjobb Powys 46 2558
Burlington Shrops 60 7711
Burlton Shrops 59 4526
Burmarsh Kent 17 1032
Burmington Warwks 48 2637
Burn N York 83 5928
Burn Cross S York 74 3496
Burn Naze Lancs 80 3443
Burn of Cambus Stirlg 124 7102
Burnage Gt Man 79 8692
Burnaston Derbys 73 2832
Burnbanks Cumb 94 5016
Burnbrae N Lans 116 8759
Burnby E R Yk 84 8346
Burndell W Susx 14 9802
Burnden Gt Man 79 7207
Burnedge Gt Man 79 9110
Burneside Cumb 87 5095
Burneston N York 89 3084
Burnett Somset 22 6665
Burnfoot Border 109 4113

Carlton

Chester Moor

Carlton S York 83 3610
Carlton Suffk 55 3764
Carlton W York 83 3327
Carlton Colville Suffk 55 5189
Carlton Curlieu Leics 50 6997
Carlton Green Cambs 53 6451
Carlton Husthwaite N York 90 4976
Carlton in Lindrick Notts 75 5883
Carlton Miniott N York 89 3981
Carlton Scroop Lincs 63 9445
Carlton-in-Cleveland N York 90 5004
Carlton-le-Moorland Lincs 76 9058
Carlton-on-Trent Notts 75 7963
Carluddon Cnwll 3 0255
Carluke S Lans 116 8450
Carlyon Bay Cnwll 3 0552
Carmacoup S Lans 107 7927
Carmarthen Carmth 31 4120
Carmel Carmth 32 5816
Carmel Flints 70 1676
Carmel Gwynd 68 4954
Carmichael S Lans 108 9238
Carminowe Cnwll 2 6623
Carmunnock C Glas 115 5957
Carmyle C Glas 116 6462
Carmyllie Angus 127 5442
Carn Brea Cnwll 2 6841
Carn-gorm Highld 138 9520
Carnaby E R Yk 91 1465
Carnbee Fife 127 5206
Carnbo P & K 125 0503
Carnbrogie Abers 143 8527
Carndu Highld 138 8827
Carnduff S Lans 116 6646
Carne Cnwll 3 7724
Carne Cnwll 3 9138
Carne Cnwll 4 9558
Carnell E Ayrs 107 4731
Carnewas Cnwll 4 8569
Carnforth Lancs 87 4970
Carnhedryn Pembks 30 8027
Carnhell Green Cnwll 2 6137
Carnie Abers 135 8005
Carnkie Cnwll 2 7134
Carnkiet Cnwll 3 7852
Carno Powys 58 9696
Carnoch Highld 130 8696
Carnock Fife 117 0489
Carnon Downs Cnwll 3 7940
Carnousie Abers 142 6650
Carnoustie Angus 127 5534
Carnwath S Lans 117 9846
Carnyorth Cnwll 2 3733
Carol Green W Mids 61 2577
Carpalla Cnwll 3 9654
Carperby N York 88 0089
Carr Gt Man 81 7816
Carr S York 75 5090
Carr Gate W York 82 3123
Carr Shield Nthumb 95 8047
Carr Vale Derbys 75 4669
Carradale Ag & B 105 8138
Carrbridge Highld 140 9022
Carrbrook Gt Man 79 9800
Carrefour Jersey 158 0000
Carreglefn IOA 68 3889
Carrhouse Lincs 84 7706
Carrick Ag & B 114 9086
Carrick Castle Ag & B 114 1994
Carriden Falk 117 0181
Carrington Gt Man 79 7492
Carrington Lincs 77 3155
Carrington Mdloth 117 3160
Carrismerry Cnwll 4 0158
Carrog Conwy 69 7647
Carrog Denbgs 70 1043
Carron Falk 116 8882
Carron Moray 141 2241
Carron Bridge Stirlg 116 7483
Carronbridge D & G 100 8698
Carronshore Falk 116 8983
Carrow Hill Mons 34 4390
Carruth House Inver 115 3566
Carrutherstown D & G 100 1071
Carrville Dur 96 3043
Carrycoats Hall Nthumb 102 9279
Carsaig Ag & B 121 5421
Carscreugh D & G 98 2260
Carse Gray Angus 127 4553
Carseriggan D & G 98 3167
Carsethorn D & G 92 9959
Carshalton Gt Lon 27 2764
Carsington Derbys 73 2553
Carskey Ag & B 104 6508
Carsluith D & G 99 4854
Carsphairn D & G 107 5693
Carstairs S Lans 116 9345
Carstairs Junction S Lans 117 9545
Carswell Marsh Oxon 36 3299
Carter's Clay Hants 23 3024
Carters Green Essex 39 5110
Carterton Oxon 36 2806
Carterway Heads Dur 95 0451
Carthew Cnwll 3 0056
Carthorpe N York 89 3083
Cartington Nthumb 103 0204
Cartland S Lans 116 8646
Cartledge Derbys 74 3276
Cartmel Cumb 87 3878
Cartmel Fell Cumb 87 4188
Carway Carmth 32 4606
Carwinley Cumb 101 4072
Cashe's Green Gloucs 35 8205
Cashmoor Dorset 11 9713
Cassington Oxon 37 4511
Cassop Colliery Dur 96 3438
Castallack Cnwll 2 4525
Castell Conwy 69 7669
Castell-y-bwch Torfn 34 2792
Casterton Lancs 87 6279
Castle Cnwll 4 0958
Castle Acre Norfk 66 8115
Castle Ashby Nhants 51 8659
Castle Bolton N York 88 0391
Castle Bromwich W Mids 61 1489
Castle Bytham Lincs 63 9818
Castle Caereinion Powys 58 1605
Castle Camps Cambs 53 6242
Castle Carrock Cumb 94 5455
Castle Cary Somset 21 6432
Castle Combe Wilts 35 8477
Castle Donington Leics 62 4427
Castle Douglas D & G 99 7662
Castle Eaton Wilts 36 1496
Castle Eden Dur 96 4238
Castle End Cambs 64 1208
Castle Frome Herefd 47 6645
Castle Gate Cnwll 2 4934
Castle Green Cumb 87 5392
Castle Green Surrey 25 9761
Castle Gresley Derbys 73 2717
Castle Hedingham Essex 53 7835
Castle Hill Kent 28 6942
Castle Hill Suffk 54 1446
Castle Kennedy D & G 98 1159
Castle Lachlan Ag & B 114 0195
Castle Morris Pembks 30 9031
Castle O'er D & G 101 2492
Castle Pulverbatch Shrops 59 4202
Castle Rising Norfk 65 6624
Castle Street W York 82 9524
Castle Stuart Highld 140 7449
Castlebay W Isls 152 6698
Castlebythe Pembks 30 0229
Castlecary Falk 116 7878
Castlecraig Highld 147 8269
Castlecroft Staffs 60 8598
Castlecroft W Mids 60 8797
Castleford W York 83 4225
Castlehill Border 109 2135
Castlehill Highld 151 1968
Castlehill W Duns 115 3875
Castlemartin Pembks 30 9198
Castlemorton Worcs 47 7937
Castleside Dur 95 0748
Castlethorpe Bucks 38 8044
Castlethorpe Lincs 84 9807
Castleton Border 101 5189
Castleton Derbys 74 1582
Castleton Gt Man 79 8810
Castleton N York 90 6807
Castleton Newpt 34 2583
Castletown Dorset 11 6874
Castletown Highld 151 1967
Castletown IOM 158 2667
Castletown T & W 96 3658
Castley N York 82 2646
Caston Norfk 66 9597
Castor Cambs 64 1298
Caswell Bay Swans 32 5987
Cat and Fiddle Ches 79 0072
Cat's Ash Newpt 34 3790
Catacol N Ayrs 105 9149
Catbrook Mons 34 5102
Catch Flints 70 2070
Catchall Cnwll 2 4228
Catchem's Corner W Mids 61 2576
Catchgate Dur 96 1652
Catcliffe S York 74 4288
Catcomb Wilts 35 0076
Catcott Somset 21 3939
Catcott Burtle Somset 21 4043
Catel Guern 158 0000
Caterham Surrey 27 3455
Catfield Norfk 67 3821
Catfield Common Norfk 67 4021
Catfirth Shet 153 4354
Catford Gt Lon 27 3773
Catforth Lancs 80 4735
Cathcart C Glas 115 5860
Cathedine Powys 45 1425
Catherine Slack W York 82 0928
Catherine-de-Barnes W Mids 61 1780
Catherington Hants 13 6914
Catherston Leweston Dorset 10 3694
Catherton Shrops 47 6578
Catisfield Hants 13 5506
Catley Herefd 47 6844
Catley Lane Head Gt Man 81 8715
Catlodge Highld 132 6392
Catlow Lancs 81 8836
Catlowdy Cumb 101 4576
Catmere End Essex 39 4939
Catmore Berks 37 4580
Caton Devon 7 7872
Caton Lancs 87 5364
Caton Green Lancs 87 5565
Cator Court Devon 8 6877
Catrine E Ayrs 107 5225
Catsfield E Susx 17 7213
Catsfield Stream E Susx 17 7113
Catsgore Somset 21 5025
Catsham Somset 21 5533
Catshill Worcs 60 9573
Catstree Shrops 60 7496
Cattadale Ag & B 105 6710
Cattal N York 83 4454
Cattawade Suffk 41 1033
Catterall Lancs 80 4942
Catteralslane Shrops 71 5640
Catterick N York 89 2397
Catterick Bridge N York 89 2299
Catterick Garrison N York 89 1897
Catterlen Cumb 94 4833
Catterline Abers 135 8678
Catterton N York 83 5145
Catteshall Surrey 25 9844
Catthorpe Leics 50 5578
Cattishall Suffk 54 8865
Cattistock Dorset 10 5999
Catton Cumb 95 8257
Catton N York 89 3678
Catton Norfk 67 2312
Catwick E R Yk 85 1345
Catworth Cambs 51 0873
Caudle Green Gloucs 35 9410
Caulcott Beds 38 0042
Caulcott Oxon 49 5024
Cauldcots Angus 127 6547
Cauldhame Stirlg 116 6493
Cauldmill Border 109 5315
Cauldon Staffs 73 0749
Cauldon Lowe Staffs 73 0747
Cauldwell Derbys 73 2517
Caulkerbush D & G 92 9257
Caulside D & G 101 4480
Caundle Marsh Dorset 11 6713
Caunsall Worcs 60 8581
Caunton Notts 75 7460
Causeway Hants 13 7422
Causeway End Cumb 87 4885
Causeway End D & G 99 4260
Causeway End Essex 40 6819
Causewayend S Lans 108 0336
Causewayhead Cumb 92 1253
Causewayhead Stirlg 116 8095
Causey Park Nthumb 103 1794
Causey Park Bridge Nthumb 103 1894
Causeyend Abers 143 9419
Cavendish Suffk 54 8046
Cavenham Suffk 53 7670
Caversfield Oxon 49 5825
Caversham Berks 24 7274
Caverswall Staffs 72 9542
Caverton Mill Border 110 7425
Cavil E R Yk 84 7730
Cawdor Highld 140 8450
Cawkwell Lincs 77 2879
Cawood N York 83 5737
Cawsand Cnwll 6 4350
Cawston Norfk 66 1323
Cawston Warwks 50 4773
Cawthorn N York 90 7788
Cawthorne S York 82 2808
Cawton N York 90 6476
Caxton Cambs 52 3058
Caxton End Cambs 52 2759
Caxton End Cambs 52 3157
Caxton Gibbet Cambs 52 2960
Caynham Shrops 46 5573
Caythorpe Lincs 76 9348
Caythorpe Notts 63 6845
Cayton N York 91 0583
Ceann a Bhaigh W Isls 152 7468
Ceannacroc Lodge Highld 131 2211
Cearsiadar W Isls 152 3320
Ceciliford Mons 34 5003
Cefn Newpt 34 2788
Cefn Berain Conwy 70 9969
Cefn Byrle Powys 33 8311
Cefn Canel Powys 58 2331
Cefn Coch Powys 58 1026
Cefn Cribwr Brdgnd 33 8582
Cefn Cross Brdgnd 33 8682
Cefn Mably Caerph 34 2283
Cefn-brith Conwy 70 9350
Cefn-bryn-brain Carmth 32 7413
Cefn-coed-y-cymmer Myr Td 33 0308
Cefn-ddwysarn Gwynd 70 9638
Cefn-Einion Shrops 58 2886
Cefn-mawr Wrexhm 70 2842
Cefn-y-bedd Wrexhm 71 3156
Cefn-y-pant Carmth 31 1925
Cefneithin Carmth 32 5513
Cefngorwydd Powys 45 9045
Cefnpennar Rhondd 33 0300
Ceint IOA 68 4875
Cellan Cerdgn 44 6149
Cellardyke Fife 127 5704
Cellarhead Staffs 72 9547
Celleron Cumb 94 4925
Celynen Caerph 33 2195
Cemaes IOA 68 3793
Cemmaes Powys 57 8406
Cemmaes Road Powys 57 8104
Cenarth Cerdgn 31 2641
Cerbyd Pembks 30 8227
Ceres Fife 126 4011
Cerne Abbas Dorset 11 6601
Cerney Wick Gloucs 36 0796
Cerrigceinwen IOA 68 4274
Cerrigydrudion Conwy 70 9548
Cess Norfk 67 4417
Ceunant Gwynd 69 5361
Chaceley Gloucs 47 8530
Chacewater Cnwll 3 7544
Chackmore Bucks 49 6835
Chacombe Nhants 49 4944
Chadbury Worcs 47 0146
Chadderton Gt Man 79 9005
Chadderton Fold Gt Man 79 9006
Chaddesden Derbys 62 3836
Chaddesley Corbett Worcs 60 8973
Chaddlehanger Devon 5 4678
Chaddleworth Berks 36 4178
Chadlington Oxon 36 3321
Chadshunt Warwks 48 3453
Chadwell Leics 63 7824
Chadwell Shrops 60 7814
Chadwell End Beds 51 0865
Chadwell Heath Gt Lon 27 4888
Chadwell St Mary Essex 40 6478
Chadwick Worcs 47 8369
Chadwick End W Mids 61 2073
Chadwick Green Mersyd 78 5299
Chaffcombe Somset 10 3510
Chafford Hundred Essex 40 6079
Chagford Devon 8 7087
Chailey E Susx 15 3919
Chainbridge Cambs 27 4200
Chainhurst Kent 28 7248
Chalbury Dorset 12 0206
Chalbury Common Dorset 12 0206
Chaldon Surrey 27 3155
Chaldon Herring or
East Chaldon Dorset 11 7983
Chale IOW 13 4877
Chale Green IOW 13 4879
Chalfont Common Bucks 26 0092
Chalfont St Giles Bucks 26 9893
Chalfont St Peter Bucks 26 0090
Chalford Gloucs 35 8903
Chalford Oxon 37 7200
Chalford Wilts 22 8650
Chalgrave Beds 38 0127
Chalgrove Oxon 37 6396
Chalk Kent 28 6773
Chalk End Essex 40 6310
Chalkhouse Green Berks 37 7178
Chalkway Somset 10 3707
Chalkwell Kent 28 8963
Challaborough Devon 7 6544
Challacombe Devon 19 6940
Challoch D & G 99 3867
Challock Lees Kent 28 0050
Chalmington Dorset 10 5900
Chalton Beds 38 0326
Chalton Beds 52 1450
Chalton Hants 13 7315
Chalvey Berks 26 9679
Chalvington E Susx 16 5109
Chambers Green Kent 28 9243
Chandler's Cross Herts 26 0698
Chandler's Ford Hants 13 4319
Chandlers Cross Worcs 47 7738
Channel's End Beds 51 1056
Chantry Somset 22 7146
Chantry Suffk 54 1443
Chapel Cumb 93 2231
Chapel Fife 117 2593
Chapel Allerton Somset 21 4050
Chapel Allerton W York 82 3037
Chapel Amble Cnwll 4 9975
Chapel Brampton Nhants 50 7266
Chapel Chorlton Staffs 72 8137
Chapel Cross E Susx 16 6120
Chapel End Beds 38 0542
Chapel End Beds 51 1058
Chapel End Cambs 52 1282
Chapel End Warwks 61 3393
Chapel Field Gt Man 79 7906
Chapel Green Warwks 61 2785
Chapel Green Warwks 49 4660
Chapel Haddlesey N York 83 5826
Chapel Hill Abers 143 0635
Chapel Hill Lincs 76 2054
Chapel Hill Mons 34 5399
Chapel Hill N York 83 3446
Chapel Lawn Shrops 46 3176
Chapel le Dale N York 88 7377
Chapel Leigh Somset 20 1229
Chapel Milton Derbys 74 0581
Chapel of Garioch Abers 142 7124
Chapel Rossan D & G 98 1044
Chapel Row Berks 24 5769
Chapel Row E Susx 16 6312
Chapel Row Essex 40 7900
Chapel St Leonards Lincs 77 5672
Chapel Stile Cumb 86 3205
Chapel Town Cnwll 3 8855
Chapel-en-le-Frith Derbys 74 0580
Chapelbridge Cambs 64 2993
Chapelend Way Essex 53 7039
Chapelgate Lincs 65 4124
Chapelhall N Lans 116 7862
Chapelhope Border 109 2318
Chapelknowe D & G 101 3173
Chapels Cumb 86 2383
Chapelton Angus 127 6247
Chapelton Devon 19 5726
Chapelton S Lans 116 6848
Chapeltown Lancs 81 7315
Chapeltown Moray 141 2320
Chapeltown S York 74 3596
Chapmans Well Devon 5 3593
Chapmanslade Wilts 22 8247
Chapmore End Herts 39 3216
Chappel Essex 40 8928
Charaton Cnwll 5 3069
Chard Somset 10 3208
Chard Junction Somset 10 3404
Chardleigh Green Somset 10 3110
Chardstock Devon 10 3004
Charfield Gloucs 35 7292
Chargrove Gloucs 35 9219
Charing Kent 28 9549
Charing Heath Kent 28 9249
Charing Hill Kent 28 9550
Charingworth Gloucs 48 1939
Charlbury Oxon 36 3519
Charlcombe Somset 22 7467
Charlcutt Wilts 35 9875
Charlecote Warwks 48 2656
Charles Devon 19 6832
Charles Tye Suffk 54 0252
Charleshill Surrey 25 8944
Charleston Angus 126 3845
Charlestown Aber C 135 9300
Charlestown Cnwll 3 0351
Charlestown Derbys 74 0392
Charlestown Dorset 11 6579
Charlestown Fife 117 0683
Charlestown Gt Man 79 8100
Charlestown Highld 144 8174
Charlestown Highld 140 6448
Charlestown W York 82 9726
Charlestown W York 82 1638
Charlesworth Derbys 79 0092
Charlinch Somset 20 2338
Charlton Gt Lon 27 4178
Charlton Hants 23 3547
Charlton Herts 39 1728
Charlton Nhants 49 5335
Charlton Nthumb 102 8184
Charlton Oxon 36 4088
Charlton Shrops 59 5911
Charlton Somset 20 2926
Charlton Somset 21 6343
Charlton Somset 22 6852
Charlton Surrey 26 0869
Charlton W Susx 14 8812
Charlton Wilts 22 9022
Charlton Wilts 35 9588
Charlton Wilts 23 1156
Charlton Worcs 60 8371
Charlton Worcs 47 0045
Charlton Abbots Gloucs 48 0324
Charlton Adam Somset 21 5328
Charlton Hill Shrops 59 5807
Charlton Horethorne Somset 22 6623
Charlton Kings Gloucs 35 9621
Charlton Mackrell Somset 21 5328
Charlton Marshall Dorset 11 9004
Charlton Musgrove Somset 22 7229
Charlton on the Hill Dorset 11 8903
Charlton-all-Saints Wilts 23 1723
Charlton-on-Otmoor Oxon 37 5616
Charlwood Hants 24 6731
Charlwood Surrey 15 2441
Charminster Dorset 11 6792
Charmouth Dorset 10 3693
Charndon Bucks 49 6724
Charney Bassett Oxon 36 3894
Charnock Green Lancs 81 5516
Charnock Richard Lancs 81 5515
Charsfield Suffk 55 2556
Chart Corner Kent 28 7950
Chart Hill Kent 28 7949
Chart Sutton Kent 28 8049
Charter Alley Hants 24 5958
Charterhall Border 110 7647
Charterhouse Somset 21 4955
Chartershall Stirlg 116 7990
Charterville Allotments Oxon 36 3110
Chartham Kent 29 1054
Chartham Hatch Kent 29 1056
Chartridge Bucks 38 9303
Chartway Street Kent 28 8350
Charwelton Nhants 49 5356
Chase Terrace Staffs 61 0309
Chasetown Staffs 61 0408
Chastleton Oxon 48 2429
Chasty Devon 18 3402
Chatburn Lancs 81 7644
Chatcull Staffs 72 7934
Chatham Caerph 33 2188
Chatham Kent 28 7567
Chatham Green Essex 40 7115
Chathill Nthumb 111 1827
Chatley Worcs 47 8561
Chattenden Kent 28 7572
Chatter End Essex 39 4725
Chatteris Cambs 52 3985
Chatterton Lancs 81 7918
Chattisham Suffk 54 0942
Chatto Border 110 7717
Chatton Nthumb 111 0528
Chaul End Beds 38 0521
Chawleigh Devon 19 7112
Chawley Oxon 37 4604
Chawston Beds 52 1556
Chawton Hants 24 7037
Chaxhill Gloucs 35 7414
Chazey Heath Oxon 37 6977
Cheadle Gt Man 79 8688
Cheadle Staffs 73 0043
Cheadle Heath Gt Man 79 8789
Cheadle Hulme Gt Man 79 8786
Cheam Gt Lon 26 2463
Cheapside Berks 25 9469
Chearsley Bucks 37 7110
Chebsey Staffs 72 8528
Checkendon Oxon 37 6683
Checkley Ches 72 7346
Checkley Staffs 73 0237
Checkley Green Ches 72 7245
Chedburgh Suffk 53 7957
Cheddar Somset 21 4553
Cheddington Bucks 38 9217
Cheddleton Staffs 72 9752
Cheddleton Heath Staffs 72 9853
Cheddon Fitzpaine Somset 20 2427
Chedglow Wilts 35 9493
Chedgrave Norfk 67 3699
Chedington Dorset 10 4805
Chediston Suffk 55 3577
Chediston Green Suffk 55 3578
Chedworth Gloucs 36 0512
Chedzoy Somset 21 3437
Cheesden Gt Man 81 8216
Cheeseman's Green Kent 28 0338
Cheetham Hill Gt Man 79 8401
Cheetwood Gt Man 79 8399
Cheldon Devon 19 7313
Chelford Ches 79 8174
Chellaston Derbys 62 3730
Chellington Beds 51 9555
Chelmarsh Shrops 60 7288
Chelmick Shrops 59 4791
Chelmondiston Suffk 55 2037
Chelmorton Derbys 74 1169
Chelmsford Essex 40 7007
Chelmsley Wood W Mids 61 1887
Chelsea Gt Lon 27 2778
Chelsfield Gt Lon 27 4864
Chelsham Surrey 27 3758
Chelston Somset 20 1521
Chelsworth Suffk 54 9748
Cheltenham Gloucs 35 9422
Chelveston Nhants 51 9969
Chelvey Somset 21 4668
Chelwood Somset 21 6361
Chelwood Common E Susx 15 4128
Chelwood Gate E Susx 15 4130
Chelworth Wilts 35 9694
Chelworth Lower Green Wilts 36 0892
Chelworth Upper Green Wilts 36 0893
Cheney Longville Shrops 59 4284
Chenies Bucks 26 0198
Chepstow Mons 34 5393
Chequerbent Gt Man 79 6706
Chequers Corner Norfk 65 4908
Cherhill Wilts 36 0370
Cherington Gloucs 35 9098
Cherington Warwks 48 2936
Cheriton Devon 19 7346
Cheriton Hants 24 5828
Cheriton Kent 29 2037
Cheriton Swans 32 4593
Cheriton Bishop Devon 8 7793
Cheriton Fitzpaine Devon 9 8606
Cheriton or
Stackpole Elidor Pembks 30 9897
Cherrington Shrops 72 6619
Cherry Burton E R Yk 84 9841
Cherry Hinton Cambs 53 4856
Cherry Orchard Worcs 47 8553
Cherry Willingham Lincs 76 0272
Chertsey Surrey 26 0466
Cheselbourne Dorset 11 7699
Chesham Bucks 26 9601
Chesham Gt Man 81 8012
Chesham Bois Bucks 26 9699
Cheshunt Herts 27 3502
Chesley Kent 28 8563
Cheslyn Hay Staffs 60 9707
Chessetts Wood Warwks 61 1873
Chessington Surrey 26 1863
Chester Ches 71 4066
Chester Moor Dur 96 2649

277

Chester-le-Street Cobley
278

Chester-le-Street Dur 96 2751
Chesterblade Somset 22 6641
Chesterfield Derbys 74 3871
Chesterfield Staffs 61 0905
Chesterhill Mdloth 118 3764
Chesters Border 110 6022
Chesters Border 110 6210
Chesterton Cambs 64 1295
Chesterton Cambs 53 4660
Chesterton Gloucs 35 0100
Chesterton Oxon 37 5621
Chesterton Shrops 60 7897
Chesterton Staffs 72 8349
Chesterton Green Warwks 48 3558
Chesterwood Nthumb 102 8364
Chestfield Kent 29 1365
Chestnut Street Kent 28 8763
Cheston Devon 7 6858
Cheswardine Shrops 72 7130
Cheswell Shrops 72 7116
Cheswick Nthumb 111 0346
Cheswick Green W Mids 61 1376
Chetnole Dorset 10 6008
Chettiscombe Devon 9 9614
Chettisham Cambs 53 5483
Chettle Dorset 11 9513
Chetton Shrops 60 6690
Chetwode Bucks 49 6429
Chetwynd Shrops 72 7321
Chetwynd Aston Shrops 72 7517
Cheveley Cambs 53 6861
Chevening Kent 27 4857
Cheverton IOW 13 4583
Chevington Suffk 53 7859
Chevington Drift Nthumb 103 2598
Chevithorne Devon 9 9715
Chew Magna Somset 21 5763
Chew Moor Gt Man 79 6607
Chew Stoke Somset 21 5561
Chewton Keynsham Somset 21 6566
Chewton Mendip Somset 21 5953
Chichacott Devon 8 6096
Chicheley Bucks 38 9046
Chichester W Susx 14 8604
Chickerell Dorset 11 6480
Chickering Suffk 55 2176
Chicklade Wilts 22 9134
Chickward Herefd 46 2853
Chidden Hants 13 6517
Chiddingfold Surrey 14 9635
Chiddingly E Susx 16 5414
Chiddingstone Kent 16 5045
Chiddingstone Causeway Kent 16 5246
Chideock Dorset 10 4292
Chidham W Susx 14 7903
Chidswell W York 82 2623
Chieveley Berks 24 4774
Chignall Smealy Essex 40 6611
Chignall St James Essex 40 6610
Chigwell Essex 27 4494
Chigwell Row Essex 27 4693
Chilbolton Hants 23 3940
Chilcomb Hants 24 5028
Chilcombe Dorset 10 5291
Chilcompton Somset 21 6451
Chilcote Leics 61 2811
Child Okeford Dorset 11 8312
Child's Ercall Shrops 72 6625
Childer Thornton Ches 71 3677
Childrey Oxon 36 3687
Childswickham Worcs 48 0738
Childwall Mersyd 78 4189
Childwick Bury Herts 38 1410
Childwick Green Herts 38 1410
Chilfrome Dorset 10 5898
Chilgrove W Susx 14 8314
Chilham Kent 29 0653
Chilhampton Wilts 23 0933
Chilla Devon 18 4402
Chillaton Devon 5 4381
Chillenden Kent 29 2753
Chillerton IOW 13 4883
Chillesford Suffk 55 3852
Chillingham Nthumb 111 0525
Chillington Devon 7 7942
Chillington Somset 10 3811
Chilmark Wilts 22 9732
Chilmington Green Kent 28 9840
Chilson Oxon 36 3119
Chilsworthy Cnwll 5 4172
Chilsworthy Devon 18 3206
Chiltern Green Beds 38 1319
Chilthorne Domer Somset 21 5219
Chilton Bucks 37 6811
Chilton Devon 9 8604
Chilton Dur 96 2829
Chilton Kent 29 2743
Chilton Oxon 37 4885
Chilton Suffk 54 8842
Chilton Candover Hants 24 5940
Chilton Cantelo Somset 21 5722
Chilton Foliat Wilts 36 3170
Chilton Polden Somset 21 3740
Chilton Street Suffk 53 7546
Chilton Trinity Somset 20 2939
Chilwell Notts 62 5135
Chilworth Hants 13 4018
Chilworth Surrey 14 0347
Chimney Oxon 36 3501
Chineham Hants 24 6555
Chingford Gt Lon 27 3894
Chinley Derbys 74 0482
Chinnor Oxon 37 7501
Chipchase Castle Nthumb 102 8775
Chipnall Shrops 72 7231
Chippenham Cambs 53 6669
Chippenham Wilts 35 9173
Chipperfield Herts 26 0401
Chipping Herts 39 3531
Chipping Lancs 81 6243
Chipping Campden Gloucs 48 1539
Chipping Hill Essex 40 8215
Chipping Norton Oxon 48 3127
Chipping Ongar Essex 39 5503
Chipping Sodbury Gloucs 35 7282
Chipping Warden Nhants 49 4948
Chipstable Somset 20 0427
Chipstead Kent 27 5056
Chipstead Surrey 27 2756
Chirbury Shrops 58 2698
Chirk Wrexhm 58 2837
Chirnside Border 119 8756
Chirnsidebridge Border 119 8556
Chirton Wilts 23 0757
Chisbury Wilts 23 2766
Chiselborough Somset 10 4614
Chiseldon Wilts 36 1880
Chisholme Border 109 4112
Chislehampton Oxon 37 5999
Chislehurst Gt Lon 27 4570
Chislet Kent 29 2264
Chisley W York 82 0028
Chiswellgreen Herts 38 1304
Chiswick Gt Lon 26 2078
Chiswick End Cambs 52 3745
Chisworth Derbys 79 9991
Chitcombe E Susx 17 8120
Chithurst W Susx 14 8423
Chittering Cambs 53 4969
Chitterne Wilts 22 9843
Chittlehamholt Devon 19 6520
Chittlehampton Devon 19 6325
Chittlehampton Devon 19 6511
Chittoe Wilts 22 9566
Chivelstone Devon 7 7838
Chivenor Devon 19 5034
Chlenry D & G 98 1260
Chobham Surrey 25 9762
Cholderton Wilts 23 2242
Cholesbury Bucks 38 9307
Chollerford Nthumb 102 9170
Chollerton Nthumb 102 9372
Cholmondeston Ches 71 6359
Cholsey Oxon 37 5886
Cholstrey Herefd 46 4659
Chop Gate N York 90 5599
Choppington Nthumb 103 2484
Chopwell T & W 95 1158
Chorley Ches 71 5751
Chorley Lancs 81 5817
Chorley Shrops 60 6983
Chorley Staffs 61 0710
Chorleywood Herts 26 0396
Chorleywood West Herts 26 0296
Chorlton Ches 72 7250
Chorlton Lane Ches 71 4547
Chorlton-cum-Hardy Gt Man 79 8193
Choulton Shrops 59 3788
Chowley Ches 71 4756
Chrishall Essex 39 4439
Chrisswell Inver 114 2274
Christchurch Cambs 65 4996
Christchurch Dorset 12 1592
Christchurch Gloucs 34 5613
Christchurch Mons 34 3489
Christian Malford Wilts 35 9678
Christleton Ches 71 4465
Christmas Common Oxon 37 7193
Christon Somset 21 3757
Christon Bank Nthumb 111 2123
Christow Devon 8 8385
Chuck Hatch E Susx 16 4733
Chudleigh Devon 9 8679
Chudleigh Knighton Devon 8 8477
Chulmleigh Devon 19 6814
Chunal Derbys 74 0390
Church Lancs 81 7429
Church Ashton Shrops 72 7317
Church Brampton Nhants 50 7165
Church Brough Cumb 95 7913
Church Broughton Derbys 73 2033
Church Crookham Hants 25 8051
Church Eaton Staffs 72 8417
Church End Beds 38 9832
Church End Beds 38 9921
Church End Beds 38 0334
Church End Beds 51 0558
Church End Beds 51 1058
Church End Beds 39 1937
Church End Cambs 51 0873
Church End Cambs 52 2082
Church End Cambs 52 3278
Church End Cambs 53 4857
Church End Essex 40 6223
Church End Essex 40 7228
Church End Essex 40 7316
Church End Gt Lon 26 2490
Church End Hants 24 6756
Church End Herts 38 1011
Church End Herts 39 2630
Church End Herts 39 4422
Church End Lincs 64 2234
Church End Lincs 77 4295
Church End Warwks 61 2490
Church End Warwks 61 2992
Church Enstone Oxon 48 3725
Church Fenton N York 83 5136
Church Green Devon 9 1796
Church Gresley Derbys 73 2918
Church Hanborough Oxon 36 4213
Church Hill Ches 72 6465
Church Hill Staffs 60 0011
Church Houses N York 90 6697
Church Knowle Dorset 11 9481
Church Laneham Notts 75 8176
Church Langton Leics 50 7293
Church Lawford Warwks 50 4576
Church Lawton Staffs 72 8255
Church Leigh Staffs 73 0235
Church Lench Worcs 48 0251
Church Mayfield Staffs 73 1544
Church Minshull Ches 72 6660
Church Norton W Susx 14 8795
Church Preen Shrops 59 5498
Church Pulverbatch Shrops 59 4303
Church Stowe Nhants 49 6357
Church Street Essex 53 7943
Church Street Kent 28 7174
Church Street Suffk 55 4883
Church Stretton Shrops 59 4593
Church Town Lincs 84 7806
Church Village Rhondd 33 0885
Church Warsop Notts 75 5668
Church Wilne Derbys 62 4431
Churcham Gloucs 35 7618
Churchbridge Staffs 60 9808
Churchdown Gloucs 35 8819
Churchend Essex 41 0093
Churchfield W Mids 60 0192
Churchgate Herts 27 3402
Churchgate Street Essex 39 4811
Churchill Devon 19 5940
Churchill Devon 10 2902
Churchill Oxon 48 2824
Churchill Somset 21 4459
Churchill Worcs 60 8879
Churchill Worcs 47 9253
Churchinford Somset 9 2112
Churchover Warwks 50 5180
Churchstanton Somset 9 1914
Churchstoke Powys 58 2794
Churchstow Devon 7 7145
Churchthorpe Lincs 77 3297
Churchtown Derbys 74 2662
Churchtown Devon 19 6744
Churchtown Lancs 80 3240
Churchtown Lancs 80 4843
Churchtown Mersyd 80 3618
Churnsike Lodge Nthumb 102 6677
Churston Ferrers Devon 7 9056
Churt Surrey 25 8538
Churton Ches 71 4156
Churwell W York 82 2729
Chwilog Gwynd 56 4338
Chyandour Cnwll 2 4731
Chyanvounder Cnwll 2 6522
Chyeowling Cnwll 3 7941
Chyvarloe Cnwll 2 6523
Cil Powys 58 1701
Cilcain Flints 70 1765
Cilcennin Cerdgn 44 5260
Cilcewydd Powys 58 2204
Cilfrew Neath 32 7700
Cilfynydd Rhondd 33 0891
Cilgerran Pembks 31 1942
Cilgwyn Carmth 44 7429
Cilgwyn Gwynd 68 4953
Ciliau-Aeron Cerdgn 44 5057
Cilmaengwyn Neath 32 7405
Cilmery Powys 45 0051
Cilrhedyn Pembks 31 2834
Cilsan Carmth 32 5922
Ciltalgarth Gwynd 57 8940
Cilycwm Carmth 44 7539
Cimla Neath 32 7696
Cinder Hill W Mids 60 9294
Cinderford Gloucs 35 6514
Cippenham Berks 26 9580
Cirencester Gloucs 35 0201
Citadilla N York 89 2299
City Gt Lon 27 3281
City V Glam 33 9878
City Dulas IOA 68 4687
Clabhach Ag & B 120 1858
Clachaig Ag & B 114 1181
Clachan Ag & B 122 7819
Clachan Ag & B 122 8543
Clachan Ag & B 113 7556
Clachan Highld 137 5436
Clachan Mor Ag & B 120 9847
Clachan na Luib W Isls 152 8163
Clachan of Campsie E Duns 116 6079
Clachan-a-Luib W Isls 152 8163
Clachan-Seil Ag & B 122 7718
Clachaneasy D & G 98 3574
Clachnaharry Highld 140 6446
Clachtoll Highld 148 0427
Clackavoid P & K 133 1463
Clackmannan Clacks 116 9191
Clackmarras Moray 141 2458
Clacton-on-Sea Essex 41 1715
Cladich Ag & B 123 0921
Cladswell Worcs 48 0558
Claggan Highld 122 7049
Claigan Highld 136 2354
Clandown Somset 22 6855
Clanfield Hants 13 6916
Clanfield Oxon 36 2801
Clannaborough Devon 8 7402
Clanville Hants 23 3148
Clanville Somset 21 6233
Claonaig Ag & B 113 8656
Clap Hill Kent 28 0537
Clapgate Dorset 11 0102
Clapgate Herts 39 4424
Clapham Beds 38 0352
Clapham Devon 9 8987
Clapham Gt Lon 27 2975
Clapham N York 88 7469
Clapham W Susx 14 0906
Clapham Folly Beds 38 0252
Clappersgate Cumb 87 3603
Clapton Somset 10 4106
Clapton Somset 21 6453
Clapton-in-Gordano Somset 34 4773
Clapton-on-the-Hill Gloucs 36 1617
Clapworthy Devon 19 6724
Clarach Cerdgn 43 6084
Claravale T & W 103 1364
Clarbeston Pembks 30 0521
Clarbeston Road Pembks 30 0121
Clarborough Notts 75 7383
Clare Suffk 53 7745
Clarebrand D & G 99 7665
Clarencefield D & G 100 0968
Clareton N York 89 3959
Clarewood Nthumb 103 0169
Clarilaw Border 109 5218
Clark's Green Surrey 15 1739
Clarken Green Hants 24 5651
Clarkston E Rens 115 5757
Clashmore Highld 148 0331
Clashmore Highld 146 7489
Clashnessie Highld 148 0530
Clashnoir Moray 141 2222
Clathy P & K 125 9920
Clathymore P & K 125 0121
Clatt Abers 142 5326
Clatter Powys 58 9994
Clatterford End Essex 40 6113
Clatworthy Somset 20 0531
Claughton Lancs 80 5342
Claughton Lancs 87 5566
Claughton Mersyd 78 3088
Clavelshay Somset 20 2531
Claverdon Warwks 48 1965
Claverham Somset 21 4566
Clavering Essex 39 4731
Claverley Shrops 60 7993
Claverton Somset 22 7864
Claverton Down Somset 22 7763
Clawdd-coch V Glam 33 0577
Clawdd-newydd Denbgs 70 0852
Clawthorpe Cumb 87 5377
Clawton Devon 18 3599
Claxby Lincs 76 1194
Claxby Lincs 77 4571
Claxton N York 90 6959
Claxton Norfk 67 3303
Clay Common Suffk 55 4681
Clay Coton Nhants 50 5976
Clay Cross Derbys 74 3963
Clay End Herts 39 3024
Claybrooke Magna Leics 50 4988
Claydon Oxon 49 4549
Claydon Suffk 54 1349
Claygate D & G 101 3979
Claygate Kent 28 7144
Claygate Surrey 26 1563
Claygate Cross Kent 27 6155
Clayhall Gt Lon 27 4390
Clayhanger Devon 20 0222
Clayhanger W Mids 61 0404
Clayhidon Devon 9 1615
Clayhill E Susx 17 8323
Clayhill Hants 12 3006
Clayhithe Cambs 53 5064
Clayock Highld 151 1659
Claypit Hill Cambs 52 3554
Claypits Gloucs 35 7606
Claypole Lincs 76 8449
Claythorpe Lincs 77 4178
Clayton S York 83 4507
Clayton W Susx 15 2914
Clayton W York 82 1231
Clayton Green Lancs 81 5723
Clayton West W York 82 2510
Clayton-le-Moors Lancs 81 7530
Clayton-le-Woods Lancs 81 5622
Clayworth Notts 75 7387
Cleadale Highld 128 4789
Cleadon T & W 96 3862
Clearbrook Devon 6 5265
Clearwell Gloucs 34 5608
Clearwell Meend Gloucs 34 5808
Cleasby N York 89 2512
Cleat Ork 153 4584
Cleatlam Dur 95 1118
Cleator Cumb 92 0113
Cleator Moor Cumb 92 0115
Cleckheaton W York 82 1825
Clee St Margaret Shrops 59 5684
Cleedownton Shrops 59 5880
Cleehill Shrops 46 5975
Cleekhimin N Lans 116 7658
Cleestanton Shrops 46 5779
Cleethorpes Lincs 85 3008
Cleeton St Mary Shrops 46 6178
Cleeve Oxon 37 6081
Cleeve Somset 21 4666
Cleeve Hill Gloucs 47 9827
Cleeve Prior Worcs 48 0849
Cleghornie E Loth 118 5983
Clehonger Herefd 46 4437
Cleish P & K 117 0998
Cleland N Lans 116 7958
Clement Street Kent 27 5370
Clement's End Beds 38 0214
Clenamacrie Ag & B 122 9228
Clench Common Wilts 23 1765
Clenchwarton Norfk 65 5920
Clenerty Abers 142 7760
Clent Worcs 60 9279
Cleobury Mortimer Shrops 60 6775
Cleobury North Shrops 59 6286
Cleongart Ag & B 105 6734
Clephanton Highld 140 8150
Clerkhill D & G 101 2697
Cleuch-head D & G 108 8200
Clevancy Wilts 36 0575
Clevedon Somset 34 4171
Cleveley Oxon 48 3923
Cleveleys Lancs 80 3143
Clevelode Worcs 47 8347
Cleverton Wilts 35 9785
Clewer Somset 21 4351
Cley next the Sea Norfk 66 0444
Cliburn Cumb 94 5824
Cliddesden Hants 24 6349
Cliff Warwks 61 2197
Cliff End E Susx 17 8813
Cliffe Dur 96 2115
Cliffe Kent 28 7376
Cliffe Lancs 81 7333
Cliffe N York 83 6631
Cliffe Woods Kent 28 7373
Clifford Herefd 46 2445
Clifford W York 83 4344
Clifford Chambers Warwks 48 1952
Clifford's Mesne Gloucs 47 7023
Cliffsend Kent 29 3464
Clifton Beds 39 1639
Clifton Bristl 34 5773
Clifton Cumb 94 5326
Clifton Derbys 73 1644
Clifton Gt Man 79 7703
Clifton Lancs 80 4630
Clifton N York 82 1948
Clifton N York 83 5953
Clifton Notts 62 5434
Clifton Nthumb 103 2082
Clifton Oxon 49 4931
Clifton S York 75 5296
Clifton W York 82 1622
Clifton Worcs 47 8446
Clifton Campville Staffs 61 2510
Clifton Dykes Cumb 44 5427
Clifton Hampden Oxon 37 5495
Clifton Reynes Bucks 38 9051
Clifton upon Dunsmore Warwks 50 5376
Clifton upon Teme Worcs 47 7161
Cliftonville Kent 29 3771
Climping W Susx 14 9902
Clink Somset 22 7948
Clint N York 89 2659
Clint Green Norfk 66 0210
Clinterty Aber C 135 8311
Clintmains Border 110 6132
Clipiau Gwynd 57 8410
Clippesby Norfk 67 4214
Clipsham Rutlnd 63 9716
Clipston Nhants 50 7181
Clipston Notts 63 6334
Clipstone Beds 38 9426
Clipstone Notts 75 5963
Clitheroe Lancs 81 7441
Clive Shrops 59 5124
Clixby Lincs 85 0904
Cloatley Wilts 35 9890
Clocaenog Denbgs 70 0854
Clochan Moray 142 4060
Clochtow Angus 127 4852
Clock Face Mersyd 78 5291
Cloddiau Powys 58 2009
Clodock Herefd 46 3227
Cloford Somset 22 7244
Clola Abers 143 0043
Clophill Beds 38 0838
Clopton Nhants 51 0680
Clopton Suffk 55 2253
Clopton Corner Suffk 55 2254
Clopton Green Suffk 53 7655
Clopton Green Suffk 54 9759
Clos du Valle Guern 158 0000
Closeburn D & G 100 8992
Closeburnmill D & G 100 9094
Closeclark IOM 158 2775
Closworth Somset 10 5610
Clothall Herts 39 2731
Clotton Ches 71 5264
Cloudesley Bush Warwks 50 4686
Clough Gt Man 79 9408
Clough Foot W York 81 9123
Clough Head N York 82 0918
Cloughton N York 91 0194
Cloughton Newlands N York 91 0096
Clousta Shet 153 3057
Clova Angus 134 3273
Clovelly Devon 18 3124
Clovenfords Border 109 4536
Clovulin Highld 130 0063
Clow Bridge Lancs 81 8228
Clowne Derbys 75 4875
Clows Top Worcs 60 7172
Cloy Wrexhm 71 3943
Cluanie Inn Highld 130 0711
Cluanie Lodge Highld 130 0910
Clubworthy Cnwll 5 2792
Clugston D & G 98 3557
Clun Shrops 59 3080
Clunas Highld 140 8846
Clunbury Shrops 59 3780
Clune Highld 140 7925
Clunes Highld 131 1988
Clungunford Shrops 46 3978
Clunie Abers 142 6350
Clunie P & K 126 1043
Clunton Shrops 59 3381
Clutton Ches 71 4654
Clutton Somset 21 6259
Clutton Hill Somset 21 6359
Clwt-y-bont Gwynd 69 5762
Clydach Mons 34 2213
Clydach Swans 32 6800
Clydach Vale Rhondd 33 9792
Clydebank W Duns 115 4970
Clydey Pembks 31 2535
Clyffe Pypard Wilts 36 0777
Clynder Ag & B 114 2484
Clynderwen Carmth 31 1219
Clyne Neath 32 8000
Clynnog-fawr Gwynd 68 4149
Clyro Powys 45 2143
Clyst Honiton Devon 9 9893
Clyst Hydon Devon 9 0301
Clyst St George Devon 9 9888
Clyst St Lawrence Devon 9 0200
Clyst St Mary Devon 9 9791
Cnoc W Isls 152 4931
Cnwch Coch Cerdgn 43 6774
Coad's Green Cnwll 5 2976
Coal Aston Derbys 74 3679
Coal Pool W Mids 60 0199
Coal Street Suffk 55 2371
Coalbrookdale Shrops 60 6604
Coalbrookvale Blae G 33 1909
Coalburn S Lans 108 8134
Coalburns T & W 96 1260
Coalcleugh Nthumb 95 8045
Coaley Gloucs 35 7701
Coalfell Cumb 94 5959
Coalhill Essex 40 7597
Coalmoor Shrops 60 6607
Coalpit Heath Gloucs 35 6780
Coalpit Hill Staffs 72 8253
Coalport Shrops 60 6902
Coalsnaughton Clacks 116 9195
Coaltown of Balgonie Fife 117 2999
Coaltown of Wemyss Fife 118 3295
Coalville Leics 62 4214
Coanwood Nthumb 94 6859
Coat Somset 21 4520
Coatbridge N Lans 116 7365
Coatdyke N Lans 116 7465
Coate Wilts 23 0462
Coate Wilts 36 1882
Coates Cambs 64 3097
Coates Gloucs 35 9701
Coates Lincs 75 8181
Coates Lincs 76 9083
Coates W Susx 14 9917
Coatham N York 97 5925
Coatham Mundeville Dur 96 2820
Cobbaton Devon 19 6126
Coberley Gloucs 35 9616
Cobhall Common Herefd 46 4535
Cobham Kent 28 6768
Cobham Surrey 26 1060
Coblers Green Essex 40 6819
Cobley Dorset 12 0220

Courteenhall

Culross

280

Courteenhall *Nhants* 49 7653
Courtsend *Essex* 41 0293
Courtway *Somset* 20 2033
Cousland *Mdloth* 118 3768
Cousley Wood *E Susx* 16 6533
Cove *Ag & B* 114 2282
Cove *Border* 119 7771
Cove *Devon* 20 9619
Cove *Hants* 25 8555
Cove *Highld* 144 8191
Cove Bay *Aber C* 135 9501
Cove Bottom *Suffk* 55 4979
Covehithe *Suffk* 55 5282
Coven *Staffs* 60 9106
Coven Lawn *Staffs* 60 9005
Coveney *Cambs* 53 4882
Covenham St Bartholomew *Lincs* 77 3394
Covenham St Mary *Lincs* 77 3394
Coventry *W Mids* 61 3378
Coverack *Cnwll* 3 7818
Coverack Bridges *Cnwll* 2 6630
Coverham *N York* 89 1086
Covington *Cambs* 51 0570
Covington *S Lans* 108 9739
Cow Green *Suffk* 54 0565
Cow Honeybourne *Worcs* 48 1143
Cowan Bridge *Lancs* 87 6376
Cowbeech *E Susx* 16 6114
Cowbit *Lincs* 64 2518
Cowbridge *V Glam* 33 9974
Cowdale *Derbys* 74 0771
Cowden *Kent* 16 4640
Cowden Pound *Kent* 16 4642
Cowden Station *Kent* 16 4741
Cowdenbeath *Fife* 117 1691
Cowers Lane *Derbys* 73 3046
Cowes *IOW* 13 4996
Cowesby *N York* 89 4689
Cowesfield Green *Wilts* 23 2523
Cowfold *W Susx* 15 2122
Cowgill *Cumb* 88 7586
Cowhill *Gloucs* 34 6091
Cowie *Stirlg* 116 8389
Cowlam *E R Yk* 91 9665
Cowley *Derbys* 74 3376
Cowley *Devon* 9 9095
Cowley *Gloucs* 35 9614
Cowley *Gt Lon* 26 0582
Cowley *Oxon* 37 5304
Cowley *Oxon* 49 6628
Cowling *Lancs* 81 5917
Cowling *N York* 82 9643
Cowling *N York* 89 2387
Cowlinge *Suffk* 53 7154
Cowmes *W York* 82 1815
Cowpe *Lancs* 81 8320
Cowpen *Nthumb* 103 2981
Cowpen Bewley *Dur* 97 4824
Cowplain *Hants* 13 6810
Cowshill *Dur* 95 8540
Cowslip Green *Somset* 21 4861
Cowthorpe *N York* 83 4252
Cox Common *Suffk* 55 4082
Coxall *Shrops* 46 3774
Coxbank *Ches* 72 6541
Coxbench *Derbys* 62 3743
Coxbridge *Somset* 21 5436
Coxford *Cnwll* 4 1696
Coxford *Norfk* 66 8529
Coxgreen *Staffs* 60 8086
Coxheath *Kent* 28 7451
Coxhoe *Dur* 96 3136
Coxley *Somset* 21 5343
Coxley *W York* 82 2717
Coxley Wick *Somset* 21 5243
Coxpark *Cnwll* 5 4072
Coxtie Green *Essex* 27 5696
Coxwold *N York* 90 5377
Coychurch *Brdgnd* 33 9379
Coylton *S Ayrs* 107 4219
Coylumbridge *Highld* 132 9111
Coytrahen *Brdgnd* 33 8885
Crab Orchard *Dorset* 12 0806
Crabbs Cross *Worcs* 48 0465
Crabtree *W Susx* 15 2125
Crabtree Green *Wrexhm* 71 3344
Crackenthorpe *Cumb* 94 6622
Crackington Haven *Cnwll* 4 1496
Crackley *Staffs* 72 8350
Crackley *Warwks* 61 2973
Crackleybank *Shrops* 60 7611
Crackpot *N York* 88 9796
Cracoe *N York* 88 9760
Craddock *Devon* 9 0812
Cradle End *Herts* 39 4521
Cradley *Herefd* 47 7347
Cradley *W Mids* 60 9485
Cradoc *Powys* 45 0130
Crafthole *Cnwll* 5 3654
Crafton *Bucks* 38 8819
Crag Foot *Lancs* 87 4873
Cragg Hill *W York* 82 2437
Cragg Vale *W York* 82 0023
Craggan *Highld* 141 0226
Craghead *Dur* 96 2150
Crai *Powys* 45 8924
Craibstone *Moray* 142 4959
Craichie *Angus* 127 5047
Craig *Angus* 127 6956
Craig *Highld* 138 0349
Craig Llangiwg *Neath* 32 7204
Craig Penllyn *V Glam* 33 9777
Craig's End *Essex* 53 7137
Craig-y-Duke *Neath* 32 7002
Craig-y-nos *Powys* 33 8415
Craigbank *E Ayrs* 107 5911
Craigburn *Border* 117 2354
Craigcefnparc *Swans* 32 6702
Craigcleuch *D & G* 101 3486
Craigdam *Abers* 143 8430
Craigdarroch *D & G* 107 7391
Craigdhu *Ag & B* 122 8205
Craigearn *Abers* 142 7214
Craigellachie *Moray* 141 2844
Craigend *P & K* 126 1120
Craigend *Rens* 115 4670
Craigendoran *Ag & B* 115 3181
Craighlaw *D & G* 98 3061
Craighouse *Ag & B* 113 5267
Craigie *P & K* 126 1143
Craigie *S Ayrs* 107 4232
Craigiefield *Abers* 143 9165
Craigley *D & G* 99 7658
Craiglockhart *C Edin* 117 2271
Craiglug *Moray* 141 3355
Craigmillar *C Edin* 117 3071
Craignant *Shrops* 58 2535
Craigneston *D & G* 107 7587
Craigneuk *N Lans* 116 7765
Craigneuk *N Lans* 116 7756
Craignure *Ag & B* 122 7236
Craigo *Angus* 135 6864
Craigrothie *Fife* 126 3810
Craigruie *Stirlg* 124 4920
Craigton *Aber C* 135 8301
Craigton *Angus* 127 5138
Craigton *E Rens* 115 4954
Craigton of Airlie *Angus* 126 3250
Crail *Fife* 127 6107
Crailing *Border* 110 6824
Craiselound *Lincs* 75 7698
Crakehall *N York* 89 2489
Crakehill *N York* 89 4273
Crakemarsh *Staffs* 73 0936
Crambe *N York* 90 7364
Cramlington *Nthumb* 103 2676
Cramond *C Edin* 117 1976
Cramond Bridge *C Edin* 117 1775
Cranage *Ches* 79 7568
Cranberry *Staffs* 72 8235
Cranborne *Dorset* 12 0513
Cranbrook *Kent* 28 7736
Cranbrook Common *Kent* 28 7838
Crane Moor *S York* 82 3001
Crane's Corner *Norfk* 66 9113
Cranfield *Beds* 38 9542
Cranford *Devon* 18 3421
Cranford *Gt Lon* 26 1076
Cranford St Andrew *Nhants* 51 9277
Cranford St John *Nhants* 51 9276
Cranham *Gloucs* 35 8913
Cranham *Gt Lon* 27 5787
Cranhill *Warwks* 48 1253
Crank *Mersyd* 78 5099
Cranleigh *Surrey* 14 0539
Cranmer Green *Suffk* 54 0171
Cranmore *IOW* 13 3990
Cranmore *Somset* 22 6643
Cranoe *Leics* 50 7695
Cransford *Suffk* 55 3164
Cranshaws *Border* 118 6861
Cranstal *IOM* 158 4602
Cranswick *E R Yk* 84 0252
Crantock *Cnwll* 4 7960
Cranwell *Lincs* 76 0349
Cranwich *Norfk* 65 7794
Cranworth *Norfk* 66 9804
Craobh Haven *Ag & B* 122 7907
Crapstone *Devon* 6 5067
Crarae *Ag & B* 114 9897
Crask Inn *Highld* 149 5224
Crask of Aigas *Highld* 139 4642
Craster *Nthumb* 111 2519
Craswall *Herefd* 46 2735
Crateford *Staffs* 60 9009
Cratfield *Suffk* 55 3175
Crathes *Abers* 135 7596
Crathie *Abers* 133 2695
Crathie *Highld* 132 5793
Crathorne *N York* 89 4407
Craven Arms *Shrops* 59 4382
Crawcrook *T & W* 103 1363
Crawford *Lancs* 78 4902
Crawford *S Lans* 108 9520
Crawfordjohn *S Lans* 108 8823
Crawick *D & G* 107 7811
Crawley *Hants* 24 4235
Crawley *Oxon* 36 3412
Crawley *W Susx* 15 2636
Crawley Down *W Susx* 15 3437
Crawley Side *Dur* 95 9940
Crawshawbooth *Lancs* 81 8125
Crawton *Abers* 135 8779
Craxe's Green *Essex* 40 9419
Cray *N York* 88 9479
Cray's Pond *Oxon* 37 6380
Crayford *Gt Lon* 27 5175
Crayke *N York* 90 5670
Craymere Beck *Norfk* 66 0631
Crays Hill *Essex* 40 7192
Craythorne *Staffs* 73 2426
Craze Lowman *Devon* 9 9814
Crazies Hill *Oxon* 37 7980
Creacombe *Devon* 18 3219
Creag Ghoraidh *W Isls* 152 7948
Creagan Inn *Ag & B* 122 9744
Creagorry *W Isls* 152 7948
Creaguaineach Lodge *Highld* 131 3068
Creamore Bank *Shrops* 59 5130
Creaton *Nhants* 50 7071
Creca *D & G* 101 2270
Credenhill *Herefd* 46 4543
Crediton *Devon* 8 8300
Creebank *D & G* 98 3477
Creebridge *D & G* 99 4165
Creech Heathfield *Somset* 20 2727
Creech St Michael *Somset* 20 2725
Creed *Cnwll* 3 9347
Creedy Park *Devon* 8 8301
Creekmouth *Gt Lon* 27 4581
Creeting St Mary *Suffk* 54 0956
Creeton *Lincs* 64 0120
Creetown *D & G* 99 4759
Cregneash *IOM* 158 1867
Cregrina *Powys* 45 1252
Creich *Fife* 126 3221
Creigiau *Cardif* 33 0781
Crelly *Cnwll* 2 6732
Cremyll *Cnwll* 6 4553
Cressage *Shrops* 59 5904
Cressbrook *Derbys* 74 1673
Cresselly *Pembks* 30 0606
Cressex *Bucks* 26 8492
Cressing *Essex* 40 7920
Cresswell *Nthumb* 103 2993
Cresswell *Pembks* 30 0506
Cresswell *Staffs* 72 9739
Creswell *Derbys* 75 5274
Creswell Green *Staffs* 61 0710
Cretingham *Suffk* 55 2260
Cretshengan *Ag & B* 113 7166
Crew Green *Powys* 59 3215
Crewe *Ches* 71 4253
Crewe *Ches* 72 7056
Crewe Green *Ches* 72 7255
Crewkerne *Somset* 10 4409
Crews Hill *Herefd* 35 6722
Crews Hill Station *Herts* 27 3000
Crewton *Derbys* 62 3733
Crianlarich *Stirlg* 123 3825
Cribbs Causeway *Gloucs* 34 5780
Cribyn *Cerdgn* 44 5250
Criccieth *Gwynd* 56 4938
Crich *Derbys* 74 3454
Crich Carr *Derbys* 74 3354
Crich Common *Derbys* 74 3553
Crichton *Mdloth* 118 3862
Crick *Mons* 34 4890
Crick *Nhants* 50 5872
Crickadarn *Powys* 45 0942
Cricket St Thomas *Somset* 10 3708
Crickheath *Shrops* 59 2922
Crickhowell *Powys* 33 2118
Cricklade *Wilts* 36 0993
Cricklewood *Gt Lon* 26 2385
Cridling Stubbs *N York* 83 5221
Crieff *P & K* 125 8621
Criggan *Cnwll* 4 0160
Criggion *Powys* 59 2915
Crigglestone *W York* 82 3116
Crimble *Gt Man* 81 8611
Crimond *Abers* 143 0556
Crimonmogate *Abers* 143 0358
Crimplesham *Norfk* 65 6503
Crimscote *Warwks* 48 2347
Crinaglack *Highld* 139 4340
Crinan *Ag & B* 113 7894
Crindledyke *N Lans* 116 8356
Cringleford *Norfk* 67 1905
Cringles *N York* 82 0448
Crinow *Pembks* 31 1214
Cripp's Corner *E Susx* 17 7721
Cripplesease *Cnwll* 2 5036
Cripplestyle *Dorset* 12 0812
Crizeley *Herefd* 46 4532
Croachy *Highld* 140 6527
Croanford *Cnwll* 4 0371
Crochmore House *D & G* 100 8977
Crock Street *Somset* 10 3213
Crockenhill *Kent* 27 5067
Crocker End *Oxon* 37 7086
Crocker's Ash *Herefd* 34 5316
Crockerhill *W Susx* 14 9206
Crockernwell *Devon* 8 7592
Crockerton *Wilts* 22 8642
Crocketford *D & G* 100 8372
Crockey Hill *N York* 83 6246
Crockham Hill *Kent* 27 4450
Crockhurst Street *Kent* 16 6245
Crockleford Heath *Essex* 41 0426
Croes-goch *Pembks* 30 8330
Croes-lan *Cerdgn* 42 3844
Croes-y-mwyalch *Torfn* 34 3092
Croes-y-pant *Mons* 34 3104
Croeserw *Neath* 33 8795
Croesor *Gwynd* 57 6344
Croesyceiliog *Carmth* 31 4016
Croesyceiliog *Torfn* 34 3096
Croft *Ches* 79 6393
Croft *Devon* 5 5296
Croft *Leics* 50 5195
Croft *Lincs* 77 5061
Croft Michael *Cnwll* 2 6637
Croft-on-Tees *Dur* 89 2809
Croftamie *Stirlg* 115 4785
Crofton *Cumb* 93 3050
Crofton *W York* 83 3817
Crofton *Wilts* 23 2562
Crofts *D & G* 99 7365
Crofts *Moray* 141 2850
Crofts Bank *Gt Man* 79 7695
Crofts of Dipple *Moray* 141 3259
Crofts of Savoch *Abers* 143 0460
Crofty *Swans* 32 5294
Crogen *Gwynd* 58 0036
Croggan *Ag & B* 122 7027
Croglin *Cumb* 94 5747
Croik *Highld* 146 4591
Cromarty *Highld* 140 7867
Crombie *Fife* 117 0584
Cromdale *Highld* 141 0728
Cromer *Herts* 39 2928
Cromer *Norfk* 67 2242
Cromford *Derbys* 73 2956
Cromhall *Gloucs* 35 6990
Cromhall Common *Gloucs* 35 6989
Cromor *W Isls* 152 4021
Crompton Fold *Gt Man* 79 9409
Cromwell *Notts* 75 7961
Cronberry *E Ayrs* 107 6022
Crondall *Hants* 25 7948
Cronk-y-Voddy *IOM* 158 3085
Cronkbourne *IOM* 158 3677
Cronton *Mersyd* 78 4988
Crook *Cumb* 87 4695
Crook *Dur* 96 1635
Crook Inn *Border* 108 1026
Crook of Devon *P & K* 117 0400
Crookdake *Cumb* 93 1943
Crooke *Gt Man* 78 5507
Crooked End *Gloucs* 35 6217
Crooked Holme *Cumb* 101 5161
Crooked Soley *Wilts* 36 3172
Crookedholm *E Ayrs* 107 4537
Crookes *S York* 74 3287
Crookhall *Dur* 95 1150
Crookham *Berks* 24 5464
Crookham *Nthumb* 110 9138
Crookham Village *Hants* 25 7952
Crooklands *Cumb* 87 5383
Cropper *Derbys* 73 2335
Cropredy *Oxon* 49 4646
Cropston *Leics* 62 5510
Cropthorne *Worcs* 47 9945
Cropton *N York* 90 7589
Cropwell Bishop *Notts* 63 6835
Cropwell Butler *Notts* 63 6837
Cros *W Isls* 152 5061
Crosbie *N Ayrs* 114 2149
Crosbost *W Isls* 152 3924
Crosby *Cumb* 92 0738
Crosby *IOM* 158 3279
Crosby *Lincs* 84 8912
Crosby *Mersyd* 78 3198
Crosby Garret *Cumb* 88 7209
Crosby Ravensworth *Cumb* 94 6214
Crosby Villa *Cumb* 92 0939
Croscombe *Somset* 21 5944
Crosemere *Shrops* 59 4329
Crosland Edge *W York* 82 1012
Crosland Hill *W York* 82 1114
Cross *Somset* 21 4154
Cross Ash *Mons* 34 4019
Cross Coombe *Cnwll* 3 7251
Cross End *Beds* 51 0658
Cross End *Essex* 54 8534
Cross Flatts *W York* 82 1040
Cross Gates *W York* 83 3534
Cross Green *Devon* 5 3888
Cross Green *Staffs* 60 9105
Cross Green *Suffk* 54 8353
Cross Green *Suffk* 54 8955
Cross Green *Suffk* 54 9852
Cross Hands *Carmth* 32 5612
Cross Hands *Pembks* 31 0712
Cross Hill *Derbys* 74 4148
Cross Hills *N York* 82 0145
Cross Houses *Shrops* 59 5307
Cross Houses *Shrops* 60 6991
Cross in Hand *E Susx* 16 5521
Cross Inn *Cerdgn* 42 3957
Cross Inn *Cerdgn* 43 5464
Cross Inn *Pembks* 31 1005
Cross Inn *Rhondd* 33 0582
Cross Keys *Ag & B* 115 3385
Cross Keys *Wilts* 35 8771
Cross Lane *IOW* 13 5089
Cross Lane Head *Shrops* 60 7195
Cross Lanes *Cnwll* 2 6921
Cross Lanes *Cnwll* 3 7642
Cross Lanes *N York* 90 5364
Cross Lanes *Wrexhm* 71 3746
Cross o' th' hands *Derbys* 73 2846
Cross Oak *Powys* 45 1023
Cross of Jackston *Abers* 142 7432
Cross Roads *Powys* 45 9756
Cross Street *Suffk* 54 1876
Cross Town *Ches* 79 7578
Cross-at-Hand *Kent* 28 7846
Crossaig *Ag & B* 113 8351
Crossapoll *Ag & B* 120 9943
Crossbush *W Susx* 14 0306
Crosscanonby *Cumb* 92 0739
Crossdale Street *Norfk* 67 2239
Crossens *Mersyd* 80 3720
Crossford *Fife* 117 0786
Crossford *S Lans* 116 8246
Crossgate *Cnwll* 5 3488
Crossgate *Lincs* 64 2426
Crossgate *Staffs* 72 9437
Crossgatehall *E Loth* 118 3669
Crossgates *E Ayrs* 115 3744
Crossgates *Fife* 117 1488
Crossgates *N York* 91 0284
Crossgates *Powys* 45 0864
Crossgill *Lancs* 87 5563
Crosshands *Carmth* 31 1923
Crosshands *E Ayrs* 107 4830
Crosshill *Fife* 117 1796
Crosshill *S Ayrs* 106 3206
Crosshouse *E Ayrs* 106 3938
Crosskeys *Caerph* 34 2292
Crosskirk *Highld* 150 0369
Crosslands *Cumb* 87 3489
Crosslanes *Shrops* 59 3218
Crosslee *Border* 109 3018
Crosslee *Rens* 115 4066
Crossley *W York* 82 2021
Crossmichael *D & G* 99 7366
Crosspost *W Susx* 15 2522
Crossroads *Abers* 134 5607
Crossroads *Abers* 135 7594
Crosston *Angus* 127 5256
Crossway *Mons* 34 4419
Crossway *Pembks* 31 1542
Crossway *Powys* 45 0558
Crossway Green *Mons* 34 5294
Crossway Green *Worcs* 47 8468
Crossways *Dorset* 11 7788
Crosswell *Pembks* 31 1236
Crosthwaite *Cumb* 87 4391
Croston *Lancs* 80 4818
Crostwick *Norfk* 67 2515
Crostwight *Norfk* 67 3430
Crouch *Kent* 28 0558
Crouch *Kent* 27 6155
Crouch End *Gt Lon* 27 3088
Crouch Hill *Dorset* 11 7010
Croucheston *Wilts* 23 0625
Crough House Green *Kent* 16 4346
Croughton *Nhants* 49 5433
Crovie *Abers* 143 8065
Crow *Hants* 12 1604
Crow Edge *S York* 82 1804
Crow End *Cambs* 52 3257
Crow Green *Essex* 27 5796
Crow Hill *Herefd* 47 6326
Crow's Green *Essex* 40 6926
Crow's Nest *Cnwll* 5 2669
Crowan *Cnwll* 2 6434
Crowborough *E Susx* 16 5131
Crowborough Town *E Susx* 16 5031
Crowcombe *Somset* 20 1436
Crowdecote *Derbys* 74 1065
Crowden *Derbys* 74 0699
Crowden *Devon* 18 4999
Crowdhill *Hants* 13 4920
Crowdleham *Kent* 27 5659
Crowell *Oxon* 37 7499
Crowfield *Nhants* 49 6141
Crowfield *Suffk* 54 1457
Crowfield Green *Suffk* 54 1458
Crowgate Street *Norfk* 67 3121
Crowhill *E Loth* 119 7374
Crowhole *Derbys* 74 3375
Crowhurst *E Susx* 17 7512
Crowhurst *Surrey* 15 3847
Crowhurst Lane End *Surrey* 15 3747
Crowland *Lincs* 64 2410
Crowland *Suffk* 54 0170
Crowlas *Cnwll* 2 5133
Crowle *Lincs* 84 7712
Crowle *Worcs* 47 9256
Crowle Green *Worcs* 47 9156
Crowmarsh Gifford *Oxon* 37 6189
Crown Corner *Suffk* 55 2570
Crownhill *Devon* 6 4858
Crownpits *Surrey* 25 9743
Crownthorpe *Norfk* 66 0803
Crowntown *Cnwll* 2 6330
Crows-an-Wra *Cnwll* 2 3927
Crowshill *Norfk* 66 9506
Crowsnest *Shrops* 59 3601
Crowthorne *Berks* 25 8464
Crowton *Ches* 71 5774
Croxall *Staffs* 61 1913
Croxby *Lincs* 76 1898
Croxdale *Dur* 96 2636
Croxden *Staffs* 73 0639
Croxley Green *Herts* 26 0795
Croxton *Cambs* 52 2460
Croxton *Lincs* 85 0912
Croxton *Norfk* 66 9831
Croxton *Norfk* 54 8786
Croxton *Staffs* 72 7832
Croxton Green *Ches* 71 5552
Croxton Kerrial *Leics* 63 8329
Croxtonbank *Staffs* 72 7832
Croy *Highld* 140 7949
Croy *N Lans* 116 7275
Croyde *Devon* 18 4439
Croyde Bay *Devon* 18 4339
Croydon *Cambs* 52 3149
Croydon *Gt Lon* 27 3265
Crubenmore *Highld* 132 6790
Cruckmeole *Shrops* 59 4309
Cruckton *Shrops* 59 4310
Cruden Bay *Abers* 143 0836
Crudgington *Shrops* 59 6318
Crudwell *Wilts* 35 9593
Crug *Powys* 45 1972
Crug-y-byddar *Powys* 58 1682
Crugmeer *Cnwll* 4 9076
Crugybar *Carmth* 44 6537
Crumlin *Caerph* 33 2197
Crumplehorn *Cnwll* 5 2051
Crumpsall *Gt Man* 79 8402
Crundale *Kent* 29 0749
Crundale *Pembks* 30 9718
Crunwear *Pembks* 31 1810
Cruwys Morchard *Devon* 19 8712
Crux Easton *Hants* 24 4256
Cruxton *Dorset* 10 6096
Crwbin *Carmth* 32 4713
Cryers Hill *Bucks* 26 8796
Crymmych *Pembks* 31 1834
Crynant *Neath* 32 7904
Crystal Palace *Gt Lon* 27 3371
Cuaig *Highld* 137 7057
Cuan Ferry Village *Ag & B* 122 7514
Cubbington *Warwks* 48 3468
Cubert *Cnwll* 4 7857
Cubley *S York* 82 2401
Cublington *Bucks* 38 8422
Cublington *Herefd* 46 4038
Cuckfield *W Susx* 15 3025
Cucklington *Somset* 22 7527
Cuckney *Notts* 75 5671
Cuckold's Green *Kent* 28 8276
Cuckoo Bridge *Lincs* 64 2020
Cuckoo's Corner *Hants* 24 7441
Cuckoo's Nest *Ches* 71 3860
Cuddesdon *Oxon* 37 5903
Cuddington *Bucks* 37 7311
Cuddington *Ches* 71 5971
Cuddington Heath *Ches* 71 4746
Cuddy Hill *Lancs* 80 4937
Cudham *Gt Lon* 27 4459
Cudliptown *Devon* 5 5279
Cudnell *Dorset* 12 0696
Cudworth *S York* 83 3808
Cudworth *Somset* 10 3810
Cudworth Common *S York* 83 4007
Cuerden Green *Lancs* 81 5525
Cuerdley Cross *Ches* 78 5486
Cufaude *Hants* 24 6557
Cuffley *Herts* 39 3003
Cuil *Highld* 122 9855
Culbokie *Highld* 140 6059
Culbone *Somset* 19 8448
Culburnie *Highld* 139 4941
Culcabock *Highld* 140 6844
Culcharry *Highld* 140 8650
Culcheth *Ches* 79 6694
Culdrain *Abers* 142 5134
Culduie *Highld* 137 7140
Culford *Suffk* 54 8370
Culgaith *Cumb* 94 6029
Culham *Oxon* 37 5095
Culkein *Highld* 148 0333
Culkein Drumbeg *Highld* 148 1133
Culkerton *Gloucs* 35 9395
Cullen *Moray* 142 5167
Cullercoats *T & W* 103 3570
Cullerlie *Abers* 135 7603
Cullicudden *Highld* 140 6463
Cullingworth *W York* 82 0636
Cullipool House *Ag & B* 122 7413
Cullivoe *Shet* 153 5402
Culloden *Highld* 140 7246
Cullompton *Devon* 9 0207
Culm Davy *Devon* 9 1215
Culmington *Shrops* 59 4982
Culmstock *Devon* 9 1013
Culnacraig *Highld* 145 0603
Culnaightrie *D & G* 92 7750
Culnaknock *Highld* 137 5162
Culpho *Suffk* 55 2149
Culrain *Highld* 146 5794
Culross *Fife* 117 9886

Culroy
Doddington
281

Culroy S Ayrs 106 3114
Culsalmond Abers 142 6532
Culscadden D & G 99 4748
Culshabbin D & G 98 3051
Culswick Shet 153 2745
Cultercullen Abers 143 9223
Cults Aber C 135 8903
Culverstone Green Kent 27 6362
Culverthorpe Lincs 64 0240
Culworth Nhants 49 5446
Cumbernauld N Lans 116 7674
Cumbernauld Village N Lans 116 7676
Cumberworth Lincs 77 5073
Cumdivock Cumb 93 3448
Cuminestown Abers 143 8050
Cumledge Border 119 7956
Cummersdale Cumb 93 3953
Cummertrees D & G 100 1366
Cummingston Moray 141 1368
Cumnock E Ayrs 107 5620
Cumnor Oxon 37 4504
Cumrew Cumb 94 5550
Cumrue D & G 100 0686
Cumwhinton Cumb 93 4552
Cumwhitton Cumb 94 5052
Cundall N York 89 4272
Cunninghamhead N Ayrs 106 3741
Cupar Fife 126 3714
Cupar Muir Fife 126 3613
Cupernham Hants 23 3622
Curbar Derbys 74 2574
Curbridge Hants 13 5211
Curbridge Oxon 36 3308
Curdridge Hants 13 5213
Curdworth Warwks 61 1792
Curland Somset 10 2717
Curridge Berks 24 4972
Currie C Edin 117 1867
Curry Mallet Somset 21 3221
Curry Rivel Somset 21 3925
Curteis Corner Kent 28 8539
Curtisden Green Kent 28 7440
Curtisknowle Devon 7 7353
Cury Cnwll 2 6721
Cushnie Abers 134 5211
Cushuish Somset 20 1930
Cusop Herefd 46 2441
Cutcloy D & G 99 4534
Cutcombe Somset 20 9339
Cutgate Gt Man 81 8614
Cuthill Highld 147 7587
Cutiau Gwynd 57 6317
Cutler's Green Essex 40 5930
Cutmadoc Cnwll 4 0963
Cutmere Cnwll 5 3260
Cutnall Green Worcs 47 8868
Cutsdean Gloucs 48 0830
Cutsyke W York 83 4224
Cutthorpe Derbys 74 3473
Cuxham Oxon 37 6695
Cuxton Kent 28 7066
Cuxwold Lincs 85 1701
Cwm Blae G 33 1805
Cwm Denbgs 70 0677
Cwm Capel Carmth 32 4502
Cwm Crawnon Powys 33 1419
Cwm Dulais Swans 32 6103
Cwm Irfon Powys 45 8549
Cwm Morgan Carmth 31 2934
Cwm Penmachno Conwy 69 7547
Cwm-bach Carmth 32 4801
Cwm-celyn Blae G 33 2008
Cwm-Cewydd Gwynd 57 8713
Cwm-cou Cerdgn 31 2942
Cwm-Ifor Carmth 44 6625
Cwm-Llinau Powys 57 8408
Cwm-y-glo Carmth 32 5513
Cwm-y-glo Gwynd 69 5562
Cwmafan Neath 32 7791
Cwmaman Rhondd 33 0099
Cwmann Carmth 44 5847
Cwmavon Torfn 34 2706
Cwmbach Carmth 31 2526
Cwmbach Powys 45 1639
Cwmbach Rhondd 33 0201
Cwmbach Llechrhyd Powys 45 0254
Cwmbelan Powys 58 9481
Cwmbran Torfn 34 2994
Cwmbrwyno Cerdgn 43 7180
Cwmcarn Caerph 34 2293
Cwmcarvan Mons 34 4707
Cwmdare Rhondd 33 9803
Cwmdu Carmth 44 6330
Cwmdu Powys 45 1823
Cwmdu Swans 32 6494
Cwmduad Carmth 31 3731
Cwmdwr Carmth 44 7132
Cwmergyr Cerdgn 43 7982
Cwmfelin Brdgnd 33 8589
Cwmfelin Myr Td 33 0901
Cwmfelin Boeth Carmth 31 1919
Cwmfelin Mynach Carmth 31 2224
Cwmfelinfach Caerph 33 1891
Cwmffrwd Carmth 31 4217
Cwmgiedd Powys 32 7911
Cwmgorse Carmth 32 7010
Cwmgwili Carmth 32 5710
Cwmgwrach Neath 33 8604
Cwmhiraeth Carmth 31 3437
Cwmisfael Carmth 32 4915
Cwmllynfell Neath 32 7412
Cwmparc Rhondd 33 9495
Cwmpengraig Carmth 31 3536
Cwmpennar Rhondd 33 0300
Cwmrhos Powys 45 1824
Cwmrhydyceirw Swans 32 6699
Cwmsychbant Cerdgn 44 4746
Cwmtillery Blae G 33 2105
Cwmyoy Mons 46 2923
Cwmystwyth Cerdgn 43 7874
Cwrt Gwynd 32 6800
Cwrt-newydd Cerdgn 44 4947
Cwrt-y-gollen Powys 34 2317
Cyfronydd Powys 58 1408
Cylibebyll Neath 32 7404
Cymer Neath 33 8695
Cymmer Rhondd 33 0290
Cynghordy Carmth 44 8040
Cynheidre Carmth 32 4907
Cynonville Neath 33 8395
Cynwyd Denbgs 70 0541
Cynwyl Elfed Carmth 31 3727

# D

Daccombe Devon 7 9068
Dacre Cumb 93 4526
Dacre N York 89 1960
Dacre Banks N York 89 1962
Daddry Shield Dur 95 8937
Dadford Bucks 49 6638
Dadlington Leics 61 4097
Dafen Carmth 32 5201
Daffy Green Norfk 66 9609
Dagenham Gt Lon 27 5084
Daglingworth Gloucs 35 9905
Dagnall Bucks 38 9916
Dagworth Suffk 54 0361
Dailly S Ayrs 106 2701
Dainton Devon 7 8566
Dairsie Fife 126 4117
Daisy Hill Gt Man 79 6504
Daisy Hill W York 82 2728
Dalabrog W Isls 152 7521
Dalavich Ag & B 122 9612
Dalbeattie D & G 100 8361
Dalbury Derbys 73 2634
Dalby IOM 158 2178
Dalby Lincs 77 4169
Dalby N York 90 6371
Dalcapon P & K 125 9754
Dalchalm Highld 147 9105
Dalchreichart Highld 131 2812
Dalchruin P & K 124 7116
Dalcrue P & K 125 0427
Dalderby Lincs 77 2565
Dalditch Devon 9 0483
Dale Cumb 94 5443
Dale Derbys 62 4338
Dale Pembks 30 8005
Dale Bottom Cumb 93 2921
Dale End Derbys 74 2161
Dale End N York 82 9645
Dale Hill E Susx 16 7030
Dalehouse N York 97 7717
Dalgarven N Ayrs 115 2846
Dalgety Bay Fife 117 1683
Dalgig E Ayrs 107 5512
Dalginross P & K 124 7721
Dalguise P & K 125 9847
Dalhalvaig Highld 150 8954
Dalham Suffk 53 7261
Daliburgh W Isls 152 7521
Dalkeith Mdloth 118 3367
Dallas Moray 141 1252
Dallinghoo Suffk 55 2655
Dallington E Susx 16 6519
Dallington Nhants 49 7362
Dallow N York 89 1971
Dalmally Ag & B 123 1627
Dalmary Stirlg 115 5195
Dalmellington E Ayrs 107 4705
Dalmeny C Edin 117 1477
Dalmigavie Highld 140 7319
Dalmigavie Lodge Highld 140 7523
Dalmore Highld 140 6668
Dalmuir W Duns 115 4871
Dalnabreck Highld 129 7069
Dalnacardoch P & K 132 7270
Dalnahaitnach Highld 140 8519
Dalnaspidal P & K 132 6473
Dalnawillan Lodge Highld 150 0340
Daloist P & K 124 7857
Dalqueich P & K 125 0804
Dalquhairn S Ayrs 106 3296
Dalreavoch Lodge Highld 147 7508
Dalry N Ayrs 115 2949
Dalrymple E Ayrs 106 3514
Dalserf S Lans 116 7950
Dalsmeran Ag & B 104 6413
Dalston Cumb 93 3650
Dalston Gt Lon 27 3384
Dalswinton D & G 100 9385
Dalton Cumb 87 5476
Dalton D & G 100 1173
Dalton Lancs 78 4908
Dalton N York 89 1108
Dalton N York 89 4376
Dalton Nthumb 103 1172
Dalton S York 75 4594
Dalton Magna S York 75 4692
Dalton Parva S York 75 4593
Dalton Piercy Dur 97 4631
Dalton-in-Furness Cumb 86 2274
Dalton-le-Dale Dur 96 4048
Dalton-on-Tees N York 89 2907
Dalveen D & G 108 8806
Dalveich Stirlg 124 6124
Dalwhinnie Highld 132 6384
Dalwood Devon 9 2400
Dam Green Norfk 54 0485
Damask Green Herts 39 2529
Damerham Hants 12 1016
Damgate Norfk 67 4009
Dan-y-Parc Powys 34 2217
Danaway Kent 28 8663
Danbury Essex 40 7805
Danby N York 90 7008
Danby Bottom N York 90 6904
Danby Wiske N York 89 3398
Dandaleith Moray 141 2846
Danderhall Mdloth 117 3069
Dane End Herts 39 3321
Dane Hills Leics 62 5604
Dane Street Kent 28 0552
Danebridge Ches 72 9665
Danegate E Susx 16 5633
Danehill E Susx 15 4027
Danemoor Green Norfk 66 0505
Danesford Shrops 60 7391
Danesmoor Derbys 74 4063
Daniel's Water Kent 28 9541
Danshillock Abers 142 7157
Danskine E Loth 118 5667
Danthorpe E R Yk 85 2532
Danzey Green Warwks 48 1269
Dapple Heath Staffs 73 0425
Darby Green Hants 25 8360
Darcy Lever Gt Man 79 7308
Daren-felen Mons 34 2212
Darenth Kent 27 5671
Daresbury Ches 78 5882
Darfield S York 83 4104
Darfoulds Notts 75 5578
Dargate Kent 29 0861
Darite Cnwll 5 2569
Darland Kent 28 7865
Darland Wrexhm 71 3757
Darlaston Staffs 72 8835
Darlaston W Mids 60 9796
Darlaston Green W Mids 60 9797
Darley N York 89 2059
Darley Abbey Derbys 62 3538
Darley Bridge Derbys 74 2661
Darley Dale Derbys 74 2663
Darley Green Warwks 61 1874
Darley Head N York 89 1959
Darleyhall Herts 38 1422
Darlingscott Warwks 48 2342
Darlington Dur 89 2814
Darliston Shrops 59 5733
Darlton Notts 75 7773
Darnford Staffs 61 1308
Darnick Border 109 5334
Darowen Powys 57 8201
Darra Abers 142 7447
Darracott Cnwll 18 2811
Darracott Devon 18 2317
Darracott Devon 18 4739
Darras Hall Nthumb 103 1570
Darrington W York 83 4820
Darsham Suffk 55 4169
Darshill Somset 21 6144
Dartford Kent 27 5474
Dartington Devon 7 7862
Dartmeet Devon 7 6773
Dartmouth Devon 7 8751
Darton S York 82 3110
Darvel E Ayrs 107 5637
Darwell Hole E Susx 16 6919
Darwen Lancs 81 6922
Datchet Berks 26 9877
Datchworth Herts 39 2619
Datchworth Green Herts 39 2718
Daubhill Gt Man 79 7007
Dauntsey Wilts 35 9782
Dauntsey Green Wilts 35 9981
Dava Highld 141 0038
Davenham Ches 79 6571
Davenport Gt Man 79 9088
Davenport Green Ches 79 8379
Davenport Green Gt Man 79 8086
Daventry Nhants 49 5762
David Street Kent 27 6464
Davidson's Mains C Edin 117 2175
Davidstow Cnwll 4 1587
Davington D & G 109 2302
Davington Hill Kent 28 0161
Daviot Abers 142 7428
Daviot Highld 140 7239
Daviot House Highld 140 7240
Davis's Town E Susx 16 5217
Davoch of Grange Moray 142 4751
Davyhulme Gt Man 79 7595
Daw End W Mids 61 0300
Daw's House Cnwll 5 3182
Dawesgreen Surrey 15 2147
Dawley Shrops 60 6808
Dawlish Devon 9 9576
Dawlish Warren Devon 9 9778
Dawn Conwy 69 8672
Daws Green Somset 20 1921
Daws Heath Essex 40 8188
Dawsmere Lincs 65 4430
Day Green Ches 72 7757
Daybrook Notts 62 5744
Dayhills Staffs 72 9532
Dayhouse Bank Worcs 60 9678
Daylesford Gloucs 48 2425
Ddol Flints 70 1471
Ddol-Cownwy Powys 58 0117
Deal Kent 29 3752
Dean Cumb 92 0725
Dean Devon 19 6245
Dean Devon 19 7048
Dean Devon 7 7364
Dean Dorset 11 9715
Dean Hants 24 4431
Dean Hants 13 5619
Dean Lancs 81 8525
Dean Oxon 36 3422
Dean Somset 22 6743
Dean Bottom Kent 27 5868
Dean Court Oxon 37 4705
Dean End Dorset 11 9717
Dean Head S York 74 2600
Dean Prior Devon 7 7363
Dean Row Ches 79 8781
Dean Street Kent 28 7453
Deanburnhaugh Border 109 3911
Deancombe Devon 7 7264
Deane Gt Man 79 6907
Deane Hants 24 5450
Deanhead W York 82 0415
Deanland Dorset 22 9918
Deanlane End W Susx 13 7412
Deanraw Nthumb 102 8162
Deans W Loth 117 0369
Deanscales Cumb 92 0926
Deanshanger Nhants 49 7639
Deanshaugh Moray 141 3550
Deanston Stirlg 116 7101
Dearham Cumb 92 0736
Dearnley Gt Man 81 9215
Debach Suffk 55 2454
Debden Essex 53 5533
Debden Essex 27 4496
Debden Green Essex 40 5831
Debenham Suffk 54 1763
Deblin's Green Worcs 47 8148
Dechmont W Loth 117 0370
Dechmont Road W Loth 117 0269
Deddington Oxon 49 4631
Dedham Essex 41 0533
Dedham Heath Essex 41 0531
Dedworth Berks 26 9476
Deene Nhants 51 9492
Deenethorpe Nhants 51 9591
Deepcar S York 74 2897
Deepcut Surrey 25 9057
Deepdale Cumb 88 7184
Deepdale N York 88 8979
Deeping Gate Lincs 64 1509
Deeping St James Lincs 64 1609
Deeping St Nicholas Lincs 64 2115
Deerhurst Gloucs 47 8730
Deerhurst Walton Gloucs 47 8828
Deerton Street Kent 28 9762
Defford Worcs 47 9143
Defynnog Powys 45 9227
Deganwy Conwy 69 7779
Degnish Ag & B 122 7812
Deighton N York 89 3801
Deighton N York 83 6244
Deighton W York 82 1519
Deiniolen Gwynd 69 5763
Delabole Cnwll 4 0683
Delamere Ches 71 5668
Delfrigs Abers 143 9620
Dell Quay W Susx 14 8302
Delley Devon 19 5424
Delliefure Highld 141 0730
Delly End Oxon 36 3513
Delmonden Green Kent 17 7330
Delnashaugh Inn Moray 141 1835
Delny Highld 146 7372
Delph Gt Man 82 9807
Delves Dur 95 1149
Delvine P & K 126 1240
Dembleby Lincs 64 0437
Demelza Cnwll 4 9763
Den of Lindores Fife 126 2616
Denaby S York 75 4899
Denaby Main S York 75 4999
Denbies Surrey 26 1450
Denbigh Denbgs 70 0566
Denbrae Fife 126 3818
Denbury Devon 7 8268
Denby Derbys 62 3946
Denby Bottles Derbys 62 3846
Denby Dale W York 82 2208
Denchworth Oxon 36 3891
Dendron Cumb 86 2470
Denel End Beds 38 0335
Denfield P & K 125 9517
Denford Nhants 51 9976
Dengie Essex 41 9802
Denham Bucks 26 0487
Denham Suffk 53 7561
Denham Suffk 55 1974
Denham End Suffk 53 7663
Denham Green Bucks 26 0488
Denham Green Suffk 55 1974
Denhead Abers 143 9952
Denhead Fife 127 4613
Denhead of Gray Dund C 126 3531
Denholm Border 110 5718
Denholme W York 82 0734
Denholme Clough W York 82 0732
Denio Gwynd 56 3635
Denmead Hants 13 6512
Denmore Aber C 135 9411
Denne Park W Susx 15 1628
Dennington Suffk 55 2867
Denny Falk 116 8082
Dennyloanhead Falk 116 8080
Denshaw Gt Man 82 9710
Denside Abers 135 8095
Densole Kent 29 2141
Denston Suffk 53 7652
Denstone Staffs 73 0940
Denstroude Kent 29 1061
Dent Cumb 87 7086
Dent-de-Lion Kent 29 3269
Denton Cambs 52 1587
Denton Dur 96 2118
Denton E Susx 16 4502
Denton Gt Man 79 9295
Denton Kent 28 6673
Denton Kent 29 2147
Denton Lincs 63 8632
Denton N York 82 1448
Denton Nhants 51 8358
Denton Norfk 55 2788
Denton Oxon 37 5902
Denver Norfk 65 6001
Denwick Nthumb 111 2014
Deopham Norfk 66 0400
Deopham Green Norfk 66 0499
Depden Suffk 53 7857
Depden Green Suffk 53 7756
Deptford Gt Lon 27 3777
Deptford Wilts 22 0138
Derby Derbys 62 3536
Derby Devon 19 5633
Derbyhaven IOM 158 2867
Derculich P & K 125 8852
Dereham Norfk 66 9913
Deri Caerph 33 1201
Derril Devon 18 3003
Derringstone Kent 29 2049
Derrington Staffs 72 8922
Derriton Devon 18 3303
Derry Hill Wilts 35 9670
Derrythorpe Lincs 84 8208
Dersingham Norfk 65 6830
Dervaig Ag & B 121 4352
Derwen Denbgs 70 0750
Derwen Fawr Carmth 44 5722
Derwenlas Powys 57 7298
Derwydd Carmth 32 6117
Desborough Nhants 51 8083
Desford Leics 62 4703
Deskford Moray 142 5061
Detchant Nthumb 111 0836
Detling Kent 28 7958
Deuxhill Shrops 60 6987
Devauden Mons 34 4898
Devil's Bridge Cerdgn 43 7376
Deviock Cnwll 5 3155
Devitts Green Warwks 61 2790
Devizes Wilts 22 0061
Devonport Devon 6 4554
Devonside Clacks 116 9196
Devoran Cnwll 3 7939
Dewarton Mdloth 118 3763
Dewlish Dorset 11 7798
Dewsbury W York 82 2421
Dewsbury Moor W York 82 2321
Deytheur Powys 58 2317
Dial Somset 21 5366
Dial Green W Susx 14 9227
Dial Post W Susx 15 1519
Dibberford Dorset 10 4504
Dibden Hants 13 4008
Dibden Purlieu Hants 13 4106
Dickens Heath W Mids 61 1176
Dickleburgh Norfk 54 1682
Didbrook Gloucs 48 0531
Didcot Oxon 37 5290
Diddington Cambs 52 1965
Diddlebury Shrops 59 5085
Didley Herefd 46 4532
Didling W Susx 14 8318
Didmarton Gloucs 35 8287
Didsbury Gt Man 79 8491
Didworthy Devon 7 6862
Digby Lincs 76 0854
Digg Highld 136 4668
Diggle Gt Man 82 0007
Digmoor Lancs 78 4905
Digswell Herts 39 2415
Digswell Water Herts 39 2514
Dihewyd Cerdgn 44 4855
Dilham Norfk 67 3325
Dilhorne Staffs 72 9743
Dillington Cambs 52 1365
Dilston Nthumb 102 9763
Dilton Wilts 22 8548
Dilton Marsh Wilts 22 8449
Dilwyn Herefd 46 4154
Dimple Derbys 74 2960
Dimple Gt Man 81 7015
Dinas Carmth 31 2730
Dinas Cnwll 4 9274
Dinas Gwynd 56 2735
Dinas Pembks 30 0138
Dinas Rhondd 33 0091
Dinas Dinlle Gwynd 68 4356
Dinas Powys V Glam 33 1571
Dinas-Mawddwy Gwynd 57 8515
Dinder Somset 21 5744
Dinedor Herefd 46 5336
Dingestow Mons 34 4510
Dingle Mersyd 78 3687
Dingleden Kent 17 8131
Dingley Nhants 50 7787
Dingwall Highld 139 5458
Dinham Mons 34 4792
Dinmael Conwy 70 0044
Dinnet Abers 134 4598
Dinnington S York 75 5285
Dinnington Somset 10 4012
Dinnington T & W 103 2073
Dinorwic Gwynd 69 5961
Dinton Bucks 37 7610
Dinton Wilts 22 0131
Dinwoodie D & G 100 1190
Dinworthy Devon 18 3015
Dipford Somset 20 2021
Dipley Hants 24 7457
Dippen Ag & B 105 7937
Dippen N Ayrs 105 0422
Dippenhall Surrey 25 8146
Dippermill Devon 18 4406
Dippertown Devon 5 4284
Dipple Moray 141 3258
Dipple S Ayrs 106 2002
Diptford Devon 7 7256
Dipton Dur 96 1554
Diptonmill Nthumb 102 9361
Dirleton E Loth 118 5184
Dirt Pot Nthumb 95 8545
Discoed Powys 46 2764
Diseworth Leics 62 4524
Dishforth N York 89 3873
Disley Ches 79 9784
Diss Norfk 54 1180
Disserth Powys 45 0358
Distington Cumb 92 0023
Ditchampton Wilts 23 0831
Ditchburn Nthumb 111 1320
Ditcheat Somset 21 6236
Ditchingham Norfk 67 3391
Ditchley Oxon 36 3820
Ditchling E Susx 15 3215
Ditherington Shrops 59 5014
Ditteridge Wilts 35 8169
Dittisham Devon 7 8655
Ditton Ches 78 4986
Ditton Kent 28 7158
Ditton Green Cambs 53 6558
Ditton Priors Shrops 59 6089
Dixton Gloucs 47 9830
Dixton Mons 34 5113
Dizzard Cnwll 4 1698
Dobcross Gt Man 82 9906
Dobroyd Castle W York 81 9323
Dobwalls Cnwll 5 2165
Doccombe Devon 8 7786
Dochgarroch Highld 140 6140
Dockenfield Surrey 25 8240
Docker Lancs 87 5774
Docking Norfk 65 7636
Docklow Herefd 46 5657
Dockray Cumb 93 2649
Dockray Cumb 93 3921
Dod's Leigh Staffs 73 0134
Dodbrooke Devon 7 7444
Dodd's Green Ches 71 6043
Doddinghurst Essex 27 5999
Doddington Cambs 52 4090
Doddington Kent 28 9357
Doddington Lincs 76 8970

283

Fife Keith
Fyfield Wick

Fife Keith Moray 142 4250
Fifehead Magdalen Dorset 22 7821
Fifehead Neville Dorset 11 7610
Fifehead St Quinton Dorset 11 7710
Fifield Berks 26 9076
Fifield Oxon 36 2418
Fifield Wilts 23 1450
Figheldean Wilts 23 1547
Filands Wilts 35 9388
Filby Norfk 67 4613
Filey N York 91 1180
Filgrave Bucks 38 8648
Filkins Oxon 36 2304
Filleigh Devon 19 6627
Filleigh Devon 19 7410
Fillingham Lincs 76 9485
Fillongley Warwks 61 2887
Filmore Hill Hants 13 6627
Filton Gloucs 34 6079
Fimber E R Yk 91 8960
Finavon Angus 127 4956
Fincham Norfk 65 6806
Finchampstead Berks 25 7963
Fincharn Ag & B 122 9003
Finchdean Hants 13 7312
Finchingfield Essex 40 6832
Finchley Gt Lon 27 2690
Findern Derbys 73 3030
Findhorn Moray 141 0364
Findhorn Bridge Highld 140 8027
Findo Gask P & K 125 0019
Findochty Moray 142 4667
Findon Abers 135 9397
Findon W Susx 14 1208
Findon Mains Highld 140 6060
Findrack House Abers 134 6004
Finedon Nhants 51 9172
Fingal Street Suffk 55 2169
Fingask P & K 126 1619
Fingest Bucks 37 7791
Finghall N York 89 1889
Fingland Cumb 93 2557
Fingland D & G 107 7517
Finglesham Kent 29 3353
Fingringhoe Essex 41 0220
Finkle Green Essex 53 7040
Finkle Street S York 74 3099
Finlarig Stirlg 124 5733
Finmere Oxon 49 6332
Finnart P & K 124 5157
Finningham Suffk 54 0669
Finningley S York 75 6799
Finsbay W Isls 152 0786
Finstall Worcs 60 9770
Finsthwaite Cumb 87 3687
Finstock Oxon 36 3616
Finstown Ork 153 3513
Fintry Abers 142 7554
Fintry Stirlg 116 6186
Finzean Abers 134 5993
Fionnphort Ag & B 120 3023
Fionnsbhagh W Isls 152 0786
Fir Tree Dur 96 1434
Firbank Cumb 87 6293
Firbeck S York 75 5688
Firby N York 89 2686
Firby N York 90 7466
Firgrove Gt Man 81 9113
Firsby Lincs 77 4562
Firsdown Wilts 23 2133
Fishbourne IOW 13 5592
Fishbourne W Susx 14 8304
Fishburn Dur 96 3632
Fishcross Clacks 116 8995
Fisher W Susx 14 8700
Fisher's Pond Hants 13 4820
Fisher's Row Lancs 80 4148
Fisherford Abers 142 6735
Fisherrow E Loth 118 3472
Fisherstreet W Susx 14 9431
Fisherton Highld 140 7451
Fisherton S Ayrs 106 2717
Fisherton de la Mere Wilts 22 0038
Fisherwick Staffs 61 1708
Fishery Estate Berks 26 8980
Fishguard Pembks 30 9537
Fishlake S York 83 6513
Fishleigh Devon 8 5405
Fishmere End Lincs 64 2837
Fishnish Pier Ag & B 121 6542
Fishpond Bottom Dorset 10 3698
Fishponds Bristl 35 6375
Fishpool Gt Man 79 8009
Fishtoft Lincs 64 3642
Fishtoft Drove Lincs 77 3148
Fishwick Border 119 9151
Fishwick Lancs 81 5629
Fiskavaig Highld 136 3334
Fiskerton Lincs 76 0471
Fiskerton Notts 75 7351
Fitling E R Yk 85 2534
Fittleton Wilts 23 1449
Fittleworth W Susx 14 0019
Fitton End Cambs 65 4313
Fitz Shrops 59 4417
Fitzhead Somset 20 1228
Fitzroy Somset 20 1927
Fitzwilliam W York 83 4115
Fiunary Highld 121 6246
Five Ash Down E Susx 16 4723
Five Ashes E Susx 16 5525
Five Bells Somset 20 0642
Five Bridges Herefd 47 6446
Five Lanes Mons 34 4490
Five Oak Green Kent 16 6445
Five Oaks Jersey 158 0000
Five Oaks W Susx 14 0928
Five Roads Carmth 32 4805
Five Wents Kent 28 8050
Fivecrosses Ches 71 5276
Fivehead Somset 21 3522
Fivelanes Cnwll 5 2280
Flack's Green Essex 40 7614
Flackwell Heath Bucks 26 8989
Fladbury Worcs 47 9946
Fladdabister Shet 153 4332
Flagg Derbys 74 1368
Flamborough E R Yk 91 2270
Flamstead Herts 38 0714
Flansham W Susx 14 9601
Flanshaw W York 82 3020
Flappit Spring W York 82 0536
Flasby N York 82 9456
Flash Staffs 74 0266
Flashader Highld 136 3453
Flaunden Herts 26 0100
Flawborough Notts 63 7842
Flawith N York 90 4865
Flax Bourton Somset 21 5069
Flaxby N York 89 3957
Flaxley Gloucs 35 6815
Flaxmere Ches 71 5572
Flaxpool Somset 20 1435
Flaxton N York 90 6762
Fleckney Leics 50 6493
Flecknoe Warwks 49 5163
Fledborough Notts 75 8072
Fleet Dorset 10 6380
Fleet Hants 13 7201
Fleet Hants 25 8053
Fleet Lincs 64 3823
Fleet Hargate Lincs 65 3925
Fleetend Hants 13 5006
Fleetwood Lancs 80 3348
Flemingston V Glam 20 0169
Flemington S Lans 116 6559
Flempton Suffk 54 8169
Fletcher Green Kent 16 5349
Fletchersbridge Cnwll 4 1065
Fletchertown Cumb 93 2042
Fletching E Susx 16 4223
Fleur-de-lis Caerph 33 1696
Flexbury Cnwll 18 2107
Flexford Surrey 25 9350
Flimby Cumb 92 0233
Flimwell E Susx 17 7131
Flint Flints 70 2472
Flint Mountain Flints 70 2470
Flint's Green W Mids 61 2680
Flintham Notts 63 7445
Flinton E R Yk 85 2136
Flishinghurst Kent 28 7537
Flitcham Norfk 65 7326
Flitton Beds 38 0535
Flitwick Beds 38 0334
Flixborough Lincs 84 8714
Flixborough Stather Lincs 84 8614
Flixton Gt Man 79 7494
Flixton N York 91 0479
Flixton Suffk 55 3186
Flockton W York 82 2314
Flockton Green W York 82 2515
Flodden Nthumb 110 9235
Flodigarry Highld 136 4671
Flookburgh Cumb 87 3675
Flordon Norfk 66 1897
Flore Nhants 49 6460
Flotterton Nthumb 103 9902
Flowers Green E Susx 16 6311
Flowton Suffk 54 0846
Flushdyke W York 82 2820
Flushing Cnwll 3 8034
Fluxton Devon 9 0893
Flyford Flavell Worcs 47 9755
Fobbing Essex 40 7183
Fochabers Moray 141 3458
Fochriw Caerph 33 1005
Fockerby Lincs 84 8519
Foddington Somset 21 5729
Foel Powys 58 9911
Foel y Dyffryn Brdgnd 33 8594
Foelgastell Carmth 32 5414
Foggathorpe E R Yk 84 7537
Fogo Border 110 7649
Fogwatt Moray 141 2356
Foindle Highld 148 1948
Folda Angus 133 1963
Fole Staffs 73 0437
Foleshill W Mids 61 3582
Foliejon Park Berks 25 8974
Folke Dorset 11 6613
Folkestone Kent 29 2336
Folkingham Lincs 64 0733
Folkington E Susx 16 5603
Folksworth Cambs 52 1489
Folkton N York 91 0579
Folla Rule Abers 142 7332
Follifoot N York 83 3452
Folly Gate Devon 8 5798
Folly Hill Surrey 25 8348
Fonmon V Glam 20 0467
Font-y-gary V Glam 20 0566
Fonthill Bishop Wilts 22 9333
Fonthill Gifford Wilts 22 9231
Fontmell Magna Dorset 11 8616
Fontmell Parva Dorset 11 8214
Fontwell W Susx 14 9407
Foolow Derbys 74 1976
Foots Cray Gt Lon 27 4770
Forbestown Abers 134 3513
Forcett N York 89 1712
Ford Ag & B 122 8603
Ford Bucks 37 7709
Ford Derbys 74 4080
Ford Devon 18 4124
Ford Devon 6 6150
Ford Devon 7 7940
Ford Gloucs 48 0829
Ford Nthumb 110 9437
Ford Shrops 59 4113
Ford Somset 20 0928
Ford Somset 21 5953
Ford Staffs 73 0653
Ford W Susx 14 9903
Ford Wilts 35 8475
Ford End Essex 40 6716
Ford Green Lancs 80 4746
Ford Heath Shrops 59 4011
Ford Street Somset 20 1518
Ford's Green Suffk 54 0666
Forda Devon 8 5390
Fordcombe Kent 16 5240
Fordell Fife 117 1588
Forden Powys 58 2201
Forder Devon 8 6789
Forder Green Devon 7 7967
Fordham Cambs 53 6370
Fordham Essex 40 9228
Fordham Norfk 65 6199
Fordham Heath Essex 40 9426
Fordingbridge Hants 12 1414
Fordon E R Yk 91 0475
Fordoun Abers 135 7475
Fordstreet Essex 40 9226
Fordton Devon 8 8399
Fordwells Oxon 36 3013
Fordwich Kent 29 1859
Fordyce Abers 142 5563
Forebridge Staffs 72 9322
Foremark Derbys 62 3326
Forest Guern 158 0000
Forest N York 89 2700
Forest Becks Lancs 81 7851
Forest Chapel Ches 79 9772
Forest Gate Gt Lon 27 4085
Forest Green Surrey 14 1241
Forest Hall Cumb 87 5401
Forest Hall T & W 103 2769
Forest Head Cumb 94 5857
Forest Hill Gt Lon 27 3672
Forest Hill Oxon 37 5807
Forest Lane Head N York 83 3356
Forest Lodge Ag & B 123 2742
Forest Mill Clacks 117 9694
Forest Row E Susx 16 4234
Forest Side IOW 13 4889
Forest Town Notts 75 5662
Forest-in-Teesdale Dur 95 8630
Forestburn Gate Nthumb 103 0696
Forestside W Susx 14 7612
Forfar Angus 127 4550
Forgandenny P & K 125 0818
Forge Powys 57 7699
Forge Hammer Torfn 34 2895
Forge Side Torfn 34 2408
Forgie Moray 141 3854
Forgieside Moray 142 4053
Forgorig Border 110 7748
Forgue Abers 142 6145
Forhill Worcs 61 0575
Formby Mersyd 78 3006
Forncett End Norfk 66 1493
Forncett St Mary Norfk 66 1694
Forncett St Peter Norfk 66 1693
Fornham All Saints Suffk 54 8367
Fornham St Martin Suffk 54 8567
Fornside Cumb 93 3220
Forres Moray 141 0358
Forsbrook Staffs 72 9641
Forse Highld 151 2234
Forse House Highld 151 2135
Forshaw Heath Warwks 61 0873
Forsinain Highld 150 9148
Forsinard Highld 150 8942
Forston Dorset 11 6695
Fort Augustus Highld 131 3709
Fort Hommet Guern 158 0000
Fort le Marchant Guern 158 0000
Fort William Highld 130 1074
Forteviot P & K 125 0517
Forth S Lans 116 9453
Forthampton Gloucs 47 8532
Fortingall P & K 124 7347
Fortnighty Highld 140 9350
Forton Hants 24 4143
Forton Lancs 80 4851
Forton Shrops 59 4316
Forton Somset 10 3307
Forton Staffs 72 7521
Fortrie Abers 142 6645
Fortrose Highld 140 7256
Fortuneswell Dorset 11 6873
Forty Green Bucks 26 9291
Forty Hill Gt Lon 27 3398
Forward Green Suffk 54 1059
Fosbury Wilts 23 3157
Foscot Oxon 36 2421
Foscote Nhants 49 6546
Fosdyke Lincs 64 3133
Fosdyke Bridge Lincs 64 3232
Foss P & K 132 7858
Foss-y-ffin Cerdgn 42 4460
Fossebridge Gloucs 36 0711
Foster Street Essex 39 4809
Fosterhouses S York 83 6514
Foston Derbys 73 1931
Foston Leics 50 6094
Foston Lincs 63 8542
Foston N York 90 6965
Foston on the Wolds E R Yk 85 1055
Fotherby Lincs 77 3191
Fothergill Cumb 92 0234
Fotheringhay Nhants 51 0593
Foul End Warwks 61 2494
Foul Mile E Susx 16 6215
Foulbridge Cumb 93 4248
Foulby W York 83 3917
Foulden Border 119 9355
Foulden Norfk 65 7699
Foulridge Lancs 81 8942
Foulsham Norfk 66 0324
Fountainhall Border 118 4249
Four Ashes Staffs 60 9108
Four Ashes Staffs 60 8087
Four Ashes Suffk 54 0070
Four Ashes W Mids 61 1575
Four Cabots Guern 158 0000
Four Crosses Powys 58 2618
Four Crosses Staffs 60 9509
Four Elms Kent 16 4648
Four Foot Somset 21 5833
Four Forks Somset 20 2336
Four Gates Gt Man 79 6407
Four Gotes Cambs 65 4516
Four Lane End S York 82 2702
Four Lane Ends Ches 71 5561
Four Lanes Cnwll 2 6838
Four Marks Hants 24 6735
Four Mile Bridge IOA 68 2778
Four Oaks E Susx 17 8524
Four Oaks Gloucs 47 6928
Four Oaks W Mids 61 1098
Four Oaks W Mids 61 2480
Four Points Berks 37 5579
Four Roads Carmth 32 4409
Four Shire Stone Warwks 48 2232
Four Throws Kent 17 7729
Four Wents Kent 27 6251
Fourlanes End Ches 72 8059
Fourpenny Highld 147 8094
Fourstones Nthumb 102 8867
Fovant Wilts 22 0028
Foveran Abers 143 9723
Fowey Cnwll 3 1251
Fowley Common Ches 79 6795
Fowlhall Kent 28 6946
Fowlis Angus 126 3233
Fowlis Wester P & K 125 9224
Fowlmere Cambs 53 4245
Fownhope Herefd 46 5834
Fox Corner Surrey 25 9654
Fox Hatch Essex 27 5798
Fox Street Essex 41 0227
Foxbar Rens 115 4561
Foxcombe Devon 5 4887
Foxcote Gloucs 35 0118
Foxcote Somset 22 7155
Foxdale IOM 158 2778
Foxearth Essex 54 8344
Foxendown Kent 27 6466
Foxfield Cumb 86 2185
Foxham Wilts 35 9777
Foxhills Hants 12 3411
Foxhole Cnwll 3 9654
Foxhole Swans 32 6694
Foxholes N York 91 0173
Foxhunt Green E Susx 16 5417
Foxley Nhants 49 6451
Foxley Norfk 66 0422
Foxley Wilts 35 8986
Foxley Green Wilts 35 8985
Foxlydiate Worcs 47 0167
Foxt Staffs 73 0348
Foxton Cambs 52 4148
Foxton Dur 96 3624
Foxton Leics 50 7089
Foxton N York 89 4296
Foxup N York 88 8676
Foxwist Green Ches 71 6268
Foxwood Shrops 47 6276
Foy Herefd 46 5928
Foyers Highld 139 4921
Foynesfield Highld 140 8953
Fraddam Cnwll 2 5834
Fraddon Cnwll 4 9158
Fradley Staffs 61 1513
Fradswell Staffs 73 9931
Fraisthorpe E R Yk 91 1561
Framfield E Susx 16 4920
Framingham Earl Norfk 67 2702
Framingham Pigot Norfk 67 2703
Framlingham Suffk 55 2863
Frampton Dorset 10 6295
Frampton Lincs 64 3239
Frampton Cotterell Gloucs 35 6682
Frampton Mansell Gloucs 35 9202
Frampton on Severn Gloucs 35 7407
Frampton West End Lincs 64 3041
Framsden Suffk 55 1959
Framwellgate Moor Dur 96 2644
Frances Green Lancs 81 6236
Franche Worcs 60 8278
Frandley Ches 71 6379
Frank's Bridge Powys 45 1156
Frankaborough Devon 5 3991
Frankby Mersyd 78 2486
Frankfort Norfk 67 3024
Franklands Gate Herefd 46 5346
Frankley Worcs 60 9980
Frankton Warwks 50 4270
Frant E Susx 16 5835
Fraserburgh Abers 143 9966
Frating Essex 41 0722
Frating Green Essex 41 0823
Fratton Hants 13 6500
Freathy Cnwll 5 3952
Freckenham Suffk 53 6672
Freckleton Lancs 80 4329
Freebirch Derbys 74 3072
Freeby Leics 63 8020
Freefolk Hants 24 4848
Freehay Staffs 73 0241
Freeland Oxon 36 4112
Freethorpe Norfk 67 4005
Freethorpe Common Norfk 67 4004
Freiston Lincs 64 3743
Fremington Devon 19 5132
Fremington N York 88 0499
French Street Kent 27 4552
Frenchay Gloucs 35 6377
Frenchbeer Devon 8 6785
Frenich P & K 132 8258
Frensham Surrey 25 8441
Freshfields Mersyd 78 2907
Freshford Somset 22 7860
Freshwater IOW 12 3487
Freshwater Bay IOW 12 3485
Freshwater East Pembks 30 0198
Fressingfield Suffk 55 2677
Freston Suffk 54 1638
Freswick Highld 151 3667
Fretherne Gloucs 35 7210
Frettenham Norfk 67 2417
Freuchie Fife 126 2806
Freystrop Pembks 30 9511
Friar Waddon Dorset 11 6486
Friar's Gate E Susx 16 4933
Friars' Hill N York 90 7485
Friday Bridge Cambs 65 4604
Friday Street E Susx 16 6203
Friday Street Suffk 55 2459
Friday Street Suffk 55 3351
Friday Street Suffk 55 3760
Friday Street Surrey 14 1245
Fridaythorpe E R Yk 90 8759
Friden Derbys 74 1660
Friendly W York 82 0524
Friern Barnet Gt Lon 27 2892
Friesland Bay Ag & B 120 1954
Friesthorpe Lincs 76 0683
Frieston Lincs 63 9347
Frieth Bucks 37 7990
Friezeland Notts 75 4750
Frilford Oxon 37 4497
Frilsham Berks 24 5473
Frimley Surrey 25 8757
Frimley Green Surrey 25 8856
Frindsbury Kent 28 7469
Fring Norfk 65 7334
Fringford Oxon 49 6029
Frinsted Kent 28 8957
Frinton-on-Sea Essex 41 2320
Friockheim Angus 127 5949
Friog Gwynd 57 6112
Frisby on the Wreake Leics 63 6917
Friskney Lincs 77 4655
Friskney Eaudike Lincs 77 4755
Friston E Susx 16 5598
Friston Suffk 55 4160
Fritchley Derbys 74 3552
Frith Bank Lincs 77 3147
Frith Common Worcs 47 6969
Fritham Hants 12 2314
Frithelstock Devon 18 4619
Frithelstock Stone Devon 18 4518
Frithend Hants 25 8039
Frithsden Herts 38 0009
Frithville Lincs 77 3150
Frittenden Kent 28 8140
Frittiscombe Devon 7 8043
Fritton Norfk 67 4600
Fritton Norfk 67 2293
Fritwell Oxon 49 5229
Frizinghall W York 82 1435
Frizington Cumb 92 0316
Frocester Gloucs 35 7803
Frodesley Shrops 59 5101
Frodsham Ches 71 5177
Frog End Cambs 52 3946
Frog End Cambs 53 5358
Frog Pool Worcs 47 8065
Frogden Border 110 7628
Froggatt Derbys 74 2476
Froghall Staffs 73 0247
Frogham Hants 12 1612
Frogham Kent 29 2550
Frogmore Devon 7 7742
Frognall Lincs 64 1610
Frogpool Cnwll 3 7540
Frogwell Cnwll 5 3468
Frolesworth Leics 50 5090
Frome Somset 22 7747
Frome St Quintin Dorset 10 5902
Frome Whitfield Dorset 11 6991
Fromes Hill Herefd 47 6846
Fron Denbgs 70 0666
Fron Gwynd 56 3539
Fron Gwynd 68 5054
Fron Powys 58 2203
Fron Powys 58 1797
Fron Isaf Wrexhm 70 2740
Fron-goch Gwynd 70 9039
Froncysyllte Denbgs 70 2640
Frostenden Suffk 55 4781
Frosterley Dur 95 0237
Froxfield Beds 38 9733
Froxfield Wilts 23 2968
Froxfield Green Hants 13 7025
Fryern Hill Hants 13 4320
Fryerning Essex 40 6300
Fryton N York 90 6874
Fulbeck Lincs 76 9450
Fulbourn Cambs 53 5256
Fulbrook Oxon 36 2513
Fulflood Hants 24 4730
Fulford N York 83 6149
Fulford Somset 20 2029
Fulford Staffs 72 9537
Fulham Gt Lon 27 2576
Fulking W Susx 15 2411
Full Sutton E R Yk 84 7455
Fullaford Devon 19 6838
Fullarton N Ayrs 106 3238
Fuller Street Essex 40 7416
Fuller Street Kent 27 5656
Fuller's End Essex 39 5325
Fuller's Moor Ches 71 4954
Fullerton Hants 23 3739
Fulletby Lincs 77 2973
Fullready Warwks 48 2846
Fullwood E Ayrs 115 4450
Fulmer Bucks 26 9985
Fulmodeston Norfk 66 9930
Fulnetby Lincs 76 0979
Fulney Lincs 64 2623
Fulstone W York 82 1709
Fulstow Lincs 77 3297
Fulwell Oxon 36 3722
Fulwood Lancs 80 5431
Fulwood Notts 75 4757
Fulwood S York 74 3085
Fulwood Somset 20 2120
Fundenhall Norfk 66 1596
Funtington W Susx 14 8008
Funtley Hants 13 5608
Funtullich P & K 124 7526
Furley Devon 10 2604
Furnace Ag & B 114 0200
Furnace Carmth 32 5001
Furnace Cerdgn 43 6895
Furnace End Warwks 61 2491
Furner's Green E Susx 15 4126
Furness Vale Derbys 79 0083
Furneux Pelham Herts 39 4327
Further Quarter Kent 28 8939
Furtho Nhants 49 7743
Furze Platt Berks 26 8782
Furzehill Devon 19 7245
Furzehill Dorset 11 0101
Furzehills Lincs 77 2572
Furzeley Corner Hants 13 6510
Furzley Hants 12 2816
Fyfett Somset 9 2314
Fyfield Essex 40 5707
Fyfield Hants 23 2946
Fyfield Oxon 36 4298
Fyfield Wilts 23 1468
Fyfield Wilts 23 1760
Fyfield Bavant Wilts 22 0125
Fyfield Wick Oxon 36 4197

285

Fylingthorpe Gorey
286

Fylingthorpe N York 91 9404
Fyning W Susx 14 8123
Fyvie Abers 142 7637

# G

Gabroc Hill E Ayrs 115 4550
Gaddesby Leics 63 6813
Gaddesden Row Herts 38 0512
Gadfa IOA 68 4689
Gadgirth S Ayrs 106 4022
Gadlas Shrops 59 3737
Gaer Powys 33 1721
Gaer-llwyd Mons 34 4496
Gaerwen IOA 68 4871
Gagingwell Oxon 48 4025
Gailes N Ayrs 106 3235
Gailey Staffs 60 9110
Gainford Dur 96 1716
Gainsborough Lincs 75 8189
Gainsford End Essex 53 7235
Gairloch Highld 144 8076
Gairlochy Highld 131 1784
Gairneybridge P & K 117 1398
Gaisby W York 82 1536
Gaisgill Cumb 87 6305
Gaitsgill Cumb 93 3846
Galashiels Border 109 4936
Galcantray Highld 140 8148
Galgate Lancs 80 4855
Galhampton Somset 21 6329
Gallanach Ag & B 120 2161
Gallanach Ag & B 122 8326
Gallantry Bank Ches 71 5153
Gallatown Fife 117 2994
Galley Common Warwks 61 3091
Galleywood Essex 40 7003
Gallovie Highld 132 5589
Gallowfauld Angus 127 4342
Gallowhill P & K 126 1635
Gallows Green Essex 40 9226
Gallows Green Worcs 47 9362
Gallowstree Common Oxon 37 6980
Gallt-y-foel Gwynd 69 5862
Galltair Highld 129 8120
Gally Hill Hants 25 8051
Gallypot Street E Susx 16 4735
Galmisdale Highld 128 4784
Galmpton Devon 7 6940
Galmpton Devon 7 8856
Galphay N York 89 2572
Galston E Ayrs 107 5036
Galton Dorset 11 7785
Gamballs Green Staffs 74 0367
Gambles Green Essex 40 7614
Gamblesby Cumb 94 6039
Gamelsby Cumb 93 2552
Gamesley Gt Man 79 0194
Gamlingay Cambs 52 2452
Gamlingay Cinques Cambs 52 2352
Gamlingay Great Heath Beds 52 2151
Gammersgill N York 88 0582
Gamrie Abers 143 7962
Gamston Notts 75 7176
Gamston Notts 62 5937
Ganarew Herefd 34 5216
Ganavan Bay Ag & B 122 8632
Gang Cnwll 5 3068
Ganllwyd Gwynd 57 7324
Gannachy Angus 134 5970
Ganstead E R Yk 85 1434
Ganthorpe N York 90 6870
Ganton N York 91 9977
Ganwick Corner Herts 27 2599
Gappah Devon 9 8677
Garbity Moray 141 3152
Garboldisham Norfk 54 0081
Garchory Abers 134 3010
Garden City Flints 71 3269
Garden Village Derbys 74 2698
Gardeners Green Berks 25 8266
Gardenstown Abers 143 8064
Garderhouse Shet 153 3347
Gardham E R Yk 84 9542
Gare Hill Somset 22 7840
Garelochhead Ag & B 114 2491
Garford Oxon 36 4296
Garforth W York 83 4033
Garforth Bridge W York 83 3932
Gargrave N York 81 9354
Gargunnock Stirlg 116 7094
Garizim Conwy 69 6975
Garlic Street Norfk 55 2183
Garlieston D & G 99 4746
Garlinge Kent 29 3369
Garlinge Green Kent 29 1152
Garlogie Abers 135 7805
Garmond Abers 143 8052
Garmondsway Dur 96 3434
Garmouth Moray 141 3364
Garmston Shrops 59 6006
Garn Gwynd 56 2834
Garn-Dolbenmaen Gwynd 56 4943
Garnant Carmth 32 6713
Garnett Bridge Cumb 87 5299
Garnkirk N Lans 116 6768
Garnswllt Swans 32 6209
Garrabost W Isls 152 5133
Garrallan E Ayrs 107 5418
Garras Cnwll 2 7023
Garreg Gwynd 57 6141
Garrigill Cumb 94 7441
Garriston N York 89 1592
Garroch D & G 99 5981
Garrochtrie D & G 98 1138
Garrochty Ag & B 114 0953
Garros Highld 136 4962
Garrowby Hall E R Yk 90 7957
Garsdale Cumb 88 7489
Garsdale Head Cumb 88 7891
Garsdon Wilts 35 9687
Garshall Green Staffs 72 9633
Garsington Oxon 37 5802
Garstang Lancs 80 4945
Garston Herts 26 1100
Garston Mersyd 78 4084
Gartachossan Ag & B 112 3461
Gartcosh N Lans 116 6967
Garth Brdgnd 33 8690
Garth Denbgs 70 2542
Garth Mons 34 3492
Garth Powys 45 9549
Garth Powys 46 2772
Garth Penrhyncoch Cerdgn 43 6484
Garth Row Cumb 87 5297
Garthamlock C Glas 116 6566
Garthbrengy Powys 45 0433
Gartheli Cerdgn 44 5856
Garthmyl Powys 58 1999
Garthorpe Leics 63 8320
Garthorpe Lincs 84 8418
Garths Cumb 87 5489
Gartly Abers 142 5232
Gartmore Stirlg 115 5297
Gartness N Lans 116 7864
Gartness Stirlg 115 5086
Gartocharn W Duns 115 4286
Garton E R Yk 85 2635
Garton-on-the-Wolds E R Yk 91 9759
Gartymore Highld 147 0114
Garvald E Loth 118 5870
Garvan Highld 130 9777
Garvard Ag & B 112 3791
Garve Highld 139 3961
Garvestone Norfk 66 0207
Garvock Inver 114 2570
Garway Herefd 34 4522
Garway Common Herefd 34 4622
Garway Hill Herefd 46 4425
Garyvard W Isls 152 3619
Gasper Wilts 22 7633
Gastard Wilts 22 8868
Gasthorpe Norfk 54 9781
Gaston Green Essex 39 4917
Gatcombe IOW 13 4985
Gate Burton Lincs 76 8382
Gate Helmsley N York 83 6955
Gatebeck Cumb 87 5485
Gateford Notts 75 5781
Gateforth N York 83 5628
Gatehead E Ayrs 106 3936
Gatehouse Nthumb 102 7889
Gatehouse of Fleet D & G 99 5956
Gatelawbridge D & G 100 9096
Gateley Norfk 66 9624
Gatenby N York 89 3287
Gates Heath Ches 71 4760
Gatesgarth Cumb 93 1915
Gateshaw Border 110 7722
Gateshead T & W 96 2562
Gateside Angus 127 4344
Gateside E Rens 115 4858
Gateside Fife 126 1809
Gateside N Ayrs 115 3653
Gateslack D & G 108 8902
Gathurst Gt Man 78 5407
Gatley Gt Man 79 8488
Gatton Surrey 27 2752
Gattonside Border 109 5435
Gaufron Powys 45 9968
Gaulby Leics 50 6900
Gauldry Fife 126 3723
Gauldswell P & K 126 2151
Gaulkthorn Lancs 81 7526
Gaultree Norfk 65 4907
Gaunt's Common Dorset 12 0205
Gaunt's End Essex 39 5525
Gaunton's Bank Ches 71 5647
Gautby Lincs 76 1772
Gavinton Border 119 7652
Gawber S York 83 3207
Gawcott Bucks 49 6831
Gawsworth Ches 79 8969
Gawthorpe W York 82 2721
Gawthrop Cumb 87 6987
Gawthwaite Cumb 86 2784
Gay Bowers Essex 40 7904
Gay Street W Susx 14 0820
Gaydon Warwks 48 3653
Gayhurst Bucks 38 8446
Gayle N York 88 8688
Gayles N York 89 1207
Gayton Mersyd 78 2780
Gayton Nhants 49 7054
Gayton Norfk 65 7219
Gayton Staffs 72 9828
Gayton le Marsh Lincs 77 4284
Gayton Thorpe Norfk 65 7418
Gaywood Norfk 65 6320
Gazeley Suffk 53 7264
Gear Cnwll 3 7224
Gearraidh Bhaird W Isls 152 3619
Geary Highld 136 2661
Gedding Suffk 54 9457
Geddinge Kent 29 2346
Geddington Nhants 51 8983
Gedling Notts 62 6142
Gedney Lincs 65 4024
Gedney Broadgate Lincs 65 4022
Gedney Drove End Lincs 65 4629
Gedney Dyke Lincs 65 4126
Gedney Hill Lincs 64 3311
Gee Cross Gt Man 79 9593
Geeston Rutlnd 63 9803
Geldeston Norfk 67 3991
Gelli Rhondd 33 9794
Gelli Torfn 34 2792
Gelli Gynan Denbgs 70 1854
Gellifor Denbgs 70 1262
Gelligaer Caerph 33 1396
Gelligroes Caerph 33 1794
Gelligron Neath 32 7104
Gellilydan Gwynd 57 6839
Gellinudd Neath 32 7303
Gelly Carmth 31 0819
Gellyburn P & K 125 0939
Gellywen Carmth 31 2723
Gelston D & G 92 7758
Gelston Lincs 63 9145
Gembling E R Yk 91 1057
Gentleshaw Staffs 61 0511
George Green Bucks 26 9981
George Nympton Devon 19 7023
Georgefield D & G 101 2991
Georgeham Devon 18 4639
Georgetown Blae G 33 1508
Georgia Cnwll 2 4836
Georth Ork 153 3625
Gerlan Gwynd 69 6366
Germansweek Devon 5 4394
Germoe Cnwll 2 5829
Gerrans Cnwll 3 8735
Gerrards Cross Bucks 26 0088
Gerrick N York 90 7012
Gestingthorpe Essex 54 8138
Geuffordd Powys 58 2114
Gib Hill Ches 79 6478
Gibraltar Lincs 77 5558
Gibsmere Notts 75 7148
Giddeahall Wilts 35 8674
Giddy Green Dorset 11 8386
Gidea Park Gt Lon 27 5290
Gidleigh Devon 8 6788
Giffnock E Rens 115 5658
Gifford E Loth 118 5368
Giffordtown Fife 126 2811
Giggleswick N York 88 8063
Gilberdyke E R Yk 84 8329
Gilbert Street Hants 24 6432
Gilbert's Cross Staffs 60 8187
Gilbert's End Worcs 47 8342
Gilchriston E Loth 118 4865
Gilcrux Cumb 92 1138
Gildersome W York 82 2429
Gildingwells S York 75 5585
Gilesgate Moor Dur 96 2942
Gileston V Glam 20 0166
Gilfach Caerph 33 1598
Gilfach Goch Brdgnd 33 9790
Gilfachrheda Cerdgn 42 4158
Gilgarran Cumb 92 0323
Gill Cumb 93 4429
Gill's Green Kent 17 7532
Gillamoor N York 90 6889
Gillan Cnwll 3 7825
Gillen Highld 136 2659
Gillesbie D & G 100 1691
Gilling East N York 90 6176
Gilling West N York 89 1805
Gillingham Dorset 22 8026
Gillingham Kent 28 7768
Gillingham Norfk 67 4191
Gillock Highld 151 2159
Gillow Heath Staffs 72 8858
Gills Highld 151 3272
Gilmanscleuch Border 109 3321
Gilmerton C Edin 117 2868
Gilmerton P & K 125 8823
Gilmonby Dur 95 9912
Gilmorton Leics 50 5787
Gilsland Nthumb 102 6366
Gilson Warwks 61 1989
Gilstead W York 82 1239
Gilston Herts 39 4413
Gilston Mdloth 118 4456
Giltbrook Notts 62 4845
Gilwern Mons 34 2414
Gimingham Norfk 67 2836
Ginclough Ches 79 9576
Gingers Green E Susx 16 6212
Gipping Suffk 54 0763
Gipsey Bridge Lincs 77 2849
Girdle Toll N Ayrs 106 3440
Girlington W York 82 1334
Girlsta Shet 153 4350
Girsby N York 89 3508
Girtford Beds 52 1649
Girthon D & G 99 6053
Girton Cambs 53 4262
Girton Notts 75 8265
Girvan S Ayrs 106 1897
Gisburn Lancs 81 8248
Gisleham Suffk 55 5188
Gislingham Suffk 54 0771
Gissing Norfk 54 1485
Gittisham Devon 9 1398
Gladestry Powys 45 2355
Gladsmuir E Loth 118 4573
Glais Swans 32 7000
Glaisdale N York 90 7705
Glamis Angus 126 3846
Glan-Duar Carmth 44 5243
Glan-Dwyfach Gwynd 56 4843
Glan-rhyd Powys 32 7809
Glan-y-don Flints 70 1679
Glan-y-llyn Rhondd 33 1183
Glan-y-nant Powys 58 9384
Glan-yr-afon Gwynd 70 9140
Glan-yr-afon Gwynd 70 0142
Glan-yr-afon IOA 69 6080
Glan-yr-afon Swans 32 6305
Glanaber Gwynd 69 6351
Glanafon Pembks 30 9617
Glanaman Carmth 32 6713
Glandford Norfk 66 0441
Glandwr Pembks 31 1928
Glandyfi Cerdgn 43 6996
Glangrwyne Powys 34 2416
Glanllynfi Brdgnd 33 8690
Glanmule Powys 58 1690
Glanrhyd Pembks 31 1442
Glanton Nthumb 111 0714
Glanton Pike Nthumb 111 0514
Glanvilles Wootton Dorset 11 6708
Glapthorn Nhants 51 0290
Glapwell Derbys 75 4766
Glasbury Powys 45 1739
Glascoed Denbgs 70 9973
Glascoed Mons 34 3301
Glascote Staffs 61 2203
Glascwm Powys 45 1552
Glasfryn Conwy 70 9250
Glasgow C Glas 115 5865
Glasinfryn Gwynd 69 5868
Glasnacardoch Bay Highld 129 6795
Glasnakille Highld 128 5313
Glaspwll Powys 43 7397
Glass Houghton W York 83 4324
Glassenbury Kent 28 7536
Glasserton D & G 99 4237
Glassford S Lans 116 7247
Glasshouse Gloucs 35 7021
Glasshouse Hill Gloucs 35 7020
Glasshouses N York 89 1764
Glasson Cumb 101 2560
Glasson Lancs 80 4456
Glassonby Cumb 94 5738
Glasterlaw Angus 127 5951
Glaston Rutlnd 51 8900
Glastonbury Somset 21 5038
Glatton Cambs 52 1586
Glazebrook Ches 79 6992
Glazebury Ches 79 6797
Glazeley Shrops 60 7088
Gleadsmoss Ches 79 8168
Gleaston Cumb 86 2570
Glebe Highld 139 5118
Gledhow W York 82 3137
Gledpark D & G 99 6250
Gledrid Shrops 59 3036
Glemsford Suffk 54 8348
Glen Auldyn IOM 158 4393
Glen Clunie Lodge Abers 133 1383
Glen Maye IOM 158 2379
Glen Mona IOM 158 4588
Glen Nevis House Highld 130 1272
Glen Parva Leics 50 5798
Glen Trool Lodge D & G 99 4080
Glen Vine IOM 158 3378
Glenallachie Highld 141 2641
Glenancross Highld 129 6691
Glenaros House Ag & B 121 5544
Glenbarr Ag & B 105 6736
Glenbarry Abers 142 5554
Glenbeg Highld 121 5862
Glenbeg Highld 141 0028
Glenbervie Abers 135 7680
Glenboig N Lans 116 7268
Glenborrodale Highld 121 6061
Glenbranter Ag & B 114 1197
Glenbreck Border 108 0521
Glenbrittle House Highld 128 4121
Glenbuck E Ayrs 107 7425
Glencally Angus 134 3562
Glencaple D & G 100 9968
Glencarron Lodge Highld 138 0650
Glencarse P & K 126 1921
Glenceitlein Highld 123 1548
Glencoe Highld 130 1058
Glencothe Border 108 0829
Glencraig Fife 117 1894
Glencrosh D & G 107 7689
Glendale Highld 136 1749
Glendaruel Ag & B 114 9983
Glendevon P & K 125 9904
Glendoe Lodge Highld 131 4009
Glendoick P & K 126 2022
Glenduckie Fife 126 2818
Gleneagles P & K 125 9208
Gleneagles Hotel P & K 125 9111
Glenegedale Ag & B 112 3351
Glenelg Highld 129 8119
Glenerney Moray 141 0146
Glenfarg P & K 126 1310
Glenfeshie Lodge Highld 132 8493
Glenfield Leics 62 5406
Glenfinnan Highld 130 9080
Glenfintaig Lodge Highld 131 2286
Glenfoot P & K 126 1815
Glenfyne Lodge Ag & B 123 2215
Glengarnock N Ayrs 115 3252
Glengolly Highld 151 1065
Glengorm Castle Ag & B 121 4457
Glengrasco Highld 136 4444
Glenholm Border 108 1033
Glenhoul D & G 107 6187
Glenisla Angus 133 2160
Glenkin Ag & B 114 1280
Glenkindie Abers 142 4314
Glenlivet Moray 141 1929
Glenlochar D & G 99 7364
Glenloig N Ayrs 105 9435
Glenlomond P & K 126 1704
Glenluce D & G 98 1957
Glenmassen Ag & B 114 1088
Glenmavis N Lans 116 7567
Glenmore Highld 136 4340
Glenmore Lodge Highld 133 9709
Glenquiech Angus 134 4261
Glenralloch Ag & B 113 8659
Glenridding Cumb 93 3817
Glenrothes Fife 117 2700
Glenshee P & K 125 9834
Glenshera Lodge Highld 132 5592
Glenstriven Ag & B 114 0878
Glentham Lincs 76 0090
Glentromie Lodge Highld 132 7897
Glentrool Village D & G 98 3578
Glentruim House Highld 132 6894
Glentworth Lincs 76 9488
Glenuig Highld 129 6677
Glenure Ag & B 123 0448
Glenurquhart Highld 140 7462
Glenvarragill Highld 136 4739
Glenwhilly D & G 98 1771
Glespin S Lans 108 8127
Glewstone Herefd 34 5521
Glinton Cambs 64 1505
Glooston Leics 50 7595
Glororum Nthumb 111 1633
Glossop Derbys 74 0393
Gloster Hill Nthumb 103 2504
Gloucester Gloucs 35 8318
Glusburn N York 82 0045
Glutt Lodge Highld 150 0036
Gluvian Cnwll 4 9164
Glympton Oxon 36 4221
Glyn Ceiriog Wrexhm 70 2038
Glyn-Neath Neath 33 8806
Glynarthen Cerdgn 42 3148
Glyncorrwg Neath 33 8798
Glynde E Susx 16 4509
Glyndebourne E Susx 16 4510
Glyndyfrdwy Denbgs 70 1442
Glyntaff Rhondd 33 0889
Glyntawe Powys 33 8416
Glynteg Carmth 31 3637
Gnosall Staffs 72 8220
Gnosall Heath Staffs 72 8220
Goadby Leics 50 7598
Goadby Marwood Leics 63 7726
Goat Lees Kent 28 0145
Goatacre Wilts 35 0276
Goatfield Ag & B 114 0100
Goatham Green E Susx 17 8120
Goathill Dorset 11 6717
Goathland N York 90 8301
Goathurst Somset 20 2534
Goathurst Common Kent 27 4952
Gobowen Shrops 59 3033
Godalming Surrey 25 9643
Godameavy Devon 6 5364
Goddard's Corner Suffk 55 2868
Goddard's Green Kent 17 8134
Godford Cross Devon 9 1302
Godington Bucks 49 6427
Godley Gt Man 79 9595
Godmanchester Cambs 52 2470
Godmanstone Dorset 11 6697
Godmersham Kent 28 0550
Godney Somset 21 4842
Godolphin Cross Cnwll 2 6031
Godre'r-graig Neath 32 7506
Godshill Hants 12 1715
Godshill IOW 13 5281
Godstone Staffs 73 0134
Godstone Surrey 27 3551
Godsworthy Devon 5 5277
Godwinscroft Hants 12 1996
Goetre Mons 34 3206
Goff's Oak Herts 27 3202
Gofilon Mons 34 2613
Gogar C Edin 117 1672
Goginan Cerdgn 43 6881
Golan Gwynd 57 5242
Golant Cnwll 3 1254
Golberdon Cnwll 5 3271
Golborne Gt Man 78 6097
Golcar W York 82 0915
Gold Hill Cambs 65 5392
Gold Hill Dorset 11 8213
Goldcliff Newpt 34 3683
Golden Cross E Susx 16 5312
Golden Green Kent 16 6348
Golden Grove Carmth 32 5919
Golden Hill Pembks 30 9802
Golden Pot Hants 24 7143
Golden Valley Derbys 74 4251
Goldenhill Staffs 72 8553
Golders Green Gt Lon 26 2487
Goldfinch Bottom Berks 24 5063
Goldhanger Essex 40 9008
Golding Shrops 59 5403
Goldington Beds 38 0750
Golds Green W Mids 60 9893
Goldsborough N York 90 8314
Goldsborough N York 83 3856
Goldsithney Cnwll 2 5430
Goldstone Kent 29 2961
Goldstone Shrops 72 7028
Goldsworth Surrey 25 9958
Goldthorpe S York 83 4604
Goldworthy Devon 18 3922
Golford Kent 28 7936
Golford Green Kent 28 7936
Gollanfield Highld 140 8053
Gollinglith Foot N York 89 1481
Golly Wrexhm 71 3358
Golsoncott Somset 20 0239
Golspie Highld 147 8300
Gomeldon Wilts 23 1835
Gomersal W York 82 2026
Gomshall Surrey 14 0847
Gonalston Notts 63 6747
Gonerby Hill Foot Lincs 63 9037
Gonfirth Shet 153 3661
Good Easter Essex 40 6212
Gooderstone Norfk 65 7602
Goodleigh Devon 19 6034
Goodmanham E R Yk 84 8843
Goodnestone Kent 28 0461
Goodnestone Kent 29 2554
Goodrich Herefd 34 5719
Goodrington Devon 7 8958
Goodshaw Lancs 81 8125
Goodshaw Fold Lancs 81 8026
Goodstone Devon 7 7872
Goodwick Pembks 30 9438
Goodworth Clatford Hants 23 3642
Goodyers End Warwks 61 3385
Goole E R Yk 84 7423
Goole Fields E R Yk 84 7520
Goom's Hill Worcs 47 0154
Goonbell Cnwll 3 7249
Goonhavern Cnwll 3 7853
Goonvrea Cnwll 2 7149
Goose Green Essex 41 1327
Goose Green Essex 41 1325
Goose Green Gloucs 35 6774
Goose Green Gt Man 78 5603
Goose Green Kent 27 6451
Goose Green Kent 28 8437
Goose Green W Susx 14 1118
Goose Pool Herefd 46 4636
Goosecruives Abers 135 7583
Gooseford Devon 8 6792
Gooseham Cnwll 18 2316
Goosehill Green Worcs 47 9361
Goosemoor Somset 20 9635
Goosey Oxon 36 3591
Goosnargh Lancs 81 5536
Goostrey Ches 79 7770
Gorddinog Conwy 69 6773
Gordon Border 110 6443
Gordon Arms Hotel Border 109 3025
Gordonstown Abers 142 5656
Gordonstown Abers 142 7138
Gore Powys 46 2558
Gore Pit Essex 40 8719
Gore Street Kent 29 2765
Gorebridge Mdloth 118 3461
Gorefield Cambs 65 4112
Gores Wilts 23 1158
Gorey Jersey 158 0000

Gulling Green

Haslington

288

Gulling Green Suffk 54 8256
Gulval Cnwll 2 4831
Gulworthy Devon 6 4572
Gumfreston Pembks 31 1001
Gumley Leics 50 6889
Gummow's Shop Cnwll 4 8657
Gun Green Kent 17 7731
Gun Hill E Susx 16 5614
Gun Hill Warwks 61 2889
Gunby E R Yk 84 7035
Gunby Lincs 63 9121
Gunby Lincs 77 4666
Gundleton Hants 24 6133
Gunn Devon 19 6333
Gunnerside N York 88 9598
Gunnerton Nthumb 102 9074
Gunness Lincs 84 8411
Gunnislake Cnwll 6 4371
Gunnista Shet 153 5043
Gunthorpe Cambs 64 1802
Gunthorpe Norfk 66 0134
Gunthorpe Notts 63 6844
Gunton Suffk 67 5395
Gunville IOW 13 4788
Gunwalloe Cnwll 2 6522
Gupworthy Somset 20 9734
Gurnard IOW 13 4795
Gurnett Ches 79 9271
Gurney Slade Somset 21 6249
Gurnos Powys 32 7709
Gushmere Kent 28 0457
Gussage All Saints Dorset 11 0010
Gussage St Andrew Dorset 11 9714
Gussage St Michael Dorset 11 9811
Guston Kent 29 3244
Gutcher Shet 153 5499
Guthrie Angus 127 5650
Guy's Marsh Dorset 22 8420
Guyhirn Cambs 65 4003
Guyhirn Gull Cambs 65 3904
Guyzance Nthumb 103 2103
Gwaenysgor Flints 70 0781
Gwalchmai IOA 68 3876
Gwastadnant Gwynd 69 6157
Gwaun-Cae-Gurwen Carmth 32 6911
Gwbert on Sea Cerdgn 42 1650
Gwealavellan Cnwll 2 6041
Gwealeath Cnwll 2 6922
Gweek Cnwll 2 7026
Gwehelog Mons 34 3804
Gwenddwr Powys 45 0643
Gwendreath Cnwll 3 7217
Gwennap Cnwll 3 7340
Gwenter Cnwll 3 7417
Gwernaffield Flints 70 2065
Gwernesney Mons 34 4101
Gwernogle Carmth 44 5333
Gwernymynydd Flints 70 2162
Gwersyllt Wrexhm 71 3153
Gwespyr Flints 70 1183
Gwindra Cnwll 3 9552
Gwinear Cnwll 2 5937
Gwithian Cnwll 2 5841
Gwredog IOA 68 4085
Gwrhay Caerph 33 1899
Gwyddelwern Denbgs 70 0746
Gwyddgrug Carmth 44 4635
Gwynfryn Wrexhm 70 2552
Gwystre Powys 45 0665
Gwytherin Conwy 69 8761
Gyfelia Wrexhm 71 3245
Gyrn-goch Gwynd 68 4048

# H

Habberley Shrops 59 3903
Habberley Worcs 60 8177
Habergham Lancs 81 8033
Habertoft Lincs 77 5069
Habin W Susx 14 8022
Habrough Lincs 85 1413
Hacconby Lincs 64 1025
Haceby Lincs 64 0236
Hacheston Suffk 55 3059
Hack Green Ches 72 6448
Hackbridge Gt Lon 27 2865
Hackenthorpe S York 74 4183
Hackford Norfk 66 0502
Hackforth N York 89 2492
Hackland Ork 153 3920
Hackleton Nhants 51 8055
Hacklinge Kent 29 3454
Hackman's Gate Worcs 60 8978
Hackness N York 91 9790
Hackness Somset 21 3345
Hackney Gt Lon 27 3484
Hackthorn Lincs 76 9982
Hackthorpe Cumb 94 5423
Hacton Gt Lon 27 5585
Hadden Border 110 7836
Haddenham Bucks 37 7308
Haddenham Cambs 53 4675
Haddington E Loth 118 5173
Haddington Lincs 76 9162
Haddiscoe Norfk 67 4497
Haddo Abers 143 8337
Haddon Cambs 64 1392
Hade Edge W York 82 1404
Hadfield Derbys 74 0296
Hadham Cross Herts 39 4218
Hadham Ford Herts 39 4321
Hadleigh Essex 40 8187
Hadleigh Suffk 54 0242
Hadleigh Heath Suffk 54 9941
Hadley Shrops 60 6711
Hadley Worcs 47 8564
Hadley End Staffs 73 1320
Hadley Wood Gt Lon 27 2698
Hadlow Kent 27 6350
Hadlow Down E Susx 16 5324
Hadnall Shrops 59 5220
Hadstock Essex 53 5644
Hadzor Worcs 47 9162
Haffenden Quarter Kent 28 8840
Hafod-y-bwch Wrexhm 71 3147
Hafod-y-coed Blae G 34 2200
Hafodunos Conwy 69 8666
Hafodyrynys Caerph 34 2298
Haggate Lancs 81 8735
Haggbeck Cumb 101 4773
Haggerston Nthumb 111 0443
Haggington Hill Devon 19 5547
Haggs Falk 116 7879
Hagley Herefd 46 5641
Hagley W Mids 60 9180
Hagmore Green Suffk 54 9539
Hagnaby Lincs 77 3462
Hagnaby Lincs 77 4879
Hagworthingham Lincs 77 3469
Haigh Gt Man 78 6009
Haighton Green Lancs 81 5634
Hail Weston Cambs 52 1662
Haile Cumb 86 0308
Hailes Gloucs 48 0430
Hailey Herts 39 3710
Hailey Oxon 37 6485
Hailey Oxon 36 3512
Hailsham E Susx 16 5909
Hainault Gt Lon 27 4591
Haine Kent 29 3566
Hainford Norfk 67 2218
Hainton Lincs 76 1884
Hainworth W York 82 0638
Haisthorpe E R Yk 91 1264
Hakin Pembks 30 8905
Halam Notts 75 6754
Halbeath Fife 117 1288
Halberton Devon 9 0112
Halcro Highld 151 2360
Hale Ches 78 4782
Hale Cumb 87 5078
Hale Gt Man 79 7786
Hale Hants 12 1818
Hale Somset 22 7427
Hale Surrey 25 8448
Hale Bank Ches 78 4784
Hale Green E Susx 16 5514
Hale Nook Lancs 80 3944
Hale Street Kent 28 6749
Halebarns Gt Man 79 7985
Hales Norfk 67 3797
Hales Staffs 72 7134
Hales Green Derbys 73 1841
Hales Place Kent 29 1459
Halesgate Lincs 64 3226
Halesowen W Mids 60 9683
Halesville Essex 40 9092
Halesworth Suffk 55 3877
Halewood Mersyd 78 4585
Halford Devon 7 8174
Halford Shrops 59 4383
Halford Warwks 48 2645
Halfpenny Cumb 87 5387
Halfpenny Green Staffs 60 8291
Halfpenny Houses N York 89 2284
Halfway Berks 24 4068
Halfway Carmth 44 6430
Halfway Carmth 44 8232
Halfway S York 75 4381
Halfway Bridge W Susx 14 9321
Halfway House Shrops 59 3411
Halfway Houses Kent 28 9372
Halifax W York 82 0925
Halkirk Highld 151 1359
Halkyn Flints 70 2171
Hall E Rens 115 4154
Hall Cliffe W York 82 2918
Hall Cross Lancs 80 4230
Hall Dunnerdale Cumb 86 2195
Hall End Beds 38 0045
Hall End Beds 38 0737
Hall End W Mids 60 0092
Hall Glen Falk 116 8978
Hall Green W Mids 61 1181
Hall's Green Essex 39 4108
Hall's Green Herts 39 2728
Hallam Fields Derbys 62 4739
Halland E Susx 16 4916
Hallaton Leics 50 7896
Hallatrow Somset 21 6357
Hallbankgate Cumb 94 5859
Hallbeck Cumb 87 6288
Hallen Gloucs 34 5580
Hallfield Gate Derbys 74 3958
Hallgarth Dur 96 3243
Hallin Highld 136 2558
Halling Kent 28 7063
Hallington Lincs 77 3085
Hallington Nthumb 102 9875
Halliwell Gt Man 79 6910
Halloughton Notts 75 6951
Hallow Worcs 47 8258
Hallow Heath Worcs 47 8259
Hallrule Border 110 5914
Hallsands Devon 7 8138
Hallthwaites Cumb 86 1885
Halltoft End Lincs 64 3645
Hallworthy Cnwll 4 1787
Hallyne Border 109 1940
Halmer End Staffs 72 7948
Halmond's Frome Herefd 47 6747
Halmore Gloucs 35 7002
Halnaker W Susx 14 9007
Halsall Lancs 78 3710
Halse Nhants 49 5640
Halse Somset 20 1428
Halsetown Cnwll 2 5038
Halsham E R Yk 85 2727
Halsinger Devon 19 5138
Halstead Essex 40 8130
Halstead Kent 27 4861
Halstead Leics 63 7505
Halstock Dorset 10 5308
Halsway Somset 20 1337
Haltcliff Bridge Cumb 93 3636
Haltham Lincs 77 2463
Halton Bucks 38 8710
Halton Ches 78 5481
Halton Lancs 87 5064
Halton Nthumb 103 9967
Halton W York 83 3533
Halton Wrexhm 71 3039
Halton East N York 82 0454
Halton Fenside Lincs 77 4263
Halton Gill N York 88 8776
Halton Green Lancs 87 5165
Halton Holegate Lincs 77 4165
Halton Lea Gate Nthumb 94 6458
Halton Quay Cnwll 5 4165
Halton Shields Nthumb 103 0168
Halton West N York 81 8454
Haltwhistle Nthumb 102 7064
Halvergate Norfk 67 4106
Halwell Devon 7 7753
Halwill Devon 18 4299
Halwill Junction Devon 18 4400
Ham Devon 9 2301
Ham Gloucs 35 9721
Ham Gloucs 35 6898
Ham Gt Lon 26 1772
Ham Kent 29 3254
Ham Somset 20 2825
Ham Somset 22 6748
Ham Wilts 23 3262
Ham Common Dorset 22 8125
Ham Green Herefd 47 7544
Ham Green Kent 28 8468
Ham Green Kent 17 8926
Ham Green Somset 34 5375
Ham Green Worcs 47 0163
Ham Hill Kent 28 6960
Ham Street Somset 21 5534
Hamble-le-Rice Hants 13 4806
Hambleden Bucks 37 7886
Hambledon Hants 13 6414
Hambledon Surrey 25 9638
Hambleton Lancs 80 3742
Hambleton N York 83 5530
Hambleton Moss Side Lancs 80 3842
Hambridge Somset 21 3921
Hambridge Somset 21 5936
Hambrook Gloucs 35 6478
Hambrook W Susx 14 7806
Hameringham Lincs 77 3167
Hamerton Cambs 52 1379
Hamilton S Lans 116 7255
Hamlet Dorset 10 5908
Hamlins E Susx 16 5908
Hammerpot W Susx 14 0605
Hammersmith Gt Lon 26 2378
Hammerwich Staffs 61 0707
Hammerwood E Susx 16 4339
Hammond Street Herts 39 3304
Hammoon Dorset 11 8114
Hamnavoe Shet 153 3735
Hamnavoe Shet 153 4971
Hampden Park E Susx 16 6002
Hampden Row Bucks 26 8501
Hamperden End Essex 40 5730
Hampnett Gloucs 36 0915
Hampole S York 83 5010
Hampreston Dorset 12 0598
Hampsfield Cumb 87 4080
Hampson Green Lancs 80 4954
Hampstead Gt Lon 27 2685
Hampstead Norrey's Berks 37 5276
Hampsthwaite N York 89 2559
Hampt Cnwll 5 3874
Hampton Devon 10 2696
Hampton Gt Lon 26 1369
Hampton Kent 29 1568
Hampton Shrops 60 7486
Hampton Wilts 36 1892
Hampton Worcs 48 0243
Hampton Bishop Herefd 46 5637
Hampton Green Ches 71 5149
Hampton Heath Ches 71 5049
Hampton in Arden W Mids 61 2080
Hampton Loade Shrops 60 7486
Hampton Lovett Worcs 47 8865
Hampton Lucy Warwks 48 2557
Hampton on the Hill Warwks 48 2564
Hampton Poyle Oxon 37 5015
Hampton Wick Gt Lon 26 1769
Hamptworth Wilts 12 2419
Hamrow Norfk 66 9124
Hamsey E Susx 15 4012
Hamsey Green Gt Lon 27 3559
Hamstall Ridware Staffs 73 1019
Hamstead IOW 13 4091
Hamstead W Mids 61 0592
Hamstead Marshall Berks 24 4165
Hamsterley Dur 95 1156
Hamsterley Dur 96 1231
Hamstreet Kent 17 0033
Hamwood Somset 21 3756
Hamworthy Dorset 11 9991
Hanbury Staffs 73 1727
Hanbury Worcs 47 9664
Hanby Lincs 64 0231
Hanchet End Suffk 53 6446
Hanchurch Staffs 72 8441
Hand and Pen Devon 9 0495
Hand Green Ches 71 5460
Handale N York 97 7215
Handbridge Ches 71 4065
Handcross W Susx 15 2629
Handforth Ches 79 8583
Handley Ches 71 4657
Handley Derbys 74 3761
Handley Green Essex 40 6501
Handsacre Staffs 73 0915
Handsworth S York 74 4186
Handsworth W Mids 61 0489
Handy Cross Bucks 26 8590
Hanford Dorset 11 8411
Hanford Staffs 72 8741
Hanging Houghton Nhants 60 7573
Hanging Langford Wilts 23 0337
Hangleton E Susx 15 2607
Hangleton W Susx 14 0803
Hanham Gloucs 35 6472
Hankelow Ches 72 6645
Hankerton Wilts 35 9790
Hankham E Susx 16 6105
Hanley Staffs 72 8847
Hanley Castle Worcs 47 8442
Hanley Child Worcs 47 6565
Hanley Swan Worcs 47 8142
Hanley William Worcs 47 6766
Hanlith N York 88 8961
Hanmer Wrexhm 71 4539
Hannaford Devon 19 6029
Hannah Lincs 77 4979
Hannington Hants 24 5355
Hannington Nhants 51 8170
Hannington Wilts 36 1793
Hannington Wick Wilts 36 1795
Hanscombe End Beds 38 1133
Hanslope Bucks 38 8046
Hanthorpe Lincs 64 0823
Hanwell Gt Lon 26 1579
Hanwell Oxon 49 4343
Hanworth Gt Lon 26 1271
Hanworth Norfk 67 1935
Happendon S Lans 108 8533
Happisburgh Norfk 67 3831
Happisburgh Common Norfk 67 3728
Hapsford Ches 71 4774
Hapton Lancs 81 7931
Hapton Norfk 66 1796
Harberton Devon 7 7758
Harbertonford Devon 7 7856
Harbledown Kent 29 1357
Harborne W Mids 60 0284
Harborough Magna Warwks 50 4879
Harbottle Nthumb 102 9304
Harbourneford Devon 7 7162
Harbours Hill Worcs 47 9565
Harbridge Hants 12 1410
Harbridge Green Hants 12 1410
Harbury Warwks 48 3759
Harby Leics 63 7431
Harby Notts 76 8770
Harcombe Devon 9 8881
Harcombe Devon 9 1590
Harcombe Bottom Devon 10 3395
Harden W Mids 60 0100
Harden W York 82 0838
Hardenhuish Wilts 35 9174
Hardgate Abers 135 7901
Hardgate D & G 100 8167
Hardgate N York 89 2662
Hardgate W Duns 115 5072
Hardham W Susx 14 0317
Hardhorn Lancs 80 3537
Hardingham Norfk 66 0403
Hardingstone Nhants 49 7657
Hardington Somset 22 7452
Hardington Mandeville Somset 10 5111
Hardington Marsh Somset 10 5009
Hardington Moor Somset 10 5112
Hardisworthy Devon 18 2320
Hardley Hants 13 4205
Hardley Street Norfk 67 3701
Hardmead Bucks 38 9347
Hardraw N York 88 8691
Hardsough Lancs 81 7920
Hardstoft Derbys 75 4363
Hardway Hants 13 6001
Hardway Somset 22 7234
Hardwick Bucks 38 8019
Hardwick Cambs 52 3758
Hardwick Lincs 76 8675
Hardwick Nhants 51 8469
Hardwick Norfk 55 2289
Hardwick Oxon 36 3806
Hardwick Oxon 49 5729
Hardwick S York 75 4885
Hardwick W Mids 61 0798
Hardwick Green Worcs 47 8133
Hardwicke Gloucs 35 7912
Hardwicke Gloucs 47 9027
Hardy's Green Essex 40 9320
Hare Croft W York 82 0835
Hare Green Essex 41 1025
Hare Hatch Berks 37 8077
Hare Street Essex 39 4209
Hare Street Essex 27 5300
Hare Street Herts 39 3929
Harebeating E Susx 16 5910
Hareby Lincs 77 3365
Harefield Gt Lon 26 0590
Harehill Derbys 73 1735
Harehills W York 82 3135
Harehope Nthumb 111 0920
Harelaw Border 109 5323
Harelaw D & G 101 4378
Harelaw Dur 96 1652
Hareplain Kent 28 8339
Harescugh Cumb 94 6042
Harescombe Gloucs 35 8310
Haresfield Gloucs 35 8010
Harestock Hants 24 4631
Harewood W York 83 3245
Harewood End Herefd 46 5227
Harford Devon 6 6359
Hargate Norfk 66 1191
Hargatewall Derbys 74 1175
Hargrave Ches 71 4862
Hargrave Nhants 51 0370
Hargrave Suffk 53 7760
Hargrave Green Suffk 53 7759
Harker Cumb 101 3960
Harkstead Suffk 54 1834
Harlaston Staffs 61 2110
Harlaxton Lincs 63 8832
Harle Syke Lancs 81 8635
Harlech Gwynd 57 5831
Harlescott Shrops 59 4916
Harlesden Gt Lon 26 2183
Harlesthorpe Derbys 75 4976
Harleston Devon 7 7945
Harleston Norfk 55 2483
Harleston Suffk 54 0160
Harlestone Nhants 49 7064
Harley S York 74 3698
Harley Shrops 59 5901
Harlington Beds 38 0330
Harlington Gt Lon 26 0877
Harlington S York 83 4802
Harlosh Highld 136 2841
Harlow Essex 39 4410
Harlow Hill Nthumb 103 0768
Harlthorpe E R Yk 84 7337
Harlton Cambs 52 3852
Harlyn Bay Cnwll 4 8775
Harman's Cross Dorset 11 9880
Harmby N York 89 1289
Harmer Green Herts 39 2515
Harmer Hill Shrops 59 4822
Harmondsworth Gt Lon 26 0577
Harmston Lincs 76 9662
Harnage Shrops 59 5604
Harnham Nthumb 103 0781
Harnhill Gloucs 36 0600
Harold Hill Gt Lon 27 5392
Harold Wood Gt Lon 27 5590
Haroldston West Pembks 30 8615
Haroldswick Shet 153 6312
Harome N York 90 6481
Harpenden Herts 38 1314
Harpford Devon 9 0990
Harpham E R Yk 91 0861
Harpley Norfk 65 7825
Harpley Worcs 47 6861
Harpole Nhants 49 6961
Harpsdale Highld 151 1355
Harpsden Oxon 37 7680
Harpswell Lincs 76 9389
Harpur Hill Derbys 74 0671
Harpurhey Gt Man 79 8501
Harraby Cumb 93 4154
Harracott Devon 19 5527
Harrapool Highld 129 6523
Harrietfield P & K 125 9829
Harrietsham Kent 28 8652
Harringay Gt Lon 27 3188
Harrington Cumb 92 9825
Harrington Lincs 77 3671
Harrington Nhants 50 7780
Harringworth Nhants 51 9197
Harriseahead Staffs 72 8655
Harriston Cumb 92 1541
Harrogate N York 82 3054
Harrold Beds 51 9457
Harrop Dale Gt Man 82 0008
Harrow Gt Lon 26 1588
Harrow Green Suffk 54 8654
Harrow on the Hill Gt Lon 26 1587
Harrow Weald Gt Lon 26 1591
Harrowbarrow Cnwll 5 4070
Harrowden Beds 38 0647
Harrowgate Village Dur 96 2917
Harston Cambs 53 4250
Harston Leics 63 8331
Harswell E R Yk 84 8240
Hart Dur 97 4734
Hart Station Dur 97 4836
Hartburn Nthumb 103 0885
Hartest Suffk 54 8352
Hartfield E Susx 16 4735
Hartford Cambs 52 2572
Hartford Ches 71 6372
Hartford Somset 20 9529
Hartford End Essex 40 6817
Hartfordbridge Hants 25 7757
Hartforth N York 89 1606
Harthill Ches 71 4955
Harthill N Lans 116 9064
Harthill S York 75 4980
Hartington Derbys 74 1260
Hartington Nthumb 103 0288
Hartland Devon 18 2524
Hartland Quay Devon 18 2224
Hartlebury Worcs 60 8471
Hartlepool Dur 97 5032
Hartley Cumb 88 7808
Hartley Kent 27 6066
Hartley Kent 17 7634
Hartley Nthumb 103 3475
Hartley Green Kent 27 6067
Hartley Green Staffs 72 9829
Hartley Wespall Hants 24 6958
Hartley Wintney Hants 24 7656
Hartlip Kent 28 8464
Hartoft End N York 90 7493
Harton N York 90 7061
Harton Shrops 59 4888
Harton T & W 103 3765
Hartpury Gloucs 47 7924
Hartshead W York 82 1822
Hartshead Moor Side W York 82 1625
Hartshill Staffs 72 8546
Hartshill Warwks 61 3194
Hartshorne Derbys 62 3221
Hartside Nthumb 111 9716
Hartsop Cumb 93 4013
Hartswell Somset 20 0827
Hartwell Nhants 38 7850
Hartwith N York 89 2161
Hartwood N Lans 116 8459
Hartwoodmyres Border 109 4324
Harvel Kent 28 6563
Harvington Worcs 60 8775
Harvington Worcs 48 0549
Harwell Notts 75 6891
Harwell Oxon 37 4989
Harwich Essex 41 2531
Harwood Dur 95 8233
Harwood Gt Man 79 7410
Harwood Nthumb 103 0189
Harwood Dale N York 91 9695
Harwood Lee Gt Man 81 7411
Harworth Notts 75 6191
Hasbury W Mids 60 9582
Hascombe Surrey 25 0039
Haselbeach Nhants 50 7177
Haselbury Plucknett Somset 10 4710
Haseley Warwks 48 2367
Haseley Green Warwks 48 2369
Haseley Knob Warwks 61 2371
Haselor Warwks 48 1257
Hasfield Gloucs 47 8227
Hasguard Pembks 30 8509
Haskayne Lancs 78 3508
Hasketon Suffk 55 2450
Hasland Derbys 74 3969
Hasland Green Derbys 74 3968
Haslemere Surrey 14 9032
Haslingden Lancs 81 7823
Haslingden Grane Lancs 81 7522
Haslingfield Cambs 52 4052
Haslington Ches 72 7355

289

High Green Hopton
290

High Green W York 82 2014
High Green Worcs 47 8745
High Halden Kent 28 8937
High Halstow Kent 28 7875
High Ham Somset 21 4231
High Harrington Cumb 92 0025
High Harrogate N York 82 3155
High Haswell Dur 96 3643
High Hatton Shrops 59 6124
High Hawsker N York 91 9207
High Hesket Cumb 93 4744
High Hoyland S York 82 2710
High Hunsley E R Yk 84 9535
High Hurstwood E Susx 16 4926
High Hutton N York 90 7568
High Ireby Cumb 93 2237
High Kilburn N York 90 5179
High Killerby N York 91 0683
High Knipe Cumb 94 5219
High Lands Dur 96 1226
High Lane Gt Man 79 9585
High Lanes Cnwll 2 5637
High Laver Essex 39 5208
High Legh Ches 79 7084
High Leven N York 89 4512
High Littleton Somset 21 6458
High Lorton Cumb 92 1625
High Marnham Notts 75 8070
High Melton S York 83 5001
High Mickley Nthumb 103 0761
High Moorsley T & W 96 3345
High Newport T & W 96 3754
High Newton Cumb 87 4082
High Nibthwaite Cumb 86 2989
High Offley Staffs 72 7826
High Ongar Essex 40 5603
High Onn Staffs 72 8216
High Park Corner Essex 41 0320
High Pennyvenie E Ayrs 107 4907
High Post Wilts 23 1536
High Roding Essex 40 6017
High Row Cumb 93 3535
High Row Cumb 93 3821
High Salter Lancs 87 6062
High Salvington W Susx 14 1206
High Scales Cumb 93 1845
High Seaton Cumb 92 0231
High Shaw N York 88 8691
High Side Cumb 93 2330
High Spen T & W 96 1359
High Stoop Dur 95 1040
High Street Cambs 52 3762
High Street Cnwll 3 9653
High Street Kent 17 7430
High Street Suffk 55 4171
High Street Suffk 55 4355
High Throston Dur 97 4833
High Town Staffs 60 9911
High Toynton Lincs 77 2869
High Trewhitt Nthumb 111 0105
High Urpeth Dur 96 2354
High Valleyfield Fife 117 0086
High Warden Nthumb 102 9067
High Westwood Dur 95 1155
High Woolaston Gloucs 34 5899
High Worsall N York 89 3809
High Wray Cumb 87 3799
High Wych Herts 39 4614
High Wycombe Bucks 26 8693
Higham Derbys 74 3859
Higham Kent 16 6048
Higham Kent 28 7171
Higham Lancs 81 8136
Higham S York 82 3107
Higham Suffk 53 7465
Higham Suffk 54 0335
Higham Dykes Nthumb 103 1375
Higham Ferrers Nhants 51 9668
Higham Gobion Beds 38 1032
Higham Hill Gt Lon 27 3590
Higham on the Hill Leics 61 3895
Highampton Devon 18 4804
Highams Park Gt Lon 27 3891
Highbridge Hants 13 4621
Highbridge Somset 21 3247
Highbrook W Susx 15 3630
Highburton W York 82 1813
Highbury Gt Lon 27 3185
Highbury Somset 22 6949
Highclere Hants 24 4359
Highcliffe Dorset 12 2193
Highcross Lancs 80 3437
Higher Alham Somset 22 6741
Higher Ansty Dorset 11 7604
Higher Ballam Lancs 80 3630
Higher Bartle Lancs 80 5033
Higher Berry End Beds 38 9834
Higher Bockhampton Dorset 11 7292
Higher Brixham Devon 7 9155
Higher Burrowton Devon 9 0097
Higher Burwardsley Ches 71 5156
Higher Chillington Somset 10 3810
Higher Clovelly Devon 18 3123
Higher Combe Somset 20 9030
Higher Coombe Dorset 10 5391
Higher Disley Ches 79 9784
Higher Gabwell Devon 7 9169
Higher Halstock Leigh Dorset 10 5107
Higher Harpers Lancs 81 8237
Higher Heysham Lancs 87 4160
Higher Hurdsfield Ches 79 9374
Higher Irlam Gt Man 79 7295
Higher Kingcombe Dorset 10 5400
Higher Kinnerton Flints 71 3261
Higher Melcombe Dorset 11 7402
Higher Muddiford Devon 19 5638
Higher Nyland Dorset 22 7322
Higher Ogden Gt Man 82 9512
Higher Pentire Cnwll 2 6525
Higher Penwortham Lancs 80 5128
Higher Studfold N York 88 8170
Higher Town Cnwll 3 8044
Higher Town Cnwll 4 0061
Higher Town IOS 2 9215
Higher Tregantle Cnwll 5 4052
Higher Walton Ches 78 5985
Higher Walton Lancs 81 5727
Higher Wambrook Somset 10 2908
Higher Waterston Dorset 11 7295
Higher Whatcombe Dorset 11 8301
Higher Wheelton Lancs 81 6022
Higher Whiteleigh Cnwll 5 2494
Higher Whitley Ches 78 6180
Higher Wraxhall Dorset 10 5601
Higher Wych Ches 71 4943
Higherford Lancs 81 8640
Highfield Devon 8 7097
Highfield E R Yk 84 7236
Highfield N Ayrs 115 3150
Highfield T & W 96 1458
Highfields S York 83 5406
Highgate E Susx 16 4234
Highgate Gt Lon 27 2887
Highgate Head Derbys 74 0486
Highgreen Manor Nthumb 102 8091
Highlane Ches 79 8868
Highlane S York 74 4081
Highlaws Cumb 92 1449
Highleadon Gloucs 47 7623
Highleigh W Susx 14 8498
Highley Shrops 60 7483
Highmoor Cumb 93 2647
Highmoor Oxon 37 7084
Highmoor Cross Oxon 37 7084
Highmoor Hill Mons 34 4689
Highnam Gloucs 35 7817
Highnam Green Gloucs 35 7920
Highridge Somset 21 5567
Highstead Kent 29 2166
Highsted Kent 28 9061
Highstreet Kent 29 0862
Highstreet Green Essex 53 7634
Highstreet Green Surrey 14 9835
Hightae D & G 100 0978
Highter's Heath W Mids 61 0879
Hightown Ches 72 8762
Hightown Hants 12 1704
Hightown Mersyd 78 3003
Hightown Green Suffk 54 9756
Highway Herefd 46 4549
Highway Wilts 36 0474
Highweek Devon 7 8472
Highwood Staffs 73 0931
Highwood Hill Gt Lon 26 2193
Highworth Wilts 36 2092
Hilcote Derbys 75 4558
Hilden Park Kent 16 5747
Hildenborough Kent 16 5648
Hildersham Cambs 53 5448
Hilderstone Staffs 72 9534
Hilderthorpe E R Yk 91 1766
Hilfield Dorset 10 6305
Hilgay Norfk 65 6298
Hill Gloucs 35 6495
Hill Warwks 50 4566
Hill Brow Hants 14 7926
Hill Chorlton Staffs 72 7939
Hill Common Norfk 67 4122
Hill Common Somset 20 1426
Hill Deverill Wilts 22 8640
Hill Dyke Lincs 77 3447
Hill End Dur 95 0136
Hill End Fife 117 0395
Hill End Gloucs 47 9037
Hill Green Kent 28 8362
Hill Head Hants 13 5402
Hill of Beath Fife 117 1590
Hill of Fearn Highld 147 8377
Hill Ridware Staffs 73 0817
Hill Side W York 82 1717
Hill Side Worcs 47 7561
Hill Top Dur 95 9924
Hill Top Hants 13 4003
Hill Top S York 74 3992
Hill Top W Mids 60 9993
Hill Top W York 82 0712
Hill Top W York 83 3315
Hillam N York 83 5028
Hillbeck Dur 95 7915
Hillborough Kent 29 2168
Hillbutts Dorset 11 9901
Hillcliffane Derbys 73 2947
Hillcott Wilts 23 1158
Hillend Fife 117 1483
Hillend Mdloth 117 2566
Hillend N Lans 116 8267
Hillend Swans 31 4190
Hillersland Gloucs 34 5614
Hillerton Devon 8 7298
Hillesden Bucks 49 6828
Hillesley Gloucs 35 7689
Hillfarrance Somset 20 1624
Hillgrove W Susx 14 9428
Hillhampton Herefd 46 5847
Hillhead Devon 7 9054
Hillhead S Lans 108 9840
Hillhead of Cocklaw Abers 143 0844
Hillhead of Durno Abers 142 7128
Hilliard's Cross Staffs 61 1511
Hilliclay Highld 151 1764
Hillingdon Gt Lon 26 0782
Hillington C Glas 115 5164
Hillington Norfk 65 7225
Hillis Corner IOW 13 4793
Hillmorton Warwks 50 5373
Hillock Vale Lancs 81 7629
Hillowton D & G 100 7763
Hillpool Worcs 60 8976
Hillpound Hants 13 5715
Hills Town Derbys 75 4869
Hillside Abers 135 9197
Hillside Angus 135 6960
Hillside Devon 7 7060
Hillstreet Hants 12 3416
Hillswick Shet 153 2877
Hilltown Devon 8 5380
Hilltown E Loth 118 3170
Hillwell Shet 153 3714
Hilmarton Wilts 35 0175
Hilperton Wilts 22 8759
Hilperton Marsh Wilts 22 8659
Hilsea Hants 13 6503
Hilston E R Yk 85 2833
Hilston Park Mons 34 4418
Hiltingbury Hants 13 4221
Hilton Border 119 8750
Hilton Cambs 52 2966
Hilton Cumb 94 7320
Hilton Derbys 73 2430
Hilton Dorset 11 7802
Hilton Dur 96 1622
Hilton Highld 147 8776
Hilton N York 89 4611
Hilton Shrops 60 7795
Himbleton Worcs 47 9458
Himley Staffs 60 8891
Hincaster Cumb 87 5084
Hinchley Wood Surrey 26 1565
Hinckley Leics 50 4294
Hinderclay Suffk 54 0276
Hinderwell N York 97 7916
Hindford Shrops 59 3333
Hindhead Surrey 14 8835
Hindle Fold Lancs 81 7332
Hindley Gt Man 78 6104
Hindley Nthumb 95 0459
Hindley Green Gt Man 79 6403
Hindlip Worcs 47 8858
Hindolveston Norfk 66 0329
Hindon Wilts 22 9132
Hindringham Norfk 66 9836
Hingham Norfk 66 0202
Hinksford Staffs 60 8689
Hinnington Shrops 60 7404
Hinstock Shrops 72 6925
Hintlesham Suffk 54 0843
Hinton Gloucs 35 6803
Hinton Gloucs 35 7376
Hinton Hants 12 2195
Hinton Herefd 46 3338
Hinton Shrops 59 4008
Hinton Shrops 59 6582
Hinton Admiral Hants 12 2096
Hinton Ampner Hants 13 6027
Hinton Blewett Somset 21 5956
Hinton Charterhouse Somset 22 7758
Hinton Green Worcs 48 0240
Hinton Marsh Hants 24 5828
Hinton Martell Dorset 11 0106
Hinton on the Green Worcs 48 0240
Hinton Parva Wilts 36 2383
Hinton St George Somset 10 4212
Hinton St Mary Dorset 11 7816
Hinton Waldrist Oxon 36 3799
Hinton-in-the-Hedges Nhants 49 5636
Hints Shrops 46 6174
Hints Staffs 61 1502
Hinwick Beds 51 9361
Hinxhill Kent 28 0442
Hinxton Cambs 53 4945
Hinxworth Herts 39 2340
Hipperholme W York 82 1225
Hipsburn Nthumb 111 2311
Hipswell N York 89 1898
Hirn Abers 135 7200
Hirnant Powys 58 0422
Hirst Nthumb 103 2787
Hirst Courtney N York 83 6124
Hirwaen Denbgs 70 1361
Hirwaun Rhondd 33 9505
Hiscott Devon 19 5426
Histon Cambs 53 4463
Hitcham Suffk 54 9851
Hitcham Causeway Suffk 54 9852
Hitcham Street Suffk 54 9851
Hitchin Herts 39 1829
Hither Green Gt Lon 27 3874
Hittisleigh Devon 8 7395
Hittisleigh Cross Devon 8 7395
Hive E R Yk 84 8230
Hixon Staffs 73 0025
Hoaden Kent 29 2759
Hoar Cross Staffs 73 1323
Hoarwithy Herefd 46 5429
Hoath Kent 29 2064
Hoathly Kent 28 6536
Hobarris Shrops 46 3178
Hobbles Green Suffk 53 7053
Hobbs Cross Essex 27 4799
Hobbs Cross Essex 39 4910
Hobkirk Border 110 5811
Hobland Hall Norfk 67 5001
Hobsick Notts 75 4549
Hobson Dur 96 1756
Hoby Leics 63 6617
Hoccombe Somset 20 1129
Hockering Norfk 66 0713
Hockerton Notts 75 7156
Hockley Ches 79 9383
Hockley Essex 40 8392
Hockley Staffs 61 2200
Hockley W Mids 61 2779
Hockley Heath W Mids 61 1572
Hockliffe Beds 38 9726
Hockwold cum Wilton Norfk 53 7388
Hockworthy Devon 20 0319
Hoddesdon Herts 39 3708
Hoddlesden Lancs 81 7122
Hoddom Cross D & G 101 1773
Hoddom Mains D & G 100 1572
Hodgehill Ches 79 8269
Hodgeston Pembks 30 0399
Hodnet Shrops 59 6128
Hodsall Street Kent 27 6263
Hodsock Notts 75 6185
Hodson Wilts 36 1780
Hodthorpe Derbys 75 5376
Hoe Hants 13 5617
Hoe Norfk 66 9916
Hoe Gate Hants 13 6213
Hoff Cumb 94 6717
Hog Hill E Susx 17 8815
Hogben's Hill Kent 28 0356
Hoggards Green Suffk 54 8856
Hoggeston Bucks 38 8024
Hoggrill's End Warwks 61 2292
Hoghton Lancs 81 6127
Hoghton Bottoms Lancs 81 6227
Hognaston Derbys 73 2350
Hogsthorpe Lincs 77 5372
Holbeach Lincs 64 3624
Holbeach Bank Lincs 64 3527
Holbeach Clough Lincs 64 3526
Holbeach Drove Lincs 64 3212
Holbeach Hurn Lincs 65 3926
Holbeach St Johns Lincs 64 3518
Holbeach St Mark's Lincs 64 3731
Holbeach St Matthew Lincs 65 4132
Holbeck Notts 75 5473
Holbeck Woodhouse Notts 75 5472
Holberrow Green Worcs 48 0259
Holbeton Devon 6 6150
Holborn Gt Lon 27 3181
Holborough Kent 28 7062
Holbrook Derbys 62 3644
Holbrook S York 75 4481
Holbrook Suffk 54 1636
Holbrook Moor Derbys 62 3645
Holburn Nthumb 111 0436
Holbury Hants 13 4303
Holcombe Devon 7 9574
Holcombe Gt Man 81 7816
Holcombe Somset 22 6749
Holcombe Brook Gt Man 81 7815
Holcombe Rogus Devon 20 0518
Holcot Nhants 50 7969
Holden Lancs 81 7749
Holden Gate W York 81 8923
Holdenby Nhants 50 6967
Holder's Green Essex 40 6328
Holdgate Shrops 59 5689
Holdingham Lincs 76 0547
Holditch Dorset 10 3402
Holdsworth W York 82 0829
Hole Devon 18 4206
Hole Park Kent 17 8332
Hole Street W Susx 15 1314
Hole-in-the-Wall Herefd 46 6128
Holehouse Derbys 79 0092
Holemoor Devon 18 4205
Holford Somset 20 1541
Holgate N York 83 5851
Holker Cumb 87 3676
Holkham Norfk 66 8943
Hollacombe Devon 18 3702
Hollam Somset 20 9232
Holland Fen Lincs 76 2349
Holland Lees Lancs 78 5208
Holland-on-Sea Essex 41 1916
Hollandstoun Ork 153 7553
Hollesley Suffk 55 3544
Hollicombe Devon 7 8962
Hollies Hill Worcs 60 9377
Hollin Green Ches 71 5952
Hollingbourne Kent 28 8455
Hollingbury E Susx 15 3107
Hollingdon Bucks 38 8727
Hollingthorpe W York 83 3831
Hollington Derbys 73 2239
Hollington Staffs 73 0538
Hollingworth Gt Man 79 0096
Hollinlane Ches 79 8384
Hollins Derbys 74 3271
Hollins Gt Man 79 8107
Hollins Staffs 73 9947
Hollins End S York 74 3883
Hollins Green Ches 79 6990
Hollins Lane Lancs 80 4951
Hollinsclough Staffs 74 0666
Hollinswood Shrops 60 7008
Hollinwood Shrops 59 5136
Hollingrove E Susx 16 6821
Hollocombe Devon 19 6311
Holloway Derbys 74 3256
Holloway Gt Lon 27 3086
Holloway Wilts 22 8730
Hollowell Nhants 50 6971
Hollowmoor Heath Ches 71 4868
Hollows D & G 101 3878
Holly End Norfk 65 4906
Holly Green Worcs 47 8641
Hollybush Caerph 33 1603
Hollybush E Ayrs 106 3915
Hollybush Herefd 47 7536
Hollyhurst Ches 71 5744
Hollym E R Yk 85 3425
Hollywood Worcs 61 0877
Holmbridge W York 82 1206
Holmbury St Mary Surrey 14 1143
Holmbush Cnwll 3 0352
Holmcroft Staffs 72 9024
Holme Cambs 52 1987
Holme Cumb 87 5278
Holme Lincs 84 9206
Holme N York 89 3582
Holme Notts 75 8059
Holme W York 82 1105
Holme Chapel Lancs 81 8728
Holme Green N York 83 5541
Holme Hale Norfk 66 8807
Holme Lacy Herefd 46 5535
Holme Marsh Herefd 46 3454
Holme next the Sea Norfk 65 7043
Holme on the Wolds E R Yk 84 9646
Holme Pierrepont Notts 62 6238
Holme St Cuthbert Cumb 92 1047
Holme upon
Spalding Moor E R Yk 84 8038
Holmer Herefd 46 5042
Holmer Green Bucks 26 9097
Holmes Chapel Ches 72 7667
Holmes Hill E Susx 16 5312
Holmesfield Derbys 74 3277
Holmeswood Lancs 80 4316
Holmethorpe Surrey 27 2851
Holmewood Derbys 75 4365
Holmfield W York 82 0828
Holmfirth W York 82 1408
Holmgate Derbys 74 3763
Holmhead E Ayrs 107 5620
Holmpton E R Yk 85 3623
Holmrook Cumb 86 0799
Holmsey Green Suffk 53 6978
Holmshurst E Susx 16 6425
Holmside Dur 96 2149
Holmwood Surrey 15 1647
Holmwrangle Cumb 94 5148
Holne Devon 7 7069
Holnest Dorset 11 6510
Holnicote Somset 20 9146
Holsworthy Devon 18 3403
Holsworthy Beacon Devon 18 3608
Holt Dorset 12 0303
Holt Norfk 66 0838
Holt Wilts 22 8661
Holt Worcs 47 8362
Holt Wrexhm 71 4053
Holt End Worcs 48 0769
Holt Fleet Worcs 47 8263
Holt Green Lancs 78 3905
Holt Heath Dorset 12 0504
Holt Heath Worcs 47 8163
Holt Street Kent 29 2551
Holtby N York 83 6754
Holton Oxon 37 6006
Holton Somset 22 6826
Holton Suffk 55 4077
Holton cum Beckering Lincs 76 1181
Holton Heath Dorset 11 9490
Holton Hill E Susx 16 6625
Holton le Clay Lincs 85 2802
Holton le Moor Lincs 76 0897
Holton St Mary Suffk 54 0536
Holtye E Susx 16 4539
Holway Flints 70 1876
Holwell Dorset 11 6911
Holwell Herts 39 1633
Holwell Leics 63 7323
Holwell Oxon 36 2309
Holwick Dur 95 9126
Holworth Dorset 11 7683
Holy Cross Worcs 60 9278
Holy Island Nthumb 111 1241
Holybourne Hants 24 7340
Holyfield Essex 39 3803
Holyhead IOA 68 2482
Holymoorside Derbys 74 3369
Holyport Berks 26 8977
Holystone Nthumb 102 9502
Holytown N Lans 116 7660
Holywell Cambs 52 3370
Holywell Cnwll 4 7659
Holywell Dorset 10 5904
Holywell Flints 70 1875
Holywell Nthumb 103 3174
Holywell Warwks 61 2066
Holywell Green W York 82 0819
Holywell Lake Somset 20 1020
Holywell Row Suffk 53 7177
Holywood D & G 100 9480
Holywood Village D & G 100 9579
Hom Green Herefd 34 5822
Homer Shrops 59 6101
Homer Green Mersyd 78 3402
Homersfield Suffk 55 2885
Homescales Cumb 87 5587
Homington Wilts 23 1226
Honey Hill Kent 29 1161
Honey Tye Suffk 54 9535
Honeyborough Pembks 30 9406
Honeybourne Worcs 48 1144
Honeychurch Devon 8 6303
Honeystreet Wilts 23 1061
Honiley Warwks 61 2372
Honing Norfk 67 3227
Honingham Norfk 66 1011
Honington Lincs 63 9443
Honington Suffk 54 9174
Honington Warwks 48 2642
Honiton Devon 9 1600
Honley W York 82 1311
Honnington Shrops 72 7215
Hoo Kent 27 2964
Hoo Kent 28 7872
Hoo End Herts 39 1820
Hoo Green Ches 79 7182
Hoo Meavy Devon 6 5265
Hoobrook Worcs 60 8374
Hood Green S York 82 3102
Hood Hill S York 74 3697
Hooe Devon 6 5052
Hooe E Susx 16 6809
Hooe Common E Susx 16 6910
Hoohill Lancs 80 3237
Hook Cambs 65 4293
Hook Devon 10 3005
Hook E R Yk 84 7625
Hook Hants 13 5105
Hook Hants 24 7254
Hook Kent 27 6170
Hook Pembks 30 9711
Hook Surrey 26 1864
Hook Wilts 36 0784
Hook Bank Worcs 47 8140
Hook Green Kent 16 6535
Hook Norton Oxon 48 3533
Hook Street Gloucs 35 6799
Hook Street Wilts 36 0884
Hookagate Shrops 59 4609
Hooke Dorset 10 5300
Hookgate Staffs 72 7435
Hookway Devon 8 8598
Hookwood Surrey 15 2643
Hooley Surrey 27 2856
Hooley Bridge Gt Man 81 8511
Hooton Ches 71 3678
Hooton Levitt S York 75 5291
Hooton Pagnell S York 83 4807
Hooton Roberts S York 75 4897
Hop Pole Lincs 64 1813
Hopcrofts Holt Oxon 49 4625
Hope Derbys 74 1783
Hope Devon 7 6740
Hope Flints 71 3058
Hope Powys 58 2507
Hope Shrops 59 3401
Hope Shrops 46 5974
Hope Staffs 73 1254
Hope Bowdler Shrops 59 4792
Hope End Green Essex 40 5720
Hope Mansell Herefd 35 6219
Hope under Dinmore Herefd 46 5052
Hopehouse Border 109 2916
Hopeman Moray 147 1469
Hopesay Shrops 59 3983
Hopetown W York 83 3923
Hopperton N York 83 4256
Hopsford Warwks 50 4284
Hopstone Shrops 60 7894
Hopton Derbys 73 2653

Inverroy Kingsdown
292

Inverroy *Highld* 131 2581
Inversanda *Highld* 130 9459
Invershiel *Highld* 138 9319
Invershin *Highld* 146 5796
Invershore *Highld* 151 2435
Inversnaid Hotel *Stirlg* 123 3308
Inverugie *Abers* 143 0948
Inveruglas *Ag & B* 123 3109
Inveruglass *Highld* 132 8000
Inverurie *Abers* 142 7721
Inwardleigh *Devon* 8 5699
Inworth *Essex* 40 8717
Iping *W Susx* 14 8522
Ipplepen *Devon* 7 8366
Ipsden *Oxon* 37 6285
Ipstones *Staffs* 73 0149
Ipswich *Suffk* 54 1644
Irby *Mersyd* 78 2584
Irby in the Marsh *Lincs* 77 4663
Irby upon Humber *Lincs* 85 1904
Irchester *Nhants* 51 9265
Ireby *Cumb* 93 2338
Ireby *Lancs* 87 6575
Ireland *Beds* 38 1341
Ireleth *Cumb* 86 2277
Ireshopeburn *Dur* 95 8638
Ireton Wood *Derbys* 73 2847
Irlam *Gt Man* 79 7294
Irnham *Lincs* 64 0226
Iron Acton *Gloucs* 35 6783
Iron Bridge *Cambs* 65 4898
Iron Cross *Warwks* 48 0552
Ironbridge *Shrops* 60 6703
Ironmacannie *D & G* 99 6675
Irons Bottom *Surrey* 15 2446
Ironville *Derbys* 75 4351
Irstead *Norfk* 67 3620
Irthington *Cumb* 101 4961
Irthlingborough *Nhants* 51 9470
Irton *N York* 91 0184
Irvine *N Ayrs* 106 3238
Isauld *Highld* 150 9865
Isbister *Shet* 153 3790
Isfield *E Susx* 16 4417
Isham *Nhants* 51 8873
Isington *Hants* 25 7842
Islandpool *Worcs* 60 8780
Isle Abbotts *Somset* 21 3520
Isle Brewers *Somset* 21 3621
Isle of Dogs *Gt Lon* 27 3779
Isle of Whithorn *D & G* 99 4736
Isleham *Cambs* 53 6474
Isleornsay *Highld* 129 7012
Islesteps *D & G* 100 9672
Islet Village *Guern* 158 0000
Isleworth *Gt Lon* 26 1575
Isley Walton *Leics* 62 4224
Islibhig *W Isls* 152 0029
Islington *Gt Lon* 27 3184
Islip *Nhants* 51 9879
Islip *Oxon* 37 5214
Islivig *W Isls* 152 0029
Isombridge *Shrops* 59 6113
Istead Rise *Kent* 27 6370
Itchen Abbas *Hants* 24 5333
Itchen Stoke *Hants* 24 5532
Itchingfield *W Susx* 15 1328
Itchington *Gloucs* 35 6587
Itteringham *Norfk* 66 1430
Itton *Devon* 8 6899
Itton *Mons* 34 4995
Ivegill *Cumb* 93 4143
Ivelet *N York* 88 9398
Iver *Bucks* 26 0381
Iver Heath *Bucks* 26 0283
Iveston *Dur* 96 1350
Ivinghoe *Bucks* 38 9416
Ivinghoe Aston *Bucks* 38 9517
Ivington *Herefd* 46 4756
Ivington Green *Herefd* 46 4656
Ivy Cross *Dorset* 22 8623
Ivy Hatch *Kent* 27 5854
Ivy Todd *Norfk* 66 8909
Ivybridge *Devon* 6 6356
Ivychurch *Kent* 17 0327
Iwade *Kent* 28 9067
Iwerne Courtney or Shroton *Dorset* 11 8512
Iwerne Minster *Dorset* 11 8614
Ixworth *Suffk* 54 9370
Ixworth Thorpe *Suffk* 54 9173

# J

Jack Green *Lancs* 81 5925
Jack Hill *N York* 82 1951
Jack's Bush *Hants* 23 2636
Jack-in-the-Green *Devon* 9 0195
Jacksdale *Notts* 75 4451
Jackson Bridge *W York* 82 1607
Jackton *S Lans* 115 5952
Jacobs Well *Surrey* 25 0053
Jacobstow *Cnwll* 5 1995
Jacobstowe *Devon* 8 5801
Jameston *Pembks* 30 0598
Jamestown *Highld* 139 4756
Jamestown *W Duns* 115 3981
Janets-town *Highld* 151 3551
Janetstown *Highld* 151 1932
Jardine Hall *D & G* 100 1088
Jarrow *T & W* 103 3364
Jarvis Brook *E Susx* 16 5329
Jasper's Green *Essex* 40 7226
Jawcraig *Falk* 116 8475
Jaywick *Essex* 41 1413
Jealott's Hill *Berks* 25 8673
Jeater Houses *N York* 89 4394
Jedburgh *Border* 110 6420
Jeffreston *Pembks* 31 0906
Jemimaville *Highld* 140 7165
Jerbourg *Guern* 158 0000
Jerusalem *Lincs* 76 9170
Jesmond *T & W* 103 2566
Jevington *E Susx* 16 5601
Jingle Street *Mons* 34 4710
Jockey End *Herts* 38 0413
Jodrell Bank *Ches* 79 7970
John O'Groats *Highld* 151 3872
John's Cross *E Susx* 17 7421
Johnby *Cumb* 93 4332
Johnshaven *Abers* 135 7967
Johnson's Street *Norfk* 67 3717
Johnston *Pembks* 30 9310
Johnstone *D & G* 109 2400
Johnstone *Rens* 115 4263
Johnstonebridge *D & G* 100 1092
Johnstown *Carmth* 31 3919
Johnstown *Wrexhm* 71 3046
Joppa *C Edin* 118 3173
Joppa *Cerdgn* 43 5666
Joppa *S Ayrs* 106 4119
Jordans *Bucks* 26 9791
Jordanston *Pembks* 30 9132
Jordanthorpe *S York* 74 3580
Joyden's Wood *Kent* 27 5072
Jubilee Corner *Kent* 28 8447
Jump *S York* 83 3801
Jumper's Town *E Susx* 16 4632
Juniper Green *C Edin* 117 1968
Jurby *IOM* 158 3598
Jurston *Devon* 8 6984

# K

Kaber *Cumb* 88 7911
Kaimend *S Lans* 117 9945
Kames *Ag & B* 114 9771
Kames *E Ayrs* 107 6926
Kea *Cnwll* 3 8142
Keadby *Lincs* 84 8311
Keal Cotes *Lincs* 77 3660
Kearby Town End *N York* 83 3447
Kearsley *Gt Man* 79 7504
Kearsley *Nthumb* 103 0275
Kearsney *Kent* 29 2844
Kearstwick *Cumb* 87 6079
Kearton *N York* 88 9999
Keasden *N York* 88 7266
Keason *Cnwll* 5 3168
Keaton *Devon* 7 6454
Keckwick *Ches* 78 5783
Keddington *Lincs* 77 3488
Keddington Corner *Lincs* 77 3589
Kedington *Suffk* 53 7046
Kedleston *Derbys* 73 3040
Keelby *Lincs* 85 1610
Keele *Staffs* 72 8045
Keele University *Staffs* 72 8144
Keeley Green *Beds* 38 0046
Keelham *W York* 82 0732
Keeston *Pembks* 30 9019
Keevil *Wilts* 22 9258
Kegworth *Leics* 62 4826
Kehelland *Cnwll* 2 6241
Keig *Abers* 142 6119
Keighley *W York* 82 0541
Keilarsbrae *Clacks* 116 8994
Keillour *P & K* 125 9725
Keiloch *Abers* 133 1891
Keils *Ag & B* 113 5268
Keinton Mandeville *Somset* 21 5430
Keir Mill *D & G* 100 8593
Keirsleywell Row *Nthumb* 94 7751
Keisby *Lincs* 64 0328
Keisley *Cumb* 94 7124
Keiss *Highld* 151 3461
Keith *Moray* 142 4250
Keithick *P & K* 126 2038
Keithock *Angus* 134 6063
Keithtown *Highld* 139 5256
Kelbrook *Lancs* 81 9044
Kelburn *N Ayrs* 114 2156
Kelby *Lincs* 63 0041
Keld *Cumb* 94 5514
Keld *N York* 88 8900
Keld Head *N York* 90 7884
Keldholme *N York* 90 7086
Kelfield *Lincs* 84 8201
Kelfield *N York* 83 5938
Kelham *Notts* 75 7755
Kelhead *D & G* 100 1469
Kellacott *Devon* 5 4088
Kellamergh *Lancs* 80 4029
Kellas *Angus* 127 4535
Kellas *Moray* 141 1654
Kellaton *Devon* 7 8039
Kelleth *Cumb* 87 6605
Kelling *Norfk* 66 0942
Kellington *N York* 83 5524
Kelloe *Dur* 96 3436
Kelloholm *D & G* 107 7411
Kells *Cumb* 92 9616
Kelly *Devon* 5 3981
Kelly Bray *Cnwll* 5 3671
Kelmarsh *Nhants* 50 7379
Kelmscot *Oxon* 36 2499
Kelsale *Suffk* 55 3865
Kelsall *Ches* 71 5268
Kelshall *Herts* 39 3336
Kelsick *Cumb* 93 1950
Kelso *Border* 110 7234
Kelstedge *Derbys* 74 3363
Kelstern *Lincs* 77 2489
Kelsterton *Flints* 70 2770
Kelston *Somset* 22 7067
Keltneyburn *P & K* 124 7749
Kelty *Fife* 117 1494
Kelvedon *Essex* 40 8619
Kelvedon Hatch *Essex* 27 5698
Kelynack *Cnwll* 2 3729
Kemacott *Devon* 19 6647
Kemback *Fife* 126 4115
Kemberton *Shrops* 60 7204
Kemble *Gloucs* 35 9897
Kemble Wick *Gloucs* 35 9895
Kemerton *Worcs* 47 9536
Kemeys Commander *Mons* 34 3404
Kemnay *Abers* 142 7316
Kemp Town *E Susx* 15 3303
Kempe's Corner *Kent* 28 0346
Kempley *Gloucs* 47 6629
Kempley Green *Gloucs* 47 6728
Kemps Green *Warwks* 61 1470
Kempsey *Worcs* 47 8549
Kempsford *Gloucs* 36 1696
Kempshott *Hants* 24 6050
Kempston *Beds* 38 0347
Kempston Hardwick *Beds* 38 0344
Kempton *Shrops* 59 3682
Kemsing *Kent* 27 5558
Kemsley *Kent* 28 9166
Kemsley Street *Kent* 28 8062
Kenardington *Kent* 17 9732
Kenchester *Herefd* 46 4342
Kencot *Oxon* 36 2504
Kendal *Cumb* 87 5192
Kenderchurch *Herefd* 46 4028
Kendleshire *Gloucs* 35 6679
Kenfig *Brdgnd* 32 8081
Kenfig Hill *Brdgnd* 33 8382
Kenidjack *Cnwll* 2 3632
Kenilworth *Warwks* 61 2871
Kenley *Gt Lon* 27 3260
Kenley *Shrops* 59 5500
Kenmore *Highld* 137 7557
Kenmore *P & K* 124 7745
Kenn *Devon* 9 9285
Kenn *Somset* 21 4268
Kennacraig *Ag & B* 113 8262
Kennards House *Cnwll* 5 2883
Kenneggy *Cnwll* 2 5628
Kennerleigh *Devon* 8 8107
Kennessee Green *Mersyd* 78 3801
Kennet *Clacks* 116 9291
Kennethmont *Abers* 142 5428
Kennett *Cambs* 53 7068
Kennford *Devon* 9 9186
Kenninghall *Norfk* 54 0386
Kennington *Kent* 28 0245
Kennington *Oxon* 37 5201
Kennoway *Fife* 126 3502
Kenny *Somset* 10 3117
Kennyhill *Suffk* 53 6679
Kennythorpe *N York* 90 7865
Kenovay *Ag & B* 120 9946
Kensaleyre *Highld* 136 4151
Kensham Green *Kent* 17 8229
Kensington *Gt Lon* 27 2579
Kensworth *Beds* 38 0319
Kensworth Common *Beds* 38 0317
Kent End *Wilts* 36 0594
Kent Green *Ches* 72 8458
Kent Street *E Susx* 17 7816
Kent Street *Kent* 28 6654
Kent's Green *Gloucs* 47 7423
Kent's Oak *Hants* 23 3224
Kentallen *Highld* 122 0057
Kentchurch *Herefd* 46 4125
Kentford *Suffk* 53 7066
Kentisbeare *Devon* 9 0608
Kentisbury *Devon* 19 6243
Kentisbury Ford *Devon* 19 6242
Kentish Town *Gt Lon* 27 2884
Kentmere *Cumb* 87 4504
Kenton *Devon* 9 9583
Kenton *Gt Lon* 26 1788
Kenton *Suffk* 55 1965
Kenton *T & W* 103 2267
Kenton Bank Foot *Nthumb* 103 2069
Kentra *Highld* 129 6569
Kents Bank *Cumb* 87 3975
Kenwick *Shrops* 59 4230
Kenwyn *Cnwll* 3 8145
Kenyon *Ches* 79 6395
Keoldale *Highld* 149 3866
Keppoch *Highld* 138 8924
Kepwick *N York* 89 4690
Keresley *W Mids* 61 3282
Keresley Green *Warwks* 61 3283
Kergilliak *Cnwll* 3 7833
Kernborough *Devon* 7 7941
Kerne Bridge *Herefd* 34 5818
Kerridge *Ches* 79 9376
Kerridge-end *Ches* 79 9475
Kerris *Cnwll* 2 4427
Kerry *Powys* 58 1490
Kerrycroy *Ag & B* 114 1061
Kersall *Notts* 75 7162
Kersbrook *Devon* 9 0683
Kerscott *Devon* 19 6329
Kersey *Suffk* 54 0044
Kersey Tye *Suffk* 54 9843
Kersey Upland *Suffk* 54 9942
Kershader *W Isls* 152 3320
Kershopefoot *Cumb* 101 4782
Kersoe *Worcs* 47 9940
Kerswell *Devon* 9 0806
Kerswell Green *Worcs* 47 8646
Kerthen Wood *Cnwll* 2 5833
Kesgrave *Suffk* 55 2245
Kessingland *Suffk* 55 5286
Kessingland Beach *Suffk* 55 5385
Kestle *Cnwll* 3 9845
Kestle Mill *Cnwll* 4 8459
Keston *Gt Lon* 27 4164
Keswick *Cumb* 93 2623
Keswick *Norfk* 67 2004
Ketsby *Lincs* 77 3676
Kettering *Nhants* 51 8678
Ketteringham *Norfk* 66 1603
Kettins *Angus* 126 2338
Kettle Green *Herts* 39 4118
Kettlebaston *Suffk* 54 9650
Kettlebridge *Fife* 126 3007
Kettlebrook *Staffs* 61 2103
Kettleburgh *Suffk* 55 2660
Kettleholm *D & G* 100 1577
Kettleness *N York* 97 8315
Kettleshulme *Ches* 79 9879
Kettlesing *N York* 82 2256
Kettlesing Bottom *N York* 89 2357
Kettlestone *Norfk* 66 9631
Kettlethorpe *Lincs* 76 8475
Kettletoft *Ork* 153 6538
Kettlewell *N York* 88 9672
Ketton *Rutlnd* 63 9704
Kew *Gt Lon* 26 1876
Kewstoke *Somset* 21 3363
Kexbrough *S York* 82 3009
Kexby *Lincs* 76 8785
Kexby *N York* 84 7050
Key Green *Ches* 72 8963
Key Green *N York* 90 8004
Key Street *Kent* 28 8764
Key's Toft *Lincs* 77 4858
Keyham *Leics* 63 6706
Keyhaven *Hants* 12 3091
Keyingham *E R Yk* 85 2425
Keymer *W Susx* 15 3115
Keynsham *Somset* 21 6568
Keysoe *Beds* 51 0762
Keysoe Row *Beds* 51 0861
Keyston *Cambs* 51 0475
Keyworth *Notts* 62 6130
Kibbear *Somset* 20 2222
Kibblesworth *T & W* 96 2456
Kibworth Beauchamp *Leics* 50 6893
Kibworth Harcourt *Leics* 50 6894
Kidbrooke *Gt Lon* 27 4176
Kidburngill *Cumb* 92 0621
Kidd's Moor *Norfk* 66 1103
Kiddemore Green *Staffs* 60 8509
Kidderminster *Worcs* 60 8376
Kiddington *Oxon* 49 4123
Kidlington *Oxon* 37 4913
Kidmore End *Oxon* 37 6979
Kidsdale *D & G* 99 4336
Kidsgrove *Staffs* 72 8454
Kidstones *N York* 88 9581
Kidwelly *Carmth* 31 4006
Kiel Crofts *Ag & B* 122 9039
Kielder *Nthumb* 102 6293
Kiells *Ag & B* 112 4168
Kilbarchan *Rens* 115 4063
Kilbeg *Highld* 129 6506
Kilberry *Ag & B* 113 7164
Kilbirnie *N Ayrs* 115 3154
Kilbride *Ag & B* 122 8525
Kilbride *Ag & B* 113 7279
Kilbride *Ag & B* 114 0367
Kilbuiack *Moray* 141 0960
Kilburn *Derbys* 62 3845
Kilburn *Gt Lon* 26 2483
Kilburn *N York* 90 5179
Kilby *Leics* 50 6295
Kilchamaig *Ag & B* 113 8060
Kilchattan *Ag & B* 112 3795
Kilchattan *Ag & B* 114 1054
Kilcheran *Ag & B* 122 8239
Kilchoan *Highld* 121 4863
Kilchrenan *Ag & B* 122 0322
Kilconquhar *Fife* 127 4802
Kilcot *Gloucs* 47 6925
Kilcoy *Highld* 139 5751
Kilcreggan *Ag & B* 114 2480
Kildale *N York* 90 6009
Kildalloig *Ag & B* 105 7518
Kildary *Highld* 147 7674
Kildavaig *Ag & B* 114 9866
Kildavanan *Ag & B* 114 0266
Kildonan *Highld* 147 9120
Kildonan *N Ayrs* 105 0321
Kildonan Lodge *Highld* 147 9022
Kildonnan *Highld* 128 4885
Kildrochet House *D & G* 98 0856
Kildrummy *Abers* 142 4617
Kildwick *N York* 82 0046
Kilfinan *Ag & B* 114 9378
Kilfinnan *Highld* 131 2795
Kilford *Denbgs* 70 0766
Kilgetty *Pembks* 31 1207
Kilgrammie *S Ayrs* 106 2502
Kilgwrrwg Common *Mons* 34 4797
Kilham *E R Yk* 91 0664
Kilham *Nthumb* 110 8832
Kilkenneth *Ag & B* 120 9444
Kilkenzie *Ag & B* 105 6724
Kilkhampton *Cnwll* 18 2511
Killamarsh *Derbys* 75 4581
Killay *Swans* 32 6092
Killearn *Stirlg* 115 5286
Killerby *Dur* 96 1919
Killerton *Devon* 9 9700
Killichonan *P & K* 132 5458
Killiechronan *Ag & B* 121 5441
Killiecrankie *P & K* 132 9162
Killilan *Highld* 138 9430
Killin *Stirlg* 124 5733
Killinghall *N York* 89 2858
Killington *Cumb* 87 6188
Killington *Devon* 19 6646
Killingworth *T & W* 103 2770
Killiow *Cnwll* 3 8042
Killivose *Cnwll* 3 8049
Killochyett *Border* 118 4545
Kilmacolm *Inver* 115 3567
Kilmahog *Stirlg* 124 6108
Kilmahumaig *Ag & B* 113 7893
Kilmaluag *Highld* 136 4374
Kilmany *Fife* 126 3821
Kilmarie *Highld* 129 5517
Kilmarnock *E Ayrs* 107 4237
Kilmartin *Ag & B* 113 8398
Kilmaurs *E Ayrs* 106 4141
Kilmelford *Ag & B* 122 8512
Kilmeny *Ag & B* 112 3965
Kilmersdon *Somset* 22 6952
Kilmeston *Hants* 13 5825
Kilmichael *Ag & B* 113 8593
Kilmichael *Ag & B* 105 6922
Kilmichael of Inverlussa *Ag & B* 113 7786
Kilmington *Devon* 10 2797
Kilmington *Wilts* 22 7736
Kilmington Common *Wilts* 22 7735
Kilmington Street *Wilts* 22 7835
Kilmorack *Highld* 139 4944
Kilmore *Ag & B* 122 8825
Kilmore *Highld* 129 6507
Kilmory *Ag & B* 113 7074
Kilmory *Highld* 128 5270
Kilmory *N Ayrs* 105 9621
Kilmuir *Highld* 136 2547
Kilmuir *Highld* 136 3770
Kilmuir *Highld* 140 6749
Kilmuir *Highld* 147 7573
Kilmun *Ag & B* 114 1781
Kiln Green *Berks* 37 8178
Kiln Pit Hill *Nthumb* 95 0355
Kilnave *Ag & B* 112 2871
Kilncadzow *S Lans* 116 8848
Kilndown *Kent* 16 7035
Kilnhill *Cumb* 93 2132
Kilnhouses *Ches* 71 6366
Kilnhurst *S York* 75 4597
Kilninver *Ag & B* 122 8221
Kilnsea *E R Yk* 85 4115
Kilnsey *N York* 88 9767
Kilnwick *E R Yk* 84 9949
Kilnwick Percy *E R Yk* 84 8249
Kiloran *Ag & B* 112 3996
Kilpatrick *N Ayrs* 105 9026
Kilpeck *Herefd* 46 4430
Kilpin *E R Yk* 84 7726
Kilpin Pike *E R Yk* 84 7626
Kilrenny *Fife* 127 5704
Kilrie *Ches* 79 7478
Kilsby *Nhants* 50 5671
Kilspindie *P & K* 126 2125
Kilstay *D & G* 98 1238
Kilsyth *N Lans* 116 7178
Kiltarlity *Highld* 139 5041
Kilton *N York* 97 7018
Kilton Thorpe *N York* 97 6917
Kilvaxter *Highld* 136 3869
Kilve *Somset* 20 1442
Kilvington *Notts* 63 8042
Kilwinning *N Ayrs* 106 3043
Kimberley *Norfk* 66 0603
Kimberley *Notts* 62 4944
Kimberworth *S York* 74 4093
Kimble Wick *Bucks* 38 8007
Kimblesworth *Dur* 96 2547
Kimbolton *Cambs* 51 1067
Kimbolton *Herefd* 46 5261
Kimcote *Leics* 50 5886
Kimmeridge *Dorset* 11 9179
Kimmerston *Nthumb* 111 9535
Kimpton *Hants* 23 2746
Kimpton *Herts* 39 1718
Kimworthy *Devon* 18 3112
Kinbrace *Highld* 150 8631
Kinbuck *Stirlg* 125 7905
Kincaple *Fife* 127 4618
Kincardine *Fife* 116 9387
Kincardine *Highld* 146 6089
Kincardine O'Neil *Abers* 134 5999
Kinclaven *P & K* 126 1538
Kincorth *Aber C* 135 9403
Kincorth House *Moray* 141 0161
Kincraig *Highld* 132 8305
Kincraigie *P & K* 125 9849
Kindallachan *P & K* 125 9949
Kinerarach *Ag & B* 113 6553
Kineton *Gloucs* 48 0926
Kineton *Warwks* 48 3350
Kinfauns *P & K* 126 1622
Kinfold *S Ayrs* 106 3634
King Sterndale *Derbys* 74 0972
King's Acre *Herefd* 46 4841
King's Bromley *Staffs* 73 1216
King's Cliffe *Nhants* 51 0097
King's Coughton *Warwks* 48 0859
King's Heath *W Mids* 61 0781
King's Hill *Warwks* 61 3274
King's Lynn *Norfk* 65 6120
King's Mills *Guern* 158 0000
King's Moss *Lancs* 78 5000
King's Newton *Derbys* 62 3825
King's Norton *Leics* 50 6800
King's Norton *W Mids* 61 0579
King's Nympton *Devon* 19 6819
King's Pyon *Herefd* 46 4450
King's Somborne *Hants* 23 3531
King's Stag *Dorset* 11 7210
King's Stanley *Gloucs* 35 8103
King's Sutton *Oxon* 49 4936
King's Walden *Herts* 39 1623
Kingarth *Ag & B* 114 0956
Kingcausie *Abers* 135 8699
Kingcoed *Mons* 34 4305
Kingerby *Lincs* 76 0592
Kingford *Devon* 18 2806
Kingham *Oxon* 48 2624
Kingholm Quay *D & G* 100 9773
Kinghorn *Fife* 117 2686
Kinglassie *Fife* 117 2298
Kingoldrum *Angus* 126 3355
Kingoodie *P & K* 126 3329
Kings Bridge *Swans* 32 5997
Kings Caple *Herefd* 46 5528
Kings Green *Gloucs* 47 7734
Kings Hill *Kent* 28 6755
Kings Hill *W Mids* 60 9896
Kings House Hotel *Highld* 123 2654
Kings Langley *Herts* 26 0702
Kings Meaburn *Cumb* 94 6221
Kings Muir *Border* 109 2539
Kings Newnham *Warwks* 50 4577
Kings Ripton *Cambs* 52 2676
Kings Weston *Bristl* 34 5477
Kings Worthy *Hants* 24 4932
Kingsand *Cnwll* 6 4350
Kingsash *Bucks* 38 8805
Kingsbarns *Fife* 127 5912
Kingsbridge *Devon* 7 7344
Kingsbridge *Somset* 20 9837
Kingsburgh *Highld* 136 3955
Kingsbury *Gt Lon* 26 1988
Kingsbury *Warwks* 61 2196
Kingsbury Episcopi *Somset* 21 4321
Kingsclere *Hants* 24 5258
Kingscote *Gloucs* 35 8196
Kingscott *Devon* 19 5318
Kingscross *N Ayrs* 105 0428
Kingsdon *Somset* 21 5126
Kingsdown *Kent* 29 3748
Kingsdown *Wilts* 22 8167
Kingsdown *Wilts* 36 1688

294

295

Lower Sheering

Marton

297

Lower Sheering *Essex* 39 4914
Lower Shelton *Beds* 38 9942
Lower Shiplake *Oxon* 37 7679
Lower Shuckburgh *Warwks* 49 4862
Lower Slaughter *Gloucs* 36 1622
Lower Soothill *W York* 82 2523
Lower Soudley *Gloucs* 35 6609
Lower Standen *Kent* 29 2340
Lower Stanton St Quintin *Wilts* 35 9180
Lower Stoke *Kent* 28 8375
Lower Stone *Gloucs* 35 6794
Lower Stonnall *Staffs* 61 0803
Lower Stow Bedon *Norfk* 66 9694
Lower Street *Dorset* 11 8399
Lower Street *E Susx* 16 7012
Lower Street *Norfk* 67 2635
Lower Street *Suffk* 53 7852
Lower Street *Suffk* 54 1052
Lower Stretton *Ches* 79 6281
Lower Stroud *Dorset* 10 4598
Lower Sundon *Beds* 38 0526
Lower Swanwick *Hants* 13 4909
Lower Swell *Gloucs* 48 1725
Lower Tadmarton *Oxon* 48 4036
Lower Tale *Devon* 9 0601
Lower Tean *Staffs* 73 0138
Lower Thurlton *Norfk* 67 4299
Lower Town *Cnwll* 2 6528
Lower Town *Devon* 7 7172
Lower Town *Herefd* 47 6342
Lower Town *Pembks* 30 9637
Lower Trebullett *Cnwll* 5 3277
Lower Tregantle *Cnwll* 5 3953
Lower Treluswell *Cnwll* 3 7735
Lower Tysoe *Warwks* 48 3445
Lower Ufford *Suffk* 55 2952
Lower Upcott *Devon* 9 8880
Lower Upham *Hants* 13 5219
Lower Upnor *Kent* 28 7571
Lower Vexford *Somset* 20 1135
Lower Walton *Ches* 78 6086
Lower Waterston *Dorset* 11 7395
Lower Weare *Somset* 21 4053
Lower Welson *Herefd* 46 2950
Lower Westmancote *Worcs* 47 9337
Lower Whatcombe *Dorset* 11 8401
Lower Whatley *Somset* 22 7447
Lower Whitley *Ches* 71 6179
Lower Wick *Gloucs* 35 7096
Lower Wick *Worcs* 47 8352
Lower Wield *Hants* 24 6340
Lower Wigginton *Herts* 38 9409
Lower Willingdon *E Susx* 16 5803
Lower Withington *Ches* 79 8169
Lower Woodend *Bucks* 37 8187
Lower Woodford *Wilts* 23 1235
Lower Wraxhall *Dorset* 10 5700
Lower Wyche *Worcs* 47 7743
Lower Wyke *W York* 82 1525
Lowerhouse *Lancs* 81 8032
Lowesby *Leics* 63 7207
Lowestoft *Suffk* 67 5493
Loweswater *Cumb* 92 1421
Lowfield Heath *W Susx* 15 2739
Lowgill *Cumb* 87 6297
Lowgill *Lancs* 87 6564
Lowick *Cumb* 86 2885
Lowick *Nhants* 51 9881
Lowick *Nthumb* 111 0139
Lowick Bridge *Cumb* 86 2986
Lowick Green *Cumb* 86 2985
Lowlands *Dur* 96 1325
Lowlands *Torfn* 34 2996
Lowsonford *Warwks* 48 1868
Lowther *Cumb* 94 5323
Lowther Castle *Cumb* 94 5223
Lowthorpe *E R Yk* 91 0860
Lowton *Devon* 8 6604
Lowton *Gt Man* 78 6197
Lowton *Somset* 20 1918
Lowton Common *Gt Man* 79 6397
Lowton St Mary's *Gt Man* 79 6397
Loxbeare *Devon* 9 9116
Loxhill *Surrey* 25 0038
Loxhore *Devon* 19 6138
Loxhore Cott *Devon* 19 6138
Loxley *Warwks* 48 2553
Loxley Green *Staffs* 73 0630
Loxter *Herefd* 47 7140
Loxton *Somset* 21 3755
Loxwood *W Susx* 14 0331
Loyal Lodge *Highld* 149 6146
Lubenham *Leics* 50 7087
Lucas Green *Surrey* 25 9460
Lucasgate *Lincs* 77 4147
Luccombe *Somset* 20 9243
Luccombe Village *IOW* 13 5879
Lucker *Nthumb* 111 1530
Luckett *Cnwll* 5 3873
Lucking Street *Essex* 54 8134
Luckington *Wilts* 35 8383
Lucknam *Wilts* 35 8272
Luckwell Bridge *Somset* 20 9038
Lucott *Somset* 19 8645
Lucton *Herefd* 46 4364
Lucy Cross *N York* 89 2112
Ludborough *Lincs* 77 2995
Ludbrook *Devon* 7 6654
Ludchurch *Pembks* 31 1411
Luddenden *W York* 82 0426
Luddenden Foot *W York* 82 0325
Luddenham Court *Kent* 28 9963
Luddesdown *Kent* 28 6666
Luddington *Lincs* 84 8316
Luddington *Warwks* 48 1652
Luddington in the Brook *Nhants* 51 1083
Ludford *Lincs* 76 1989
Ludford *Shrops* 46 5174
Ludgershall *Bucks* 37 6517
Ludgershall *Wilts* 23 2650
Ludgvan *Cnwll* 2 5033
Ludham *Norfk* 67 3818
Ludlow *Shrops* 46 5175
Ludney *Somset* 10 3812
Ludwell *Wilts* 22 9122
Ludworth *Dur* 96 3641
Luffenhall *Herts* 39 2928
Luffincott *Devon* 5 3394
Luffness *E Loth* 118 4780
Lugar *E Ayrs* 107 5921
Lugg Green *Herefd* 46 4462
Luggate Burn *E Loth* 118 5974
Luggiebank *N Lans* 116 7672
Lugsdale *Ches* 78 5285
Lugton *E Ayrs* 115 4152
Lugwardine *Herefd* 46 5540
Luib *Highld* 137 5627
Lulham *Herefd* 46 4141
Lullington *Derbys* 61 2412
Lullington *E Susx* 16 5202
Lullington *Somset* 22 7851
Lulsgate Bottom *Somset* 21 5165
Lulsley *Worcs* 47 7455
Lulworth Camp *Dorset* 11 8381
Lumb *Lancs* 81 8324
Lumb *W York* 82 0221
Lumbutts *W York* 82 9523
Lumby *N York* 83 4830
Lumloch *E Duns* 116 6370
Lumphanan *Abers* 134 5804
Lumphinnans *Fife* 117 1792
Lumsden *Abers* 142 4722
Lunan *Angus* 127 6851
Lunanhead *Angus* 127 4752
Luncarty *P & K* 125 0929
Lund *E R Yk* 84 9647
Lund *N York* 83 6532
Lundford Magna *Lincs* 76 1989
Lundie *Angus* 126 2836
Lundie *Stirlg* 124 7304
Lundin Links *Fife* 126 4002
Lundin Mill *Fife* 126 4102
Lundy Green *Norfk* 67 2392
Lunna *Shet* 153 4869
Lunsford *Kent* 28 6959
Lunsford's Cross *E Susx* 17 7210
Lunt *Mersyd* 78 3402
Luntley *Herefd* 46 3955
Luppitt *Devon* 9 1606
Lupridge *Devon* 7 7153
Lupset *W York* 82 3119
Lupton *Cumb* 87 5581
Lurgashall *W Susx* 14 9326
Lurley *Devon* 9 9215
Lusby *Lincs* 77 3467
Luscombe *Devon* 7 7957
Luson *Devon* 6 6050
Luss *Ag & B* 115 3692
Lusta *Highld* 136 2656
Lustleigh *Devon* 8 7881
Luston *Herefd* 46 4863
Luthermuir *Abers* 135 6568
Luthrie *Fife* 126 3319
Lutley *Worcs* 60 9382
Luton *Beds* 38 0921
Luton *Devon* 9 0802
Luton *Devon* 9 9076
Luton *Kent* 28 7766
Lutterworth *Leics* 50 5484
Lutton *Devon* 6 5959
Lutton *Devon* 7 6961
Lutton *Dorset* 11 8980
Lutton *Lincs* 65 4325
Lutton *Nhants* 52 1187
Luxborough *Somset* 20 9738
Luxulyan *Cnwll* 4 0558
Luzley *Gt Man* 79 9600
Lybster *Highld* 151 2435
Lydbury North *Shrops* 59 3486
Lydcott *Devon* 19 6936
Lydd *Kent* 17 0420
Lydden *Kent* 29 2645
Lydden *Kent* 29 3567
Lyddington *Rutlnd* 51 8797
Lyde Green *Hants* 24 7057
Lydeard St Lawrence *Somset* 20 1332
Lydford *Devon* 5 5185
Lydford on Fosse *Somset* 21 5630
Lydgate *Gt Man* 82 9516
Lydgate *W York* 81 9225
Lydham *Shrops* 59 3391
Lydiard Green *Wilts* 36 0885
Lydiard Millicent *Wilts* 36 0986
Lydiard Tregoze *Wilts* 36 1085
Lydiate *Mersyd* 78 3604
Lydiate Ash *Worcs* 60 9775
Lydlinch *Dorset* 11 7413
Lydney *Gloucs* 35 6303
Lydstep *Pembks* 31 0898
Lye *W Mids* 60 9284
Lye Cross *Somset* 21 4962
Lye Green *Bucks* 38 9703
Lye Green *E Susx* 16 5134
Lye Green *Warwks* 48 1965
Lye Head *Worcs* 60 7573
Lye's Green *Wilts* 22 8146
Lyford *Oxon* 36 3994
Lymbridge Green *Kent* 29 1244
Lyme Regis *Dorset* 10 3492
Lyminge *Kent* 29 1641
Lymington *Hants* 12 3295
Lyminster *W Susx* 14 0204
Lymm *Ches* 79 6887
Lympne *Kent* 17 1135
Lympsham *Somset* 21 3354
Lympstone *Devon* 9 9984
Lynbridge *Devon* 19 7248
Lynch *Somset* 20 9047
Lynch Green *Norfk* 66 1505
Lynchat *Highld* 132 7801
Lyndhurst *Hants* 12 3008
Lyndon *Rutlnd* 63 9004
Lyndon Green *W Mids* 61 1485
Lyne *Border* 109 2041
Lyne *Surrey* 26 0166
Lyne Down *Herefd* 47 6431
Lyne of Skene *Abers* 135 7610
Lyneal *Shrops* 59 4433
Lyneham *Devon* 8 8579
Lyneham *Oxon* 36 2720
Lyneham *Wilts* 35 0278
Lyneholmford *Cumb* 101 5172
Lynemouth *Nthumb* 103 2991
Lyness *Ork* 153 3094
Lyng *Norfk* 66 0617
Lyng *Somset* 21 3329
Lynhales *Herefd* 46 3255
Lynmouth *Devon* 19 7249
Lynn *Shrops* 72 7815
Lynn *Staffs* 61 0704
Lynn of Shenval *Moray* 141 2129
Lynsted *Kent* 28 9460
Lynstone *Cnwll* 18 2005
Lynton *Devon* 19 7249
Lyon's Gate *Dorset* 11 6505
Lyonshall *Herefd* 46 3355
Lytchett Matravers *Dorset* 11 9495
Lytchett Minster *Dorset* 11 9693
Lyth *Highld* 151 2762
Lytham *Lancs* 80 3627
Lytham St Anne's *Lancs* 80 3427
Lythbank *Shrops* 59 4607
Lythe *N York* 90 8413
Lythmore *Highld* 150 0566

# M

Mabe Burnthouse *Cnwll* 3 7634
Mabie *D & G* 100 9570
Mablethorpe *Lincs* 77 5085
Macclesfield *Ches* 79 9173
Macduff *Abers* 142 7064
Macharioch *Ag & B* 105 7309
Machen *Caerph* 33 2189
Machire *Ag & B* 112 2164
Machrie *N Ayrs* 105 8934
Machrihanish *Ag & B* 104 6320
Machrins *Ag & B* 112 3693
Machynlleth *Powys* 57 7400
Machynys *Carmth* 32 5198
Mackworth *Derbys* 62 3137
Macmerry *E Loth* 118 4372
Maddaford *Devon* 8 5494
Madderty *P & K* 125 9522
Maddington *Wilts* 23 0744
Maddiston *Falk* 116 9476
Madehurst *W Susx* 14 9810
Madeley *Shrops* 60 6904
Madeley *Staffs* 72 7744
Madeley Heath *Staffs* 72 7845
Madford *Devon* 9 1411
Madingley *Cambs* 52 3960
Madley *Herefd* 46 4238
Madresfield *Worcs* 47 8047
Madron *Cnwll* 2 4531
Maen-y-groes *Cerdgn* 42 3858
Maenaddwyn *IOA* 68 4684
Maenan *Conwy* 69 7965
Maenclochog *Pembks* 31 0827
Maendy *V Glam* 33 0076
Maenporth *Cnwll* 3 7829
Maentwrog *Gwynd* 57 6640
Maer *Cnwll* 18 2008
Maer *Staffs* 72 7938
Maerdy *Carmth* 44 6527
Maerdy *Rhondd* 33 9798
Maes-glas *Newpt* 34 2985
Maesbrook *Shrops* 59 3021
Maesbury *Shrops* 59 3026
Maesbury Marsh *Shrops* 59 3125
Maesgwynne *Carmth* 31 2024
Maeshafn *Denbgs* 70 2061
Maesllyn *Cerdgn* 42 3644
Maesmynis *Powys* 45 0146
Maesmynis *Powys* 45 0350
Maesteg *Brdgnd* 33 8590
Maesybont *Carmth* 32 5616
Maesycwmmer *Caerph* 33 1594
Magdalen Laver *Essex* 39 5108
Maggieknockater *Moray* 141 3145
Maggots End *Essex* 39 4827
Magham Down *E Susx* 16 6011
Maghull *Mersyd* 78 3703
Magor *Mons* 34 4286
Maiden Bradley *Wilts* 22 8038
Maiden Head *Somset* 21 5666
Maiden Law *Dur* 96 1749
Maiden Newton *Dorset* 10 5997
Maiden Wells *Pembks* 30 9799
Maidencombe *Devon* 7 9268
Maidenhayne *Devon* 10 2795
Maidenhead *Berks* 26 8980
Maidens *S Ayrs* 106 2107
Maidens Green *Berks* 25 8972
Maidenwell *Lincs* 77 3179
Maidford *Nhants* 49 6052
Maids Moreton *Bucks* 49 7035
Maidstone *Kent* 28 7555
Maidwell *Nhants* 50 7476
Maindee *Newpt* 34 3288
Mains of Balhall *Angus* 134 5163
Mains of Balnakettle *Abers* 134 6274
Mains of Dalvey *Highld* 141 1132
Mains of Haulkerton *Abers* 135 7172
Mainsforth *Dur* 96 3131
Mainsriddle *D & G* 92 9456
Mainstone *Shrops* 58 2787
Maisemore *Gloucs* 35 8121
Major's Green *Worcs* 61 1077
Makeney *Derbys* 62 3544
Malborough *Devon* 7 7139
Malcoff *Derbys* 74 0782
Malden *Surrey* 26 2166
Malden Rushett *Gt Lon* 26 1761
Maldon *Essex* 40 8506
Malham *N York* 88 9063
Mallaig *Highld* 129 6796
Mallaigvaig *Highld* 129 6897
Malleny Mills *C Edin* 117 1665
Mallows Green *Essex* 39 4726
Malltraeth *IOA* 68 4068
Mallwyd *Gwynd* 57 8612
Malmesbury *Wilts* 35 9387
Malmsmead *Somset* 19 7947
Malpas *Ches* 71 4847
Malpas *Cnwll* 3 8442
Malpas *Newpt* 34 3090
Maltby *Lincs* 77 3183
Maltby *N York* 89 4613
Maltby *S York* 75 5392
Maltby le Marsh *Lincs* 77 4681
Malting Green *Essex* 41 9720
Maltman's Hill *Kent* 28 9043
Malton *N York* 90 7871
Malvern Link *Worcs* 47 7947
Malvern Wells *Worcs* 47 7742
Malzie *D & G* 99 3754
Mamble *Worcs* 60 6871
Mamhilad *Mons* 34 3003
Manaccan *Cnwll* 3 7624
Manafon *Powys* 58 1102
Manais *W Isls* 152 1089
Manaton *Devon* 8 7581
Manby *Lincs* 77 3986
Mancetter *Warwks* 61 3296
Manchester *Gt Man* 79 8497
Mancot *Flints* 71 3167
Mandally *Highld* 131 2900
Manea *Cambs* 53 4789
Maney *W Mids* 61 1195
Manfield *N York* 89 2113
Mangerton *Dorset* 10 4995
Mangotsfield *Gloucs* 35 6676
Mangrove Green *Herts* 38 1224
Manhay *Cnwll* 2 6930
Manish *W Isls* 152 1089
Mankinholes *W York* 82 9523
Manley *Ches* 71 5071
Manmoel *Caerph* 33 1803
Mannel *Ag & B* 120 9840
Manning's Heath *W Susx* 15 2028
Manningford Bohune *Wilts* 23 1357
Manningford Bruce *Wilts* 23 1358
Manningham *W York* 82 1435
Mannington *Dorset* 12 0605
Manningtree *Essex* 41 1031
Mannofield *Aber C* 135 9104
Manor Park *Gt Lon* 27 4285
Manorbier *Pembks* 30 0697
Manorbier Newton *Pembks* 30 0400
Manordeilo *Carmth* 44 6726
Manorhill *Border* 110 6632
Manorowen *Pembks* 30 9336
Mansell Gamage *Herefd* 46 3944
Mansell Lacy *Herefd* 46 4245
Mansergh *Cumb* 87 6082
Mansfield *E Ayrs* 107 6214
Mansfield *Notts* 75 5361
Mansfield Woodhouse *Notts* 75 5363
Mansriggs *Cumb* 86 2980
Manston *Dorset* 11 8115
Manston *Kent* 29 3466
Manston *W York* 83 3634
Manswood *Dorset* 11 9708
Manthorpe *Lincs* 63 9137
Manthorpe *Lincs* 64 0715
Manton *Lincs* 84 9302
Manton *Notts* 75 6078
Manton *Rutlnd* 63 8704
Manton *Wilts* 23 1768
Manuden *Essex* 39 4926
Manwood Green *Essex* 39 5412
Maperton *Somset* 22 6726
Maple Cross *Herts* 26 0393
Maplebeck *Notts* 75 7060
Mapledurham *Oxon* 37 6776
Mapledurwell *Hants* 24 6851
Maplehurst *W Susx* 15 1824
Maplescombe *Kent* 27 5664
Mapleton *Derbys* 73 1647
Mapleton *Kent* 16 4649
Mapperley *Derbys* 62 4342
Mapperley Park *Notts* 62 5842
Mapperton *Dorset* 10 5099
Mappleborough Green *Warwks* 48 0866
Mappleton *E R Yk* 85 2243
Mapplewell *S York* 83 3210
Mappowder *Dorset* 11 7306
Marazanvose *Cnwll* 3 7950
Marazion *Cnwll* 2 5130
Marbury *Ches* 71 5645
March *Cambs* 65 4196
March *S Lans* 108 9914
Marcham *Oxon* 37 4596
Marchamley *Shrops* 59 5929
Marchamley Wood *Shrops* 59 5831
Marchington *Staffs* 73 1330
Marchington Woodlands *Staffs* 73 1128
Marchros *Gwynd* 56 3125
Marchwiel *Wrexhm* 71 3547
Marchwood *Hants* 12 3810
Marcross *V Glam* 20 9269
Marden *Herefd* 46 5146
Marden *Kent* 28 7444
Marden *Wilts* 23 0857
Marden Ash *Essex* 27 5502
Marden Beech *Kent* 28 7442
Marden Thorn *Kent* 28 7642
Mardens Hill *E Susx* 16 5032
Mardlebury *Herts* 39 2618
Mardy *Mons* 34 3015
Marefield *Leics* 63 7407
Mareham le Fen *Lincs* 77 2761
Mareham on the Hill *Lincs* 77 2867
Marehay *Derbys* 62 3947
Marehill *W Susx* 14 0618
Maresfield *E Susx* 16 4624
Marfleet *E R Yk* 85 1429
Marford *Wrexhm* 71 3556
Margam *Neath* 32 7887
Margaret Marsh *Dorset* 22 8218
Margaret Roding *Essex* 40 5912
Margaretting *Essex* 40 6701
Margaretting Tye *Essex* 40 6800
Margate *Kent* 29 3571
Margnaheglish *N Ayrs* 105 0332
Margrie *D & G* 99 5950
Margrove Park *N York* 97 6515
Marham *Norfk* 65 7009
Marhamchurch *Cnwll* 18 2203
Marholm *Cambs* 64 1401
Marian-glas *IOA* 68 5084
Mariansleigh *Devon* 19 7422
Marine Town *Kent* 28 9274
Marionburgh *Abers* 135 7006
Marishader *Highld* 136 4963
Maristow *Devon* 6 4764
Marjoriebanks *D & G* 100 0883
Mark *D & G* 98 1157
Mark *Somset* 21 3847
Mark Causeway *Somset* 21 3547
Mark Cross *E Susx* 16 5010
Mark Cross *E Susx* 16 5831
Mark's Corner *IOW* 13 4692
Markbeech *Kent* 16 4742
Markby *Lincs* 77 4878
Markeaton *Derbys* 62 3237
Market Bosworth *Leics* 62 4002
Market Deeping *Lincs* 64 1310
Market Drayton *Shrops* 72 6734
Market Harborough *Leics* 50 7387
Market Lavington *Wilts* 22 0154
Market Overton *Rutlnd* 63 8816
Market Rasen *Lincs* 76 1089
Market Stainton *Lincs* 76 2279
Market Weighton *E R Yk* 84 8741
Market Weston *Suffk* 54 9877
Markfield *Leics* 62 4809
Markham *Caerph* 33 1601
Markham Moor *Notts* 75 7173
Markinch *Fife* 126 2901
Markington *N York* 89 2865
Markle *E Loth* 118 5777
Marks Tey *Essex* 40 9023
Marksbury *Somset* 22 6662
Markwell *Cnwll* 5 3758
Markyate *Herts* 38 0616
Marl Bank *Worcs* 47 7840
Marlborough *Wilts* 23 1868
Marlbrook *Herefd* 46 5154
Marlbrook *Worcs* 60 9774
Marlcliff *Warwks* 48 0950
Marldon *Devon* 7 8663
Marle Green *E Susx* 16 5816
Marlesford *Suffk* 55 3258
Marley *Kent* 29 1850
Marley *Kent* 29 3353
Marley Green *Ches* 71 5845
Marley Hill *T & W* 96 2058
Marlingford *Norfk* 66 1309
Marloes *Pembks* 30 7908
Marlow *Bucks* 26 8486
Marlow *Herefd* 46 4076
Marlpit Hill *Kent* 16 4347
Marlpits *E Susx* 16 4528
Marlpits *E Susx* 16 7013
Marlpool *Derbys* 62 4345
Marnhull *Dorset* 22 7818
Marple *Gt Man* 79 9588
Marple Bridge *Gt Man* 79 9688
Marr *S York* 83 5105
Marrick *N York* 88 0798
Marros *Carmth* 31 2008
Marsden *T & W* 103 3964
Marsden *W York* 82 0411
Marsden Height *Lancs* 81 8636
Marsett *N York* 88 9085
Marsh *Bucks* 38 8109
Marsh *Devon* 10 2510
Marsh *W York* 82 0235
Marsh Baldon *Oxon* 37 5699
Marsh Chapel *Lincs* 77 3599
Marsh Gibbon *Bucks* 37 6422
Marsh Green *Devon* 9 0493
Marsh Green *Kent* 16 4344
Marsh Green *Shrops* 59 6014
Marsh Green *Staffs* 72 8858
Marsh Lane *Derbys* 74 4079
Marsh Lane *Gloucs* 34 5807
Marsh Street *Somset* 20 9944
Marshall's Heath *Herts* 39 1614
Marshalswick *Herts* 39 1608
Marsham *Norfk* 67 1923
Marshborough *Kent* 29 3057
Marshbrook *Shrops* 59 4489
Marshfield *Gloucs* 35 7873
Marshfield *Newpt* 34 2582
Marshgate *Cnwll* 4 1592
Marshland Green *Gt Man* 79 6899
Marshland St James *Norfk* 65 5209
Marshside *Mersyd* 80 3619
Marshwood *Dorset* 10 3899
Marske *N York* 89 1000
Marske-by-the-Sea *N York* 97 6322
Marston *Ches* 79 6775
Marston *Herefd* 46 3557
Marston *Lincs* 63 8943
Marston *Oxon* 37 5208
Marston *Staffs* 60 8313
Marston *Staffs* 72 9227
Marston *Warwks* 61 2094
Marston *Wilts* 22 9656
Marston Green *W Mids* 61 1785
Marston Jabbet *Warwks* 61 3788
Marston Magna *Somset* 21 5922
Marston Meysey *Wilts* 36 1297
Marston Montgomery *Derbys* 73 1337
Marston Moretaine *Beds* 38 9941
Marston on Dove *Derbys* 73 2329
Marston St Lawrence *Nhants* 49 5341
Marston Stannett *Herefd* 46 5655
Marston Trussell *Nhants* 50 6985
Marstow *Herefd* 34 5518
Marsworth *Bucks* 38 9114
Marten *Wilts* 23 2860
Marthall *Ches* 79 7975
Martham *Norfk* 67 4518
Martin *Hants* 12 0619
Martin *Kent* 29 3447
Martin *Lincs* 76 1259
Martin *Lincs* 77 2466
Martin Dales *Lincs* 76 1762
Martin Drove End *Hants* 12 0520
Martin Hussingtree *Worcs* 47 8860
Martindale *Cumb* 93 4319
Martinhoe *Devon* 19 6648
Martinscroft *Ches* 79 6589
Martinstown *Dorset* 11 6489
Martlesham *Suffk* 55 2547
Martletwy *Pembks* 30 0310
Martley *Worcs* 47 7560
Martock *Somset* 21 4619
Marton *Ches* 71 6267
Marton *Ches* 79 8568

Milton Street Neatham


Milton Street *E Susx* 16 5304
Milton-under-Wychwood *Oxon* 36 2618
Milverton *Somset* 20 1225
Milverton *Warwks* 48 3166
Milwich *Staffs* 72 9632
Milwr *Flints* 70 1974
Minard Ag & B 114 9796
Minchington *Dorset* 11 9614
Minchinhampton *Gloucs* 35 8700
Mindrum *Nthumb* 110 8432
Mindrum Mill *Nthumb* 110 8533
Minehead *Somset* 20 9646
Minera *Wrexhm* 70 2751
Minety *Wilts* 36 0290
Minffordd *Gwynd* 57 5938
Mingarrypark *Highld* 129 6869
Miningsby *Lincs* 77 3264
Minions *Cnwll* 5 2671
Minishant *S Ayrs* 106 3314
Minllyn *Gwynd* 57 8514
Minnigaff *D & G* 99 4166
Minnis Bay *Kent* 29 2869
Minnonie *Abers* 142 7760
Minskip *N York* 89 3864
Minstead *Hants* 12 2811
Minsted *W Susx* 14 8520
Minster *Kent* 28 9573
Minster *Kent* 29 3064
Minster Lovell *Oxon* 36 3111
Minsteracres *Nthumb* 95 0156
Minsterley *Shrops* 59 3705
Minsterworth *Gloucs* 35 7817
Minterne Magna *Dorset* 11 6504
Minterne Parva *Dorset* 11 6603
Minting *Lincs* 76 1873
Mintlaw *Abers* 143 9948
Minto *Border* 109 5620
Minton *Shrops* 59 4390
Minwear *Pembks* 30 0413
Minworth *W Mids* 61 1691
Mirehouse *Cumb* 92 9715
Mirfield *W York* 82 2019
Miserden *Gloucs* 35 9308
Miskin *Rhondd* 33 0480
Miskin *Rhondd* 33 0498
Misson *Notts* 75 6895
Misterton *Leics* 50 5583
Misterton *Notts* 75 7694
Misterton *Somset* 10 4508
Mistley *Essex* 41 1231
Mistley Heath *Essex* 41 1230
Mitcham *Gt Lon* 27 2768
Mitchel Troy *Mons* 34 4910
Mitcheldean *Gloucs* 35 6618
Mitchell *Cnwll* 3 8554
Mitchellslacks *D & G* 100 9696
Mitford *Nthumb* 103 1786
Mithian *Cnwll* 3 7450
Mitton *Staffs* 72 8815
Mixbury *Oxon* 49 6033
Mixenden *W York* 82 0629
Mixon *Staffs* 74 0457
Moats Tye *Suffk* 54 0455
Mobberley *Ches* 79 7879
Mobberley *Staffs* 73 0041
Moccas *Herefd* 46 3542
Mochdre *Conwy* 69 8278
Mochdre *Powys* 58 0788
Mochrum *D & G* 98 3446
Mockbeggar *Hants* 12 1609
Mockbeggar *Kent* 28 7146
Mockerkin *Cumb* 92 0923
Modbury *Devon* 7 6651
Moddershall *Staffs* 72 9236
Moel Tryfan *Gwynd* 68 5156
Moelfre *IOA* 68 5186
Moelfre *Powys* 58 1828
Moffat *D & G* 108 0805
Mogerhanger *Beds* 52 1449
Moira *Leics* 62 3115
Mol-chlach *Highld* 128 4513
Molash *Kent* 28 0251
Mold *Flints* 70 2363
Moldgreen *W York* 82 1516
Molehill Green *Essex* 40 5624
Molehill Green *Essex* 40 7120
Molescroft *E R Yk* 84 0140
Molesden *Nthumb* 103 1484
Molesworth *Cambs* 51 0775
Molland *Devon* 19 8028
Mollington *Ches* 71 3870
Mollington *Oxon* 49 4447
Mollinsburn *N Lans* 116 7171
Monachty *Cerdgn* 44 5061
Monday Boys *Kent* 28 9045
Mondynes *Abers* 135 7779
Monewden *Suffk* 55 2358
Moneydie *P & K* 125 0629
Moneyrow Green *Berks* 26 8977
Moniaive *D & G* 107 7890
Monifieth *Angus* 127 4932
Monikie *Angus* 127 4938
Monimail *Fife* 126 2914
Monington *Pembks* 42 1344
Monk Bretton *S York* 83 3607
Monk Fryston *N York* 83 5029
Monk Sherborne *Hants* 24 6056
Monk Soham *Suffk* 55 2165
Monk Soham Green *Suffk* 55 2066
Monk Street *Essex* 40 6128
Monk's Gate *W Susx* 15 2027
Monken Hadley *Gt Lon* 26 2497
Monkhide *Herefd* 46 6144
Monkhill *Cumb* 93 3458
Monkhopton *Shrops* 59 6293
Monkland *Herefd* 46 4557
Monkleigh *Devon* 18 4520
Monknash *V Glam* 33 9170
Monkokehampton *Devon* 8 5805
Monks Eleigh *Suffk* 54 9647
Monks Heath *Ches* 79 8474
Monks Horton *Kent* 29 1139
Monks Kirby *Warwks* 50 4683
Monks Risborough *Bucks* 38 8104
Monkseaton *T & W* 103 3472
Monksilver *Somset* 20 0737
Monkspath *W Mids* 61 1376
Monksthorpe *Lincs* 77 4465
Monkswood *Mons* 34 3402
Monkton *Devon* 9 1803
Monkton *Kent* 29 2964
Monkton *S Ayrs* 106 3527
Monkton *T & W* 103 3363
Monkton *V Glam* 33 9270
Monkton Combe *Somset* 22 7762
Monkton Deverill *Wilts* 22 8537
Monkton Farleigh *Wilts* 22 8065
Monkton Heathfield *Somset* 20 2526
Monkton Up Wimborne *Dorset* 11 0113
Monkton Wyld *Dorset* 10 3396
Monkwearmouth *T & W* 96 3958
Monkwood *Hants* 24 6630
Monmore Green *W Mids* 60 9297
Monmouth *Mons* 34 5012
Monnington on Wye *Herefd* 46 3743
Monreith *D & G* 98 3541
Mont Saint *Guern* 158 0000
Montacute *Somset* 10 4916
Montcliffe *Gt Man* 81 6611
Montford *Shrops* 59 4114
Montford Bridge *Shrops* 59 4215
Montgarrie *Abers* 142 5717
Montgarswood *E Ayrs* 107 5227
Montgomery *Powys* 58 2296
Montgreenan *N Ayrs* 106 3343
Monton *Gt Man* 79 7699
Montrose *Angus* 135 7157
Monxton *Hants* 23 3144
Monyash *Derbys* 74 1566
Monymusk *Abers* 142 6815
Monzie *P & K* 125 8725
Moodiesburn *N Lans* 116 6970
Moonzie *Fife* 126 3317
Moor Allerton *W York* 82 3038
Moor Crichel *Dorset* 11 9908
Moor End *Beds* 38 9719
Moor End *Devon* 19 6609
Moor End *E R Yk* 84 8137
Moor End *Lancs* 80 3744
Moor End *N York* 83 6038
Moor End *W York* 82 0528
Moor Green *Herts* 39 3226
Moor Head *W York* 82 2329
Moor Monkton *N York* 83 5156
Moor Row *Cumb* 92 0014
Moor Row *Cumb* 93 2149
Moor Row *Dur* 96 1515
Moor Side *Lancs* 80 4935
Moor Side *Lancs* 80 4334
Moor Side *Lincs* 77 2557
Moor Street *Kent* 28 8265
Moor Street *W Mids* 60 9982
Moorbath *Dorset* 10 4395
Moorby *Lincs* 77 2964
Moorcot *Herefd* 46 3555
Moordown *Dorset* 12 0994
Moore *Ches* 78 5784
Moorend *Gloucs* 35 7303
Moorends *S York* 83 6915
Moorgreen *Hants* 13 4815
Moorgreen *Notts* 62 4847
Moorhall *Derbys* 74 3074
Moorhampton *Herefd* 46 3746
Moorhead *W York* 82 1337
Moorhouse *Cumb* 93 2551
Moorhouse *Cumb* 93 3356
Moorhouse *Notts* 75 7566
Moorhouse *W York* 83 4810
Moorhouse Bank *Surrey* 27 4353
Moorland *Somset* 21 3332
Moorlinch *Somset* 21 3936
Moorsholm *N York* 90 6814
Moorside *Cumb* 86 0701
Moorside *Dorset* 22 7919
Moorside *Gt Man* 79 9407
Moorside *W York* 82 2436
Moorstock *Kent* 29 1038
Moorswater *Cnwll* 5 2364
Moorthorpe *W York* 83 4611
Moortown *Devon* 6 5274
Moortown *Hants* 12 1503
Moortown *IOW* 13 4283
Moortown *Lincs* 76 0798
Moortown *Shrops* 59 6118
Moortown *W York* 82 2939
Morangie *Highld* 147 7683
Morar *Highld* 129 6793
Morborne *Cambs* 64 1391
Morchard Bishop *Devon* 8 7707
Morcombelake *Dorset* 10 4094
Morcott *Rutlnd* 51 9200
Morda *Shrops* 58 2827
Morden *Dorset* 11 9195
Morden *Gt Lon* 27 2666
Mordiford *Herefd* 46 5737
Mordon *Dur* 96 3226
More *Shrops* 59 3491
Morebath *Devon* 20 9525
Morebattle *Border* 110 7724
Morecambe *Lancs* 87 4364
Moredon *Wilts* 36 1487
Morefield *Highld* 145 1195
Morehall *Kent* 29 2136
Moreleigh *Devon* 7 7652
Morenish *P & K* 124 6035
Moresby *Cumb* 92 9921
Moresby Parks *Cumb* 92 9919
Morestead *Hants* 13 5025
Moreton *Dorset* 11 8089
Moreton *Essex* 39 5307
Moreton *Herefd* 46 5064
Moreton *Mersyd* 78 2689
Moreton *Oxon* 37 6904
Moreton *Staffs* 72 7817
Moreton *Staffs* 73 1429
Moreton Corbet *Shrops* 59 5623
Moreton Jeffries *Herefd* 46 6048
Moreton Morrell *Warwks* 48 3155
Moreton on Lugg *Herefd* 46 5045
Moreton Paddox *Warwks* 48 3154
Moreton Pinkney *Nhants* 49 5749
Moreton Say *Shrops* 59 6334
Moreton Valence *Gloucs* 35 7809
Moreton-in-Marsh *Gloucs* 48 2032
Moretonhampstead *Devon* 8 7586
Moretonmill *Shrops* 59 5723
Morfa *Cerdgn* 42 3053
Morfa Bychan *Gwynd* 57 5437
Morfa Dinlle *Gwynd* 68 4358
Morfa Glas *Neath* 33 8606
Morfa Nefyn *Gwynd* 56 2840
Morgan's Vale *Wilts* 12 1920
Morganstown *Cardif* 33 1281
Morham *E Loth* 118 5571
Moriah *Cerdgn* 43 6279
Morland *Cumb* 94 6022
Morley *Ches* 79 8282
Morley *Derbys* 62 3940
Morley *Dur* 96 1227
Morley *W York* 82 2627
Morley Green *Ches* 79 8281
Morley St Botolph *Norfk* 66 0799
Mornick *Cnwll* 5 3272
Morningside *C Edin* 117 2470
Morningside *N Lans* 116 8355
Morningthorpe *Norfk* 67 2192
Morpeth *Nthumb* 103 1986
Morphie *Abers* 135 7164
Morrey *Staffs* 73 1218
Morridge Side *Staffs* 73 0254
Morridge Top *Staffs* 74 0365
Morriston *Swans* 32 6697
Morston *Norfk* 66 0043
Mortehoe *Devon* 18 4545
Morthen *S York* 75 4788
Mortimer *Berks* 24 6564
Mortimer Common *Berks* 24 6565
Mortimer West End *Hants* 24 6363
Mortimer's Cross *Herefd* 46 4263
Mortlake *Gt Lon* 26 2075
Morton *Cumb* 93 3854
Morton *Cumb* 93 4539
Morton *Derbys* 74 4060
Morton *IOW* 13 6085
Morton *Lincs* 75 8091
Morton *Lincs* 64 0923
Morton *Norfk* 66 1216
Morton *Notts* 75 7251
Morton *Shrops* 59 2924
Morton Hall *Lincs* 76 8863
Morton Tinmouth *Dur* 96 1821
Morton-on-Swale *N York* 89 3291
Morvah *Cnwll* 2 4035
Morval *Cnwll* 5 2556
Morvich *Highld* 138 9621
Morville *Shrops* 60 6794
Morville Heath *Shrops* 60 6893
Morwenstow *Cnwll* 18 2015
Mosborough *S York* 74 4281
Moscow *E Ayrs* 107 4840
Mose *Shrops* 60 7590
Mosedale *Cumb* 93 3532
Moseley *W Mids* 60 9498
Moseley *W Mids* 61 0783
Moseley *Worcs* 47 8159
Moses Gate *Gt Man* 79 7306
Moss *Ag & B* 120 9544
Moss *S York* 83 5914
Moss *Wrexhm* 71 3053
Moss Bank *Mersyd* 78 5197
Moss Edge *Lancs* 80 4243
Moss End *Ches* 79 6778
Moss Side *Cumb* 93 1952
Moss Side *Lancs* 80 3730
Moss Side *Mersyd* 78 3802
Moss Side *Mersyd* 78 3107
Moss-side *Highld* 140 8555
Mossat *Abers* 142 4719
Mossbank *Shet* 153 4575
Mossbay *Cumb* 92 9927
Mossblown *S Ayrs* 106 4024
Mossbrow *Gt Man* 79 7089
Mossburnford *Border* 110 6616
Mossdale *D & G* 99 6670
Mossdale *E Ayrs* 107 4904
Mossend *N Lans* 116 7460
Mosser Mains *Cumb* 92 1125
Mossgiel *E Ayrs* 107 4828
Mossknowe *D & G* 101 2769
Mossley *Ches* 72 8861
Mossley *Gt Man* 82 9701
Mosspaul Hotel *Border* 109 3999
Mosstodloch *Moray* 141 3259
Mossy Lea *Lancs* 80 5312
Mossyard *D & G* 99 5451
Mosterton *Dorset* 10 4505
Moston *Gt Man* 79 8701
Moston *Shrops* 59 5626
Moston Green *Ches* 72 7261
Mostyn *Flints* 70 1580
Motcombe *Dorset* 22 8525
Mothecombe *Devon* 6 6047
Motherby *Cumb* 93 4228
Motherwell *N Lans* 116 7457
Motspur Park *Gt Lon* 26 2267
Mottingham *Gt Lon* 27 4272
Mottisfont *Hants* 23 3226
Mottistone *IOW* 13 4083
Mottram in Longdendale *Gt Man* 79 9995
Mottram St Andrew *Ches* 79 8778
Mouilpied *Guern* 158 0000
Mouldsworth *Ches* 71 5071
Moulin *P & K* 132 9459
Moulsecoomb *E Susx* 15 3307
Moulsford *Oxon* 37 5883
Moulsoe *Bucks* 38 9141
Moultavie *Highld* 146 6371
Moulton *Ches* 79 6569
Moulton *Lincs* 64 3023
Moulton *N York* 89 2303
Moulton *Nhants* 50 7866
Moulton *Suffk* 53 6964
Moulton *V Glam* 33 0770
Moulton Chapel *Lincs* 64 2918
Moulton Seas End *Lincs* 64 3227
Moulton St Mary *Norfk* 67 3907
Mount *Cnwll* 3 7856
Mount *Cnwll* 4 1468
Mount *W York* 82 0917
Mount Ambrose *Cnwll* 2 7043
Mount Bures *Essex* 40 9032
Mount Hawke *Cnwll* 2 7147
Mount Hermon *Cnwll* 2 6915
Mount Lothian *Mdloth* 117 2757
Mount Pleasant *Ches* 72 8456
Mount Pleasant *Derbys* 74 3448
Mount Pleasant *Dur* 96 2634
Mount Pleasant *E Susx* 16 4216
Mount Pleasant *Norfk* 66 9994
Mount Pleasant *Suffk* 53 7347
Mount Pleasant *Worcs* 47 0064
Mount Sorrel *Wilts* 23 0324
Mount Tabor *W York* 82 0527
Mountain *W York* 82 0930
Mountain Ash *Rhondd* 33 0499
Mountain Cross *Border* 117 1547
Mountain Street *Kent* 29 0652
Mountfield *E Susx* 17 7320
Mountgerald House *Highld* 139 5661
Mountjoy *Cnwll* 4 8760
Mountnessing *Essex* 40 6297
Mounton *Mons* 34 5193
Mountsorrel *Leics* 62 5814
Mousehill *Surrey* 25 9441
Mousehole *Cnwll* 2 4626
Mouswald *D & G* 100 0672
Mow Cop *Ches* 72 8557
Mowhaugh *Border* 110 8120
Mowmacre Hill *Leics* 62 5807
Mowsley *Leics* 50 6489
Mowtie *Abers* 135 8388
Moy *Highld* 140 7634
Moy *Highld* 131 4282
Moye *Highld* 138 8818
Moyles Court *Hants* 12 1608
Moylgrove *Pembks* 42 1144
Muasdale *Ag & B* 105 6840
Much Birch *Herefd* 46 5030
Much Cowarne *Herefd* 46 6147
Much Dewchurch *Herefd* 46 4831
Much Hadham *Herts* 39 4219
Much Hoole *Lancs* 80 4723
Much Hoole Town *Lancs* 80 4722
Much Marcle *Herefd* 47 6532
Much Wenlock *Shrops* 59 6299
Muchalls *Abers* 135 9092
Muchelney *Somset* 21 4224
Muchelney Ham *Somset* 21 4423
Muchlarnick *Cnwll* 5 2156
Mucking *Essex* 40 6881
Muckingford *Essex* 40 6779
Muckleford *Dorset* 10 6393
Mucklestone *Staffs* 72 7237
Muckley *Shrops* 59 6495
Muckton *Lincs* 77 3781
Mucomir *Highld* 131 1884
Mud Row *Kent* 28 0072
Muddiford *Devon* 19 5638
Muddles Green *E Susx* 16 5413
Mudeford *Dorset* 12 1892
Mudford *Somset* 21 5719
Mudford Sock *Somset* 21 5519
Mudgley *Somset* 21 4545
Mugdock *Stirlg* 115 5577
Mugeary *Highld* 136 4439
Mugginton *Derbys* 73 2842
Muggintonlane End *Derbys* 73 2844
Muggleswick *Dur* 95 0449
Muir of Fowlis *Abers* 134 5612
Muir of Miltonduff *Moray* 141 1859
Muir of Ord *Highld* 139 5250
Muir of Thorn *P & K* 125 0637
Muirden *Abers* 142 7054
Muirdrum *Angus* 127 5637
Muiresk *Abers* 142 6948
Muirhead *Angus* 126 3434
Muirhead *Fife* 126 2805
Muirhead *N Lans* 116 6869
Muirhouses *Falk* 117 0180
Muirkirk *E Ayrs* 107 6927
Muirmill *Stirlg* 116 7283
Muirshearlich *Highld* 131 1380
Muirtack *Abers* 143 9937
Muirton *P & K* 125 9211
Muirton Mains *Highld* 139 4553
Muirton of Ardblair *P & K* 126 1643
Muker *N York* 88 9097
Mulbarton *Norfk* 67 1901
Mulben *Moray* 141 3550
Mulfra *Cnwll* 2 4534
Mullacott Cross *Devon* 19 5144
Mullion *Cnwll* 2 6719
Mullion Cove *Cnwll* 2 6617
Mumby *Lincs* 77 5174
Munderfield Row *Herefd* 47 6451
Munderfield Stocks *Herefd* 47 6550
Mundesley *Norfk* 67 3136
Mundford *Norfk* 66 8093
Mundham *Norfk* 67 3397
Mundon Hill *Essex* 40 8602
Mungrisdale *Cumb* 93 3630
Munlochy *Highld* 140 6453
Munnoch *N Ayrs* 114 2548
Munsley *Herefd* 47 6640
Munslow *Shrops* 59 5287
Murchington *Devon* 8 6888
Murcot *Worcs* 48 0640
Murcott *Oxon* 37 5815
Murcott *Wilts* 35 9591
Murkle *Highld* 151 1668
Murlaggan *Highld* 130 0192
Murrell Green *Hants* 24 7455
Murroes *Angus* 127 4635
Murrow *Cambs* 64 3707
Mursley *Bucks* 38 8128
Murston *Kent* 28 9264
Murthill *Angus* 134 4657
Murthly *P & K* 126 1038
Murton *Cumb* 94 7221
Murton *Dur* 96 3847
Murton *N York* 83 6452
Murton *Nthumb* 111 9748
Murton *T & W* 103 3270
Musbury *Devon* 10 2794
Muscoates *N York* 90 6879
Musselburgh *E Loth* 118 3472
Muston *Leics* 63 8237
Muston *N York* 91 0979
Mustow Green *Worcs* 60 8774
Muswell Hill *Gt Lon* 27 2889
Mutehill *D & G* 99 6848
Mutford *Suffk* 55 4888
Muthill *P & K* 125 8717
Mutterton *Devon* 9 0205
Muxton *Shrops* 60 7114
Mybster *Highld* 151 1652
Myddfai *Carmth* 44 7730
Myddle *Shrops* 59 4623
Mydroilyn *Cerdgn* 42 4555
Mylor *Cnwll* 3 8135
Mylor Bridge *Cnwll* 3 8036
Mynachlog ddu *Pembks* 31 1430
Myndd-llan *Flints* 70 1572
Myndtown *Shrops* 59 3989
Mynydd Buch *Cerdgn* 43 7276
Mynydd Isa *Flints* 70 2563
Mynydd Llandygai *Gwynd* 69 6065
Mynydd-bach *Mons* 34 4894
Mynydd-Bach *Swans* 32 6597
Mynyddgarreg *Carmth* 31 4208
Mynytho *Gwynd* 56 3031
Myrebird *Abers* 135 7398
Myredykes *Border* 102 5998
Mytchett *Surrey* 25 8855
Mytholm *W York* 82 9827
Mytholmroyd *W York* 82 0126
Mythop *Lancs* 80 3634
Myton-on-Swale *N York* 89 4366


# N


Na Buirgh *W Isls* 152 0394
Naast *Highld* 144 8283
Nab's Head *Lancs* 81 6229
Naburn *N York* 83 5945
Naccolt *Kent* 28 0544
Nackington *Kent* 29 1554
Nacton *Suffk* 55 2240
Nafferton *E R Yk* 91 0559
Nag's Head *Gloucs* 35 8898
Nailbridge *Gloucs* 35 6415
Nailsbourne *Somset* 20 2128
Nailsea *Somset* 34 4770
Nailstone *Leics* 62 4106
Nailsworth *Gloucs* 35 8499
Nairn *Highld* 140 8856
Nalderswood *Surrey* 15 2445
Nancegollan *Cnwll* 2 6332
Nancledra *Cnwll* 2 4936
Nanhoron *Gwynd* 56 2731
Nannerch *Flints* 70 1669
Nanpantan *Leics* 62 5017
Nanpean *Cnwll* 3 9556
Nanquidno *Cnwll* 2 3629
Nanstallon *Cnwll* 4 0367
Nant Gwynant *Gwynd* 69 6350
Nant Peris *Gwynd* 69 6058
Nant-ddu *Powys* 33 0014
Nant-glas *Powys* 45 9965
Nant-y-Bwch *Blae G* 33 1210
Nant-y-caws *Carmth* 32 4518
Nant-y-derry *Mons* 34 3306
Nant-y-gollen *Shrops* 58 2428
Nant-y-moel *Brdgnd* 33 9392
Nant-y-pandy *Conwy* 69 6973
Nanternis *Cerdgn* 42 3756
Nantgaredig *Carmth* 32 4921
Nantgarw *Rhondd* 33 1285
Nantglyn *Denbgs* 70 0061
Nantgwyn *Powys* 45 9776
Nantlle *Gwynd* 68 5153
Nantmawr *Shrops* 58 2524
Nantmel *Powys* 45 0366
Nantmor *Gwynd* 57 6046
Nantwich *Ches* 72 6552
Nantyffyllon *Brdgnd* 33 8492
Nantyglo *Blae G* 33 1910
Naphill *Bucks* 26 8496
Napleton *Worcs* 47 8648
Nappa *N York* 81 8553
Napton on the Hill *Warwks* 49 4661
Narberth *Pembks* 31 1015
Narborough *Leics* 50 5497
Narborough *Norfk* 65 7412
Narkurs *Cnwll* 5 3255
Nasareth *Gwynd* 68 4749
Naseby *Nhants* 50 6978
Nash *Bucks* 38 7833
Nash *Gt Lon* 27 4063
Nash *Herefd* 46 3062
Nash *Newpt* 34 3483
Nash *Shrops* 46 6071
Nash End *Worcs* 60 7781
Nash Lee *Bucks* 38 8408
Nash Street *Kent* 27 6469
Nash's Green *Hants* 24 6745
Nassington *Nhants* 51 0696
Nastend *Gloucs* 35 7906
Nasty *Herts* 39 3524
Nateby *Cumb* 88 7706
Nateby *Lancs* 80 4644
Natland *Cumb* 87 5289
Naughton *Suffk* 54 0249
Naunton *Gloucs* 48 1123
Naunton *Worcs* 47 8739
Naunton Beauchamp *Worcs* 47 9652
Navenby *Lincs* 76 9858
Navestock *Essex* 27 5397
Navestock Side *Essex* 27 5697
Navidale House Hotel *Highld* 147 0316
Navity *Highld* 140 7864
Nawton *N York* 90 6584
Nayland *Suffk* 54 9734
Nazeing *Essex* 39 4106
Nazeing Gate *Essex* 39 4105
Neacroft *Hants* 12 1896
Neal's Green *Warwks* 61 3384
Neap *Shet* 153 5058
Near Cotton *Staffs* 73 0646
Near Sawrey *Cumb* 87 3795
Neasden *Gt Lon* 26 2185
Neasham *Dur* 89 3210
Neath *Neath* 32 7597
Neatham *Hants* 24 7440


299

**300**

Nightcott

Old Harlow

301

Nightcott *Somset* 19 8925
Nimlet *Somset* 35 7470
Nine Elms *Wilts* 36 1085
Nine Wells *Pembks* 30 7924
Ninebanks *Nthumb* 94 7853
Nineveh *Worcs* 47 6265
Ninfield *E Susx* 16 7012
Ningwood *IOW* 13 3989
Nisbet *Border* 110 6725
Nisbet Hill *Border* 119 7950
Niton *IOW* 13 5076
Nitshill *C Glas* 115 5260
No Man's Heath *Ches* 71 5148
No Man's Heath *Warwks* 61 2808
No Man's Land *Cnwll* 4 9470
No Man's Land *Cnwll* 5 2756
Noah's Ark *Kent* 27 5557
Noak Bridge *Essex* 40 6990
Noak Hill *Essex* 27 5494
Noblethorpe *W York* 82 2805
Nobold *Shrops* 59 4710
Nobottle *Nhants* 49 6763
Nocton *Lincs* 76 0564
Nogdam End *Norfk* 67 3900
Noke *Oxon* 37 5413
Nolton *Pembks* 30 8618
Nolton Haven *Pembks* 30 8618
Nomansland *Devon* 19 8313
Nomansland *Wilts* 12 2517
Noneley *Shrops* 59 4828
Nonington *Kent* 29 2552
Nook *Cumb* 101 4679
Nook *Cumb* 87 5481
Norbiton *Gt Lon* 26 1969
Norbreck *Lancs* 80 3140
Norbridge *Herefd* 47 7144
Norbury *Ches* 71 5547
Norbury *Derbys* 73 1241
Norbury *Gt Lon* 27 3069
Norbury *Shrops* 59 3692
Norbury *Staffs* 72 7823
Norbury Common *Ches* 71 5548
Norbury Junction *Staffs* 72 7923
Norchard *Worcs* 47 8568
Norcott Brook *Ches* 78 6080
Norcross *Lancs* 80 3341
Nordelph *Norfk* 65 5501
Norden *Gt Man* 81 8614
Nordley *Shrops* 60 6996
Norham *Nthumb* 110 9047
Norland Town *W York* 82 0622
Norley *Ches* 71 5772
Norleywood *Hants* 12 3597
Norlington *E Susx* 16 4413
Norman Cross *Cambs* 52 1690
Norman's Bay *E Susx* 16 6805
Norman's Green *Devon* 9 0503
Normanby *Lincs* 84 8816
Normanby *Lincs* 76 9988
Normanby *N York* 97 5418
Normanby *N York* 90 7381
Normanby le Wold *Lincs* 76 1295
Normandy *Surrey* 25 9351
Normanton *Derbys* 62 3433
Normanton *Leics* 63 8140
Normanton *Lincs* 63 9446
Normanton *Notts* 75 7054
Normanton *Rutlnd* 63 9305
Normanton *W York* 83 3822
Normanton *Wilts* 23 1340
Normanton le Heath *Leics* 62 3712
Normanton on Soar *Notts* 62 5122
Normanton on the Wolds *Notts* 62 6232
Normanton on Trent *Notts* 75 7868
Normoss *Lancs* 80 3437
Norney *Surrey* 25 9444
Norrington Common *Wilts* 22 8864
Norris Green *Cnwll* 5 4169
Norristhorpe *W York* 82 2123
North Anston *S York* 75 5184
North Aston *Oxon* 49 4828
North Baddesley *Hants* 13 3920
North Ballachulish *Highld* 130 0560
North Barrow *Somset* 21 6129
North Barsham *Norfk* 66 9135
North Benfleet *Essex* 40 7588
North Bersted *W Susx* 14 9201
North Berwick *E Loth* 118 5485
North Bitchburn *Dur* 96 1732
North Blyth *Nthumb* 103 3082
North Boarhunt *Hants* 13 6010
North Bockhampton *Hants* 12 1797
North Bovey *Devon* 8 7484
North Bradley *Wilts* 22 8555
North Brentor *Devon* 5 4881
North Brewham *Somset* 22 7236
North Bridge *Surrey* 14 9636
North Brook End *Cambs* 39 2944
North Buckland *Devon* 18 4840
North Burlingham *Norfk* 67 3609
North Cadbury *Somset* 21 6327
North Carlton *Lincs* 76 9477
North Carlton *Notts* 75 5984
North Cave *E R Yk* 84 8932
North Cerney *Gloucs* 35 0107
North Charford *Hants* 12 1919
North Charlton *Nthumb* 111 1622
North Cheam *Gt Lon* 26 2365
North Cheriton *Somset* 22 6925
North Chideock *Dorset* 10 4294
North Cliffe *E R Yk* 84 8736
North Clifton *Notts* 75 8272
North Close *Dur* 96 2532
North Cockerington *Lincs* 77 3790
North Common *E Susx* 15 3921
North Connel *Ag & B* 122 9034
North Cornelly *Brdgnd* 33 8181
North Corner *Cnwll* 3 7818
North Corry *Highld* 122 8353
North Cotes *Lincs* 77 3400
North Country *Cnwll* 2 6943
North Cove *Suffk* 55 4689
North Cowton *N York* 89 2803
North Crawley *Bucks* 38 9244
North Cray *Gt Lon* 27 4872
North Creake *Norfk* 66 8538
North Curry *Somset* 21 3125
North Dalton *E R Yk* 84 9351
North Deighton *N York* 83 3951
North Duffield *N York* 83 6837
North Duntulm *Highld* 136 4274
North Elham *Kent* 29 1844
North Elkington *Lincs* 77 2890
North Elmham *Norfk* 66 9820
North Elmsall *W York* 83 4712
North End *Cumb* 93 3259
North End *Dorset* 22 8427
North End *E R Yk* 85 1941
North End *E R Yk* 85 2831
North End *Essex* 40 6618
North End *Hants* 12 1016
North End *Hants* 24 5828
North End *Hants* 13 6502
North End *Leics* 62 5715
North End *Lincs* 85 1022
North End *Lincs* 85 3101
North End *Lincs* 76 0499
North End *Lincs* 64 2341
North End *Lincs* 77 4289
North End *Mersyd* 78 3004
North End *Nhants* 51 9668
North End *Norfk* 66 9992
North End *Nthumb* 103 1301
North End *Somset* 21 4266
North End *W Susx* 14 9703
North End *W Susx* 14 1109
North Erradale *Highld* 144 7480
North Evington *Leics* 62 6204
North Fambridge *Essex* 40 8597
North Ferriby *E R Yk* 84 9826
North Frodingham *E R Yk* 85 1053
North Gorley *Hants* 12 1611
North Green *Norfk* 55 2288
North Green *Suffk* 55 3162
North Green *Suffk* 55 3966
North Grimston *N York* 90 8467
North Halling *Kent* 28 7065
North Hayling *Hants* 13 7303
North Hazelrigg *Nthumb* 111 0533
North Heasley *Devon* 19 7333
North Heath *W Susx* 14 0621
North Hele *Somset* 20 0323
North Hill *Cnwll* 5 2776
North Hillingdon *Gt Lon* 26 0784
North Hinksey *Oxon* 37 4905
North Huish *Devon* 7 7156
North Hykeham *Lincs* 76 9465
North Kelsey *Lincs* 84 0401
North Kessock *Highld* 140 6548
North Killingholme *Lincs* 85 1417
North Kilvington *N York* 89 4285
North Kilworth *Leics* 50 6183
North Kingston *Hants* 12 1603
North Kyme *Lincs* 76 1552
North Landing *E R Yk* 91 2471
North Lee *Bucks* 38 8308
North Lees *N York* 89 2973
North Leigh *Kent* 29 1347
North Leigh *Oxon* 36 3813
North Leverton with
Habblesthorpe *Notts* 75 7882
North Littleton *Worcs* 48 0847
North Lopham *Norfk* 54 0382
North Luffenham *Rutlnd* 63 9303
North Marden *W Susx* 14 8016
North Marston *Bucks* 37 7722
North Middleton *Mdloth* 118 3559
North Middleton *Nthumb* 111 9924
North Milmain *D & G* 98 0852
North Molton *Devon* 19 7329
North Moreton *Oxon* 37 5689
North Mundham *W Susx* 14 8702
North Muskham *Notts* 75 7958
North Newbald *E R Yk* 84 9136
North Newington *Oxon* 49 4240
North Newnton *Wilts* 23 1257
North Newton *Somset* 20 3031
North Nibley *Gloucs* 35 7495
North Oakley *Hants* 24 5354
North Ockendon *Gt Lon* 27 5985
North Ormesby *N York* 97 5119
North Ormsby *Lincs* 77 2893
North Otterington *N York* 89 3689
North Owersby *Lincs* 76 0594
North Perrott *Somset* 10 4709
North Petherton *Somset* 20 2833
North Petherwin *Cnwll* 5 2789
North Pickenham *Norfk* 66 8606
North Piddle *Worcs* 47 9654
North Pool *Devon* 7 7741
North Poorton *Dorset* 10 5298
North Poulner *Hants* 12 1606
North Quarme *Somset* 20 9236
North Queensferry *C Edin* 117 1380
North Radworthy *Devon* 19 7534
North Rauceby *Lincs* 76 0246
North Reston *Lincs* 77 3883
North Rigton *N York* 82 2749
North Ripley *Hants* 12 1699
North Rode *Ches* 72 8866
North Row *Cumb* 93 2232
North Runcton *Norfk* 65 6416
North Scale *Cumb* 86 1869
North Scarle *Lincs* 76 8466
North Seaton *Nthumb* 103 2986
North Seaton Colliery *Nthumb* 103 2986
North Shian *Ag & B* 122 9143
North Shields *T & W* 103 3568
North Shoebury *Essex* 40 9286
North Shore *Lancs* 80 3037
North Side *Cambs* 64 2799
North Side *Cumb* 92 9929
North Skelton *N York* 97 6718
North Somercotes *Lincs* 77 4296
North Stainley *N York* 89 2876
North Stainmore *Cumb* 95 8314
North Stifford *Essex* 40 6080
North Stoke *Oxon* 37 6186
North Stoke *Somset* 35 7069
North Stoke *W Susx* 14 0110
North Street *Berks* 24 6371
North Street *Cambs* 53 5868
North Street *Hants* 12 1518
North Street *Hants* 24 6433
North Street *Kent* 28 8174
North Street *Kent* 28 0157
North Sunderland *Nthumb* 111 2131
North Tamerton *Cnwll* 5 3197
North Tawton *Devon* 8 6601
North Third *Stirlg* 116 7589
North Thoresby *Lincs* 77 2998
North Tidworth *Wilts* 23 2349
North Town *Berks* 26 8882
North Town *Devon* 19 5109
North Town *Somset* 21 5642
North Tuddenham *Norfk* 66 0314
North Walbottle *T & W* 103 1767
North Walsham *Norfk* 67 2830
North Waltham *Hants* 24 5646
North Warnborough *Hants* 24 7351
North Weald Basset *Essex* 39 4904
North Wheatley *Notts* 75 7585
North Whilborough *Devon* 7 8766
North Wick *Somset* 21 5865
North Widcombe *Somset* 21 5758
North Willingham *Lincs* 76 1688
North Wingfield *Derbys* 74 4065
North Witham *Lincs* 63 9221
North Wootton *Dorset* 11 6514
North Wootton *Norfk* 65 6424
North Wootton *Somset* 21 5641
North Wraxall *Wilts* 35 8175
North Wroughton *Wilts* 36 1481
Northacre *Norfk* 66 9598
Northall *Bucks* 38 9520
Northall Green *Norfk* 66 9914
Northallerton *N York* 89 3694
Northam *Devon* 18 4529
Northam *Hants* 13 4312
Northampton *Nhants* 49 7560
Northampton *Worcs* 47 8365
Northaw *Herts* 27 2702
Northay *Somset* 10 2811
Northborough *Cambs* 64 1507
Northbourne *Kent* 29 3352
Northbridge Street *E Susx* 17 7324
Northbrook *Hants* 24 5139
Northbrook *Oxon* 37 4922
Northchapel *W Susx* 14 9529
Northchurch *Herts* 38 9708
Northcott *Devon* 9 0912
Northcott *Devon* 9 1209
Northcott *Devon* 5 3392
Northcourt *Oxon* 37 4998
Northdown *Kent* 29 3770
Northedge *Derbys* 74 3665
Northend *Bucks* 37 7392
Northend *Warwks* 48 3952
Northend Woods *Bucks* 26 9089
Northenden *Gt Man* 79 8289
Northfield *Aber C* 135 9008
Northfield *E R Yk* 84 0326
Northfield *W Mids* 60 0279
Northfields *Lincs* 64 0208
Northfleet *Kent* 27 6374
Northiam *E Susx* 17 8324
Northill *Beds* 52 1446
Northington *Gloucs* 35 7008
Northington *Hants* 24 5637
Northlands *Lincs* 77 3453
Northleach *Gloucs* 36 1114
Northleigh *Devon* 19 6034
Northleigh *Devon* 9 1995
Northlew *Devon* 19 5099
Northload Bridge *Somset* 21 4939
Northmoor *Oxon* 36 4202
Northmoor *Somset* 20 9028
Northmuir *Angus* 126 3854
Northney *Hants* 13 7303
Northolt *Gt Lon* 26 1384
Northop *Flints* 70 2468
Northop Hall *Flints* 70 2667
Northorpe *Lincs* 76 8997
Northorpe *Lincs* 64 0917
Northorpe *Lincs* 64 2036
Northorpe *W York* 82 2221
Northover *Somset* 21 4838
Northover *Somset* 21 5223
Northowram *W York* 82 1126
Northport *Dorset* 11 9288
Northrepps *Norfk* 67 2439
Northton *W Isls* 152 9989
Northway *Somset* 20 1329
Northway *Swans* 32 5889
Northwich *Ches* 79 6673
Northwick *Gloucs* 34 5686
Northwick *Somset* 21 3548
Northwick *Worcs* 47 8458
Northwold *Norfk* 65 7597
Northwood *Derbys* 74 2664
Northwood *Gt Lon* 26 0990
Northwood *IOW* 13 4992
Northwood *Shrops* 59 4633
Northwood *Staffs* 72 8949
Northwood Green *Gloucs* 35 7216
Norton *Ches* 78 5581
Norton *Cnwll* 4 0869
Norton *Dur* 96 4421
Norton *E Susx* 16 4701
Norton *Gloucs* 47 8524
Norton *Herts* 39 2334
Norton *IOW* 12 3488
Norton *Mons* 34 4420
Norton *N York* 90 7971
Norton *Nhants* 49 5963
Norton *Notts* 75 5771
Norton *Powys* 46 3067
Norton *S York* 83 5415
Norton *S York* 74 3681
Norton *Shrops* 59 5609
Norton *Shrops* 60 7200
Norton *Shrops* 59 4681
Norton *Shrops* 59 6382
Norton *Somset* 21 3463
Norton *Suffk* 54 9565
Norton *Swans* 32 6188
Norton *W Susx* 14 9206
Norton *Wilts* 35 8884
Norton *Worcs* 47 8751
Norton *Worcs* 48 0447
Norton Bavant *Wilts* 22 9043
Norton Bridge *Staffs* 72 8630
Norton Canes *Staffs* 60 0107
Norton Canon *Herefd* 46 3847
Norton Corner *Norfk* 66 0928
Norton Disney *Lincs* 76 8859
Norton Ferris *Wilts* 22 7936
Norton Fitzwarren *Somset* 20 1925
Norton Green *IOW* 12 3488
Norton Green *Staffs* 60 0107
Norton Hawkfield *Somset* 21 5964
Norton Heath *Essex* 40 6004
Norton in Hales *Shrops* 72 7038
Norton in the Moors *Staffs* 72 8951
Norton Lindsey *Warwks* 48 2263
Norton Little Green *Suffk* 54 9766
Norton Malreward *Somset* 21 6064
Norton Mandeville *Essex* 40 5804
Norton St Philip *Somset* 22 7755
Norton sub Hamdon *Somset* 10 4615
Norton Subcourse *Norfk* 67 4198
Norton Wood *Herefd* 46 3648
Norton-Juxta-Twycross *Leics* 61 3207
Norton-le-Clay *N York* 89 4071
Norwell *Notts* 75 7761
Norwell Woodhouse *Notts* 75 7362
Norwich *Norfk* 67 2308
Norwick *Shet* 153 6414
Norwood *Clacks* 116 8793
Norwood *Kent* 17 0530
Norwood *S York* 75 4681
Norwood End *Essex* 40 5608
Norwood Green *Gt Lon* 26 1378
Norwood Green *W York* 82 1326
Norwood Hill *Surrey* 15 2343
Norwoodside *Cambs* 65 4197
Noseley *Leics* 50 7398
Noss Mayo *Devon* 6 5547
Nosterfield *N York* 89 2780
Nosterfield End *Cambs* 53 6344
Nostie *Highld* 138 8527
Notgrove *Gloucs* 36 1020
Nottage *Brdgnd* 33 8177
Notter *Cnwll* 5 3960
Nottingham *Notts* 62 5739
Nottington *Dorset* 11 6682
Notton *W York* 83 3413
Notton *Wilts* 35 9169
Nottswood Hill *Gloucs* 35 7018
Nounsley *Essex* 40 7910
Noutard's Green *Worcs* 47 8066
Nowton *Suffk* 54 8660
Nox *Shrops* 59 4110
Nuffield *Oxon* 37 6687
Nun Monkton *N York* 90 5057
Nunburnholme *E R Yk* 84 8447
Nuncargate *Notts* 75 5054
Nunclose *Cumb* 94 4945
Nuneaton *Warwks* 61 3691
Nuneham Courtenay *Oxon* 37 5599
Nunhead *Gt Lon* 27 3475
Nunkeeling *E R Yk* 85 1449
Nunney *Somset* 22 7345
Nunney Catch *Somset* 22 7344
Nunnington *Herefd* 46 5543
Nunnington *N York* 90 6679
Nunnykirk *Nthumb* 103 0793
Nunsthorpe *Lincs* 85 2607
Nunthorpe *N York* 83 6050
Nunthorpe *N York* 97 5314
Nunthorpe Village *N York* 90 5413
Nunton *Wilts* 23 1526
Nunwick *N York* 89 3274
Nunwick *Nthumb* 102 8774
Nup End *Bucks* 38 8619
Nupdown *Gloucs* 35 6395
Nupend *Gloucs* 35 7806
Nuptow *Berks* 25 8873
Nursling *Hants* 12 3716
Nursted *Hants* 13 7521
Nursteed *Wilts* 23 0260
Nurton *Staffs* 60 8399
Nutbourne *W Susx* 14 7705
Nutbourne *W Susx* 14 0718
Nutfield *Surrey* 27 3050
Nuthall *Notts* 62 5243
Nuthampstead *Herts* 39 4034
Nuthurst *W Susx* 15 1925
Nutley *E Susx* 16 4427
Nutley *Hants* 24 6044
Nuttal Lane *Gt Man* 81 7915
Nutwell *S York* 83 6304
Nybster *Highld* 151 3663
Nyetimber *W Susx* 14 8998
Nyewood *W Susx* 14 8021
Nymet Rowland *Devon* 19 7108
Nymet Tracey *Devon* 8 7200
Nympsfield *Gloucs* 35 8000
Nynehead *Somset* 20 1422
Nythe *Somset* 21 4234
Nyton *W Susx* 14 9305

# O

Oad Street *Kent* 28 8762
Oadby *Leics* 50 6200
Oak Cross *Devon* 8 5399
Oak Tree *Dur* 89 3613
Oakall Green *Worcs* 47 8161
Oakamoor *Staffs* 73 0444
Oakbank *W Loth* 117 0766
Oakdale *Caerph* 33 1898
Oake *Somset* 20 1525
Oaken *Staffs* 60 8602
Oakenclough *Lancs* 80 5447
Oakengates *Shrops* 60 7010
Oakenholt *Flints* 70 2571
Oakenshaw *Dur* 96 1937
Oakenshaw *W York* 82 1727
Oaker Side *Derbys* 74 2760
Oakerthorpe *Derbys* 74 3854
Oakford *Cerdgn* 42 4558
Oakford *Devon* 20 9121
Oakfordbridge *Devon* 20 9122
Oakgrove *Ches* 79 9169
Oakham *Rutlnd* 63 8608
Oakhanger *Ches* 72 7754
Oakhanger *Hants* 14 7635
Oakhill *Somset* 21 6347
Oakhurst *Kent* 27 5550
Oakington *Cambs* 52 4164
Oaklands *Powys* 45 0450
Oakle Street *Gloucs* 35 7517
Oakley *Beds* 51 0153
Oakley *Bucks* 37 6412
Oakley *Dorset* 11 0198
Oakley *Fife* 117 0289
Oakley *Hants* 24 5650
Oakley *Oxon* 37 7500
Oakley *Suffk* 54 1677
Oakley Green *Berks* 26 9276
Oakley Park *Powys* 58 9886
Oakridge *Gloucs* 35 9103
Oaks *Dur* 96 1525
Oaks *Lancs* 81 6733
Oaks *Shrops* 59 4204
Oaks Green *Derbys* 73 1533
Oaksey *Wilts* 35 9993
Oakshaw *Cumb* 101 5176
Oakshott *Hants* 13 7427
Oakthorpe *Leics* 61 3212
Oakwood *Derbys* 62 3738
Oakwood *Nthumb* 102 9465
Oakwoodhill *Surrey* 15 1337
Oakworth *W York* 82 0338
Oare *Kent* 28 0063
Oare *Somset* 19 7947
Oare *Wilts* 23 1563
Oasby *Lincs* 63 0039
Oath *Somset* 21 3827
Oathlaw *Angus* 127 4756
Oatlands Park *Surrey* 26 0865
Oban *Ag & B* 122 8629
Obley *Shrops* 46 3377
Obney *P & K* 125 0237
Oborne *Dorset* 11 6518
Obthorpe *Lincs* 64 0914
Occold *Suffk* 54 1570
Occumster *Highld* 151 2635
Ochiltree *E Ayrs* 107 5021
Ockbrook *Derbys* 62 4235
Ocker Hill *W Mids* 60 9793
Ockeridge *Worcs* 47 7762
Ockham *Surrey* 26 0756
Ockle *Highld* 129 5570
Ockley *Surrey* 15 1440
Ocle Pychard *Herefd* 46 5945
Octon *E R Yk* 91 0369
Odcombe *Somset* 10 5015
Odd Down *Somset* 22 7462
Oddingley *Worcs* 47 9159
Oddington *Gloucs* 48 2225
Oddington *Oxon* 37 5515
Odell *Beds* 51 9657
Odham *Devon* 18 4703
Odiham *Hants* 24 7451
Odsal *W York* 82 1529
Odsey *Herts* 39 2938
Odstock *Wilts* 23 1426
Odstone *Leics* 62 3907
Offchurch *Warwks* 48 3565
Offenham *Worcs* 48 0546
Offerton *T & W* 96 3455
Offham *E Susx* 15 4012
Offham *Kent* 28 6557
Offham *W Susx* 14 0208
Offleymarsh *Shrops* 72 7829
Offord Cluny *Cambs* 52 2267
Offord Darcy *Cambs* 52 2266
Offton *Suffk* 54 0649
Offwell *Devon* 9 1999
Ogbourne Maizey *Wilts* 36 1871
Ogbourne St Andrew *Wilts* 36 1872
Ogbourne St George *Wilts* 36 2074
Ogden *W York* 82 0730
Ogle *Nthumb* 103 1378
Oglet *Mersyd* 78 4481
Ogmore *V Glam* 33 8876
Ogmore Vale *Brdgnd* 33 9390
Ogmore-by-Sea *V Glam* 33 8675
Ogwen Bank *Gwynd* 69 6265
Okeford Fitzpaine *Dorset* 11 8010
Okehampton *Devon* 8 5995
Olchard *Devon* 9 8777
Old *Nhants* 50 7872
Old Aberdeen *Aber C* 135 9407
Old Alresford *Hants* 24 5834
Old Auchenbrack *D & G* 107 7597
Old Basford *Notts* 62 5543
Old Basing *Hants* 24 6652
Old Bewick *Nthumb* 111 0621
Old Bolingbroke *Lincs* 77 3565
Old Bracknell *Berks* 25 8668
Old Bramhope *W York* 82 2343
Old Brampton *Derbys* 74 3371
Old Bridge of Urr *D & G* 100 7767
Old Buckenham *Norfk* 66 0691
Old Burghclere *Hants* 24 4657
Old Byland *N York* 90 5585
Old Cassop *Dur* 96 3339
Old Castle *Brdgnd* 33 9079
Old Church Stoke *Powys* 58 2894
Old Clee *Lincs* 85 2808
Old Cleeve *Somset* 20 0441
Old Clipstone *Notts* 75 6064
Old Colwyn *Conwy* 69 8678
Old Dailly *S Ayrs* 106 2299
Old Dalby *Leics* 63 6723
Old Dam *Derbys* 74 1179
Old Deer *Abers* 143 9747
Old Ditch *Somset* 21 5049
Old Edlington *S York* 75 5397
Old Eldon *Dur* 96 2427
Old Ellerby *E R Yk* 85 1637
Old Felixstowe *Suffk* 55 3135
Old Fletton *Cambs* 64 1997
Old Forge *Herefd* 34 5518
Old Furnace *Herefd* 46 4923
Old Glossop *Derbys* 74 0494
Old Goole *E R Yk* 84 7422
Old Grimsby *IOS* 2 8915
Old Hall Green *Herts* 39 3722
Old Hall Street *Norfk* 67 3033
Old Harlow *Essex* 39 4711

302

303

304

# Q

# R

305

Rodmarton St Wenn
306

Rodmarton Gloucs 35 9498
Rodmell E Susx 15 4106
Rodmersham Kent 28 9261
Rodmersham Green Kent 28 9161
Rodney Stoke Somset 21 4849
Rodsley Derbys 73 2040
Rodway Somset 20 2540
Roe Cross Gt Man 79 9896
Roe Green Gt Man 79 7501
Roe Green Herts 39 2107
Roe Green Herts 39 3133
Roecliffe N York 89 3765
Roehampton Gt Lon 26 2273
Roffey W Susx 15 1932
Rogart Highld 146 7202
Rogate W Susx 14 8023
Roger Ground Cumb 87 3597
Rogerstone Newpt 34 2787
Roghadal W Isls 152 0483
Rogiet Mons 34 4587
Roke Oxon 37 6293
Roker T & W 96 4058
Rollesby Norfk 67 4416
Rolleston Leics 50 7300
Rolleston Notts 75 7452
Rolleston Staffs 73 2327
Rolston E R Yk 85 2144
Rolstone Somset 21 3962
Rolvenden Kent 17 8431
Rolvenden Layne Kent 17 8530
Romaldkirk Dur 95 9922
Romanby N York 89 3693
Romanno Bridge Border 117 1647
Romansleigh Devon 19 7220
Romden Castle Kent 28 8941
Romesdal Highld 136 4053
Romford Dorset 12 0709
Romford Gt Lon 27 5188
Romiley Gt Man 79 9490
Romney Street Kent 27 5561
Romsey Hants 12 3521
Romsley Shrops 60 7883
Romsley Worcs 60 9680
Ronachan Ag & B 113 7454
Rookhope Dur 95 9342
Rookley IOW 13 5084
Rookley Green IOW 13 5083
Rooks Bridge Somset 21 3652
Rooks Nest Somset 20 0933
Rookwith N York 89 2086
Roos E R Yk 85 2830
Roose Cumb 86 2269
Roosebeck Cumb 86 2567
Roothams Green Beds 51 0957
Ropley Hants 24 6431
Ropley Dean Hants 24 6232
Ropley Soke Hants 24 6533
Ropsley Lincs 63 9933
Rora Abers 143 0650
Rorrington Shrops 59 3000
Rosarie Moray 141 3850
Roscroggan Cnwll 2 6542
Rose Cnwll 3 7754
Rose Ash Devon 19 7921
Rose Green Essex 40 9028
Rose Green Suffk 54 9337
Rose Green Suffk 54 9744
Rose Green W Susx 14 9099
Rose Hill E Susx 16 4516
Rose Hill Lancs 81 8231
Roseacre Lancs 80 4336
Rosebank S Lans 116 8049
Rosebush Pembks 31 0729
Rosecare Cnwll 4 1695
Rosecliston Cnwll 4 8159
Rosedale Abbey N York 90 7296
Roseden Nthumb 111 0321
Rosehall Highld 146 4702
Rosehearty Abers 143 9267
Rosehill Shrops 59 4715
Roseisle Moray 141 1466
Roselands E Susx 16 6200
Rosemarket Pembks 30 9508
Rosemarkie Highld 140 7357
Rosemary Lane Devon 9 1514
Rosemount P & K 126 1843
Rosenannon Cnwll 4 9566
Rosenithon Cnwll 3 8021
Roser's Cross E Susx 16 5420
Rosevean Cnwll 4 0258
Rosevine Cnwll 3 8736
Rosewarne Cnwll 2 6036
Rosewell Mdloth 117 2862
Roseworth Dur 96 4221
Roseworthy Cnwll 2 6139
Rosgill Cumb 94 5316
Roshven Highld 129 7078
Roskhill Highld 136 2744
Roskorwell Cnwll 3 7923
Roskrow Cnwll 3 7635
Rosley Cumb 93 3245
Roslin Mdloth 117 2763
Rosliston Derbys 73 2416
Rosneath Ag & B 114 2583
Ross D & G 99 6444
Ross Nthumb 111 1337
Ross-on-Wye Herefd 46 5923
Rossett Wrexhm 71 3657
Rossett Green N York 82 2952
Rossington S York 75 6298
Rosskeen Highld 146 6869
Rossland Rens 115 4370
Roster Highld 151 2639
Rostherne Ches 79 7483
Rosthwaite Cumb 93 2514
Roston Derbys 73 1340
Rosudgeon Cnwll 2 5529
Rosyth Fife 117 1082
Rothbury Nthumb 103 0501
Rotherby Leics 63 6716
Rotherfield E Susx 16 5529
Rotherfield Greys Oxon 37 7282
Rotherfield Peppard Oxon 37 7182
Rotherham S York 75 4392
Rothersthorpe Nhants 49 7156
Rotherwick Hants 24 7156
Rothes Moray 141 2749
Rothesay Ag & B 114 0864
Rothiebrisbane Abers 142 7437
Rothiemay Moray 142 5548
Rothiemurchus Lodge Highld 133 9407
Rothienorman Abers 142 7235
Rothley Leics 62 5812
Rothley Nthumb 103 0488
Rothmaise Abers 142 6832
Rothwell Lincs 76 1499
Rothwell Nhants 51 8181
Rothwell W York 83 3428
Rothwell Haigh W York 83 3328
Rotsea E R Yk 84 0651
Rottal Lodge Angus 134 3769
Rottingdean E Susx 15 3602
Rottington Cumb 92 9613
Roucan D & G 100 0277
Roud IOW 13 5180
Rough Close Staffs 72 9239
Rough Common Kent 29 1259
Rougham Norfk 66 8320
Rougham Green Suffk 54 9061
Roughlee Lancs 81 8440
Roughley W Mids 61 1399
Roughpark Abers 134 3412
Roughton Lincs 77 2464
Roughton Norfk 67 2136
Roughton Shrops 60 7594
Roughway Kent 27 6153
Round Bush Herts 26 1498
Round Green Beds 38 1022
Round Street Kent 28 6568
Roundbush Essex 40 8501
Roundbush Green Essex 40 5814
Roundham Somset 10 4209
Roundhay W York 83 3337
Rounds Green W Mids 60 9889
Roundstreet Common W Susx 14 0528
Roundway Wilts 22 0163
Roundyhill Angus 126 3750
Rous Lench Worcs 47 0153
Rousdon Devon 10 2991
Rousham Oxon 49 4724
Rout's Green Bucks 37 7898
Routenbeck Cumb 93 1930
Routenburn N Ayrs 114 1961
Routh E R Yk 85 0942
Row Cnwll 4 0976
Row Cumb 94 6234
Row Cumb 87 4589
Row Ash Hants 13 5413
Row Green Essex 40 7420
Row Town Surrey 26 0363
Rowanburn D & G 101 4177
Rowardennan Hotel Stirlg 115 3698
Rowardennan Lodge Stirlg 115 3598
Rowarth Derbys 79 0189
Rowberrow Somset 21 4558
Rowborough IOW 13 4684
Rowde Wilts 22 9762
Rowden Devon 8 6499
Rowen Conwy 69 7671
Rowfield Derbys 73 1948
Rowfoot Nthumb 102 6860
Rowford Somset 20 2327
Rowhedge Essex 41 0221
Rowhook W Susx 14 1234
Rowington Warwks 48 2069
Rowland Derbys 74 2172
Rowland's Castle Hants 13 7310
Rowland's Gill T & W 96 1658
Rowledge Surrey 25 8243
Rowley Dur 95 0848
Rowley E R Yk 84 9732
Rowley Shrops 59 3006
Rowley Green W Mids 61 3483
Rowley Hill W York 82 1914
Rowley Regis W Mids 60 9787
Rowlstone Herefd 46 3727
Rowly Surrey 14 0440
Rowner Hants 13 5801
Rowney Green Worcs 61 0471
Rownhams Hants 12 3817
Rowrah Cumb 92 0518
Rows of Trees Ches 79 8379
Rowsham Bucks 38 8417
Rowsley Derbys 74 2565
Rowstock Oxon 37 4789
Rowston Lincs 76 0856
Rowthorne Derbys 75 4764
Rowton Ches 71 4464
Rowton Shrops 59 3612
Rowton Shrops 59 6119
Rowton Shrops 59 4180
Roxburgh Border 110 6930
Roxby Lincs 84 9116
Roxby N York 97 7616
Roxton Beds 52 1554
Roxwell Essex 40 6408
Roy Bridge Highld 131 2681
Royal Oak Dur 96 2023
Royal Oak Lancs 78 4103
Royal's Green Ches 71 6242
Roydhouse W York 82 2112
Roydon Essex 39 4010
Roydon Norfk 65 7023
Roydon Norfk 54 1080
Roydon Hamlet Essex 39 4107
Royston Herts 39 3540
Royston S York 83 3611
Royton Gt Man 79 9107
Rozel Jersey 158 0000
Ruabon Wrexhm 71 3043
Ruaig Ag & B 120 0747
Ruan High Lanes Cnwll 3 9039
Ruan Lanihorne Cnwll 3 8942
Ruan Major Cnwll 2 7016
Ruan Minor Cnwll 2 7115
Ruardean Gloucs 35 6217
Ruardean Hill Gloucs 35 6317
Ruardean Woodside Gloucs 35 6216
Rubery Worcs 60 9977
Ruckcroft Cumb 94 5344
Ruckhall Herefd 46 4637
Ruckhall Common Herefd 46 4539
Ruckinge Kent 17 0233
Ruckland Lincs 77 3378
Ruckley Shrops 59 5300
Rudby N York 89 4706
Rudchester Nthumb 103 1167
Ruddington Notts 62 5732
Ruddle Gloucs 35 6811
Ruddlemoor Cnwll 3 0054
Rudford Gloucs 35 7721
Rudge Somset 22 8251
Rudgeway Gloucs 35 6386
Rudgwick W Susx 14 0834
Rudhall Herefd 47 6225
Rudheath Ches 79 6772
Rudley Green Essex 40 8303
Rudloe Wilts 35 8470
Rudry Caerph 33 2086
Rudston E R Yk 91 0967
Rudyard Staffs 72 9557
Ruecastle Border 110 6120
Rufford Lancs 80 4615
Rufforth N York 83 5251
Rug Denbgs 70 0543
Rugby Warwks 50 5075
Rugeley Staffs 73 0418
Ruggaton Devon 19 5545
Ruishton Somset 20 2625
Ruislip Gt Lon 26 0987
Ruletownhead Border 110 6113
Rumbach Moray 141 3852
Rumbling Bridge P & K 117 0199
Rumburgh Suffk 55 3481
Rumby Hill Dur 96 1634
Rumford Cnwll 4 8970
Rumford Falk 116 9377
Rumney Cardif 33 2178
Rumwell Somset 20 1923
Runcorn Ches 78 5182
Runcton W Susx 14 8802
Runcton Holme Norfk 65 6109
Runfold Surrey 25 8647
Runhall Norfk 66 0507
Runham Norfk 67 4610
Runham Norfk 67 5108
Runnington Somset 20 1221
Runsell Green Essex 40 7905
Runshaw Moor Lancs 80 5319
Runswick N York 97 8016
Runtaleave Angus 133 2867
Runwell Essex 40 7594
Ruscombe Berks 37 7976
Rush Green Ches 79 6987
Rush Green Essex 41 1515
Rush Green Gt Lon 27 5187
Rush Green Herts 39 2123
Rush Green Herts 39 3325
Rushall Herefd 47 6435
Rushall Norfk 55 1982
Rushall W Mids 60 0200
Rushall Wilts 23 1255
Rushbrooke Suffk 54 8961
Rushbury Shrops 59 5191
Rushden Herts 39 3031
Rushden Nhants 51 9566
Rushenden Kent 28 9071
Rusher's Cross E Susx 16 6028
Rushett Common Surrey 14 0242
Rushford Devon 5 4576
Rushford Norfk 54 9281
Rushlake Green E Susx 16 6218
Rushmere Suffk 55 4986
Rushmere St Andrew Suffk 55 1946
Rushmoor Surrey 25 8740
Rushock Herefd 46 3058
Rushock Worcs 60 8871
Rusholme Gt Man 79 8594
Rushton Ches 71 5863
Rushton Nhants 51 8482
Rushton Shrops 59 6008
Rushton Spencer Staffs 72 9362
Rushwick Worcs 47 8254
Rushyford Dur 96 2728
Ruskie Stirlg 116 6200
Ruskington Lincs 76 0851
Rusland Cumb 87 3488
Rusper W Susx 15 2037
Ruspidge Gloucs 35 6611
Russ Hill Surrey 15 2240
Russel's Green Suffk 55 2572
Russell Green Essex 40 7413
Russell's Green E Susx 16 7011
Russell's Water Oxon 37 7089
Rusthall Kent 16 5639
Rustington W Susx 14 0402
Ruston N York 91 9583
Ruston Parva E R Yk 91 0661
Ruswarp N York 90 8809
Ruthall Shrops 59 5990
Rutherford Border 110 6430
Rutherglen S Lans 116 6161
Ruthernbridge Cnwll 4 0166
Ruthin Denbgs 70 1258
Ruthrieston Aber C 135 9204
Ruthven Abers 142 5046
Ruthven Angus 126 2848
Ruthven Highld 140 8132
Ruthven Highld 132 7699
Ruthven House Angus 126 3047
Ruthvoes Cnwll 4 9260
Ruthwaite Cumb 93 2336
Ruthwell D & G 100 0967
Ruxley Corner Gt Lon 27 4770
Ruxton Green Herefd 34 5419
Ruyton-XI-Towns Shrops 59 3922
Ryal Nthumb 103 0174
Ryall Dorset 10 4095
Ryall Worcs 47 8640
Ryarsh Kent 28 6660
Rycote Oxon 37 6705
Rydal Cumb 87 3606
Ryde IOW 13 5992
Rye E Susx 17 9220
Rye Cross Worcs 47 7735
Rye Foreign E Susx 17 8922
Rye Harbour E Susx 17 9319
Rye Street Worcs 47 7835
Ryebank Shrops 59 5131
Ryeford Herefd 35 6322
Ryehill E R Yk 85 2225
Ryeish Green Nhants 24 7267
Ryhall Rutlnd 64 0310
Ryhill W York 83 3814
Ryhope T & W 96 4152
Rylah Derbys 75 4667
Ryland Lincs 76 0179
Rylands Notts 62 5335
Rylstone N York 88 9658
Ryme Intrinseca Dorset 10 5810
Ryther N York 83 5539
Ryton N York 90 7975
Ryton Shrops 60 7602
Ryton T & W 103 1564
Ryton Warwks 61 4086
Ryton Woodside T & W 96 1462
Ryton-on-Dunsmore Warwks 61 3874

# S

Sabden Lancs 81 7837
Sabine's Green Essex 27 5496
Sacombe Herts 39 3319
Sacombe Green Herts 39 3419
Sacriston Dur 96 2447
Sadberge Dur 96 3416
Saddell Ag & B 105 7832
Saddington Leics 50 6691
Saddle Bow Norfk 65 6015
Saddlescombe W Susx 15 2711
Sadgill Cumb 87 4805
Saffron Walden Essex 39 5438
Sageston Pembks 30 0503
Saham Hills Norfk 66 9003
Saham Toney Norfk 66 8901
Saighton Ches 71 4462
St Abbs Border 119 9167
St Agnes Border 118 6763
St Agnes Cnwll 2 7150
St Albans Herts 38 1407
St Allen Cnwll 3 8250
St Andrew Guern 158 0000
St Andrew's Major V Glam 33 1371
St Andrews Fife 127 5116
St Andrews Well Dorset 10 4793
St Ann's D & G 100 0793
St Ann's Chapel Cnwll 5 4170
St Ann's Chapel Devon 7 6647
St Anne's Lancs 80 3228
St Anthony Cnwll 3 7825
St Anthony's Hill E Susx 16 6201
St Arvans Mons 34 5296
St Asaph Denbgs 70 0374
St Athan V Glam 20 0167
St Aubin Jersey 158 0000
St Austell Cnwll 3 0152
St Bees Cumb 86 9711
St Blazey Cnwll 3 0654
St Blazey Gate Cnwll 3 0653
St Boswells Border 110 5930
St Brelade Jersey 158 0000
St Brelade's Bay Jersey 158 0000
St Breock Cnwll 4 9771
St Breward Cnwll 4 0977
St Briavels Gloucs 34 5604
St Bride's Major V Glam 33 8974
St Brides Pembks 30 8010
St Brides Netherwent Mons 34 4289
St Brides super-Ely V Glam 33 0977
St Brides Wentlooge Newpt 34 2982
St Budeaux Devon 6 4558
St Buryan Cnwll 2 4025
St Catherine Somset 35 7769
St Catherines Ag & B 123 1207
St Chloe Gloucs 35 8401
St Clears Carmth 31 2816
St Cleer Cnwll 5 2468
St Clement Cnwll 3 8543
St Clement Jersey 158 0000
St Clether Cnwll 5 2084
St Colmac Ag & B 114 0467
St Columb Major Cnwll 4 9163
St Columb Minor Cnwll 4 8362
St Columb Road Cnwll 4 9159
St Combs Abers 143 0563
St Cross South Elmham Suffk 55 2984
St Cyrus Abers 135 7464
St David's P & K 125 9420
St David's Pembks 30 7525
St Day Cnwll 3 7242
St Decumans Somset 20 0642
St Dennis Cnwll 4 9557
St Devereux Herefd 46 4431
St Dogmaels Cerdgn 42 1645
St Dogwells Pembks 30 9727
St Dominick Cnwll 5 4067
St Donats V Glam 20 9368
St Edith's Marsh Wilts 22 9764
St Endellion Cnwll 4 9978
St Enoder Cnwll 3 8956
St Erme Cnwll 3 8449
St Erney Cnwll 5 3759
St Erth Cnwll 2 5535
St Erth Praze Cnwll 2 5735
St Ervan Cnwll 4 8970
St Ewe Cnwll 3 9746
St Fagans Cardif 33 1277
St Fergus Abers 143 0952
St Fillans P & K 124 6924
St Florence Pembks 31 0801
St Gennys Cnwll 4 1497
St George Conwy 70 9775
St George's V Glam 33 1076
St George's Hill Surrey 26 0862
St Georges Somset 21 3762
St Germans Cnwll 5 3657
St Giles in the Wood Devon 19 5319
St Giles-on-the-Heath Cnwll 5 3690
St Gluvia's Cnwll 3 7834
St Harmon Powys 45 9872
St Helen Auckland Dur 96 1826
St Helena Norfk 66 1816
St Helens Cumb 92 0232
St Helens E Susx 17 8212
St Helens IOW 13 6289
St Helens Mersyd 78 5195
St Helier Gt Lon 27 2567
St Helier Jersey 158 0000
St Hilary Cnwll 2 5431
St Hilary V Glam 33 0173
St Hill Devon 9 0908
St Hill W Susx 15 3835
St Illtyd Blae G 34 2201
St Ippollitts Herts 39 1927
St Ishmael's Pembks 30 8307
St Issey Cnwll 4 9271
St Ive Cnwll 5 3167
St Ives Cambs 52 3171
St Ives Cnwll 2 5140
St Ives Dorset 12 1204
St James Norfk 67 2720
St James South Elmham Suffk 55 3281
St James's End Nhants 49 7460
St John Cnwll 5 4053
St John Jersey 158 0000
St John's IOM 158 2781
St John's Chapel Devon 19 5329
St John's Chapel Dur 95 8837
St John's Fen End Norfk 65 5312
St John's Highway Norfk 65 5214
St John's Kirk S Lans 108 9836
St John's Town of Dalry D & G 99 6281
St John's Wood Gt Lon 27 2683
St Johns Dur 95 0633
St Johns Kent 27 5356
St Johns Surrey 25 9857
St Johns Worcs 47 8454
St Jude's IOM 158 3996
St Just Cnwll 2 3731
St Just Lane Cnwll 3 8535
St Just-in-Roseland Cnwll 3 8435
St Katherines Abers 142 7834
St Keverne Cnwll 3 7921
St Kew Cnwll 4 0276
St Kew Highway Cnwll 4 0375
St Keyne Cnwll 5 2461
St Lawrence Cnwll 4 0466
St Lawrence Essex 41 9604
St Lawrence IOW 13 5376
St Lawrence Jersey 158 0000
St Lawrence Kent 29 3665
St Leonard's Street Kent 28 6756
St Leonards Bucks 38 9007
St Leonards Dorset 12 1103
St Leonards E Susx 17 8009
St Levan Cnwll 2 3822
St Lythans V Glam 33 1072
St Mabyn Cnwll 4 0473
St Madoes P & K 126 1921
St Margaret South Elmham Suffk 55 3183
St Margaret's at Cliffe Kent 29 3544
St Margarets Herefd 46 3533
St Margarets Herts 39 3811
St Margarets Hope Ork 153 4493
St Marks IOM 158 2974
St Martin Cnwll 5 2555
St Martin Guern 158 0000
St Martin Jersey 158 0000
St Martin's P & K 126 1530
St Martin's Green Cnwll 3 7323
St Martin's Moor Shrops 59 3135
St Martins Shrops 59 3236
St Mary Jersey 158 0000
St Mary Bourne Hants 24 4250
St Mary Church V Glam 33 0071
St Mary Cray Gt Lon 27 4768
St Mary Hill V Glam 33 9678
St Mary in the Marsh Kent 17 0627
St Mary's Ork 153 4701
St Mary's Bay Kent 17 0827
St Mary's Grove Somset 21 4669
St Mary's Hoo Kent 28 8076
St Marychurch Devon 7 9166
St Maughans Mons 34 4617
St Maughans Green Mons 34 4717
St Mawes Cnwll 3 8433
St Mawgan Cnwll 4 8765
St Mellion Cnwll 5 3965
St Mellons Cardif 34 2281
St Merryn Cnwll 4 8874
St Mewan Cnwll 3 9951
St Michael Caerhays Cnwll 3 9642
St Michael Church Somset 20 3030
St Michael Penkevil Cnwll 3 8541
St Michael South Elmham Suffk 55 3483
St Michael's on Wyre Lancs 80 4641
St Michaels Kent 17 8835
St Michaels Worcs 46 5865
St Minver Cnwll 4 9677
St Monans Fife 127 5201
St Neot Cnwll 4 1868
St Neots Cambs 52 1860
St Nicholas Pembks 30 9035
St Nicholas V Glam 33 0974
St Nicholas at Wade Kent 29 2666
St Ninians Stirlg 116 7991
St Olaves Norfk 67 4599
St Osyth Essex 41 1215
St Ouen Jersey 158 0000
St Owens Cross Herefd 46 5324
St Paul's Walden Herts 39 1922
St Pauls Cray Gt Lon 27 4768
St Peter Jersey 158 0000
St Peter Port Guern 158 0000
St Peter's Guern 158 0000
St Peter's Kent 29 3868
St Peter's Hill Cambs 52 2372
St Petrox Pembks 30 9797
St Pinnock Cnwll 5 2063
St Quivox S Ayrs 106 3723
St Ruan Cnwll 2 7115
St Sampson Guern 158 0000
St Saviour Guern 158 0000
St Saviour Jersey 158 0000
St Stephen Cnwll 3 9453
St Stephen's Coombe Cnwll 3 9451
St Stephens Cnwll 5 3285
St Stephens Cnwll 5 4158
St Teath Cnwll 4 0680
St Tudy Cnwll 4 0676
St Twynnells Pembks 30 9597
St Veep Cnwll 3 1455
St Vigeans Angus 127 6443
St Wenn Cnwll 4 9664

Sockbridge

Stapleford Tawney

309

Sockbridge Cumb 94 4926
Sockburn Dur 89 3406
Sodom Denbgs 70 0971
Sodylt Bank Shrops 71 3439
Soham Cambs 53 5973
Soham Cotes Cambs 53 5775
Solas W Isls 152 8074
Solbury Pembks 30 8912
Soldon Devon 18 3210
Soldon Cross Devon 18 3210
Soldridge Hants 24 6535
Sole Street Kent 28 6567
Sole Street Kent 29 0949
Solihull W Mids 61 1679
Sollers Dilwyn Herefd 46 4255
Sollers Hope Herefd 46 6132
Sollom Lancs 80 4518
Solva Pembks 30 8024
Solwaybank D & G 101 3077
Somerby Leics 63 7710
Somerby Lincs 84 0606
Somercotes Derbys 74 4253
Somerford Dorset 12 1793
Somerford Keynes Gloucs 35 0195
Somerley W Susx 14 8198
Somerleyton Suffk 67 4897
Somersal Herbert Derbys 73 1335
Somersby Lincs 77 3472
Somersham Cambs 52 3678
Somersham Suffk 54 0848
Somerton Oxon 49 4928
Somerton Somset 21 4928
Somerton Suffk 54 8153
Somerwood Shrops 59 5614
Sompting W Susx 15 1505
Sonning Berks 37 7575
Sonning Common Oxon 37 7180
Sonning Eye Oxon 37 7476
Sontley Wrexhm 71 3347
Sopley Hants 12 1596
Sopworth Wilts 35 8286
Sorbie D & G 99 4346
Sordale Highld 151 1462
Sorisdale Ag & B 120 2763
Sorn E Ayrs 107 5526
Sortat Highld 151 2863
Sosgill Cumb 92 1024
Sotby Lincs 76 2078
Sots Hole Lincs 76 1264
Sotterly Suffk 55 4484
Soughton Flints 70 2466
Soulbury Bucks 38 8826
Soulby Cumb 93 4625
Soulby Cumb 88 7411
Souldern Oxon 49 5231
Souldrop Beds 51 9861
Sound Muir Moray 141 3652
Soundwell Gloucs 35 6575
Sourton Devon 8 5390
Soutergate Cumb 86 2281
South Acre Norfk 66 8114
South Alkham Kent 29 2441
South Allington Devon 7 7938
South Alloa Falk 116 8791
South Ambersham W Susx 14 9120
South Anston S York 75 5183
South Ascot Berks 25 9268
South Ashford Kent 28 0041
South Baddesley Hants 12 3596
South Bank N York 97 5320
South Bank N York 83 5950
South Barrow Somset 21 6028
South Beddington Gt Lon 27 2863
South Beer Cnwll 5 3091
South Benfleet Essex 40 7787
South Bersted W Susx 14 9300
South Bockhampton Dorset 12 1795
South Bowood Dorset 10 4498
South Bramwith S York 83 6211
South Brent Devon 7 6960
South Brewham Somset 22 7236
South Broomhill Nthumb 103 2499
South Burlingham Norfk 67 3807
South Cadbury Somset 21 6325
South Carlton Lincs 76 9476
South Carlton Notts 75 5883
South Cave E R Yk 84 9230
South Cerney Gloucs 36 0497
South Chard Somset 10 3205
South Charlton Nthumb 111 1620
South Cheriton Somset 22 6924
South Church Dur 96 2128
South Cleatlam Dur 96 1218
South Cliffe E R Yk 84 8735
South Clifton Notts 75 8270
South Cockerington Lincs 77 3888
South Cornelly Brdgnd 33 8280
South Cove Suffk 55 4981
South Creake Norfk 66 8536
South Crosland W York 82 1112
South Croxton Leics 63 6810
South Dalton E R Yk 84 9645
South Darenth Kent 27 5669
South Duffield N York 83 6833
South Elkington Lincs 77 2988
South Elmsall W York 83 4711
South End E R Yk 85 3918
South End Hants 12 1015
South End Herefd 47 7444
South End Lincs 85 1120
South End Norfk 54 9990
South Erradale Highld 137 7471
South Fambridge Essex 40 8694
South Fawley Berks 36 3880
South Ferriby Lincs 84 9820
South Field E R Yk 84 0225
South Godstone Surrey 15 3648
South Gorley Hants 12 1610
South Gosforth T & W 103 2467
South Green Essex 41 0319
South Green Essex 40 6893
South Green Kent 28 8560
South Green Norfk 66 0510
South Green Suffk 54 1775
South Gyle C Edin 117 1871
South Hanningfield Essex 40 7497
South Harting W Susx 14 7819
South Hayling Hants 13 7299
South Hazelrigg Nthumb 111 0532
South Heath Bucks 26 9101
South Heighton E Susx 16 4402
South Hetton Dur 96 3845
South Hiendley W York 83 3912
South Hill Cnwll 5 3272
South Hill Somset 21 4726
South Hinksey Oxon 37 5104
South Hole Devon 18 2220
South Holmwood Surrey 15 1744
South Hornchurch Gt Lon 27 5183
South Huish Devon 7 6941
South Hykeham Lincs 76 9364
South Hylton T & W 96 3556
South Kelsey Lincs 76 0498
South Kessock Highld 140 6547
South Killingholme Lincs 85 1416
South Kilvington N York 89 4284
South Kilworth Nhants 50 6081
South Kirkby W York 83 4410
South Knighton Devon 7 8172
South Kyme Lincs 76 1749
South Lawn Oxon 36 2814
South Leigh Oxon 36 3909
South Leverton Notts 75 7881
South Littleton Worcs 48 0746
South Lopham Norfk 54 0481
South Luffenham Rutlnd 63 9301
South Malling E Susx 16 4210
South Marston Wilts 36 1987
South Merstham Surrey 27 2952
South Middleton Nthumb 111 9923
South Milford N York 83 4931
South Milton Devon 7 7042
South Mimms Herts 26 2201
South Molton Devon 19 7125
South Moor Dur 96 1951
South Moreton Oxon 37 5688
South Mundham W Susx 14 8700
South Muskham Notts 75 7957
South Newbald E R Yk 84 9035
South Newington Oxon 48 4033
South Newton Wilts 23 0834
South Normanton Derbys 75 4456
South Norwood Gt Lon 27 3368
South Nutfield Surrey 15 3049
South Ockendon Essex 27 5983
South Ormsby Lincs 77 3675
South Ossett W York 82 2819
South Otterington N York 89 3787
South Owersby Lincs 76 0693
South Park Surrey 15 2448
South Perrott Dorset 10 4706
South Petherton Somset 10 4316
South Petherwin Cnwll 5 3181
South Pickenham Norfk 66 8504
South Pill Cnwll 6 4259
South Pool Devon 7 7740
South Poorton Dorset 10 5297
South Quarme Somset 20 9236
South Queensferry C Edin 117 1378
South Radworthy Devon 19 7432
South Rauceby Lincs 64 0245
South Raynham Norfk 66 8723
South Reddish Gt Man 79 8891
South Reston Lincs 77 4083
South Runcton Norfk 65 6308
South Scarle Notts 76 8463
South Shian Ag & B 122 9042
South Shields T & W 103 3666
South Shore Lancs 80 3033
South Somercotes Lincs 77 4193
South Stainley N York 89 3063
South Stifford Essex 27 5978
South Stoke Lincs 63 9127
South Stoke Oxon 37 5983
South Stoke Somset 22 7461
South Stoke W Susx 14 0209
South Stour Kent 28 0338
South Street E Susx 15 3918
South Street Kent 27 6363
South Street Kent 28 0557
South Street Kent 29 1265
South Tarbrax S Lans 117 0353
South Tawton Devon 8 6594
South Thoresby Lincs 77 4076
South Thorpe Dur 95 1013
South Tidworth Wilts 23 2347
South Town Hants 24 6536
South Walsham Norfk 67 3613
South Warnborough Hants 24 7247
South Weald Essex 27 5694
South Weston Oxon 37 7098
South Wheatley Cnwll 5 2492
South Widcombe Somset 21 5856
South Wigston Leics 50 5897
South Willesborough Kent 28 0240
South Willingham Lincs 76 1983
South Wingate Dur 96 4134
South Wingfield Derbys 74 3755
South Witham Lincs 63 9219
South Wonston Hants 24 4636
South Woodham Ferrers Essex 40 8097
South Wootton Norfk 65 6422
South Wraxall Wilts 22 8364
South Zeal Devon 8 6593
Southall Gt Lon 26 1279
Southam Gloucs 47 9725
Southam Warwks 49 4161
Southampton Hants 13 4112
Southborough Gt Lon 27 4267
Southborough Kent 16 5842
Southbourne Dorset 12 1491
Southbourne W Susx 14 7705
Southbrook Dorset 11 8494
Southburgh Norfk 66 0005
Southburn E R Yk 84 9854
Southchurch Essex 40 9086
Southcott Cnwll 5 1995
Southcott Devon 18 4416
Southcott Devon 8 5495
Southcott Devon 8 7580
Southcott Wilts 23 1659
Southcourt Bucks 38 8112
Southease E Susx 16 4205
Southend Ag & B 105 6908
Southend Wilts 36 1973
Southend-on-Sea Essex 40 8885
Southernby Cumb 93 3639
Southernden Kent 28 8645
Southerndown V Glam 33 8873
Southerness D & G 92 9754
Southerton Devon 9 0790
Southery Norfk 65 6194
Southfield Falk 116 8472
Southfleet Kent 27 6171
Southford IOW 13 5179
Southgate Gt Lon 27 2994
Southgate Norfk 65 6833
Southgate Norfk 66 8635
Southgate Norfk 66 1324
Southgate Swans 32 5587
Southill Beds 39 1542
Southington Hants 24 5049
Southleigh Devon 9 2093
Southminster Essex 40 9599
Southmoor Oxon 36 3998
Southmuir Angus 126 3852
Southoe Cambs 52 1864
Southolt Suffk 55 1968
Southorpe Cambs 64 0803
Southover Dorset 10 6294
Southover E Susx 16 6525
Southowram W York 82 1123
Southport Mersyd 80 3317
Southrepps Norfk 67 2536
Southrey Lincs 76 1366
Southrop Gloucs 36 1903
Southrope Hants 24 6644
Southsea Hants 13 6599
Southsea Wrexhm 71 3051
Southside Dur 95 1026
Southtown Norfk 67 5106
Southtown Somset 10 3216
Southwaite Cumb 93 4445
Southwark Gt Lon 27 3279
Southwater W Susx 15 1526
Southwater Street W Susx 15 1427
Southway Somset 21 5242
Southwell Dorset 11 6870
Southwell Notts 75 6953
Southwick Hants 13 6208
Southwick Nhants 51 0292
Southwick Somset 21 3646
Southwick T & W 96 3758
Southwick W Susx 15 2405
Southwick Wilts 22 8355
Southwold Suffk 55 5076
Southwood Norfk 67 3905
Southwood Somset 21 5533
Sowe Common W Mids 61 3782
Sower Carr Lancs 80 3743
Sowerby N York 89 4380
Sowerby W York 82 0423
Sowerby Bridge W York 82 0523
Sowerby Row Cumb 93 3940
Sowerhill Somset 19 8924
Sowhill Torfn 34 2700
Sowley Green Suffk 53 7050
Sowood W York 82 0818
Sowton Devon 6 5065
Sowton Devon 9 9792
Soyland Town W York 82 0320
Spa Common Norfk 67 2930
Spain's End Essex 53 6637
Spalding Lincs 64 2422
Spaldington E R Yk 84 7633
Spaldwick Cambs 52 1372
Spalford Notts 76 8369
Spanby Lincs 64 0938
Spanish Green Hants 24 6958
Sparham Norfk 66 0719
Sparhamill Norfk 66 0818
Spark Bridge Cumb 86 3084
Sparket Cumb 93 4325
Sparkford Somset 21 6025
Sparkhill W Mids 61 1083
Sparkwell Devon 6 5857
Sparrow Green Norfk 66 9414
Sparrowpit Derbys 74 0880
Sparrows Green E Susx 16 6332
Sparsholt Hants 24 4331
Sparsholt Oxon 36 3487
Spartylea Cumb 95 8548
Spath Staffs 73 0835
Spaunton N York 90 7289
Spaxton Somset 20 2237
Spean Bridge Highld 131 2281
Spear Hill W Susx 15 1317
Spearywell Hants 23 3127
Speen Berks 24 4567
Speen Bucks 26 8499
Speeton N York 91 1574
Speke Mersyd 78 4383
Speldhurst Kent 16 5541
Spellbrook Herts 39 4817
Spelmonden Kent 28 7037
Spelsbury Oxon 36 3421
Spen W York 82 1925
Spen Green Ches 72 8160
Spencers Wood Berks 24 7166
Spennithorne N York 89 1388
Spennymoor Dur 96 2533
Spernall Warwks 48 0862
Spestos Devon 8 7298
Spetchley Worcs 47 8953
Spetisbury Dorset 11 9102
Spexhall Suffk 55 3780
Spey Bay Moray 141 3565
Speybridge Highld 141 0326
Speyview Moray 141 2541
Spilsby Lincs 77 4066
Spindlestone Nthumb 111 1533
Spinkhill Derbys 75 4578
Spinningdale Highld 146 6789
Spirthill Wilts 35 9976
Spital Berks 26 9675
Spital Mersyd 78 3482
Spital Hill S York 75 6193
Spital in the Street Lincs 76 9690
Spithurst E Susx 16 4217
Spittal E Loth 118 4677
Spittal E R Yk 84 7652
Spittal Highld 151 1654
Spittal Nthumb 119 0051
Spittal Pembks 30 9723
Spittal of Glenmuick Abers 134 3085
Spittal of Glenshee P & K 133 1070
Spittal-on-Rule Border 110 5819
Spittalfield P & K 126 1040
Spixworth Norfk 67 2415
Splatt Cnwll 4 9476
Splatt Cnwll 5 2288
Splatt Devon 8 6005
Splayne's Green E Susx 16 4224
Splottlands Cardif 33 2077
Spodegreen Ches 79 7385
Spofforth N York 83 3651
Spon Green Flints 70 2863
Spondon Derbys 62 4036
Spooner Row Norfk 66 0997
Sporle Norfk 66 8411
Spott E Loth 118 6775
Spottiswoode Border 110 6049
Spratton Nhants 50 7169
Spreakley Surrey 25 8341
Spreyton Devon 8 6996
Spriddlestone Devon 6 5351
Spridlington Lincs 76 0084
Spring Gardens Dur 96 1726
Spring Vale S York 82 2502
Springburn C Glas 116 6068
Springfield D & G 101 3268
Springfield Essex 40 7208
Springfield Fife 126 3411
Springhill Staffs 60 9704
Springhill Staffs 61 0705
Springholm D & G 100 8070
Springkell D & G 101 2575
Springside N Ayrs 106 3738
Springthorpe Lincs 76 8789
Springwell T & W 96 2858
Sproatley E R Yk 85 1934
Sproston Green Ches 72 7366
Sprotbrough S York 83 5301
Sproughton Suffk 54 1244
Sprouston Border 110 7535
Sprowston Norfk 67 2512
Sproxton Leics 63 8524
Sproxton N York 90 6181
Sprytown Devon 5 4185
Spunhill Shrops 59 4133
Spurstow Ches 71 5556
Spyway Dorset 10 5293
Squirrel's Heath Gt Lon 27 5389
Stableford Shrops 60 7598
Stableford Staffs 72 8138
Stacey Bank Derbys 74 2890
Stackhouse N York 88 8165
Stackpole Pembks 30 9896
Stacksford Norfk 54 0590
Stacksteads Lancs 81 8521
Stadbury Devon 7 6846
Staddiscombe Devon 6 5151
Staddlethorpe E R Yk 84 8328
Staden Derbys 74 0771
Stadhampton Oxon 37 6098
Stadhlaigearraidh W Isls 152 7638
Staffield Cumb 94 5442
Staffin Highld 136 4967
Stafford Staffs 72 9223
Stagsden Beds 38 9848
Stainborough S York 83 3203
Stainburn Cumb 92 0129
Stainburn N York 82 2548
Stainby Lincs 63 9022
Staincross S York 83 3210
Staindrop Dur 96 1220
Staines Surrey 26 0371
Stainfield Lincs 64 0824
Stainfield Lincs 76 1172
Stainforth N York 88 8267
Stainforth S York 83 6411
Staining Lancs 80 3436
Stainland W York 82 0719
Stainsacre N York 91 9108
Stainsby Derbys 75 4565
Stainton Cumb 93 3857
Stainton Cumb 94 4828
Stainton Cumb 87 5285
Stainton Dur 95 0718
Stainton N York 97 4714
Stainton N York 89 1096
Stainton S York 75 5593
Stainton by Langworth Lincs 76 0677
Stainton le Vale Lincs 76 1794
Stainton with Adgarley Cumb 86 2472
Staintondale N York 91 9998
Stair Cumb 93 2321
Stair E Ayrs 107 4423
Stair Haven D & G 98 2153
Stairfoot S York 83 3705
Staithes N York 97 7818
Stake Pool Lancs 80 4147
Stakeford Nthumb 103 2685
Stakes Hants 13 6808
Stalbridge Dorset 11 7317
Stalbridge Weston Dorset 11 7116
Stalham Norfk 67 3725
Stalham Green Norfk 67 3824
Stalisfield Green Kent 28 9552
Stallen Dorset 10 6016
Stalling Busk N York 88 9186
Stallingborough Lincs 85 1911
Stallington Staffs 72 9439
Stalmine Lancs 80 3745
Stalmine Moss Side Lancs 80 3845
Stalybridge Gt Man 79 9698
Stambourne Essex 53 7238
Stambourne Green Essex 53 6938
Stamford Lincs 64 0307
Stamford Nthumb 111 2219
Stamford Bridge Ches 71 4667
Stamford Bridge E R Yk 84 7155
Stamford Hill Gt Lon 27 3387
Stamfordham Nthumb 103 0771
Stanah Lancs 80 3542
Stanborough Herts 39 2211
Stanbridge Beds 38 9624
Stanbridge Dorset 11 0004
Stanbury W York 82 0137
Stand Gt Man 79 7905
Stand N Lans 116 7668
Standburn Falk 116 9274
Standeford Staffs 60 9107
Standen Kent 28 8540
Standen Street Kent 17 8030
Standerwick Somset 22 8150
Standford Hants 14 8134
Standingstone Cumb 92 0533
Standish Gloucs 35 7908
Standish Gt Man 78 5610
Standish Lower Ground Gt Man 78 5507
Standlake Oxon 36 3903
Standon Hants 13 4226
Standon Herts 39 3922
Standon Staffs 72 8135
Standon Green End Herts 39 3620
Standwell Green Suffk 54 1369
Stane N Lans 116 8859
Stanfield Norfk 66 9320
Stanford Beds 39 1640
Stanford Kent 29 1238
Stanford Shrops 59 3313
Stanford Bishop Herefd 47 6851
Stanford Bridge Shrops 72 7024
Stanford Bridge Worcs 47 7265
Stanford Dingley Berks 24 5771
Stanford in the Vale Oxon 36 3493
Stanford le Hope Essex 40 6882
Stanford on Avon Nhants 50 5978
Stanford on Soar Notts 62 5421
Stanford on Teme Worcs 47 7065
Stanford Rivers Essex 27 5301
Stanfree Derbys 75 4773
Stanghow N York 97 6715
Stanground Cambs 64 2097
Stanhill Lancs 81 7227
Stanhoe Norfk 66 8036
Stanhope Border 108 1229
Stanhope Dur 95 9939
Stanhope Bretby Derbys 73 2921
Stanion Nhants 51 9186
Stanklin Worcs 60 8574
Stanley Derbys 62 4140
Stanley Dur 96 1953
Stanley Notts 75 4662
Stanley P & K 126 1033
Stanley Shrops 60 7483
Stanley Staffs 72 9352
Stanley W York 83 3422
Stanley Common Derbys 62 4042
Stanley Crook Dur 96 1637
Stanley Ferry W York 83 3522
Stanley Gate Lancs 78 4405
Stanley Moor Staffs 72 9251
Stanley Pontlarge Gloucs 47 0030
Stanmer E Susx 15 3309
Stanmore Berks 37 4778
Stanmore Gt Lon 26 1692
Stanmore Hants 24 4628
Stannersburn Nthumb 102 7286
Stanningley W York 82 2234
Stannington Nthumb 103 2179
Stannington S York 74 2987
Stannington Station Nthumb 103 2181
Stansbatch Herefd 46 3461
Stansfield Suffk 53 7852
Stanshope Staffs 73 1253
Stanstead Suffk 54 8449
Stanstead Abbots Herts 39 3811
Stanstead Street Suffk 54 8448
Stansted Kent 27 6062
Stansted Mountfitchet Essex 39 5125
Stanton Derbys 73 2718
Stanton Devon 7 7050
Stanton Gloucs 48 0634
Stanton Mons 34 3021
Stanton Nthumb 103 1390
Stanton Staffs 73 1245
Stanton Suffk 54 9673
Stanton Butts Cambs 52 2372
Stanton by Bridge Derbys 62 3726
Stanton by Dale Derbys 62 4637
Stanton Drew Somset 21 5963
Stanton Fitzwarren Wilts 36 1790
Stanton Harcourt Oxon 36 4105
Stanton Hill Notts 75 4760
Stanton in Peak Derbys 74 2364
Stanton Lacy Shrops 46 4978
Stanton Lees Derbys 74 2562
Stanton Long Shrops 59 5791
Stanton on the Wolds Notts 63 6330
Stanton Prior Somset 22 6762
Stanton St Bernard Wilts 23 0961
Stanton St John Oxon 37 5709
Stanton St Quintin Wilts 35 9079
Stanton Street Suffk 54 9566
Stanton under Bardon Leics 62 4610
Stanton upon Hine Heath Shrops 59 5624
Stanton Wick Somset 21 6162
Stantway Gloucs 35 7313
Stanwardine in the Field Shrops 59 4124
Stanwardine in the Wood Shrops 59 4227
Stanway Essex 40 9424
Stanway Gloucs 48 0632
Stanway Green Essex 40 9523
Stanway Green Suffk 55 2470
Stanwell Surrey 26 0574
Stanwell Moor Surrey 26 0474
Stanwick Nhants 51 9771
Stanwix Cumb 93 4057
Staoinebrig W Isls 152 7532
Stape N York 90 7994
Stapehill Dorset 12 0500
Stapeley Ches 72 6749
Stapenhill Staffs 73 2521
Staple Kent 29 2756
Staple Somset 20 1141
Staple Cross Devon 20 0320
Staple Cross E Susx 17 7822
Staple Fitzpaine Somset 10 2618
Staple Hill Worcs 60 9773
Staplefield W Susx 15 2728
Stapleford Cambs 53 4751
Stapleford Herts 39 3117
Stapleford Leics 63 8018
Stapleford Lincs 76 8857
Stapleford Notts 62 4837
Stapleford Wilts 23 0737
Stapleford Abbotts Essex 27 5194
Stapleford Tawney Essex 27 5099

Staplegrove Suisnish
310


Staplegrove *Somset* 20 2126
Staplehay *Somset* 20 2121
Staplehurst *Kent* 28 7843
Staplers *IOW* 13 5189
Staplestreet *Kent* 29 0660
Staplet *Cumb* 101 5071
Stapleton *Herefd* 46 3265
Stapleton *Leics* 50 4398
Stapleton *N York* 89 2612
Stapleton *Shrops* 59 4704
Stapleton *Somset* 21 4621
Stapley *Somset* 9 1913
Staploe *Beds* 52 1560
Staplow *Herefd* 47 6941
Star *Fife* 126 3103
Star *Pembks* 31 2434
Star *Somset* 21 4358
Starbeck *N York* 83 3255
Starbotton *N York* 88 9574
Starcross *Devon* 9 9781
Stareton *Warwks* 61 3371
Starkholmes *Derbys* 74 3058
Starling *Gt Man* 79 7710
Starlings Green *Essex* 39 4631
Starr's Green *E Susx* 17 7615
Starston *Norfk* 55 2384
Start *Devon* 7 8044
Startforth *Dur* 95 0415
Startley *Wilts* 35 9482
Statenborough *Kent* 29 3155
Statham *Ches* 79 6787
Stathe *Somset* 21 3728
Stathern *Leics* 63 7731
Station Town *Dur* 96 4036
Staughton Green *Cambs* 52 1365
Staughton Highway *Cambs* 52 1364
Staunton *Gloucs* 34 5512
Staunton *Gloucs* 47 7829
Staunton Green *Herefd* 46 3661
Staunton in the Vale *Notts* 63 8043
Staunton on Arrow *Herefd* 46 3660
Staunton on Wye *Herefd* 46 3644
Staveley *Cumb* 87 3786
Staveley *Cumb* 87 4698
Staveley *Derbys* 75 4374
Staveley *N York* 89 3662
Staverton *Devon* 7 7964
Staverton *Gloucs* 47 8923
Staverton *Nhants* 49 5361
Staverton *Wilts* 22 8560
Staverton Bridge *Gloucs* 35 8722
Stawell *Somset* 21 3738
Stawley *Somset* 20 0622
Staxigoe *Highld* 151 3852
Staxton *N York* 91 0179
Staylittle *Cerdgn* 43 6489
Staylittle *Powys* 43 8891
Staynall *Lancs* 80 3643
Staythorpe *Notts* 75 7554
Stead *W York* 82 1446
Stean *N York* 89 0973
Steane *Nhants* 49 5538
Stearsby *N York* 90 6171
Steart *Somset* 20 2745
Stebbing *Essex* 40 6624
Stebbing Green *Essex* 40 6823
Stebbing Park *Essex* 40 6524
Stechford *W Mids* 61 1287
Stede Quarter *Kent* 28 8738
Stedham *W Susx* 14 8622
Steel *Nthumb* 95 9458
Steel Cross *E Susx* 16 5331
Steel Green *Cumb* 86 1679
Steel Heath *Shrops* 59 5436
Steele Road *Border* 101 5293
Steelend *Fife* 117 0392
Steen's Bridge *Herefd* 46 5357
Steep *Hants* 13 7425
Steep Lane *W York* 82 0223
Steephill *IOW* 13 5477
Steeple *Dorset* 11 9080
Steeple *Essex* 40 9303
Steeple Ashton *Wilts* 22 9056
Steeple Aston *Oxon* 49 4725
Steeple Barton *Oxon* 49 4424
Steeple Bumpstead *Essex* 53 6841
Steeple Claydon *Bucks* 49 7026
Steeple Gidding *Cambs* 52 1381
Steeple Langford *Wilts* 23 0337
Steeple Morden *Cambs* 39 2842
Steeton *W York* 82 0344
Stein *Highld* 136 2656
Stella *T & W* 103 1763
Stelling Minnis *Kent* 29 1447
Stembridge *Somset* 21 4220
Stenalees *Cnwll* 3 0156
Stenhouse *D & G* 100 8093
Stenhousemuir *Falk* 116 8783
Stenigot *Lincs* 77 2480
Stenscholl *Highld* 136 4767
Stenton *E Loth* 118 6274
Steornabhagh *W Isls* 152 4232
Stepaside *Pembks* 31 1407
Stepney *Gt Lon* 27 3681
Stepping Hill *Gt Man* 79 9187
Steppingley *Beds* 38 0035
Stepps *N Lans* 116 6568
Sternfield *Suffk* 55 3861
Sterridge *Devon* 19 5545
Stert *Wilts* 23 0259
Stetchworth *Cambs* 53 6459
Steven's Crouch *E Susx* 17 7115
Stevenage *Herts* 39 2325
Stevenston *N Ayrs* 106 2742
Steventon *Hants* 24 5447
Steventon *Oxon* 37 4691
Steventon End *Essex* 53 5942
Stevington *Beds* 51 9853
Stewartby *Beds* 38 0142
Stewartfield *S Lans* 116 6255
Stewarton *E Ayrs* 115 4245
Stewkley *Bucks* 38 8526
Stewley *Somset* 10 3118
Stewton *Lincs* 77 3587
Steyne Cross *IOW* 13 6487
Steyning *W Susx* 15 1711
Steynton *Pembks* 30 9107
Stibb *Cnwll* 18 2210
Stibb Cross *Devon* 18 4314
Stibb Green *Wilts* 23 2262
Stibbard *Norfk* 66 9828
Stibbington *Cambs* 51 0898
Stichill *Border* 110 7138
Sticker *Cnwll* 3 9750
Stickford *Lincs* 77 3560
Sticklepath *Devon* 8 6494
Sticklepath *Somset* 20 0436
Stickling Green *Essex* 39 4732
Stickney *Lincs* 77 3457
Stiff Street *Kent* 28 8761
Stiffkey *Norfk* 66 9742
Stifford's Bridge *Herefd* 47 7347
Stile Bridge *Kent* 28 7547
Stileway *Somset* 21 4641
Stilligarry *W Isls* 152 7638
Stillingfleet *N York* 83 5940
Stillington *Dur* 96 3723
Stillington *N York* 90 5867
Stilton *Cambs* 52 1689
Stinchcombe *Gloucs* 35 7298
Stinsford *Dorset* 11 7091
Stiperstones *Shrops* 59 3600
Stirchley *Shrops* 60 6907
Stirchley *W Mids* 61 0581
Stirling *Abers* 143 1242
Stirling *Stirlg* 116 7993
Stirtloe *Cambs* 52 1966
Stirton *N York* 82 9752
Stisted *Essex* 40 8024
Stitchcombe *Wilts* 36 2369
Stithians *Cnwll* 3 7336
Stivichall *W Mids* 61 3376
Stixwould *Lincs* 76 1765
Stoak *Ches* 71 4273
Stobo *Border* 109 1837
Stoborough *Dorset* 11 9286
Stoborough Green *Dorset* 11 9285
Stobs Castle *Border* 109 5008
Stobswood *Nthumb* 103 2195
Stock *Essex* 40 6998
Stock *Somset* 21 4561
Stock Green *Worcs* 47 9859
Stock Wood *Worcs* 47 0058
Stockbridge *Hants* 23 3535
Stockbriggs *S Lans* 107 7936
Stockbury *Kent* 28 8461
Stockcross *Berks* 24 4368
Stockdale *Cnwll* 3 7837
Stockdalewath *Cumb* 93 3845
Stocker's Hill *Kent* 28 9650
Stockerston *Leics* 51 8397
Stocking *Herefd* 47 6230
Stocking Green *Bucks* 38 8047
Stocking Pelham *Herts* 39 4529
Stockingford *Warwks* 61 3391
Stockland *Devon* 9 2404
Stockland Bristol *Somset* 20 2443
Stockland Green *Kent* 16 5642
Stockleigh English *Devon* 8 8506
Stockleigh Pomeroy *Devon* 9 8703
Stockley *Wilts* 22 9967
Stockley Hill *Herefd* 46 3738
Stocklinch *Somset* 10 3817
Stockmoor *Herefd* 46 3954
Stockport *Gt Man* 79 8990
Stocksbridge *S York* 74 2698
Stocksfield *Nthumb* 103 0561
Stockstreet *Essex* 40 8222
Stockton *Herefd* 46 5261
Stockton *Norfk* 67 3894
Stockton *Shrops* 58 2601
Stockton *Shrops* 72 7716
Stockton *Shrops* 60 7299
Stockton *Warwks* 49 4363
Stockton *Wilts* 22 9838
Stockton Brook *Staffs* 72 9151
Stockton Heath *Ches* 78 6185
Stockton on Teme *Worcs* 47 7167
Stockton on the Forest *N York* 83 6556
Stockton-on-Tees *Dur* 96 4419
Stockwell *Gloucs* 35 9414
Stockwell End *W Mids* 60 8900
Stockwell Heath *Staffs* 73 0521
Stockwood *Bristl* 21 6368
Stockwood *Dorset* 10 5906
Stodday *Lancs* 87 4658
Stodmarsh *Kent* 29 2260
Stody *Norfk* 66 0535
Stoer *Highld* 148 0328
Stoford *Somset* 10 5613
Stoford *Wilts* 23 0835
Stogumber *Somset* 20 0937
Stogursey *Somset* 20 2042
Stoke *Devon* 18 2324
Stoke *Hants* 24 4051
Stoke *Hants* 13 7202
Stoke *Kent* 28 8274
Stoke *W Mids* 61 3778
Stoke Abbott *Dorset* 10 4500
Stoke Albany *Nhants* 51 8088
Stoke Ash *Suffk* 54 1170
Stoke Bardolph *Notts* 63 6441
Stoke Bliss *Worcs* 47 6563
Stoke Bruerne *Nhants* 49 7449
Stoke by Clare *Suffk* 53 7443
Stoke Canon *Devon* 9 9398
Stoke Charity *Hants* 24 4839
Stoke Climsland *Cnwll* 5 3674
Stoke Cross *Herefd* 47 6250
Stoke D'Abernon *Surrey* 26 1258
Stoke Doyle *Nhants* 51 0286
Stoke Dry *Rutlnd* 51 8596
Stoke Edith *Herefd* 46 6040
Stoke End *Warwks* 61 1797
Stoke Farthing *Wilts* 23 0525
Stoke Ferry *Norfk* 65 7000
Stoke Fleming *Devon* 7 8648
Stoke Gabriel *Devon* 7 8557
Stoke Gifford *Gloucs* 35 6279
Stoke Golding *Leics* 61 3997
Stoke Goldington *Bucks* 38 8348
Stoke Green *Bucks* 26 9882
Stoke Hammond *Bucks* 38 8829
Stoke Heath *Shrops* 72 6529
Stoke Heath *W Mids* 61 3681
Stoke Heath *Worcs* 47 9468
Stoke Holy Cross *Norfk* 67 2301
Stoke Lacy *Herefd* 47 6249
Stoke Lyne *Oxon* 49 5628
Stoke Mandeville *Bucks* 38 8310
Stoke Newington *Gt Lon* 27 3386
Stoke Orchard *Gloucs* 47 9128
Stoke Poges *Bucks* 26 9783
Stoke Pound *Worcs* 47 9667
Stoke Prior *Herefd* 46 5256
Stoke Prior *Worcs* 47 9467
Stoke Rivers *Devon* 19 6335
Stoke Rochford *Lincs* 63 9127
Stoke Row *Oxon* 37 6884
Stoke St Gregory *Somset* 21 3427
Stoke St Mary *Somset* 20 2622
Stoke St Michael *Somset* 22 6646
Stoke St Milborough *Shrops* 59 5682
Stoke sub Hamdon *Somset* 10 4717
Stoke Talmage *Oxon* 37 6799
Stoke Trister *Somset* 22 7428
Stoke upon Tern *Shrops* 59 6328
Stoke Wake *Dorset* 11 7606
Stoke Wharf *Worcs* 47 9567
Stoke-by-Nayland *Suffk* 54 9836
Stoke-on-Trent *Staffs* 72 8847
Stoke-upon-Trent *Staffs* 72 8745
Stokeford *Dorset* 11 8687
Stokeham *Notts* 75 7876
Stokeinteignhead *Devon* 7 9170
Stokenchurch *Bucks* 37 7696
Stokenham *Devon* 7 8042
Stokesay *Shrops* 59 4381
Stokesby *Norfk* 67 4310
Stokesley *N York* 90 5208
Stolford *Somset* 20 0332
Stolford *Somset* 20 2345
Ston Easton *Somset* 21 6253
Stondon Massey *Essex* 27 5800
Stone *Bucks* 37 7812
Stone *Gloucs* 35 6895
Stone *Kent* 27 5774
Stone *Kent* 17 9427
Stone *S York* 75 5589
Stone *Somset* 21 5834
Stone *Staffs* 72 9034
Stone *Worcs* 60 8675
Stone Allerton *Somset* 21 3951
Stone Bridge Corner *Cambs* 64 2700
Stone Chair *W York* 82 1227
Stone Cross *E Susx* 16 5128
Stone Cross *E Susx* 16 6104
Stone Cross *E Susx* 16 6431
Stone Cross *Kent* 16 5239
Stone Cross *Kent* 28 0236
Stone Cross *Kent* 29 3257
Stone Hill *S York* 83 6809
Stone House *Cumb* 88 7685
Stone Street *Kent* 27 5754
Stone Street *Suffk* 54 9639
Stone Street *Suffk* 54 0143
Stone Street *Suffk* 55 3882
Stone-edge-Batch *Somset* 34 4671
Stonea *Cambs* 65 4593
Stonebridge *Norfk* 54 9290
Stonebridge *Somset* 21 3859
Stonebridge *W Mids* 61 2182
Stonebroom *Derbys* 74 4059
Stonecross Green *Suffk* 54 8257
Stonecrouch *Kent* 16 7033
Stoneferry *E R Yk* 85 1031
Stonefield Castle Hotel *Ag & B* 113 8671
Stonegarthside *Cumb* 101 4780
Stonegate *E Susx* 16 6628
Stonegate *N York* 90 7708
Stonegrave *N York* 90 6577
Stonehall *Worcs* 47 8848
Stonehaugh *Nthumb* 102 7976
Stonehaven *Abers* 135 8786
Stonehill Green *Gt Lon* 27 5070
Stonehouse *Ches* 71 5070
Stonehouse *D & G* 100 8268
Stonehouse *Devon* 6 4654
Stonehouse *Gloucs* 35 8005
Stonehouse *Nthumb* 94 6958
Stonehouse *S Lans* 116 7546
Stoneleigh *Warwks* 61 3372
Stoneley Green *Ches* 71 6151
Stonely *Cambs* 52 1167
Stoner Hill *Hants* 13 7225
Stones Green *Essex* 41 1626
Stonesby *Leics* 63 8224
Stonesfield *Oxon* 36 3917
Stonestreet Green *Kent* 29 0637
Stonethwaite *Cumb* 93 2613
Stonewells *Moray* 141 2865
Stonewood *Kent* 27 5972
Stoney Cross *Hants* 12 2611
Stoney Middleton *Derbys* 74 2375
Stoney Stanton *Leics* 50 4994
Stoney Stoke *Somset* 22 7032
Stoney Stratton *Somset* 21 6539
Stoney Stretton *Shrops* 59 3809
Stoneybridge *W Isls* 152 7532
Stoneybridge *Worcs* 60 9476
Stoneyburn *W Loth* 117 9862
Stoneygate *Leics* 62 6002
Stoneyhills *Essex* 40 9597
Stoneykirk *D & G* 98 0853
Stoneywood *Aber C* 135 8811
Stoneywood *Falk* 116 7982
Stonham Aspal *Suffk* 54 1359
Stonnall *Staffs* 61 0603
Stonor *Oxon* 37 7388
Stonton Wyville *Leics* 50 7395
Stony Cross *Herefd* 46 5466
Stony Cross *Herefd* 47 7247
Stony Houghton *Derbys* 75 4966
Stony Stratford *Bucks* 38 7840
Stonyford *Hants* 12 3215
Stonywell *Staffs* 61 0712
Stoodleigh *Devon* 19 6532
Stoodleigh *Devon* 20 9218
Stopham *W Susx* 14 0219
Stopsley *Beds* 38 1023
Stoptide *Cnwll* 4 9475
Storeton *Mersyd* 78 3084
Storeyard Green *Herefd* 47 7144
Stormy Corner *Lancs* 78 4707
Stornoway *W Isls* 152 4232
Storridge *Herefd* 47 7548
Storrington *W Susx* 14 0814
Storth *Cumb* 87 4779
Storwood *E R Yk* 84 7144
Stotfield *Moray* 141 2270
Stotfold *Beds* 39 2136
Stottesdon *Shrops* 60 6782
Stoughton *Leics* 63 6402
Stoughton *Surrey* 25 9851
Stoughton *W Susx* 14 8011
Stoul *Highld* 129 7594
Stoulton *Worcs* 47 9049
Stour Provost *Dorset* 22 7921
Stour Row *Dorset* 22 8221
Stourbridge *W Mids* 60 8983
Stourpaine *Dorset* 11 8609
Stourport-on-Severn *Worcs* 60 8171
Stourton *Staffs* 60 8684
Stourton *W York* 83 3230
Stourton *Warwks* 48 2936
Stourton *Wilts* 22 7734
Stourton Caundle *Dorset* 11 7115
Stout *Somset* 21 4331
Stove *Shet* 153 4224
Stoven *Suffk* 55 4481
Stow *Border* 118 4544
Stow *Lincs* 76 8882
Stow Bardolph *Norfk* 65 6206
Stow Bedon *Norfk* 66 9596
Stow cum Quy *Cambs* 53 5260
Stow Longa *Cambs* 51 1070
Stow Maries *Essex* 40 8399
Stow-on-the-Wold *Gloucs* 48 1925
Stowbridge *Norfk* 65 6007
Stowe *Gloucs* 34 5606
Stowe *Shrops* 46 3173
Stowe by Chartley *Staffs* 73 0026
Stowehill *Nhants* 49 6458
Stowell *Somset* 22 6822
Stowey *Somset* 21 5959
Stowford *Devon* 5 4398
Stowford *Devon* 19 6541
Stowford *Devon* 5 4387
Stowford *Devon* 9 1189
Stowlangtoft *Suffk* 54 9568
Stowmarket *Suffk* 54 0458
Stowting *Kent* 29 1242
Stowting Common *Kent* 29 1243
Stowupland *Suffk* 54 0760
Straanruie *Moray* 141 9916
Strachan *Abers* 135 6792
Strachur *Ag & B* 114 0901
Stradbroke *Suffk* 55 2373
Stradbrook *Wilts* 22 9152
Stradishall *Suffk* 53 7552
Stradsett *Norfk* 65 6605
Stragglethorpe *Lincs* 76 9152
Stragglethorpe *Notts* 63 6537
Straight Soley *Wilts* 36 3172
Straiton *Mdloth* 117 2766
Straiton *S Ayrs* 106 3804
Straloch *Abers* 143 8620
Straloch *P & K* 133 0463
Stramshall *Staffs* 73 0735
Strang *IOM* 158 3578
Strangford *Herefd* 46 5827
Stranraer *D & G* 98 0560
Strata Florida *Cerdgn* 43 7465
Stratfield Mortimer *Berks* 24 6664
Stratfield Saye *Hants* 24 6861
Stratfield Turgis *Hants* 24 6959
Stratford *Beds* 52 1748
Stratford *Gt Lon* 27 3884
Stratford St Andrew *Suffk* 55 3560
Stratford St Mary *Suffk* 54 0434
Stratford sub Castle *Wilts* 23 1332
Stratford Tony *Wilts* 23 0926
Stratford-upon-Avon *Warwks* 48 2055
Strath *Highld* 144 7978
Strathan *Highld* 145 0821
Strathan *Highld* 149 5764
Strathan *Highld* 130 9791
Strathaven *S Lans* 116 7044
Strathblane *Stirlg* 115 5679
Strathcanaird *Highld* 145 1501
Strathcarron Station *Highld* 138 9442
Strathcoil *Ag & B* 122 6830
Strathdon *Abers* 134 3512
Strathkinness *Fife* 127 4516
Strathloanhead *W Loth* 116 9272
Strathmashie House *Highld* 132 5891
Strathmiglo *Fife* 126 2109
Strathpeffer *Highld* 139 4858
Strathtay *P & K* 125 9153
Strathwhillan *N Ayrs* 105 0235
Strathy *Highld* 150 8464
Strathy Inn *Highld* 150 8365
Strathyre *Stirlg* 124 5617
Stratton *Cnwll* 18 2306
Stratton *Dorset* 11 6593
Stratton *Gloucs* 35 0103
Stratton Audley *Oxon* 49 6025
Stratton St Margaret *Wilts* 36 1786
Stratton St Michael *Norfk* 67 2093
Stratton Strawless *Norfk* 67 2220
Stratton-on-the-Fosse *Somset* 22 6650
Stravithie *Fife* 127 5313
Stream *Somset* 20 0639
Streat *E Susx* 15 3515
Streatham *Gt Lon* 27 3071
Streatley *Beds* 38 0728
Streatley *Berks* 37 5980
Street *Devon* 9 1888
Street *Lancs* 80 5252
Street *N York* 90 7304
Street *Somset* 21 4836
Street Ashton *Warwks* 50 4582
Street Dinas *Shrops* 71 3338
Street End *E Susx* 16 6023
Street End *Kent* 29 1453
Street End *W Susx* 14 8599
Street Gate *T & W* 96 2159
Street Houses *N York* 97 7419
Street Houses *N York* 83 5245
Street Lane *Derbys* 74 3848
Street on the Fosse *Somset* 21 6239
Streethay *Staffs* 61 1410
Streetlam *N York* 89 3098
Streetly *W Mids* 61 0898
Streetly End *Cambs* 53 6148
Strefford *Shrops* 59 4485
Strelitz *P & K* 126 1836
Strelley *Notts* 62 5141
Strensall *N York* 90 6360
Strensham *Worcs* 47 9140
Stretcholt *Somset* 20 2943
Strete *Devon* 7 8446
Stretford *Gt Man* 79 7994
Stretford *Herefd* 46 4455
Stretford *Herefd* 46 5257
Strethall *Essex* 39 4839
Stretham *Cambs* 53 5174
Strettington *W Susx* 14 8907
Stretton *Ches* 71 4452
Stretton *Ches* 79 6282
Stretton *Derbys* 74 3961
Stretton *Rutlnd* 63 9415
Stretton *Staffs* 60 8811
Stretton *Staffs* 73 2526
Stretton en le Field *Leics* 61 3011
Stretton Grandison *Herefd* 47 6344
Stretton Heath *Shrops* 59 3610
Stretton on Fosse *Warwks* 48 2238
Stretton Sugwas *Herefd* 46 4642
Stretton under Fosse *Warwks* 50 4581
Stretton Westwood *Shrops* 59 5998
Stretton-on-Dunsmore *Warwks* 61 4072
Strichen *Abers* 143 9455
Strines *Gt Man* 79 9786
Stringston *Somset* 20 1742
Strixton *Nhants* 51 9061
Stroat *Gloucs* 34 5797
Stromeferry *Highld* 138 8634
Stromness *Ork* 153 2508
Stronachlachar *Stirlg* 123 4010
Stronafian *Ag & B* 114 0281
Stronchrubie *Highld* 145 2419
Strone *Ag & B* 114 1980
Strone *Highld* 131 1481
Stronenaba *Highld* 131 2084
Stronmilchan *Ag & B* 123 1528
Strontian *Highld* 130 8161
Strood *Kent* 28 7268
Strood *Kent* 17 8532
Strood Green *Surrey* 15 2048
Strood Green *W Susx* 14 0224
Strood Green *W Susx* 15 1332
Stroud *Gloucs* 35 8505
Stroud *Hants* 13 7223
Stroud Green *Essex* 40 8590
Stroud Green *Gloucs* 35 8007
Stroude *Surrey* 25 0068
Stroxton *Lincs* 63 9030
Struan *Highld* 136 3438
Struan *P & K* 132 8065
Strubby *Lincs* 77 4582
Strumpshaw *Norfk* 67 3407
Strutherhill *S Lans* 116 7649
Struthers *Fife* 126 3709
Struy *Highld* 139 4040
Stryd-y-Facsen *IOA* 68 3383
Stryt-issa *Wrexhm* 70 2845
Stuartfield *Abers* 143 9745
Stubbers Green *W Mids* 61 0401
Stubbington *Hants* 13 5503
Stubbins *N York* 81 7918
Stubbs Green *Norfk* 67 2598
Stubhampton *Dorset* 11 9113
Stubley *Derbys* 74 3378
Stubshaw Cross *Gt Man* 78 5899
Stubton *Lincs* 76 8748
Stuchbury *Nhants* 49 5643
Stuckeridge *Devon* 20 9221
Stuckton *Hants* 12 1613
Stud Green *Berks* 26 8877
Studfold *N York* 88 8169
Studham *Beds* 38 0215
Studholme *Cumb* 93 2556
Studland *Dorset* 12 0382
Studley *Warwks* 48 0764
Studley *Wilts* 35 9671
Studley Common *Warwks* 48 0664
Studley Roger *N York* 89 2970
Studley Royal *N York* 89 2770
Stump Cross *Cambs* 39 5044
Stuntney *Cambs* 53 5578
Stunts Green *E Susx* 16 6213
Sturbridge *Staffs* 72 8330
Sturgate *Lincs* 76 8888
Sturmer *Essex* 53 6943
Sturminster Common *Dorset* 11 7812
Sturminster Marshall *Dorset* 11 9500
Sturminster Newton *Dorset* 11 7814
Sturry *Kent* 29 1760
Sturton *Lincs* 84 9604
Sturton by Stow *Lincs* 76 8980
Sturton le Steeple *Notts* 75 7883
Stuston *Suffk* 54 1377
Stutton *N York* 83 4841
Stutton *Suffk* 54 1534
Styal *Ches* 79 8383
Stydd *Lancs* 81 6536
Stynie *Moray* 141 3360
Styrrup *Notts* 75 6090
Succoth *Ag & B* 123 2905
Suckley *Worcs* 47 7251
Suckley Green *Worcs* 47 7253
Sudborough *Nhants* 51 9682
Sudbourne *Suffk* 55 4153
Sudbrook *Lincs* 63 9744
Sudbrook *Mons* 34 5087
Sudbrooke *Lincs* 76 0376
Sudbury *Derbys* 73 1631
Sudbury *Gt Lon* 26 1685
Sudbury *Suffk* 54 8741
Sudden *Gt Man* 81 8812
Suddie *Highld* 140 6554
Suddington *Worcs* 47 8463
Sudgrove *Gloucs* 35 9308
Suffield *N York* 91 9890
Suffield *Norfk* 67 2232
Sugdon *Shrops* 59 6015
Sugnall *Staffs* 72 7931
Sugwas Pool *Herefd* 46 4541
Suisnish *Highld* 129 5816

Sulby Thelbridge Cross
311

Sulby IOM 158 3894
Sulgrave Nhants 49 5544
Sulham Berks 24 6474
Sulhamstead Berks 24 6368
Sulhamstead Abbots Berks 24 6467
Sulhamstead Bannister Berks 24 6368
Sullington W Susx 14 0913
Sullom Shet 153 3573
Sullom Voe Shet 153 4075
Sully V Glam 20 1568
Summer Heath Bucks 37 7490
Summer Hill Wrexhm 71 3153
Summerbridge N York 89 2062
Summercourt Cnwll 3 8856
Summerfield Norfk 65 7538
Summerfield Worcs 60 8473
Summerhouse Dur 96 2019
Summerlands Cumb 87 5386
Summerley Derbys 74 3778
Summersdale W Susx 14 8606
Summerseat Gt Man 81 7914
Summertown Oxon 37 5009
Summit Gt Man 79 9109
Summit N York 82 9418
Sunbiggin N York 87 6608
Sunbury Surrey 26 1168
Sundaywell D & G 100 8284
Sunderland Ag & B 112 2464
Sunderland Cumb 93 1735
Sunderland Lancs 80 4255
Sunderland T & W 96 3957
Sunderland Bridge Dur 96 2637
Sundhope Border 109 3325
Sundon Park Beds 38 0525
Sundridge Kent 27 4855
Sunk Island E R Yk 85 2619
Sunningdale Berks 25 9567
Sunninghill Surrey 25 9367
Sunningwell Oxon 37 4900
Sunniside Dur 96 1438
Sunniside T & W 96 2059
Sunny Bank Lancs 81 7720
Sunny Brow Dur 96 1934
Sunnyhill Derbys 62 3432
Sunnyhurst Lancs 81 6722
Sunnylaw Stirlg 116 7998
Sunnymead Oxon 37 5009
Sunton Wilts 23 2454
Sunwick Border 119 9052
Surbiton Gt Lon 26 1867
Surfleet Lincs 64 2528
Surfleet Seas End Lincs 64 2628
Surlingham Norfk 67 3106
Surrex Essex 40 8722
Sustead Norfk 66 1837
Susworth Lincs 84 8302
Sutcombe Devon 18 3411
Sutcombemill Devon 18 3411
Suton Norfk 66 0999
Sutterby Lincs 77 3872
Sutterton Lincs 64 2835
Sutton Beds 52 2247
Sutton Cambs 51 0998
Sutton Cambs 53 4479
Sutton Devon 8 7202
Sutton Devon 7 7042
Sutton E Susx 16 4999
Sutton Gt Lon 27 2564
Sutton Kent 29 3349
Sutton Mersyd 78 5393
Sutton N York 83 4925
Sutton Norfk 67 3823
Sutton Notts 75 6784
Sutton Notts 63 7637
Sutton Oxon 36 4106
Sutton Pembks 30 9115
Sutton S York 83 5512
Sutton Shrops 59 3527
Sutton Shrops 59 5010
Sutton Shrops 72 6631
Sutton Shrops 60 7386
Sutton Staffs 72 7622
Sutton Suffk 55 3046
Sutton W Susx 14 9715
Sutton at Hone Kent 27 5569
Sutton Bassett Nhants 50 7790
Sutton Benger Wilts 35 9478
Sutton Bingham Somset 10 5410
Sutton Bonington Notts 62 5024
Sutton Bridge Lincs 65 4721
Sutton Cheney Leics 50 4100
Sutton Coldfield W Mids 61 1295
Sutton Courtenay Oxon 37 5094
Sutton Crosses Lincs 65 4321
Sutton Fields Notts 62 4926
Sutton Grange N York 89 2873
Sutton Green Oxon 36 4107
Sutton Green Surrey 25 0054
Sutton Green Wrexhm 71 4048
Sutton Howgrave N York 89 3179
Sutton in Ashfield Notts 75 4958
Sutton in the Elms Leics 50 5193
Sutton Lane Ends Ches 79 9270
Sutton Maddock Shrops 60 7201
Sutton Mallet Somset 21 3736
Sutton Mandeville Wilts 22 9828
Sutton Manor Mersyd 78 5190
Sutton Marsh Herefd 46 5544
Sutton Montis Somset 21 6224
Sutton on Sea Lincs 77 5281
Sutton on the Hill Derbys 73 2333
Sutton on Trent Notts 75 7965
Sutton Poyntz Dorset 11 7083
Sutton Scotney Hants 24 4639
Sutton St Edmund Lincs 64 3613
Sutton St James Lincs 65 3918
Sutton St Nicholas Herefd 46 5245
Sutton Street Kent 28 8055
Sutton upon Derwent E R Yk 84 7047
Sutton Valence Kent 28 8149
Sutton Veny Wilts 22 9041
Sutton Waldron Dorset 11 8615
Sutton Weaver Ches 71 5479
Sutton Wick Oxon 37 4894
Sutton Wick Somset 21 5759
Sutton-in-Craven N York 82 0043
Sutton-on-Hull E R Yk 85 1232
Sutton-on-the-Forest N York 90 5864
Sutton-under-Brailes Warwks 48 3037
Sutton-under-Whitestonecliffe N York 90 4882
Swaby Lincs 77 3877
Swadlincote Derbys 73 2919
Swaffham Norfk 66 8108
Swaffham Bulbeck Cambs 53 5562
Swaffham Prior Cambs 53 5764
Swafield Norfk 67 2832
Swainby N York 89 4701
Swainshill Herefd 46 4641
Swainsthorpe Norfk 67 2101
Swainswick Somset 22 7668
Swalcliffe Oxon 48 3737
Swalecliffe Kent 29 1367
Swallow Lincs 85 1703
Swallow Beck Lincs 76 9467
Swallow Nest S York 75 4585
Swallowcliffe Wilts 22 9627
Swallowfield Berks 24 7264
Swallows Cross Essex 40 6198
Swampton Hants 24 4150
Swan Green Ches 79 7373
Swan Street Essex 40 8927
Swan Village W Mids 60 9892
Swanage Dorset 12 0378
Swanbourne Bucks 38 8026
Swanbridge V Glam 20 1667
Swancote Shrops 60 7494
Swanland E R Yk 84 9928
Swanley Kent 27 5168
Swanley Village Kent 27 5369
Swanmore Hants 13 5716
Swannington Lincs 62 4116
Swannington Norfk 66 1319
Swanpool Garden Suburb Lincs 76 9569
Swanscombe Kent 27 6074
Swansea Swans 32 6592
Swanton Abbot Norfk 67 2625
Swanton Morley Norfk 66 0117
Swanton Novers Norfk 66 0231
Swanton Street Kent 28 8759
Swanwick Derbys 74 4053
Swanwick Hants 13 5109
Swarby Lincs 64 0440
Swardeston Norfk 67 2002
Swarkestone Derbys 62 3728
Swarland Nthumb 103 1602
Swarland Estate Nthumb 103 1603
Swarraton Hants 24 5636
Swartha W York 82 0546
Swarthmoor Cumb 86 2777
Swaton Lincs 64 1337
Swavesey Cambs 52 3668
Sway Hants 12 2798
Swayfield Lincs 63 9922
Swaythling Hants 13 4416
Sweet Green Worcs 47 6462
Sweetham Devon 9 8899
Sweethaws E Susx 16 5028
Sweetlands Corner Kent 28 7845
Sweets Cnwll 4 1595
Sweetshouse Cnwll 4 0861
Swefling Suffk 55 3463
Swepstone Leics 62 3610
Swerford Oxon 48 3731
Swettenham Ches 72 8067
Swffryd Blae G 33 2198
Swift's Green Kent 28 8744
Swiftsden E Susx 17 7328
Swilland Suffk 54 1852
Swillbrook Lancs 80 4834
Swillington W York 83 3830
Swimbridge Devon 19 6230
Swimbridge Newland Devon 19 6030
Swinbrook Oxon 36 2812
Swincliffe N York 89 2458
Swincliffe W York 82 2027
Swincombe Devon 19 6941
Swinden N York 81 8554
Swinderby Lincs 76 8663
Swindon Gloucs 47 9325
Swindon Nthumb 102 9799
Swindon Staffs 60 8690
Swindon Wilts 36 1484
Swine E R Yk 85 1335
Swinefleet E R Yk 84 7621
Swineford Gloucs 35 6969
Swineshead Beds 51 0565
Swineshead Lincs 64 2340
Swineshead Bridge Lincs 64 2242
Swiney Highld 151 2335
Swinford Leics 50 5679
Swinford Oxon 37 4408
Swingfield Minnis Kent 29 2142
Swingfield Street Kent 29 2343
Swingleton Green Suffk 54 9647
Swinhill S Lans 116 7748
Swinhoe Nthumb 111 2128
Swinhope Lincs 76 2196
Swinithwaite N York 88 0489
Swinmore Common Herefd 47 6741
Swinscoe Staffs 73 1247
Swinside Cumb 93 2421
Swinstead Lincs 64 0122
Swinthorpe Lincs 76 0680
Swinton Border 110 8347
Swinton Gt Man 79 7701
Swinton N York 89 2179
Swinton N York 90 7573
Swinton S York 75 4599
Swithland Leics 62 5512
Swordale Highld 139 5765
Swordland Highld 129 7891
Swordly Highld 150 7463
Sworton Heath Ches 79 6884
Swyddffynnon Cerdgn 43 6966
Swynnerton Staffs 72 8535
Swyre Dorset 10 5288
Sycharth Powys 58 2025
Sychnant Powys 45 9777
Sychtyn Powys 58 9907
Sydallt Flints 71 3055
Syde Gloucs 35 9511
Sydenham Gt Lon 27 3671
Sydenham Oxon 37 7301
Sydenham Damerel Devon 5 4176
Sydenhurst Surrey 14 9534
Syderstone Norfk 66 8332
Sydling St Nicholas Dorset 10 6399
Sydmonton Hants 24 4857
Sydnal Lane Shrops 60 8005
Syerston Notts 63 7447
Syke Gt Man 81 8915
Sykehouse S York 83 6316
Syleham Suffk 55 2078
Sylen Carmth 32 5106
Symbister Shet 153 5462
Symington S Ayrs 106 3831
Symington S Lans 108 9935
Symonds Yat Herefd 34 5515
Symondsbury Dorset 10 4493
Sympson Green W York 82 1838
Synderford Dorset 10 3803
Synod Inn Cerdgn 42 4054
Syre Highld 149 6943
Syreford Gloucs 35 0220
Syresham Nhants 49 6241
Syston Leics 62 6211
Syston Lincs 63 9240
Sytchampton Worcs 47 8466
Sywell Nhants 51 8267

# T

Tabley Hill Ches 79 7379
Tackley Oxon 37 4719
Tacolneston Norfk 66 1495
Tadcaster N York 83 4843
Taddington Derbys 74 1471
Taddington Gloucs 48 0831
Taddiport Devon 18 4818
Tadley Hants 24 6061
Tadlow Cambs 52 2847
Tadmarton Oxon 48 3937
Tadwick Somset 35 7470
Tadworth Surrey 26 2257
Tafarn-y-bwlch Pembks 31 0834
Tafarn-y-Gelyn Denbgs 70 1961
Tafarnaubach Blae G 33 1210
Taff's Well Cardif 33 1283
Tafolwern Powys 57 8902
Tai'r Bull Powys 45 9925
Taibach Neath 32 7788
Tain Highld 151 2266
Tain Highld 147 7781
Tairbeart W Isls 152 1500
Takeley Essex 40 5621
Takeley Street Essex 39 5421
Tal-y-Bont Conwy 69 7668
Tal-y-bont Gwynd 57 5921
Tal-y-bont Gwynd 69 6070
Tal-y-Cafn Conwy 69 7871
Tal-y-coed Mons 34 4115
Tal-y-garn Rhondd 33 0379
Tal-y-llyn Gwynd 57 7109
Tal-y-Waun Torfn 34 2604
Talachddu Powys 45 0833
Talacre Flints 70 1183
Talaton Devon 9 0699
Talbenny Pembks 30 8411
Talbot Green Rhondd 33 0382
Talbot Village Dorset 12 0793
Taleford Devon 9 0997
Talerddig Powys 58 9300
Talgarreg Cerdgn 42 4251
Talgarth Powys 45 1533
Taliesin Cerdgn 43 6591
Talisker Highld 136 3230
Talke Staffs 72 8253
Talke Pits Staffs 72 8353
Talkin Cumb 94 5557
Talla Linnfoots Border 108 1320
Talladale Highld 144 9170
Tallaminnock S Ayrs 106 4098
Tallarn Green Wrexhm 71 4444
Tallentire Cumb 92 1035
Talley Carmth 44 6332
Tallington Lincs 64 0908
Tallwrn Wrexhm 71 2947
Talmine Highld 149 5863
Talog Carmth 31 3325
Talsarn Cerdgn 44 5456
Talsarnau Gwynd 57 6135
Talskiddy Cnwll 4 9165
Talwrn IOA 68 4877
Talwrn Wrexhm 71 3847
Talybont Cerdgn 43 6589
Talybont-on-Usk Powys 33 1122
Talysarn Gwynd 68 4952
Talywern Powys 57 8200
Tamer Lane End Gt Man 79 6401
Tamerton Foliot Devon 6 4761
Tamworth Staffs 61 2003
Tamworth Green Lincs 64 3842
Tan Hill N York 88 8906
Tan Office Green Suffk 53 7858
Tan-y-Bwlch Gwynd 57 6540
Tan-y-fron Conwy 70 9564
Tan-y-fron Wrexhm 71 2952
Tan-y-groes Cerdgn 42 2849
Tancred N York 89 4558
Tancredston Pembks 30 8826
Tandlemuir Rens 115 3361
Tandridge Surrey 27 3750
Tanfield Dur 96 1855
Tanfield Lea Dur 96 1854
Tangiers Pembks 30 9518
Tangley Hants 23 3252
Tangmere W Susx 14 9006
Tankerness Ork 153 5109
Tankersley S York 74 3499
Tankerton Kent 29 1166
Tannach Highld 151 3247
Tannachie Abers 135 7884
Tannadice Angus 134 4758
Tanner's Green Worcs 61 0874
Tannington Suffk 55 2467
Tannochside N Lans 116 7061
Tansley Derbys 74 3259
Tansor Nhants 51 0590
Tantobie Dur 96 1754
Tanton N York 90 5210
Tanwood Worcs 60 9074
Tanworth in Arden Warwks 61 1170
Tanygrisiau Gwynd 57 6945
Taobh Tuath W Isls 152 9989
Taplow Bucks 26 9182
Tarbert Ag & B 113 6551
Tarbert Ag & B 113 8668
Tarbert W Isls 152 1500
Tarbet Ag & B 123 3104
Tarbet Highld 148 1649
Tarbet Highld 129 7992
Tarbock Green Mersyd 78 4687
Tarbolton S Ayrs 107 4327
Tarbrax S Lans 117 0255
Tardebigge Worcs 47 9969
Tardy Gate Lancs 80 5425
Tarfside Angus 134 4879
Tarland Abers 134 4804
Tarleton Lancs 80 4520
Tarlscough Lancs 80 4314
Tarlton Gloucs 35 9599
Tarnock Somset 21 3752
Tarns Cumb 92 1248
Tarnside Cumb 87 4390
Tarporley Ches 71 5562
Tarr Somset 19 8632
Tarr Somset 20 1030
Tarrant Crawford Dorset 11 9203
Tarrant Gunville Dorset 11 9213
Tarrant Hinton Dorset 11 9311
Tarrant Keyneston Dorset 11 9204
Tarrant Launceston Dorset 11 9409
Tarrant Monkton Dorset 11 9408
Tarrant Rawston Dorset 11 9306
Tarrant Rushton Dorset 11 9305
Tarring Neville E Susx 16 4403
Tarrington Herefd 46 6140
Tarskavaig Highld 129 5810
Tarves Abers 143 8631
Tarvie P & K 133 0164
Tarvin Ches 71 4966
Tarvin Sands Ches 71 4967
Tasburgh Norfk 67 1996
Tasley Shrops 60 6894
Taston Oxon 36 3521
Tatenhill Staffs 73 2021
Tathall End Bucks 38 8246
Tatham Lancs 87 6069
Tathwell Lincs 77 3182
Tatsfield Surrey 27 4156
Tattenhall Ches 71 4858
Tatterford Norfk 66 8628
Tattersett Norfk 66 8429
Tattershall Lincs 76 2157
Tattershall Bridge Lincs 76 1956
Tattershall Thorpe Lincs 76 2159
Tattingstone Suffk 54 1337
Tattingstone White Horse Suffk 54 1338
Tatworth Somset 10 3205
Tauchers Moray 141 3749
Taunton Somset 20 2224
Taverham Norfk 66 1613
Taverners Green Essex 40 5618
Tavernspite Pembks 31 1812
Tavistock Devon 6 4874
Taw green Devon 8 6597
Tawstock Devon 19 5529
Taxal Derbys 79 0079
Taychreggan Hotel Ag & B 123 0421
Tayinloan Ag & B 105 6946
Taynton Gloucs 35 7222
Taynton Oxon 36 2313
Taynuilt Ag & B 122 0031
Tayport Fife 127 4628
Tayvallich Ag & B 113 7487
Tealby Lincs 76 1590
Team Valley T & W 103 2459
Teangue Highld 129 6609
Teanord Highld 140 5964
Tebay Cumb 87 6104
Tebworth Beds 38 9926
Tedburn St Mary Devon 8 8194
Teddington Gloucs 47 9633
Teddington Gt Lon 26 1670
Tedstone Delamere Herefd 47 6958
Tedstone Wafer Herefd 47 6759
Teesport N York 97 5423
Teesside Park N York 97 4618
Teeton Nhants 50 6970
Teffont Evias Wilts 22 9931
Teffont Magna Wilts 22 9932
Tegryn Pembks 31 2233
Teigh Rutlnd 63 8615
Teigncombe Devon 8 6787
Teigngrace Devon 7 8574
Teignmouth Devon 7 9473
Teindside Border 109 4408
Telford Shrops 60 6908
Tellisford Somset 22 8055
Telscombe E Susx 15 4003
Telscombe Cliffs E Susx 15 4001
Tempar P & K 124 6857
Templand D & G 100 0886
Temple C Glas 115 5469
Temple Cnwll 4 1473
Temple Mdloth 117 3158
Temple Balsall W Mids 61 2076
Temple Bar Cerdgn 44 5354
Temple Cloud Somset 21 6257
Temple End Suffk 53 6650
Temple Ewell Kent 29 2844
Temple Grafton Warwks 48 1255
Temple Guiting Gloucs 48 0928
Temple Hirst N York 83 6024
Temple Normanton Derbys 74 4167
Temple Pier Highld 139 5330
Temple Sowerby Cumb 94 6127
Templecombe Somset 22 7022
Templeton Devon 19 8813
Templeton Pembks 31 1111
Templetown Dur 95 1050
Tempsford Beds 52 1653
Ten Mile Bank Norfk 65 5996
Tenbury Wells Worcs 46 5968
Tenby Pembks 31 1300
Tendring Essex 41 1424
Tendring Green Essex 41 1325
Tendring Heath Essex 41 1326
Tenpenny Heath Essex 41 0820
Tenterden Kent 17 8833
Terling Essex 40 7715
Tern Shrops 59 6216
Ternhill Shrops 59 6332
Terregles D & G 100 9377
Terrington N York 90 6770
Terrington St Clement Norfk 65 5520
Terrington St John Norfk 65 5314
Terry's Green Warwks 61 1073
Teston Kent 28 7053
Testwood Hants 12 3514
Tetbury Gloucs 35 8993
Tetbury Upton Gloucs 35 8895
Tetchill Shrops 59 3932
Tetcott Devon 5 3396
Tetford Lincs 77 3374
Tetney Lincs 77 3100
Tetney Lock Lincs 85 3402
Tetsworth Oxon 37 6801
Tettenhall W Mids 60 8800
Tettenhall Wood W Mids 60 8899
Teworth Cambs 52 2253
Teversal Notts 75 4861
Teversham Cambs 53 4958
Teviothead Border 109 4005
Tewel Abers 135 8085
Tewin Herts 39 2714
Tewkesbury Gloucs 47 8932
Teynham Kent 28 9662
Thackley W York 82 1738
Thackthwaite Cumb 92 1423
Thackthwaite Cumb 93 4225
Thakeham W Susx 14 1017
Thame Oxon 37 7005
Thames Ditton Surrey 26 1567
Thamesmead Gt Lon 27 4780
Thanington Kent 29 1356
Thankerton S Lans 108 9738
Tharston Norfk 66 1894
Thatcham Berks 24 5167
Thatto Heath Mersyd 78 5093
Thaxted Essex 40 6131
The Bank Ches 72 8457
The Bank Shrops 59 6199
The Beeches Gloucs 36 0302
The Biggins Cambs 53 4788
The Blythe Staffs 73 0428
The Bog Shrops 59 3597
The Bourne Worcs 47 9856
The Braes Highld 137 5234
The Bratch Staffs 60 8693
The Broad Herefd 46 4961
The Brunt E Loth 118 6873
The Bungalow IOM 158 3986
The Bush Kent 28 6649
The Butts Gloucs 35 8916
The Camp Gloucs 35 9109
The Chequer Wrexhm 71 4840
The City Beds 52 1159
The City Bucks 37 7896
The Common Oxon 48 2927
The Common Wilts 35 0285
The Common Wilts 23 2432
The Corner Kent 28 7041
The Corner Shrops 59 4387
The Cronk IOM 158 3395
The Den N Ayrs 115 3251
The Flatt Cumb 101 5678
The Forge Herefd 46 3459
The Forstal E Susx 16 5435
The Forstal Kent 28 8946
The Forstal Kent 28 0438
The Fouralls Shrops 72 6831
The Green Cumb 86 1884
The Green Essex 40 7719
The Green N York 90 7705
The Grove Worcs 47 8741
The Haven W Susx 14 0830
The Haw Gloucs 47 8427
The Hill Cumb 86 1783
The Holt Berks 37 8078
The Hundred Herefd 46 5264
The Leacon Kent 17 9833
The Lee Bucks 38 9004
The Lhen IOM 158 3801
The Lochs Moray 141 3062
The Marsh Powys 59 3197
The Middles Dur 96 2051
The Moor Kent 17 7529
The Mumbles Swans 32 6187
The Murray S Lans 116 6353
The Mythe Gloucs 47 8934
The North Mons 34 5206
The Neuk Abers 135 7397
The Quarry Gloucs 35 7499
The Quarter Kent 28 8844
The Reddings Gloucs 35 9121
The Rookery Staffs 72 8555
The Ross P & K 124 7621
The Sands Surrey 25 8846
The Shoe Wilts 35 8074
The Smithies Shrops 60 6897
The Spike Cambs 53 4848
The Spring Warwks 61 2873
The Square Torfn 34 2796
The Stair Kent 16 6047
The Stocks Kent 17 9127
The Straits Hants 25 7839
The Strand Wilts 22 9259
The Thrift Herts 39 3139
The Towans Cnwll 2 5538
The Vauld Herefd 46 5349
The Wyke Shrops 60 7206
Theakston N York 89 3085
Thealby Lincs 84 8917
Theale Berks 24 6471
Theale Somset 21 4646
Thearne E R Yk 85 0736
Theberton Suffk 55 4365
Thedden Grange Hants 24 6839
Theddingworth Leics 50 6685
Theddlethorpe All Saints Lincs 77 4688
Theddlethorpe St Helen Lincs 77 4788
Thelbridge Cross Devon 19 7911

Tovil
Uckerby
313

Tovil Kent 28 7554
Tow Law Dur 95 1138
Towan Cnwll 4 8774
Towan Cnwll 3 0148
Toward Ag & B 114 1368
Toward Quay Ag & B 114 1167
Towcester Nhants 49 6948
Towednack Cnwll 2 4838
Towersey Oxon 37 7305
Towie Abers 134 4312
Town End Cambs 65 4195
Town End Cumb 86 2692
Town End Cumb 87 3406
Town End Cumb 94 6325
Town End Cumb 87 3687
Town End Cumb 87 4483
Town Green Lancs 78 4005
Town Green Norfk 67 3612
Town Head Cumb 87 4103
Town Head N York 88 8258
Town Head N York 82 1748
Town Kelloe Dur 96 3536
Town Lane Gt Man 79 6999
Town Littleworth E Susx 15 4117
Town of Lowdon Mersyd 78 6196
Town Row E Susx 16 5630
Town Street Suffk 53 7785
Town Yetholm Border 110 8128
Townend W Duns 115 3976
Towngate Cumb 94 5246
Towngate Lincs 64 1310
Townhead Cumb 92 0735
Townhead Cumb 94 6334
Townhead D & G 100 0088
Townhead S York 82 1602
Townhead of Greenlaw D & G 99 7464
Townhill Fife 117 1089
Townlake Devon 5 4074
Towns End Hants 24 5659
Townsend Somset 10 3614
Townshend Cnwll 2 5932
Townwell Gloucs 35 7090
Towthorpe E R Yk 91 8962
Towthorpe N York 90 6258
Towton N York 83 4839
Towyn Conwy 70 9779
Toxteth Mersyd 78 3588
Toy's Hill Kent 27 4651
Toynton All Saints Lincs 77 3963
Toynton Fen Side Lincs 77 3961
Toynton St Peter Lincs 77 4063
Trabboch E Ayrs 107 4421
Trabbochburn E Ayrs 107 4621
Traboe Cnwll 3 7421
Tracebridge Somset 20 0621
Tradespark Highld 140 8656
Traethsaith Cerdgn 42 2851
Trafford Park Gt Man 79 7896
Trallong Powys 45 9629
Tranent E Loth 118 4072
Tranmere Mersyd 78 3187
Trannack Cnwll 2 5633
Trantelbeg Highld 150 8952
Trantlemore Highld 150 8953
Tranwell Nthumb 103 1883
Trap's Green Warwks 48 1069
Trapp Carmth 32 6518
Traprain E Loth 118 5975
Trapshill Berks 23 3763
Traquair Border 109 3334
Trash Green Berks 24 6569
Traveller's Rest Devon 19 6127
Trawden Lancs 81 9138
Trawscoed Cerdgn 43 6672
Trawsfynydd Gwynd 57 7035
Tre Aubrey V Glam 33 0372
Tre'r-ddol Cerdgn 43 6692
Tre-gagle Mons 34 5207
Tre-Gibbon Rhondd 33 9905
Tre-groes Cerdgn 42 4044
Tre-Mostyn Flints 70 1479
Tre-Vaughan Carmth 31 3921
Tre-wyn Mons 34 3222
Trealaw Rhondd 33 0092
Treales Lancs 80 4332
Treamble Cnwll 3 7856
Trearddur Bay IOA 68 2579
Treaslane Highld 136 3953
Treator Cnwll 4 9075
Trebanog Rhondd 33 0190
Trebanos Neath 32 7103
Trebartha Cnwll 5 2677
Trebarvah Cnwll 2 7130
Trebarwith Cnwll 4 0586
Trebeath Cnwll 5 2587
Trebehor Cnwll 2 3724
Trebelzue Cnwll 4 8464
Trebetherick Cnwll 4 9378
Treborough Somset 20 0136
Trebudannon Cnwll 4 8961
Trebullett Cnwll 5 3278
Treburgett Cnwll 4 0579
Treburick Cnwll 4 8971
Treburley Cnwll 5 3577
Treburrick Cnwll 4 8670
Trebyan Cnwll 4 0763
Trecastle Powys 45 8829
Trecogo Cnwll 5 3080
Trecott Devon 8 6300
Trecwn Pembks 30 9632
Trecynon Rhondd 33 9903
Tredaule Cnwll 5 2381
Tredavoe Cnwll 2 4528
Tredegar Blae G 33 1408
Tredethy Cnwll 4 0672
Tredington Gloucs 47 9029
Tredington Warwks 48 2543
Tredinnick Cnwll 4 9270
Tredinnick Cnwll 4 0459
Tredinnick Cnwll 4 1666
Tredinnick Cnwll 5 2357
Tredinnick Cnwll 5 2957
Tredomen Powys 45 1231
Tredrissi Pembks 31 0742
Tredrizzick Cnwll 4 9577
Tredunhock Mons 34 3794
Tredustan Powys 45 1332
Treen Cnwll 2 4337
Treen Cnwll 2 3923
Treesmill Cnwll 3 0855
Treeton S York 75 4387
Trefasser Pembks 30 8938
Trefdraeth IOA 68 4170
Trefecca Powys 45 1431
Trefeglwys Powys 58 9690
Trefenter Cerdgn 43 6068
Treffgarne Pembks 30 9523
Treffgarne Owen Pembks 30 8625
Trefforest Rhondd 33 0888
Treffynnon Pembks 30 8528
Trefil Blae G 33 1212
Trefilan Cerdgn 44 5456
Treflach Wood Shrops 58 2625
Trefnannau Powys 58 2316
Trefnant Denbgs 70 0570
Trefonen Shrops 58 2526
Trefor Gwynd 56 3746
Trefor IOA 68 3780
Treforda Cnwll 4 0988
Trefrew Cnwll 4 1084
Trefriw Conwy 69 7863
Tregadillett Cnwll 5 2983
Tregaian IOA 68 4580
Tregare Mons 34 4110
Tregarne Cnwll 3 7823
Tregaron Cerdgn 44 6759
Tregarth Gwynd 69 6067
Tregaswith Cnwll 4 8962
Tregatta Cnwll 4 0587
Tregawne Cnwll 4 0066
Tregear Cnwll 3 8650
Tregeare Cnwll 5 2486
Tregeiriog Wrexhm 58 1733
Tregele IOA 68 3592
Tregellist Cnwll 4 0177
Tregenna Cnwll 3 8743
Tregenna Cnwll 4 0973
Tregeseal Cnwll 2 3731
Tregew Cnwll 3 8034
Tregidden Cnwll 3 7523
Tregiddle Cnwll 2 6723
Tregidgeo Cnwll 3 9647
Tregiskey Cnwll 3 0146
Treglemais Pembks 30 8229
Tregole Cnwll 5 1998
Tregolls Cnwll 3 7335
Tregonce Cnwll 4 9373
Tregonetha Cnwll 4 9563
Tregony Cnwll 3 9244
Tregoodwell Cnwll 4 1183
Tregoose Cnwll 2 6823
Tregoss Cnwll 4 9660
Tregowris Cnwll 3 7722
Tregoyd Powys 45 1937
Tregrehan Mills Cnwll 3 0453
Tregullon Cnwll 4 0664
Tregunna Cnwll 4 9673
Tregunnon Cnwll 5 2283
Tregurrian Cnwll 4 8565
Tregustick Cnwll 4 9866
Tregynon Powys 58 0998
Trehafod Rhondd 33 0490
Trehan Cnwll 5 4058
Treharris Myr Td 33 0996
Treharrock Cnwll 4 0178
Trehemborne Cnwll 4 8773
Treherbert Carmth 44 5847
Treherbert Rhondd 33 9498
Treheveras Cnwll 3 8046
Trehunist Cnwll 5 3263
Trekelland Cnwll 5 3480
Trekenner Cnwll 5 3478
Treknow Cnwll 4 0586
Trelan Cnwll 3 7418
Trelash Cnwll 4 1890
Trelassick Cnwll 3 8752
Trelawne Cnwll 5 2154
Trelawnyd Flints 70 0979
Treleague Cnwll 3 7821
Treleaver Cnwll 3 7716
Trelech Carmth 31 2830
Trelech a'r Betws Carmth 31 3026
Treleddyd-fawr Pembks 30 7528
Trelew Cnwll 3 8135
Trelewis Myr Td 33 1096
Treligga Cnwll 4 0484
Trelights Cnwll 4 9979
Trelill Cnwll 4 0478
Trelinnoe Cnwll 5 3181
Trelion Cnwll 3 9252
Trelissick Cnwll 3 8339
Trelleck Mons 34 5005
Trelleck Grange Mons 34 4901
Trelogan Flints 70 1180
Trelonk Cnwll 3 8941
Trelow Cnwll 4 9269
Trelowarren Cnwll 2 7124
Trelowia Cnwll 5 2956
Treluggan Cnwll 3 8838
Trelystan Powys 58 2503
Tremadog Gwynd 57 5640
Tremail Cnwll 4 1686
Tremain Cerdgn 42 2348
Tremaine Cnwll 5 2389
Tremar Cnwll 5 2568
Trematon Cnwll 5 3959
Trembraze Cnwll 5 2565
Tremeirchion Denbgs 70 0873
Tremethick Cross Cnwll 2 4430
Tremollett Cnwll 5 2975
Tremore Cnwll 4 0164
Trenance Cnwll 3 8022
Trenance Cnwll 4 8568
Trenance Cnwll 4 9270
Trenance Cnwll 2 6718
Trenarren Cnwll 3 0348
Trenault Cnwll 5 2683
Trench Shrops 60 6912
Trench Green Oxon 37 6877
Trencreek Cnwll 4 8260
Trencreek Cnwll 4 1896
Trendeal Cnwll 3 8952
Trendrine Cnwll 2 4739
Treneague Cnwll 4 9871
Trenear Cnwll 2 6731
Treneglos Cnwll 5 2088
Trenerth Cnwll 2 6035
Trenewan Cnwll 4 1753
Trenewth Cnwll 4 0778
Trengothal Cnwll 2 3724
Trengune Cnwll 4 1893
Treninnick Cnwll 4 8160
Trenowah Cnwll 4 7959
Trenoweth Cnwll 3 7533
Trent Dorset 10 5918
Trent Port Lincs 76 8381
Trent Vale Staffs 72 8643
Trentham Staffs 72 8740
Trentishoe Devon 19 6448
Trentlock Derbys 62 4831
Treoes V Glam 33 9478
Treorchy Rhondd 33 9597
Trequite Cnwll 4 0377
Trerhyngyll V Glam 33 0077
Trerulefoot Cnwll 5 3358
Tresahor Cnwll 3 7431
Tresawle Cnwll 3 8846
Trescott Staffs 60 8597
Trescowe Cnwll 2 5731
Tresean Cnwll 4 7858
Tresham Gloucs 35 7991
Tresillian Cnwll 3 8646
Tresinney Cnwll 4 1081
Treskinnick Cross Cnwll 5 2098
Treslea Cnwll 4 1368
Tresmeer Cnwll 5 2387
Tresparrett Cnwll 4 1491
Tressait P & K 132 8160
Tresta Shet 153 3650
Tresta Shet 153 6090
Treswell Notts 75 7879
Treswithian Cnwll 2 6241
Trethawle Cnwll 5 2662
Trethevey Cnwll 4 0789
Trethewey Cnwll 2 3823
Trethomas Caerph 33 1888
Trethosa Cnwll 3 9454
Trethurgy Cnwll 3 0355
Tretio Pembks 30 7829
Tretire Herefd 46 5123
Tretower Powys 33 1821
Treuddyn Flints 70 2557
Trevadlock Cnwll 5 2679
Trevague Cnwll 5 2379
Trevalga Cnwll 4 0890
Trevalyn Wrexhm 71 3856
Trevanger Cnwll 4 9677
Trevanson Cnwll 4 9773
Trevarrack Cnwll 2 4731
Trevarren Cnwll 4 9160
Trevarrian Cnwll 4 8566
Trevarrick Cnwll 3 9843
Trevarth Cnwll 3 7240
Trevaughan Carmth 31 2015
Treveal Cnwll 2 4740
Treveal Cnwll 4 7858
Treveale Cnwll 3 8751
Treveighan Cnwll 4 0779
Trevellas Downs Cnwll 3 7452
Trevelmond Cnwll 5 2063
Trevemper Cnwll 4 8159
Treveneague Cnwll 2 5432
Treveor Cnwll 3 9841
Treverbyn Cnwll 3 8849
Treverbyn Cnwll 4 0157
Treverva Cnwll 3 7531
Trevescan Cnwll 2 3524
Trevethin Torfn 34 2801
Trevia Cnwll 4 0983
Trevigro Cnwll 5 3369
Trevilla Cnwll 3 8239
Trevilledor Cnwll 4 8867
Trevilson Cnwll 3 8455
Trevine Pembks 30 8432
Treviscoe Cnwll 3 9455
Treviskey Cnwll 3 9340
Trevissick Cnwll 3 0248
Trevithal Cnwll 2 4626
Trevithick Cnwll 4 8862
Trevithick Cnwll 3 9645
Trevivian Cnwll 4 1785
Trevoll Cnwll 4 8358
Trevone Cnwll 4 8975
Trevor Denbgs 70 2742
Trevorgans Cnwll 2 4025
Trevorrick Cnwll 4 8672
Trevorrick Cnwll 4 9273
Trevose Cnwll 4 8675
Trew Cnwll 2 6129
Trewalder Cnwll 4 0782
Trewalkin Powys 45 1531
Trewarlett Cnwll 5 3380
Trewarmett Cnwll 4 0686
Trewarthenick Cnwll 3 9044
Trewassa Cnwll 4 1486
Trewavas Cnwll 2 5926
Treween Cnwll 5 2182
Trewellard Cnwll 2 3733
Trewen Cnwll 5 2583
Trewen Cnwll 4 0577
Trewennack Cnwll 2 6728
Trewent Pembks 30 0197
Trewern Powys 58 2811
Trewetha Cnwll 4 0080
Trewethern Cnwll 4 0076
Trewidland Cnwll 5 2559
Trewillis Cnwll 3 7717
Trewince Cnwll 3 8633
Trewint Cnwll 4 1072
Trewint Cnwll 5 2180
Trewint Cnwll 5 2963
Trewirgie Cnwll 3 8845
Trewithian Cnwll 3 8737
Trewoodloe Cnwll 5 3271
Trewoofe Cnwll 2 4425
Trewoon Cnwll 2 6819
Trewoon Cnwll 3 9952
Treworgan Cnwll 3 8349
Treworlas Cnwll 3 8938
Treworld Cnwll 4 1190
Treworthal Cnwll 3 8839
Treyarnon Cnwll 4 8673
Treyford W Susx 14 8218
Triangle W York 82 0422
Trickett's Cross Dorset 12 0800
Triermain Cumb 102 5966
Triffleton Pembks 30 9724
Trillacott Cnwll 5 2689
Trimdon Dur 96 3634
Trimdon Colliery Dur 96 3735
Trimdon Grange Dur 96 3635
Trimingham Norfk 67 2838
Trimley Suffk 55 2737
Trimley Heath Suffk 55 2738
Trimley Lower Street Suffk 55 2636
Trimpley Worcs 60 7978
Trims Green Herts 39 4717
Trimsaran Carmth 32 4504
Trimstone Devon 19 5043
Trinafour P & K 132 7264
Trinant Caerph 33 2099
Tring Herts 38 9211
Tring Wharf Herts 38 9212
Tringford Herts 38 9113
Trinity Angus 134 6061
Trinity Jersey 158 0000
Trinity Gask P & K 125 9618
Triscombe Somset 20 9237
Triscombe Somset 20 1535
Trislaig Highld 130 0874
Trispen Cnwll 3 8450
Tritlington Nthumb 103 2092
Troan Cnwll 4 8957
Trochry P & K 125 9740
Troedrhiwfuwch Caerph 33 1204
Troedyraur Cerdgn 42 3245
Troedyrhiw Myr Td 33 0702
Trofarth Conwy 69 8571
Trois Bois Jersey 158 0000
Troon Cnwll 2 6638
Troon S Ayrs 106 3230
Troston Suffk 54 8972
Troswell Cnwll 5 2592
Trotshill Worcs 47 8855
Trottiscliffe Kent 27 6460
Trotton W Susx 14 8322
Trough Gate Lancs 81 8821
Troughend Nthumb 102 8692
Troutbeck Cumb 93 3927
Troutbeck Cumb 87 4002
Troutbeck Bridge Cumb 87 4000
Troway Derbys 74 3879
Trowbridge Wilts 22 8558
Trowell Notts 62 4839
Trowle Common Wilts 22 8458
Trowse Newton Norfk 67 2406
Troy W York 82 2439
Trudoxhill Somset 22 7443
Trull Somset 20 2122
Trumfleet S York 83 6011
Trumpan Highld 136 2261
Trumpet Herefd 47 6539
Trumpington Cambs 53 4454
Trumpsgreen Surrey 25 9967
Trunch Norfk 67 2834
Trunnah Lancs 80 3442
Truro Cnwll 3 8244
Truscott Cnwll 5 2985
Trusham Devon 8 8582
Trusley Derbys 73 2535
Trusthorpe Lincs 77 5183
Trysull Staffs 60 8594
Tubney Oxon 36 4399
Tuckenhay Devon 7 8156
Tuckhill Shrops 60 7888
Tuckingmill Cnwll 2 6540
Tuckingmill Wilts 22 9329
Tuckton Dorset 12 1492
Tucoyse Cnwll 3 9645
Tuddenham Suffk 53 7371
Tuddenham Suffk 55 1948
Tudeley Kent 16 6245
Tudhoe Dur 96 2535
Tudorville Herefd 46 5922
Tudweiloig Gwynd 56 2436
Tuesley Surrey 25 9642
Tuffley Gloucs 35 8314
Tufton Hants 24 4546
Tufton Pembks 30 0428
Tugby Leics 63 7601
Tugford Shrops 59 5587
Tughall Nthumb 111 2126
Tullibody Clacks 116 8595
Tullich Ag & B 123 0815
Tullich Highld 140 6328
Tullich Highld 147 8576
Tulliemet P & K 125 0052
Tulloch Abers 143 8031
Tulloch Stirlg 124 5120
Tulloch Station Highld 131 3580
Tullochgorm Ag & B 114 9695
Tullybeagles Lodge P & K 125 0136
Tullynessle Abers 142 5519
Tulse Hill Gt Lon 27 3172
Tumble Carmth 32 5411
Tumbler's Green Essex 40 8025
Tumby Lincs 76 2359
Tumby Woodside Lincs 77 2757
Tummel Bridge P & K 132 7659
Tunbridge Wells Kent 16 5839
Tundergarth D & G 101 1780
Tungate Norfk 67 2629
Tunstall E R Yk 85 3031
Tunstall Kent 28 8961
Tunstall Lancs 87 6073
Tunstall N York 89 2196
Tunstall Norfk 67 4107
Tunstall Staffs 72 7727
Tunstall Staffs 72 8651
Tunstall Suffk 55 3655
Tunstall T & W 96 3953
Tunstead Derbys 74 1074
Tunstead Norfk 67 2921
Tunstead Milton Derbys 79 0180
Tunworth Hants 24 6748
Tupsley Herefd 46 5340
Tur Langton Leics 50 7194
Turgis Green Hants 24 6959
Turkdean Gloucs 36 1017
Turleigh Wilts 22 8060
Turleygreen Shrops 60 7685
Turn Lancs 81 8118
Turnastone Herefd 46 3536
Turnberry S Ayrs 106 2005
Turnchapel Devon 6 4953
Turnditch Derbys 73 2946
Turner Green Lancs 81 6030
Turner's Green E Susx 16 6319
Turner's Green Warwks 48 1969
Turner's Hill W Susx 15 3435
Turners Puddle Dorset 11 8393
Turnford Herts 39 3604
Turnhouse C Edin 117 1674
Turnworth Dorset 11 8207
Turriff Abers 142 7250
Turton Bottoms Gt Man 81 7315
Turves Cambs 64 3396
Turvey Beds 38 9452
Turville Bucks 37 7691
Turville Heath Bucks 37 7490
Turweston Bucks 49 6037
Tushielaw Inn Border 109 3017
Tushingham cum Grindley Ches 71 5246
Tutbury Staffs 73 2128
Tutnall Worcs 60 9970
Tutshill Gloucs 34 5494
Tuttington Norfk 67 2227
Tutwell Cnwll 5 3875
Tuxford Notts 75 7471
Twatt Ork 153 2724
Twatt Shet 153 3253
Twechar E Duns 116 6975
Tweedmouth Nthumb 119 9952
Tweedsmuir Border 108 1024
Twelve Oaks E Susx 16 6820
Twelveheads Cnwll 3 7542
Twemlow Green Ches 79 7868
Twenty Lincs 64 1520
Twerton Somset 22 7264
Twickenham Gt Lon 26 1673
Twigworth Gloucs 35 8422
Twineham W Susx 15 2519
Twineham Green W Susx 15 2520
Twinhoe Somset 22 7559
Twinstead Essex 54 8636
Twiss Green Ches 79 6595
Twitchen Devon 19 7930
Twitchen Shrops 46 3779
Twitham Kent 29 2656
Two Bridges Devon 6 6174
Two Dales Derbys 74 2763
Two Gates Staffs 61 2101
Two Mile Oak Cross Devon 7 8468
Two Pots Devon 19 5344
Two Waters Herts 38 0505
Twycross Leics 62 3304
Twyford Berks 37 7976
Twyford Bucks 49 6626
Twyford Hants 13 4824
Twyford Leics 63 7210
Twyford Lincs 63 9323
Twyford Norfk 66 0123
Twyford Common Herefd 46 5135
Twyn-carno Caerph 33 1108
Twyn-y-Sheriff Mons 34 4005
Twyn-yr-Odyn V Glam 33 1173
Twynholm D & G 99 6654
Twyning Gloucs 47 8936
Twyning Green Gloucs 47 9036
Twynllanan Carmth 44 7524
Twywell Nhants 51 9578
Ty'n-dwr Denbgs 70 2341
Ty'n-y-bryn Rhondd 33 0087
Ty'n-y-coedcae Caerph 33 1988
Ty'n-y-Groes Conwy 69 7771
Ty-nant Conwy 70 9944
Ty-nant Gwynd 58 9026
Tyberton Herefd 46 3839
Tyburn W Mids 61 1391
Tycroes Carmth 32 6010
Tycrwyn Powys 58 1018
Tydd Gote Lincs 65 4518
Tydd St Giles Cambs 65 4216
Tydd St Mary Lincs 65 4418
Tye Hants 13 7302
Tye Green Essex 39 5424
Tye Green Essex 53 5935
Tye Green Essex 40 7821
Tyersal W York 82 1932
Tyldesley Gt Man 79 6802
Tyler Hill Kent 29 1461
Tyler's Green Essex 39 5005
Tylers Green Bucks 26 9093
Tylers Green Surrey 27 3552
Tylorstown Rhondd 33 0095
Tylwch Powys 58 9780
Tyn-y-nant Rhondd 33 0685
Tyndrum Stirlg 123 3230
Tyneham Dorset 11 8880
Tynemouth T & W 103 3669
Tynewydd Rhondd 33 9398
Tyninghame E Loth 118 6179
Tynron D & G 100 8093
Tynygongl IOA 68 5082
Tynygraig Cerdgn 43 6969
Tyringham Bucks 38 8547
Tyseley W Mids 61 1184
Tythegston Brdgnd 33 8578
Tytherington Ches 79 9175
Tytherington Gloucs 35 6688
Tytherington Somset 22 7644
Tytherington Wilts 22 9141
Tytherleigh Devon 10 3103
Tytherton Lucas Wilts 35 9474
Tywardreath Cnwll 3 0854
Tywardreath Highway Cnwll 3 0755
Tywyn Conwy 69 7878
Tywyn Gwynd 57 5800

## U

Ubbeston Green Suffk 55 3271
Ubley Somset 21 5258
Uckerby N York 89 2402

Uckfield Walton

314


Uckfield *E Susx* 16 4721
Uckinghall *Worcs* 47 8637
Uckington *Gloucs* 47 9124
Uckington *Shrops* 59 5709
Uddingston *S Lans* 116 6960
Uddington *S Lans* 108 8633
Udimore *E Susx* 17 8719
Udny Green *Abers* 143 8726
Udny Station *Abers* 143 9024
Uffcott *Wilts* 36 1277
Uffculme *Devon* 9 0612
Uffington *Oxon* 36 3089
Uffington *Shrops* 59 5313
Ufford *Cambs* 64 0903
Ufford *Suffk* 55 2952
Ufton *Warwks* 48 3762
Ufton Nervet *Berks* 24 6367
Ugadale *Ag & B* 105 7828
Ugborough *Devon* 7 6755
Uggeshall *Suffk* 55 4480
Ugglebarnby *N York* 90 8707
Ughill *Derbys* 74 2590
Ugley *Essex* 39 5228
Ugley Green *Essex* 39 5227
Ugthorpe *N York* 90 7911
Uig *Ag & B* 120 1654
Uig *Highld* 136 1952
Uig *Highld* 136 3963
Uig *W Isls* 152 0533
Uigshader *Highld* 136 4346
Uisken *Ag & B* 121 3919
Ulbster *Highld* 151 3241
Ulcat Row *Cumb* 93 4022
Ulceby *Lincs* 85 1014
Ulceby *Lincs* 77 4272
Ulceby Cross *Lincs* 77 4173
Ulceby Skitter *Lincs* 85 1215
Ulcombe *Kent* 28 8448
Uldale *Cumb* 93 2437
Uley *Gloucs* 35 7898
Ulgham *Nthumb* 103 2392
Ullapool *Highld* 145 1294
Ullenhall *Warwks* 48 1267
Ullenwood *Gloucs* 35 9416
Ulleskelf *N York* 83 5239
Ullesthorpe *Leics* 50 5087
Ulley *S York* 75 4687
Ullingswick *Herefd* 46 5949
Ullinish Lodge Hotel *Highld* 136 3237
Ullock *Cumb* 92 0724
Ulpha *Cumb* 86 1993
Ulpha *Cumb* 87 4581
Ulrome *E R Yk* 85 1656
Ulsta *Shet* 153 4680
Ulting Wick *Essex* 40 8009
Ulverley Green *W Mids* 61 1382
Ulverston *Cumb* 86 2878
Ulwell *Dorset* 12 0280
Umachan *Highld* 137 6050
Umberleigh *Devon* 19 6023
Unapool *Highld* 148 2333
Under Burnmouth *Border* 101 4783
Under River *Kent* 27 5552
Underbarrow *Cumb* 87 4692
Undercliffe *W York* 82 1834
Underdale *Shrops* 59 5013
Underley Hall *Cumb* 87 6179
Underling Green *Kent* 28 7546
Underwood *Notts* 75 4750
Undley *Suffk* 53 6981
Undy *Mons* 34 4386
Union Mills *IOM* 158 3577
Union Street *E Susx* 16 7031
Unstone *Derbys* 74 3777
Unstone Green *Derbys* 74 3776
Unsworth *Gt Man* 79 8207
Unthank *Cumb* 93 3948
Unthank *Cumb* 93 4536
Unthank *Cumb* 94 6040
Unthank *Derbys* 74 3075
Unthank *Nthumb* 111 9848
Unthank End *Cumb* 93 4535
Up Cerne *Dorset* 11 6502
Up Exe *Devon* 9 9402
Up Holland *Lancs* 78 5205
Up Marden *W Susx* 14 7913
Up Mudford *Somset* 10 5718
Up Nately *Hants* 24 6951
Up Somborne *Hants* 23 3932
Up Sydling *Dorset* 10 6201
Upavon *Wilts* 23 1354
Upchurch *Kent* 28 8467
Upcott *Devon* 19 5838
Upcott *Devon* 19 7529
Upcott *Herefd* 46 3250
Upcott *Somset* 20 9025
Updown Hill *Surrey* 25 9363
Upend *Cambs* 53 7058
Upgate *Norfk* 66 1318
Upgate Street *Norfk* 66 0992
Upgate Street *Norfk* 67 2891
Uphall *Dorset* 10 5502
Uphall *W Loth* 117 0671
Upham *Devon* 19 8808
Upham *Hants* 13 5320
Uphampton *Herefd* 46 3963
Uphampton *Worcs* 47 8364
Uphill *Somset* 21 3158
Uplawmoor *E Rens* 115 4355
Upleadon *Gloucs* 47 7527
Upleatham *N York* 97 6319
Uplees *Kent* 28 0064
Uploders *Dorset* 10 5093
Uplowman *Devon* 9 0115
Uplyme *Devon* 10 3293
Upminster *Gt Lon* 27 5686
Upottery *Devon* 9 2007
Uppaton *Devon* 5 4380
Upper Affcot *Shrops* 59 4486
Upper Ardchronie *Highld* 146 6188
Upper Arley *Worcs* 60 7680
Upper Arncott *Oxon* 37 6117
Upper Astrop *Nhants* 49 5137
Upper Basildon *Berks* 37 5976
Upper Batley *W York* 82 2325
Upper Beeding *W Susx* 15 1910
Upper Benefield *Nhants* 51 9789
Upper Bentley *Worcs* 47 9966
Upper Bighouse *Highld* 150 8856
Upper Birchwood *Derbys* 75 4355
Upper Boat *Rhondd* 33 1086
Upper Boddington *Nhants* 49 4852
Upper Borth *Cerdgn* 43 6088
Upper Brailes *Warwks* 48 3039
Upper Breakish *Highld* 129 6823
Upper Breinton *Herefd* 46 4640
Upper Broadheath *Worcs* 47 8056
Upper Broughton *Notts* 63 6826
Upper Bucklebury *Berks* 24 5468
Upper Burgate *Hants* 12 1516
Upper Bush *Kent* 28 6966
Upper Caldecote *Beds* 52 1645
Upper Canada *Somset* 21 3658
Upper Canterton *Hants* 12 2612
Upper Catesby *Nhants* 49 5259
Upper Catshill *Worcs* 60 9674
Upper Chapel *Powys* 45 0040
Upper Cheddon *Somset* 20 2328
Upper Chicksgrove *Wilts* 22 9529
Upper Chute *Wilts* 23 2953
Upper Clapton *Gt Lon* 27 3487
Upper Clatford *Hants* 23 3543
Upper Clynnog *Gwynd* 56 4646
Upper Coberley *Gloucs* 35 9816
Upper Cokeham *W Susx* 15 1605
Upper Cotton *Staffs* 73 0547
Upper Cound *Shrops* 59 5505
Upper Cudworth *S York* 83 3909
Upper Cumberworth *W York* 82 2008
Upper Cwmtwrch *Powys* 32 7511
Upper Dallachy *Moray* 141 3662
Upper Deal *Kent* 29 3651
Upper Dean *Beds* 51 0467
Upper Denby *W York* 82 2207
Upper Denton *Cumb* 102 6165
Upper Dicker *E Susx* 16 5509
Upper Dinchope *Shrops* 59 4583
Upper Dounreay *Highld* 150 0065
Upper Dovercourt *Essex* 41 2330
Upper Drumbane *Stirlg* 124 6606
Upper Dunsforth *N York* 89 4463
Upper Eashing *Surrey* 25 9543
Upper Egleton *Herefd* 47 6344
Upper Elkstone *Staffs* 74 0558
Upper Ellastone *Staffs* 73 1043
Upper End *Derbys* 74 0875
Upper Enham *Hants* 23 3650
Upper Ethie *Highld* 140 7662
Upper Farmcote *Shrops* 60 7791
Upper Farringdon *Hants* 24 7135
Upper Framilode *Gloucs* 35 7510
Upper Froyle *Hants* 24 7543
Upper Godney *Somset* 21 4842
Upper Gravenhurst *Beds* 38 1136
Upper Green *Berks* 23 3763
Upper Green *Essex* 53 5935
Upper Green *Mons* 34 3818
Upper Green *Suffk* 53 7464
Upper Grove Common *Herefd* 46 5526
Upper Hackney *Derbys* 74 2861
Upper Hale *Surrey* 25 8349
Upper Halliford *Surrey* 26 0968
Upper Halling *Kent* 28 6964
Upper Hambleton *Rutlnd* 63 9007
Upper Harbledown *Kent* 29 1158
Upper Hardres Court *Kent* 29 1550
Upper Hardwick *Herefd* 46 4057
Upper Hartfield *E Susx* 16 4634
Upper Hartshay *Derbys* 74 3850
Upper Hatherley *Gloucs* 35 9220
Upper Hatton *Staffs* 72 8237
Upper Haugh *S York* 74 4297
Upper Hayton *Shrops* 59 5181
Upper Heaton *W York* 82 1719
Upper Helmsley *N York* 83 6956
Upper Hergest *Herefd* 46 2654
Upper Heyford *Nhants* 49 6659
Upper Heyford *Oxon* 49 4925
Upper Hiendley *W York* 83 3913
Upper Hill *Herefd* 46 4753
Upper Hockenden *Kent* 27 5069
Upper Hopton *W York* 82 1918
Upper Howsell *Worcs* 47 7848
Upper Hulme *Staffs* 73 0160
Upper Ifold *Surrey* 14 0033
Upper Inglesham *Wilts* 36 2096
Upper Kilcott *Gloucs* 35 7988
Upper Killay *Swans* 32 5892
Upper Kinchrackine *Ag & B* 123 1627
Upper Lambourn *Berks* 36 3080
Upper Landywood *Staffs* 60 9805
Upper Langford *Somset* 21 4659
Upper Langwith *Derbys* 75 5169
Upper Largo *Fife* 127 4203
Upper Leigh *Staffs* 73 0136
Upper Ley *Gloucs* 35 7217
Upper Littleton *Somset* 21 5564
Upper Longdon *Staffs* 61 0614
Upper Ludstone *Shrops* 60 8095
Upper Lybster *Highld* 151 2537
Upper Lydbrook *Gloucs* 34 6015
Upper Lyde *Herefd* 46 4944
Upper Lye *Herefd* 46 3965
Upper Maes-coed *Herefd* 46 3334
Upper Midhope *Derbys* 74 2199
Upper Milton *Worcs* 60 8172
Upper Minety *Wilts* 35 0091
Upper Moor *Worcs* 47 9747
Upper Moor Side *W York* 82 2430
Upper Mulben *Moray* 141 3551
Upper Netchwood *Shrops* 59 6092
Upper Nobut *Staffs* 73 0335
Upper Norwood *W Susx* 14 9317
Upper Padley *Derbys* 74 2478
Upper Pennington *Hants* 12 3095
Upper Pickwick *Wilts* 35 8571
Upper Pollicott *Bucks* 37 7013
Upper Pond Street *Essex* 39 4636
Upper Poppleton *N York* 83 5553
Upper Quinton *Warwks* 48 1846
Upper Ratley *Hants* 23 3223
Upper Rochford *Worcs* 47 6367
Upper Ruscoe *D & G* 99 5661
Upper Sapey *Herefd* 47 6863
Upper Seagry *Wilts* 35 9480
Upper Shelton *Beds* 38 9843
Upper Sheringham *Norfk* 66 1441
Upper Shuckburgh *Warwks* 49 5061
Upper Skelmorlie *N Ayrs* 114 2067
Upper Slaughter *Gloucs* 48 1523
Upper Soudley *Gloucs* 35 6510
Upper Spond *Herefd* 46 3152
Upper Standen *Kent* 29 2139
Upper Staploe *Beds* 52 1459
Upper Stepford *D & G* 100 8681
Upper Stoke *Norfk* 67 2502
Upper Stondon *Beds* 38 1435
Upper Stowe *Nhants* 49 6456
Upper Street *Hants* 12 1518
Upper Street *Norfk* 67 3217
Upper Street *Norfk* 67 3616
Upper Street *Norfk* 54 1779
Upper Street *Suffk* 53 7851
Upper Street *Suffk* 54 1050
Upper Street *Suffk* 54 1434
Upper Strensham *Worcs* 47 8939
Upper Sundon *Beds* 38 0428
Upper Swell *Gloucs* 48 1726
Upper Tankersley *S York* 74 3499
Upper Tasburgh *Norfk* 67 2095
Upper Tean *Staffs* 73 0139
Upper Threapwood *Ches* 71 4345
Upper Town *Derbys* 73 2351
Upper Town *Derbys* 74 2361
Upper Town *Dur* 95 0737
Upper Town *Herefd* 46 5848
Upper Town *Somset* 21 5265
Upper Town *Suffk* 54 9267
Upper Tysoe *Warwks* 48 3343
Upper Ufford *Suffk* 55 2952
Upper Upham *Wilts* 36 2277
Upper Upnor *Kent* 28 7570
Upper Victoria *Angus* 127 5336
Upper Vobster *Somset* 22 7049
Upper Wardington *Oxon* 49 4945
Upper Weald *Bucks* 38 8037
Upper Weedon *Nhants* 49 6258
Upper Wellingham *E Susx* 16 4313
Upper Weston *Somset* 22 7267
Upper Weybread *Suffk* 55 2379
Upper Wick *Worcs* 47 8252
Upper Wield *Hants* 24 6238
Upper Winchendon *Bucks* 37 7414
Upper Woodford *Wilts* 23 1237
Upper Wootton *Hants* 24 5754
Upper Wraxall *Wilts* 35 8074
Upper Wyche *Worcs* 47 7643
Upperby *Cumb* 93 4153
Upperglen *Highld* 136 3151
Uppermill *Gt Man* 82 9905
Upperthong *W York* 82 1208
Upperthorpe *Derbys* 75 4580
Upperthorpe *Lincs* 84 7500
Upperton *W Susx* 14 9522
Uppertown *Derbys* 74 3264
Uppertown *Highld* 151 3576
Upperup *Gloucs* 36 0496
Upperwood *Derbys* 73 2956
Uppincott *Devon* 9 9006
Uppingham *Rutlnd* 51 8699
Uppington *Dorset* 12 0206
Uppington *Shrops* 59 5909
Upsall *N York* 89 4586
Upsettlington *Border* 110 8846
Upshire *Essex* 27 4101
Upstreet *Kent* 29 2263
Upthorpe *Suffk* 54 9772
Upton *Berks* 26 9779
Upton *Bucks* 37 7711
Upton *Cambs* 64 1000
Upton *Cambs* 52 1778
Upton *Ches* 71 4069
Upton *Ches* 78 5087
Upton *Cnwll* 18 2004
Upton *Cnwll* 5 2772
Upton *Cumb* 93 3139
Upton *Devon* 9 0902
Upton *Devon* 7 7043
Upton *Dorset* 11 7483
Upton *Dorset* 11 9893
Upton *E R Yk* 85 1454
Upton *Hants* 23 3555
Upton *Hants* 12 3716
Upton *Leics* 61 3699
Upton *Lincs* 76 8686
Upton *Mersyd* 78 2788
Upton *Nhants* 49 7159
Upton *Norfk* 67 3912
Upton *Notts* 75 7354
Upton *Notts* 75 7476
Upton *Oxon* 36 2312
Upton *Oxon* 37 5187
Upton *Pembks* 30 0204
Upton *Somset* 20 9928
Upton *Somset* 21 4526
Upton *W York* 83 4713
Upton *Warwks* 48 1257
Upton *Wilts* 22 8731
Upton Bishop *Herefd* 47 6527
Upton Cheyney *Gloucs* 35 6970
Upton Cressett *Shrops* 59 6592
Upton Crews *Herefd* 47 6427
Upton Cross *Cnwll* 5 2872
Upton End *Beds* 38 1234
Upton Grey *Hants* 24 6948
Upton Heath *Ches* 71 4169
Upton Hellions *Devon* 8 8403
Upton Lovell *Wilts* 22 9440
Upton Magna *Shrops* 59 5512
Upton Noble *Somset* 22 7139
Upton Pyne *Devon* 9 9198
Upton Scudamore *Wilts* 22 8647
Upton Snodsbury *Worcs* 47 9454
Upton St Leonards *Gloucs* 35 8615
Upton Towans *Cnwll* 2 5740
Upton upon Severn *Worcs* 47 8540
Upton Warren *Worcs* 47 9267
Upwaltham *W Susx* 14 9413
Upware *Cambs* 53 5470
Upwell *Norfk* 65 4902
Upwey *Dorset* 11 6685
Upwick Green *Herts* 39 4524
Upwood *Cambs* 52 2582
Urchfont *Wilts* 23 0357
Urdimarsh *Herefd* 46 5248
Ure Bank *N York* 89 3172
Urlay Nook *Dur* 89 4014
Urmston *Gt Man* 79 7694
Urquhart *Moray* 141 2862
Urra *N York* 90 5601
Urray *Highld* 139 5052
Usan *Angus* 127 7254
Ushaw Moor *Dur* 96 2242
Usk *Mons* 34 3700
Usselby *Lincs* 76 0993
Usworth *T & W* 96 3057
Utkinton *Ches* 71 5564
Utley *W York* 82 0542
Uton *Devon* 8 8298
Utterby *Lincs* 77 3093
Uttoxeter *Staffs* 73 0933
Uwchmynydd *Gwynd* 56 1525
Uxbridge *Gt Lon* 26 0584
Uyeasound *Shet* 153 5901
Uzmaston *Pembks* 30 9714


## V


Vale *Guern* 158 0000
Valley *IOA* 68 2979
Valley End *Surrey* 25 9564
Valley Truckle *Cnwll* 4 0982
Valtos *Highld* 137 5163
Valtos *W Isls* 152 0936
Van *Caerph* 33 1686
Vange *Essex* 40 7186
Varteg *Torfn* 34 2606
Vatsetter *Shet* 153 5389
Vatten *Highld* 136 2843
Vaynor *Myr Td* 33 0410
Vazon Bay *Guern* 158 0000
Velindre *Powys* 45 1836
Vellow *Somset* 20 0938
Velly *Devon* 18 2924
Venn *Cnwll* 18 2608
Venn *Devon* 7 8549
Venn Ottery *Devon* 9 0891
Venngreen *Devon* 18 3711
Vennington *Shrops* 59 3309
Venny Tedburn *Devon* 8 8297
Venterdon *Cnwll* 5 3675
Ventnor *IOW* 13 5677
Venton *Devon* 6 5956
Vernham Dean *Hants* 23 3356
Vernham Street *Hants* 23 3457
Vernolds Common *Shrops* 59 4780
Verwood *Dorset* 12 0809
Veryan *Cnwll* 3 9139
Veryan Green *Cnwll* 3 9140
Vickerstown *Cumb* 86 1868
Victoria *Blae G* 33 1707
Victoria *Cnwll* 4 9861
Victoria *S York* 82 1705
Vidlin *Shet* 153 4765
Viewfield *Moray* 141 2864
Viewpark *N Lans* 116 7061
Vigo *Kent* 27 6361
Ville la Bas *Jersey* 158 0000
Villiaze *Guern* 158 0000
Vinehall Street *E Susx* 17 7520
Vines Cross *E Susx* 16 5917
Virginia Water *Surrey* 25 0067
Virginstow *Devon* 5 3792
Virley *Essex* 40 9414
Vobster *Somset* 22 7048
Voe *Shet* 153 4062
Vowchurch *Herefd* 46 3636
Vulcan Village *Lancs* 78 5894


## W


Wackerfield *Dur* 96 1522
Wacton *Norfk* 66 1791
Wadborough *Worcs* 47 9047
Waddesdon *Bucks* 37 7416
Waddeton *Devon* 7 8756
Waddicar *Mersyd* 78 3999
Waddingham *Lincs* 76 9896
Waddington *Lancs* 81 7343
Waddington *Lincs* 76 9764
Waddon *Devon* 9 8879
Waddon *Dorset* 10 6285
Wadebridge *Cnwll* 4 9972
Wadeford *Somset* 10 3110
Wadenhoe *Nhants* 51 0183
Wadesmill *Herts* 39 3617
Wadhurst *E Susx* 16 6431
Wadshelf *Derbys* 74 3170
Wadswick *Wilts* 22 8467
Wadworth *S York* 75 5696
Waen *Denbgs* 70 9962
Waen *Denbgs* 70 1065
Waen *Powys* 58 2319
Waen Fach *Powys* 58 2017
Waen-pentir *Gwynd* 69 5766
Waen-wen *Gwynd* 69 5768
Wagbeach *Shrops* 59 3602
Wainfelin *Torfn* 34 2701
Wainfleet All Saints *Lincs* 77 4959
Wainfleet Bank *Lincs* 77 4759
Wainford *Norfk* 55 3490
Wainhouse Corner *Cnwll* 4 1895
Wains Hill *Somset* 34 3970
Wainscott *Kent* 28 7470
Wainstalls *W York* 82 0428
Waitby *Cumb* 88 7508
Waithe *Lincs* 77 2800
Wake Green *W Mids* 61 0982
Wakefield *W York* 83 3320
Wakerley *Nhants* 51 9599
Wakes Colne *Essex* 40 8928
Wal-wen *Flints* 70 2076
Walberswick *Suffk* 55 4974
Walberton *W Susx* 14 9705
Walbottle *T & W* 103 1666
Walbutt *D & G* 99 7468
Walby *Cumb* 101 4460
Walcombe *Somset* 21 5546
Walcot *Lincs* 84 8720
Walcot *Lincs* 64 0635
Walcot *Lincs* 76 1356
Walcot *Shrops* 59 5912
Walcot *Shrops* 59 3485
Walcot *Warwks* 48 1358
Walcot *Wilts* 36 1684
Walcot Green *Norfk* 54 1280
Walcote *Leics* 50 5683
Walcott *Norfk* 67 3532
Walden *N York* 88 0082
Walden Head *N York* 88 9880
Walden Stubbs *N York* 83 5516
Walderslade *Kent* 28 7663
Walderton *W Susx* 14 7910
Walditch *Dorset* 10 4892
Waldley *Derbys* 73 1236
Waldridge *Dur* 96 2549
Waldringfield *Suffk* 55 2845
Waldron *E Susx* 16 5419
Wales *S York* 75 4882
Wales *Somset* 21 5824
Walesby *Lincs* 76 1392
Walesby *Notts* 75 6870
Walford *Herefd* 46 3872
Walford *Herefd* 34 5820
Walford *Shrops* 59 4320
Walford *Staffs* 72 8133
Walford Heath *Shrops* 59 4419
Walgherton *Ches* 72 6948
Walgrave *Nhants* 51 8071
Walhampton *Hants* 12 3396
Walk Mill *Lancs* 81 8729
Walkden *Gt Man* 79 7302
Walker *T & W* 103 2864
Walker Fold *Lancs* 81 6741
Walker's Green *Herefd* 46 5247
Walker's Heath *W Mids* 61 0578
Walkerburn *Border* 109 3637
Walkeringham *Notts* 75 7792
Walkerith *Lincs* 75 7892
Walkern *Herts* 39 2826
Walkerton *Fife* 126 2301
Walkford *Dorset* 12 2194
Walkhampton *Devon* 6 5369
Walkington *E R Yk* 84 9936
Walkley *S York* 74 3388
Walkwood *Worcs* 48 0364
Wall *Cnwll* 2 6036
Wall *Nthumb* 102 9168
Wall *Staffs* 61 1006
Wall End *Cumb* 86 2383
Wall End *Herefd* 46 4457
Wall Heath *W Mids* 60 8889
Wall Houses *Nthumb* 103 0368
Wall under Haywood *Shrops* 59 5092
Wallacetown *S Ayrs* 106 2703
Wallacetown *S Ayrs* 106 3422
Wallands Park *E Susx* 15 4010
Wallasey *Mersyd* 78 2992
Wallend *Kent* 28 8775
Waller's Green *Herefd* 47 6739
Wallhead *Cumb* 101 4660
Wallingford *Oxon* 37 6089
Wallington *Gt Lon* 27 2864
Wallington *Hants* 13 5806
Wallington *Herts* 39 2933
Wallington Heath *W Mids* 60 9903
Wallis *Pembks* 30 0125
Wallisdown *Dorset* 12 0694
Walliswood *W Susx* 14 1138
Walls *Shet* 153 2449
Wallsend *T & W* 103 2966
Wallthwaite *Cumb* 93 3526
Wallyford *E Loth* 118 3671
Walmer *Kent* 29 3750
Walmer Bridge *Lancs* 80 4724
Walmersley *Gt Man* 81 8013
Walmestone *Kent* 29 2559
Walmley *W Mids* 61 1393
Walmley Ash *W Mids* 61 1492
Walmsgate *Lincs* 77 3677
Walpole *Somset* 20 3042
Walpole *Suffk* 55 3674
Walpole Cross Keys *Norfk* 65 5119
Walpole Highway *Norfk* 65 5114
Walpole St Andrew *Norfk* 65 5017
Walpole St Peter *Norfk* 65 5016
Walrow *Somset* 21 3447
Walsall *W Mids* 60 0198
Walsall Wood *W Mids* 61 0403
Walsden *W York* 81 9321
Walsgrave on Sowe *W Mids* 61 3881
Walsham le Willows *Suffk* 54 0071
Walshaw *Gt Man* 81 7711
Walshaw *W York* 82 9731
Walshford *N York* 83 4153
Walsoken *Norfk* 65 4710
Walston *S Lans* 117 0545
Walsworth *Herts* 39 1930
Walter's Ash *Bucks* 37 8398
Walters Green *Kent* 16 5140
Walterston *V Glam* 33 0671
Walterstone *Herefd* 46 3425
Waltham *Kent* 29 1048
Waltham *Lincs* 85 2603
Waltham Abbey *Essex* 27 3800
Waltham Chase *Hants* 13 5614
Waltham Cross *Herts* 27 3600
Waltham on the Wolds *Leics* 63 8024
Waltham St Lawrence *Berks* 37 8276
Waltham's Cross *Essex* 40 6930
Walthamstow *Gt Lon* 27 3689
Walton *Bucks* 38 8936
Walton *Cambs* 64 1702
Walton *Cumb* 101 5264
Walton *Derbys* 74 3568
Walton *Leics* 50 5987
Walton *Powys* 46 2559

315

# Y

# Z

# mileage chart

The distances between towns on the mileage chart are given to the nearest mile, and are measured along the normal AA-recommended routes. It should be noted that AA-recommended routes do not necessarily follow the shortest distance between places but are based on the quickest travelling time, making maximum use of motorways and dual carriageways.

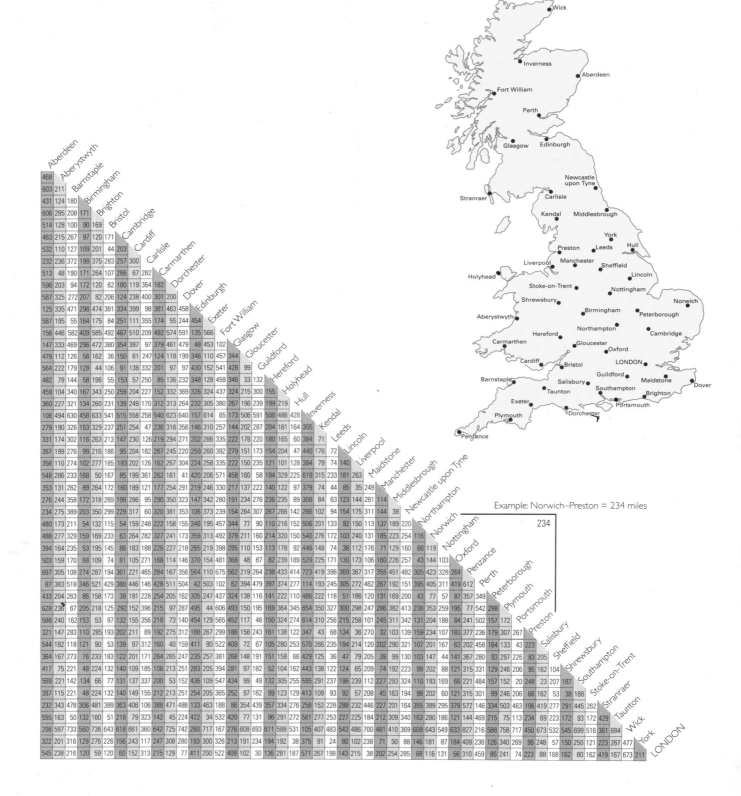

Example: Norwich–Preston = 234 miles

Mileage chart (triangular distance table). The diagonal labels read, in order: Aberdeen, Aberystwyth, Barnstaple, Birmingham, Brighton, Bristol, Cambridge, Cardiff, Carlisle, Carmarthen, Dorchester, Dover, Edinburgh, Exeter, Fort William, Glasgow, Gloucester, Guildford, Hereford, Holyhead, Hull, Inverness, Kendal, Leeds, Lincoln, Liverpool, Maidstone, Manchester, Middlesbrough, Newcastle upon Tyne, Northampton, Norwich, Nottingham, Oxford, Penzance, Perth, Peterborough, Plymouth, Portsmouth, Preston, Salisbury, Sheffield, Shrewsbury, Southampton, Stoke-on-Trent, Stranraer, Taunton, Wick, York, LONDON.

| City | Distances to preceding towns |
| --- | --- |
| Aberystwyth | 468 |
| Barnstaple | 603 211 |
| Birmingham | 431 124 180 |
| Brighton | 606 285 208 171 |
| Bristol | 514 128 100 90 169 |
| Cambridge | 463 215 267 97 120 171 |
| Cardiff | 532 110 127 109 201 44 203 |
| Carlisle | 232 236 372 199 375 283 257 300 |
| Carmarthen | 513 48 190 171 264 107 266 67 282 |
| Dorchester | 596 203 94 172 120 62 180 119 364 182 |
| Dover | 587 325 272 207 82 206 124 238 400 301 200 |
| Edinburgh | 125 335 471 298 474 381 334 399 98 381 463 458 |
| Exeter | 587 195 55 164 175 84 251 111 355 174 55 244 454 |
| Fort William | 156 446 582 409 585 492 467 510 209 492 574 591 135 566 |
| Glasgow | 147 333 469 296 472 380 354 397 97 379 461 479 48 453 102 |
| Gloucester | 479 112 126 56 162 36 150 61 247 124 118 199 346 110 457 344 |
| Guildford | 564 222 179 128 44 106 91 138 332 201 97 97 430 152 541 428 99 |
| Hereford | 482 79 144 58 196 55 153 57 250 85 136 232 348 128 459 346 33 132 |
| Holyhead | 459 104 340 167 343 250 259 204 227 152 332 369 326 324 437 324 215 300 155 |
| Hull | 360 227 321 134 260 231 139 249 170 312 313 264 232 305 380 267 196 239 199 219 |
| Inverness | 106 494 630 458 633 541 515 558 258 540 623 640 157 614 65 173 506 591 508 486 428 |
| Kendal | 279 190 326 153 329 237 251 254 47 236 318 356 146 310 257 144 202 287 204 181 164 305 |
| Leeds | 331 174 302 116 263 213 147 230 126 219 294 271 202 286 335 222 178 220 180 165 60 384 71 |
| Lincoln | 387 199 276 99 216 186 95 204 182 226 227 218 265 219 398 285 110 153 119 178 92 440 176 72 |
| Liverpool | 358 110 274 102 277 185 193 202 126 162 267 304 224 258 335 222 150 235 121 101 128 384 79 74 140 |
| Maidstone | 548 286 233 168 50 167 85 199 361 262 161 41 420 206 571 458 160 58 194 329 225 619 315 233 181 263 |
| Manchester | 353 131 262 89 264 172 160 189 121 177 254 291 219 246 330 217 137 222 140 122 97 379 74 44 85 35 249 |
| Middlesbrough | 276 244 358 172 318 269 198 286 95 290 350 323 147 342 280 191 234 276 236 235 89 308 84 63 123 144 281 114 |
| Newcastle upon Tyne | 234 275 389 203 350 299 229 317 60 320 381 353 106 373 239 154 264 307 267 266 102 266 102 94 154 175 311 144 38 |
| Northampton | 480 173 211 54 132 115 54 159 248 222 158 155 346 195 457 344 77 90 110 216 152 506 201 133 92 150 113 137 189 220 |
| Norwich | 488 277 329 159 169 233 63 264 282 327 241 173 359 211 160 214 320 540 276 172 103 240 131 185 223 254 116 |
| Nottingham | 394 164 235 53 195 145 86 163 288 227 218 265 219 398 285 110 153 119 178 92 275 71 129 160 66 119 |
| Oxford | 503 159 170 68 109 74 81 105 271 168 114 146 370 154 481 368 48 67 82 239 189 529 225 171 130 173 106 160 226 257 43 144 103 |
| Penzance | 697 305 108 274 287 194 361 221 465 284 167 356 564 110 675 562 219 264 238 433 414 723 419 396 369 367 317 355 451 482 305 423 328 264 |
| Perth | 87 383 518 346 521 429 380 446 146 428 511 504 42 503 102 62 394 479 397 374 277 114 193 245 305 272 462 267 192 151 395 405 311 419 612 |
| Peterborough | 433 204 86 158 173 38 191 228 254 205 162 305 247 437 324 138 116 141 222 110 486 222 118 51 186 120 131 169 200 43 77 57 87 357 349 |
| Plymouth | 628 236 67 205 218 125 292 152 396 215 97 287 495 44 606 493 150 195 169 364 345 654 350 327 300 298 247 286 382 413 236 353 259 195 77 542 288 |
| Portsmouth | 588 240 162 153 53 97 132 155 356 218 73 140 454 129 565 452 117 46 150 324 274 614 310 256 215 258 101 245 311 342 131 204 188 84 241 502 157 172 |
| Preston | 321 147 283 110 285 193 202 211 89 192 275 312 188 267 299 186 158 243 161 138 122 347 43 38 112 79 103 139 159 230 163 208 183 377 236 137 271 429 |
| Salisbury | 544 182 118 121 90 53 139 97 312 160 40 159 411 90 522 409 72 67 105 280 253 570 266 235 194 214 120 202 290 321 107 201 167 63 202 458 164 133 43 223 |
| Sheffield | 364 167 273 76 233 183 122 201 171 264 265 247 235 257 381 268 148 191 151 158 66 429 125 36 47 79 205 39 99 130 103 147 44 141 367 280 93 297 226 83 205 |
| Shrewsbury | 417 75 221 48 224 132 140 109 185 108 213 251 283 205 394 281 97 182 52 184 443 138 122 64 65 209 74 192 223 98 202 88 121 315 331 129 246 206 95 162 104 |
| Southampton | 569 221 142 134 66 77 131 137 337 200 53 152 436 109 547 434 99 49 132 305 295 595 291 237 196 239 112 220 293 324 110 193 169 66 221 484 157 152 20 248 23 207 187 |
| Stoke-on-Trent | 387 115 221 48 224 132 140 149 155 212 213 251 254 205 365 252 97 182 99 123 129 413 109 93 92 57 208 45 163 194 98 202 60 121 315 301 90 246 206 66 162 53 38 188 |
| Stranraer | 232 343 478 306 481 389 363 406 106 388 471 488 133 463 188 86 354 439 357 334 276 258 153 228 288 232 446 207 201 164 355 389 295 379 572 146 334 503 463 196 419 277 291 445 262 |
| Taunton | 555 163 50 132 160 51 218 79 323 142 45 224 422 34 532 420 77 131 96 291 272 581 277 252 227 225 184 212 309 340 163 280 183 177 238 159 234 69 223 172 93 172 429 |
| Wick | 208 597 733 560 736 643 618 661 360 642 725 742 260 717 167 276 608 693 611 588 531 105 407 483 543 486 700 481 410 369 609 643 549 633 827 216 588 758 757 450 673 532 599 516 361 684 |
| York | 322 201 316 129 278 226 156 243 117 247 308 280 193 300 326 213 191 234 194 192 38 375 91 24 80 102 238 71 50 88 146 181 87 184 409 238 126 340 269 96 248 57 150 250 121 223 267 477 |
| LONDON | 545 238 216 120 59 120 60 152 313 215 129 77 411 200 522 409 102 30 136 281 187 571 267 198 143 216 38 200 254 285 68 116 131 56 310 459 86 241 74 223 88 168 162 80 162 419 167 673 211 |